# GLOBAL DISCORD

# Global Discord

## VALUES AND POWER IN A
## FRACTURED WORLD ORDER

PAUL TUCKER

PRINCETON UNIVERSITY PRESS

PRINCETON & OXFORD

Published by Princeton University Press
41 William Street, Princeton, New Jersey 08540
99 Banbury Road, Oxford OX2 6JX

press.princeton.edu

All Rights Reserved

Library of Congress Control Number: 2022937782

ISBN 9780691229317
ISBN (e-book) 9780691232096

British Library Cataloging-in-Publication Data is available

Editorial: Hannah Paul, Joe Jackson, Josh Drake
Jacket Design: Karl Spurzem
Production: Erin Suydam, Lauren Reese
Publicity: James Schneider, Kate Farquhar-Thomson

This book has been composed in Arno Pro

Printed on acid-free paper. ∞

Printed in the United States of America

10 9 8 7 6 5 4 3 2 1

For Jacques de Larosière and the memory of Paul Volcker,
international monetary titans

# CONTENTS

# PREFACE

IN THE MIDST of the Global Financial Crisis, a colleague walked into my then office at the Bank of England to say that the US Federal Reserve had refused India a secured line of credit (known as a swap line) to help them navigate the fallout from the collapse of the West's banking system. My response was something like, "But India will be a power!" I was left wondering how my world of economic policymaking had become detached from geopolitics when, only a generation before, titans like the late Paul Volcker had lived the connections.[1]

A few years later, at the beginning of 2016, I used the Tacitus Lecture in London to explore this question, setting out four possible scenarios.[2] At the time, the world still seemed to be lingering in the status quo of US leadership, but with superpower rivalry becoming ever more apparent. By 2020, when a media commentator drew on the framework, we were pretty well already in that second scenario.[3] Writing this in early 2022, we edge ever closer to a new cold war, and conceivably some kind of hot war if the People's Republic of China takes military action to control Taiwan, or too obviously comes to Russia's aid. Who knows where things will stand when the book is published, underlining the need to think about international institutions in the context of a fracturing world order. That is one of two impetuses behind this book.

The other is a loose end in my 2018 book, *Unelected Power*, about whether central banks, and other independent agencies insulated from day-to-day politics, can find a decent place in healthy constitutional democracies. That book merely gestured toward the question of how far pooling authority in international organizations, and delegating to their staff, can be legitimate for nations and peoples who think of themselves as self-governing.

---

1. Citing transcripts, Sahasrabuddhe, "Drawing the Line," p. 474, reveals that the Fed did weigh "diplomatic perspectives" (perhaps myopically).
2. Tucker, "Geopolitics."
3. Nixon, "Rival Superpowers."

This book is, then, about where geopolitics and legitimacy meet, or maybe collide: How can what is legitimate for *us* survive a changing balance of power? It is therefore also about how the boundaries between policy fields that usually keep a distinct distance from each other—the international monetary system, national security, trade, human rights, humanitarian intervention, the environment, pandemic control, even war and peace—unavoidably blur as governments confront problems of geopolitical grand strategy and domestic political authority. When more or less any public policy instrument can be "weaponized," geoeconomics becomes integral to foreign policy.

The common theme of the two books, amounting to an underlying project, is how far our political values should constrain rational-choice institutional design. Institutions that are, as economists put it, incentive compatible— meaning all actors have incentives that make the institution sustainable—are not much use if those same incentives create conduct and outcomes that are at odds with the political values that supposedly animate them. To give a concrete example, the US system of government creates incentives for Congress to delegate a lot of lawmaking to unelected administrative agencies, and for the Supreme Court both to acquiesce and join in. But that is hardly consistent with the values that animated a constitution founded on the republican value of political representation via an elected legislature. The resulting system of government is incentive compatible, but teeters on the edge of values incompatibility.[4] *Global Discord* is partly about whether combined *values-incentives compatibility* is feasible in international cooperation, and how international policy regimes and organizations might have to change to bring incentives into line with *our* deep political values without that driving states with different values and systems into hostile conflict with us. Some of its prescriptions on bringing national security and local legitimacy considerations into international economic policy have become mainstream since I first drafted them (before COVID) but are none the worse for that given the world's fractures are likely to persist for decades.

As the risk of hostilities faces great powers rooted in very different civilizations, I want to say here that it is one of my life's great blessings that many years ago I was able to taste something of the wonders of other civilizations when I traveled (and read my way) around China, the Indian subcontinent, and parts of the Middle East and Southeast Asia. The emphasis is on "able to," because that blessing was bestowed by peace. What, following the late

4. Tucker, *Unelected Power*, pp. 337–40, 551–52.

philosopher Bernard Williams, I call the problem of the First Political Question—how governance can be legitimized so that excessive coercive power does not have to be used to maintain security and stability—looms large in the book because it is not something we should ever take for granted. After Russia's invasion of Ukraine, that, grotesquely, is now more obvious than while I was writing.

Finally, *Global Discord* is for Jacques de Larosière and the late Paul Volcker, who led the International Monetary Fund and the Fed during the 1980s in extraordinary careers in international economic diplomacy. It is dedicated to them as tribute, in gratitude for their friendship and support, and because, of course, the Titans were overthrown by their successors, the Gods.

# 1

# Introduction

## GEOPOLITICS AND LEGITIMACY IN
## A GLOBALIZED WORLD

You are pivoting to Asia, but we're already there.

RUSSIA'S AMBASSADOR TO THE UNITED STATES, 2014[1]

The situation of one lot of people terrorizing another lot of people is not a political situation; it is, rather, the situation which the existence of the political is in the first place supposed to alleviate (replace).

BERNARD WILLIAMS, *IN THE BEGINNING WAS THE DEED*[2]

IN LATE 1971 at a meeting in Rome, US president Richard Nixon's treasury secretary, John Connally, famously told his international peers, the world's leading finance ministers, that the dollar "is our currency, but your problem."[3] Whatever he had in mind, he had a point.

By his own admission not an economist, Connally, a former governor of Texas who had survived serious wounds when President John F. Kennedy was assassinated, was widely regarded as a formidable politician. Almost a decade earlier, President Charles de Gaulle had exercised France's right, under the

---

1. Quoted in Blackwill and Harris, *War by Other Means*, p. 39.

2. Williams, "Realism and Moralism in Political Theory," in *In the Beginning*, p. 5.

3. Volcker and Gyohten, *Changing Fortunes*, p. 81. Volcker writes, "I cringed at putting it that way." Before my 2016 Tacitus Lecture, I discussed these events with Volcker, a US Treasury official during the period.

Bretton Woods international monetary system, to demand that the United States redeem its dollars for gold. Coming not long after the Suez debacle, and shortly before de Gaulle temporarily pulled France out of the North Atlantic Treaty Organization (NATO), it signaled not only Paris's discomfort with US leadership but also a growing sense that Washington would not be able to sustain the dollar's international value given its escalating Vietnam War and the social welfare programs judged necessary to maintain a semblance of domestic order.

Faced with European and Japanese reluctance to revalue their currencies, Connally asserted, "My philosophy is that the foreigners are out to screw us. Our job is to screw them first."[4] While the swagger suggests a man out of his depth, he certainly sensed the paucity of options available to his international partners. Import tariffs were imposed, and duly challenged by Europe in the Geneva-based trade body crafted by an earlier generation of US policymakers. National Security Adviser Henry Kissinger warned the president of the diplomatic costs, including a descent back into protectionism, but Nixon was initially more taken by their domestic popularity.[5]

On the monetary side, which was the show's point, Washington suspended gold convertibility—without consulting the International Monetary Fund (IMF), another of its postwar babies—exposing its counterparts to substantial losses on their large dollar reserves. The main targets were not London or Paris, but the booming economies of World War II's losers, Germany and Japan. With the Cold War near its peak, however, West Germany in particular was dependent on the United States to protect it from the Soviet Union. But that cut both ways. While a US Treasury study of options included reducing the military presence in Europe and Japan, it was hardly credible.[6]

The key was that since no other country was remotely ready to provide a substitute world reserve currency, the dollar's preeminence was not at risk. Nevertheless, finding a credible new monetary regime was a heck of a problem for the United States. Their first solution, the December 1971 Smithsonian pact, was celebrated by Nixon as "the most significant monetary agreement in the history of the world." Perhaps, though its glory blazed for less than eighteen months. From the spring of 1973, the Europeans floated their currencies.[7]

4. Irwin, *Clashing over Commerce*, p. 543.

5. Irwin, *Clashing over Commerce*, pp. 546, 752–53n88.

6. Irwin, "Nixon Shock," p. 34.

7. Irwin, *Clashing over Commerce*, pp. 546–47; Eichengreen, *Globalizing Capital*, pp. 133–34. (Canada floated in the 1950s.)

At that point, the underlying vulnerabilities were dramatically exposed. With oil priced in dollars, the inevitable depreciation put pressure on the incomes of the big Middle Eastern producers, who eventually imposed an embargo, pushing prices up, in the wake of the Yom Kippur War. Unable or unwilling to control the resulting domestic inflation and so stabilize medium-term inflation expectations, the United States saw its economic performance deteriorate. Stagflation (rising inflation, falling activity and jobs) compounded the political turmoil brought by Watergate and withdrawal from Southeast Asia. Eventually, a backbreaking recession and resumed fiscal discipline restored internal monetary order, and so underpinned the dollar's role in US global leadership. Over much the same period, Washington recast its policies on oil exploration and energy dependencies.

Closing the episode with an unexpected twist, the Geneva trade machinery rejected an IMF finding that the US import surcharge had been a legitimate balance-of-payments measure. Highlighting a tension latent in fragmentation of the international monetary and trade regimes and their secretariats, the rules were changed to avoid this happening again (chapter 3).[8]

That old story underlines the often-neglected intertwining of international monetary affairs with trade and geopolitics; how those connections can play back into domestic politics; and how they reverberate through international organizations. Occasionally, the fields of economic policy and foreign policy converge. We are back in one of those phases of history and will remain so for some considerable time.

After prolonged geopolitical peace, that will challenge specialist policymakers used to inhabiting segmented spheres: distinct tribes, trained separately, operating via their own networks of power and influence, and often distant from one another in government. With the deep architecture of the international economy in flux for the first time in decades, the big issues are not easily parceled out to different buildings. With diverse fields coming together, whether in collision or concord, high policy—"grand strategy" is a better expression—needs to be framed, explained, and executed accordingly. This book will, accordingly, traverse the international economy, security (war and peace), human rights and humanitarian interventions, and the global commons (climate change and pandemic disease) before drilling down into the first.

At its heart are the complexities and hazards produced by the conjunction of economic globalization, discordant geopolitics, and strains in the legitimacy

8. Irwin, "Nixon Shock," pp. 51–52.

of domestic and international governance. How can the West and other constitutional democracies maintain their liberal traditions in the face of interdependencies with rising (or revived) authoritarian states? Can peaceful coexistence be sustained without the Powers retreating into free-world and authoritarian blocs? Can Western-style states reconcile legitimacy at home with legitimate international cooperation?

While serious tensions were already present in globalization's trajectories, they have been raised to a new level by Beijing's ambitions, Moscow's opportunism, Washington's long-standing sclerosis morphing into corrosive disarray, and Europe's presumption of stability. In the remainder of this introductory chapter, we sketch some of the background to globalization, geopolitics, and legitimacy.

## Globalization: Different This Time Around, but the Same Too

The period leading up to World War I is often described as the first globalization. Its unraveling involved the reintroduction of controls on trade, immigration, and, eventually, flows of capital.[9] In recent years, we have already seen the first and second, and a version of the third has been creeping back (chapter 16). But the late twentieth and early twenty-first century's "second globalization" is not a simple replay, being distinct in its economic structure, international institutions, and breadth of participation.

### The First Globalization's Emergence: Technology and Politics

Until modernity, trade flows had since time immemorial been largely in goods (alongside some personally delivered services, such as religion, ideas, and some arts and crafts). Nearly all that goods trade was in raw materials and precious commodities. If you were a ruler, you could obtain building materials from afar: ancient Egypt famously imported cedar from Mount Lebanon, sometimes coercively. If you were a wealthy family, you could eat or wear things from outside your locality—even spices and silks.[10] They were transported across Eurasia's famous ancient Silk Road, and much later via coastal routes developed by Europe's commercial empires. Both highways also transmitted deadly pathogens: most famously the bubonic plague, wreaking havoc

9. James, *End of Globalization*.
10. Drawing on Baldwin, *Great Convergence*.

across western Eurasia through the fourteenth century's Black Death and spo-radically thereafter.

Later, northern Europe's (and then North America's) Industrial Revolution delivered two profound changes: it mechanized production and, thanks at first to the steam engine, crushed land and sea transportation costs (for people as well as things). Finished goods no longer needed to be produced close to where they were consumed. Making something of their natural endowments and capabilities, localities—and in due course whole countries—could now specialize, increasing cross-border trade and opening a door to economies of scale and the clustering of skills.

All that took off only after the Napoleonic Wars, ushering in peace among the European powers. Where external trade expanded, exporters tended to prosper relative to import-competing businesses, increasing their clout in poli-tics. In Britain, the (all-male) franchise was gradually expanded from the 1830s, and trade liberalized from the 1840s. Meanwhile, Europe's absolute monarchies (and the United States) maintained high tariffs, power lying with landowners, courtiers, and administrators. In Prussia, its (selectively) reforming leader, Count Bismarck, erected external tariffs around a new German customs union, and later his new nation-state. With successful industrialization fueling a military caste's appetite for power, his successors helped tip the world into a war bringing the curtain down on the first globalization.

There is a view—plausible enough for policymakers to take seriously—that the first globalization undid itself. Trade created winners and losers, and mas-sive movements of working-age people put downward pressure on incum-bents' wages in some areas, sparking varieties of populism. Flows of finance and technology amplified the arms race. Later, flawed monetary and financial regimes fueled a credit-led asset-price bubble and exacerbated the costs, in-cluding across borders, when it burst. Neither the politics nor the economics of the international order had proved resilient (see below).[11]

### *The Second Globalization: Multinational Corporations and Cross-Border Services*

An integrated international economy was not rebuilt until after the second of Germany's wars against the world (chapter 3). Initially, patterns of trade were not so different. After the twentieth century's assembly-line revolution,

11. O'Rourke, "Economic History."

manufacturers bought in more component parts, including increasingly from industrialized neighbors. Nevertheless, design, assembly, quality control, and sales and marketing—and hence most value added and jobs—stayed at home. More notably, Japan and then South Korea showed it was possible to join the club of rich industrialized countries.

Then two things changed everything. First, the now familiar standard boxlike containers used on cargo ships improved loading and unloading times and reliability, helping factories avoid the previous flip-flop between idleness and bottlenecks. Multinational businesses moved labor-intensive production—via subcontracting agreements, joint ventures, and wholly owned subsidiaries—to orderly but poorer economies (with lower wages).[12]

The second change, in communications technology, was closer to revolution. A business's headquarters could now specify exactly what they wanted down to every last detail, track physically distant production processes in real time, and, crucially, stipulate and monitor the quality of outputs. In effect, technical know-how was transmitted from home base to entities and workforces in other countries. As trade economist Richard Baldwin puts it, "High tech with low wages beats low tech with low wages."[13]

Over time, this offshoring, as it became known, became more and more ambitious. A lead business might choose to do only design and some global marketing back at base, and even some of that could shift as emerging-market-economy workforces tooled up. The main host countries were initially relatively few and often physically close to the North American, European, or Japanese domicile of the offshoring multinationals (e.g., Mexico or Poland), but not always (notably China).

Then services companies started moving back-office processes to places like Slovakia (a member of the European Union) and Bangalore in India. And as hosts' workforces became more skilled, more central functions shifted too—for example, the credit analysis conducted by banks. It was like moving operations from expensive cities to cheaper provinces, but across national borders.

Measured by location, rich countries' share in global manufacturing output dropped sharply. But much of the return from geographical dispersion accrued to multinationals' shareholders and top management (but not always the corresponding tax authorities). Meanwhile, wages rose in host countries, but came under pressure among those North American and European communities

---

12. Krugman, "Globalization."
13. Baldwin, *Great Convergence*, p. 149.

whose relatively unskilled jobs could now be done more cheaply elsewhere. Oversimplifying, interstate inequality narrowed while, in some advanced economies, intrastate inequality increased.[14] When domestic politics became toxic in rich states, especially the United States, the explanations implicated trade, technology, and immigration (which, in economic terms, moves low-cost labor to capital rather than vice versa).

## Capital and Globalization

Where there is trade, there is financing. Where there is cross-border investment, there is a capital flow (known as foreign direct investment). Here too there are similarities and differences between the first and second globalizations.

Just as the first economic globalization ended with a bubble bursting during the interwar years, so the 2007/8 implosion of Western banking might mark a switching point in world history. Hot money's pathologies are, sadly, familiar. Similarly, just as sterling's role in world finance underpinned the Pax Britannica (and vice versa), so the dollar and the Pax Americana. An extraordinary proportion of world trade is invoiced in dollars (even when neither importer nor exporter is US based).[15] And foreign sovereigns and companies from all over borrow in dollar capital markets, as they once did in pounds.

But there are big differences too. First, derivative markets—in currencies, interest rates, default risk, and equities—have separated cross-border flows of funds from flows of risk, complicating voluntary sovereign-debt workouts. Second, after accumulating vast sovereign wealth funds, some states have acquired great influence in global capital allocation. They include energy exporters (Saudi Arabia, other Gulf states, and Russia), those East Asian states that built defensive war chests after their late-1990s crises, and China. Taken with some powers' state-owned enterprises, state-capitalist actors on this scale have not been seen since Europe's merchant companies traded and intervened around the planet half a millennium ago. Third, today's infrastructure for cross-border financial transactions creates vulnerabilities that not only preoccupy central bankers but, in a cyber world, can be weaponized.[16] As we progress through that list, existing fora such as the Group of 20 (G20), whose members include Russia, seem built for a happier age.

14. For a review and defense of economic globalization, see Kolb, "What Is Globalization?"
15. Gopinath, "International Price System."
16. Farrell and Newman, "Weaponized Interdependence."

## Institutions and Globalization: Rule by International Organizations?

The first globalization emerged against a background of norms, mainly rooted in customary law, providing rules of the road for trade, monetary affairs, diplomacy, and war. Many were refined during the nineteenth century, which grafted onto this proto-international system various technical conventions to oil the wheels of commerce (chapter 2). There were, however, few international organizations to speak of. By contrast, the second globalization has been presided over by a rash of powerful international organizations. Perhaps best known are the World Trade Organization (WTO), the IMF, the World Bank, and, since COVID, the World Health Organization (WHO).

There is no body for international investment or the environment, but they are not ungoverned. The geographic dispersion of production described above has been underpinned by regional trade agreements constraining "behind-the-border" regulatory policies,[17] and by bilateral pacts protecting cross-border investors against local discrimination.[18] Environmental measures have been promoted by a mixture of hard and soft law, with varying success.

Away from specific regimes, the plethora of judicial and arbitral tribunals, from the International Court of Justice downward, mostly have only voluntary jurisdiction. Nevertheless, human rights and other conventions aim to diffuse universal norms. All told, these various features of the second globalization have delighted many internationalists while horrifying its opponents.

## Globalization's Challenges: The Commons, Geopolitics, Legitimacy

The edifice faces three major problems. The first is what to do about shared threats, requiring deep but so far elusive international cooperation. During the first globalization, industrial production was limited to only a few parts of the world, and pollution seemed local. With the second, pollution itself went global, climate change becoming the existential poster child for the global commons.

---

17. Competition policy, state aid and subsidies, public-procurement processes, intellectual property rights, and so on. See Baldwin, *Great Convergence*, table 5, pp. 106–7.

18. Running at around 150 per year from the mid-1990s to the mid-2000s, they total around 3,000. See Bonnitcha et al., *Political Economy*, fig. 1.1, p. 2; fig. 1.5, p. 20; fig. 1.7, p. 25.

But it is not the only one. With more people traveling to more places than ever before, in 2020 the second globalization faced a pandemic, the first since 1918, at the tail end of the first globalization. The WHO could barely coordinate, let alone lead. The most powerful capitals on the planet hurled accusations at each other.

The second problem is precisely that dislocation in international politics rendered by the rise of new economic powers and already, in China, an economic and (almost) military superpower. Cooperation is partly about managing (resolving or side-stepping) disagreement, containing the risk of its spiraling into hostile conflict. This disagreement-conflict distinction will recur.

It shapes the third problem: legitimacy. In liberal states, there have been long-standing complaints that globalization has gone too far (mainly on the economic side), and not far enough (the environment, human rights, poverty). Now there are pressing questions about whether the current constellation of international regimes and organizations is in China's sights; whether it permitted China's rise as an illiberal power; and, more elementally, whether there are any reasonable terms on which peaceful coexistence can be secured.

The international world needs to adapt, but we, people living in constitutional democracies, need to take care if we are to remain who we have managed to become. The book will land on prescriptions for the main international economic regimes and organizations (covering currencies, trade, investment, and finance), but by examining the conditions under which international cooperation is feasible and, for us, decent. First we need some scene setting on geopolitics, international relations, and legitimacy.

## Geopolitics: From World War II's Grand Bargain to the Thucydides Trap?

In the grand sweep of history, the postwar international economic order can be viewed as predicated on two grand bargains. First was the bargain between, on the one hand, the United States and, on the other hand, Western Europe and the free states of East Asia. The dollar succeeded sterling as the world's reserve currency, and the European and East Asian powers abandoned their colonial projects—delivering world leadership to Washington, DC. In exchange, Europe and East Asia essentially outsourced their defense, and thus their external stability, to the United States, via NATO in the West and bilateral treaties in the East. The second de facto bargain, cemented during the 1970s, was between Washington and Middle Eastern oil producers. The marginal supply of oil, coming from Saudi Arabia, was to be invoiced and traded in dollars, and in exchange the new world hegemon armed its rulers and acquiesced in their continuing accommodation (dating back, with bumps, to the eighteenth century) with local Wahhabi religious authorities. These were all fateful choices.[19]

While reality is hugely more complex, that stylized account captures the vital truth that, baldly, the baton of leadership passed between allies who, despite family differences and aggravations, drew on shared histories and cultures. For nearly three-quarters of a century, Europeans have been able to pursue their affairs while taking the global order as a given, allowing local preferences for leisure and the good life to be expressed as never before.

Now that settled world might be changing, with the remarkable growth during the 1990s and 2000s of emerging-market economies that are, by now, rather more than emerging. Even though their per capita income levels remain well below those of Western and East Asian democracies, China and India are already big parts of global output and trade, and officials from countries as widely dispersed as Brazil and Mexico, Indonesia and South Korea, and Saudi Arabia sit at the G20 table.

### China and the West: Like Germany versus Britain around the Turn of the Twentieth Century?

Over recent years, many have compared the current geopolitical predicament to that prevailing between Britain and Germany before World War I. The general idea is that it is hard to avoid conflict, even war, between a rising state and the established power: a thought going back to Thucydides's account of the Peloponnesian War between Sparta and Athens in the fifth century BCE.[20] Because the rising state cannot credibly commit not to turn the tables if and when it becomes preeminent (a problem known to economists as moral

---

19. Major Saudi oil fields, discovered in 1938, were licensed to a US operator and became larger than the Persian and other fields initially under British control-cum-influence. Washington's acquiescing in religious fundamentalism might have reflected a Cold War wish to distinguish itself from Soviet atheism.

20. "What made war inevitable was the growth of Athenian power and the fear which this caused in Sparta" (Thucydides, *History*, I.23, p. 49). In fact, much of his account concerns contingencies, including allies or friends drawing the powers into war. On World War I's contingencies, see Ferguson, *Pity of War*.

hazard: see chapters 6 and 7), the established power has incentives to preempt things while it can.

The ancient and modern analogies are not crazy. Germany's rise *did* disturb the prevailing balance of power. Its investment in Anatolian and Mesopotamian railways—the age's critical infrastructure for economic development—triggered anxieties in rival capitals not dissimilar to those prompted by China's Belt and Road Strategy (chapter 4). Just as today, those concerns were not only about commerce. All sides prized maintaining access to the Mesopotamian and Gulf oil fields and ports, and they were variously concerned about whether the crumbling but still massive Ottoman Empire was becoming Berlin's pupil or finally falling apart.[21] With Germany increasing its military assistance to the Porte, Moscow had geopolitical reasons to fret about the crucial Bosphorus and Dardanelles, as well as its role in Persia, and wanted its Entente partners (London and Paris) to apply financial sanctions or take more aggressive measures. Anyone making a case for imperial Germany being modernity's instructive rising state for contemporary geopolitics could, perhaps, point to the support given by the People's Republic of China (PRC) to Iran (and others) today.

But while instructive, the parallels are not complete. In the first place, quite unlike both the ancient and modern comparators, there is not (yet) in the wings some still greater power that might intervene to swing the outcome between Washington and Beijing (as Persia eventually did against Athens, and the United States did against the Second Reich's western front).

Second, at the turn of the twentieth century, there was more than one rising power, and multiple established powers. Fearing Russia's rise and intentions, Germany accelerated its military buildup, amplifying London's concerns about Berlin.[22] But Britain was sometimes more preoccupied by Russia's "awesome expansion of . . . economic power and military strength." Reciprocating, Moscow was frustrated about the naval support Britain was providing to the Porte. Paris, meanwhile, concerned that Moscow would outgrow their alliance against Germany, oiled its appeal with gigantic loans for railways that enabled Russia to mobilize troops toward the west. In consequence, while the Entente powers did, as classical International Relations theory posits, effectively rebalance against Germany, trust among them was low, scrambling whatever signals

---

21. Drawing on C. Clark, *Sleepwalkers*, pp. 334–49. The Ottomans disastrously sided with Germany in World War I.

22. Myerson, "Game Theory."

their various confidential pacts were intended to deliver to Berlin.[23] Today things are simpler, with only two full-purpose superpowers; India might eventually join them. Russia is a major actor below power's all-purpose summit. While pointedly reminding the Obama administration it was already in Asia, only a few years later Moscow needed (at least) tacit acceptance from Beijing when it invaded Ukraine (chapters 3 and 10).

A third reason for being wary of modern Thucydides Trap comparisons is the mutualized threat provided by nuclear weapons. Nothing like that has prevailed before: when the Roman Republic totally destroyed Carthage, there was hardly a question of reciprocal annihilation. The constraint of mutual destruction applied through the recent Cold War but, as already noted, economic globalization means the PRC currently touches the West in immeasurably more ways than the Soviets ever did, giving both sides myriad opportunities to harm each other in ways that, as yet, would not trespass the legal boundaries of war (part I).

Finally, nearly all the instances typically cited as examples of the Thucydides Trap were fairly brief—half a century or so[24]—and very much about raw power, or its commercial cousin, rather than ideology. By contrast, the contest between China and the West is likely to go on for much longer, a century or more, and is partly about how peoples and communities should live and govern themselves.

### France and Britain's Long-Eighteenth-Century Struggle: A Strategic and Ideological Contest

For that reason, an instructive parallel is Britain and France over the long eighteenth century.[25] The tensions between them persisted from immediately after Britain's 1688 constitutional transformation through to the end of the Napoleonic Wars in 1815, with persistent aftershocks. Three features of their struggle resonate today.

First, it was partly about ideology and culture. The British resisted successive variants of universalism: at the outset, the universal absolutist monarchy sought by Louis XIV; at the end, the political and social revolution declared

---

23. C. Clark, *Sleepwalkers*, pp. 324, 333, 349, 351–52, 557. On capital flows, technology, and prerevolutionary Russia's rise, see O'Rourke, "Economic History."

24. Allison, *Destined for War.*

25. Pincus, *1688*, chap. 11; Simms, *Britain's Europe*, chaps. 2–5.

in the name of universal rights but prosecuted through terror at home and proselytizing war abroad. When, at the end of the seventeenth century, the newly liberated English (in multiconfessional alliance with the very Catholic Holy Roman Empire, as well as the Protestant Dutch) went to war with France, they feared a Europe "submitted to the French yoke."[26] When, a century later, Edmund Burke, having taken the American side in their war of independence, warned of the French Revolution's dangers, it was because it ushered in the wrong kind of power (chapter 9).[27] Similarly, some in the West conceive of their current strategic competition as being, ultimately, between the universalism of the authoritarian Chinese Communist Party and the pluralism inscribed into the constitutionalism of the West, while Beijing might see the proselytizing universalist shoe on the other foot. This first parallel is, then, about legitimation principles: the kind of world we shall live in.

Second, the French-British struggle was also a contest for markets and market dominance.[28] Britons feared that universal monarchy would herald captive markets for France, not dissimilar to the sentiment that had driven Britain's pursuit of overseas territories but closer to home.[29] This is what the Scottish British Enlightenment philosopher David Hume, writing during the mid-eighteenth-century Seven Years' War, disapprovingly called the "jealousy of trade."[30] Reason-of-state strategic thinking about national interests absorbed the economic realm: the glory of a state could be commercial as well as martial, and so it was worth fighting for.

Linking those first and second issues, contemporaries fretted over whether the structures of domestic power would affect the contestants' relative capabilities. In particular, Hume and others worried that, in accumulating debt to finance war, absolutist France would have more degrees of freedom than republican (mixed-government) Britain, since London was constrained by its need to respect the interests and property rights of its citizens in order to preserve its system of government: "Either the nation must destroy public credit, or public credit will destroy the nation."[31] This is uncannily similar to

26. Pincus, *1688*, p. 354, quoting Whig pamphleteer Robert Molesworth.

27. Armitage, "Edmund Burke."

28. Hont, *Jealousy of Trade*, pp. 23–24.

29. Hont, *Jealousy of Trade*, p. 59.

30. Hume, "Jealousy of Trade," in *Political Essays*.

31. Hume, "Of Public Credit," in *Political Essays*, p. 174. Hume worried absolutist France could survive reneging on its debt by simply putting down any insurrection: see Hont, *Jealousy of Trade*, p. 86. Over the course of the struggle, Britain's public debt rose from zero to around

the parade of modern public intellectuals, Asian and Western, proclaiming or fretting that the PRC's absolutism will give it a clear edge in policy agility, ambition, and execution.

Third, because Britain's and France's commercial ambitions had taken them almost everywhere, the underlying contest could be waged everywhere. And so it was: not only in every corner of Europe, but in North America and the West Indies, the Levant, North Africa, coastal India, and the East Indies. Similarly, the United States and China confront each other across the world. Surely that will continue, in every imaginable way, in every conceivable field: in trade, finance, cyber, technology, education, propaganda, polar exploration, outer space, and arenas hardly yet conceived. Today's extraordinary connectivity is a vulnerability once states (and rogue actors) turn against each other, as is belatedly recognized.[32]

For precisely these reasons, accommodations and alliances (formal and informal) with third-party states will be vital today. But if the French-British contest is anything to go by, they will also be shifting. Whereas Britain was initially, as noted, allied with Habsburg Austria and the (then) minor Prussian state, during the middle of the eighteenth century the Austrian house moved to side with France, only to find its thousand-year-old Germanic Empire abolished a few decades later by Napoleon, who at the denouement could, in turn, be defeated only by the combined forces of Britain and a now mighty Prussia ("Give me night or give me Blucher," Wellington implores the heavens in, for Brits, the 1970s movie's central scene). On a long view, think India, Indonesia, and Brazil, as well as, conceivably, a rearmed Europe or Japan.

### Four Scenarios

Summing up, a problem with the Thucydidean picture of the US-PRC predicament is that it too easily beckons assumptions that it is all about power, and one way or another it will be all over quite soon. Maybe. But I want to suggest this latest geopolitical standoff is just as likely to be going on long after China is ensconced as a great power. For Britain and France, facing each other at the dawn of commercial society three centuries ago, the eighteenth century was

---

twice GDP but it did not default. Its prevailing against France, despite a smaller population, is sometimes attributed to innovations in public finance. See Slater, *National Debt*, fig. 4, p. 46, and chap. 4.

32. Leonard, *Age of Unpeace*, chap. 4.

punctuated by efforts to separate economic competition from existential struggle, only for jealousies of trade to regain traction before the revolutionary denouement.[33] Relations began to regularize only as the nineteenth century progressed (chapter 2), with plenty of later betrayals (London's conduct during Suez), fractures (General de Gaulle twice vetoing Britain's admission to the European Union), and misapprehensions.

Since predictions are foolhardy, this book offers four scenarios: *Lingering Status Quo*; *Superpower Struggle* (that most resembling Britain and France's eighteenth-century contest); *New Cold War* (retreat to autarkic blocs); and *Reshaped World Order* (with a new top table reconfiguring international regimes and organizations). This leaves space for Washington and Beijing to emulate their eighteenth-century predecessors by occasionally trying to put boundaries around their contest, for other powers to rise, and for Europe or Japan to reassert themselves as hard powers.

## "International Relations" on International Relations

Naturally, all this is crawled over by policymakers, commentators, and academics, especially in the discipline of International Relations.[34]

For some of the latter, globalization heralded not merely mundane economic integration but a deep transformation of political life. With the state itself set to be eclipsed by processes marginalizing the familiar realms of diplomacy, treaty-making, and intergovernmental cooperation, we were on the threshold of global governance. This was to be the *real* New World Order delivered by the end of the Cold War—presided over by transnational networks of, in the main, unelected technocrats.[35] As description-cum-prediction, it proved mixed, truer in some fields than others. As normative project, however, it hardly lacked ambition: "Sovereignty itself could be disaggregated, that is attached to . . . courts, regulatory agencies, legislators or legislative committees. . . . The core characteristic . . . would shift from [states'] autonomy from outside interference to the capacity to participate in trans-governmental networks."[36] Others maintained it was delusional to fancy that the basics of

33. Shovlin, *Trading with the Enemy*, disinters the attempted compromises.

34. Capitals used for the academic discipline.

35. "New world order" was a phrase of President George H. W. Bush's, with a later intellectual manifesto in Slaughter, *New World Order* (elaborating a 1997 *Foreign Affairs* piece).

36. Slaughter, *New World Order*, p. 34.

interstate relations had changed. But that did not deter a veritable avalanche of visions and programs, in varying degrees of Olympian ambition or granular prescription. Just three very different normative agendas will serve as illustrations.

The first aims for a holistic global constitutional order.[37] Juridically, it might be hierarchical, culminating in a new world court with mandatory universal jurisdiction across all states and fields. Gone would be the currently unresolvable conflicts between different regimes (trade, sovereign default, the environment, human rights, war and peace, and so on). Gone would be the limited jurisdiction of the existing international courts over international organizations (the World Bank, UN peacekeepers, and humanitarian aid teams). This would be the realm of law: rights trump choice, judges trump politics.

A second vision—libertarian internationalism—also looks to international law but to entrench an international economy that is free and open, thereby constraining the nationalist or welfare-statist urges of populist or democratic states. With ideational roots in mid-nineteenth-century classical liberalism and its early engine room in Geneva's post–World War II community of trade officials and intellectuals, the goal is an international libertarian order buttressed by heavily constrained global institutions. Any international organizations would have minimal agency, impeding bureaucratic activism.[38]

A third vision—the restoration of sovereignty—embraces the second's technocratic parsimony while jettisoning the rest. Since, on this view, international agreements unavoidably qualify states' sovereignty, especially when delegating to international organizations or courts, they are presumptively a bad thing (chapter 11). Paradoxically but unacceptably, they jeopardize the very authority on which they depend, and that must stop.[39]

The headlines—global constitutionalism, libertarianism, unalloyed sovereignty—are less interesting than the background values. The first would rely on values and norms being shared across the globe, implying cosmopolitan commitments to all humans (of equal concern), with the rights of the individual paramount, trumping those of the territorial state. By contrast, the second—libertarian economic constitutionalism—can dispense with

---

37. Essays in Dunoff and Trachtman, *Ruling the World?*, especially the survey chapter, Dunoff and Trachtman, "Functional Approach."

38. Sully, *Classical Liberalism*. For a critical history, see Slobodian, *Globalists*.

39. Rabkin, *Law without Nations?*

convergence of deep values in the interest of promoting efficiency via a freedom to choose that is constrained only insofar as it infringes on others' choices; a globalized regime of negative liberty. Cooperative institutions would exist not as the instantiation of global justice but rather as a means for individuals and businesses to pursue their rational self-interest subject to agreed limits.[40] Nevertheless, libertarian constitutionalism would most likely be expected to drive convergence in states' economic structures, including freedom to trade and protections from discriminatory (municipal) state laws. In sharp contrast, the third—sovereignty restored in substance, not merely legal form—has the flavor of aiming for no more than peaceful coexistence among states.

If you are thinking all this is slightly loopy, I agree (and varnished all three for that effect). But lying in the background is something genuinely important: different explanations of what international relations are about.

### *The Power of Old Ideas: Hobbesian, Lockean-Grotian, and Kantian Theories*

Is what *really* matters power, material capabilities, and war and peace, as insisted by "International Relations realists"?[41] Or is it interdependence, cooperation, and hence international regimes and organizations, as maintained by liberal international institutionalists of various stripes? Or is it values, norms, and hence, at root, ideas and identities, as claimed by constructivist social theorists?[42] The debate is spirited, and long standing, as nicely captured on the eve of World War II by the classical realist E. H. Carr: "Utopians . . . think in terms of ethics, and realists . . . in terms of power."[43]

Today's three schools—they are nothing less—often seem to pledge allegiance to venerable traditions of European thought embodied in the work of,

40. Some temper this vision with commitments to human rights: e.g., Petersmann, "Justice in International Economic Law?" Left-progressives think they spy a Trojan horse: see Alston, "Resisting the Merger."

41. In scare quotes because I draw on, and try to develop, a different political realist tradition.

42. The contemporary US set texts are, respectively, Waltz, *Theory of International Politics*; Keohane, *After Hegemony*; and Wendt, *Social Theory*.

43. Carr, *Twenty Years Crisis*, p. 161. But given Carr's appeasement (largely scrubbed from the 1945 second edition) and later affection for Stalinism, we might question the quality of his "realism." The barbed contest has been revived by Russia's invasion of Ukraine: see Tooze, "John Mearsheimer."

in turn, Thomas Hobbes (1588–1679, a translator of Thucydides), John Locke (1632–1704), and Immanuel Kant (1724–1804) and their followers.[44] As such, the lives of states and their peoples in the international arena are destined to be, variously, inalienably nasty and brutish (if not always short); amenable to rational, self-interested cooperation; and capable of pacification through public reason.

Among many strange things about this, one stands out: which among power, rational calculation, and values one wants to emphasize depends (surely?) on what question in international relations or policy one is trying to address. Unsurprisingly, realists talk mostly about war and peace; internationalist liberals mainly about the regimes for trade, the environment, and other technical collective-action problems; and constructivists about human rights, the role of international law in promoting convergence in norms and values, and so on. In terms that will, when developed in part II, do a lot of work in this book, these positions could be associated with, respectively, Order, System, and Society.

But if, as here, one is interested in how globalization has affected geopolitics and the legitimacy of international regimes and organizations, we need to attend to the whole: to power and conflict, selfish interests, rational calculation, norms and values, and so to each of material capabilities, policy regimes, international law, and opinion. In taking that on, the book will draw on part of our intellectual heritage that is relatively neglected in political theory: the writings of Kant's contemporary David Hume (1711–76), whom we have encountered already. Unlike his peers, Hume did not allocate politics and economics, or ethics and politics, to separate spheres. He can help us think about coordination and cooperation problems, in remarkably modern game-theoretic terms, in ways that are not detached from questions of political authority.

Indeed, this book is partly an effort to help recover a lost opportunity in International Relations. It does so by marrying Hume to the twentieth-century

---

44. See Wight, "Anatomy of International Thought," in *International Relations*; and Bull, *Anarchical Society*, pp. 23–26. This is not nostalgia. Whereas science's relationship with its own history does not entail studying Isaac Newton's or Albert Einstein's papers to become a physicist, International Relations scholarship and international political theory do not have an account of their own earlier errors and progress, leaving them, like other humanistic disciplines, forever in dialogue with their past. See the title essay in Williams, *Philosophy as a Humanistic Discipline*.

philosopher Bernard Williams (1929–2003) who, after a career spent upending various parts of ethical theory, turned tantalizingly in his final years to political philosophy, espousing a kind of realism. It is a realism that studiously avoids erecting political theory on a foundational morality system, but without, importantly, ejecting moral considerations.[45] And a central message it takes from Thucydides, of whom both Hume and Williams were big fans, is not the inevitability of this or that, or of might beating right, but rather the dangers of wishful thinking.[46]

## The State and International "Anarchy"

A central realist tenet is that states remain elemental to international politics. Those who expected or wished for their disappearance have, for the moment, been derailed by Beijing's assertion of state power. But there is more to it than that. We live in a world where local order and stability (where they prevail) are maintained mainly by states, with their formal and de facto monopoly over coercive power in a defined territory.

Many International Relations realists draw from this the inference that, without world government—leaving a state of "anarchy," as some like to call it—international cooperation is a sham, or problematic, and probably both. But that argument is at best incomplete. The absence of a higher power does not *of itself* prevent states—even enemies—from entering bargains and agreements among themselves to avoid the heavy costs of war, secure some public goods, and mitigate certain other shared problems.[47] The point, rather, is that many such bargains are unlikely to hold, and, grasping that, leaders and peoples act (or don't) accordingly. Deep down, the central problem of cooperation among any set of wholly autonomous actors is what to do about

45. See the essays in Williams, *In the Beginning*. For those unfamiliar with Williams, among many other things he articulated a devastating critique of Utilitarianism as a normative creed (which goes well beyond giving weight to usefulness) and aimed to dismantle Kantian deontological morality systems. He served on various British public policy commissions, just as Hume was an aide to senior British diplomats and military commanders, and for a while an undersecretary in what today is the Foreign Office.

46. Geuss, "Thucydides, Nietzsche, and Williams." Less romantic than Nietzsche about the ancient historian, Williams observes, "The psychology he deploys in his explanations is not at the service of his ethical beliefs" (*Shame and Necessity*, p. 161). (Thucydides is, though, partly trying to prop up the reputation of Athens's early leader, Pericles, who had been lost to plague.)

47. Precisely registered in Fearon, "Rationalist Explanations for War."

dissembling, lying, and broken promises. These are problems of accuracy and sincerity, which, as Williams brilliantly set out, are twin facets of truthfulness.[48]

Seen thus, part of the puzzle of international cooperation becomes why truthfulness is especially challenging among states. After all, it is a problem faced and sometimes overcome in other nonhierarchical contexts, including for example among merchants transacting at great distances in the medieval world without a state's oversight and enforcement.[49] In the international case, is the underlying problem the scale of the international community (it's not so big), or is it something to do with the nature of the actors (states)? I am going to argue that it is partly the latter: that needing to maintain their home monopoly over legitimate coercive power, they can face incredibly tough trade-offs when bargaining and cooperating with each other.

## Legitimacy: History and Civilizations

Preserving order is the First Political Question, as Williams put it, because answering it can liberate us from fear, a precondition for widespread cooperation in large, complex societies. But it does not follow that any old order will do. To avoid resistance and spur participation, an order needs to be accepted, in some sense, by a state's citizen-subjects.[50] As exhibited at the chapter head, legitimacy marks the dividing line between political relations and the quite different situation of tyranny or excessively coercive domination (chapter 12).

While not condemning states and peoples to an inevitably fragile international anarchy (although I shall have to argue for that), the vital role of the domestic state does have important implications for international cooperation. When a state pools or delegates power and authority in an international regime or organization, it is vitally important that its legitimacy at home is not undermined. An international system's legitimacy has two dimensions: among states, and between individual states and their peoples. In both, institutions and policy regimes will need to be resilient to adverse shocks—and not aim for more than can be resilient—if an order or system is to avoid unraveling under pressure.[51] Resilience and legitimacy will be running themes.

48. Williams, *Truth and Truthfulness*, especially chap. 5 on sincerity.
49. Milgrom et al., "Role of Institutions."
50. I use "citizen-subjects" when the discussion is not confined to (broadly) liberal states, and "citizens" when it is.
51. Brunnermeier, *Resilient Society*.

## History and Vindicatory Genealogies

The book also takes history to matter to its central questions because our deep political values, meaning the values embedded in *our* core political institutions, are partly a product of the problems we have faced and the opportunities we have reached for. Those values, and hence our history, including how we make sense of it, shape the resources we have to navigate new challenges and opportunities.

Although not cashed out with Williams's habitual élan, that kind of thinking is found in a fourth approach to international relations—known as the English School, mainly signifying its typical absence from US campuses. Their patron saint has been the seventeenth-century Dutch lawyer and diplomat—and "miracle of Holland," as France's Henri IV once described him—Hugo de Groot (Grotius, 1583–1645), who was taken to combine pragmatism with moral rationalism, connecting him with Locke (chapter 2).[52]

As well as introducing useful distinctions between international order, system, and society that will be developed here, Hedley Bull and other English School writers, notably Ian Clark, draw heavily on history in accounts of the norms and institutions that (might) both constitute and hold together any international society. Consistent with that, Bull avoids calling on a universal morality that stipulates categorical imperatives for states and peoples, but at the cost of being criticized, with other Grotians, for not providing solid foundations that securely foreclose relativism. Hume and Williams offer a way of escaping from both Hobbesians and Kantians, and of prioritizing history and locality, without being cornered into moral skepticism or left hanging in the air. Both prudence and morals matter, but the search for ultimate foundations—for a grounding in some version of the morality system—goes away. What the English School has needed is a Scotsman.[53]

There is more going on here, however, than histories of how we happen to have gotten to where we happen to be, whether that be a balance of power or elements of customary law. Some stylized histories are about how conventions, norms, and practices become internalized. Pace Friedrich Nietzsche,

52. The set text is Bull, *Anarchical Society*. On connections between Grotius and Locke, see Tuck, *Rights of War*, pp. 170–75.

53. On criticisms of Bull's ungrounded Grotianism, see Harris, "Order and Justice." (Incidentally, the English School is not exclusively English; Bull himself was born and initially educated in Australia.) On the three traditions, see Doyle and Carlson, "Silence of the Laws?"

such genealogies need not inevitably undermine our institutions: sometimes they can be, as Williams emphasized, vindicatory. In his hands, truthfulness first evolves as a socially useful practice but becomes internalized as something intrinsically valuable, enhancing its utility precisely because people are not consciously motivated by its functionality: the origins story drops out of sight.[54] A similar kind of story was told by Hume for promising, but with an important rider for promises between states (chapter 5).

## Legitimacy and Civilizational Competition

Despite its apparent high abstraction, that emphasis on the genealogy of institutions and norms highlights a deep fracture in the current environment. Institutionalized norms that evolved locally are not always shared across great distances—where distance might be civilizational as well as geographic. Whatever the merits of my eighteenth-century France-Britain analogue with the West and the PRC today, those earlier protagonists did not face a civilizational airgap: Europe's (and North America's) classically educated politicians and diplomats were familiar with Greek, Roman, and biblical texts; to a lesser extent with the premodern scholastic and humanist writers; and with each other.[55] All of which made things easier after 1815, but harder with the Porte. Today, a crunch issue facing the West somewhere down the road—certainly under the *Reshaped World Order* scenario—is where, in order to preserve ways of life, lines should be drawn in reforming international institutions. As Williams put the general point, "Historical understanding . . . can help with the business . . . of distinguishing between different ways in which various of our ideas and procedures can seem to be such that we cannot get beyond them, that there is no conceivable alternative."[56]

That could hardly matter more given a geopolitical conjuncture in which we meet rising states and superpowers with quite different histories, embedded values, and institutions; in other words, states, with different civilizational histories, that were less designers than recipients of the current international

54. Craig, "Genealogies"; Queloz, "Williams's Pragmatic Genealogy." Hume did something similar, on a grander scale, in his six-volume history of Britain's political institutions: see Sabl, *Hume's Politics*.

55. Adam Smith visited France during the Seven Years' War, meeting Voltaire. Hume and Jean-Jacques Rousseau knew each other, and fell out.

56. From the title essay of Williams, *Philosophy as a Humanistic Discipline*, p. 191.

order and system.[57] No trivial matter, this is apparent in tensions over human rights norms, regimes, and conduct.

If the West has, since World War II, been rediscovering those parts of its roots associated with ideas of an essential shared humanity and of universally binding "natural" or higher law (chapters 2 and 3), some rising powers, notably the PRC, remain attached to the international legal doctrines prevailing during the first globalization, when East Asian states joined "international society." That was an international law for coexistence among sovereign states entitled to territorial integrity, and to noninterference, without qualification. This matters hugely to our story because if individuals are taken to have inalienable rights, then states and their rulers no longer enjoy inviolable sovereignty (chapter 11).

Bringing things together, globalization's costs have become salient just as societies face dislocation from technological change, war, and mass migrations, and as international institutions are challenged by civilizational geopolitics. Great uncertainty about the future combines with legitimacy strains at home and abroad.[58]

## Economics versus Political Theory?

Before continuing, it is worth asking whether the book is careering headlong into a fundamental clash between economics and political theory. It is true that economists (and political scientists), seeking to make sense of the world in terms of choices rationally made by individuals, businesses, and governments, would approach questions of institutional design through the lens of preferences (including yearnings for power and glory) and constraints. At a high level, this goes to a methodological feature of economics, which often proceeds by identifying a social welfare problem and working out how a benign social planner would cure the problem efficiently. All government functions are in the hands of the benign planner, subject only to whether delegation can help to overcome any problems in credibly committing to the socially optimal plan.

57. The great surviving and widely operating civilizational cultures might be taken to be Confucian-Chinese, Persian, Sanskrit, Arab-Islamic, and European. There is obviously overlap: India, for example, is a Sanskrit-Persian (and European?) fusion. Other civilizations—e.g., Tibetan-Buddhist, Chinggisid-Mongol—currently subsist on the margins of more dominant ones.

58. For similar themes, see King, *Grave New World*.

By contrast, the starting point for much political and constitutional theory is that the greatest threat to the people's well-being is arbitrary or oppressive government by an all-powerful unitary sovereign. The values of the rule of law and of constitutionalism, including notably the separation of powers, are directed at keeping those problems at bay. In summary, one discipline, economics, positing a benign sovereign, sets out to achieve a flourishing society in which well-being (on some measure) is maximized, while the other, political and constitutional theory, alert to the possibility of a malign sovereign, aims to avoid tyranny (or, in an international context, war and tyranny).

That would be a forlorn prospect. In fact, we are going to see that, despite being rather neglected even in game-theoretic International Relations, the modern economics of "mechanism design" has things to say—about conditions for rules being enforceable and so credible, about institutional equilibria, and hence about design—that will mesh in profoundly helpful ways with Williams's realist political theory. In some ways, Hume is the intellectual ancestor of both traditions, which lost track of each other during the nineteenth century.

## Structure of the Book

The book has five parts, ranging over history, political economy, geopolitics, political theory, and policy diagnosis and prescription. It has high and low roads. The former, traveled mainly via chapters 2, 5–8, and 11–14, develops and applies realist political theory and mechanism-design economics to international relations and cooperative regimes. Schematically, the argument builds a chain beginning with conventions that solve coordination problems and can sometimes help cooperation. Some of those conventions become social norms, some of which in turn are internalized as values, and some of those values stand up under critical reflection (normativity). This part of the argument will dissolve some distinctions between power, interests, and values.

The lower road, traveled mainly via chapters 3, 4, 9, 10, and 15–19, addresses current geopolitical tensions, the rise of geoeconomic strategy, vulnerabilities in the international economy, and legitimacy issues challenging international regimes and organizations. Obviously I believe the roads intersect in vital ways, even though those traversing them outside this book rarely look for each other.

Part I offers a stylized history of the evolution, design, and, lately, fracturing of the international sphere. It aims to convey, especially for nonspecialists and policymakers, the ways that practices and ideas around sovereignty, war and peace, the economy, and a lot more are intertwined. For example, during the first globalization, a state could, in the last resort, enforce a debt claim by going to war, but unprovoked interference with another state's commerce could be an illegal act of war. It is now the other way around. Another example is the rise, since World War II's crimes against humanity, of some human rights laws held to stand above all other concerns. Part I closes by summarizing current superpower tensions and introducing the Four Scenarios.

Part II is about the (Humean) conditions under which interstate cooperation can be feasible, and how organizations can sometimes help. Deploying ideas of organic versus designed institutions, and of self-enforcing versus dependent institutional equilibria, it builds a bridge from game-theoretic accounts of cooperative regimes to the English School framework of international order, system, and society (of various kinds). This helps resolve ambiguities in lamentations for a "rules-based international order" or "system."[59] Each chapter in part II leaves loose ends, with one, legitimacy, left hanging until part IV.

Part III turns to power, geopolitics, and civilizational difference. It looks at whether the norms underlying the post–World War II Order-System can be squared with values embedded in China's core institutions and the legacy of its old Tribute System of international relations. Fleshing out the Four Scenarios, it concludes that a robust geopolitical strategy will need to be sensitive to *our* core values given the ideological element in the contest-cum-struggle.

Part IV, after vainly searching for answers in the values and practices of sovereignty, turns to a realist account of political legitimacy, which takes seriously the need for high-level institutions to be self-enforcing and rejects a top-down morality-first approach but not morality.[60] The connection between self-enforcing equilibria and history-dependent legitimation principles is the book's analytical engine: a demand for *incentives-values compatibility*. Thus armed, it pivots, in chapter 13, to posing a first *international* political question. Then, beginning the descent from the high ground, principles are articulated

59. Even officials sometimes pause when asked what they mean by "system" or "order," and which rules are lamented.

60. On realist political theory, see Rossi and Sleat, "Realism." For important morality-led analyses of international cooperation that take institutions seriously and treat states as elemental actors, see Christiano, "Legitimacy of International Institutions," and Buchanan, "Institutional Legitimacy" and other writings.

for pooling and delegating power in international regimes and organizations: *Principles for Participation and Delegation* by constitutional democracies in international System.

Finally, after summarizing vulnerabilities and design flaws in the current international economy and how they affect the Four Scenarios, part V applies those principles to the international monetary order / the IMF, the trade system / the WTO, the investment order / bilateral investment treaties, and the international financial system / Basel. None escapes unscathed. The ubiquity of political judgment is stressed.

Before moving on, I should underline, because it might occasionally seem otherwise, especially in parts II and III, that I do not think the state is a monolithic, unitary rational actor. States are obviously made up of different branches of government, and many organizations within them, each subject to its own pressures, incentives, and pathologies, not least because they are led and operated by people.

# PART I

# History

## INTERNATIONAL ORDER, LAW, AND ORGANIZATIONS IN A EUROCENTRIC WORLD

There really is, as everyone to some extent divines, a natural justice and injustice that is binding on all men, even those who have no association or covenant with each other.

ARISTOTLE, *RHETORIC*, FOURTH CENTURY BCE

# 2

# A European Order

## FROM CHRISTENDOM TO THE LEAGUE

[Grotius] secularized the law of nature. He gave it added authority and dignity by making it an integral part of the exposition of a system of law which became essential to civilized life. By doing this he laid, more truly than any other writer before him, the foundations of international law.

HERSCH LAUTERPACHT, 1946[1]

AS FAR BACK as it is possible to go, people, goods, services, and capital have moved about geographically, traversing natural and political borders—peacefully, opportunistically, too often desperately, and sometimes aggressively.

In the modern era, this has meant mobility across the borders of sovereign states, whose emergence in Europe is typically tied to the 1648 Peace of Westphalia marking the formal end of the Thirty Years' War in the Germanic Empire and its neighbors. Starting there, this chapter and the next trace the arrival of modern international organizations through a history of power and ideas, of law and other institutions. The historical focus is Eurocentric, because a European and Euro–North American outlook shaped the mores and institutions of the international order and system that has prevailed since World War II.

We will see that as well as people, goods, services, and capital, the international movement of ideas, waste, and pathogens matters too, and that the idea of international relations as governed in some way by morality has ebbed and

---

1. Lauterpacht, "Grotian Tradition," p. 24. Re-secularized might be more accurate.

flowed over the centuries. The story will also bring out some of the often obscured connections between the economic sphere and, respectively, security, human rights, and environmental policy. And it will highlight both the demands of states to be left alone, as well as the claims of individuals and groups to be protected from tyranny and worse: tensions between pluralism and universalism.

This chapter's installment takes the story up to the twentieth century's tragic interwar years. Beginning with some history of power and ideas, it then traces the evolution of the interconnected practices and norms around war and peace, and international commerce and finance.[2]

## "Westphalian" States: Power (and Ideas)

The shift toward a world of sovereign states was neither sharp nor clean.[3] It was not suddenly inaugurated by the Westphalian negotiations and treaties, the earlier 1555 Peace of Augsburg (another junction in Europe's confessional wars) having already marked a significant erosion of a locally complex but continent-wide feudal hierarchy, rising to Holy Roman emperor and pope. Arguably, that had begun with the "freedom" of the northern Italian city-states in the twelfth century. And, earlier still, the emergence of towns and Cluny's international monastic network signified strains in feudalism's capacity to maintain order given developments in military technology and trade.[4]

Nor, second, did the path to independent statehood end with Westphalia; a multitude of princely estates and free cities accepted the authority of the Holy Roman Empire's juridical bodies until it was finally overthrown by Napoleon in 1806. As one leading historian puts it, within the empire itself, "the Peace . . . reaffirmed the rights, liberties, and privileges of the Imperial and territorial estates in all their medieval complexity. At the same time, some of the larger imperial territories pursued a rapid buildup of quintessentially modern state structures."[5] Even so, envoys of the queen of Sweden, who through

---

2. Thanks to Stephen Neff for comments on this and the next chapter.

3. Stollberg-Rilinger, *Holy Roman Empire*, chaps. 4–7, pp. 60–115; Osiander, "Sovereignty, International Relations"; I. Clark, *Legitimacy in International Society*, chap. 3.

4. Spruyt, *Sovereign State*.

5. Stollberg-Rilinger, *Holy Roman Empire*, p. 121. There were two Westphalian treaties— between the Empire and, respectively, France and Sweden—and the constitution-like material in them largely concerned the Empire's internal affairs. Even the more autonomous imperial territories remained part of its system. Meanwhile, some imperial electors were autonomous

conquest had become a prince of the Empire, were attending imperial councils within a decade of Westphalia.[6] Peculiar though it may seem, those details of that most complex edifice—famously skewered by Voltaire as neither holy, Roman, nor an empire—matter because they are part of the history of modern Europe's devotion to international relations via law and adjudicatory tribunals.

Three-quarters of a century later, the treaty of Utrecht (1713/14), closing the War of Spanish Succession, signaled a newly emerging antipathy among many European sovereign states toward continental hegemony (the Bourbons). Rather than dynastic legitimacy pure and simple, there is an element of compromise and reciprocity, with succession potentially a matter for mutual agreement when materially affecting the balance of power.[7] Whether or not each of the parties especially liked it, the agreed-on course had to look sustainable for all them: an equilibrium (part II), which was a necessary condition for what one author calls the "consensus about proceeding on the basis of consensus."[8]

In Utrecht's wake, the leading states moved to maintaining permanently resident ambassadors in each other's capitals, a practice initiated among Italian city-states a few centuries earlier. The common drivers were a desire for formal equality and avoiding dominance from without or within. Writing a little later, the period's leading international legal scholar—Prussian Swiss Emmerich de Vattel (1714–67), sometime adviser to Augustus of Saxony—described this ambassadorial institution as enabling "continual negotiations . . . for the maintenance of order and the preservation of liberty."[9]

However drawn out and complex the process, sovereign states had emerged in Europe and eventually spread, including much later through resistance to colonialism, to the rest of the world. Unsurprisingly, as the new order matured, the idea of the *sovereign state*—first expressly articulated by the sixteenth-century French political theorist Jean Bodin—became a structural

---

monarchs elsewhere (including Hannover being King George I of Great Britain and Ireland; Saxony, the king of Poland; and Brandenburg, the king of Prussia).

6. Stoye, *Europe Unfolding*, pp. 17–18.

7. Spain's European empire was broken up, with no question of the same person occupying the Spanish and French thrones: see I. Clark, *Legitimacy in International Society*, chap. 4.

8. I. Clark, *Legitimacy in International Society*, p. 83. On consensus as a precondition for legitimacy, see Kissinger, *World Restored* (and *World Order*, pp. 9–10).

9. Vattel, *Law of Nations*, III.iii.46, quoted in Tuck, *Rights of War and Peace*, pp. 193–94.

pillar of international law.[10] It included a commitment to noninterference in each other's affairs, and a conception of foreign policy and international relations as the sphere in which formally equal sovereign states interact with each other, bilaterally and sometimes multilaterally, in a host of ways, seeking peaceful coexistence but not much more. As Vattel put it, "A small republic is no less a sovereign state than the most powerful kingdom."[11]

Certainly, the "post-Westphalian" European world was not politically and juridically hierarchical in the manner of a national domestic state. It was a set of repeated, and so anticipated, engagements among states that were notionally equal under the canons of international law, but they were mostly unequal in pretty well every material dimension.

That became apparent when Europe succumbed to a struggle for supremacy among its now autonomous states, culminating in the cataclysmic Napoleonic Wars at the turn of the nineteenth century (decades-long pancontinental hostilities that somehow escape the label "world war"). The ensuing Congress of Vienna brought the next great shift, seeking to maintain order by giving some institutional structure to the balance of power. The Concert of Europe, as it became known, comprised the victorious powers—Britain, Habsburg Austria, Prussia, and Russia—together, significantly, with the defeated France after monarchy was restored. The balance of power was now more clearly a designed collective security system operating among the Great Powers (with capital letters).

Britain and France did not join the narrower, less liberal Holy Alliance (Russia, Prussia, and Habsburg Austria) seeking to maintain absolutist monarchy. Within the Concert, there were different levels of ambition, expressed partly in terms of legitimacy. Whereas Austria's Prince Metternich promoted a specific principle of legitimate domestic rule (hereditary monarchy), for Britain's Lord Castlereagh the collective scheme was merely a device for preserving European order.[12]

It succeeded in containing some eruptions—notably, Belgium's establishment and Greek uprisings against their Ottoman overlords. At other times, deeper forces emerged from the shadows. In 1840 the age's key protagonists seemed to cross a vital symbolic threshold to amity when, at the request of

10. Hinsley, *Sovereignty*.

11. Vattel, *Law of Nations*, Preliminaries, proposition 18, articulating formal equality during the 1750s.

12. Kissinger, *Diplomacy*, chap. 4.

French prime minister Adolphe Thiers, Britain returned Napoleon's body from St. Helena, to public joy in Paris. But in the very same year, France backed Mehmet Ali's Egyptian revolt against the Ottoman sultan, taking it close to war with Britain (and the other Powers). Two great liberals, John Stuart Mill and Alexis de Tocqueville, fell out over French belligerence, but hostilities were avoided—in what was described, by a Frenchman, as "the Waterloo of French diplomacy."[13]

Its power increasing, by midcentury Britain's Lord Palmerston was willing to go further than his predecessors (and some colleagues, notably Aberdeen), sometimes favoring intervention to promote constitutional liberties (think US Wilsonians and twenty-first-century neoconservatives).[14] But this was for weaker states, his broader policy still constrained by the balance of power, as evidenced in a message to Russia's Czar Nicholas I (during early 1840s concerns about France):[15]

> One of the general principles which her majesty's government wish to observe as a guide for their conduct in dealing with the relations between England [sic] and other States, is, that changes which foreign nations may chuse to make to their internal Constitution and form of Government, are to be looked upon as matters with which England has no business to interfere by force of arms.

That left open interfering in others' domestic politics by nonmilitary means, a policy countenanced by the prevailing norms of international law. We pick up the story below, but it is already clear that the Concert more than genuflected in the direction of (selective) multilateralism. Embracing diplomacy, the 1815 treaty had provided for the Powers to "renew their meeting at fixed periods for consulting on their common interests [of] prosperity . . . and the maintenance of peace in Europe."[16] The resulting interstate relations could be orderly or disorderly; rules based or not; and informed by some sense of shared values and substantive norms or, alternatively, solely by interests—the first leg of each of those three pairs corresponding, with escalating demands,

13. Tombs and Tombs, *That Sweet Enemy*, pp. 335–37; Clinton, "Tocqueville." (Thiers was replaced by Francois Guizot, historian and sometime-liberal statesman.)

14. Kissinger, *World Order*, pp. 27, 30; D. Hurd and Young, "Aberdeen and Palmerston," in *Choose Your Weapons*, pp. 69–116.

15. Kissinger, *Diplomacy*, p. 96.

16. Quadruple Alliance Treaty, Article VI.

to ideas of international order, international system, and international society (chapter 7).

## "Anarchy" in Succession to a Post-Roman Christendom

All that—whatever its variations: Westphalia, Utrecht, Vienna, and so on—is known to academics as "anarchy," in some ways a silly turn of phrase given normal usage.[17] Jargon aside, however, the absence of an ultimate authority in modern international affairs plainly matters. In the sense of seventeenth-century political theorist Thomas Hobbes, there is no empowered and legitimate sovereign who maintains order, can command obedience, and so is capable of having the final word on any dispute. In other words, there is no world government.[18]

In this sense, the Westphalian moment *did* alter Europe somewhat. Prior to the fifteenth-century humanist Renaissance and the sixteenth-century confessional Reformation, Europe—conceived as Christendom—was held together by a complex hierarchy of authority operating partly via a continent-wide legal order. While leaving space for local variation, it embodied a higher-level set of transnational norms—meaning norms prevailing, or intended to prevail, within communities as well as between them. They drew on the eleventh- and twelfth-century rediscovery of the legal *Digests* assembled under the late-Roman emperor Justinian (a civilizing moment, celebrated in David Hume's *History* for helping escape feudalism) and the twelfth- and thirteenth-century discursive compilation of canon law (Gratian's *Decretals*), used to extend the church's translocal authority.[19]

17. Not anarchy as in the Sex Pistols' "Anarchy in the UK." Or the Anarchy, Norman England's twelfth-century civil war. Or Bernard Williams's "disorder which is at the limit anarchy" (*In the Beginning*, "Human Rights and Relativism," p. 69).

18. Immanuel Kant accepted Hobbes's analysis: "Peoples who have grouped themselves into nation states may be judged in the same way as individual men living in a state of nature, independent of external laws; for they are a standing offence to one another" (Kant, "Perpetual Peace," in *Political Writings*, p. 102).

19. Neff, "Short History"; Siedentop, *Inventing the Individual*. Also, 1054's great schism between the Western and Eastern (Orthodox) Churches left the Catholic hierarchy self-contained given that the other ancient sees (Alexandria, Antioch, Constantinople, and Jerusalem) were in the Near East (Byzantium).

It was a world that, although foreign to us in many ways, echoes down to today in three respects that matter to our inquiry because of the contrast with some other civilizations' political institutions (chapter 9). First, it was a world of law, in which kings and other rulers could not count on being above the law—a central element of our idea of the rule of law (chapter 14).[20] Second, the dual hierarchy of pope and Germanic emperor delivered a kind of separation of powers, rivaling and checking each other. That was especially so once, early in the twelfth century, the Western Church wrested from secular powers the right to appoint its own bishops, creating a unitary ecclesiastic hierarchy leading to Rome.[21] Third, it was a world where the morality of laws was debated within the church, and also in the new universities that sprang up from the late eleventh century.

## The Tradition of Natural Law: From Rationalist Higher Authority to Positivist Practice (Ideas and Power)

Those first European universities—Bologna, Paris, Oxford and Cambridge, and Salamanca, joined later by Heidelberg—also taught the new systematic rationalist philosophy fostered by the rediscovery of Aristotle's scientific writings (via Arabic translations), and rendered compatible with Christianity by the (posthumously canonized) Dominican friar Tommaso d'Aquino (Thomas Aquinas, 1225–74).

In consequence, even while disappearing, the old world bequeathed to the new modern Europe of states, and onto us, a debate—going back to the Greek Stoics, Cicero and Roman Stoics such as Seneca and Emperor Marcus Aurelius, and the medieval Christian scholastics—about whether, alongside what today is termed positive (human) law, governments and their peoples should properly be thought of as being subject to a universally binding "natural law."[22]

20. Fukuyama, *Origins of Political Order*, pp. 272–73.

21. Concordat of Worms (1122) between the pope and the Holy Roman emperor, following a slightly earlier agreement with the English Crown (reinforced locally in 1215 by the Magna Carta's first provision: "The English Church shall be free, and shall have its rights undiminished, and its liberties unimpaired"). Within Germany (but not elsewhere), the emperor maintained a residual role in choosing bishops or abbots when there were multiple candidates.

22. This combines two thoughts: that there *is* a natural law, an idea going back to Plato and Aristotle, who held individuals could be intrinsically unequal; and that all humans are in fact equal under natural law, going back to some Roman Stoics and Christian scholastics.

Variously regarded as rooted in divine authority, immutable laws of nature, or imperatives accessible to human reason, natural law was held to govern all activities, within political communities and between them. This is perhaps because what today we call international relations was then in part still conceived as relations among people, as in the Roman jus gentium (law of peoples), which purported to capture what, given human nature and the world as we find it, were common norms and practices across the empire (and so the whole world).

As Christianity gained hold, it was concluded natural law and the more practical human laws could conflict, with accountability for breaches of the former in a higher realm.[23] Indeed, medieval and early modern writers grappled with various possible hierarchies of law: divine, moral, and natural, through to the voluntaristic (later, positive) law of nations and local civil law. What matters for us is the recurrent notion, in Europe, of a possible wedge between binding moral norms and human voluntary law.

While the work of human hands, the jus gentium, like its higher-order counterpart, still applied universally. A millennium after Rome's fall, the Dominican jurist-theologian Francisco Vitoria (1483–1546)—University of Salamanca, and sometime adviser to Charles V, Holy Roman emperor, king of Spain, and hence the most powerful person in the West—was still holding, early in his career, that this law of peoples "does not have the force merely of pacts or agreements between men, but has the validity of a positive enactment (*lex*)." In other words, as legal historian Stephen Neff points out, this was notionally legislation *for all*, and so a forerunner of doctrines regarded today as *erga omnes*: duties owed to the international community as a whole, and binding with or without agreement (chapters 3 and 11).[24]

## A Search for New Sources of Law's Moral Authority

Whether pure natural law or jus gentium, this was a realm of norms and values claiming to govern or guide the conduct of relations among princes and, later, states. Central to the tradition were successive rearticulations of the doctrine of "just war" fought for a just cause by just means—a form of organized killing

23. Graphically documented in the *Justinian Institutes*: "Slavery is an institution of the *jus gentium*, against nature subjecting one man to the dominion of another" (I.iii.2), since in nature men [*sic*] were born free.

24. Vitoria's 1528 "On Civil Power" (Neff, "Consent," p. 132). According to Tuck, *Rights of War and Peace*, p. 74, he later retreated from the notion of a lawmaking "world commonwealth" (perhaps because of its humanist and imperialist connotations).

legalized under certain conditions.[25] They gained salience from Spain's and Portugal's imperial conquests in the Americas and Indies, Europe's Reformation, and Dutch commerce. Two things warrant special mention.

First, during sixteenth-century debates on imperialism's legality, Vitoria held, after rejecting other grounds, that Spain was legally entitled to intervene in the Americas against "human sacrifice practiced on innocent people or the killing of condemned criminals for cannibalism." This was conquest justified as, in today's terms, a kind of humanitarian intervention.[26]

Second, the Western Church's schism pressed the question of what norms bound both Protestant and Catholic princes and peoples in their relations with each other. Most urgently, without a shared hierarchy of authority, how could one tell which side had the "just cause," entitling them to greater freedom in combat? Alberico Gentili (1552–1608), an Italian-born humanist professor of civil law at Oxford, and a Protestant, argued that maybe there was no way of telling, even objectively. Norms of conduct *within* war (*jus in bello*) became the central issue.

Driving this search for norms covering war and peace, binding irrespective of creed, is the thought—a legacy of ancient Rome's rediscovery—that only a universal moral code enshrined in law can adequately substitute for the universal authority previously found in a universal sovereign (and, interestingly, continuing for centuries longer in the old Far East: the Son of Heaven, Tianzi, ruler of the whole world). Over the following centuries, the fortunes of this "universal moral law" waxed and waned, becoming marginalized during the doctrinally positivist nineteenth century but reviving after World War II in formal commitments to human rights.

### The Journey to Positivism: From Deduction to Induction

That history has an interesting dynamic. Once law could no longer be regarded as descending from an earthly but divinely mandated power, accounts of law's authority could affect what was proclaimed to be law. Many of the modern era's

25. Going back to the Romans and Saint Augustine (third to fourth century CE). As later articulated by Aquinas, just war required proper authorization, a just cause, and good conduct during hostilities (and, later, a just peace).

26. Hathaway and Shapiro, *Internationalists and Their Plan*, pp. 48–49, 451n83. In line with Dominican opposition to the conquest, Vitoria rejected the legality of an earlier papal grant (the pope was, he held, not ruler of the world) and other grounds such as enslavement (Tuck, *Rights of War and Peace*, pp. 70–75) . . . but still found a way.

earliest treatise writers accordingly inhabited a space between pure practitioners and the political philosophers whose names are more familiar today.

Starting before the break, for Aquinas and later scholastics natural law's authority was unambiguously divine but it was apprehended not via revelation but rationally: God-given human reason for sure, but human nonetheless. That belief-cum-doctrine (inadvertently) laid a bridge from a theological to a secular world.

When, early in the seventeenth century, Gentili's fellow Protestant Grotius issued his foundational treatise—*On the Law of War and Peace*, written and published a couple of decades *before* Westphalia—he made two vital moves.[27] Walking a tightrope of constructive ambiguity, he suggested that while the moral law enjoyed divine backing, its strictures would hold without God.[28] Then, adapting the neoscholastic Jesuit Francisco Suárez (1548–1617), Grotius broke from the established view that positive law captured and applied, imperfectly, the precepts of natural law. Despite best efforts, there was no *necessary* connection between the two. Whereas natural law bound individuals and rulers (and therefore nations) indistinguishably, positive law had separate fields for local civil law and the law of nations.[29] Eclectically synthesizing scholastic and humanist thought, whereas rulers would be accountable in the life to come for breaching natural law (scholastic), their first priority in this life was self-preservation (the humanists' reason of state).

That was anathema to the Lutheran Saxon professor Samuel Pufendorf (1632–94), an old-style right-reason natural lawyer through and through when it came to the law of nations.[30] Writing during the 1660s in the post-Westphalian

27. Grotius's was the first fairly comprehensive thesis, but it had been preceded on international community by Vitoria and Francisco Suárez, and on war by Gentili. Lauterpacht, "Grotian Tradition," p. 17; Tuck, *Rights of War and Peace*, chap. 1.

28. Tuck, *Rights of War and Peace*, pp. 99–101.

29. Suárez had distinguished between two senses of "jus gentium," a term used since ancient Rome to cover both those internal laws common to many states (e.g., murder laws) and laws regulating relations *between* nations and peoples as distinct political communities. Neff, *Justice among Nations*, pp. 153–58.

30. Lesaffer, "Classical Law of Nations." On *domestic* governance, Pufendorf stresses positive law and utility in fostering society: see Sagar, *Opinion of Mankind*, pp. 92–93. Many of these new treatise writers were moderate Protestants, seeking grounds for a moral law in reason, including observation, rather than authority (morality without a papal communications department). While scattered across different churches, they each resisted the purist Reform doctrine, reminiscent of Saint Augustine, that since grace could not be earned, what passed for earthly morality was a matter of convention alone. Their relation to Calvinism is thus not dissimilar to that

Germanic Empire, he maintained that among states there was no binding voluntary law distinct from the higher moral law. Left needing an explanation for why states would comply with any law of nations, he argued, against Hobbes (and possibly Grotius), that left to their own devices—in the contrivance known as "the state of nature"—people (and hence rulers) were not simply self-interested but could (and should) develop a bent toward natural sociability (chapter 5 on Hume).[31]

A century after Pufendorf, Vattel also maintained (civilized) states were bound by natural law to help each other to advance "human society."[32] But he reverted to distinguishing those imperatives that applied to states universally via a "necessary law of nations" from human voluntary law, which elaborated natural law for the world's complex richness, and was found in the law (treaties and tacitly accepted customary law) agreed on among states that were equal juridically, and accordingly entitled to territorial integrity (noninterference). While any lingering echoes of Vitoria's proto-right of humanitarian intervention had retreated, something else had survived, for the time being: that some parts of natural law simply had to find their way into man-made law, and all states could be taken to have consented, whether or not they had.[33] (Hold onto this thought, vanquished during the nineteenth century, for when we reach our world.)

Vattel's *Law of Nations* (1758), with less philosophizing than earlier tracts, not written in Latin, and rapidly translated from French into other vernacular languages, quickly became a standard in practical affairs. It was famously read by US founding fathers, and cited by American courts during their republic's early years.[34] Helped by his celebrity, the idea of a plurality of sovereign

---

of the Hellenistic Stoics to the Epicureans (a designation later bestowed on Hobbes). Those older contests were familiar and real to these seventeenth- and eighteenth-century writers, many of whom worked as political or legal advisers, rather as, slightly earlier, ancient Confucian debates were real for neo-Confucians (chapter 9)—the point for us being that some traditions of thought run through state administration and relations.

31. This is a "state of nature" more in the style of John Locke, where people are quite friendly, rather than of Hobbes, where they are rather horrid and life is, infamously, "solitary, poor, nasty, brutish and short"—the anarchy of the International Relations realists.

32. Tuck, *Rights of War and Peace*, pp. 192–93.

33. A thought Vattel took from Christian Wolff, one of Germany's leading eighteenth-century thinkers (who also influenced Kant). Neff, *Justice among Nations*, pp. 195–97.

34. According to Benjamin Franklin, the book had "been continually in the hands of the members of our Congress now sitting" (Hathaway and Shapiro, *Internationalists and Their Plan*, p. 449). George Washington owned a copy.

states, with different capabilities and interests but equal at law, was firmly on the map.

### Bifurcation: Revolutionary Moralism versus Positivist "Realism"

Since Vattel demanded codified elaboration of natural law, he heralded movement toward the view that international law and relations become whatever we (states) make of them. At this point, there was a major bifurcation, resonating loudly today.

On the one hand, following Immanuel Kant (on whom more below), some argued universal and egalitarian rights could (and should) be deduced from natural law reconceived in terms of our shared humanity. Inspiring many, this is manifest in, famously, Thomas Paine's "rights of man," Jefferson's Declaration of Independence ("All men are created equal"), and the proclamations of the French Revolution, which were cosmopolitan in spirit even if bloody and militaristic in their prosecution.

On the other hand, if morally valid law depended on human reason, it became possible to argue that the only prevailing *law* was human law (part of the nineteenth-century doctrine of legal positivism), with questions of morality lying in a separate sphere. Since, as a matter of fact, different human laws applied to relations between states than to those within them, this unambiguously implied there existed a separate realm of *international law*, a term coined by the positivist Utilitarian Jeremy Bentham (1748–1832), who declared natural rights "nonsense on stilts."

That was, however, assuming international law could be regarded as "law" at all given that it was not backed by the coercive force of a sovereign power (a skeptical tradition finding inspiration in Hobbes, whose political theory of sovereign states had appeared shortly after Westphalia and the parallel English Civil Wars). Those nineteenth-century positivists committed to the idea of international law were left to embark on their own search for its warrant. The three main contenders, which chapter 6 will reshape, were that customary law did the work since the conditions of its emergence provided its grounds, via some kind of tacit consent (a rather Humean thought ending in a distinctly un-Humean flourish); that open agreement via multilateral treaties or codes did the trick; or that law's authority turned on the voluntary self-restraint of autonomous state actors (a familiar idea of self-binding, going back to at least the sixteenth century, and detachable from its Hegelian baggage).[35]

35. Drawing on Neff, *Justice among Nations*, chap. 6, with my glosses.

After a long ascendency, positivism was confronted by the horrors of the twentieth century, reviving the feeling that, surely, sovereign states could not self-legalize crimes against humanity, or disregard the opinion of mankind [*sic*] when articulated through appropriate procedures. Men and women can suffer the stench of only so much evil before they turn back, with hope and conviction, to the idea of universal moral absolutes. In some ways, the post–World War II dispensation has represented a partial return to earlier ideas of cosmopolitan natural rights but now stripped, sometimes, of the metaphysics.[36]

### Four Models of the Authority and Viability of an International System of Law

Running through that history, then, are two great issues concerning international relations and law. First, do authoritative international norms descend from on high (via some kind of a moral or political imperium) or, more prosaically, are they rooted in the practices and customs of states and peoples? Second, are states sociable and so cooperative (by nature or interest), or basically just out for themselves in a dangerous world and so inherently unreliable? We have a two-by-two matrix, and the main strains of opinion fall into three of the cells.[37]

|  | No sociability | Sociability |
|---|---|---|
| Top-down authority | Hobbes (so no effective international authority) | Natural-law and Rationalist Grotians, including Pufendorf Kant (via Reason's authority) |
| Bottom-up authority | Some Positivists (via consent) | Hume |

For Hobbes, states are notionally bound by top-down natural law, but since there is no enforcing international sovereign, they are tragically left in a state of incipient or actual conflict: rationalist realism, with moral pessimism. For his nineteenth-century and modern followers, nonsociability is retained but natural law rejected for positivism: bottom-up consent. This is realism with a moral shrug.

36. For one history, see Griffin, *On Human Rights*, pp. 9–14. Scholars differ on whether natural rights were entertained first in the twelfth, fourteenth, or seventeenth century, and thus whether the idea is attributable to early canon lawyers, scholarly Franciscans (Ockham), or John Locke.

37. Adapting Neff, *Justice among Nations*, chap. 5, but framed in two-by-two terms and emphasizing the Humean cell.

For Pufendorf, Locke, and others of a broad Grotian disposition, embracing some kind of natural or induced sociability, there can and should be an international society of states, with the positive law of nations serving the moral purpose, demanded by reason's natural law, of fostering cooperation: constrained communal self-help, with more than a nod to justice.[38] This is a crowded space, inhabited by pluralists as well as some moral and political cosmopolitans—many finding inspiration in Kant.

Tucked away toward the Baltics, Kant labeled the whole lot of treatise writers—Grotius, Pufendorf, and Vattel—"sorry comforters," since they give grounds for war checked by notional constraints with no practical force (a distinctly Hobbesian thought).[39] But all was not lost. Since the moral law's normative authority was, although objective, sourced ultimately in reason itself, we both impose it on ourselves and must (morally) do so. In consequence, a system of universal international morality could be erected (by reason) so long as states chose—as, of course, they must—to constitute themselves as republics and enter into a pact (substituting for higher law) committing to peaceful relations. While seeming to require an efflorescence of revolutionary reform that, to date, has defied history, it lives on as an idealist benchmark, in the multiplicative moral "shoulds" of some International Relations theory, and more concretely in various security pacts and the projects of universalist liberal internationalism.

Those standard International Relations traditions ignore our matrix's fourth cell: that moral authority is not top-down but sociability nevertheless feasible, while not inevitable. The new idea is that the originating source of law's authority might lie in usefulness rather than in its moral content (the claim of old-style natural law and Kantian reason), or in the authority of its maker (Hobbes), but might be sustained partly through normative convictions (opinion).[40] It is the notion this book explores drawing on Hume and Bernard Williams. That must wait, other than to stress the importance it gives to the practical operation of law and policy in particular fields, and thus to their history.

---

38. Beitz, *Political Theory*, pp. 59–63. On whether Grotius was "Grotian," Tuck, *Rights of War and Peace,* argues he was closer to Hobbes, and that Pufendorf was the instigator of the notion of interstate cooperation rooted in extensive natural sociability. Kingsbury and Straumann, "State of Nature," disagree, while underlining Pufendorf's significance. (I use "Grotian" in the now standard way.)

39. Kant, "Perpetual Peace," in *Political Writings,* p. 103. Given unsocial sociability, Kant starts in the same matrix cell as Hobbes but escapes via Reason.

40. Hont, *Jealousy of Trade,* p. 45, placing Pufendorf in this tradition.

# History of Substantive International Law and Institutions up to World War I

It is best to begin with international law, which preceded both overt multilateralism and international organizations. Today, it has two variants—treaties and custom.

Treaties are explicit, documented agreements between states, and are surrounded by a paraphernalia of process—negotiation, agreement, signing ceremonies, ratification. By contrast, customary law is not formally codified and has no formalized ex ante process but, rather, comprises embedded norms of practice widely accepted, by international jurists, as being legally binding (*opinio juris*).

## Treaties

Treaties go back millennia, in the ancient world mainly drawing a line under war and regulating its aftermath. Perhaps the most famous is the settlement, a dozen years after the Battle of Kadesh, between the Egyptian pharaoh Ramesses II and the Hittite king Hattusili III (1258 BCE), saved for posterity on the walls of the Temple of Karnak in Luxor and tablets in the Istanbul Museum of Archeology. A replica of the Akkadian (Anatolian) version is prominently displayed in the UN's New York headquarters.

Half a millennium later, there were many treaties among the groups struggling for supremacy in China before it was finally unified, and centralized, under the Qin (whose emperor was interred with the magnificent terracotta soldiers in Xian).[41] During that extended Warring States period (722–221 BCE), some pacts cemented sporadic peace, while others constituted alliance leagues for ongoing struggle.[42] Similarly among the Greek city-states, which also shared some customary norms of warfare (e.g., not desecrating each other's holy sites). But classical China and Europe differed in other respects. Whereas Chinese emperors entered into very few treaties with other nations (perhaps, given nomadic neighbors, seeing themselves as the known world's apex), treaty writing was a staple of the foreign affairs of the Greeks, Macedonians, and Romans (perhaps because they bordered great nations: Persians, Carthaginians, and so on).

---

41. The Qin were quickly succeeded by the Han, who restored Confucianism and ruled for over four hundred years.

42. Drawing on Neff, *Justice among Nations*, chap. 1.

Since those ancient times, treaties have periodically provided for third-party arbitration or adjudication.[43] Greek disputes were sometimes arbitrated by third-party city-states. In medieval Europe, where treaties were regarded as personal contracts between princes sworn before God, many documented obligations fell under canon law, meaning the parties could resort to church lawyers for their interpretation and adjudication, with enforcement powers ultimately including excommunication.[44] That ended with the fragmentation and erosion of Rome's spiritual and legal authority: while the 1648 treaties notionally embraced arbitration, the principal instrument for seeking to enforce agreements was collective armed force.[45]

Developing distinct political identities, states increasingly entered into treaties of alliance (to head off war) and of friendship, commerce, and navigation (to help underpin peace). This involved two innovations. Pacts were now regarded as binding on successors, not personal to the signatories, and they extended beyond the military, to commerce and economic interdependence.

Leaping another few hundred years, the treaties and conventions that structured the end of the Napoleonic Wars marked another point of departure.[46] First, they stipulated that the many state boundaries redrawn by the Congress of Vienna could be revisited only if the original signatories agreed, formalizing a hierarchy whose leadership group comprised the Great Powers.[47] The idea of a top table has persisted ever since. Second, the treaties incorporated what might be the first human rights–like provision of international diplomacy and law: a declaration against the slave trade.[48] Third, they set up one of the first transnational regulatory regimes: rules for navigating the river Rhine (and, later,

---

43. O'Connell and VanderZee, "History of International Adjudication."

44. This instrument was sometimes accompanied by a bar on church services in a prince's nation, depriving whole communities of the sacraments and, therefore, exposing individuals to eternal damnation if they passed away before the interdict was lifted. Beliefs underpinned the sanction's traction.

45. Lesaffer, "Classical Law of Nations."

46. Collectively termed the 1815 Treaty of Paris, agreeing to peace between France and each of Austria, Britain, Prussia, and Russia.

47. Spain and Sweden, declining, were not included at the top table. On hierarchy, see chapters 8 and 11.

48. Subsequently, Britain entered into a series of bilateral treaties giving its navy rights to intercept, board, and seize suspect vessels. In a protracted struggle, perceived morality occasionally drove interventions beyond the letter of the law, reflecting public opinion in the United Kingdom: see Krasner, *Sovereignty*, pp. 106–9.

the Danube, Po, and others). But like private law contracts, at this stage inter-state treaties created reciprocal rights and obligations *using* the general law rather than legislating or articulating that higher law. Big picture, the only general international law was what today we call customary law.

## Customary Law

Thus, it was already a very long-standing norm that formal agreements should be honored (*pacta sunt servanda*). As with much else in the West, that, and wider notions of customary law, had late Roman-Christian origins. The *Digests* had recognized the force of custom. High-medieval commentaries on Roman and canon law had acknowledged reliance on custom after Rome's fall. But while those sources were treated as authoritative by imperial, ecclesiastical, and other tribunals until the fifteenth- and sixteenth-century revolutions, they too were casualties of Christendom's undoing.[49] Although knowledge of earlier means for maintaining order was hardly lost, there was initially more agonizing about authority's grounds (see above) than recording how practices adapted to the new political and material circumstances.

That changed approaching the turn of the nineteenth century, reflecting the efforts of more practically oriented scholar-officials—perhaps most prominently Georg Friedrich von Martens (1756–1821), who rather splendidly worked briefly for the king of Westphalia, Bonaparte's younger brother—to document the common principles running through the rapidly multiplying modern-era treaties ("a general convention," as Martens called them), together with the customs recognized and applied as law in national courts handling interstate issues. While an opaque source of higher authority lurked in the background, the method for identifying law was now inductive rather than the natural-law tradition's rationalist deductions.[50]

For that period, "customary law" operates as shorthand for any uncodified provisions of law. Since there was neither a higher power nor, yet, a practice of multilateral treaty making, no general principles were codified. Hence customary law covered both general principles and field-specific norms. In the latter, narrower sense, such laws derived from those norms of practice bearing

49. Drawing on Kadens, "Custom's Past," and Lesaffer, "Roman Law."
50. Drawing on Neff, *Justice among Nations*, pp. 189–94, 198–205, 227 (Martens quote, p. 200). Conventions, a very Humean notion, are central to parts II and IV.

on wars, navigation of the seas, diplomacy, and cross-border commerce that were regarded as legally binding, rather than morally so, or as mere habit.[51]

To work effectively, legal binding depends on a degree of normative pull plus sanctions of some kind for noncompliance. Notwithstanding the gulf between the early treatise writers and nineteenth-century doctrinal positivists, who had neither Grotius's appetite nor need to track norms back to antiquity or Thomism, even at the end of the nineteenth century there persisted a doctrine-cum-practice that profoundly distinguishes their shared world from ours. Namely, breaches of positive law could provide grounds, in law, for war: states were in principle free to try to enforce legal claims by force if other methods failed.

### Decentralized Enforcement of International Responsibilities: From Warlike Reprisals to Nonviolent Countermeasures

With the church's application of canon law no longer universal, and the West-phalian treaties' arbitral provisions largely in abeyance, enforcement reverted to self-help.[52] How that worked is tied up with the history of norms of state responsibility. Once princes were regarded as rulers, they effectively demanded their subjects be properly treated by foreign powers. In effect, whether or not states (as they became) had responsibilities to their own citizen-subjects, a great late twentieth-century cause (see the next chapter), they had responsi-bilities to each other's—to foreign envoys, merchants, even travelers. "Whoever uses a citizen ill, indirectly offends the state, which is bound to protect this citizen," as Vattel put it: a doctrine of diplomatic protection that survives, more or less, to this day.[53] Around that basic norm—essentially, a principle of reciprocity—grew all sorts of substantive and procedural conventions.

When one of those conventions was violated, the party in the wrong was expected to stop, and either to make restitution of some kind (undoing or compensating for the wrong suffered) or to accept retaliatory measures of various kinds as lawful. In broad outline, that remains at the heart of today's law, notably in international trade: if X raises tariffs on Y in violation of an

51. Lowe, *International Law*, pp. 20–23. On medieval customary maritime and merchant law, see Neff, *Justice among Nations*, pp. 80–91.

52. Verosta, "History of International Law," para. 39.

53. Vattel, *Law of Nations*, II.vi.71.

agreement, Y can reciprocate, which is why newspapers report befuddling stories of the WTO authorizing, say, the United States or the European Union to impose tariffs on the other.

The interesting part of the history comes in what happens if those essentially peaceful or friendly measures do not resolve the problem. In the past, something more intrusive—reprisals—could be applied, but what, and by whom? Before Westphalia—a world lacking a neat private-public split given its complex overlapping authorities—private actors were in the habit of enforcing the law against others once a ruling of some kind had been given. Even afterward, when sovereign states' capabilities were increasing, they might still outsource reprisals to harmed citizens or corporations: a form of publicly authorized private war. This continued until the late 1700s.[54]

During the nineteenth century, enforcement became a matter reserved to states, but reprisals remained an exercise in force: the legal use of armed force warranted by injury or unsatisfied wrong. That did not end until our era.[55] This has two implications for our inquiry. First, throughout the period covered in the rest of this chapter, aggression was an instrument of law enforcement in commerce as well as diplomacy, not merely of conquest or defense. Second, since aggression or outright war is definitely interference (in any normal sense), the post-Vattelian positivist doctrine of sovereignty did not mean noninterference *tout court* but required noninterference so long as a state was meeting its obligations under international law. That being so, states were bound to resist any suggestion they had such obligations toward their citizen-subjects. While egregious conduct might affect the opinion of mankind (today, world opinion), morality (natural law) was not necessarily reflected in positive law, and so was not as such enforceable between states and peoples.

All that has changed, with profound effects for economic statecraft. Moral imperatives are now incorporated into positive international law, and states are no longer free to police the law with unauthorized force. But, where not constrained by legal obligations, they may withdraw benefits; and they can employ economic instruments as countermeasures (nonviolent reprisals) when illegally violated. The stories of rights, war, and commerce are, therefore, entangled in striking ways. We start with war.

54. Crawford, *Brownlie's Principles*, p. 595.

55. Paddeau, "Countermeasures"; Hathaway and Shapiro, *Internationalists and Their Plan*, pp. 77–81.

## War and Peace: Toward Multilateral Codification

Well before the great break, the Powers embarked on multilateral codification of some areas of customary international law, most notably concerning war and peace. At the Vienna Congress, as part of their half step toward multilateralism, the parties recommitted themselves in writing to diplomatic immunities that had long featured in customary law: effectively an act of reaffirmation after prolonged struggle. A few decades later, after the bloody 1859 Battle of Solferino between French-backed Italian partisans and the Austro-Hungarian Empire, the multilateral Geneva Conventions on the conduct of war famously documented the rights of wounded and sick combatants, and of those looking after them.

Just over thirty years after that, some laws of war were incorporated into the dozen or so multilateral Hague conventions and declarations of 1899 and 1907—an extraordinary effort during peacetime to fix, reshape, and disseminate norms of war and peace. Notwithstanding the enthusiasm of local and transnational peace movements, however, their substantive provisions were comprehensively violated when, only a little later, Germany invaded Belgium without notice at the beginning of World War I (notwithstanding its neutrality under an 1839 treaty: chapter 4), and again when all sides used poisonous gas against enemies. Nevertheless, the gatherings left a legacy, not least in the provision that, even where the conventions were silent, citizen-subjects were protected by "the laws of humanity and the dictates of the public conscience"—a kind of secular resummoning of the spirit of a bygone natural law for modernity's emerging world of public opinion.[56]

## Commerce, Economic Statecraft, and the Laws of War

While the peace conferences took slow-motion steps on war crimes (next chapter), they had rather faster effects on commerce. When long before— prior to Westphalia but after the initiation of Europe's trading empires— Grotius had recast some of the doctrines of the law of war in his famous treatise, he was recycling material from earlier work commissioned to help justify the seizure by the Dutch East India Company of treasure from a

---

56. This Martens clause, named after the czar's adviser, addressed silence over the rights of formally noncombatant citizen-subjects who resisted occupying forces (I. Clark, *International Legitimacy and World Society*, pp. 77–82).

Portuguese ship just off modern Singapore.[57] Unsurprisingly, perhaps, given those sponsors, he edged positive law away from the more moralistic strictures of late Christendom's scholastics, instead making use of the harder-edged reason-of-state thinking associated with the humanists (most famously Machiavelli, 1469–1527), who held, like Romans of old,[58] that for glory and preservation a prince or state could violate both positive and natural law (for us, law and morality: a view sporadically echoed in modern US claims to legal exceptionalism). A "just cause" under natural law (with accountability in the life to come) could include defense, enforcing property rights after all else had failed, and punishment for breaching agreements or other obligations.[59] Substantively, in this world, as Gentili had already argued, that made room, when prudentially necessary, for preemptive strikes against other states, including in Grotius's time by private bodies such as his erstwhile merchant-adventurer client.

Before the seventeenth century, war as enforcement could be precise in focus and limited in scope, permitting trade and commerce to continue between nonbelligerent private individuals while the warring parties (public and private) battled away. As time passed, however, positive law came to conceive of war more broadly in scope but narrowly in personalities. War now characterized a state of relations in toto between sovereign states, implying legal authority to take measures against their opponent's people and their property, including barring trade. During the Napoleonic Wars, France boycotted British goods, while Britain mounted wide-ranging blockades (including on parts of the American Atlantic coast).

There were parallel changes in the norms applying to neutral states. So long as it was believed that, objectively viewed, one side in a conflict would have a just cause, neutral states were under a natural-law duty not to get in that state's way, whereas they were under no duties to the other belligerent (a thought that resonates again today: chapter 3).[60] But as the community retreated from discerning who had justice on their side, third parties were instead regarded as being under an obligation to stay neutral in all matters.

57. Drawing on Hathaway and Shapiro, *Internationalists and Their Plan*, pp. 6–9 and following; and Lesaffer, "Too Much History." Grotius's *On the Law of War and Peace* was published in 1625.

58. The non-Stoic Romans, notably Tacitus (Tuck, *Rights of War and Peace*, chaps. 1–3).

59. Neff, *Justice among Nations*, p. 164. Having distinguished natural and positive law as distinct realms (earlier), Grotius, writing with the Reformation in full swing, needed to articulate doctrine for both.

60. Neff, "Law of Armed Conflict."

By the middle of the nineteenth century, it was still regarded as legal to take armed reprisal measures in order to enforce claims or right wrongs. What is more, agreements between states reached under duress (gunboat diplomacy) could be valid, and thus their breach a basis for war.[61] With natural law eclipsed, Might and Right blurred somewhat. Neutral states were, however, now precluded from applying economic sanctions to warring states unless they had been illegally wronged.[62] In summary, this was a world in which debt collection by force was lawful but imposing certain sanctions to alter another state's actions or policies could be held to be an act of war. Bearing in mind 2022's barrage of sanctions against Russia, how things have changed!

In what became a series of incremental steps, the transformation began in earnest with one of the 1907 Hague conventions, barring force to collect debts owed to a state or its citizens unless arbitration had been refused or ignored.[63] After stumbling with the 1909 London Declaration (on blockades, prizes, and other elements of naval warfare), which was never ratified, the transformation hit the headlines with the 1919 Covenant of the League of Nations, whose signatories signaled "acceptance of obligations not to resort to war" (Preamble) and, more concretely, that they would act collectively in response to "external aggression [against] the territorial integrity and existing political independence of all Members" (Articles 10 and 11).[64] Finally (for the moment), and

61. Hathaway and Shapiro, *Internationalists and Their Plan*, p. 51, citing the way the Sioux Indians were handled after the discovery of gold on their traditional lands during the 1870s. On Britain taking control of Egypt at the end of the century being justified as debt collection, see Neff, *Friends but No Allies*, p. 59.

62. "Neutrals" discriminating in trade was also an act of war: see Hathaway and Shapiro, *Internationalists and Their Plan*, pp. 90–92; Lowe and Tzanakopoulos, "Economic Warfare." Note, however, that so-called pacific blockades against weaker states, not considered legal equals of the European states, were regarded differently during the nineteenth century (under colonialism, as a form of policing rather than war): see Mulder, "Rise and Fall."

63. The 1907 Convention Respecting the Limitation of the Employment of Force for the Recovery of Contract Debts, responding to Argentinian calls for debt claims to be resolved in local courts and without resort to force (the Drago Doctrine opposing armed debt collection, a narrow version of the Calvo Doctrine discussed later). That story is told in terms of both strong claims of sovereignty and noninterference (Neff, *Friends but No Allies*, pp. 69–70), and also rights for the weak, anticipating later human rights (Sikkink, *Evidence for Hope*, pp. 60–61).

64. A little later, Britain and France proposed that disputes should be arbitrated by the League's new Permanent Court (see below), with nonsubmission and noncompliance with its findings deemed to be acts of aggression. This was incorporated into the Geneva Protocol for

most emphatically, in 1928 the Kellogg-Briand Pact, promoted by the eponymous American and French foreign ministers, "condemn[ed] recourse to war
for the solution of international controversies and renounce[d] it as an instrument of national policy." Instead, the grounds for war were limited to self-
defense, removing any warrant for debt collection by the armed services.[65]

But if gunboat diplomacy and debt collection by force were out, sanctions
(economic and financial) were in.[66] Identified as an instrument the League
could ask members to deploy in response to unlawful aggression (Article 16),
they were admitted to the repertoire of measures a state may legally take to
fend off war or other threats (or, in certain circumstances, to respond to a
counterpart state's breaches of obligations). Although sanctions were not
frequently used during the interwar years (including ineffectively against Italy
for invading Abyssinia), these legislative measures marked a doorway to *our*
world of widespread lawful but coercive economic diplomacy (chapter 4 and
part III). Geoeconomic statecraft exited by one door only to reenter via another. Given the history of trade, this cannot be a surprise.

### Commercial Society: From Merchant Law via Mercantilism to the Emergence of International Economic Organizations in the Late Nineteenth Century

Trade is as ancient as war. In Europe, the medieval law of merchants (*lex mer-
catoria*) developed to adjudicate commercial disputes speedily. Enforced by
guilds and fairs, it was customary law but not law regulating relations between
states. Nevertheless, states (and earlier types of political community) were
involved. From the medieval Italian cities and Byzantine Empire onward, they
entered into agreements allowing merchants to trade in each other's markets.[67]
As well as setting tariffs on goods moving into or out of a territory, these pacts
promised foreign merchant communities certain legal rights and protections.
Often those included settling each "nation" in its own dedicated quarter of

---

the Pacific Settlement of International Disputes, which was not ratified after Britain's government changed in 1924.

65. Lowe, *International Law*, pp. 64–68. (Britain insisted the new self-defense doctrine include resisting attacks on its empire.)

66. Hathaway and Shapiro, *Internationalists and Their Plan*, pp. 304–5.

67. Drawing on Neff, *Justice among Nations*, pp. 86–91, 201–3; and Neff, "Peace and
Prosperity."

town, permitting them a degree of self-government (and sometimes religious freedoms) under their home laws. Among the world's tourist attractions, the Genovese Galata Tower in modern Istanbul (Byzantium's capital, Constantinople) reminds us of this.

By the early modern period, these pacts had evolved into interstate treaties of amity and commerce (later known in the United States as friendship, commerce, and navigation agreements). Like bilateral investment treaties today, they provided private citizens with legal rights against their host governments. They were typically annulled upon entry into a state of war, and later renegotiated as part of the peace, with the terms of trade (the ratio of export prices to import prices) often shifting to the victor's advantage.

Treaties were not the only instrument of commercial policy. They were struck in the context of an emergent norm of customary international law, recognized from at least the seventeenth century, that aliens (residents and visitors who are not citizen-subjects) are entitled to a minimum standard of treatment, which excludes denial of justice. Cutting through a lot of subtlety, in the economic sphere this "international minimum standard" meant states could not simply expropriate the property of foreigners even if exactly the same was being meted out to locals. If they did, as described above, reprisals were permitted, international law claiming to trump domestic law (still hotly contested: chapter 18).[68]

Meanwhile, the doctrine suited priorities bequeathed by the age of exploration, when statecraft had embraced granting monopoly rights over external commerce in particular geographies. These were the merchant-adventurer companies, most famously the East India companies of Holland and Britain. Trade policy (along with the public finances, discussed below) had become an arm of foreign policy, intended both to project power and to help finance a nation's security. Beginning among the commercial republics (the Netherlands and Britain), this lasted well into the period that Europeans call the Enlightenment, forming a core element of the policy of absolutist France, whose chief minister, Jean-Baptiste Colbert, famously wrote to Louis XIV in 1669 that "commerce is a perpetual and peaceable war of wit and energy among notions."[69]

For international lawyers, these developments tracked shifts in presumptive doctrine concerning the high seas and trade.[70] Traditionally, it had been held

68. Bonnitcha et al., *Political Economy*, pp. 11–13; Dickerson, "Minimum Standards."

69. Hume, "Jealousy of Trade," in *Political Essays*; Colbert quote from Hont, *Jealousy of Trade*, p. 23.

70. Drawing on Tuck, *Rights of War and Peace*, including pp. 63–65, 72–77, and 90–93.

that the emperor exercised imperium over the oceans, a notion reflected in papal bulls, around the turn of the sixteenth century, dividing up the Indies, East and West, between the two great maritime empires, Portugal and Spain. Even when, sweeping aside higher authority, the two powers settled outstanding differences via a bilateral treaty (1529), their asserted rights were not confined to land. In a spectacular example of a rising state asserting itself, the aspirant maritime commercial power—the Dutch—would not put up with that. Thus, Grotius—a hired hand, remember—argued that since the oceans could hardly be private property, nor could they belong to states, establishing freedom on the high seas for trading nations: a core customary law doctrine to this day.

The shifts did not stop there. At the dawn of modernity, Vitoria, other late scholastics, and natural lawyers had still been holding that people, as people, had rights to trade and presumptively, therefore, could properly retaliate against refusals to trade.[71] A little later, however, first Gentili and then Grotius maintained, as part of the emerging state-centric law of nations, that political communities had some discretion over trading counterparts. After all, Grotius needed to rationalize the right of East Asian and Indonesian peoples to stop trading with the Portuguese if they were to be free (narrowly) to flip to commerce with the Dutch.

By the time of Pufendorf and, a little later, Vattel, states were held to be free to exclude foreign merchants, and to decline to trade with anyone at all; a right China famously exercised under the Ming dynasty (chapter 9). As material conditions and political circumstances had changed, there was in effect a transition from a cosmopolitan disposition toward noninterference in exchange among individuals to something like the articulation of state economic policy conducted according to perceptions of national interest. Doctrinally, it marked a shift from the spirit of a universal law of peoples (Rome's jus gentium, framing relations and exchange among people scattered across a vast empire with different local civil laws) to the contingent realities of a post-Westphalian law of nations. The preoccupation of rulers, meanwhile, was now less exclusively focused on the basic goal of preserving food (especially grain) stocks in order to underpin internal stability and their own legitimacy, and more on gathering specie in order to be free to manage their trade and pursue riches via external expansion.

For economists, this was mercantilism: designed to produce a surplus, and in effect to operate in the interests of exporters while protecting domestic

71. Drawing on Neff, *Friends but No Allies*, pp. 11–28.

enterprises exposed to competition from importers. For eighteenth-century political economists, it fostered the "jealousy of trade," as Hume called it (chapter 1). Provoked by Britain's financial revolution—introducing paper money and public financing under merchant control—France famously fought back with John Law's doomed Mississippi Company's financial engineering, in a "jealousy of credit" not matched until, perhaps, today's digital-currency race.[72]

In ways that remain instructive (chapter 4), the incorporation of trade and finance into an essentially competitive and hostile geoeconomic strategy—devoted to achieving relative prestige and power—frequently tipped over into outright war, fought out across the planet, and subordinating the potential mutual benefits of trade to the winner-loser logic of military conflict. That, as emphasized in chapter 1, is the story of British-French relations from the late seventeenth century until well into the nineteenth century. Given domestic interests and forces, only war itself could change things, and it did.

By then, however, the new political economists—Hume, Adam Smith (1723–90), and their followers—had begun to turn the tides of thought.[73] As Hume pointed out, international commerce, which changed nearly everything, had not featured in Machiavelli's reason-of-state thinking (nor, he might have added, in Hobbes's).[74]

While subscribing to a balance-of-power account of international order, this new generation rejected the inescapability of Hobbesian fearfulness, instead emphasizing the possibility (not inevitability) of an empathetic sociability among nations. It was not sourced in natural virtue (Pufendorf's response to Hobbes and Grotius a century earlier) but, instead, could arise organically from the mutual interests and shared experience of trade and exchange: an acquired virtue under commercial society (chapters 5 and 7). For them, a distinctive feature of modernity was that while previously liberty had enabled trade, now commerce could promote liberty in the world at large,

72. On Britain's financial revolution, see North and Weingast, "Constitutions and Commitment." On Law's venture (not dissimilar to Britain's South Sea Company and bubble) and the jealousy of credit, see Shovlin, *Trading with the Enemy*.

73. Drawing on Hont, *Jealousy of Trade*, introduction. Hume and Smith were participants, alongside Voltaire and Montesquieu, in a broader Enlightenment inquiry into political order's history.

74. Hume, "On Civil Liberty," in *Political Essays*, pp. 51–52. Hume says of Machiavelli, often thought the canonical realist, "A great genius; but . . . his reasonings . . . have been found extremely defective" (p. 51), because confined in space and time.

as well as prosperity at home: the pendulum was swinging to a kind of incipient international liberalism.[75] Whereas a craving for luxury had (rightly or
wrongly) been thought to undermine the public virtue sustaining ancient
Rome and, later, Florence and other Italian republics (a view held by Vattel,
since imports threatened the trade balance), it was now suggested that demand for luxury could be beneficial by enhancing the political power of
merchants and others, and so acting as a check on top-down (land-based)
political power and ambition—an argument twenty-first-century Asia suggests is contingent on whether a rising commercial middle class gains a
strong foothold in the political assembly (chapter 9). With that condition
on its way to being satisfied in some parts of Europe, Vattel (an Anglophile)
thought Britain a healthy check on the aspirations of the Continent's absolutist monarchies.[76]

But why didn't the merchants use their vast wealth to capture and corrupt
the state? What check stood in the way of their purchasing politicians? For
Smith, the answer was the rule of law (chapter 14).[77] That is, best thought of
as an orthogonal axis of ideas and authority that was part of a healthy domestic
equilibrium—one notably lacking in, say, a post-Soviet Russia that embraced
commerce without law's virtues. Commercial society—meaning an economy
where most people live by selling their labor and purchasing what they want
to consume—was insufficient alone.

As to any tolerable equilibrium among nations, Smith argued that a state
harmed itself and its people if it undermined the prosperity of its neighbors—a
thought going back to late seventeenth-century Whigs.[78] Emulation was to
be preferred over envy. Jealousy of state, manifested in early modernity as jealousy of trade, could be harnessed and turned (sometimes, given a fair wind).
In France, Montesquieu had struck a similar note: agreeable manners both
fostered and were fostered by commerce. (Somewhat typically, Kant went

75. Part of the history of liberalism, Hume was not a modern liberal, as exemplified by the
notorious racist footnote in "Of National Character" (*Political Essays*, p. 86), which met contemporary opposition. That contrasts but is not inconsistent with his condemning slavery, ancient and modern: it "trample[s] upon human nature" and "disgusts us with that unbounded
dominium," turning masters into "petty tyrants" ("Of the Populousness," pp. 283–84).

76. Whatmore, "Vattel, Britain and Peace." For Vattel on luxury, see Neff, *Friends but No
Allies*, p. 25.

77. Sagar, *Adam Smith Reconsidered*, chap. 5.

78. A. Smith, *Wealth of Nations*, IV.iii.c.11. On Whig political economy, see Pincus, "Revolution in Political Economy," in *1688*.

further still: trade could *and should* underpin peace.) For these writers, commercial sociability was not inevitably narrowly nationalistic: while war was zero-sum (a winner and a loser), trade could be win-win, producing net benefits for all trading nations (famously articulated a few decades later by David Ricardo as comparative advantage).

Back in the world of affairs, while the newly independent United States pursued a Hamiltonian commercial policy behind a wall of tariffs, things began to move in Europe.[79] Britain, on achieving commercial preeminence in the aftermath of the Napoleonic Wars, changed tack, legislating domestically in the 1830s to broaden the franchise and, during the 1840s, to repeal various tariffs (most famously the Corn Laws) and unilaterally embrace free trade (splitting the Tory party for a generation). Others held back from unilateral commercial disarmament but pursued bilateral pacts. By 1860, Britain and France—economically liberal but politically and socially illiberal during the Bonapartist Second Empire—were embarking on mutual tariff reductions via the Cobden-Chevalier Treaty, which, crucially, included a "most-favored-nation" clause pledging that neither would receive worse treatment than other trading counterparts.[80] A wave of similar bilateral treaties followed, and the multilateral 1856 Declaration of Paris, expressly open to signature by any state, tightened the net on licensed piratical interference with commerce: effectively a collective measure to maintain freedom of navigation for commerce (a principle finally accepted by Britain).[81] Big picture, just as railways were transforming the material possibilities for economic and cultural exchange (and security), these various steps created the formal rudiments of a multilateral trading regime. British-French rivalry was constrained by structure and the norms that underpinned it.

79. After founding father Alexander Hamilton. Mead, *Special Providence*, also labels three other US foreign policy traditions: Jeffersonian (pastoral isolationism), Jacksonian (spiky isolationism), and Wilsonian (missionary).

80. Brown, *Reluctant Partners*, pp. 53–56. The British-French eighteenth-century Eden Treaty contained a most-favored-nation clause for some goods but was short lived, drowning in the mercantilism accompanying renewed war. Sustained free trade was a product of peace.

81. This treaty accompanied that settling the end of the Crimean War (which admitted the Ottoman Empire into what remained of the Concert's system: chapter 7). The Declaration Respecting Maritime Law (1) explicitly aimed to clarify maritime law by outlawing privateering (government-sponsored piracy to intercept enemy commerce); and, for us most significantly, (2) invited other states to join as signatories. The United States stood aside, until its own civil war. Lemnitzer, "'Moral League of Nations.'"

Things unraveled toward the end of the century under the pressure of the fallout from the Franco-Prussian War (in many ways, the century's unfortunate pivot), subsequent macroeconomic shocks, and intensified imperial, perhaps especially UK-German, rivalries (chapters 1 and 8). But some of the new institutions persisted, especially within colonial trade blocs, and the underlying liberal principles of the mid-nineteenth-century reformers provided a lodestar for system builders a century later.

Notably, not long after the British and French had clinched their trade deal, the first international organizations were established through multilateral treaties.[82] In 1865 the International Telegraph (later Telecommunications) Union replaced the nonsystem of bilateral agreements that had grown up to cope with the telegraphic messages sent from one country to another. The 1874 Treaty of Bern established the Universal Postal Union, a multilateral mechanism, initially among twenty states, for agreeing on conventions for handling letters and parcels sent across borders. Over the same decades, prompted by cholera epidemics, the first international sanitary conventions had been promulgated. And during the 1880s, the Paris and Bern conventions on industrial patents and artistic copyrights were agreed on, supported by a small bureau that later grew into the World Intellectual Property Organization, based in Geneva under the umbrella of the UN.

These were the original international standard setters, responding to challenges produced by new technology and increased international commerce. They were addressing problems that have a special quality (coordination: chapter 5) and gathered participants as interests converged. In a tremendous example of that, while the United States had joined the industrial patent pact, it stayed outside the artistic copyright convention, much to the frustration of Charles Dickens, until its own cultural output needed protection across the world—in 1988.[83]

More important, importers of capital had a different perspective on Europe's commercial project for international law. This came to a head, and did not really go away, when toward the end of the nineteenth century the Argentinian jurist Carlos Calvo challenged the customary law norm that foreign investors were entitled to special treatment, enunciating instead his eponymous

---

82. A couple of years earlier (1863), alongside the Geneva conduct-of-war conventions, the International Committee of the Red Cross had been established, in Geneva, as a private body. (It was joined in federation by the Red Crescent in 1919.)

83. D. Vagts, "International Economic Law," p. 773.

doctrine that states could expropriate so long as foreigners did not suffer discrimination. The rival views—an international minimum standard versus national treatment—persisted, getting resolved (sort of) only much later via bilateral investment treaties (next chapter).

### Europe's Positivist Law of Nations: Arbitral Machinery and Professionalization

With Europe's and North America's economic dynamism transforming the world, and international law carried along in its wake, this was the period when another now-familiar institution was revived and regularized: arbitral tribunals, a mechanism for resolving specific disputes turning on states formally committing to abide by the findings.[84] While, as already noted, the ancient and medieval worlds had used third-party arbitration when secular power was broadly dispersed, it was rarely employed under hegemony (notably, the Roman Empire) or when power was delicately balanced (eighteenth-century Europe). It was gradually revived after the 1794 Jay Treaty between Britain and the newly independent United States. Mixed-claims commissions, comprising representatives of the disputing parties, were widely used during the nineteenth century, notably to settle claims between Latin American states and, on the other side, European states or the United States after independence struggles and subsequent civil wars.[85] Then, in the 1870s, after the United States' own civil war, London and Washington set up a tribunal to determine whether Britain had breached its proclaimed neutrality by building ships it knew (or should have known) would be used by the Confederates against the Union. Not only did Britain end up honoring the finding that it should pay compensation, the *Alabama* claims case triggered a rash of new treaties incorporating similar dispute-settlement machinery.

Arbitration was also employed to resolve boundary disputes (including some bearing on the United States' Monroe Doctrine of hemispherical autonomy), and more widely to bring closure to contested claims on the natural environment, or where competitive overuse would leave everyone worse off (the problem of the commons: chapter 5).[86] It was not, then, a big leap to

---

84. Drawing on Fraser, "Sketch of the History"; and O'Connell and VanderZee, "History of International Adjudication."

85. Dolzer, "Mixed Claims Commissions."

86. Sand, "Evolution of International Environmental Law." The case relevant to the Monroe Doctrine concerned a US-British dispute over the border between Guiana and Venezuela. (Think of today's China Sea disputes: chapter 9.)

institutionalize voluntary but (purportedly) binding arbitration. In 1899 the leading states established the Permanent Court of Arbitration in The Hague. It was, and remains, a voluntary venue for countries to settle disputes, with tribunals constituted ad hoc but supported by a permanent secretariat. Since the arbitral mechanism itself no longer needed to be established as each dispute arose, its proponents believed tribunals could be deployed more effectively before the clamor of public opinion and media impeded compromise.[87] While that failed to prevent World War I, it was a major step toward our world.

The growth of arbitration in the closing decades of the nineteenth century reflected and fostered the development of a community of practicing international lawyers, no longer confined to the schoolroom and treatise writing. The first international law journal was established in 1869, and a professional association in 1873 (in Belgium and Paris). Crystallizing and accelerating the role of legal scholars and activists in international affairs, one notable upshot was a call for some kind of coordinating-cum-normative framework for the intensifying colonial competition on the continent of Africa.[88]

That became a critical moment for international law's trajectory through the 1884/85 Conference on Africa, hosted in Berlin by Otto von Bismarck, Prussian chancellor of the only recently unified Germany. A late-century avatar of the old Concert, it was attended by Europe's Great Powers (including the fading Ottomans), its lesser powers, and the United States. Whatever its effect on the subsequent scramble for Africa, its main formal output, the General Act, a longish treaty with thirty-eight articles, crystallized certain ideas on the point and reach of European international law. At a substantive level, the treaty created rights for free commerce and river navigation (the point of the shindig); committed to using the Postal Union conventions agreed on a decade before; formally introduced into law the ideas of "spheres of influence" and, for coastal areas, "effective occupation," which therefore did not require a treaty with the conquered people ("natives" in the language of the act) but instead had to be notified to fellow signatories (Article 34); and, among other things, committed signatories to suppressing slavery (and, yet again, the slave trade).

87. Mazower, *Governing the World*, pp. 88–89, citing William Randal Cremer, British peace activist and trade unionist.

88. Rasilla, "Very Short History."

## Europe's Law of Nations under Late Imperialism:
### A "Standard of Civilization"

Perhaps most important here, Berlin effectively codified the notion that international law was the law prevailing among civilized nations; only they could be its subjects, carrying the duties it imposed as well as, of course, the rights it conferred. Needless to say, the European-American powers got to decide which states-cum-peoples counted as "civilized," "barbarian" (a term historically applied by the Greeks to non-Greek speakers, and by the Romans to Germanic tribes), and "savage," which became terms of art as well as bearers of cultural heritage, interest, and prejudice.[89]

That lack of sovereign equality was, however, somehow, and sometimes, to be squared with certain rights of individuals (given a lingering inheritance from natural law). In other words, the apportionment of other states and peoples to categories outside that of "sovereign equals" was to be conceived paternalistically, and therefore patronizingly.[90]

That was very much the view of the central nineteenth-century liberal theorist and commentator John Stuart Mill (1806–73), who held that other places and peoples could not be treated as equals where not yet capable of sticking to a norm of reciprocity. In those cases, intervention and hence empire, as in India, could be warranted by its expected civilizing effects (!). Otherwise, as if trying to find a position between Palmerston and Aberdeen (see above and chapter 13 on Robert Peel), Mill suggested that a power might intervene to help a freedom-loving people resist a foreign despot, but not a local one, and even then only when the measure would work. So, in this revival of just war theory, there was no general license to protect a people against tyranny.[91]

89. "Barbarian" connoted difference rather than a state or people being uncivilized in some deeper sense: so, for the ancient Greeks, the Persians, the Near East's most powerful people, were barbarian. Other civilizations had similar terms—e.g., a Sanskrit epic describes the Ghaznavids, forerunners of the Delhi sultanate, marauding from (today's) Afghanistan, as *mlechhas* (foreign or barbarian): see Eaton, *India in the Persianate Age*, p. 5. In the European lexicon, "savage" was even nastier, connoting lack of political order and more.

90. Drawing on Onuma, "When Was the Law . . . ?," pp. 39–50; and Koskenniemi, *Gentle Civilizer of Nations*, pp. 121–32.

91. Mill, "Few Words on Non-intervention"; and Walzer, "Mill's 'A Few Words.'" (Under those tests, the British could not have justified intervening in India as helping lift the yoke of earlier Moghul and Persianate conquests unless they planned, quickly, to make way for local rule.)

In practice, and bizarrely in law, Japan, China, and Persia were seen by Europeans as almost civilized, and so might be treated as states, at least for some purposes.[92] Whether those peoples' leaders thought about each other in this way mattered to which ordering framework governed their own approach to international relations: whether interacting under the categories (and terms) of European international law or, alternatively, via their own historical conceptions of themselves, their near neighbors, and distant peoples. That makes it significant that just a few years after the Berlin conference, on the other side of the world another treaty delivered an epoch-confirming globalization of (European-style) international law. The 1895 Treaty of Shimonoseki, marking the end of a war between Japan and Qing China, asserted the independence of Korea.[93] Since Korea had long been under Chinese suzerainty, this effectively signaled the end of Beijing's tribute system of international relations (chapter 9).[94] European international law was now, in some sense, hegemonic.

What were its central precepts by this stage? Not, in contrast to the practice of earlier empires, formal or symbolic acceptance of imperial power, or religious conversion. Rather, the following essentially instrumental concerns: that individuals' property rights and physical integrity be respected when engaging in international trade; that those interests be safeguarded in some way by domestic law; and that state-to-state relations be conducted under (European) international law. When this was in doubt, Western states demanded extraterritorial authority via so-called capitulations (with the Ottoman Empire) and unequal treaties (in East Asia, starting with the 1842 Treaty of Nanjing), which granted their merchants immunity from local law and substituted consular jurisdiction in its place. As one author puts it,

> Western expansion changed the concept of "civilization" from one dominated by "Christianity, chivalry, and trade" to one focused on whether a State "was sufficiently stable to undertake binding commitments under international law and whether it was able and willing to protect the life, liberty and property of foreigners." . . . Whether a country was civilized was

92. Donnelly, "Human Rights," pp. 3–8. Remarkably by today's mores, during the 1870s the members of the Institute du Droit Internationale surveyed its members on how best to think about civilized Oriental peoples under international law (Koskenniemi, *Gentle Civilizer of Nations*, pp. 132–36). As late as 1912, Lassa Oppenheim's leading textbook listed states deemed "half sovereign" (Nardin, "International Legal Order," p. 159).

93. Other articles ceded Taiwan to Japan (chapter 9).

94. Onuma, "When Was the Law . . . ?," pp. 51–54.

more a question of the adoption of Westphalian mechanics than the acceptance of Western culture.[95]

## Monetary Regimes and Public Finances before the Middle of the Twentieth Century

We have gotten this far and hardly mentioned money. Perhaps the longest-standing rule of international economic law is that a state may criminalize the counterfeiting of its money by foreigners outside its own territory.[96] Otherwise, while there has long existed an international monetary order, it persisted for centuries without bilateral treaties, let alone a multilateral agreement of the kind adopted in 1944 at Bretton Woods. Convergence in national monetary systems had occurred partly through Smith's process of emulation.

From sometime in the sixteenth century, developments in military technology (pistols and other portable firearms) increased the costs of war and defense, which, no longer spread across a military nobility, fell directly on the sovereign state. Like trade, managing the public finances became integral to statecraft. By the eighteenth century, Hume was worrying default would be a greater threat to Britain's republic than to France's absolutist state, and so hated the accumulating debt mountain (chapter 1).

He had it the wrong way around. Combined with a somewhat more developed system of taxation, the parliamentary constraints on executive government and innovations in public finance (including the Bank of England) ushered in by Britain's 1688 revolution enhanced the credibility of its promise to repay. The struggle with France was underpinned by materially lower debt-servicing costs.[97] Such was the advantage, Hume's near (and more idealistic) contemporary Immanuel Kant concluded international order depended on rejecting debt as an instrument of statecraft. In his 1795/96 tract *Perpetual Peace*, the fourth of six preliminary articles for establishing and maintaining peace was the following: "No national debt shall be contracted in connection with the

95. Fidler, "Return of the Standard," p. 144. In 1894, Britain (followed by others) formally relinquished consular jurisdiction rights in Japan, subject to its incorporating various property rights and conventions into its reforming system of domestic law. The system of Ottoman concessions ended after World War I (with the breakup of the empire, and various League of Nations mandates for its component parts). For China, however, changes took longer (chapter 9).

96. Lowe, *International Law*, p. 97.

97. At times two percentage points (roughly a third) lower than for France, helping Britain spend more during military peaks: see Schulz and Weingast, "Democratic Advantage."

external affairs of the state."[98] That, of course, did not remotely happen. Instead, France's monarchical state having collapsed into revolution and inflationary crisis, states prioritized combining fiscal sustainability and flexibility
with a monetized economy. They moved, at varying speeds, toward backing
their national currencies with gold.

Since ancient times, domestic and foreign trade had been settled in precious metals, especially silver (because it is light) and gold. For centuries,
many states minted coins in both (bimetallism). Early in the eighteenth
century, partly thanks to Isaac Newton, Britain moved to a gold-only domestic
system.[99] Within little more than a generation, Hume had explained how the
gold-standard mechanism works. Essentially, a country that was running an external trade deficit paid in gold (or notes convertible into gold), with the consequent domestic monetary contraction bringing about a fall in the prices of local
goods and services relative to those abroad: in today's language, this is a real-
exchange-rate depreciation, which helps return the economy to balance. Like a
balance of power, on which Hume also wrote, this balance-of-payments mechanism is organic, not planned. It sets up self-fulfilling expectations so long as
states' commitments to their gold parities are highly credible (chapter 16).[100]

Over the century and a half following Newton's measure, Britain's industrial
revolution increased its share of trade, and the steam engine reduced the costs
of transporting the heavy metal. Other major states emulated London. By the
1870s, the new Bismarckian Reich had adopted gold, and France abandoned
its attachment to silver. Such domestic measures were underpinned by domestic legislation, *not* international law. The monetary order emerged rather than
being a jointly planned or stipulated treaty-based system (see chapter 6 on the
important distinction between spontaneous and designed institutions).

The process was not smooth, and there were international discussions.
Given the expansion and geographical broadening in trade, there were coordination problems and frictions among centers using different standards.
During an era when, under norms-cum-habits promoted by the Concert, some
great issues were taken at diplomatic conferences, monetary affairs became

98. Kant, *Political Writings*, p. 95.

99. When not discovering laws of nature or coinventing the calculus, Newton was Master
of the Mint. In 1717 he priced gold too cheaply relative to silver, causing silver to disappear,
which left the emergent commercial power uniquely on a de facto gold standard (Eichengreen,
*Globalizing Capital*, pp. 9–15).

100. Eichengreen, *Globalizing Capital*, pp. 25–27.

one of them. Between 1867 and 1892, four monetary conferences were held, revolving around whether to peg to gold (the instigator France's strong preference), silver, or both. They were attended not only by the European powers (with selective absences during wider tensions) but also by the United States, where bimetallism was a salient domestic issue. Indeed, as the period's rising economic power, the United States requested the last three conferences. India and smaller European states, such as the Netherlands and Spain, participated in some.

Divergent short-term interests were not a game-stopper, initially. As leading economic historian Barry Eichengreen puts it, "Discussions [at the 1867 conference] were informed by the shared values of classical liberalism: limited government, individual liberty, and free markets. Delegates shared a belief that monetary standardization would foster international commerce, economic growth, and world peace."[101] With shared values and a common interest in maintaining monetary order, it is perhaps not so surprising that during the last quarter of the nineteenth century and into the twentieth, the major monetary states frequently provided material support to each other. Perhaps most notably, France lent gold to Britain, its historical rival, on more than one occasion in order to keep the monetary ship afloat. There was no obligation or entitlement to this, whether in customary international law or otherwise (chapter 16).[102]

Multilateral monetary deliberations stalled as liberalism frayed (on the Continent) and relations soured in the run-up to World War I but resumed afterward as the underlying monetary strains had not gone a way. Initially under the umbrella of the newly established League of Nations, monetary officials met during the 1920s in Brussels and, later, in Genoa. Again, nothing was agreed formally, but the world shuffled into what became known as the gold-exchange standard (involving most advanced economies now holding part of their reserves in sterling or dollars, which the United Kingdom and the United States promised to convert on demand into gold).[103]

Separately, to assist with the mechanics of paying German reparations, the main powers established the Bank for International Settlements in Basel, Switzerland. In time this became headquarters for an international community of central bankers (chapter 19).

101. Eichengreen, "International Policy Coordination," p. 51.
102. Speaking in the Banque de France's magnificent Salle D'Or, I once thanked my hosts for this.
103. Pauly, "League of Nations."

## The League

Over that part of the story hovers the ghost of the League of Nations, US president Woodrow Wilson's *grand projet* after World War I, committing the world to national self-determination, territorial integrity, peace, disarmament, and a return to multilateral free trade among signatories.[104] As with Metternich's conception of European order a century before, Wilson viewed world order as needing to be buttressed by a principle of legitimacy, albeit a rather different one rejecting the balance of power.[105]

The foundational element was collective security: the central idea of the old Concert recast, universalized, and bound in law. Peace was to be maintained via deliberation and arbitration. If one signatory state went to war against another, notwithstanding the outcome of League-sponsored arbitration, members undertook to participate in economic and financial sanctions, and to assist (via free passage or more) whatever military measures were recommended by the League's council (Article 16). Among signatories, neutrality, once seen as limiting conflict, was over. Arbitration could be compulsory and was presumptively to be tried first in all circumstances. The parameters were set by international law, which was declaring its own high tide (the episode's enduring significance).

Otherwise, this was to be a world of group rights rather than the individual rights emphasized after World War II. But only some group rights. Faced with opposition from Britain's dominions (not so much the metropolis itself) and, at best, indifference from Wilson, Japan failed in its effort to get racial equality recognized in the covenant.[106] Instead, a concern for minority communities emerged from the commitment to self-determination, which in practice became identified with unwinding colonialism and, closer to home, breaking up the defeated European land empires (Habsburg and Ottoman). Former

104. The covenant did not mention *national* self-determination, which was pursued via a series of plebiscites and the mandate system (see below). On the commitment to free trade, see Article 23(e) of the covenant; and House, "Interpretation of President Wilson's," point 3. Eichengreen, "Versailles," notes the covenant's silence on a gold standard and free capital flows, both implicitly assumed.

105. Kissinger, *Diplomacy*.

106. A sad and shaming story, possibly exacerbating Japanese nationalism: see MacMillan, *Paris 1919*, pp. 316–21. (Later China failed to get antiracism expressly included in the UN Charter: see Sikkink, *Evidence for Hope*, p. 67. But a soft-law covenant followed once the UN was functioning.)

colonies joined the family of sovereign states only if deemed ready for it, otherwise falling under a new mandate system.[107]

Among the new central and eastern European states, the question of minority protections could not be ducked because while the states themselves were
products of nationalist and confessional sentiment, ethnic and religious communities had become widely dispersed across the empire after the 1848 and
1867 reforms (a lost mobility later lamented by the novelist Joseph Roth).
Notwithstanding minorities elsewhere, only new nations carved out of the
empires or otherwise conjured up had to pledge to treat their own minorities
decently. Processes and machinery (organizations) were established by the
League to give this force. They did not work.[108]

Conditions for the new League's success were vanquished partly by the
economic and social dislocation unleashed by stock market crashes and banking crises in the late 1920s and early 1930s. Far from healthy cooperation, the end
of the first wave of globalization ushered in trade protectionism, restrictions on
migration, and controls on the flow of capital across borders—in other words,
a prolonged suspension of international economic connectivity.[109]

And far from delivering collective security, within a few years Japan had
invaded Manchuria (1931). Nor did the American states gathering to declare
states' rights and duties—the 1933 Montevideo Convention, outlawing recognition of territory acquired by force (Article 11)—make a difference to the
wider world: Italy invaded Abyssinia (Ethiopia, 1935), Russia invaded Finland
(1939, leading to the Soviets' expulsion from the League), and then Nazi Germany declared war on as many states as it possibly could (and worse).

Of course, it was not just the turn from financial boom to bust that felled
the League. It rested too much on goodwill and left everything that really
mattered, when it mattered most, to individual states. It relied heavily on voluntarism, notably submitting disputes to League arbitration, and each interested party having a right of veto. The French had wanted the League to be
capable of projecting force, whereas that was left as a decision for each individual member.[110]

---

107. Established states with administrative capacity were, in the language of the day, held to
be trustees helping a new state prepare for sovereign nationhood—e.g., France in the Levant,
and (de facto) Britain in Mesopotamia.

108. Krasner, *Sovereignty*, pp. 90–96.

109. James, *End of Globalization*.

110. Drawing on MacMillan, *Paris 1919*, pp. 83–97.

Nor was the mood music great. Countries outside the Great Powers' magic circle were skeptical. Of those definitely inside, the British, many of its top officials lukewarm, thought Wilson a bully and vain. The exclusion of Germany reflected a will to punish the war's main belligerent. The US administration insisted that the Monroe Doctrine, claiming hegemony in the western Atlantic, be expressly recognized but would not permit others' similar zones of influence to be entrenched in international law. Since many types of decision required unanimity, these various asymmetries mattered. On top of all of which, notwithstanding Wilson's high-flown rhetoric, the US Congress declined to approve the treaty, leaving the great powers of the day without a structural majority of votes in the eight-member executive council empowered to make recommendations.

Even so, Wilson's vision was apparent, fatefully, in the principle of self-determination (except for the Great War's losers).[111] On top of sounding the slow-motion death knell for colonialism, it left ideas of sovereignty in a contest with more cosmopolitan values, initiating a path back toward a more natural law–like conception of international law (next chapter).

More important, the League's machinery and processes amounted to nothing less than a prototype for what came later: a potentially universal organization formally dedicated to peace, with a small executive council, a permanent secretariat housed in a building, a general assembly, and the Permanent International Court of Justice.[112]

## A World Court

The World Court, as it was known to aficionados, was the outcome of a long campaign.[113] Reformers, convinced that independent judges could preserve peace by applying international law without fear or favor, had two, sometimes three, aims: a permanent body of jurists to hear cases rather than The Hague's pick-and-mix arbitral panels, viewed as only a halfway house away from

111. Among the many peoples emerging from the old Austro-Hungarian Empire, those who identified as ethnic Germans were not permitted a self-determining plebiscite (perhaps not crazy given the later *Anschluss*): see MacMillan, *Paris 1919*, pp. 243–56.

112. Under Article 19, the assembly could recommend that past bilateral treaties be revisited in the interests of peace or if outdated. It was not used, although China tried (Neff, *Justice among Nations*, p. 352).

113. O'Connell and VanderZee, "History of International Adjudication," including the possibility of a criminal court (created decades later).

diplomatic negotiation; compulsory jurisdiction; and, for some, jurisdiction over individuals and international organizations, not only state-to-state relations. Other than the first, it was not to be—for all sorts of reasons, not least Wilson's greater faith in political institutions.[114] The British, notwithstanding reservations about the man, agreed, which mattered given the large role they played in drafting the covenant, including the League's structure and processes—a striking example of a declining Power's lingering clout and capability in shaping institutions (chapter 8).

During those interwar years, the court took fewer cases than some had expected, but one in particular had lasting significance.[115] In 1928, in its *Lotus* judgment, the new court effectively backed legal positivism's manifesto commitments: that international law was the law "govern[ing] relations between independent states . . . from their own free will. . . . Restrictions upon the independence of states therefore cannot be presumed."[116] This matters because it was the prevailing doctrine when—and therefore implicitly set the terms on which—non-European countries such as China, Japan, and Siam (Thailand's predecessor) joined the League and, so, the international community being assembled by the West—a point running through the book.

### The League Secretariat, Economic Institutions, and Legal Codification

Meanwhile, if the court proved less than its proponents campaigned for, the permanent secretariat, based in Geneva, might have become more than anyone bargained on. While the League's plenary assembly met only once per year, the secretariat was active each day. In such circumstances, a lot depends on individuals and structure. Jean Monnet (architect, later, of the European Community) and Per Jacobson (head, subsequently, of the International Monetary Fund) are only the two most illustrious members of the first cohort. Apparently well drilled, this remarkable group might have forged the first active international organization, shifting the sense of possibility for the next generation of internationalist officials and politicians.[117]

---

114. Mazower, *Governing the World*, pp. 118–36.

115. From 1922 to 1940, twenty-five judgments and twenty-seven advisory opinions, mostly on technical issues: see Neff, *Justice among Nations*, p. 356.

116. *S.S. Lotus* (France v. Turkey), PCIJ, Ser. A, No. 10, 1927.

117. Mazower, *Governing the World*, pp. 143–53.

As well as ushering in standardization of passports and visas, the new universal organization's less salient accomplishments, significantly for this inquiry, included moves toward a novel world of specialist international bodies tucked under its broad umbrella. Those surviving include the WHO and the International Labor Organization (which, constitutionally, was semidetached, having representatives of employers and employees, as well as national governments, on its governing body).

Just as significant, although marginalized in policy folk memory, was the League's Economic and Financial Organisation (EFO), established after the 1920 Brussels conference, and whose wide-ranging activities prefigured some of the roles later taken up by the IMF, the secretariat of the General Agreement on Tariffs and Trade (GATT), and others.[118] As well as searching for a credible monetary regime, in the mid-1920s the EFO organized and oversaw economic support operations for the flailing nations spun out of Austria-Hungary, a few years later tried to negotiate a "tariff truce" to arrest creeping protectionism, and during the 1930s promoted debate on Eastern European underdevelopment, migration, and poverty, and started to publish an annual survey of the world economy. Notwithstanding mixed results, the EFO was an "actor, rather than a stage."[119]

Finally, although the covenant was silent on codifying international law, the assembly was persuaded by its legal advisers to establish The Hague 1930 Codification Conference. With descent toward war, it achieved nothing substantive, but the baton had passed from the various international law associations to a new international technocracy. Their great project was dormant, not dead.[120]

## Moving On

Looking back on that first part of the history of international institutions, three persistent threads are striking. First, the survival from the High Middle Ages, through the Enlightenment, and into our world of some separation of political

118. Later additions to the League's star-studded economics team included Jacques Polak, who became a seminal figure in IMF policy, and James Meade, who during World War II wrote a paper for the British government proposing an international commercial union based on a tariff-reducing multilateral trade system, helping pave the way to the GATT (and who won the 1977 Nobel Prize).

119. Baughan, review of *Securing the World Economy*; Pauly, "League of Nations."

120. Rosenne, "Codification Revisited."

and adjudicatory powers, checking unfettered unitary rule and distinguishing the European tradition from those of some other great civilizations (chapter 9). Second, the recurrent tension between autonomous lawmaking and a higher morality—in one version, between reason of state and inalienable rights; in another, between legality and legitimacy. And third, the entanglement of the world of war and peace with the world of commerce and finance. None disappeared after World War II, but the resolutions and tensions were transformed.

# 3

# A Leadership-Based International System Is Built and Adapts

## FROM WORLD WAR II AND ITS HORRORS TO JUDICIALIZED INTERNATIONAL LAW, FINANCIAL CRISIS, AND WAR

In that [old] world, conquest is permissible, aggression is not a crime, neutrals must stay impartial (thus economic sanctions against aggressors are illegal), and agreements may be coerced. In [the new world] . . . states agree that war is illegal and refuse to recognize it as a source of legal entitlements, even when used to right wrongs. In that world, conquest is illegal, aggression a crime, economic sanctions are an essential tool of statecraft, and agreements cannot be coerced . . . moreover, trade plays an essential role not only as a source of beneficial collaboration but also as a collective tool for constraining illegal behavior.

OONA HATHAWAY AND SCOTT SHAPIRO,
*THE INTERNATIONALISTS AND THEIR PLAN
TO OUTLAW WAR*[1]

TO THIS STARK CONTRAST between the old and new worlds, we can add that the old had few international regimes, organizations, and tribunals, whereas ours is swimming in them. In a crescendo of activity, the threads of multilateralism, treaty-making, and organization building came together in a

1. Hathaway and Shapiro, *Internationalists and Their Plan*, p. 421.

comprehensive redesign of international relations spanning war and peace, human rights, trade, monetary affairs, and development.

It was a response to material and moral desolation. As the end of World War II came within sight, there was no escaping the wreckage in many states, or the need for a new kind of world. The international monetary system had unraveled in the 1930s, international trade was decimated, and the productive capacity of mainland Europe and Japan was literally shattered. Meanwhile, the peoples of Asia and Africa were demanding release from colonial shackles, and unspeakable horrors had been committed by the leaders and followers of a country, Germany, that had been central to Europe's supposed Enlightenment.

The foundational work was done at international conferences held before the war's end at venues—Washington, DC, and New Hampshire's White Mountains—that were both far away from theaters of war, and signified the United States' emerging preeminence. Over the next thirty or so years, the number of international organizations soared.[2] The edifice was more elaborate than before, attempting to delineate separate spheres for economic institutions and their political counterparts. But the wedge was incomplete, as time and circumstances revealed.[3]

## The United Nations and Nuremberg: Security and Rights

At their Moscow summit in October 1943, the United States, Britain, the Soviet Union, and the Republic of China (ruled by Chiang Kai-shek's Kuomintang) committed to exploring the establishment "at the earliest possible date of a general international organization."[4] The outcome, after conferences at Dumbarton Oaks in Washington, DC, and San Francisco, was the UN, comprising the General Assembly of all members; the Security Council of eleven (later fifteen) members; and a secretariat.

The UN's treaty is more exhaustive than that of the League of Nations—111 articles, compared with 26. Its declared purposes are grand:

> to maintain international peace and security . . . ; develop friendly relations among nations based on respect for the principle of equal rights and self-determination of peoples . . . ; to achieve international co-operation in

2. Zurn, *Theory of Global Governance*, fig. 5.2, p. 111.

3. Drawing on I. Hurd, *International Organizations*; Frieden et al., *World Politics*; Neff, *Friends but No Allies*.

4. Moscow Conference Communique, October 1943.

solving international problems of an economic, social, cultural, or humanitarian character, and in promoting and encouraging respect for human rights and for fundamental freedoms for all without distinction as to race, sex, language, or religion. (Article 1)

That is the language of international liberalism, but the charter is not comprehensively cosmopolitan: "The Organization is based on the principle of the sovereign equality of all of its members" (Article 2[1]); plus "Nothing . . . shall impair the inherent right of individual or collective self-defense" (Article 51); and "Nothing . . . shall authorize the UN to intervene in matters which are essentially within the domestic jurisdiction of any state" (Article 2[7]).

That left intact customary law doctrines of sovereignty and reciprocal duties, including that states were free to choose whether and how to trade with other nations but owed a minimum standard of protection to foreigners (and their property). On the face of it, then, the UN was an institution for coordination and cooperation among states.

## Coordinator versus Lawmaker: Hierarchy and Opinion

But it was to be no ordinary mechanism. First, signatories agreed that charter obligations and commitments trump all other international agreements in the event of a conflict (Article 103), giving the UN the formal appearance of the summit of summits.

Second, the Security Council stands above the rest of the membership. Whereas the General Assembly's motions are advisory or an expression of opinion, some council decisions bind UN members irrespective of whether they agree (Article 25). Qualifying freedoms in self-defense (including inaction), the council is empowered to determine "the existence of any threat to the peace, breach of the peace, or act of aggression," and to decide what measures are appropriate (Chapter VII). It is, at least formally, akin to a trustee for peace and security, for which the charter gives it "primary responsibility" (Article 24). Further, it can require members to effect "complete or partial interruption of economic relations and . . . means of communication" and, if such steps are inadequate, nonenumerated actions (Articles 41, 42). In other words, economic relations can be weaponized on the council's say-so, adding a ratchet to the pre–World War II relaxations of the laws of neutrality during war (chapter 2).[5]

5. Steil and Litan, *Financial Statecraft*, pt. 1. On law, see Lowe and Tzanakopoulos, "Economic Warfare."

Third, it therefore matters that the Security Council's membership is not wholly rotational or electoral but, rather, has five permanent members, each wielding a veto: they—senior trustees, as it were—are the great-power victors of World War II: Britain, China, France, Russia, and the United States.[6] The charter's declaration of "sovereign equality" could mislead the unwary (chapters 8 and 11).

Fourth, the zone preserved by the charter for "domestic jurisdiction"—for sovereignty free from involuntary intervention—turned out to be fluid, depending on how international law developed (as the League's Permanent Court had flagged in 1929).[7] The law did anything but stay still. The UN was empowered to pursue its enumerated ends by acting as midwife to covenants, treaties, and subsidiary bodies, licensing bursts of activity initially lasting into the 1970s and resuming after the Cold War. We begin with the law's higher reaches—moral and architectural—since they affect opinion on states' geoeconomic strategies (next chapter) and how the purely economic regimes should operate.

## From Nuremberg to Codified Human Rights and Humanitarian Law

A watershed came at the 1945–46 Nuremberg war crimes trials, described by US counsel as "the first trial in history for crimes against the peace of the world."[8]

While the tribunal carefully avoided basing its findings entirely on either positive or natural law, the indictment and trial seemed to reassert the meaningfulness of a higher law, applicable to all. Specifically, the tribunal determined the Hague conventions were part of the customary laws of war, "recognised by all civilised nations" and so binding whether or not a state had signed up.[9]

6. The PRC assumed China's seat during 1971.

7. Crawford, *Brownlie's Principles*, pp. 438–39; Ratner, *Thin Justice*, p. 126.

8. US chief prosecutor Robert Jackson, who had stepped down from the Supreme Court to undertake this service (Hathaway and Shapiro, *Internationalists and Their Plan*, p. 280).

9. International Military Tribunal, *Trial of the Major War Criminals*, pp. 253–54. The tribunal held the London Agreement and Charter of the International Military Tribunal, August 8, 1945—a multilateral treaty among the Western victors (France, the Soviet Union, the United Kingdom, and the United States) and ratified by many others—articulated legal rules that, notwithstanding any provisions of German law, were binding on the war criminals by virtue of provisions of international law and doctrines of humanity prevailing before the war.

Second, the accused were tried not only for breaching the laws of war (war crimes) but also for crimes against peace (starting a war of aggression, as per the Kellogg-Briand Pact, which Germany had signed in 1928) and crimes against humanity. The indictment (count three, war crimes) included among its particulars "deliberate and systematic genocide" against particularly "Jews, Poles, and Gypsies" as well as others. This, together with the term "genocide" being used by some of the prosecutors during the trial, was a step toward crystallizing the idea that *groups* of people, not only individuals, could have rights in international law.[10]

And third, the prosecution's case aimed to tear away the veil between the state and its individual officials. In the tribunal's own words, "Crimes against international law are committed by men, not by abstract entities."[11] Nor were crimes against Germany's citizens excluded. As Britain's chief prosecutor put it, when Germany's crimes affected the international community, they were "not mere matters of domestic law but crimes against the law of nations."[12] Nuremberg and its counterpart for Japan (the 1946 International Military Tribunal for the Far East) represented, then, a possibility: that something we call the international community would not always leave the leaders of states immune from accountability for atrocities, whether committed at home or abroad. While that was set aside during the Cold War, its spirit lives today in the International Criminal Court (ICC) (see below).[13]

Around the same time as those climactic tribunals, the UN Charter (1945, Article 55) told the new international organization to promote, among other things, not only living standards, social progress, development, and solutions to cooperative problems but also human rights and fundamental freedoms. This was quite something because it broadened the focus of international law from

10. On the indictment, see Yale Law School, "Nuremberg Trial Proceedings." The notion of crimes against peace was pushed by the Soviet party, drawing on A. N. Trainin: see Neff, *Justice among Nations*, p. 397. Genocide was part of the description of war crimes, not of crimes against humanity. Raphael Lemkin coined the term in 1944, compiled a good deal of the evidence, and campaigned for it to be recognized as a crime in its own right.

11. Neff, *Justice among Nations*, p. 399. The tribunal's charter also precluded a defense of acting on orders.

12. Hartley Shawcross, drawing on Hersch Lauterpacht's work (Vrdoljak, "Human Rights and Genocide," p. 1189).

13. For the extraordinary history of Lauterpacht's and Lemkin's contributions to, respectively, the "human rights" and "genocide" elements of the trial, and modern international law generally, see Vrdoljak, "Human Rights and Genocide."

state-to-state relations and the protection of minority groups to state-citizen relations. The centerpiece became the 1948 Universal Declaration of Human Rights, issued by the General Assembly (before the change of regime in China). In the same year, states signed up to the Genocide Convention, giving this crime formal existence (including during peacetime) and committing signatories to punish perpetrators.[14]

Those steps—leaps, really—were followed by the 1951 Convention Relating to the Status of Refugees, which pledged humane treatment for refugees with a "well-founded fear of persecution" in their home state; the 1965 Convention on the Elimination of All Forms of Racial Discrimination; and the 1966 Covenants on Civil and Political Rights and, separately, Economic, Social and Cultural Rights.

Taken together, the package amounted to something approaching an international bill of liberal rights. While beginning life as resolutions of the General Assembly, the components became treaties ratified by a number of states over the following decade—but with notable exceptions, including China for political rights and the United States for economic and social rights.[15] There have been subsequent additions, including the 1985 Convention on the Elimination of All Forms of Discrimination against Women (signed but not ratified by the United States).

The global declaratory edifice works in parallel with a series of regional rights treaties, initiated by the Bogota Declaration of the Rights and Duties of Man, passed by the Latin American states a year before the UN declaration; and most famously including the 1953 European Convention for the Protection of Human Rights and Fundamental Freedoms.[16] Whereas the UN declaration was essentially exhortation—attempting to harness world opinion—some regional measures went further. The Europeans created the Court of Human Rights, and an investigatory commission, which can receive complaints from individuals, not only states. Some twenty to thirty years later, the Latin American states created similar monitoring and enforcement machinery

14. Because of the need to demonstrate intent to destroy all or part of a group, genocide is harder to prove, but generally regarded as the gravest horror.

15. On the United States' signing (President Carter, 1977) and eventually ratifying (1992, with multiple reservations, etc.) the political rights convention and a few other treaties (e.g., against genocide and torture), see Donnelly and Whelan, *International Human Rights*, pp. 126–28, 148–50. China has signed (1998) but not ratified the civil-political covenant.

16. Sikkink, *Evidence for Hope*.

in a new convention (1969, in force since 1978).[17] In effect, the institution of human rights norms was buttressed with organizations.

### Law's Codification and Development: The Treaty on Treaties, and Peremptory Norms

Human rights were one project, but not the only one. Picking up the work of the 1930 Hague conference (previous chapter), the UN Charter (Article 13) told the General Assembly to promote the progressive development and codification of international law. Alongside ad hoc exercises, this saw the creation in 1947 of the International Law Commission, which proposes conventions for the General Assembly to declare should become or be treated as law. Outputs have covered the law of the sea, diplomatic conventions, states' responsibilities for wrongful acts (see below), and, vitally, the law of treaties.[18]

The seventy-five articles of the 1969 Vienna Convention on the Law of Treaties, effective since 1980, codified and honed various customary law doctrines governing treaties among states. While superficially tedious legal plumbing, it is important at almost every level of our inquiry. Its provisions include, broadly expressed, an obligation to comply with treaties to which a state has consented (Preamble and Article 26, headed *pacta sunt servanda*); the inadmissibility of domestic law provisions as justification for failure to honor a treaty (Article 27);[19] the invalidity of treaties where consent was procured coercively in ways that violated principles of international law (an important qualification; Articles 51–52);[20] the obligation to comply being subject, in some cases, to domestic ratification, not only executive branch signing (Article 14);[21] the need to interpret

17. Venezuela issued a denunciation and withdrawal notice in 2012 and, after criticism, later left the Organization of American States.

18. Rosenne, "Codification Revisited."

19. Bearing on UK 2020 measures, eventually withdrawn, to legislate itself out of parts of its EU exit treaty.

20. Certainly physical coercion, but not (all) economic or political pressure, which developing countries failed to get included as grounds for nullity. A nonbinding declaration condemning such pressure was issued instead: see Ratner, *Thin Justice*, p. 206.

21. States determine their internal processes for agreement (signing, ratification). The United States employs both "treaties" (approved by the Senate for presidential ratification) and, more frequently, "executive agreements." If deemed "self-executing," both automatically become domestic law, giving citizens rights of redress for breaches. By contrast, under legacy prerogative powers, the British executive government may strike binding international agreements without

a treaty in the light of its object and purpose, and taking account of any sub-sequent overt or tacit agreement among the parties on interpretation (Articles 31–32); a general inability to exit a treaty lacking express or implied termina-tion provisions (which the charter itself lacks; Article 56); but the right to exit or suspend compliance with bilateral treaties, except provisions protecting certain human rights, in the face of breaches by others undermining the pur-pose of a treaty (Article 60).

The convention also codified the right of states to add reservations to any treaty so long as doing so is not expressly precluded, at odds with its basic purpose, or opposed by other states objecting to how the reservation affects relations with them (Articles 19–23).[22] That right is regularly exercised, leav-ing many multilateral treaties operating in different forms. More than merely cautious statecraft, such measures create ambiguities in the overall edifice because a number of states have lodged reservations to various provisions of the "bill of rights" covenants, pointing toward a deep cleavage in modern inter-national affairs. States are said to be sovereign but, according to international law, only if they stay within international law, incentivizing dissenting states to try to circumscribe the international law that applies to them, and to furnish themselves with exit routes.

In one vital respect, however, the Vienna treaty limited states' freedom to do that. In Article 53, it asserts the unqualified priority of peremptory norms of international law (*jus cogens*), voiding any treaty that violates them. Now held to be preeminent also in customary law (at least by some tribunals: see below), these special norms are currently regarded as including the bars on genocide, torture, slavery, and other crimes against humanity. So, after the long nineteenth century's positivist interregnum, we find an updated version— focused on a subset of positive human rights—of earlier jurists' efforts to con-strain absolute monarchs and other rulers with law, as when Vattel maintained that some parts of man-made law echoing natural law were binding whether or not a state had consented (chapter 2).

Practically, however, that left a good deal hanging in the air. While the Se-curity Council clearly had legal authority to decide that action should be taken

---

the sanction of Parliament, except where implementation materially alters domestic legal rights and obligations.

22. Also, exit can be followed by re-ratification subject to reservations when a state wishes to extricate itself from a particular provision rather than a whole regime: see Helfer, "Taking Stock," pp. 109–10.

against an aggressor, what if a state breached its own citizen-subjects' basic human rights? Could the "international community" invade or take other deterrent action? And did human rights place constraints on the Security Council itself, and other UN organs? Those questions-cum-claims, picked up later in the story, highlight a tension at the heart of the UN-led part of the international order: between an individual-centric notion of human rights and a state-centric notion of sovereignty. The latter was emphatically the line taken in the Five Principles of Peaceful Existence drawn up by China and India in 1954 and backed a year later by the Bandung conference of Asian and African states leading to the nonaligned movement.[23]

One thing, perhaps, was clear. Uncertainty could not be resolved by the Security Council alone because, as a matter of international law, it exercises the authority of a political body, not a judicial one. For example, under Article 39, it determines whether there are "threats to the peace," not whether a state has illegally violated the obligation to preserve peace. It does not authoritatively resolve disputes in law.[24] That happens, to the extent it does, elsewhere.

## The International Court of Justice

The International Court of Justice (ICJ) is unambiguously a judicial body. Established by the UN Charter in 1945, as successor to the League's Permanent Court of International Justice, and opening a year later, it is housed, alongside the earlier Court of Arbitration, in The Hague's Peace Palace. It heard its first case (a dispute between Britain and Albania) in 1947.[25]

The ICJ is an organ of the UN, its fifteen judges appointed by the General Assembly and Security Council. Its judgments are "final and without appeal" (Article 60, ICJ Statute), UN members are obliged to comply "in any case to which [they are] a party," and a state not receiving its declared redress may look to the Security Council, appearing now in the guise of an executive enforcement agency (Article 94[2], UN Charter).

23. Akin to early twentieth-century "Westphalian" norms, they are (1) mutual respect for others' territorial integrity and sovereignty, (2) mutual nonaggression, (3) mutual noninterference in others' internal affairs, (4) equality and mutual benefit, and (5) peaceful coexistence (Chesterman, "Asia's Ambivalence").

24. I. Hurd, *How to Do Things*, p. 40.

25. Concerning responsibilities for safeguarding shipping in the Corfu Channel. Albania lost, finally paying the prescribed damages in the 1990s (Wikipedia, accessed August 9, 2019).

The court is charged with applying international law, which, in terms essentially the same as those governing its predecessor, is defined (at least for its purposes) in Article 38(1) as

a) International conventions, whether general or particular, establishing rules expressly recognized by the contesting states;
b) International custom, as evidence of a general practice accepted as law;
c) The general principles of law recognized by civilized states;
d) ... judicial decisions and the teachings of the most highly qualified publicists of the various nations.

That seemingly dry list is, in fact, rather more, given paragraph (c)'s echoes of the natural-law tradition, and the implication that the court can fill in gaps in the positive law of treaties and established custom. Taken together with the various human rights treaties and conventions, a new substantive "standard of civilization" was being raised from World War II's ashes, separating the new world from the thinner formalism of the late nineteenth century's classical liberal commercial priorities.

Given that UN organs may seek advisory opinions from the court, which is not therefore restricted to the flow of bilateral disputes, it is positioned to fill in, and develop, the rules of the game for international relations, and even states' relations with their own citizen-subjects. Two cases are relevant to our inquiry.

In 1970 the court held that, for some matters, a state owes duties to all other states: not merely to specific parties' (under a treaty or customary law) but responsibilities to the international community as such (*erga omnes*: toward all).[26] This, again, summoned pre-nineteenth-century ideas of natural law (Grotius) and international society (Pufendorf), but it did so without clarifying which responsibilities fall into this category, or how they might be enforced.[27] An important question is whether, for lawyers, this class of duties might include responding to any natural existential threats to our species or planetary home, or broadly upholding those general principles of international law necessary for the system to function at all (part IV).

---

26. Barcelona Traction, Light and Power Co., Ltd, Second Phase, ICJ Reports 1970, p. 32, paras. 33–34 (Crawford, *Brownlie's Principles*, pp. 566–75; Koskenniemi, *Fragmentation of International Law*, pp. 193–206).

27. Examples like genocide and slavery imply a redundant equivalence with *jus cogens* norms, but *erga omnes* is probably about who can intervene.

The second case seems, however, to go in the other direction. In 1986 the ICJ held that US help to the Nicaraguan Contra rebels had been illegal.[28] Since it had involved not only military measures but trade embargoes, the ICJ was fleshing out the scope of the bar on unwelcome intervention. In doing so, it echoed a 1970 General Assembly motion, marking the UN's twenty-fifth anniversary, affirming the right of states "freely to determine, without external interference, their political status and to pursue their economic, social and cultural development."[29] Apart from shining an uncomfortable light on later IMF programs (chapter 16), that seems to strengthen sovereignty.

The reconciliation, if there is one, is that so far as international law is concerned, sovereignty's freedoms must be exercised within the law. Where a state is not complying with its international legal obligations, adversely affected states may, without consent, take countermeasures of various kinds (the basis for the mechanics of trade pacts: see below). This leaves much in the air, however, including what responsibility for improperly exercised sovereignty means (on which the International Law Commission worked for decades), and the reconciliation of conflicting norms.

It would be a mistake to think decisive answers come from the court. In the first place, it has jurisdiction over only states (Article 34), not international organizations (including the UN itself), people, nongovernmental organizations, or corporations. Second, both state parties have to agree to take a dispute to the court, unless its jurisdiction has been preagreed in a subject-specific treaty, or follows from a state having made a general declaration of jurisdiction, subject to reservations (Article 36, ICJ Statute).[30] Third, its decisions do not, formally, create binding precedent (general law binding other states; Article 59). And, fourth, any motion to the Security Council to enforce an ICJ judgment is subject to the permanent members' veto powers.[31]

28. *Nicaragua*, 1986, Rep. 108 (205). On other aspects of the case, see I. Hurd, *International Organizations*, pp. 199, 208.

29. Resolution 2625: 1970 Declaration on Principles of International Law on Friendly Relations and Cooperation among States in Accordance with the UN Charter (adopted by consensus).

30. Of permanent Security Council members, only the United Kingdom has accepted the court's general jurisdiction (most recently in 2017 for disputes arising after 1987, and excepting cases concerning nuclear weapons). Until 1986, the United States maintained a heavily qualified formal acceptance of jurisdiction, which it rescinded after the *Nicaragua* case (see above and chapter 9). France did the same in 1974. Other states, including Germany and India, have signed up with heavy exceptions.

31. Which Washington exercised after the *Nicaragua* case.

Summing up, on the one hand, the international community sought to maintain the doctrine of state sovereignty via parts of the charter, ICJ voluntarism, case-by-case jurisprudence, and some kind of political oversight: a world of positivism. On the other, a combination of the Nuremberg trials, the declaratory "bill of rights," and the court has ushered in preemptory and universal norms: a world of higher law.

## The Economic Sphere

Turning to commerce and finance, they too experienced a spasm of activity into the 1970s. The UN quickly spawned the Economic and Social Council (1945); the Commission on Trade and Development (UNCTAD, 1964), which produces annual reports; the Commission on International Trade Law (UNCITRAL, 1966); and others. It also entered into "specialized agency agreements" with the IMF and the World Bank, which obtained rights to seek advisory opinions from the ICJ and UN international diplomatic immunities for their staff, while recognizing the supremacy of the Security Council and giving the UN the right to participate in agenda setting. In other words, while formally independent organizations, the IMF and the World Bank were somehow to fit under the UN's umbrella.

Although things did not work out like that, it was not always obvious they wouldn't. Major developing countries spent a couple of decades pursuing the nonaligned movement's Bandung agenda.[32] During the 1960s, UNCTAD provided a forum for articulating a development-centered approach to international economic affairs, and in 1974 the General Assembly voted by majority for the New International Economic Order and the Charter of Economic Rights and Duties of States. Together, they promoted a different set of norms for international commercial and political relations: no economic coercion in international relations, no interference in economic affairs, absolute sovereignty over natural resources (implying no obligation to export essential materials),[33] and a Calvo Doctrine right to nationalize or seize foreign-owned enterprises (with domestic law determining any compensation, and no counterpart right to reprisals). They also called for fair prices and more assistance, technology transfers, and a regime governing exploitation of

---

32. Drawing on Neff, *Friends but No Allies*, pp. 180–96; D. Vagts, "International Economic Law"; and Frieden et al., *World Politics*, p. 451.

33. Already espoused in a moderate 1962 declaration, for which the United States voted.

oceanic seabeds. Tonally, it was social democratic nationalism, with cosmopolitan help.

None of it was binding in international law, and not much of it found its way into customary law. While some themes were picked up in particular fields, any impetus was derailed by political revolutions and coups, the Arab oil embargoes (a kind of super-sovereign use of economic coercion on rich and poor alike), stagflation, and developing-country sovereign debt crises during the late 1970s and 1980s. By the time the world economy stabilized, the various UN bodies were talking shops. While that occasionally affected the tone of international politics, the substantive action has, in the main, been elsewhere, with high policy driven not by the UN but by the Bretton Woods institutions, trade negotiators, the various informal Gs (Group of 7, 20, etc.), and latterly Basel.

## The Atlantic Charter and Bretton Woods

Their agenda goes back to the earliest years of World War II, when Winston Churchill and his advisers sailed in secret to see President Franklin D. Roosevelt in Newfoundland. In the Atlantic Charter issued after their meeting, alongside clauses on relations during the war, the great men committed themselves to a geopolitical-cum-economic vision to "further the enjoyment by all States, great or small, victor or vanquished, of access, on equal terms to the trade and to the raw materials of the world which are needed for their economic prosperity ... [and to] bring about the fullest collaboration between all nations in the economic field."[34]

When, later, the world's monetary experts gathered in New Hampshire, that owed a good deal to US grand strategy framed under Secretary of State Cordell Hull, an avowed free trader. In the style of Alexander Hamilton, he was committed to reopening markets for US firms, but in the manner of Hume and Smith he saw expectations of increased commerce as part of a path to peace among nations.[35] Looking toward the war's end, this meant reembracing the most-favored-nation principle championed by London and Paris a century before, and also dismantling Britain's sterling-area system of imperial preference: Roosevelt, perhaps closer to an economic nationalist than a free trader,

---

34. Atlantic Charter, Clauses 4–5.

35. Hull's 1930s bilateral-treaties project was authorized by the 1934 Reciprocal Trade Act.

had not taken the United States into the war for American troops to return home with Britain's global empire and power intact.[36] Washington having been frustrated in getting their way through the 1941 Atlantic Charter or Lend-Lease financing, Britain's desperate need for credit after the war provided the decisive opportunity. The famous monetary conference could go ahead.

Its history is typically told in terms of the (frustrated) grand designs and intellectual brilliance of Britain's John Maynard Keynes, the policy realism and strategic and managerial acumen of America's Harry Dexter White, the competition between them, and the question of whether White was moonlighting as a Soviet agent. Prosaically, the outcome was an international monetary regime under which the United States pledged to maintain the dollar's value against gold, while everyone else pledged to peg their currencies to the dollar. The agreement entered international law in 1944, before the war's end, perhaps reflecting White's view, informed by the previous Washington generation's problems with the League, that the chances of getting congressional approval "would be better during the war than after it."[37]

The IMF was established to police the signatories' commitments, and help manage any needed adjustments in fixed exchange rates. The International Bank for Reconstruction and Development (World Bank) was created to help postwar reconstruction (which morphed into economic development in poorer countries). In both, the United States wielded a veto on crucial issues (chapter 16).[38]

What remains striking is not formal recognition that the dollar had supplanted the pound sterling, after its nearly two centuries as the proximate anchor of the world monetary system. That had been more or less inevitable. No, the novelty is the creation of an organization to manage the new international monetary order. From now on, international economic institutions seemed to need international organizations, with buildings, staff, written rules, and regular meetings.

36. By ensuring trade within the empire was settled in sterling, international demand for the dollar was reduced. In consequence, in an otherwise tense relationship, the State Department's free-trade goals were aligned with the Treasury's aim for the dollar to supplant sterling. Steil, *Battle of Bretton Woods*, pp. 114–18.

37. July 1942 cable from Britain's Washington, DC, embassy to Keynes reporting a conversation with White (Ikenberry, "World Economy Restored," p. 303).

38. A de facto veto capability was also available to the British Commonwealth if they acted as a bloc and, later, to the EU's IMF members.

## The GATT and Postponed Aspirations for a Trade Organization

But just as that seemed to be the direction of travel, the victors' efforts stalled. The General Agreement on Tariffs and Trade (GATT), produced in Geneva under the auspices of the UN's Conference on Trade and Employment during 1947, had only twenty-three signatories. A wider cast participated in talks that began in Cuba later that year on how to police the new trading system. Fifty-six states signed the 1948 Havana Charter committing to establish an International Trade Organization, but it never got off the ground thanks to the US Congress (see below).

Even Washington's hopes for trade liberalization proved harder to land than anticipated. By the late 1940s, it had become apparent that continental Europe's economy was in emergency, that Britain was close to bankruptcy, that Stalin was not the benign partner Roosevelt had fancied, and that Washington therefore had bigger priorities than economic principle.

The GATT's leading clauses did formally enshrine the most-favored-nation principle and combat free-riding. But it went on to enumerate a series of provisions the Europeans had demanded for near-term survival, and a set of permanent exceptions for public order (Article XX), national security (Article XXI), and so on. It was liberal in aspiration but tailored to the circumstances of the day.[39]

The new Truman administration had recognized the vacuity of its predecessor's strategy of cooperating with Moscow, forcing German economic pacification, and quickly dismantling Britain's remaining imperial pretensions. When, suffering financial strains exacerbated by the terms of the US postwar loan, Britain signaled it would withdraw from Greece—a country that remained part of the West largely thanks to Churchill facing down Stalin—Washington finally grasped that the Roosevelt Treasury's policy would create a vacuum for Moscow to fill as it wished; a friendly fading empire replaced by an unfriendly rising one. As the Central Intelligence Agency advised, "The greatest danger to the security of the United States [is] the possibility of economic collapse in western Europe and the consequent accession to power of communist elements." More precisely, the State Department concluded, "British abdication from the Middle East . . . [meant that] if Russian expansion

---

39. On the GATT's inherent liberalism, see Mavroidis and Sapir, *China and the WTO*; and chapters 17 and 18.

was to be checked, the United States [would have to] move into the defaulted position."[40]

As power moved away from Roosevelt's myopic Treasury, US policy became less parochial. Economically, the action moved from the modestly resourced Bretton Woods institutions to the Marshall Plan, seeking to underpin Western Europe's security by reviving its economy. The Organization for European Economic Cooperation was established in Paris in 1948 to help coordinate reconstruction, with a key objective of avoiding inconsistency among countries' local macroeconomic plans. Two years later, there followed the European Payments Union, enabling multilateral month-end settlement of trade-related debts in currencies that were not convertible. It lasted until 1958.

## Keeping the Sea-Lanes Open and Shipping Safe

As well as monetary settlement, trade in goods and fossil fuels needs transport, linking commerce to policy in a quite different field. Shortly after its founding, the UN established another body: the International Maritime Organization, focusing mainly on the safety and soundness of commercial shipping. It also commissioned work to recodify the law of the sea. While taking many decades to complete (see below), the focus quickly broadened from the traditional preoccupations of naval war and prize to who had what rights to seas and oceans and, in particular, to passage.

That gained edge from plans to increase states' territorial waters from three nautical miles (an old cannon's range) to twelve. In consequence, some of the world's most important cargo routes—notably the Straits of Malacca and Singapore, which today see much more traffic than the Suez or Panama canals—would no longer be part of the high seas, with their established customary-law freedom of navigation. As a matter of law, the answer was to introduce codified rights of innocent and transit passage through straits and archipelagic islands (especially Indonesia and the Philippines), an approach, germinating during the 1950s and 1960s, not so far from Grotius's (chapter 2).[41]

In practice, however, those conventions have relied on the United States and others keeping the sea-lanes open, via what are known as Freedom of Navigation Operations. It is another way, invisible to most consumers and

---

40. Key figures were Dean Acheson and George Kennan: see Steil, *Marshall Plan*, pp. 21–32. CIA quote from p. 12; State Department memoir quote from p. 32.

41. Rothwell, "Sea Lanes."

producers, in which the second globalization depended on the Pax Americana. That is up for grabs today given the contest across the South China Sea and beyond (chapter 4), which ought to revive interest in how economic and security policies and institutions fitted together during the Cold War, subjects many thought behind us.

## Segmented Cold War Blocs: Security Pacts and a Wider Commercial Circle

The Cold War provides an instructive example of the gap—chasm even— between form and substance in international law and relations. As a matter of form, the leading communist states did not dissent from the law of nations' orthodoxies. The Soviet Union was wedded to state sovereignty, noninterference, overt consent (treaties) as the basis for binding law, and the subjects of international law being states not individuals; a Russian jurist even sat on the world court during its early years.[42]

Substantively, meanwhile, the world split into security and ideological blocs, and the international economy bent its shape to fit in. Form did align with substance, however, in the view, advanced at various points by both the Soviets and Americans, that interventions could be permissible *within* their own blocs—an assertion of legitimate hierarchy within their ideological locality (chapter 8).[43]

### *The Security Sphere*

Of the thousands of treaties lodged with the UN, many concern security. Among the most important are collective-defense military alliances, including the 1949 North Atlantic Treaty and the 1951 treaties between the United States and, respectively, Japan, South Korea, and Australia and New Zealand, which extended the Pax Americana to the western Pacific. These treaties are typically short, broad brush, and bold. The NATO treaty had just fourteen articles, but they are profound. After genuflecting to the UN Charter, Article 5 commits the signatories, as a matter of hard law, to be ready to come to each other's aid in the face of external attack. Each member, however great and powerful, undertakes to consider an attack on any member, however weak or small, an

42. Drawing on Neff, *Justice among Nations*, pp. 419–22.
43. Neff, *Justice among Nations*, pp. 407–10.

attack on all. (It was invoked for the first time after the September 11 attacks on New York City and Washington, DC, in a manifestation of European solidarity with the United States.) Almost as important here, Article 9 creates a council with, among other things, a power to set up subsidiary bodies. This the council did when, during the 1950s, it created a permanent secretariat, headed by a secretary general, and established the Supreme Headquarters Allied Powers Europe, which in effect delivered some pooling of military resources under NATO command (just as then-general Dwight Eisenhower had been supreme Allied commander after the D-Day Normandy landings in 1944).[44]

Very differently, another kind of security treaty commits the parties to limit an arms race. The most famous has been the Nuclear Non-proliferation Treaty (NPT), agreed on when both Washington and Moscow were feeling the financial and political costs of their Vietnamese proxy war. Since 1970 it has committed its nearly two hundred signatory states not to hold nuclear weapons, with derogations only for the five permanent Security Council members, which pledge not to help other states acquire nuclear capability other than for peaceful purposes. Initially in force for twenty-five years, since 1995 the NPT has applied in perpetuity, subject to each signatory giving three months' notice of exit. India, Israel, and Pakistan never signed up, and North Korea withdrew in 2003—far fewer holdouts than predicted.

The NPT also commits all signatories, including the nuclear powers, to pursue disarmament in good faith (Article VI). As such, it provided an umbrella for the bilateral agreements between the United States and Russia. Those began, during the 1960s and 1970s, with the Strategic Arms Limitation Talks (SALT) and the Anti-ballistic Missile Treaty, and continued with the 1987 treaty on intermediate-range forces.

Given powerful incentives to cheat, agreements of that kind present formidable monitoring problems. That vital function falls, under the NPT's Article III, to the International Atomic Energy Agency, an international organization created in the 1950s, and headquartered in Vienna, with a director general and large staff. Each NPT signatory is obliged to enter into more specific agreements with the International Atomic Energy Agency, whose role is broadly analogous to (but graver than) the IMF's in monitoring compliance with economic standards and codes: verification. The agency also facilitates a formal review of the NPT every five years (the next one has twice been delayed by COVID).

---

44. NATO headquarters moved from Paris to Brussels after President de Gaulle suspended French participation in 1966.

The NPT and the SALT agreement were central to 1970s efforts intended to de-escalate US-Soviet relations, known as détente. This too begat a new international forum, the Conference on Security and Cooperation in Europe, bringing Moscow and Washington together with Northern Hemisphere states from both blocs. Its key output was the 1975 Helsinki Accords, a set of multi-lateral agreements among (initially) thirty-five countries recognizing, among other things, the prevailing borders in Europe, territorial integrity, sovereign equality, and nonintervention, which taken together effectively acquiesced in the de facto division of the continent (and so Soviet bloc legitimacy). But, in a different register, the accords also affirmed respect for human rights, includ-ing freedom to emigrate, giving succor to Soviet bloc dissidents.[45] The Final Act accords were not treaties, and so were not binding under international law. Nothing like them exists today with Beijing.

### Cold War Economic Order: Porous Autarky

By contrast, economic relations were much simpler than today. They had not been easy since the Russian Revolution. The Bolsheviks' first acts included repudiating Russia's debts and expropriating foreign-owned assets— international economic taboos. Unlike London, Washington did not recognize the new regime until the mid-1930s and would not accept gold that originated in the Soviet Union. Some private trade persisted nonetheless, partly under the umbrella of bilateral treaties with Britain and Germany.[46]

When World War II came, the United States provided its ideological rival with financial assistance, but relations refrosted after the war was won. During the late 1940s and early 1950s, against the backdrop of communist victory in China, the Korean War, and the descent of the Iron Curtain, the United States, the United Kingdom, and the founding members of what became the European Union (EU) established a process for controlling the export of arms, nuclear material, and sensitive industrial goods to communist states. Subsequently extended to most other European countries, Australia, Japan, and Turkey, this became the Coordinating Committee on Export Controls.

Naturally enough, this commercial cold war was symmetric, with the Soviet Gosplan (State Planning Committee, overseeing the Ministry of Foreign

45. In 1974, the US Congress had made freedom to emigrate a condition, subject to annual presidential waivers, for granting most-favored-nation trade status.

46. Neff, *Friends but No Allies*, pp. 89–90.

Trade) controlling external trade with the noncommunist bloc. Residual trade was small and concentrated: exports of natural gas and petroleum products to Western Europe (little of anything to the United States), and imports of grain and other foodstuffs from Australia, Canada, and the United States.[47] Payment required some financial linkages. Imports were paid for via the Soviet Bank for Foreign Trade and various overseas banking satellites that it or Gosbank controlled.

The setup was approximately autarkic, with a commercial funnel for essential trade and associated financial flows. Consistent with that, the Soviet Union declined to ratify the Bretton Woods agreements it had helped shape.[48] A few years later Poland, Czechoslovakia (as it then was), and Cuba pulled out of the IMF, realizing they had made the wrong choice once the Soviet Union consolidated its power over them. Their currencies were not convertible, and trade with Western Europe and North America shrank sharply.

That was not one-sided. In 1946 the US-led World Bank wriggled out of lending to Poland.[49] Four decades later, the USSR's overtures to the GATT were turned away on the grounds that it was not a market economy (nor is the PRC: chapter 17). For similar (given) reasons, for decades the United States blocked the PRC from joining the IMF. What used to be called the Second World lay outside the international system of multilateral economic institutions.

By the early 1970s, however, under détente, there were Soviet banks in London, Paris, Zurich, and Singapore, with a few branches elsewhere. They held dollars needed for trade, probably because they were less likely to be seized in Europe than if under the United States' direct jurisdiction.[50] Soviet bloc banks acted elsewhere via correspondent banks, and over time became participants in the London markets.

During the 1970s, some of the USSR's central and Eastern European satellites (Warsaw Pact security system members) borrowed heavily from Western banks in dollars and other convertible currencies. By 1981, facing the oil price shocks and the Volcker Federal Reserve's monetary contraction, they were

47. Under its Ostpolitik, West Germany sought greater engagement and accounted for a big share of European–Soviet bloc trade.

48. I was once allocated the Bretton Woods hotel room used by the Soviets during the 1944 negotiations.

49. Neff, *Friends but No Allies*, p. 109.

50. US Central Intelligence Agency, "Soviet International Banking," para. 19. Partly in consequence, the euro-dollar deposit (and, later, bond) markets developed in London.

struggling to repay, and the lending banks were struggling to cover their losses (a financial stability problem for the West). Finding a shared interest in pragmatic solutions, Poland's debt was rescheduled by the Paris Club of official-sector creditors and also by the banks, sparing them heavy write-offs. A little later, in 1986, after martial law had ended, Washington lifted its veto on Poland joining the IMF. Romania, which had joined the IMF in an act of semi-independence from Moscow, had already received IMF program assistance in the 1970s and did so again in the 1980s. By contrast, Hungary, which was mildly liberalizing its economy, turned first to the Bank for International Settlements in Basel, which provided loans bridging to IMF membership (1982) and a support program.[51] They had both become GATT members during the 1960s and 1970s, well before the collapse of the Berlin Wall and the Soviet Union, which never itself became a member.[52]

## The "Western" International Economic System

A vital thing about this period is that whether Cold War relations were frozen or thawing, non-Western, relatively undeveloped, and nonaligned states all participated in the "Western" international economic system. As time passed, this spawned regimes and bodies outside the UN's orbit, just a few of which are mentioned here because they feature in later chapters.

As early as 1961, the Marshall Plan's Organization for European Economic Cooperation was opened up to non-European industrialized countries. Renamed the Organization for Economic Cooperation and Development (OECD), it quickly reissued in its own name the Code of Liberalization of Capital Movements, developed just a couple of years earlier for Europe. It is, so far as international law is concerned, a nonbinding public commitment among the members of a club, and exists to this day (chapter 16).

The trade regime struggled to get going, but once the European economy began to function without life support, liberalization picked up steam, starting with the Kennedy Round in 1964 and continuing with Tokyo (1973) and, momentously, Uruguay (1986), which, forty years after the first attempts, finally delivered the WTO (including a binding, judicial dispute-settlement system). Uruguay also extended the GATT's reach well beyond trade in goods to, for

51. Boughton, *Silent Revolution*, pp. 320–21, 986–92.

52. Soviet Moscow could not guarantee to trade on commercial considerations only (chapter 17). Kennedy, "Accession of the Soviet Union."

example, some trade in services, subsidies, intellectual property, and product regulation. Step by step, these changes transformed the economics and politics of international commerce (chapters 17 and 18).

By contrast, on the monetary front, the Bretton Woods system began tolerably well but then foundered. Immediately after the war, few countries' currencies were freely convertible into each other, and extensive controls limited cross-border capital flows given the risks of flight. The return to something like normality was prolonged, arduous, and, at times, fraught with geopolitics. That was most visible when London was forced to abandon its 1956 Suez adventure as a precondition for Washington's help with its stretched external financing. An IMF program followed. France also borrowed from the IMF and via central bank swap lines with European peers.[53]

Even once currency convertibility had gradually been restored—by the Europeans in 1958 and by Japan in 1964, when it hosted the Olympic Games—the exchanges mostly remained protected by capital controls. To underpin the new regime, the IMF's resources were enlarged (again in the early 1960s) by a borrowing facility from a group of industrialized countries, which became the Group of 10 (G10), an informal gathering of finance ministers and governors.[54] The US Federal Reserve provided swap lines to its main peers, effectively guaranteeing a supply of dollars in case countries experienced dollar shortages.[55] And in 1969, the IMF was authorized to create the Special Drawing Right in case the world as a whole suffered a serious liquidity shortage (chapter 16).[56]

If anything, as told in chapter 1, the opposite became the problem, with the dollar unable to maintain its gold parity. Before long—in a move underlining the links between defense, arms sales, trade invoicing, and international monetary affairs—Washington sought to underpin the dollar's role by obtaining a

53. Eichengreen, "International Policy Coordination."

54. The General Agreement to Borrow (phased out after 2018). The G10 had eleven members. Its composition was essentially the same as the board of the Bank for International Settlements.

55. Cooper, "Almost a Century." Years later they were terminated for everyone other than Canada and Mexico, theirs continuing under the (informal) 1994 North American Framework Agreement. A Bank of Canada press release of April 26, 1994 confirms this was connected to the North American Free Trade Agreement (chapter 18).

56. Eichengreen, *Globalizing Capital*, pp. 119–20. The Special Drawing Right is a strange beast (chapter 16).

Saudi, then wider Gulf, promise to invoice oil in dollars.[57] These were the tumultuous years—of runaway inflation and recession—during which the leaders of the largest economies began to meet regularly with their finance ministers in what became the important Group of 7 (G7): an informal institution born of desperation.[58]

Similar angst, triggered by banking crises on both sides of the Atlantic, was gripping the G10 central bank governors, meeting at the Bank for International Settlements in Basel. It put them on the path to becoming informal standard setters for banks (the Basel Committee on Banking Supervision [BCBS]), core financial infrastructure, and today rather more (chapter 19).

At the other end of the financial world, the lifting of capital controls accelerated the need to find rules of the road for cross-border investment (generally known as foreign direct investment [FDI]). No longer permitted by international law to protect their businesses against (perceived) abuse through gunboat diplomacy (previous chapter), the rich countries looked for protections in treaty law. The International Trade Organization regime proposed by Washington back in the mid-1940s would have included protections for foreign investors (from actions like expropriation, and nationalization without fair compensation). Indeed, the project collapsed partly because it lost the support of US business when Washington's negotiators agreed to drop the FDI provisions in the face of the developing world's concerted opposition to incorporating customary law's "international minimum standard" of protection, favoring instead the Calvo Doctrine (see above and chapter 2).[59] This was nothing less than a standoff over basic principles of international law and relations; one echoing down to today (chapter 18).

What emerged was a world of bilateral investment treaties (BITs), initially building on the older US Friendship, Navigation and Commerce agreements and taken forward by West Germany's postwar efforts to make credible promises to treat foreign investors fairly. In terms of international law, the distinctive thing about BITs is that they are hard-law treaties between states, but any litigation is between host states and the investing companies themselves (not their home states). Mechanisms for arbitrating disputes were set up in 1966 by the World Bank (the International Centre for Settlement of Investment

57. Momani, "Gulf Cooperation Council."

58. The initial meeting involved only Britain, France, Germany, and the United States. Japan joined in 1973, Italy in 1974, and Canada in 1975. G. Smith, "G7 to G8 to G20."

59. Bonnitcha et al., *Political Economy*, pp. 182–83.

Disputes). Things began to take off only from the 1980s, when it seemed de-mandeurs for capital had to accept terms of engagement that would not deter its supply.

In between banking and FDI lie the capital markets themselves: the mar-kets in equities, sovereign bonds, corporate bonds, and from the mid-1980s, derivatives on those instruments. Building on a loose grouping of national market regulators in the Americas, the International Organization of Securities Commissions was established in 1986, with a staff and headquarters (Madrid). Like the BCBS, it is not a treaty organization, and its members are not states (or representatives of central government). Unlike the BCBS, it is a universal organ-ization with over two hundred members (all regulatory bodies).

On a separate tack, just a few years later, the G7 set up the Financial Action Task Force to combat the growth in drug-money laundering facilitated by the international financial system. Supported by a secretariat based in the Organization for Economic Cooperation and Development, it has grown from sixteen to thirty-nine members, issues nonbinding minimum standards, and has black (or gray)listed some offshore and other financial centers (chapter 16).

## Cold War Pandemics and Environmental Policy

The construction of that international financial system did not involve the Soviet Union, whose organs and satellite states were merely passive users of the banks and markets in the West, Tokyo, Hong Kong (returned to Britain after World War II), and elsewhere. The same could hardly be said, however, of pandemic risk and environmental issues: in one case, the superpower was as exposed as anyone else, and in the other it obviously was as much of a polluter as any Western European or North American country.

Even before détente (usually dated to the 1971/72 Nixon–Brezhnev ex-changes and summit), from 1966 the Americans and Soviets collaborated, via the WHO, on a long and eventually successful campaign to contain and eradicate smallpox.[60] The International Health Regulations were issued in 1969.[61]

A few years later, however, notwithstanding having participated in the pre-paratory work, the Soviets declined to attend the UN's groundbreaking 1972 Stockholm Conference on the Human Environment. This on the grounds that

60. Carroll, "Mission." The Soviet Union and satellites left the WHO in 1949 but, following Stalin's death, rejoined in 1956.

61. For their history, see World Health Organization, "Frequently Asked Questions."

the German Democratic Republic (East Germany) was not invited, which was because it was not internationally recognized as a state. China, meanwhile, did attend—in the same year as US president Nixon made his historic visit to Chairman Mao Zedong in Beijing.

Stockholm generated high-level principles, scores of action points, and machinery for monitoring progress and catalyzing action (the UN Environmental Programme, which is not an organization). Its greatest legacy is probably the multilateral 1987 Montreal Protocol on the ozone layer, which incorporated what is now known as the "precautionary principle" (taking action against low-probability or imperfectly understood but high-impact risks). Helped by careful regime design (chapter 6), it has been ratified by almost every country in the world. The Soviet Union signed up in 1988, the same year as the United States, Japan, and the major European states. China followed in 1991.

## After the Cold War

Such was the state of things on the eve of the Cold War's conclusion in 1989. It had been a world in which North Atlantic multilateral and Pacific Rim bilateral security treaties opened and preserved space for a Western-style economic system; where the West's leading actors had been free to pursue their own domestic priorities, and somewhat different international visions, but where glimpses of more truly global collective-action problems were emerging.

As nearly half a century of geopolitical struggle and détente seemed to come to a close, US president George H. W. Bush proclaimed his New World Order (an expression launching a thousand conspiracies). The security landscape apparently transformed, there were calls-cum-predictions, including from International Relations realists, for NATO to be disbanded. Instead, it expanded in geography (including into Afghanistan) and membership. From 1999, former Soviet states in central Europe, the Baltics, and the Balkans joined, with others, including Ukraine, slated as future possibles—to Moscow's lasting fury.

On the other side of the world, Laos, Myanmar, and then Cambodia joined the Association of Southeast Asian Nations. Beijing convened the Shanghai Cooperation Organization, initially loosely (1996) with Russia and some central Asian states but later, after being formalized in 2001, adding India and Pakistan (2017), with Afghanistan, Belarus, and Iran as observers, and dialogue with Turkey, Cambodia, Nepal, and Sri Lanka. Nevertheless, for a while the United States seemed (to itself) to have a free hand.

## State Building?

The Soviets having (temporarily) vacated the stage, Washington—accompanied, with varying enthusiasm, by allies and friends—could deploy what levers it had, covering the gamut from hard to soft power, to spread market-economy-based constitutional democracy's core institutions.[62]

Its most audacious measures were attempts to introduce democracy into "postconflict" zones, notably Afghanistan and Iraq. These had something of the style of Palmerstonian interventionism, but conjoined with Wilsonian idealism, and perhaps lacking nineteenth-century Britain's focus on results (reflected in chapter-head quotes scattered through the book). It usually ended without success on the ground, but nevertheless signaled a US political generation's interest in redesigning the world in its (slightly imagined) image.

## Institution Building

That was displayed to somewhat greater effect in adapting international institutions to US-led globalization. The informal top table shifted from G7 to G20.[63] Regime building mushroomed, as illustrated by a catalog of landmarks:

- 1992: Twenty years after Stockholm, the UN staged the Rio de Janeiro Earth Summit on environmental sustainability, attended by over a hundred heads of government, and involving thousands of activists and scores of nongovernmental organizations in a moment of globalism with world society. One key output was the 1994 UN Framework Convention on Climate Change, the legal foundation for later, more specific agreements.
- 1993: The Vienna World Conference on Human Rights agrees, by consensus, on its Declaration and Programme of Action, appoints a UN high commissioner, and calls for national action plans.
- 1994: Following a 1982 agreement, the UN Convention on the Law of the Sea (UNCLOS) comes into effect, with 320 articles plus annexes covering coastal sovereignty, freedom of navigation, resource management, overflight rights, and more. Two years later its tribunal, based in Hamburg, starts operating. The International Seabed Authority, based in Jamaica, is established to regulate the exploitation of minerals in

62. On soft power, see Nye, *Future of Power*, chap. 4.

63. Among finance ministers, G20 followed a G22, and a G33 after the late 1990s Asian crises. There was also an interlude with Russia in a G8. G. Smith, "G7 to G8 to G20."

international waters. (The United States has not ratified the treaty, but most administrations follow UNCLOS substance as measures of customary law.) [64]

- In the same year and in a neighboring field: The San Remo Manual documents the consensus understanding of international law on armed conflict at sea.
- Also in the same year: The Cold War–era Conference on Security and Cooperation in Europe becomes the Organization for Security and Cooperation in Europe, with a large, Vienna-based permanent secretariat and parliamentary assembly.
- 1995: Implementing the previous year's Marrakesh treaty, the WTO opens, with a binding appellate body. Unlike the IMF and the World Bank, it is not formally part of the UN system.
- In the same year: The Wassenaar Arrangement replaces the West's Cold War Coordinating Committee on Export Controls (see above). Roughly forty states, supported by a secretariat in Vienna, police the export of arms and other restricted technologies, which since 2013 have included various high-tech surveillance systems. (India joined in 2017. China is not a member.)
- 1995 (and 1999): In a broadening of its mission, NATO forces intervene in the Balkans to keep peace and prevent continuing atrocities.
- 1997: Following a widespread rise in bankruptcies, UNCITRAL finalizes its model law on cross-border insolvency but excludes international banking (chapter 19).
- In the same year: The Kyoto Protocol, produced under the UN Framework Convention on Climate Change, sees nearly two hundred states, but not the United States, set themselves binding targets, coming into force in 2005, for reducing greenhouse-gas emissions.
- 1998: The ICC is established by the Treaty of Rome to try war crimes, crimes against humanity, genocide, and the crime of aggression. Starting work four years later, some 120 states have signed up to its jurisdiction, not including the United States or China.
- 2001: China joins the WTO as a "developing country" (chapter 17).
- In the same year: After nearly half a century's work, the International Law Commission publishes Draft Articles on the Responsibility of

64. UNCLOS is included here because it might not have garnered the requisite signatories during the Cold War. Coastal sovereignty is complicated but, roughly, comprises 12 nautical miles (nm) territorial rights and 200 nm exclusive economic zone rights.

States for Internationally Wrongful Acts, among other things looking
inside the state. It is later described, by a leading author and ICJ justice,
as "part of the mental landscape of international lawyers."[65]

- In the same year: After the 9/11 attacks, the Financial Action Task
Force's mission broadens to combat terrorist financing.
- In the same year: National and regional competition authorities form
the International Competition Network, an informal forum for
exploring policy convergence and cooperating around specific cross-
border cases, particularly multinational mergers.
- 2002: The (deeply flawed) second Basel Capital Accord for banks is
finalized, in hundreds of pages of detail.
- 2007: Responding to the SARS epidemic of 2002/3, the WHO's
reformed International Health Regulations come into force, binding
each non-opting-out member to report "within 24 hours . . . all events
which may constitute a public health emergency of international
concern within its territory" (Article 6.1).[66]
- Throughout the period: Thousands of bilateral investment treaties are
signed, promoting, alongside some preferred trade agreements, convergence toward liberal economic structures around the world (chapter 18).

One obvious pattern is that, with a few massive exceptions (WTO), the post–
Cold War years did not spawn lots of new international organizations. Instead,
existing ones expanded their reach.[67] That, combined with other trends, led
to problems.

## Tensions in the Edifice

Among the late twentieth century's more important below-the-radar developments was the accelerating role of international organizations as makers
of policy and law. In 1949 the ICJ had ruled that the powers of the UN (and so
presumptively any international organization) were not limited to those

---

65. Crawford, "Revising the Draft Articles," p. 435.

66. Barrett, *Why Cooperate?*, pp. 62–67. Opt-out rather than sign-up fits with providing a
weakest-link public good (chapter 5). Remarkably given the subsequent delays in alerting the
world to COVID-19, the prompt to tighten the regulations was the PRC not reporting its SARS
outbreak. (Comment: the regulations strike me as poorly constructed, often merging substance
and modalities, leaving headline obligations buried in dense text.)

67. Zurn, *Theory of Global Governance*, fig. 5.2, p. 111; fig. 5.3, p. 127.

expressly conferred (or plainly implied)—the pre–World War II doctrine—but extended to measures "essential to the performance of its duties."[68] Power was to follow purpose and function. Later, the 1969 Vienna Convention on treaties (Article 5) recognized the capacity for treaties to be made "within" international organizations, not solely among states meeting autonomously. In consequence, except where the contrary was clear, international organizations could agree and promulgate hard-law multilateral conventions, issue binding standards, and make soft-law recommendations.

Analogously to the way broad-brush delegations can unleash domestic administrative agencies, the effect was to untether international organizations. According to one leading textbook, examples include the WHO's binding 2005 International Health Regulations; the International Civil Aviation Organization's standards on air traffic control; the International Atomic Energy Agency's standards on nuclear technology; and the regulation-making power effectively granted by UNCLOS to the International Maritime Organization.[69]

Pursuing the analogy with the municipal administrative state, whether an organization's member states retain or relinquish control depends in part on whether, at the beginning of the chain of delegation, they sign up to lawmaking and standard setting by majority vote rather than unanimity. In other words, international organizations face delegation's standard hazards, including mission creep and drift (chapter 6).

### Fragmented Law and Policymakers

That is one issue. Another has been fragmentation. This is partly about gaps—for example, there are cooperative regimes for passports and visas, and for refugees (sort of), but not for economic migrants (perhaps wisely), and incentives complicate the coordination of border controls.[70] At another level, it is about potential conflicts among regimes that do exist.

Perhaps the most salient emerged among trade, investment, and environmental policy and law. Since environmental (and public health) policies sometimes erect what amount to nontariff barriers to trade, the WTO Appellate Body can end up having the last word. Similarly, arbitral tribunals have made

68. Klabbers, *Advanced Introduction*, chaps. 2, 4; Alvarez, *International Organizations as Law-Makers*.

69. Klabbers, *Advanced Introduction*, 4.2.

70. Koslowski, "Global Mobility Regimes."

findings that, in effect, required Canada to dismantle a local environmental measure to avoid discriminating against US companies wanting to invest there.[71] Those examples highlight the other big development.

## Judicialization, Rights, and Civilizational Agendas

That was the rise of international courts and tribunals: from just a handful to over twenty (plus many more arbitral bodies), and from back-foot to front-foot actors. Virtually all fields are covered, from trade to human rights; and, in a striking shift, some permit nonstate actors, including individuals, to initiate proceedings against states. Four have global reach (the ICJ, the ICC, the WTO, and the International Tribunal of the Law of the Sea), while others serve groups of states and policy regimes in Africa, Europe, and Latin America.[72] This was set to "considerably shift lawmaking from states to international tribunals."[73] While eventually blowing up at the WTO (chapter 17), another key arena has been human rights.

Here it becomes necessary to distinguish between policy (as conceived by signatories) and law. For example, following an earlier initiative of the African Union, the UN's 1986 Declaration on the Right to Development asserts an inalienable right "to participate in, contribute to, and enjoy economic, social, cultural and political development, in which all human rights and fundamental freedoms can be fully realized," but there is effectively silence on where any reciprocal duties lie. The UN's Committee on Economic, Social and Cultural Rights declared (1988) that human rights should always have priority, but that is exhortatory.[74] Some regional conventions, meanwhile, took a different tack, reflecting local priorities and norms. The Association of Southeast Asian Nations' 2012 declaration of rights includes commitments to minimum sanitary and environmental standards but seeks to reconcile individual freedoms and well-being with rulers' prerogatives and states' sovereignty.[75]

There were similar differences among courts. During the mid-2000s, the Inter-American Court of Human Rights and the EU's Court of First Instance

---

71. Wirth, "Environment"; Esty, "Bridging the Trade-Environment Divide."

72. Alter, "Multiplication of International Courts."

73. Shelton, "Normative Hierarchy," p. 312.

74. Shelton, "Human Rights," p. 269n136.

75. The Association of Southeast Asian Nations' intergovernmental human rights commission had been established in 2009. Donnelly and Whelan, *International Human Rights*, pp. 102–3.

each held that various provisions of human rights conventions are peremptory norms (*jus cogens*) in international law, trumping not only treaties but also other provisions of the customary law of nations, and in the European case the Security Council itself (*Kadi* case, chapter 11). They argued, moreover, this hierarchy of norms was grounded in the dignity of the individual, without which it was not possible to conceive of a system of law at all (parts III and IV). But any priority for human dignity did not govern the conduct of international organizations themselves, notably UN peacekeepers and aid workers who (allegedly) abused the trust of people they were meant to be helping: because, broadly, they are not subjects of international law.

Elsewhere, the ICJ (sensibly) declined to rule on whether the threat or use of nuclear weapons was barred by human rights even when self-defense was otherwise permitted by the charter ("neither allowed nor forbidden"). The revealed gap in the law prompted calls from global constitutionalists (chapter 1) for international judges to maintain the integrity of the system as a whole by deploying their own view of community interest where necessary.[76] Closer to terra firma, there were issues around the legality of economic sanctions and humanitarian intervention.

## *The Fuzzy World of Sanctions: Economics, Geopolitics, and Individuals*

Earlier we noted the UN Charter conferred on the Security Council a power to apply economic sanctions in certain circumstances. That did not alter states' own customary-law rights (summarized by Vattel) to restrict trade or take other unfriendly measures against other states (retorsion), or to retaliate without violence against illegal injury, violated agreements, and so on (countermeasures).[77] Retorsionary acts, which are intrinsically lawful, cannot step over the line barring coercive intervention, or abuse human rights or humanitarian law. Countermeasures, by contrast, are rendered lawful only where taken to right a wrong, and must be proportional. Importantly, the International Law Commission's Draft Articles on State Responsibility leave it unclear whether, in the Commission's view, states may respond with countermeasures to violations of peremptory norms (*jus cogens*) owed to all (*erga omnes*) when their own people were not directly harmed (Article 54). We return to this in chapter 13.

76. Paulus, "International Adjudication."
77. Alexander, *Economic Sanctions*, chap. 3; Giegerich, "Retorsion."

After World War II, those customary law freedoms and rights were voluntarily limited when states joined the GATT, the IMF, and other regimes, which generally provided dispute-settlement procedures for issues within their domain. But they also included important carve outs enabling states to step away from regime-specific matters to safeguard more elemental interests (see above). Thus, some western states invoked national security when suspending Russia's most-favored-nation status after it invaded Ukraine in 2022.

In practice, economic sanctions have become a staple instrument of modern geoeconomics (chapter 4), variously applied collectively, by single states, or by small groups of states. Compared with the nineteenth century, physical war (as ordinarily understood) might be a lot more legally constrained, but de facto economic combat seems not to be.[78] This is underlined by the prevalence of secondary sanctions applied to states that continue to trade in various ways with the target of primary sanctions. Largely a matter of removing benefits, secondary sanctions are applied when the sanctioning state wants to stop the target state circumventing its sanctions by importing or exporting elsewhere, or using its currency offshore. They are often resented when not cooperatively agreed.

During wartime, sanctions may be directed by third parties against the aggressor, because it has committed a crime; and secondary sanctions would be justified in terms of others not aiding and abetting an aggressor. Although there sometimes remains uncertainty as to which of the warring parties is the aggressor, the legal position seems closer to the old natural-law doctrine that neutrals should not impede the just party's cause than to the nineteenth-century positivist preference for strict impartiality (chapter 2).

During peacetime, economic sanctions are lawful only if they lie outside the UN Charter's bar on the threat or use of force against states (Article 2.4), do not breach specific treaty obligations (e.g., under the GATT, IMF articles, regional free-trade agreements, or bilateral investment treaties), do not violate specific customary-law duties (such as the minimum standard of local protection owed to foreigners), and do not coercively interfere with a target state's basic choices about its political, economic, or social system (see above on "friendly relations" and chapter 16).[79] Not everyone accepts that sanctions always pass those tests.

---

78. The constraints on war, including legal liabilities, affect incentives to cast hostilities as war: the United States has not declared war on another state since 1942 (against Balkan Axis members). Mulder, "Rise and Fall," p. 147.

79. See above on the *Nicaragua* case. On the legality of sanctions, see Lowe and Tzanakopoulos, "Economic Warfare." On blurred lines between political and economic aggression, see Neff, *Friends but No Allies*, pp. 124–51.

Both the General Assembly and the UN Human Rights Council—neither a lawmaking body—have argued, generally, that sanctions are illegal "coercive measures" designed to interfere with a sovereign state's domestic policy choices.[80] More specifically, there were complaints that the 2012 suspension of Iranian banks from the SWIFT global payments-messaging system harmed the Iranian people more than the government regime itself (chapter 10). But when the Security Council targeted sanctions against named individuals (rather than their home states), there were claims that lack of due process—for example, no appeal mechanism—violated their human rights (see chapter 11 on the *Kadi* case).[81]

One of many big issues here is whether judges and lawyers can determine states' measures to protect themselves, their way of life, or their interests (not the same things).

### Humanitarian Intervention and "Responsibility to Protect"

Similar issues, but the other way around, were posed by the three-pillar Responsibility to Protect (R2P) policy-cum-doctrine declared early in the new millennium. Maintaining, first, that each state is responsible for protecting its citizens and, second, that states have a responsibility to assist others struggling to do so, it goes on to state that, if peaceful measures are inadequate, the international community, via and under the authority of the Security Council, has a right to intervene in a country seriously and irreparably harming its people (and so manifestly failing in its Responsibility).

That followed a striking episode in international law prompted by NATO's 1999 interventions against atrocities in Kosovo. Since they had not been authorized by the Security Council, and were hardly "self-defence" under Article 51 of the UN Charter, the measures were dubbed "illegal but legitimate," with calls for the gap to be closed through law reform.[82] After reports and negotiations, R2P was included in the General Assembly's unanimous but nonbinding resolution—a 178-paragraph communiqué—at the UN's 2005 World Summit. Compared with initial proposals, this narrowed its scope to genocide, ethnic

---

80. E.g., UN General Assembly Resolution 68/180.

81. Happold, "Economic Sanctions"; Farrell and Newman, "Weaponized Interdependence," pp. 67–69.

82. Sweden-appointed Independent International Commission on Kosovo, *Kosovo Report*, pp. 5, 10. Separately, the prosecutor for the Yugoslav war crimes tribunal concluded NATO should not be prosecuted. Ratner, *Thin Justice*, p. 386.

cleansing, war crimes, and crimes against humanity (roughly, *jus cogens* norms); inserted veto rights for the Security Council's permanent members; and omitted conditions on military action deriving from the West's just-law traditions (proportionality, prospect of success, and last resort), partly because China objected that they could sideline Security Council voluntarism.[83]

Although R2P is neither a binding pact nor (clearly) customary international law, for a while it was affirmed as policy in various Security Council resolutions, but then apparently sidelined. Having been deployed for the 2011 intervention in Libya (China voting in favor or abstaining), it fell by the wayside a year later for Syria (China and Russia vetoing).[84]

All of which matters greatly here because as articulated, if R2P's third pillar survives, the doctrine amounts to a political commitment that qualifies the meaning of states' sovereignty, the Westphalian starting point for part I's potted history of international relations, institutions, and organizations.

## To Today's Discordant Geopolitics

As chapter 1 flagged, by the turn of the millennium there were calls for "constitutional" reform of the global system to cure problems of fragmentation, competing norms, and incompleteness. In other words, the very process of internationalization seemed to generate pressure for still more. But just as international law's ambitions seemed to soar, the world was afflicted by two big policy failures in quick succession.

The first, in 2003, was the second Iraq war, which the United States embarked on without a clear UN mandate, and in the face of opposition from a Security Council ally (France). While Saddam Hussein was quickly dispatched, the aftermath did not work out well, revealing unrealistic planning in Washington. Then, when no weapons of mass destruction were found, it turned out both Washington and London had treated intelligence as a political output, at the service of public presentation, rather than a technical and highly uncertain input to policymaking. The combination of incompetence, apparent mendacity, and sidelining of UN processes did not do much for confidence in the international system.

---

83. GA Resolution 60/1, October 24, 2005, paras. 138–39; Garwood-Gowers, "China and the Responsibility."

84. Shelton, "Human Rights," pp. 280–81; Ratner, *Thin Justice*, pp. 307–10; Chesterman, "Responsibility to Protect."

Just as that was sinking in, the financial crises of 2007–8 and, in Europe, 2011–12 exposed the hopeless inadequacy of the Basel-centered regime on which global financial stability had supposedly rested. Whatever one thinks of the subsequent reforms, this surely counted as one of the most abject failures of the modern international liberal order.

## Politicization: Fracture to Hostilities

By then, fractures in the edifice of international cooperation were more than apparent both within and between states. The internationalization of governance had not escaped politicians, or some citizens, leaving the quiet technocratic world of international meetings and initiatives politicized back home.[85] Some political leaders, reflecting and channeling domestic discontent, responded with a major course change. Washington walked away from the Kyoto climate change treaty (and later the 2015 Paris Agreement), ditched the Iranian nuclear pact, called for rich European states to contribute more to NATO, and started pulling out of arms control treaties. Across the Atlantic, Britain voted to leave the EU, heralding years of acrimonious negotiations, while Europe itself continued to dither over the further integration needed to underpin its monetary union.

Those legitimacy strains, one of the book's two themes, were manifest before the incipient US-China geopolitical contest, its second, was widely appreciated. In actual fact, cracks in the international order had been emerging for a while. In 2008, when liberal capitals were preoccupied with the Global Financial Crisis, Russia waged war on Georgia. Six years later it annexed the Crimea region and occupied eastern Ukraine, and it intervened to support the Syrian regime. Elsewhere in the Middle East, Sunni/Shia proxy wars persisted, with neither Saudi Arabia nor Iran having consistently comfortable relations with the West. Meanwhile, the United States, and more slowly Europe, began to see Beijing as a strategic competitor. People contemplated how to preserve or change the world order.

And then, in 2022, Vladimir Putin altered the dynamics by going to war in Europe. Western capitals and their friends having mainly sat on their hands while troops amassed on Ukraine's borders, they responded to the invasion with more determination and cohesion than many, including possibly Putin

85. Zurn et al., "International Authority and Politicization"; Zurn, *Theory of Global Governance*, chap. 6.

and Xi Jinping, had thought possible. Divisions among Washington, Brussels, and London receded as they unleashed sanctions on a scale not seen for a long time against a power. Perhaps just as significantly, they were joined by the leading East Asian democracies, Korea and Japan, and by states such as Singapore and Switzerland, whose prosperity has long depended on being perceived as neutral safe havens for money and wealth.

Internationally, the UN General Assembly voted overwhelmingly to condemn Russia's aggression. The ICJ held a preliminary hearing of a case brought by Ukraine, under the Genocide Convention, challenging Russia's statements that they had intervened to prevent genocide. The Court concluded on a 13–2 vote (the Chinese and Russian justices in the minority) that Russia should suspend its military operations (getting close to designating it an aggressor, in law). The ICC's chief prosecutor announced an investigation into alleged Russian war crimes. NATO became the focal point for strategic cooperation to help Ukraine resist. Were international institutions back in business just as they had seemed to be crumbling? In one obvious sense, yes. But that hardly touched the growing tensions with Beijing, to which we now turn.

# 4

# Geoeconomics within Geopolitics

## CHINA AND THE WEST TODAY, AND SCENARIOS FOR TOMORROW

*Definition of Geo-economics:* The use of economic instruments to promote and defend national interests, and to produce beneficial geopolitical results; and the effects of other nations' economic actions on a country's geopolitical goals.

ROBERT BLACKWILL AND JENNIFER HARRIS,
*WAR BY OTHER MEANS*[1]

OF ALL THE twentieth-century transformations of international law and institutions summarized in the previous chapter—human rights, nonproliferation pacts, multilateral regimes and organizations, judicialization, and so on—one had the effect of placing economic policy within the orbit of geopolitical strategy. This is geoeconomics (defined above), unleashed by the topsy-turvy reforms of the laws of war.

After some background, this chapter shows how, unlike the old Cold War, geoeconomics suffuses the tense relationship between the United States and China. It then introduces the book's four geopolitical-cum-commercial scenarios.

## Geoeconomics

While the early nineteenth-century Prussian general and military theorist Carl von Clausewitz famously held that war is the continuation of politics by other means, geoeconomics is the conduct of competitive foreign policy by economic

1. Blackwill and Harris, *War by Other Means*, p. 20 (on which this chapter draws).

means. It must be distinguished from military and political action designed to reap economic benefits—for example, the old British empire's grabbing refueling ports across the world to serve its merchant fleet. Nor is it the same as the forced acquisition of strategic economic assets, as during London and Washington's post–World War II contest to control Middle Eastern oil fields.[2]

What defines geoeconomic policy is the deployment of economic *instruments*. They include sanctions (general or targeted embargoes, asset freezes, ejections from critical infrastructure such as SWIFT, exclusion from markets, travel bans, and more); tariffs and other trade barriers; expanding a regional trade pact to add to pressure on neighboring states to converge; regulatory constraints and inducements; aggressive currency devaluations; withholding or granting economic assistance to states in persistent or urgent need; vetting inward investment for security and other risks; purchasing foreign assets to defend interests or use them against their home state and others; the terms of foreign aid and development finance; rationing the export of energy, rare earths (vital to cell phones, high-powered batteries, and more), or other essential intermediate inputs; and on and on.[3] Lying in the blurred space between geoeconomics and geopolitics is cyber interference in domestic or international commercial infrastructure (cloud information storage, financial clearing systems), which spans straightforward attack and measures disabling another country's geoeconomic armory, and might come from within or outside internationally networked technology.

Geoeconomic instruments can be used to coerce, cajole, support, or perturb another state's incentives, capabilities, and economy. They can be used reactively (as against Moscow in 2022), or proactively; to deter or to punish. They can buttress some foreign factions while weakening others, sow confusion and disorder, or help solve national problems. Their effectiveness depends on how far the dial is turned by how many states acting together for how long (chapter 10).

In kind, none of this is new. In the late nineteenth century Washington acquired Pearl Harbor, for use as a naval base, as a precondition for renewing a trade pact with the then independent Hawaii.[4] What has changed is the armory's breadth, and the trails of evasion left in modern communications

2. J. Barr, *Lords of the Desert*.

3. On rare earths, see Nakano, *Geopolitics of Critical Minerals* (e.g., China holds a majority of the world's cobalt and lithium).

4. After the initial 1876 treaty, Hawaii's productive capacity shifted toward sugar production, leaving it exposed if the United States did not renew in 1883. Carnegie, *Power Plays*, p. 1.

technology. That became plain when the response to Vladimir Putin's 2022 war on Ukraine included freezing Russia's substantial foreign exchange reserves (I had wondered what would be the threshold for that step) and the participation of traditionally neutral banking centers that can no longer, as during World War II, rely on being shielded by paper book entries and physical settlement of bearer instruments.

### Geoeconomic Capabilities: Nature and Nurture

States' geoeconomic capabilities and vulnerabilities vary enormously. While some are acquired through economic performance (via growth and modern trade networks), many reflect natural endowments (and deficiencies). Who controls the supply of energy and other mineral resources has mattered to geopolitics since the age of industrialization, prompting powers to control or, in the post-imperial world, have strong influence over states with scarce but vital resources, if only to exclude their rivals.[5] But energy supply is also a geoeconomic instrument, since it can be rationed or cut off. Today, the main suppliers of exported energy (oil and gas) are the Persian Gulf states and Russia, together with the United States (which, broadly, is self-sufficient when prices are above fracking's break-even threshold). German and southern European reliance on Russia has long been a bugbear within NATO. Elsewhere, if, frustrated by a less solicitous Washington and sensitive to the scale of Chinese demand for its oil, Riyadh stopped invoicing in dollars (part of the 1970s deal described in chapters 1 and 3), the US economic armory would be less complete.

Other geoeconomic strengths and weaknesses are influenced by international regimes, a striking case being telecommunications standards (chapter 5), which modern history shows materially affect a state's offensive and defensive capabilities. The 1906 International Radiotelegraph Convention banned some of the market-dominating practices of Marconi (a British company), which had impeded Germany's various geoeconomic and political aims.[6] Today, with a different cast, the superpower telecom race continues, with a similar focus on entrenching advantages (see below).

Regimes have also mattered to the US dollar's position as the world's premier reserve currency. Although currently entrenched by powerful network effects (chapter 5), it initially cemented its status through the Bretton Woods

---

5. Drawing on Thompson, *Disorder*.

6. Doshi and McGuiness, *Huawei Meets History*. Britain signed up to the 1912 version.

treaties. With veto power (and corresponding management influence) over IMF and World Bank policies, this provided the conditions for articulating the so-called Washington Consensus, which, as well as calling for macroeconomic prudence, prescribed trade liberalization, market deregulation, and privatization of production, distribution, and exchange.[7] Originally informed by Latin America's 1980s crises, it developed into an informal reform script for the multilateral institutions, whose main shareholders no longer fretted over a developing state's geopolitical alignment after the Cold War was over.

But while the macro community provided the urtext, the terms of IMF rescues or World Bank development finance might have driven less change than the mushrooming bilateral investment and regional trade treaties. They effectively required a much larger group of noncrisis states to adopt market economics, including reducing subsidies and embracing antitrust policies, prompting a good deal of disquiet (chapter 18).

As well as creating or distributing geoeconomic capabilities, international regimes and pacts occasionally try to tame them. Thus, formally at least, some sanctions can be applied only with the consent of the UN Security Council; retaliatory trade measures are permitted only with a green light from the WTO's disputes procedure; and currency manipulation is illegal (chapter 16). To work, those and other constraints depend on the great powers playing ball. This matters when, in contrast to Cold War autarkic economic relations but not unlike Britain and France's long-eighteenth-century contest (chapters 1 and 2), the United States and PRC are competing everywhere, with whatever means come to hand.

## The United States and China's Engagement Today

Here I merely sketch some of the contest's theaters in order to illustrate crisscrossing connections between economic policy, geopolitics, security policy, technology, and the treatment of citizen-subjects.[8]

### Mercantilism

One long-running sore has been China's mercantilism: export-led growth underpinned, for some years, by an undervalued exchange rate. Western economists argued this was not in China's own longer-term interests, which

7. Williamson, "What Washington Means." For a retrospective account, see Fischer, "Washington Consensus."
8. Economy, *Third Revolution*, chap. 7.

would be better served by more balanced growth, with greater household consumption. "Mercantilism doesn't work" was the refrain. But as, many years ago, I used to respond to Bank of England staff, rather to their bemusement I suspect, "Mercantilism works for the mercantilists. If you doubt that, go and look at the family homes of some of our own former mercantilists." Whatever its disadvantages for the population as a whole, mercantilism generally works well for the coalition of businesspeople (getting rich) and political leaders (getting powerful) who operate it. Indeed, mercantilism tends to get displaced only when a rising middle class demands change (as in nineteenth-century Britain), and to be revived when their livelihoods come under threat.

Anyway, that was the backdrop to President Trump's complaints about the United States' negative trade balance with China—an eighteenth-century-style jealousy of trade (chapter 2). As macroeconomics, it was illiterate. What matters, narrowly, is not a country's bilateral trade balance with each of its trading partners but its aggregate trade balance with the rest of the world. For the United States, that overall deficit largely reflects its own (poor) national saving and investment choices (chapter 15).

But the then president's very public concerns underlined the asymmetric access of American and Chinese firms to each other's markets, the extent of involuntary technology transfers, and the implications of the Communist Party having reinserted itself into commerce.[9]

### Economics and Geography: The Belt and Road Strategy

While macroeconomic policymakers were preoccupied with imbalances and alleged "currency manipulation" (chapter 16), the way Beijing deployed a vast pool of external assets was arguably of greater geopolitical significance. Though hardly the first state to find itself with foreign exchange reserves exceeding any plausible monetary policy need, the PRC made external investment an arm of foreign policy.

The Belt and Road Strategy has created land and sea trading routes that summon images of the old Silk Road.[10] The largest official creditor to developing countries, its investments create potential dependencies across Asia and

9. McGregor, *Xi Jinping*, pp. 64–76.

10. I use the term employed domestically ("strategy") rather than for foreign audiences ("initiative"). Yan, *Leadership and the Rise* (pp. 29, 219n12), records that, in 2017, the Xinhua News Agency proscribed "strategy" for international situations.

Africa, a platform for debt diplomacy, and so the basis for geographically dispersed spheres of influence, Europe not excluded.[11]

Looked at from Washington, DC, that is underlined by the concentrations on communications infrastructure, including ports, which could in principle be used for security purposes, enabling the PRC to project power around the world, and to play a role in keeping open (or shut) the world's sea-lanes. (As Western capitals, including in Europe, contemplate similar strategies, they will encounter the difference between investing surplus national savings and borrowing from abroad to do so: a kind of state-based leveraged finance underlying the significance of the dollar's reserve-currency role.)

### Geography and Security: The China Seas, Indo-Pacific, Eurasia, and Beyond

That security interests feature in China's strategic thinking is hardly in doubt. Unlike other large nations that have enjoyed conspicuous economic success since World War II (notably Germany and Japan), China has built up a very large military that, as Leader Xi has stressed, needs to be capable of "fighting and winning wars."[12]

For some years, this has been on display in the South and East China Seas, with Beijing laying claim to a host of disputed reefs and islands within a "nine-dash line" drawn in the 1930s and first used in Kuomintang maps in the mid-1940s. Some now have airstrips.[13] Other than Taiwan (claimed as patrimony), China can maintain this is merely trying to insert into the global order an East Asian equivalent of the Monroe Doctrine of hemispherical autonomy declared by the United States in the middle of the nineteenth century after Latin American states had achieved independence from Spain and Portugal. One not insignificant difference, however, is that for many decades the United States' declaration mattered, objectively and in the minds of Latin American leaders, only because the United Kingdom, with a vastly superior navy, acquiesced.[14] By

---

11. S. Horn et al., "China's Overseas Lending"; Gelpern et al., *How China Lends*; Le Corre, *China's Rise.*

12. Quoted in Economy, *Third Revolution*, p. 190.

13. Kaplan, *Asia's Cauldron*; Economy, *Third Revolution*, p. 200.

14. This tests the doctrine of International Relations realists that no superpower ever deliberately aids another's rise. Britain managed to peel Washington away from Paris, notwithstanding the latter's vital help in the US War of Independence and its burning down the White House in 1812 during the war over Canadian territory. (As late as 1895, Prime Minister Salisbury

contrast, few East Asian states are soliciting Chinese suzerainty, and the United States, with extensive alliances and partnerships in the region, is unhappy. Supported by Japan, Australia, France, and Britain, it has conducted regular Freedom of Navigation Operations (chapter 3) in these waters to assert rights of free passage. The PRC regards them as a violation of its sovereignty, but that has not deterred closer defense ties between Washington and Canberra.

All this will become grave if China ever tries to assert hegemony over the Malacca Strait—through which passes a vast proposition of the world's goods trade—in order to secure its access to Middle Eastern oil, and then moves on to parity in the Indian Ocean. That very possibility led to 2017's revival of the Indo-Pacific Quad (United States, India, Japan, and Australia), criticized by Beijing for "inciting discord."[15]

Only a little farther afield, the PRC has a military base near the Red Sea (and Suez Canal) at Djibouti, which also hosts US and French bases in a setup reminiscent of older contests. Across the Arabian Sea, it operates western Pakistan's Gwadar port, a gateway to the Karakorum highway's land-based alternative to transportation via the Straits. On the other side of the world, it has large port facilities at either end of the Panama Canal, which is operated by Panama under a treaty of permanent neutrality. There are no military facilities there but, as signaled by a security deal Beijing reached in early 2022 with the South Pacific Solomon Islands, more bases around the world are likely to follow—just as they did for earlier commercial empires. The United States has around eight hundred.

On land, there have been border skirmishes with India (maybe 2020's most significant moment). And not far from land disputed with Delhi, settlements have been built at or over the border with smaller states (even though China had previously renounced Qing claims on Bhutan).[16] By contrast, looking across Eurasia, Beijing's relations with Moscow have grown closer, leaders Xi and Putin celebrating "no limits" cooperation during the 2022 Winter Olympics—just a few weeks before Russia invaded Ukraine.

---

doubted the Monroe Doctrine's validity, noting Washington did not accept responsibility for Latin American states: see D. Hurd and Young, *Choose Your Weapons*, p. 212.)

15. The Quad first met, on Japanese prime minister Shinzo Abe's initiative, in 2007 but fell into abeyance for a decade. Marlow, "What Is the 'Quad'?"

16. Barnett, "China Is Building." (A scholar of Tibet, Barnett might be regarded as hostile by Beijing.)

## Security and Technology

In an age when the information technology of day-to-day commerce and investments can be weaponized, the United States has become concerned about China's leading edge in 5G telecoms and, more broadly, about the security vulnerabilities inscribed into the mechanics of trade and finance. For over a decade Beijing has been seeking to shape a new multilateral approach toward the internet (permitting local variation), and to lead on standards for artificial intelligence, while tailoring its explanations to home and foreign audiences.[17] It aims to be largely independent in most key technologies by 2025.

Apart from joining this technology "arms race"—notably in semiconductors (where Taiwan is dominant), quantum computing, and artificial intelligence—Washington has responded with controls on sensitive imports, exports, and inward investments, and by upping subsidies for R&D (chapter 18).

## Technology, Surveillance, and Opinion

Already, Beijing employs the new technology to place its subjects under almost continuous surveillance, via a system of social credit (and debit) it offers to other states. Consistent with a state-led media, an internet firewall impedes access to news and opinions from elsewhere, and wolf-warrior diplomacy broadcasts aggressive lines to be absorbed as opinion.

When, in 2020, the world was desperate to learn more about Wuhan's role in the pandemic, the PRC retaliated against the United States ejecting some Chinese state journalists by withdrawing credentials from major US newspapers—a move simultaneously assertive but fragile. Given much greater transparency in the United States, the most predictable effect was an asymmetric decline in news flowing from east to west.[18]

## World Opinion and UN Bodies

Away from censoring the domestic circulation of information, Beijing is active in seeking to shape the expression of "world opinion" at the UN and its various offshoots. Assiduous in seeking to lead UN organizations or departments

---

17. Kissinger, *World Order*, pp. 341–47; Doshi et al., *China as a "Cyber Great Power"*; Letwin, *China vs. America*, pp. 85–89.

18. McGregor, "Increasingly Powerful."

(e.g., Civil Aviation, Food and Agriculture, and Telecoms Union), it regularly tables General Assembly motions promoting its views.[19] As though equating this with developing-world protests via the assembly during the 1960s (chapter 3), and long frustrated by UN bureaucracy, Washington passively watched. But any such analogy would be mistaken. Until recently poor, Beijing brandishes credentials unavailable to Moscow during the old Cold War. Today, when it wants others' votes, that soft power works in tandem with economic leverage. This is reminiscent of the United States itself.

## Four Scenarios for the Next Quarter to Half Century

On where this multidimensional contest ends up, it would be foolhardy to make hard predictions. Better, I suggest, to contemplate four broad scenarios, which I have labeled *Lingering Status Quo* (continuing US international leadership); *Superpower Struggle* (the scenario most resembling the long eighteenth century's French-British contest); *New Cold War* (autarkic rival blocs); and *Reshaped World Order* (more Vienna 1815 than Washington 1990). Although the edges cannot be sharp, the Four Scenarios' defining traits are outlined here, with color added in chapter 10 (after discussions of cooperative institutions and geopolitics in parts II and III), and more still on their economic content in chapter 15's introduction to part V.

A maintained assumption is that there will not be a superpower war with a clear winner or loser. That is despite the plausibility of nuclear deterrence (if it holds) expanding the envelope for conventional aggression and cyber conflict, as evidenced by Russia's invasion of Ukraine. And it is despite Beijing so far declining to agree to deescalation protocols with Washington, in contrast to the old Cold War's mature phase and so raising the stakes around skirmishes of all kinds.

### Scenario 1: Lingering Status Quo—*Continuing but Constrained US-Led System*

This would be a world in which the United States remained the greatest of great powers, but with the potency of its leadership checked somewhat by the rise of new powers of a different ideological cast.

---

19. Doshi, *Long Game*, pp. 282–84 (He is now in the Biden administration).

The United States would remain a power in the western Pacific, and its navy would continue to keep the sea-lanes open around the world. The dollar would still be the world's predominant reserve currency. The trade regime would become less favorable to state-sponsored and subsidized capitalism. US banks would remain preeminent.

As for international regimes and organizations, there would be only incremental change in policy and governance. But unless their trajectory stalled, Beijing and others would push for a bigger say and some redesign.

### *Scenario 2:* Superpower Struggle—*Prolonged Strategic, Ideological, and Commercial Competition*

The second scenario is a world of vigorously competing superpowers, but with peaceful coexistence somehow sustained. As with Paris and London in the eighteenth century (chapter 1), there would be occasional attempts to cooperate as well as some decoupling. It could last a long time—maybe a century—but that would not be inevitable, as it could transition into either the third or fourth scenario.

As the struggle played out, trade—with its attendant jealousies—would continue in those goods and services that did not compromise security. Jealousy of credit would be intense: sooner or later, there would be rival reserve currencies and overlapping zones of financial influence.

Every step, however arcane, in trade, energy, macroeconomic, and regulatory policy might be a move in this twenty-first-century contest—something occasionally lost in public musings about, for example, digital currencies. Specialists would learn to heed diplomats, and vice versa. The security of trade routes and access to key materials would become salient.

The UN Security Council would be hobbled by vetoes. As already evident, G20 meetings would veer between platitudinous and tense. Stretched between rival principals, the main international economic organizations would flounder, or retreat to the anodyne.

### *Scenario 3:* New Cold War—*Semiautarkic Blocs*

In the third scenario, the dynamics of superpower competition induce a retreat to bloc-based protectionism: insulated spheres of influence for Washington and Beijing, and conceivably Moscow if it can sustain itself without relying on its former communist underling. Some kind of fragile stability would, as during the old Cold War, depend on bloc membership reaching an equilibrium.

Importantly, the degree of commercial insulation would depend on whether it arrived in a sharp jump—perhaps driven by secondary sanctions during a proxy war—or via a more graduated retreat from overdependence (chapter 10).

Military protection of key foreign facilities would be overt continuously. Trade's jealousies would hardly seem to matter anymore; credit's jealousy would be coercive. The multinational corporation would become less multi, and Davos princes would no longer roam the planet (physical or virtual). Compared with previous episodes of hostility or war, many so-called neutral states would find business conditions less congenial given the capacity of modern states to track evasion and duplicity.

Superpower pacts would not get beyond attempts, where verifiable, to contain spiraling escalation, and perhaps shared existential threats (chapter 10). Otherwise, the more humdrum international organizations would mainly be moribund unless reconfigured to serve one bloc or another. The Security Council would, as after World War II, be largely marginalized as a forum for action.

All that assumes two semiautarkic blocs. But they could multiply if the United States' domestic politics propelled it into a parochial Jacksonian nationalism (chapter 2), reflected in transactional (and therefore abrasive) relationships with Europe and key East Asian allies, prompting them to rearm.

This third scenario is, then, a dangerous and somewhat impoverished world, as the economic and (sometimes) civilizing benefits of international trade erode, and resources get diverted into defense and struggle. It is not a world anyone would design, but one into which we might be slipping.

### Scenario 4: A (Truly) Reshaped World Order—a Multipolar Top Table in a World of Checks and Balances and Reformed International Organizations

The fourth scenario is a world in which a number of other countries are successful enough to demand a seat at a new top table, together with some reconfiguring of international institutions. Putting aside reconstruction in the aftermath of conclusive superpower hostilities, it would come about through other rising or rearming states gradually accumulating enough power to demand places alongside Washington and Beijing.

It would risk generating something like the late nineteenth-century jostling among Britain, France, Russia, Germany, a declining Austria-Hungary and Sublime Porte, and a rising Japan and United States (chapter 2). Except this time around, rather than a few rising powers joining an already plural top table, the arrival of many new de facto powers would perturb security bipolarity and the current established hierarchy in international organizations (chapter 8).

In this world, sooner or later, and perhaps as a condition for its creation, the UN Security Council's permanent membership would change, as would the distribution of veto powers in the IMF and other international regimes. Leadership of international organizations would likely either rotate among the powers or, alternatively, move to a marzipan layer of countries not quite big enough to command a top-table seat.

## Moving On: A Framework Addressing Cooperative Institutions, Geopolitics, and Legitimacy

Even that sketch of the Four Scenarios raises a host of questions, ranging from how international institutions fit with domestic governance to how realistic it is to assume peaceful existence will last. The next three parts of the book, drawing on part I's histories, aim gradually to address the former.

Regarding the maintained assumption of superpower peace, conditional on the currently expected path of technology, capabilities, and alliances, I would put the probability of there not being a decisive conflict over the next half century at somewhere over 90 percent, leaving a nearly 10 percent chance of disaster. In that nonnegligible case, afterward the relevant international-system scenarios would be a variant of the first (the United States comfortably prevails), the fourth (a free-world alliance prevails, and helps accommodate a reformed China), and a PRC hegemonic world order. Readers, who will have their own probabilities, might have those alternative scenarios in the back of their minds.

# PART II

# Framework

## INTERNATIONAL INSTITUTIONS, REGIMES, ORGANIZATIONS, AND SOCIETY

What we have very frequently performed from certain motives, we are apt likewise to continue mechanically, without recalling, on every occasion, the reflections which first determined us.

DAVID HUME, *AN ENQUIRY CONCERNING THE PRINCIPLES OF MORALS*, 1751

# 5

# International Policy Coordination and Cooperation

## HUMEAN CONVENTIONS AND NORMS

[A convention induces the members of society] to regulate their conduct by certain rules . . . since the actions of each of us have reference to those of the other and are perform'd upon the supposition, that something is to be perform'd on the other part. . . . [Each basic rule for a community is] deriv'd from human conventions, it arises gradually, and acquires force by a slow progression, and by our repeated experience of the inconvenience of transgressing it.

DAVID HUME, *A TREATISE OF HUMAN NATURE*, 1739/40[1]

PART II'S JOB is to give shape to the string of "internationals" that recurred through part I's history—institutions, norms, law, regimes, organizations, and so on.[2]

We begin with an account of why states might enter into agreements at all, and whether it is feasible for them to make meaningful cooperative pacts when they want to. It draws on game-theoretic approaches to strategic interaction to distinguish between coordination and cooperation, initially assuming each state knows what it cares about, knows what is going on, and pursues its goals rationally.[3] Hume, a proto–game theorist in his mid-twenties, makes his first

---

1. Hume, *Treatise*, III.ii.ii, p. 490.

2. Thanks to Allen Buchanan for reading a late version of these chapters.

3. Notwithstanding its limitations, game-theoretic analysis can illuminate the shape or structure of problems and opportunities facing states in their international relations.

serious appearance here: more as social scientist than philosopher, who waits until part IV. A lot is going to turn on the social institution of promising, and in particular the special kind of promising effected via the social institution known as law.

## The Challenge: Do International Institutions Matter?

Theorists and practitioners of international relations, law, and policy have rather different views of how things hang together. Among some International Relations realists, international law and regimes are irrelevant. Either states do not comply, or if they do that signifies nothing. In the jargon, the "law" in international legal agreements is epiphenomenal, adding nothing to whether states choose to honor commitments.[4]

This is because there is no higher (Hobbesian) sovereign to enforce compliance, which must, therefore, be voluntary in practice. What is more, partly for the same reason, there is no meaningful obligation to follow international law even in principle. So given compliance occurs (and need occur) only if it suits the parties' perception of their interests, the law, pact, or standard cannot be doing any meaningful work.

But the lack of a higher power (an effective sovereign) to issue and enforce international law is not the same as showing that international agreements and international organizations do not matter. That would be to claim that formalizing international accords makes no difference, that their degree of precision barely matters, and that any delegation to an international organization never leads to any loss of control, or at least that any such agreements, pooling, and delegations never have a material effect on states' prosperity, safety, or security. In fact, as I shall describe over the course of part II, the absence of a higher authority does not preclude decentralized enforcement processes, nor some centralized coordination of any such decentralized enforcement. In a separate register, to claim international institutions do not matter would, putting it mildly, shine a strange light on US complaints about international institutions, including organizations it has not joined (such as the International Criminal Court) and others it got worked up about. If they never mattered, walking away would be a rather calm affair, or so one might think.[5]

---

4. Mearsheimer, "False Promise"; Goldsmith and Posner, *Limits of International Law*.

5. An epiphenomenalist might riposte that law does not matter for a hegemon, but that assumes (and so gambles) its hegemony is so secure it will *never* need friends (part III).

Taking the point seriously, however, some illumination is available from domestic law (municipal law, in the language of international lawyers). If compliance with international law cannot be explained by a higher authority's enforcement powers, much the same can be said for domestic executive government's compliance with constitutional and administrative law. Since the judiciary and parliamentary assembly have no enforcement capacities of their own, those of their legal decisions (court judgments, legislative statutes) that go against the wishes of the executive rely on executive branch voluntarism. Yet, plainly, in most constitutional states most of the time, executive governments do enforce the law against themselves. Why? Partly because of the reputational cost of not doing so, and partly because high officialdom internalizes the values of the law (chapter 14).

The international relations analogue would be the reputation of government at home and with its foreign peers for honoring treaties and complying with customary law. The analogy is not exact, however. Domestically, reputational costs can be operationalized via the ballot box (in democracies), whereas that is not so internationally. This leaves hanging whether retaliation and reciprocity are the only forces at work, or whether violations of a norm of fidelity carry meaningful costs.[6]

Those issues are central to our account: a kind of anti-impossibility or anti-irrelevance thesis. With Hume pitched against Hobbes, the later thinker prevails.

## Why Might States Want to Enter into Lasting Agreements with Other States?

The first question is why states might want to build international institutions (and organizations) at all. Plainly, they would need to think they get something out of it.

---

6. An illuminating example is the response, in the fall of 2020, to the British government's plan to introduce legislation to override parts of its EU withdrawal treaty, which ministers conceded would breach international law. It was fourfold: that the EU could retaliate against the specific breach (bilateral retaliation); from the Speaker of the US House of Representatives, that Congress would not approve a UK-US trade deal if it endangered peace in Ireland (third-party retaliation); but also that the measure would damage Britain's credibility with other potential international partners (peer-group reputation); and that it would undermine Britain's condemnation of other states for breaching international law (diluted international authority).

If asked the purpose of international law, many practicing lawyers would probably respond that it is to enable low-cost resolution of disputes between states and other international actors. But that plainly will not do. Of the regimes enumerated in chapter 3, some were indeed designed to head off disputes (e.g., maritime laws), but others were aimed at securing common benefits (cross-border postal services) or guarding against common harms (piracy, financial instability, pandemics), and others still were dedicated to heading off threats to the values of civilization (prohibitions on war crimes).

## International and Global Public Goods, Common Resources, and Club Goods

In their great variety, many such policies (but not all) are responses to collective-action problems entailed in providing "public goods" or preventing "public bads," containing harmful "externalities," or realizing potential mutual benefits via "network externalities." These terms need explaining.

What economists call a public good can be enjoyed by everyone—so everyone locally for a local public good, everyone in the world for a global one—and cannot be eroded by anyone, so its use by one state or group does not leave less for others.[7] A lighthouse is the canonical example of a local public good, defense of a national one, and scientific knowledge of a global one. Generally speaking, because the benefits accrue universally, individual actors, whether people and firms within a state, or states themselves in the global environment, have weak incentives to supply public goods. They need to work together, somehow, whether spontaneously or by designing schemes that alter incentives.

A key thing to stress about the economist's "public goods" is that they are not, in evaluative or normative terms, always good, or good for everyone; the word "good" is being used in two senses. For example, a highly infectious deadly pathogen is neither excludable nor depletable: it can affect anyone, and your chances are not improved if I catch it. It is easier to call such things "public bads."

---

7. Whether a good is excludable or rivalrous makes for four kinds. Private goods are both, public goods neither. Common goods (not excludable but rivalrous) and club goods (nonrivalrous but excludable) are explained in the main text. (I sometimes use "public goods" to include common goods.)

Some goods are available to all but eroded by use. They are known as "common goods," or "common resources" after the problem of overusing common grazing land or fisheries. Here the challenge is how to stop each other from consuming too much, leaving less for the community as a whole, including future generations. Global common resources play an important part in this book, since they include international peace, a resilient international financial system, and a clean atmosphere.[8]

Conversely, a third type, club goods, are excludable but nonrivalrous: benefits accrue only to a club's members so long as it can police access. A movie club is a trivial example: if admitted, everyone can view the film, but membership can be refused. A regional trade pact is a serious example, especially since they became more prevalent (chapter 18).

When thinking about each of these kinds of goods, it is important to distinguish between the character of a policy (or policy institution) designed to affect the world and the character of the stuff being affected. For example, the Basel banking standards are public goods: any state can adopt them, and no state is precluded from doing so by others already having done so, because the standard is like public knowledge. But financial system resilience—the property of the world that is the object of those Basel standards—is a common resource, because the resilience of the international system is available to all but can be eroded through exploitation (chapter 19).

## Adverse Spillovers: Negative Externalities

Public goods are a special, because analytically extreme, case of what economists call externalities. As a general matter, externalities arise when the parties to an activity or agreement of some kind (commercial or public, between private actors or governments) do not take into account (internalize) its effect, for good or ill, on others. Externalities are often local, as when a loud concert disturbs neighbors, but they are regional, international, or global when those third parties are the residents of near or far states, which have no power to regulate the activity or agreement affecting them.

Examples of harmful international externalities include atmospheric pollution, loss of water supply because other territories dammed a river, loss of income or market share because another state released international merchandise at artificially low prices (known as dumping), and impaired welfare from

8. Ostrom, *Governing the Commons*.

another state employing systematic beggar-thy-neighbor macroeconomic policies (gaining from hurting others). Broadly, many national policies can be inefficient once foreigners are taken into account.

The most notorious example is imposing a tariff on imports, which harms foreign exporters even if, domestically, the costs suffered by consumers are outweighed by benefits to local businesses and government revenues (and so the provision of local public goods). Those spillovers will be meaningful when the economy of the protectionist state is large enough for its measures to affect world prices, and its government might have incentives to do just that if business managers and workers in exposed sectors influence policy.[9] But it invites retaliation from similarly sized economies, often targeted to affect workers in marginal electoral districts. Trade wars are not always a simple zero-sum game where the first mover secures a win.

As those examples illustrate, externalities can flow from either proactive or defensive policy actions, but none can be cured without mechanisms inducing states to avoid or contain adverse effects on others. For example, the symmetry of the terms-of-trade predicament motivates cooperation of some kind, whether codified or not (chapter 17).

### Network Benefits: Positive Externalities

Some externalities are positive but still require collective action. The standard example is a communication system (e.g., telephones) where the benefit of signing up increases with the number of other people who do so. Such positive network externalities drove the various nineteenth-century conventions, and prototype international organizations, described in chapter 2.[10]

They are also a vital ingredient in any one international reserve currency being used in preference to others (chapter 16). Currently, the dollar's role derives from its use as a unit of account in invoicing many raw materials (a network externality), as a medium of exchange for international payments (another network externality), and as a store of value (a positive liquidity externality in capital markets).

All this merely suggests there are problems and opportunities that many states cannot solve or secure on their own. We need to be clear, though, why the responses involve institutions, policy regimes, and, especially since World

---

9. Grossmann and Horn, "Why the WTO?," secs. 2.1, 4.1, and 4.2.
10. Abbott and Snidal, "International 'Standards.'"

War II, permanent international organizations. To make headway, it is useful to distinguish between what are known as pure coordination problems in which there are no losers (among the participants), coordination problems where some give and take is involved, and cooperation problems.[11]

## Solutions to Some Problems and Opportunities: Coordination via Conventions

Starting with vanilla coordination, the standard example is deciding on which side of the road to drive. The solution is merely a convention but, crucially, it is self-enforcing: it is in no one's interests to buck the convention-cum-rule by driving on the wrong side of the road headlong into oncoming traffic! Moreover, no one really cares which solution (driving on the right or left) is chosen, so long as there is definitely a rule, and the rule is clear.

### Coordination Problems with Distributional Bargaining

Other coordination problems also have self-enforcing solutions but are less readily overcome because the parties have different interests or preferences and so favor different solutions, making negotiation unavoidable. A classic example is a couple committed to going on holiday together but wanting to go to different places (there is no uncertainty: each knows both their own mind and the other's, and the options are well defined). Once they have chosen, the loser has weak incentives to decamp to the other possible destination (assuming the two options are far apart).[12] This type of coordination problem involves distributional issues: the agreed bargain, wherever it lands, will be closer to one party's first choice than to the other's.

In the international sphere, examples include the simplest technical standards for cross-border traffic in postal and telecom services mentioned above, which are inherently multilateral. While largely self-enforcing, they might take an effort to get started since the net benefits to any party depend on how far they have to adapt their domestic systems. Sometimes the choice might turn

11. Stein, "Coordination and Collaboration"; and Snidal, "Coordination versus Prisoners' Dilemma," which both consider a variety of game structures.

12. In game theory, strategic interactions with this structure are known as a "Battle of the Sexes." For a survey of game types in international relations, see Aggarwal and Dupont, "Collaboration and Cooperation."

out to be straightforward because one state already dominates the relevant market. While the agreement entrenches their distributional advantage, it is the obvious solution for everyone given the starting conditions: it has in effect already established a latent convention. In new technologies, this prompts races to establish dominance in order to become the de facto standard setter.

## The Centrality of Conventions: Focal Points and Spontaneous Coordination

Those simple examples point to a much broader phenomenon. Conventions and convention-based behavior are ubiquitous. The standard example is language, as its written and phonic signs, while used in a rule-like way, are essentially arbitrary.[13] Money is another. Conventions might be chosen, as with technical standards, or they might emerge. Sometimes we are conscious of using them, sometimes not (as with many rules of language).

It was part of Hume's genius, reflected in the quote at the chapter head, to spot and explain how some useful societal practices and institutions emerge to help solve recurring coordination problems, and function by becoming rooted in habits as behavioral conventions. Some might be codified, or at least documented in some way (e.g., dictionaries), but that is not always necessary.

A little over two centuries after Hume, social scientists rediscovered this when they spotted how people sometimes navigate interactive problems with many possible solutions by alighting on one that seems obvious to them. A famous example is of out-of-town visitors to New York City being asked what they would do if they had forgotten to agree on a rendezvous: go to Grand Central Station at noon. Such focal points, as they became known, function as reference points around which conduct can revolve.[14] Vitally, they draw on people's prior knowledge of the environment, so that some conventions are in effect dependent on the path of a community's history.

We do not have to romanticize the wonders of an "invisible hand" to take this seriously. In a wide range of situations, coordination, via ongoing compliance with a convention, is endogenous and stable. While there is "anarchy" in the narrow sense of no all-powerful enforcer (Hobbes's sovereign), that does not greatly matter.

13. Lewis, *Convention* (published in 1969, though the thought is older).

14. Focal points were introduced into modern social science in the early 1960s by the Nobel economist Thomas Schelling's *Strategy of Conflict*, offering a route to finding solutions to multiple-equilibria games without a top-down rational rule. Myerson, "Learning from Schelling's *Strategy.*"

## Cooperation: A More Difficult Nut to Crack?

Cooperation problems are different and inherently more difficult, because each actor (here, mainly a state) would ideally prefer a different outcome from the one that prevails from their acting on the basis of rational calculation: in the language of game theory, the optimal outcome for the community is often not the equilibrium outcome that is incentive compatible for the parties.

### Free-Riding Defectors and Taking the Easier Option

The classic problem of cooperation has become known as the prisoner's dilemma. It arises when, whatever others do, an actor will do better by not cooperating. So even if everyone had agreed to cooperate, ex post they each stand to achieve a better outcome for themselves by defecting (variously described as breaking ranks, cheating, reneging, or seeking to free ride on the others' provision of a public good), rather than being the patsy who stuck to the agreement. Where that incentive is widely understood, it very obviously obstructs the best agreement being struck in the first place, so the cooperative project either never gets going or collapses under the weight of defection. Even though all would be better off if none defected, a narrow rationalist calculus defeats them.[15] The prisoner's dilemma does not just afflict bad people trying to escape justice, but can infect cooperation among groups of all kinds, including states wishing to collaborate in supplying a global or regional public good (or preventing a harm).

That kind of free-rider problem does not exhaust the litany of collective-action challenges. Whereas in a one-shot prisoner's dilemma–type situation, each actor's rational choice does not depend on what others do, in other situations it does, as illustrated by the eighteenth-century political theorist Jean-Jacques Rousseau's parable of the stag hunt. A small group decides to take on something that only a team working together can execute (say, hunting a stag). That task is risky, and each member has opportunities to peel off and instead pursue some other goal she or he can achieve alone with less risk and effort (say, shooting a hare). If even just one of them does so, the collective task is no longer achievable, so all the others default to tackling the easier task on their own (each gaining a hare). This lies somewhere between coordination and cooperative problems. Unlike in a prisoner's dilemma situation, each person's rational course now very much depends on what the others are expected

---

15. This is a *one-shot* prisoner's dilemma game, with the future casting no shadow.

to do. So, like some of the coordination problems discussed above, there are two possible outcomes (all hunt stag, or all hunt hares), but the better one is not self-enforcing, so the actors need a mechanism to help them stick to the more rewarding collective task. Each member of the group has to trust the others. Some ambitious international endeavors have this structure, including choosing between neutrality and a security pact against a common threat, and cooperating to defeat smallpox or concentrating on local mitigation.[16]

The picture of prisoner's dilemma free riding and stag hunt take-the-easier-option collective-action problems signals the importance of the size of the group that needs to collaborate to deliver an international public good or prevent an international public harm: can the group try to police themselves, or do they need a third party? Writing at roughly the same time as Rousseau, Hume, in his rather similar (and more appealing) parable of villagers cooperating to drain a meadow, observed, "But 'tis difficult, and indeed impossible, that a thousand persons shou'd agree in any such action."[17] His answer for cooperation among really large groups was government, with powers of coercion but sustained by allegiance rather than omnipresent force (which will be central to part IV). It matters to our inquiry, therefore, that there are more than a handful but far fewer than a thousand states.

So how do small or modestly large groups manage to cooperate internationally? In general, cooperation without a sovereign owes something to the material forces of reciprocity and retaliation, and something to the more elusive forces of reputation and social norms.

## Cooperation via the Forces of Reciprocity and Retaliation in Ongoing Relations

Reciprocity and retaliation are plainly important mechanisms, sometimes working in tandem, but sometimes not, as we can see by returning to various of the policy fields covered in part I. Obviously, international trade policy is all about the benefits of reciprocity and the costs of retaliation: I will open

16. In contrast to a prisoner's dilemma, one of a stag hunt's possible equilibrium outcomes is also the social optimum. Because the problem revolves around whether the players can trust each other, it is also known as an assurance game. Skyrms, "Trust, Risk, and the Social Contract," argues such situations are underexplored in social science, including International Relations.

17. Hume, *Treatise*, III.ii.vii, p. 538, "Of the origin of government." (The stag hunt game, properly speaking, asserts itself when the next defection is at the boundary of the ambitious task's feasibility.)

up my markets if you do the same, but if you renege on your promise, I can retaliate by changing the terms of your access to my market. The prospect of retaliation—modeled as a repeated game—can sometimes help to induce cooperative behavior if states both care about the future and can tell what their counterpart is doing: tit-for-tat in trade protectionism is an example.[18] Such interactions have multiple possible cooperative equilibria, meaning that focal points of the kind introduced earlier matter as a selection device.[19]

The power and significance of tit-for-tat (and similar strategies) depend somewhat on whether soft benefits or absolute harms are at stake. The widely used term "interdependence" is misleading insofar as there is a world of difference between relying on another country for luxuries (spices, say, or more abstractly, cheaper imports) and really depending on them for essentials, such as vital medical supplies, water, or security equipment. The former is mutual reciprocity without basic dependence; the latter is not. We return to this in parts III and V.

More generally, tit-for-tat does not work easily in some fields and can be perverse in others. At the far end of the spectrum from trade policy, international laws and norms on human rights are not about reciprocity, and retaliation would be worse than perverse: since you have outrageously abused the human rights of your citizens, I shall abuse the rights of my citizens (!).

In between those poles are fields like international humanitarian and criminal law against war crimes, the slave trade, piracy, and so on. In common with human rights laws, these laws typically express deep values, but additionally, in some cases, compliance is incentivized by reciprocity and policed by its (mild) retaliatory cousin: for example, during war I will treat your captured troops well (more than decently) if you treat mine well.

Meanwhile, environmental policy alerts us to the distinction between reciprocity and retaliation. Reciprocity might sometimes help since our both bearing the short-run economic costs of acting to halt climate change might make it easier for each of us to do so if we think our domestic standing depends on relative growth rates (and especially if we perceive ourselves as in competition for

18. The happy outcome of tit-for-tat retaliation, when parties care about the future, is often known as the folk theorem, because it was widely assumed in academia before being demonstrated or formally proved. The incentives and dynamics are different if players expect the game to end, or do not care about the future beyond a certain point (e.g., a political leader who cares only about their own period of office). See Axelrod, *Evolution*.

19. Myerson, "Learning from Schelling's *Strategy*."

regional or global economic primacy). But like-for-like retaliation is impotent: I am unlikely to persuade you to stop polluting the planet by continuing to do so myself. In such areas, retaliation-cum-deterrence needs to come via other regimes—for example, cutting trade access in response to breaches of environmental agreements (but that can be hazardous once security issues are also weighed: see below).

### The Cooperative Mechanisms of Reputation and Learning

The potential force of cross-issue responses to free riding, reneging, and, by opting for the easy course, constraining international peers from doing as well as they could (leaving them having to settle for the hare rather than going for the stag) points us toward the mechanism of reputation. Indeed, it seems likely that reputation does quite a lot of work if the *law* in international law matters. Indeed, it must do so in areas like human rights, both in mobilizing domestic support for potentially costly responses in other fields and in trying to shame a foreign state into changing course.

Since, however, the idea of "the state" is obviously an abstraction, its reputation will not necessarily be damaged by one particular head of government, let alone one specialist agency, refusing to join in a new collective endeavor or walking away from a commitment its predecessors entered into.[20] If reputation is to be potent for states rather than for specific individuals, administrations, or agencies, it must turn on the medium-to-long-run benefits and costs of a state developing a reputation for keeping or breaking promises, honoring or violating widely shared norms, or being generally social or antisocial (chapter 7).

As such, reputation is a broad social mechanism affecting collective action. While any grip it has over a particular state operates via the shadow of the future, it is informed by the light of the past. It is important, therefore, to separate whether (or in what respects) a state cares about its reputation from how other states form and effect their views. For example, a state might care about only the instrumental effects: how other states concretely react to its developing a reputation for unreliability, not joining in, or whatever. In those cases, reputation is merely part of the transmission mechanism for the forces of retaliation and reciprocity.[21] Other states, however, may care not merely instrumentally (about losing some cooperative gains) but intrinsically (about

20. Brewster, "Unpacking the State's Reputation."
21. Guzman, *How International Law Works.*

promises broken or community effort spurned). And some states might care about how they themselves are regarded, per se, wanting to be esteemed, not shamed, and so on.[22]

An example brings some of these disparate points together. Rather like people in a village or small town, states (or, more accurately, their particular departments and agencies) can learn over time which of their peers they can rely on to join in pursuing ambitious but, given cooperation, achievable objectives rather than to take the course of least resistance.[23] Where such joint endeavors bear fruit, other states may end up feeling driven by their interests to join in. The origin of the groundbreaking mid-1980s Basel capital accord for internationally active banks fits that pattern, with the Federal Reserve and Bank of England acting as a vanguard that first recruited Japan before going to their wider peer group (chapter 19). But Basel is also interesting for operating under a kind of community norm: to be admitted into its core groups is to be inducted into a circle of trust (not necessarily of agreement). The role of such norms points to important features in the background of some attempts at cooperation.

## Cooperation via Social Norms: The Institution of Promising and Its Limitations

So far I have highlighted the role of conventions—some evolved, others stipulated—in solving coordination problems, and public reciprocity-cum-retaliation strategies in overcoming some ongoing cooperation problems. Some of the examples, including technical standards and trade, might well seem small beer. But that would mislead. Take one of the most fraught and dangerous sources of friction between political communities, a dispute over contiguous territory.

The precise location of a land border is often somewhat arbitrary. The groups (or their leaders) might much prefer to expand the natural resources

22. A wide range of such attributes—glory, honor, prestige, respect, and a counterpart critical catalog—play a role in the history of international relations. Marking a contrast with guilt and its association with others' (notably victims') anger, Williams highlights shame's association with fear of being exposed, failing, or losing power (to which I add, losing respect). Williams, *Shame and Necessity*, pp. 219–23.

23. On an evolutionary-style story about identifying cooperators and learning, see Skyrms, "Evolution and the Social Contract."

available to them by moving the border into the other's territory, but each might also face the risk of grave losses from armed conflict if they try.[24] The problem is how to avoid a situation where each and every day the neighboring groups fret about whether today is the day a border skirmish starts—think of contemporary China and India in Arunachal Pradesh and Aksai Chin— potentially taking them toward outright war. At some point in the distant past, something like this must have beset many land borders. In problems of this broad kind, help sometimes comes in the form of a higher-level convention: in this case, that territory be treated as belonging to whoever has traditionally occupied it. This will not resolve all tensions—for example, where the application of the convention is disputed. But where the relevant facts are not easily disputed, such a convention can provide assurance as long as each group believes that the other lives by the same conventional rules of the game.

## Humean Institutions

This, broadly, is how Hume explained the institution of property rights: as a set of conventions for recognized ownership and transfer that arose, over time, as an equilibrium from repeated interactions among members of a community (via more or less spontaneous or organic processes discussed in the next chapter).[25] The suggestion is that some conventions operate like a special kind of norm, and that they develop to help communities address collective problems.

They are norm-like because when, for example, one state violates a border, we often say they have done something wrong, not merely that they have taken a risk or made a mistake in the rational pursuit of their interests (although we might say those things too). Behind that lies an account of sovereignty as a special kind of collective property right, entailing a norm of (routine) noninterference: property rights among states. Like personal property, then, sovereignty functions as an institution that emerged in specific conditions—the breakdown of hierarchical authority in early modern Europe (chapter 2)—as a solution to coordination problems among territorial rulers. Furnished with

---

24. If they have roughly equal destructive power, this is like the game of hawk-dove, also known as chicken. Imagine two teenage drivers, as in the film *Rebel without a Cause*, accelerating toward each other: peer esteem is high for a driver who does not chicken out and survives, but if neither chickens out, they are both dead.

25. Hume, *Treatise*, III.ii.ii–iv, pp. 484–516.

the idea and norm of sovereignty, borders can function as focal points, guiding states where they can and cannot levy taxation, conscript labor, and so on.[26]

## Promising and Promises

We return to sovereignty in chapter 11. Meanwhile, and vitally important here, another of Hume's high-level problem-solving institutions is promising.[27] The social practice of promising—of making and keeping promises—is fundamental to any kind of society because promises reach between people and organizations *across time*: A commits to B that he or she will do something in the future. The Humean genealogy of promising is that it develops because it is useful, and hence we come to internalize its demands (for people, as a virtue; for society, as a norm or value).

Indeed, without this institution, it is hard to see how we would get on at all; we would be stuck in a purely transactional world. As Bernard Williams, this book's other philosophical anchor, puts it, "Promising . . . is supposed to protect the promisee against the possibility that the agent fails to deliver simply because he has changed his mind. . . . Promises are meant to provide a hedge against such changes."[28] Trustworthiness and reliability are useful qualities associated with the institution of promising (and implied promises). The institution of promising can, then, be viewed as functional before it is moral: it serves our individual and collective interests as a device for attempting to escape from myopia, fickleness, and time inconsistency. But it becomes moral. We do not have to remember its origins in utility; indeed, perhaps it is best we do not.[29]

26. Weingast, "Rational Choice Perspective."

27. Hume, *Treatise*, III.ii.v, pp. 516–26. Hume calls the basic norm-based institutions of property, promising, etc. "justice," entailing some shared sense of mutual advantage or approval. They are associated with *artificial* virtues. See Wiggins, "Natural and Artificial Virtues"; and Cohon, *Hume's Morality*.

28. Williams, *Truth and Truthfulness*, p. 80.

29. Hume is not saying that promises literally emerged in the way he describes; state-of-nature stories are "a mere philosophical fiction" (Hume, *Treatise*, p. 493). The point is to have a naturalistic, functional story rather than a foundational one. Promising is given a vindicatory genealogy of the kind flagged in chapter 1: a functional institution that works partly because people are not consciously motivated by its functionality, the origin story having dropped out of sight. (While Hume was focused on the usefulness [utility] of institutions and practices, he was not a normative Utilitarian in the sense of believing that all moral considerations and obligations derive from some kind of welfarist calculus.)

This exposes my earlier casual use of "promise" in discussing retaliation, reputation, and so on as mechanisms for incentivizing cooperation. Hume's account of promising challenges the standard Hobbesian assumption that, absent an enforcing sovereign, promising does no more than relocate a prisoner's dilemma: from vanilla noncooperation to noncooperation in breaking promises, as when Hobbes's Foole breaches the (imaginary) people's covenant.[30] If Hume is right, as big picture he surely is, there is more at stake for the defector in the second case. Because it involves violating the higher-level institution of promise-making and promise-keeping, the reputational hit from breaking a particular solemn promise is greater—partly because wider—than that from just not turning up when it would have been better for everyone to do so.

Generalizing across such institutions—property rights, promising, and others—the Humean account has societies sometimes coming to internalize, and so give real-world normative force to, such norm-like conventions. To carry any such normative force, they must be common knowledge, at least among some relevant subset of the community. For that reason, they can usefully be called *social norms*.

In the background, the force of such norms might rest on their usefulness in achieving the community's *longer-term* goals, including keeping the community together, or, alternatively, maybe even on an attachment to a particular norm for its own sake, amounting to intrinsic value (chapter 7).[31] In terms of motivational mechanics, however, they work on the basis that, as a member of some group aiming to address a collective-action problem, I expect you to comply with the norm and, further, believe that you ought to do so, and that is what you think about me, and I accept that, and so on. Normative expectation fuses with warranted predictability.[32]

What is going on here can be cashed out in the game-theoretic terms employed to delineate the strategic obstacles to cooperation. Broadly, where social norms—whether evolved or stipulated, codified or not—are embedded

---

30. Hobbes, *Leviathan*, XV.3–5, pp. 100–102.

31. Whether we (or outsiders) *should* always applaud the moral or normative force of particular social norms is a separate matter, deferred to part IV's discussion of institutional legitimacy (chapter 12).

32. Bicchieri, *Grammar of Society*. Since they rely on public (or communal) normative expectations, such social norms are distinct from those latent conventions that need not be recognized for what they are so long as they provide focal points guiding conduct. For a review of different frameworks for thinking about conventions and norms, see Paternotte and Grose, "Social Norms."

in a community, they (and their associated conventions) aid cooperation by changing the relative payoffs of participating and defecting. If the payoffs shift enough, a collective endeavor is transformed into a coordination problem, which, as we saw, should be solvable.[33] In his account of cooperation, Hume the social scientist anticipated parts of modern game theory without the technical apparatus![34]

He is clear, furthermore, that this general game-theoretic account of the role of social norms bears on relations among states (or princes, as he revealingly terms them):

> The three fundamental rules of justice, the stability of possession, its transference by consent, and the performance of promises, are duties of princes, as well as of subjects. The same interest produces the same effect in both cases. Where possession has no stability, there must be perpetual war. Where property is not transferr'd by consent, there can be no commerce. Where promises are not observ'd, there can be no leagues nor alliances. The advantages, therefore, of peace, commerce, and mutual succour, make us extend to different kingdoms the same notions of justice, which take place among individuals.[35]

## Promising in International Society: International Law?

This story of societal norms around promising risks promising too much. We must be careful not to wield a sledgehammer to crack the cooperative nut. An attempt to make "Always cooperate" some kind of formal pledge would be unlikely to work.

33. This point was made in Ullmann-Margalit, *Emergence of Norms*. Like Bicchieri, I use "convention" for solutions to coordination games and "social norm" for a mechanism via which cooperative games sometimes become resolvable. A convention is self-enforcing (e.g., driving on the wrong side of the road risks death); in English, not using the word "tree" for tree risks incomprehension. A social norm combines warranted predictability with normative expectation, needing the additional force of social (or internal) sanction. That is different from widespread approval, as people could feel stuck with a norm (without knowing others feel similarly). Some social norms carry *moral* social sanctions but not all (e.g., norms of etiquette).

34. Among others highlighting this, see Binmore, "David Hume"; Lewis, *Convention*; Hardin, *David Hume*, chap. 2; Myerson, "Learning from Schelling's *Strategy*"; Sugden, "Normative Expectations"; Vanderschraaf, "Informal Game Theory"; and Young, "Evolution of Social Norms."

35. Hume, *Treatise*, III.ii.xi, pp. 567–68, "Of the laws of nations."

In political societies, law seeks to address this by distinguishing between merely moral obligations and those given a mark of legal obligation—a special kind of social institution (separating, as Hume puts it, private from public duties).[36] Legal contracts and, in the international realm, treaties constitute a special kind of promise. They are each formal (solemn), documented, specific, and sometimes detailed with conditions and get-out clauses. They are also, crucially, each governed by background norms of an equally special kind: respectively, contract law (and more) and general international law, each of which frames the circumstances in which a legal promise is recognized and, up to a point, deters frivolous promises. On a Humean account, general international law emerges as a kind of high-level coordination device to facilitate ground-level international and transnational cooperation (on which more will be said in chapter 12).[37]

Those background conditions differ, of course, for private contracts versus formal international pacts. Most notably, international law lacks central enforcement (the nub of the International Relations realist argument that it amounts to nothing much). But that does not preclude mechanisms delivering decentralized enforcement via some kind of delegated coordinating device (next chapter). Nor does it vanquish reputational costs from reneging on treaties and other interstate promises, now conceived as a violation of background norms rather than just of the particular undertakings. Even without centralized enforcement, whenever a state enters into a formal promise (a treaty), it is acting to expose itself to reputational loss if, later, it defects. The force, if any, of that reputational compliance-inducing mechanism depends, then, on whether general international law does, in fact, constitute a social norm among states and their officials.

### Hume's Force of "Sympathy" and His Sensible Knave

In the more familiar domestic setting, Hume's account of cooperative institutions turns on individuals having some regard for the opinion of fellows, so that they occasionally try to put themselves in the shoes of others when evaluating a course of action, and in particular whether their choices will generate esteem or shame. While the instinct might be rooted in self-interest—taking

36. Hume, *Treatise*, III.ii.viii, p. 546.

37. A similar point is made in Pavel, "Hume's Dynamic Coordination," but coupled with a (Kantian) normative demand to complete law's functionality in certain morally imperative ways.

account of one's capacity to find contracting partners in the future—the effect is what Hume called an imaginative "sympathy," which can sometimes (not must) pull things together.

Since this capacity-cum-inclination, which we would term empathy, develops from learning how to pursue one's interests in a community (tight or loose), Hume has naturalized Pufendorf's insight that Hobbes cannot explain trading relations (as opposed to one-off transactions) or trade-supporting institutions, such as credit, which operate over time. But he differs from Pufendorf by not relying on "sociability" as a natural virtue in some prepolitical condition (a "state of nature") and by not precluding free riding. Consistent with his liking the way Cicero seemed to position himself between the Epicureans (law of all kinds is man-made convention) and the Stoics (higher morality), Hume claimed to have reconciled Grotius and Pufendorf, at least to his own liking (chapter 2).[38]

Sympathy-empathy is accordingly central to containing the problem posed by what Hume later calls the "sensible knave," who counts on the continuing fidelity of others—on their habitual desire to fit in—for her own free riding or exploitative conduct to be feasible. As he puts it when discussing the norm of honesty: "That *honesty is the best policy*, may be a good general rule; but is liable to many exceptions: And [the sensible knave], it may, perhaps, be thought, conducts himself with most wisdom, who observes the general rule, and takes advantage of all the exceptions."[39] Unlike the Foole in Hobbes's *Leviathan*, who irrationally reneges on the whole shebang, the knave's conduct is finely calibrated. To benefit from her own defection, she cannot afford to trigger defection by others: something like a bank run on social norms. The background norms reemerge, then, as something like an economist's "common good" in that none can be excluded from benefiting from the cooperative goods they facilitate, but they can be eroded by the exploitative if, despite each individual knave's expectations, her actual or expected conduct does induce copycat behavior in others.

Cooperation via social norms depends, therefore, on how far the norms are entrenched. As Hume says, it matters whether a repeat offender is exposed to

38. Hume, *Treatise*, p. 316 onward, and p. 577. A letter to Francis Hutchinson of September 17, 1739, mentions the natural lawyers and the ancients: see Stuart-Buttle, *From Moral Theology*, pp. 195–99.

39. Hume, *Enquiry*, IX.22, p. 81. This sensible knave is not the bad person Machiavelli warns princes about: the knave is a (potentially costly) free rider, not an enemy.

"a total loss of reputation, and the forfeiture of all future trust and confidence."[40] If the threat is credible and enough people—or, here, states—care, the run on norms is averted, leaving only a few sensible knaves operating, harmlessly, in the margins. For that to be feasible, the knave's conduct must be visible: promise but verify, a familiar refrain in international pacts.

But something else, running deeper, matters too. If social norms are to shift actors' strategic calculus around whether to cooperate in collective ventures, it is very important not to overburden them, because a critical mass of actors has to remain committed to preserving the benefits of cooperation in general. Excessive or reckless cooperative ambition—too many stag hunts—would not merely jeopardize those specific ventures that seemed to go too far but, more significantly, would erode the background norms themselves. Staying with the bank run analogy, an increasing mismatch between the manifest benefits delivered by the norms and the costs demanded by them introduces a fragility that leaves cooperation exposed to something like a legitimacy run: each state that defects does so because it suspects others are moving toward the view that the system has overreached itself.

This reveals the incompleteness of an exclusively functional genealogy of background norms and institutions. The missing ingredient is, indeed, how far—how broadly and deeply—a community has internalized a particular set of norms (or values), harnessing approval and disapproval, and hence reputation. In Hume's hands, "sympathy"—members of a community each somewhat internalizing the perspective of others, and coming to think they should—disposes us to disapprove of distant violations that do not directly affect our immediate interests: a characteristic *of* a society, which is itself fostered through education and other mechanisms *by* society (chapter 7).[41]

## How Different Is the International Realm?

Some of this can make sense in international settings. Where, for example, a transnational initiative relies on only a few vanguard states, led by a handful of key officials who care about mutual esteem, the dynamics of small groups reenter (as with my Basel example). But that is by no means the pattern. Typically,

---

40. *Enquiry*, IX.24, p. 82. Whereas Hume spots how the knave's incentives can be contained by the future's shadow without top-down control, Hobbes relies on a sovereign's sanctions to generate similar rational reasons for desisting: the Foole "cannot be received into any Society, that unite themselves for Peace and Defence" (*Leviathan*, XV.5, p. 102).

41. Hume, *Treatise*, III.ii.ii, p. 499; Cohon, *Hume's Morality*, pp. 172–79.

weaker ties and sentiments prevail among nations (and other international actors), as Hume himself pointed out: "Tho' the morality of princes has the same *extent*, yet it has not the same *force* as that of private persons, and may lawfully be transgress'd from a more trivial motive."[42] While sometimes presented as an absolute rejection of international cooperation, it is a relative statement:

> Tho' the intercourse of different states be advantageous, and even some times necessary, yet it is not so necessary nor advantageous as that among individuals, without which 'tis utterly impossible for human nature ever to subsist. Since, therefore, the *natural* obligation to justice, among different states, is not so strong as among individuals, the *moral* obligation, which arises from it, must take of its weakness.[43]

While discussion of moral obligations (or, as I shall recast them, political responsibilities) can wait until part IV, what matters here is that the distinctiveness of relations among states depends on the facts on the ground, and those might have changed somewhat in the 250 years since Hume lived given the globalization of commerce. This means attending to the variety and significance of ongoing interdependence across different fields, common existential threats, and so on. In other words, the force of Hume's observation about norms of international coexistence and cooperation turns on how much, today and prospectively, different states need each other (part III and chapter 13).

## Global Public Goods Redux: Cooperating under Different Technologies

Against that background, we can revisit the challenges presented by international and global public goods, including standards to preserve common resources. Incentives, and therefore the demands placed on norms, will vary according to a public good's production technology.

Some international public goods can, under some circumstances, be supplied by a single leading state (sometimes termed a hegemon).[44] Maintaining open sea-lanes is sometimes an example. So, significantly here, is issuing a

---

42. Hume, *Treatise*, III.ii.xi, p. 568.

43. Hume, *Treatise*, III.ii.xi, p. 569.

44. Barrett, *Why Cooperate?* The three main types of public-good supply are known as single best effort, weakest link, and aggregation. Hirshleifer, "From Weakest-Link"; Sandler, *Global Collective Action*, pp. 60–68.

world reserve currency. Discovering a vital vaccine might often be too. Whether such goods are actually supplied depends on the benefits a single supplier stands to accrue relative to its costs of production and maintenance, and how far it can spread costs across noncontributing beneficiaries. The single supplier might be exposed to free riding by others—"exploitation of the great by the small."[45] US frustration with Europe's contributions to NATO has that flavor (chapter 8).

Very differently, some other hazards require effort from every territory, however small: the venture hinges on its weakest link. Examples include completely eradicating deadly diseases and eliminating piracy (a big nineteenth-century cause). Where a weak-link state lacks capacity, better-endowed states can help, as for example with some environmental problems (next chapter). But where a state is unwilling, there is a "holdout" problem. In some fields, the rest of the world can seal off the recalcitrant state, but not in all.

That can also afflict a third type of global or international public good—most topically, climate change—where the solution relies on the aggregated actions of participants. What matters is not that every state joins in but that the actions of the main states—for climate change, the biggest polluters—add up to enough to solve the problem. If one or more of those states will not play ball, a solution is either technically impossible or prohibitively expensive for the others.

We are encountering the important difference between keeping promises once made and making them in the first place; between reneging and holding out. A social norm of honoring (verifiable) formal promises is very different from a norm pushing actors toward joining collective endeavors to tackle important global public harms. One potential remedy lies in the willing putting pressure on the unwilling by withdrawing benefits from other schemes, such as trade, or applying coercive pressure of some kind. But whatever its merits, that strategy's feasibility depends on the relative power of the holdout states.

Here we find a deeper contrast between domestic and international politics, going beyond enforcement problems. Whereas most domestic governments can launch and structure local cooperative projects of almost any kind, in the international arena there is frequently a search for the willing, with many collective-good works exposed to veto or foot dragging. As climate change and the early-2020s pandemic showed, each new kind of international venture becomes an exploration of the bounds of feasible cooperation: a search for institutions that can align incentives with goals and values.

45. Olson, *Logic of Collective Action*, p. 29.

## Summing Up

This first ground-clearing chapter has aimed to establish the possibility of meaningful interstate cooperation: collective endeavors that make a difference.

The high-level analytical core of the Humean account is twofold. First, although cooperation among groups might not come easily and is certainly not inevitable, it is not impossible. Second, people and states do not simply leap straight out of some anarchic state of nature to a cooperative society via some kind of rationalist Hobbesian constitutional moment but, rather, get there, to the extent they do, organically via the contingencies of problems and opportunities. As a Nobel economist put it, the "focal-point effect opens the door for cultural and environmental factors to influence rational behavior."[46]

This is naturalism without natural law's rationalist appeal to higher authority, and so without claims to unique solutions.[47] It offers the outline of a vindicatory functional genealogy without maintaining that institutions are sustained solely by their functional attributes; the value of some, such as honoring formal promises, becomes internalized. The internalized social norms that do some of the work are, in this chapter's jargon, part of a higher-level game: the game of life, or society. Such was Hume's genius that he not only anticipated elementary game theory (Hobbes does that too) but intuited that some games are embedded in other, more profound ones.

### Self-Binding via Audience Costs

We have also seen that international initiatives differ in the types of collective-action problems they present: bargaining over the distribution of a convention's spoils, credible commitment, embracing a substantive norm of a kind that cannot be enforced via retaliation in kind.

In the tough cases, states (and other bodies) are seeking to bind themselves and each other to a particular course, which might be refraining from imposing certain barriers to trade (the WTO), implementing a particular regulatory standard (Basel), or treating their citizen-subjects and other people in line

46. Myerson, "Learning from Schelling's *Strategy*," p. 1111. The broader account is stressed in Blackburn, *Ruling Passions*, p. 196.

47. Naturalism as in a "view that stems from the general attitude that man is part of nature" so without appeal to any transcendental authority (Williams, *Ethics and the Limits*, p. 135). Not Grotian because there is no one right answer: see Westerman, "Hume's Reception of Grotius."

with certain values (international human rights law). The commitment device works (if it does) by exposing the parties to what political scientists call "audience costs" if they renege, free ride, and so on.[48] Credible institutions need mechanisms that generate those audience costs for relevant officials (and perhaps others) in states that walk away. Norms play a role in this. Crucially, the audience who is bothered when a state breaks a formal promise is often wider than those directly affected by the particular promise's substance.

## Loose Ends

While that identifies some threads of an explanatory story of cooperative institutions, it leaves plenty of loose ends.

Some concern how audience costs work. Who is the relevant audience (is it foreign or domestic, or both)? Who in a state incurs the costs, and how do the costs manifest themselves (retaliation, withdrawal of reciprocal benefits, loss of esteem, or exposure to shame)? What does it mean for a political community to internalize cooperative norms? What if they are merely unexamined habits (and so in effect self-deceptions), liable to collapse if people come to reflect?[49] And can norms possibly cure the problem of powerful states declining to help supply vital public goods? Some of those issues—around the meaning of an international society—are addressed in chapter 7.

Other loose ends concern distributional issues, and how bargaining is affected by the balance of influence and hard power across leading states, rising powers, and others. Do geopolitical shifts dilute the norms that underpin compliance? Do they lead to demands for reform—for different distributional bargains and different norms? These issues recur over the next couple of chapters, but mainly wait until part III.

Others still concern uncertainty among actors about each other: they do not always know what each other wants, thinks, or is capable of; or they have different interpretations of some loosely defined focal points or norms. Those loose ends are related to the functional purpose of international organizations. Do they exist to help bargaining, or compliance, or what? The next chapter takes up how regimes and organizations fit into an account of coordination and cooperation.

48. In a domestic context, see Lohmann, "Why Do Institutions Matter?"; and Tucker, *Unelected Power*, chaps. 5 and 18.
49. Williams, *Truth and Truthfulness*, pp. 88–93.

# 6

# Institutions for Cooperation

## EQUILIBRIA, REGIMES, AND ORGANIZATIONS

[International policy] regimes create a more favorable institutional environment for cooperation than would otherwise exist; it is easier to maintain than it would be to create new ones. Such regimes are important not because they constitute centralized quasi-governments, but because they can facilitate agreements, and *decentralized enforcement* of disagreements, among governments. They enhance the likelihood of cooperation by *reducing the costs of making transactions* that are consistent with the principles of the regime. They create the conditions for orderly multilateral negotiations, legitimate and delegitimate different types of state action, and *facilitate linkages among issues* within regimes and between regimes. They increase the symmetry and *improve the quality of the information governments receive.* By clustering issues together in the same forums over a long period of time, they help to bring governments into continuing interaction with one another, reducing incentives to cheat and *enhancing the value of reputation.* By establishing legitimate standards of behavior for states to follow and by providing *ways to monitor compliance,* they create the basis for decentralized enforcement founded on the principle of reciprocity.

ROBERT KEOHANE, *AFTER HEGEMONY,* 1984[1]

CELEBRATING INTERDEPENDENCE, that is the intellectual manifesto for international regimes and organizations articulated by American political

1. Keohane, *After Hegemony,* pp. 244–45 (my emphases). Interdependence had been stressed by economists in the 1960s: see Cooper, "Macroeconomic Policy Adjustment."

scientist Robert Keohane nearly four decades ago. It invites many questions: What is meant by legitimacy? On what grounds is international delegation's legitimacy asserted? Is reputational damage enough to deter free riding by all who matter to particular regimes, whatever the field? How can we be assured a regime's managers do not wander off the ranch? What material conditions are necessary for cooperative ventures to stand a chance? If regimes promote compliance, does that assist or hinder bargaining over the policy's terms? Will the distribution of benefits be sustainable as relative power capabilities shift around?

Some of those questions were tackled in the voluminous institutionalist literature that followed, not least by Keohane himself. But whether or not the manifesto was robust to all seasons, and notwithstanding techno-speak, this is an authentic voice of the liberalism of hope. Later, this book will argue that no hopeful liberalism is worth its salt unless underpinned by something approaching a liberalism of fear (to protect us from fear), but for now we will approach the manifesto on its own terms: a prosaic but vital world of rationalistic cost-benefit analysis, coupled with attempts to shape incentives to generate cooperation among states with unequal power and capabilities.

This chapter will, accordingly, look more closely at how international regimes and organizations fit into the previous chapter's Humean account of the feasibility of cooperation across borders. Picking up the analytical claims italicized in the chapter head's quotation, its key themes are institutional equilibria, design, and delegation.

## Institutions: Spontaneity versus Design, Self-Enforcement versus Higher Forces

Institutions run through our social, civil, and civic lives: marriage, codes of courtesy and etiquette, and customary law, but also pegged exchange rates, a traffic code, and high-level things such as representative democracy and the laws and practices of contracts and treaties. The list goes on and on, but needs a bit of care. Driving on the left (or right) is a rule-based convention but hardly an institution. The institution is the traffic code.

Sticking for the time being with the previous chapter's game-theoretic metaphor for strategic interaction and collective action, one can think of a social institution as providing or embodying a stable equilibrium of some kind—for example, a balance of power, or money. Some institutions are constituted by rules; notably, any system of formal authority, such as a court system.[2] Even where that is not so, most are shaped (regulated) by rules of some kind, whether formal or informal, and if informal, whether explicit, or implicit as regularities.[3] Many institutions involve a cocktail of different kinds of rules; for example, modern bond markets are shaped by contract law, overt technical conventions on things like settlement periods, formal and informal codes of conduct, and more.

Since the work done by rules and equilibria is unclear, it will help to unpack things. Think of any strategic-game-like set of social interactions as having the following four elements: the players (actors), who have preferences, interests, endowments, and so on; constraints from the environment in which the game occurs (the state of technology, available natural resources, etc.); the rules and structure of the game itself; and finally, within-game equilibrium strategies.[4] To generate something recognizable as a social institution, not only would the rules of the game need to be capable of generating equilibrium outcomes (good or bad) within the game, but also, since often alternative sets of rules could serve the same broad function, the rules need to be stable, meaning that the prevailing rules of the game are, more or less, themselves a stable equilibrium too. In how this is achieved—how they operate and emerged—institutions differ profoundly.

Some are self-enforcing (self-implementing): behavior accords with the (implicit or explicit) rules of the game because they are incentive compatible for all actors given only the rules of the game. But not all institutions are like that; the rules of chess do not enforce themselves, and players might cheat (quietly steal pieces).[5] Such institutions need outside enforcement machinery

2. In the 1990s, economists defined institutions as "rules of the game in a society or, more formally, . . . the *humanly devised* constraints that shape human interaction" (North, *Institutions*, p. 3 [my emphasis]). While catering for both formality and informality (laws, conventions, social norms), it left hanging why any game's rules were followed (enforcement), prompting an emphasis on equilibria: see Greif and Kingston, "Institutions."

3. Since following almost any convention or norm can be framed as following a rule (e.g., speaking a language), it is more useful to distinguish spontaneity from design than to try to distinguish merely rule-like practices from express rules.

4. It is important to distinguish between, on the one hand, the players and environmental constraints and, on the other hand, the structure and rules of the game (e.g., number of players, whether moves are simultaneous or sequential, whether it is played once or repeatedly, and so on), known as the game form (or mechanism). Hurwicz, "Who Will Guard the Guardians?"

5. Greif, "Commitment, Coercion, and Markets." For grounding, see Myerson, "Fundamental Theory of Institutions."

of some kind—applying physical, economic, or reputational sanctions. That machinery forms part of a higher-level institution, maybe a general law-enforcement institution. If that institution is not itself self-enforcing, it must call, in turn, on a still higher-level institution, and so on. In the previous chapter, we saw the audience that cares about formal promise-keeping is often wider than the group that cares about a particular promise's content. The point is general. In chess, the referee might go AWOL, and a partisan audience close their eyes, leaving fair play to an external appeal mechanism of some kind. Soccer managers and pundits blame defeat on poor refereeing (sometimes a legitimacy accusation), triggering postmatch TV action replays and debates among audiences bigger than those physically present.

Ultimately, the regress reaches a level where an institution is itself directly self-enforcing: because, at that level, the enforcers are incentivized to demand or do what is meant to be done but not what should not be, and that is what everyone expects, and acts on. That final stage might, for example, turn on the public applying or withholding reputational rewards or sanctions (honor, shame) on primary enforcers who have done their job or shirked.[6] Wherever free riding or defection can undermine an endeavor or institution, ultimately we find glue in norms or fear (including of shame). Even in authoritarian societies, the leaders are exposed to disloyalty from those they depend on: a group credibly applying fear to a larger population will often itself be held together by norms, as well as fear of others in their group.

At each level—the ground-level "game," primary enforcement, appeal processes, higher-level norm enforcement, and much in between—any institution might have evolved organically or be the product of conscious design. The highest-level ones are likely to be organic in the previous chapter's Humean sense, since they almost have to be self-enforcing. By contrast, the design of a planned institution is constrained to heed the interest-driven incentives and capabilities of the actors (and the institution's effect on the evolution of those capabilities and perceived interests). This is the incentive compatibility emphasized in the previous chapter and explored in the economics of mechanism design.[7] It was anticipated by Hume—too often thought of as a supporter of only organic institutions—when he said that "in contriving [i.e., designing] any system of government, and fixing the several checks and controls of the

---

6. Akin to the social and constitutional guardrails in Levitsky and Ziblatt, *How Democracies Die.*

7. Hurwicz, "Who Will Guard the Guardians?"

constitution, every man ought to be supposed a *knave*, and to have no other end, in all his actions, but private interest . . . [even though that] is false in *fact*."[8]

The higher reaches of a system of government—the constitutional level—are a special kind of institution because, among other things, they authorize and help underpin lower institutions. The metaconventions they embody need to be highly stable, and self-enforcing, in order for reform and development in those lower-level institutions to be a dynamic equilibrium. This is important to Hume's story[9]—and to ours because geopolitical transformation can challenge the constitution of international system and society.

In summary, any social institution can be characterized in two dimensions: whether it emerged organically, and whether it is directly self-enforcing.[10] This is a two-by-two matrix, implying four kinds of institutions.

The first are self-enforcing institutions that evolved—for example, a balance of power without any supporting infrastructure, or some ancient tokens used as money without any law saying so. The second category are institutions that evolved but involve outside enforcement—historically, common-law jurisdictions' prohibitions against theft and murder, and perhaps parts of customary international law. The third are self-enforcing institutions that were designed—for example, some auction systems, the gold-exchange standard, and perhaps the decentralized enforcement of early trade pacts. And the fourth are institutions where both the primary rules and the immediate enforcement technology are the product of planning and design but rely on a higher-level institution—for example, many contemporary international policy regimes or organizations that rely on willing backing and contributions from major powers.

Over time an institution might move from one category to another. For example, a system of authority might have emerged organically (as an equilibrium) before being formally constituted, with various changes introduced. More profoundly, once the possibility of institutional design is embraced by

8. Hume, "Of the Independency of Parliament," in *Political Essays*, p. 24. In France, Emmanuel-Joseph Sieyes's similar thoughts got mangled by the Revolution's totalizing impulses: see Whatmore, "Enlightenment Political Philosophy." Much later, Friedrich Hayek's advocacy of purely spontaneous orders prayed in aid Hume but neglected his acceptance of design: see Binmore, "David Hume."

9. Sabl, *Hume's Politics*. (A special type of dynamic equilibrium change operates when the highest level of authority transfers smoothly from one body [say, a monarch] to another [say, a parliament]. E.g., England's 1688 constitutional rupture.)

10. Normativity is a third dimension (part IV).

the higher institutions of a political community (a legislature, say), the options shift dramatically. Ill-judged initiatives might destabilize that higher institution, but good redesign might sometimes help preserve the basic functions of core social-cum-political institutions in the face of profound shifts in the material environment (e.g., the advent of nuclear weapons, or cyber-attack capabilities) or major changes in the population of players, whether the revival of old ones (Europe and Japan after World War II) or the entry of new ones (China today).

Those rather abstract distinctions structure the next chapter's separation of Order, System, and Society; are central to part IV's discussion of legitimacy; and help make sense of some of part I's history. In particular, they cut through nineteenth-century positivism's three candidates for the grounds of international law: custom, overt agreement to multilateral codification, and (Hegelian) self-binding by states (chapter 2). The last is not credible (not self-enforcing) if it can be cast aside on a whim, so the question of law's authority is pushed back onto what, if any, mechanism generates costs that make commitments incentive compatible. The same goes for overt agreement, because *pacta sunt servanda*'s force cannot be bootstrapped via a pact, whereas it might be via internalizing a norm born from a functionally useful habit (Hume again). That leaves intact the possibility of self-enforcing customary norms of general law that, by creating the possibility of self-binding, enable express pacts both to codify parts of general law (chapter 12) and to develop legal norms and conventions for specific fields—*international policy regimes*.

## Regimes versus Organizations

I define a policy regime as a body of rules steering or seeking to promote desired equilibrium behavior within a particular field, together (sometimes) with procedural rules for making and amending those primary rules, and (sometimes) for monitoring and enforcing compliance with them.

In terms of our morphology of institutions, regimes (seek to) set the structure and rules of the game, including entry criteria and what counts as legitimate behavior.[11] They take as given the wider environment and participants' endowments and preferences, while possibly seeking to influence them. Unlike some other institutions (e.g., language), many modern policy regimes involve collective intentionality, being the product of either design or a choice to

11. Regimes are, in the jargon, about game forms.

codify preexisting practices as express rules. Those rules (substantive and procedural) might be legally binding (directly or via states) or not; formal or informal; precise or vague; simple or complex. But they are manifest in the sense
that everyone knows what they are.[12]

While one could quibble about how to distinguish this subset of institutions,[13]
there is a simple but profound difference between regimes and organizations.
Organizations have buildings, staff, and a degree of agency. They might be
stewards of regimes, but they are not the same.

Part I's historical survey furnishes us with plenty of examples to illustrate
the differences. In the security field, the undocumented eighteenth-century
balance of power was an informal institution but, after the Vienna Congress
and treaties, the nineteenth-century Concert of Europe was a regime. Neither,
however, was an organization. The Concert operated via occasional diplomatic
conferences but was not supported by a permanent secretariat, and it did not
have a settled headquarters. By contrast, NATO is a regime and an organization, with headquarters in Brussels.

In the trade field, the world of nondiscriminatory free trade that waxed and
waned after Britain's Corn Laws was initially a wholly informal and organic
institution. After the bilateral 1860 French-British treaty's incorporation of the
doctrine of most-favored nation, it was in effect an organic regime sparked by
bilateral design. The GATT, by contrast, was a formal multilateral regime but
not an organization, whereas today's WTO is—showing that an international
organization is sometimes created only well after a regime is firmly established
but can then transform the regime (chapter 17). In the monetary field, the gold
standard first became an institution and later, after it was legislated in some
countries, an organic regime, but it was never in the hands of an international
organization. The same goes for today's regime of floating exchange rates. Central bank independence is an institution; central banks themselves are organizations; and, to take two examples, inflation targeting and monetary-aggregate

12. Abbott et al., "Concept of Legalization," offers a scheme of classification, also covering
delegation, that does not distinguish between precision and simplicity (e.g., the first Basel capital accord was both precise and simple). Also, Abbott and Snidal, "Hard and Soft Law."

13. Political scientist Stephen Krasner, "Structural Causes," p. 185: "Implicit or explicit principles, norms, rules, and decision-making procedures around which actor expectations converge
in a given issue-area." Mine differs because (1) while some norms (e.g., around interpreting
some regime-specific rules) might be within-regime, others usually lie outside any policy regime
(few are self-enforcing); and (2) while regimes aim to generate equilibria, success is not
guaranteed.

targeting are types of monetary policy regimes operated by central banks at various points over the past half century.

Finally, at the top of contemporary international governance, interstate summitry has become institutionalized through the regular, scheduled meetings of the G7 and G20 (and regional groupings), but there is neither formal regime nor organization. From the outset in the 1970s, the participating governments have deliberately chosen not even to have a permanent secretariat, with the support function rotating with the chair. This gives the incumbent some agenda-setting power, but overall leaves participants with great flexibility in what they do and do not discuss over time.[14]

## What Regimes Do

While the Humean social norms (of promise-keeping or whatever) emphasized in the previous chapter help create the possibility of overcoming cooperative problems, they obviously do not dictate the solution in any particular ground-level endeavor. Precisely because they will have many options, the parties have to find a way of coordinating on just one (that chapter's focal-points story).[15] A regime constitutes a policy by documenting and promulgating that choice.

Choosing to self-bind internationally is no small matter. If exercising free will, a state will rationally agree to a technical convention or cooperative regime only if it is expected to bring (net) benefits. In economists' jargon, the agreed-on regime must be expected to deliver what is termed a Pareto improvement (after the Italian political economist Vilfredo Pareto), meaning some parties will be better off and none worse off—if necessary, after compensation, and taking into account access to other regimes. The result might even be Pareto efficient, meaning that any change in the regime would be bad for at least one state.

The parties face various challenges in coalescing *on* a pact or regime, which will drive its degrees of formality, precision, simplicity, and so on.[16] Among

14. Reynolds, "Summitry as a Way of Life: From the G7 to Bush and Blair," in *Summits*, pp. 370–403.

15. Garrett and Weingast, "Ideas, Interests, and Institutions."

16. For example, in the field of war and peace, the NATO treaty entails binding obligations to stand by one another (Article 5), but the triggering criteria are vague. By contrast, arms control treaties tend to be precise and subject to elaborate monitoring regimes. The differences turn on trust being reasonably strong among habitual allies but utterly lacking between enemies.

many important issues, I will touch here on just four: decentralized enforcement, bargaining over the spoils, exit, and whether to delegate stewardship to an organization.[17]

## Decentralized Enforcement and Incentives

Architects and designers will try to cater for problems likely to arise when a regime is up and running. They do this by, more or less, making clear what is demanded by the regime, and what should happen if its provisions are breached. That might involve codifying what counts as a material defection, what information should be revealed about each party's conduct in order to track compliance, and what is a legitimate response for which other parties (a directly wronged party, or others too).

This is about constructing a regime's focal-point effects. A regime might, for example, provide a framework for coordinated and controlled retaliation by a collective of states. If, for example, country A is formally found to have defected from an agreed-on standard for trade or banking, other states might be entitled by the agreement's terms to, say, raise their own tariffs or withhold, withdraw, or restrict a local banking license.

That is *decentralized enforcement*—without a Hobbesian sovereign, so under anarchy![18]

## Bargaining over a Regime's Terms and Benefits: The Shadow of Geopolitics

Finding credible commitment technology (the cooperation problem of defection) does not deliver a regime's substance. Except where collective action emerges organically, that must be agreed on. Far more time is typically spent— certainly in Basel—on the contents of international standards than on whether members will implement them. But credible commitment technology certainly raises the stakes in such bargaining as it means the outcome is real.[19]

17. On rationalist design choices, see Koremenos, *Continent of International Law*.

18. Formalized in Hadfield and Weingast, "Microfoundations of the Rule of Law," and a series of other important papers. (In *Limits of International Law*, Goldsmith and Posner stress that retaliation is always bilateral, but that does not preclude decentralized enforcement being centrally coordinated and policed.)

19. On this neglected feedback from enforcement to content, see Fearon, "Bargaining, Enforcement, and International Cooperation."

A lot of bargaining is about distributional issues (relative winners and losers). For example, reprising Rousseau's problem of reliability, it is not only a matter of somehow committing to hunt stag (his example's ambitious endeavor) but also whether the group does so on land much closer to some of them than others, and whether they rotate venues in a repeated cooperative program. All of that remains to be settled even where there is trust.

Who reaps the greater share of the spoils might reflect who else most needs a regime, who is indispensable, whether there is a read across to other interdependencies, and whether it is possible for key states to hold hands in establishing a regime. A good example is the 1987 Montreal convention to protect the ozone layer (chapter 3). It provided for rich countries to cover the costs of poor countries, decentralized trade sanctions against defectors, and ongoing amendment as the underlying science progressed. In order to meet the collective-action problem of getting started, the regime kicked in only if supported by a supermajority (states accounting for at least two-thirds of the problem), so that a signatory incurred the treaty's obligations only if in good company.[20]

There are plenty of examples that go the other way. With the passage of time, regimes can come unstuck for all sorts of reasons. Prosaically, incumbent beneficiaries can resist updating self-enforcing technical conventions that need adapting to new technology. More dramatically, shifting geopolitics can upend the tables if an earlier choice between different Pareto-efficient options was driven by little more than who was top dog at the time. The complainant might be a rising state. But it can be the established leading states if they failed to factor in the benefits a regime would confer on future powers (think the WTO). So when the pecking order shifts, various parties might want reform or exit.

### Exit

The costs of exiting a regime affect its credibility.[21] Where they are too low (and the goods provided by the regime are not excludable), the benefits of free riding could be reaped by a state walking out once the regime is up and running, reducing incentives for others to sign up in the first place. But if, instead, exit costs are prohibitively high, the parties face a big problem if the conditions that initially

---

20. Barrett, *Why Cooperate?*, pp. 77–83.

21. On the incentive structure of multilateral-treaty exit technology, see Helfer, "Taking Stock."

warranted willing cooperation diminish over time. In those circumstances, the net running loss from continuing to participate in what turns out to be an unexpectedly poor regime for the aggrieved states has to be balanced against the disruption of exit and the costs of either establishing any successor regime on new terms or, alternatively, living without one.[22]

Those various costs might be regime specific, or they might be incurred in a state's international relations more widely if exit from a particular regime calls into question any high-level social norms about fidelity to formal promises, or the feasibility of a cooperative international System (next chapter). Those issues are obviously topical after the period of Trump-family government.

### Enter International Organizations: Uncertainty and the Problem of Incomplete Contracts

The key ingredients of regimes—stable requirements, with authoritative devices for signaling violations—inevitably do not cater for every circumstance; and even where they have something to say about a particular situation, the provisions will not always be unambiguous. Rather than providing rules that can be applied mechanically—in the sense that in every case, everyone would automatically agree on how the agreement should be applied—they are what economists call "incomplete contracts."[23]

Enter international organizations: as the manifesto at the chapter head proclaimed, they might sometimes help to reduce the transaction costs of establishing and managing ongoing cooperation.[24]

---

22. For major international regimes, this is akin to the costs of transitioning, domestically, from one constitutional setup to another. See Hardin, *Liberalism, Constitutionalism, and Democracy*. Think of an archconservative as someone for whom the costs of almost any transition are or seem infinite, and of an armchair revolutionary as someone for whom they are zero.

23. They might be incomplete for at least three reasons: the prohibitive amount of time it would take to document a complete contract; the impossibility of specifying all future states of the world; and the difficulties in verifying some states of the world. O. Hart, "Incomplete Contracts."

24. This took its cue from economists' accounts of why, in commerce, some activities are bundled together and organized in firms rather than effected via independent market transactions. The basic idea is that, where market transactions are costly to find and execute, the total costs of making multiple transactions in the market might exceed the agency (management) costs of delegation within a firm. In the international sphere, states might incur the costs and

A regime's participants might cede or contingently transfer four kinds of authority to an organization: framing agendas, to get parties to the table; an ex ante role in formally determining some of a regime's parameters or applications; an ex post role in monitoring compliance, via collecting and disseminating information; and an ex post role in adjudicating disputes and coordinating decentralized enforcement. In each case, the authority might be delegated either to a subgroup of participants (like a club's committee) or to some kind of dedicated bureaucracy. We have a four-by-two matrix of possibilities, with more power being shed—to leading members, a permanent staff, a judicial panel, or all three—the more the original agreement needs to be developed or interpreted.

The effect is to generate applications or interpretations that authoritatively clarify the meaning of a regime's provisions, and so give substance to its purpose. That reinforces a regime's or code's role in providing focal points around which participants can coordinate in order to sustain their collective project, as an example from commercial life can illustrate.[25] Even without the shadow of coercive punishment, participants in a market want to know its trading and settlement conventions in order for the market to function tolerably well. They accordingly need to be clear about whose interpretations of the market's "rule book" they should take to be definitive, and typically want it kept up to date. Delegation can, therefore, be a device for enhancing the credibility of their willingness to participate in the market. The same goes for some international regimes but is not so straightforward.

## The Constitution, Operation, and Pathologies of International Organizations

Such is the rise since World War II of international organizations that, taken as a class, they have pretty well become an institution in their own right. Something needs to be said about their legal constitution before going on to the hazards of delegation, their membership structures, and their decision-making processes.

---

risks (effort, compromises, moral hazard, etc.) of establishing an organization if those risk-adjusted costs are lower than those of trying to cooperate without it.

25. On adjudication's role in facilitating coordination, see Ginsburg and McAdams, "Adjudicating in Anarchy." On Jeremy Bentham identifying that gap in then standard accounts of law, see Nardin, *Law, Morality*, pp. 76–83.

## Legal Status and Modalities

Some international policy bodies and other organs are formally recognized as "international organizations" under international law. This matters since it determines whether a body has various rights, obligations, and capabilities, including being able to enter into multilateral and bilateral treaties with other international organizations and with states (chapter 3).[26] While not affecting whether a body is capable of establishing international norms and policies, being an international organization as a matter of law also determines whether they are entitled, under international law, to claim that any such standards or policies are binding law. Many do, checked only by broad constraints on vires.[27]

Irrespective of whether they are recognized as subjects by (and of) international law, many international organs, fora, and policy bodies have some kind of legal personality, but not all do. Examples of formal international organizations include, most famously, the UN and various of its offshoots, but also the IMF, World Bank, WTO, and WHO. Examples of important groupings with no legal personality include, most notably, the G7 and G20. Among standard setters, the International Organization of Securities Commissions has legal personality, but although the first two words of its name are "international organization," it is not an intergovernmental body established by multilateral treaty; it is an organization under private law domiciled in Madrid.[28] By contrast, the Basel Tower's main standard setters—the bank supervisors' committee and the market infrastructure committee—are neither international organizations nor even legal persons, but are both hosted by an international organization, the Bank for International Settlements.

26. Broadly, international organizations in the narrow sense have legal personality; enjoy various immunities; can undertake activities that are integral to their function, whether or not that is clear in the text of their founding document; can enter into contracts under private law; can be held legally liable for certain things, including debts, without their membership also being liable; and are not uniformly subject to a compulsory system of judicial review of their acts and decisions. Crawford, *Brownlie's Principles*, pt. 2, chap. 7.

27. Alvarez, *International Organizations as Law-Makers*, esp. chap. 10.

28. The International Organization of Securities Commissions has a Headquarters Agreement with Spain establishing certain rights and obligations there. The Financial Stability Board, housed within the Bank for International Settlements and financed by it, has a similar agreement with Switzerland.

Except where the context requires otherwise, I will mainly use "international organization" in a looser sense to cover norm-issuing and norm-implementing international policy bodies regardless of their status under international law.

## The Varieties and Hazards of Delegation: Agents, Trustees, and Guardians

International organizations are mechanisms for states and others to pool and delegate, which I shall take to mean a grant of authority by two or more states to an international body to make decisions or take actions.[29] If, as discussed, this solves some problems, it creates others.

One is whether an organization is capable of delivering its mission. For example, a body charged with supplying public goods will struggle if every action requires unanimity, or if it is financed by voluntary grants. The latter problem afflicts the WHO, which is largely funded by project-specific donations from states, nongovernmental organizations, and rich individuals—a weakness exposed by the COVID pandemic.[30]

That is one kind of design problem. Another is leaving a body unconstrained. Any delegation, whether to a subset of leading members or to a technocracy, entails what political scientists call agency risk or drift: the risk that the agent pursues its own interests, or what it thinks its principals want, or what it believes they ought to want (think of IMF management seeming to prioritize climate change over providing a solution to the problem of spillovers from international capital flows). Involving what economists call moral hazard, this problem of hidden actions can arise through poor monitoring by principals (unleashing the agent) or lack of effective sanctions.[31] It is compounded if an agent can choose how to allocate effort across two or more tasks, as in multiple-mission organizations.

Even where some formal powers are retained by part or all of the membership, delegations matter. To give just three examples from part I, the UN Security Council may compel all UN members to act collectively against a state; the management and staff of the IMF negotiate and apply country

29. That is sufficiently broad to cover delegations that are themselves effected by hard or soft law and give authority to issue hard- or soft-law standards. Bradley and Kelley, "Concept of International Delegation," p. 3.

30. Okonjo-Iweala et al., *Global Deal.*

31. Holmstrom, "Moral Hazard and Observability."

adjustment programs (signed off at the board); and the WTO Appellate Body rules definitively on the meaning of the regime's terms. These cases alert us to different varieties of delegation.

There are four broad cases. First, an agent intended to remain under the principals' ongoing control, as domestically with the military or internationally (up to a point) with the IMF. Second, an agent that is formally independent but charged with executing only a specific, time-limited task, such as arbitrating a particular cross-border investment dispute. Third, an independent agency that—acting like a trustee, and so accountable mainly to beneficiaries (and their representatives) rather than principals or settlors—delivers credible commitment for a particular regime: as with central banks for price stability, the judiciary for ordinary domestic law, and some international tribunals for parts of international law. And fourth, going still further, a guardian-like body that, insulated not only from day-to-day interference but from reform, is somehow responsible for preserving the integrity of the whole show: as with a domestic constitutional court or, internationally, at least in conception, the Security Council for order among states.[32]

The costs of agency pathologies increase from the first to the last of those four models. Errant generals can be sacked, a wayward arbitrator not used again. But a trustee wandering off the ranch can undermine the regime entrusted to it, while a guardian that does so morphs into a formally unconstrained ruler. This underlines the importance both of principals being clear about which model they want and of design landing things where intended (issues central to chapters 17 and 18's discussion of the trade and investment regimes).

If each of a multilateral organization's multiple principals were to try to cure drift by incentivizing a bureaucracy or court to prioritize its particular interests over those of its peers, the effects are liable to be weak; under some conditions, everyone would be left worse off. That is partly why delegation often comes in tandem with pooling, meaning member states try to synthesize themselves into a unified principal for monitoring and controlling their agent or regime.[33] At least for organizations under the jurisdiction of international law, there are also avenues for checking crazy overreach. For example, in 1996 the ICJ ruled that the WHO was not entitled to address the legality of nuclear weapons on the grounds they are a health hazard (!).[34]

---

32. On domestic agents, trustees, and guardians, see Tucker, *Unelected Power*, pp. 72–91.

33. Dixit, *Making of Economic Policy*, pp. 98–104, 157–71.

34. Crawford, *Brownlie's Principles*, p. 177.

But mishaps happen, as with the furor around whether WTO judges or principals should have the final word over the trade regime's forward-looking elements (chapter 17). This is the age-old question of who guards the guardians.

## Membership and Decision-Making Processes

Partly reflecting those hazards, international organizations and regimes vary enormously in their membership and decision-making protocols. Some have universal membership, others narrow membership, which might reflect deliberate policy (a club with high entry barriers), or just where things happen to stand even though the door is open. Those members might make decisions by one member, one vote; consensus; weighted voting; or restricted veto.

Those choices about membership and decision-making norms are related to the nature of the goods provided or preserved (public, common, club), how far members trust each other (the cooperation problem), and the nature of their organization (the delegation problem). For example, membership might be selective where an organization supplies (or preserves) "club goods" that are available only or mainly to its members. Or even with wide membership, voting power might be skewed toward particular states that pick up a lion's share of the organization's or regime's costs (financial and other), and so claim moral-political leadership rights (chapter 8 on hierarchy in international relations).[35]

To put flesh on those bones, as we saw in part I, the UN is a universal organization, open (more or less) to all, but with different decision-making processes in its different bodies: one member, one vote in the General Assembly, but veto (for the five permanent members) in the Security Council. By contrast, NATO is a selective-membership security alliance providing a club good, with decisions taken by consensus. In the economic sphere, the old GATT regime was effectively a "first world" body with special informal norms on decision-making, whereas the WTO membership is universal and effectively operates via veto (chapters 17 and 18). By contrast, the IMF is universal with weighted voting, and the Basel standard setters have (expanding) club-like membership and proceed by consensus, with a social norm against holding out (chapter 19).

35. Sandler, *Global Collective Action*, esp. chap. 4.

## Specific Pathologies in the Current Setup

With that ground-clearing, some of the legitimacy challenges faced by international organizations and regimes are not so surprising. Three examples suffice.

First, for those international organizations with club-like membership and consensus processes, the challenge will be whether, by acting as a club, they are in effect depriving other states (and peoples) of benefits, and so simply sustaining their dominance. That has been a recurrent issue for the Basel Tower.

Second, for those international organizations with wide membership but weighted voting, it is likely any problems will lie in smaller states feeling on the end of ideological projects, and rising powers chafing at the incumbency of established powers. The first played out in the 1990s Asian crises, and the second is, in effect, the predicament of China at the IMF.

By contrast, third, and most interesting, for international organizations with more or less universal membership, a vetoist franchise, and strong delegation, it will likely be disaffected large states that threaten the regime's viability. This will especially be so where the strong delegation is to an independent adjudicatory body, because both incumbent and rising powers can suffer policy losses they find hard to reverse by amending the regime. The classic contemporary example is the United States at the WTO.

The dynamics of those three examples, among many other candidates, reveal the intertwining of legitimacy challenges and geopolitics as they play out in even ostensibly technocratic international regimes.

## Do International Regimes Matter Too Much for Comfort?

Even without problems inherent in the distribution among states of benefits and power, the *international administrative state*, as one might label it, already faced plenty of complaints from within the liberal democratic states that created it.[36]

Those challenges come at different levels. At what might be termed a constitutional level, they include whether there is a proper basis for international bodies exercising normative authority and power, including making law (not mentioned as a source of international law in Article 38 of the UN Charter) and intervening behind states' boundaries.

36. Alvarez, *International Organizations as Law-Makers*, pp. 627–45.

At a second, roughly legislative level, concerns include whether the bargaining process to establish, develop, and reform particular international policy regimes is open and fair, subject to proper review by states' domestic legislators, and whether it leads to treaties with vague, open-ended provisions that delegate or cede too much power to international organizations with unbalanced governance. And at a third level, analogous to domestic administrative law, some complaints focus on bad or iniquitous outcomes, while others concern the integrity of decision-making processes and a lack of ex post accountability for misdeeds (chapter 14).

Those three complaints, which are familiar from often heated debates about the domestic administrative state, amount to saying that the problem-solving capabilities of international regimes and organizations can decently be harnessed only if they do, in fact, succeed in solving problems, and only if they do not cut across, let alone undermine, the values, norms, and conventions of constitutional democracy. Were they the limits of the problem, the task ahead of us would be a slightly more complicated version of identifying principles for legitimate delegation *within* constitutional democracies (of the kind offered for independent agencies in my *Unelected Power*). Indeed, something along those lines has effectively been the default assumption of others taking on these questions: transposing constitutional or administrative precepts to the international and transnational realms. That is, indeed, part of where we are going (chapter 14). But it cannot suffice, because the distributional issues highlighted by some of our examples—at the IMF and perhaps especially the WTO—concern the read across from the division of the spoils from cooperative endeavors to the conditions for universalist multilateral cooperation being feasible at all; or, put another way, from the innocence of subject-specialist technocracy to the higher calculations and hazards of realpolitik.

## Geopolitics: Revenge of the International Relations Realists

This is where International Relations realists get to shout, "told you so." A few did maintain that the kind of approach taken in the first two-thirds of this chapter—unbundling Keohane's 1984 manifesto—is fundamentally mistaken. Whereas cooperative internationalism, distilled through rational-choice institutionalist design, is driven by states trying to improve their lot—and that of some or all of their citizen-subjects—in absolute terms (mutual gains from trade and so on), some American International Relations realists say this is so much rot. States care not about near or far prospective absolute gains but, instead, about what they stand to gain or lose *relative* to other states, and in particular to rivals. In consequence, in one version of the argument, states will not rationally cooperate when they expect to be (or are materially at risk of ending up) relative losers or overly dependent on others.[37]

In some respects, ruminating over whether states care about absolute or relative gains and losses was a muddle.[38] And as a prediction that states would not enter into lots of cooperative ventures, it was fairly useless (chapter 3). But had it been framed as a cautionary tale of the need to be farsighted about the conditions necessary for enduring cooperation and peaceful coexistence, it would be celebrated as a perhaps tragically mislaid piece of wisdom: a warning against myopia, as later chapters discuss.

## Summing Up

Having in the previous chapter offered a Humean refutation of the impossibility of international cooperation, I have now introduced the vital importance of self-enforcing institutions and explored the role of articulated policy regimes and organizations.

Taking the two chapters together, we have seen that there are three, sometimes four, levels of coordination. First, at the highest level, there is de facto coordination (often via evolution) on Humean social norms, which are self-enforcing and can help flip a cooperative game into a coordination game. We might usefully think of them as metacoordination norms or conventions, since they are necessary for all lower-level coordination.[39]

Second, there is the coordination problem of alighting on high-level institutions that, via an evolved or designed functionality, create or police ground-level

37. Grieco, "Anarchy and the Limits of Cooperation"; and Waltz, *Theory of International Politics*, pp. 105–6, which expresses aversion to overdependence as a law of nature (false) rather than prudent maxim. (This is distinct from the epiphenomenalist argument, mentioned in chapter 5, that international institutions do not matter.)

38. For International Relations realism, it matters whether relative power is incorporated directly into the welfare function or as a constraint on maximizing utility. If the former, a state seeks to maximize relative power in all circumstances, subject only to trade-offs with anything else it cares about. By contrast, where relative power is a constraint, it matters only where it might bind. (This basic distinction crops up across analytical disciplines; famously so in monetary economics.) Powell, "Absolute and Relative Gains" (and other essays).

39. This bears a family resemblance to the metacoordination of Buchanan, "Institutional Legitimacy" (chapter 12).

regimes. Multilateral conferences, summits, and some pacts can serve that purpose. Some designed international organizations do so too.

Third, in any particular ground-level endeavor, the parties face the separate coordination problem of choosing what precisely to coordinate around. In policy fields, they coordinate *on* a regime. Except where a self-enforcing regime has evolved, that means either bargaining about the distribution of benefits and costs in a multilaterally agreed regime or choosing whether to go along with a de facto leadership group's regime (such as the old gold standard). Fourth, once established and operating, the participant signatories coordinate *within* the regime, creating bits of organizational machinery to help them do so.

To the extent any parties become dissatisfied, they might flip back to the third level (regime authorization) if there is no provision for within-regime renewal. To the extent the practice of cooperation erodes generally, the second- and even first-level norms are at stake since they are losing their grip on conduct. One can think of Trumpism in that way: a kind of assault on the highest-level rules of the game.

Less abstractly, at the third and fourth levels, regimes and organizations sometimes reduce the transaction costs—in bargaining, making credible promises, monitoring compliance, and so on—faced by states trying to find each other in the marketplace of international relations with a view to committing to certain courses of action. Just as firms have a place in commerce, so multilateral organizations can be useful to states pursuing their interests.

But just as firms are exposed to myriad internal agency problems—how do shareholders know what management is up to; how does top management know what junior management is doing?—international organizations create agency problems (or, for the technocrats, opportunities). Some of these hazards can be mitigated by careful design, but the available options depend on whether a regime must be universal to work at all, or can operate as some kind of open-ended club, and so on. That rich menu is, we noted, clearly observable in the international economy's most important multilateral organizations, the IMF, the WTO, and Basel.

### Loose Ends

Our account still has ugly loose ends. At the level of legitimacy, it remains unclear who internalizes the self-enforcing norms that are a precondition for designed international institutions. What if there is tension between the audience costs incurred domestically and abroad (part IV)?

At the level of regimes, it is left vague whether relative benefits should be conceived in terms of wealth and capabilities, or also vulnerabilities embedded in network linkages and overdependencies (chapter 10).

And at the level of geopolitics, the framework so far fails to engage with whether the distribution of benefits and influence inscribed into international regimes is sustainable when the balance of material power in the world changes. The posthegemonic future of international system depends, perhaps, on what (and who) is maintaining order in the world (part III).

To help approach those issues, we turn next to part II's final chapter, to the distinct but related realms of power, incentives, and values.

# 7

# Order, System, and Society

## FROM SELF-ENFORCING ORDER TO AN INTERNATIONAL SOCIETY OF DESIGNED SUBSTANTIVE LAW?

A society of states (or international society) exists when a group of states, conscious of certain common interests and common values, form a society in the sense that they conceive themselves to be bound by a common set of rules in their relations with one another, and share in the working of common institutions. . . . An international society in this sense presupposes an international system, but an international system may exist that is not an international society.

HEDLEY BULL, *THE ANARCHICAL SOCIETY*, 1977[1]

[The Concert is for the] liberation of a great proportion of the Continent of Europe from the military dominion of France. . . . It never was, however, intended as a Union for the Government of the World or for the Superintendence of the Internal Affairs of other States.

PAPER BY CASTLEREAGH, MAY 18, 1820[2]

THE PREVIOUS TWO CHAPTERS sketched a micro, rational-choice framework for thinking about why international institutions and organizations exist and what they do, but we are still short of an account of whether (and how) they make a difference to the bigger picture of international relations, the

1. Bull, *Anarchical Society*, p. 13.
2. Quoted in Kissinger, *Diplomacy*, p. 91.

contours of globalization, and the exercise of political power. This chapter moves to a more macro (or top-down) way of thinking. Peace and stability cannot be kept in the background.

It addresses how institutions and organizations fit into international order, international system, and international society, terms I adopt (and adapt) from the English School of International Relations. Probably the most significant contribution came from Hedley Bull, who, seeking to salvage the feasibility of international order in the absence of a world sovereign, drew on the Grotian tradition (chapter 2). This was, he suggested, more realistic than the absolutist moral universalism of Kantian cosmopolitanism since it placed states at the center of things (hence, inter-national), but did so while avoiding the structural pessimism of the Hobbesians, whom he described as viewing peace as a mere interlude between the wars to which states are inevitably driven in conditions of anarchy. Rather than cooperation being morally mandatory or practically impossible, in Bull's terms, "international politics tak[es] place within an international society."[3]

Departing somewhat from the definitions and usage of Bull and his colleagues, I am going to map ideas of order and system into the earlier game-theoretic and Humean accounts of coordinating and cooperative institutions, and I will also distinguish between different types of society by drawing on Bernard Williams. Capitalized as Order, System, and (thin, thick, and deep) Society—as realms of power and fear, planning and designed regimes, and norms and opinions—those refashioned categories are then used to give some structure to a retelling of part I's history of international institutions. This will reveal the gap, discussed in part III, between what many Western thinkers and policymakers desire, and the world as it is now that China, India, and others are capable of projecting power.

## Order versus System

Here, drawing on the previous chapter, the institutions of System are designed, whereas those of Order are not. System building involves a deliberate act of top-down or collective authority. Whether, as in the past, issued by canon lawyers or an emperor with authority over many political communities, or, as

3. Bull, *Anarchical Society*, pp. 23–26, drawing on Martin Wight (e.g., "Western Values in International Relations," in *International Relations*). The "Grotian" appellation is perhaps extravagant given contextualized readings (see Tuck, *Rights of War and Peace*, chap. 3).

today, by a table of national authority delegates, System's codes and regimes frame the equilibria for strategic conduct of actors in their relevant fields.

Order, by contrast, achieves equilibrium via forces and interactions that could be described as evolutionary, spontaneous, and organic, which is to say without a plan or conscious design.[4] The process of convergence might be kicked off by unilateral actions or bilateral pacts of various kinds, inducing copycat agreements among other actors, but it was not precooked.

### Peaceful Coexistence via Order: Self-Enforcing Equilibria Redux

A central premise of this book is that peaceful coexistence among great powers is the product of Order, not System. In other words, I will assume that order (with a small $o$) as an international state of affairs is the product of Order (with a capital $O$) as a self-enforcing organic mechanism, not of designed cooperative regimes or organizations.[5]

That is because the costs and benefits of being conquered or conquering are so great, so immediate, and, potentially, so long lasting that cooperation-inducing mechanisms operating via the shadow of the future—whether tit-for-tat retaliation or social norms—are not sufficient. My intending to respond in kind tomorrow to your breaking security promises today is not like retaliating against trade tariffs. In war and peace, planned retaliation or stigma is not much use if I am knocked out by your initial strike. Meanwhile, ex ante diplomatic bargains that might, assuming rationality, spare us both the costs of war face a massive commitment problem given that a won or lost war would massively alter our relative postwar bargaining power, rendering ex ante promises of dubious value (an elemental example of moral hazard).[6]

As Rousseau observed, precisely because the state delivers a platform for domestic cooperation, it can organize for defense and war against other states, making international instability and disorder more likely, other things being

---

4. This does not entail Hayek's normative contention that only "spontaneous order" can be good (or right): see *Law, Legislation and Liberty*, vol. 1, *Rules and Order*, where "construction" is set up in overwrought opposition to "evolution" (pp. 9–10).

5. That System and Society are insufficient to produce and sustain order is the basic claim of the International Relations realists. Bull does not make the distinction between outcome (order) and mechanism (Order). It is implicit when Kissinger writes, "An order whose structure is accepted by all major powers is 'legitimate'" (*World Restored*, p. 145).

6. Lipson, "International Cooperation"; and, analytically, Fearon, "Rationalist Explanations for War."

equal.[7] On this view, never mind achieving System, states present a problem even for basic order. Especially where others might harbor threatening desires or intentions—not necessarily for territory but to reshape the terms of cooperation, and so the division of the spoils, internationally—order requires states to incur defense costs that are sufficiently high to deliver a credible deterrent and maintain bargaining clout. The severity of those costs (reducing consumption and leisure), depends on whether technology favors attack or defense, relative capabilities, the nature of distance (e.g., geographic versus cyber), and so on.[8]

Where the actors have a sense of the spontaneous mechanisms affecting order, Order does not preclude attempts to stipulate equilibria among the great powers—as, for example, when territorial boundaries are refixed after conflict or war. But any such conventions gain traction only through stronger background forces beyond the reach of planners or law—for example, a credible balance of power, or policing by a preeminent superpower (chapter 8).

Since order (peaceful coexistence) is a precondition for cooperative endeavors, particularly planned ones, among large groups, this makes a basic Order a precondition for System, including many of the main international economic regimes.

## System as Designed Regimes and Organizations

System is, then, the realm of institutions as express rules in which the rules lead and equilibria (sometimes) follow: rules of the game agreed on by rational calculators prudent enough to allow for bouts of irrationality, imperfect information, the possibility of defection, and other hazards. With each state aiming to enhance its longer-term welfare or other goals, they seek to steer their myriad strategic interactions down sustainably benign paths by promising to comply with the terms of specific regimes.

Does System exist?[9] It exists wherever there are designed regimes framing equilibrium behavior in their fields, and some of those regimes call on common higher-level institutions for their generation or enforceability. Those

7. Rousseau, "State of War" (rediscovered only in 1896; see Tuck, *Rights of War and Peace*, pp. 202–7).

8. Fearon, "Cooperation, Conflict."

9. One reading of modern Hobbesian International Relations realists—including their creedal text, Waltz, *Theory of International Politics*—is "no."

regimes do not need themselves to be self-enforcing for System to matter. It matters if the fields matter, directly, to the realization of goals and values; and it matters a lot if, on any time scale, they materially affect (say, via relative wealth) the terms or sustainability of the higher-level self-equilibrating Order.

While System can reach far and wide—security-enhancing, economic, environmental regimes, and so on—on its own it provides no glue beyond the calculated effects of reciprocity, retaliation, and the material consequences of reputation, with future benefits and costs all the while discounted to a greater or lesser extent. In consequence, to be sustainable under adversity, any System seems to depend on some rather higher-level rules of the game around states' conduct toward each other, in the sense that states need to believe other states will comply with those norms and, normatively, believe they should do so themselves given that expectation. In addition to honoring agreements, such System-underpinning social norms might include, most obviously, negotiating in good faith, not lying to each other in ways that undermine agreed-on regimes, and so on. This is a bridge of some kind—rickety or sturdy—to Society.

At its simplest, under Society, states—now conceived of as members of a community, not merely instrumentalist participants in those collective endeavors that happen to suit them—share some important norms, goals, and, perhaps, values. In contrast to System, Society—if it exists—might be able to mobilize forces like esteem or shame, which depend on some shared (societal) ideas of virtue, decency, and professionalism. If states (leaders, officials, people) do desire to fit in, as I like to put it, Society is where that happens.

## Thin, Thick, and Deep Society: Ethics, Institutionalized Morality, and Law

This notion of Society bears a family resemblance to that articulated forty years ago by Bull, quoted at the chapter head. Emphasizing the importance of history, and identifying trade as a sphere Hobbesians and Kantians struggle to say anything about, Bull might have drawn on Hume.[10] Instead, he attaches "international society" to the traditions of international law bequeathed by the parade of "right reason" theorists encountered in chapter 2 (Vitoria, Suárez, Gentili, Grotius, Pufendorf) and also, rather differently, Emmerich de Vattel and the later positivists.[11] This leaves him, and followers, wanting to distinguish

---

10. Bull, *Anarchical Society*, p. 25; hinted at in Bull, "Natural Law and International Relations."
11. Bull, *Anarchical Society*, pp. 27, 31.

between two kinds of international society, solidarist and pluralist, according to whether one comprehensive moral-legal doctrine binds all states (edging toward the Kantians), or each does its own thing within a looser communal framework of law. Since the former is often associated with a social-democratic policy disposition, and the latter with libertarian policy preferences, this categorization does not do enough to distinguish between feasibility conditions for different degrees of cooperation, and substantive policy agendas.[12]

In consequence, I depart somewhat from Bull's formulation of international society since it glosses over too much. If, instead, we think of a society as characterized partly by its internalized norms and institutions for handling disagreement, its everyday evaluative concepts, and the justificatory repertoire underpinning its institutions, there emerges a richer picture of different kinds of society, including any international society.

## Internalized Norms: Instrumental versus Intrinsic Value

If Society is to act as a vehicle via which social norms reshape some cooperation problems into coordination problems, that raises the question, hanging in the air since chapter 5, of how internalized norms can themselves escape incentives to defect and free ride if their origins lie in their functional or instrumental value. More precisely, if people, after reflecting on particular internalized norms, come to think of them as purely a means to an end, then it is hard to see how the defection problem is not simply relocated (as International Relations Hobbesians claim). The importance of whether a norm is valued instrumentally or intrinsically lies in the force of the constraint it applies; if perceived as a means to an end, it is more likely to be overridden than if viewed as worthwhile in itself. So if certain basic social norms facilitate cooperation only where reflection is suspended, cooperation's foundations risk cracking once disturbed.[13]

To have intrinsic value, examination must reach a satisfactory terminus in the norm or institution itself. As Bernard Williams puts the matter, the value of an intrinsically valued norm or institution "must make sense [to people] from the inside, so to speak; it must be possible for them to relate [it] to other things they value, and to their ethical emotions . . . [so] that they can

12. On English School uses of "solidarism," see Hurrell, *Global Order*, p. 58.
13. Williams, *Truth and Truthfulness*, pp. 90–91.

coherently treat it as an intrinsic good. This means that it is stable under reflection."[14]

That fabric of internalized norms—valued intrinsically for their own sake, and so not reducible to something ostensibly more basic, while still performing necessary problem-solving functions—is part of what characterizes a society. As Williams makes clear, the precise demands and expectations generated by any particular norm will vary according to how it relates to other internalized values and norms, and so the institutionalized practices with which it comes bundled in a society. That does not mean all values and norms are given identical weight or form a neat, coherent whole without conflict, but to make sense together they do need to include norms associated with institutions for resolving or sidestepping conflicts among values, delivering some kind of equilibrium between the private and public.[15] So a norm's grip and application will, in degree, be culturally specific, reflecting the problems and opportunities encountered in the community's material circumstances and history, and the institutions they gave rise to.

Taking this to our inquiry, for an "international society of states" (or of peoples) to hang together meaningfully as a society, some norms and values need to be internalized in broadly similar ways across the states that are putatively its members. If, for example, a supposed international society's internalized norms amounted only to "honor formal promises," the societal element in international relations would not amount to much, but nor would it be nothing. Where other norms and institutions are part of a society's fabric—say, trustworthiness or sincerity—it would amount to more; and more still if the value of institutions like the rule of law were internalized (chapter 14). A drawback of Bull's definition of international society, then, is that it is monolithic.

### Societies Characterized by Evaluative Resources and Justificatory Doctrines

In exploring the possibility of international society, the question becomes not shared instrumental interests but, rather, whether groups of states internalize and intrinsically value any, or many, essential or useful functional norms

14. Williams, *Truth and Truthfulness*, pp. 91–92, discussing trustworthiness. (This leaves open whether the norm *should* have normative force—see chapter 12.)

15. Williams, "Conflicts of Values," p. 82. (Williams does not himself reconcile conflicts and internalization, but I think they can be.)

and practices (institutions) bearing on international and transnational cooperation.

I suggest that that is more likely, the more states and peoples share ways of evaluating (and so being in) the world, and of justifying their institutions, commitments, and projects. Since those dimensions of society drive the "thin, thick, deep" categorization central to later parts of the book, they need elucidation (with their relations to philosophy, English School International Relations theory, and some political theory offered in footnotes for interested readers).

One way of thinking about shared evaluative resources and frameworks is to ask whether the peoples of some, many, or any states share (and use in much the same way) thick evaluative concepts such as cruel, humane, and so on.[16] If not, do they at least apply thin evaluative concepts—wrong, right, bad, and good—in broadly the same ways? If they differ, systematically, in how they apply thin evaluations to straightforwardly descriptive statements, then it seems likely that, in the background, some in the group simply do not have certain thick concepts or use them in different ways. Because thick moral concepts mix description with evaluation, they rely on a broadly shared, ethical sense of their meaning. Lifted from the micro to the macro, a community employing thick concepts bears a family resemblance to what Hume called a "common point of view." Sharing a range of thick concepts implies—and in some ways constitutes—thicker social relations than having in common only the standard repertoire of thin evaluations. To matter (affect conduct), things like honor and shame depend on shared thick evaluative resources.[17]

Trying forcibly to homogenize a group's ethical outlook (imposing a dominant thick ethics) risks becoming a form of civilizational imperialism, a point

16. On thick evaluative concepts, see Williams, *Ethics and the Limits*, pp. 143–45. Thick moral concepts combine description with evaluation (e.g., betrayal, courageous, cruel, truthful, and perhaps legitimate/illegitimate, just/unjust, and fair/unfair). They are different from both purely descriptive ones (e.g., complied, disobeyed, reneged, legal) and thin evaluative ones (good, bad, wrong, right). For thick concepts, perceived fact and value are in some way intermingled—although, I would add, some thick concepts are more strongly descriptive than others: e.g., cruel versus just or fair. For both strongly and weakly descriptive thick concepts, making sense of them presumes thicker social relations than needed for thin evaluative concepts, so "an important difference between ethical cultures concerns what thick ethical concepts do any work in them" (Williams, "Truth in Ethics," p. 237).

17. This finds an echo in Avishai Margalit's mapping of thick (close) and thin (more distant) social relations into, respectively, ethics and morality (*On Betrayal*).

we return to.[18] But on Hume's genealogy of the common point of view, we become inducted into an ethical outlook because it is convenient or useful—for example, assisting in cooperation because it improves our predictions of how others will respond in various situations. Hence it becomes habitual, and perhaps internalized as valuable in itself.[19]

In the international arena, this suggests that where actors in a community share thick concepts and so are better able to adopt a common point of view, they can be more ambitious, other things being equal, in their collective endeavors. This without ditching their sense of their particular interests.

Conversely, cooperative regimes (System) effectively seek to summon thicker relations when their central provisions rely on participants sharing a sense of how various thick evaluative concepts should and will be interpreted and applied. For example, see the thick terms in this central provision of the European Human Rights Convention: "No one shall be subjected to torture or to *inhuman* or *degrading* treatment or punishment."[20] Breaches do not invite the response, "They did not comply, here is the penalty, now move on," but instead produce severe judgment of the perpetrators, so the signatories need to be confident they apply those thick terms in broadly the same way. That is part and parcel of agreeing (or if privately disagreeing, nevertheless accepting) that there has, in fact, been a violation in particular cases.

Beyond states' evaluative resources, there is the separate question of whether any of them share deep justifications—moral, philosophical, religious—for their moral and political institutions and commitments. The nature or roots of participants' collective commitment to any institutions and regimes can range from shallow to deep (which is not the same as weak and strong). The underpinning of a regime can be said to be collectively deep when participating states all justify the institution in terms of shared deep beliefs—beliefs that form another part of the texture of a shared way of life, even a common sense of identity.

18. As Williams, "Truth in Ethics" (p. 242), points out, to maintain that underneath it all "there is really only one set of virtues that contribute to human flourishing" is, at this stage of our knowledge, a scholarly bluff. (See chapter 9's discussion of West-Chinese relations.)

19. Cohon, *Hume's Morality*, chap. 5, esp. pp. 150–55. His story is similar to that for promising, but for something a step further back.

20. European Convention on Human Rights, Article 3 (my emphases). The European Human Rights Court has stated (*Ireland v. UK* (1978) 2 EHRR 25, pp. 39–40) that torture is "deliberate *inhuman* treatment causing very serious and *cruel* suffering" (my emphasis of thick terms).

By contrast, the shared commitment is shallow (but not necessarily weak locally) when individual states have different deep reasons for signing up: agreement and cooperation operate at the level only of the institutionalized regimes themselves rather than summoning a shared sense of identity.[21] Quite apart from deep doctrinal differences across states, shallow common justifications might be the only option when some significant signatories are themselves locally so thoroughly pluralistic (today the United States, as well as parts of Europe?) that only thinned-out justifications can work for them.[22]

Using those distinctions, we have a two-by-two matrix, with three meaningful cells.[23] Hence, I want to suggest that international Society can in principle take two, maybe even three, broad forms—thin, thick, and deep—depending on the thinness or thickness of relations among states and their peoples, and how deeply those relations and projects are grounded and justified. As Bull observed, "States obey international law in part because of habit and inertia; they are, as it were, programmed to operate within the framework of established principles."[24] But where does that rather Humean point leave law's (System's) reach and ambition? We say it depends on the thinness, thickness, or deepness of international society, which could be thought of as spanning from Vattel's world via Grotius's to Pufendorf's (chapters 2 and 13).

## Thin Society

Among the three meaningful cells of the evaluative-justificatory matrix for Society's variants, the first possibility—substantively thin agreements and codes with shared but shallow-reasons commitment—is quite different from the purely transactional benchmark because, as I am defining it, it is underpinned

21. Each participating state's background reasons for participating might run deep, but the shared part of the justification is shallow. A similar distinction is drawn in J. Cohen, "Minimalism about Human Rights," via a contrast between justificatory minimalism that works in pluralist settings and a shared comprehensive (philosophical or religious) doctrine grounding everything (a schoolroom version of a close-knit way of life).

22. Williams, "Modernity and the Substance of Ethical Life," in *In the Beginning*, esp. pp. 47–51.

23. A System-Society comprising only thin cooperative institutions but with shared deep (doctrinal) commitments can, I suggest, be ignored because, given modernity's options, states and peoples sharing a way of life (a civilization) are unlikely to be modest in their cooperative endeavors once a noncoercive Order is secured. (That is the history of modern Europe.)

24. Bull, *Anarchical Society*, p. 113.

by some social norms to which the participants feel some degree of normative commitment. Fidelity to an agreement's provisions is maintained because participants are, to some extent, attached to the value of fidelity to such agreements for its (and so their) own sake. That was part of chapter 5's Humean account of the feasibility of sustained cooperation among largish groups.

This is *thin Society*: some commitments can become credible because a norm of fidelity has become *internalized*.[25] Here, however, reputation is only instrumental. While a state's accomplishments might be esteemed, any respect for its character is formalistic (thin). When many people, particularly economists, refer to the importance of a "rules-based international order" or "rules-based system," I think that at a high level this is often what they are getting at.

It will immediately be clear that System (as I define it) always involves at least thin Society because a social norm of fidelity to formal promises—and of promises remaining binding until formally revoked via some preagreed process—aids cooperation where states are aiming to cooperate (chapter 5). But that is not to say much at all, because the formal promises that states are prepared to enter into via international law or other pacts might be substantively thin, and few in number. Thin cooperative Society prevails without, contrary to Bull, any sharing of basic substantive values and no higher-level common interests beyond the instrumental utility (and internalized value) of making credible promises in the pursuit of interests (which means keeping a promise when, at least in the short run, reneging would be preferred).[26] It is a world of thin morality, and so of thin obligations cast in positive law.

25. This *thin Society* seems even thinner than the community of "moral minimalism" espoused in Walzer, *Thick and Thin* (pp. 1–19), since that posits some minimal, cross-cultural political commitments to truth and justice and so implicitly assumes some universally shared evaluations. At other points, Walzer's argument is close to Williams's analysis, with an emphasis on history and contingency: "Maximalism [local ethics] precedes minimalism" (p. 13). (Walzer attributes the thin-thick distinction to the method of cultural analysis developed during the 1970s by anthropologist Clifford Geertz, who drew it from Oxford philosopher Gilbert Ryle's late 1940s papers on *thick descriptions*, which are context dependent but *not* always evaluative [e.g., military saluting]. It seems a richer Oxonian notion of "thickness" trickled down to Williams, who encountered the Wittgensteinian idea that grasping an evaluative concept requires sharing its evaluative interest in the 1950s Philippa Foot–Iris Murdoch seminars attacking a fact-value dichotomy; see Williams, *Ethics and the Limits*, p. 263n7.)

26. This seems similar to how, within a decade of *Anarchical Society*, Bull redefined society in a book with Adam Watson, dropping the earlier reference to common values: "a group of states . . . which not merely form a system, in the sense that the behavior of each is a necessary factor in the calculations of the others, but also have established by dialogue and common

For System with thin Society (which, when the context is clear, I will some-times just call System) to be sustained, breaches of a regime need to be expli-cable in terms of the particular circumstances without calling into question the reliability of the promise-maker's broader commitment to the specific regime, or to System in general. It is a world of peaceful coexistence with some commerce, among states with a plurality of conceptions of the right or good.

## Thick and Deep Society

That is quite different from a world in which states sign up to codes and agree-ments that are substantively thick in terms of their moral ambition (and evalu-ative demands). While states might agree to such regimes for differing deep reasons, they each need to be confident that they will make broadly the same evaluations of the situations or cases the international regime or organization confronts. They are capable of sharing, in Hume's terms, a common point of view (see above).

Such convergence might be apparent ex ante, or forged through an explor-atory bargaining process, or entrusted to a group of empowered adjudicators, but it needs either to exist or to develop. For example, in the case of human rights violations cited above, their leaders and peoples need broadly to agree on what counts as a violation, and that it is very wrong. This is what I mean by *thick Society*: a society of states that has internalized more than a norm of keep-ing formal promises, perhaps including norms of truthfulness (sincerity and accuracy) among members.[27]

A thick Society is capable of adopting and sustaining policy regimes based on thick moral concepts, operating as focal points, but without universal jus-tification in terms of shared deep doctrinal commitments.[28] So although we

---

consent rules and institutions for the conduct of their relations and *recognize their common interest in maintaining these arrangements*" (quoted in Simpson, *Great Powers*, p. 231 [my emphasis]).

27. The central theme of Williams, *Truth and Truthfulness*, especially chaps. 5 and 9.

28. English School ideas of solidarity seem to lie between thick and deep versions of Society, and tend toward universalism (within a society), whereas one could have a thick Society that embraced some version of pluralism, as indeed must be so for all thick societies that are not deep. Buzan, *From International to World Society?*, expressly relates pluralism and solidarism to points on a spectrum between "thin and thick sets of shared norms, rules and institutions" (p. 139), and usefully maps that to a spectrum between coexistence and greater ambition (citing, via constructivist John Ruggie, the Geertz-Rylean literature on thick descriptions).

are now beyond a society held together merely by a norm of keeping formal promises, and although reputation for its own sake begins to gain traction, a thick Society can still comprise communities with very different deep beliefs about humanity, life, or whatever. Within a domestic state, a thick society might comprise communities with different religious or secular identities (and commitments) but that apply concepts such as cruelty or chastity in similar ways. Internationally, a thick society might in principle comprise states and peoples with, for example, secular humanist, Christian, Confucian, and Persian-Sanskrit identities and heritages but, even so, capable of (more or less) ambitious cooperation. Or it might comprise states with similar domestic institutions—democracy and the rule of law or, very differently, party rule—while grounding them in different deep doctrines. Whether any such thick Society exists is an empirical question.

Third and finally—in a big step—there is a world of cooperation on substantively thick codes and agreements that is rooted in shared deep identity-constituting doctrinal commitments among the participating states and peoples. Where that sense of shared interests and internalized norms and values runs very deep, forming part of a common identity, the sharing itself will have some intrinsic value for members: a world of shared political ethics, and of some communal solidarity extending beyond the formality and comprehensibility of codified obligations. I shall refer to this as *deep Society*; it would be described by some as a form of civilization.

All deep societies are thick, but not all thick societies are deep. In deep Society, breaking ranks on some shared commitment is not merely an aggravating defection by peers that signals unreliability, possibly wrecking a regime, but is also, sometimes, betrayal.[29] This is apparent in how we might respond to violations of basic human rights (beyond the question of whether international law has been breached, and what that signifies). If perpetrated by distant country X with which we do not share deep society, we might well feel disgust, perhaps expecting our leaders to explore what, if anything, we can do to help the victims (chapters 9 and 13). By contrast, if basic rights are horribly violated by a country or people with which we do share in deep society—a shared way of life, a formative history—our feelings of disgust are likely to be

---

29. On thin morality versus thicker ethics, see Margalit, *On Betrayal*. Breaking a commercial contract would not routinely be described as betrayal. But it might be if one partner in a business sells their share to a rival without consulting their lifelong business partner with whom they created, built, and managed the firm every day for many years without conflict.

accompanied by distress prompted by feelings of betrayal: how could part of *our* world have done that! And, looking outward to other communities, perhaps feelings of shame. (This—disgust, betrayal, and some shame in civilizational association—is how, I think, some non-German Europeans feel about the perpetrators of the Holocaust.) Here, then, reputation operates as an intrinsic, not merely instrumental, force.

### International Society as a Society of State-Societies

In discussing conditions for order, Bull stressed that historically identifiable international societies "were all founded upon a common culture or civilization, or at least on some of the elements of such a civilization: a common language, a common epistemology and understanding of the universe, a common religion, a common ethical code, a common aesthetic or artistic tradition."[30] While blurring thick and deep society, and not catering for a thin society of law, this usefully underlines conditions for mutual comprehension and justification and points to the profound difference of any modern global society. Any international Society is a society of state-societies, and any transnational Society—or "world society" of peoples, as it is sometimes called—is a society comprising people who are part of different local civil societies. Those state-cum-civil societies are each themselves thin, thick, or deep, and each has its own particular history of values, organic and designed institutions, and foreign relations. And in each, there might be tensions between the state and any civil society. So the dynamics of international Society play out both among Order and System, and also within the multitude of local societal norms and values. This is central to the legitimation tensions (inward and outward) at the heart of part IV.

## Relations among Order, System, and Society

Employing a framework containing only system and society, Bull says society presupposes system but not vice versa.[31] In our terms, that is not quite so. Since cooperative regimes rely on peaceful coexistence, and order requires

---

30. Bull, *Anarchical Society*, p. 15, and reprised in the conclusions (pp. 304–5) noting diversity today. On his moves between pluralism and solidarism, see Bull, "Grotian Conception"; and Alderson and Hurrell, *Hedley Bull*, chap. 1.

31. Bull, *Anarchical Society*, p. 13.

Order, we can say Order is a precondition for System: managed disagreements rather than hostile conflict.[32] Further, System needs a thin Society's fidelity norm.

Does everything look different if, for historical reasons, Society among some group of leading states happens to be thick (or even deep)? Well, assuming order, that would likely lead, under modernity, to an ambitious System, as otherwise various cooperative benefits and shared moral causes would be left on the pavement. But would thick society make order itself more likely? This is a generalized version of the "democratic peace" theory that democracies are less likely to go to war with each other; it is general because, assuming they shared thick society, perhaps communist states would be less likely to go to war with each other. Plausibly, a thickly or deeply shared way of life helps states interpret each other's actions and statements, avoiding at least some of the costly misunderstandings that can lead to arms races and conflict (next chapter). But that carries no guarantees because misperceptions are hardly the only road to ruin: conflicts of interest (real and imagined) can trump common heritage and ethics. In any case, today, the major powers do not share a heritage, so Order is a precondition for any kind of *global* Society.

Still more of a general nature can be said about these complex dynamics. First, an organic Order can gravitate toward conventions of various kinds that help to maintain order. They do so by functioning as focal points that guide states on when they can act against others without incurring reciprocal damage or countervailing action from third parties. The emergence of borders and some just-war conventions can be viewed thus.

Second, to the extent that peaceful coexistence, safety, and some degree of (limited-scope) trust foster conditions for cooperation, Order can create a door to a System of planned regimes. It might or might not be opened—or only selectively to allies and friends.[33] In a genealogy of System, a first plausible step is codification of some of the just-mentioned organic norms and conventions that help preserve an Order.[34] Once codified, amendment and

---

32. Bull makes a similar point: "By order in social life I mean a pattern of human activity that *sustains* elementary, primary or universal goals of social life" (*Anarchical Society*, p. 5 [my emphasis]).

33. Davis and Pratt, "Forces of Attraction."

34. Perhaps the most famous in Western history is the Magna Carta (initially 1215), which drew on an accession oath by the Norman Henry I and earlier Anglo-Saxon kings' coronation oaths (Bingham, *Rule of Law*, pp. 11–12). It operated like a high-level convention that repeated violations could not displace (Sabl, *Hume's Politics*, p. 143).

development become possible. So, staying with just-war norms, the post–World War II declaration, in international law, that force is permissible only in self-defense against armed attack was a massive shift in the focal point coordinating the reputational and material consequences of warlike conduct (chapter 3). But new focal points will not gel unless congruent with, even while somewhat reconfiguring, the more elemental balance of forces underpinning an Order.

Third, because any such code will be incomplete, its ongoing interpretation shapes its meaning. That might occur via machinery for producing authorized applications (the UN Security Council for "aggression") or via procedures for a code's amendment and development. Since in some places courts and legislative assemblies emerged themselves in a rather Humean way before becoming constituted as organizations, System sometimes gives overt structure to an Order's institutions. Codification marks, then, a qualitative and temporal transition from pure Order to Order with System (assuming some institutional equilibria are now framed by the overt, designed rules and associated organizations).

Fourth, it seems likely that the modalities and substance of any designed regimes will depend, perhaps heavily, on the particular mechanisms and actors that sustain and characterize the enabling international (whether regional or global) Order. To the extent System is a child of an Order, it will tend to underpin that Order. That means that disturbances to an Order—say, from a change in the population of powers or in technology—might be contained by features of the prevailing System. It also means that a new Order of things might put the underlying System of policy regimes into play, although not inevitably: while dynastic change in old England often triggered regime change in the state (1066, the Tudors, 1688), the history of China is one of continuity in the system of government under changing (including foreign) ruling dynasties. This turns partly on Society.

Fifth, a Society's thinness or thickness affects not only the scope of ambition (the problem of trust among Rousseau's aspirant stag hunters) but also how ambitions are pursued. A Society's conventions and norms provide focal points that help select among the multiple candidate solutions to a cooperative problem. How a Society handles conflicts among norms and values affects System's scope to put a wedge between disagreement and hostile conflict. In this way, Society influences the feasible functional scope and coherence of a System of regimes. Norms generate macro effects beyond any simple aggregation of their micro uses.

Sixth, Society is enabling, endogenous, and constraining. Other things being equal, members of thick Society might be more substantively ambitious, but perhaps only among themselves. A thin Society increases the feasibility of pacts among civilizationally distant states: a different form of ambition. They are likely to have fairly thin content, revolving around mutually beneficial bargains that neither summon deeper moral commitments nor risk upsetting the prevailing Order.[35] But they widen commercial and cultural exchange.

Designed regimes can thereby influence Society (although not always as planned). There is feedback between the evolution of values and the development of rules-based institutions.[36] That is a complex process because, except in the face of massive shocks—war, a calamitous natural disaster—a Society's norms, values, and opinions are typically slow moving.

Pulling things together, two broad conclusions can be drawn. First, the more the identity and orientation of a System's designers reflect a Society shaped by the underlying Order, the more a later rising state might want to turn over the whole lot, unless it happens to share in the same deep or thick Society.

Second, while in principle a System could outgrow, and so outlive, its origins in a particular confluence of powers (an Order), that is not destiny because the values of the state-societies making up any international Society are likely to evolve even more slowly than international norms. Many state-societies have long histories, which are much more likely to be taught in school and discussed at home than the history and achievements (and failures) of international regimes and organizations. An international System is in jeopardy if it outruns the local values of its participating states and peoples—particularly those vital to the prevailing Order—even as it tries, in effect, to reshape them.

The first of those conclusions conjures China, the second the United States. And so, after three rather abstract chapters providing the first installment of our framework, we can now retell part I's history of international institutions so as to bring out its underlying structure.

---

35. Tabellini, "Scope of Cooperation," shows that the more people care about distant peoples, the less efforts to cooperate will be undone by the prisoner's dilemma problem of ex post defection. I am positing, separately, that the *way* one cares about them might affect the *substance* of what can be agreed.

36. Persson and Tabellini, "Culture, Institutions and Policy."

# Making Sense of International Coordination and Cooperation since Westphalia

At one level (a Eurocentric level), the history of international cooperation is of movement from a pre-Reformation civilizational (deep) Society to a mere basic Order of Westphalian states, and then gradually back toward a thicker Society of universal (human) rights and shared trusteeship of a global commons, but this time with a System of designed regimes and organizations, triggering a complex backlash among both leading and rising states. The remainder of the chapter gives that historical procession some color.

## From Christendom's Society and System to the "Westphalian" Order

The starting point is Christendom, a complex European society with overlapping authorities, held together by norms associated with a hierarchy culminating, for many, in the emperor and, for all, in the pope. The church's system of canon law institutionalized elements of that hierarchy, operationalizing a belief that some kind of higher or moral law should bind rulers and peoples. While the hierarchy is long gone, echoes of the idea of moral law have survived the succeeding centuries, sometimes only dimly, at other times more strongly.

Challenged by the humanism of the Renaissance, and upended by the political Reformation, that deep and thickish European Society gave way to a mere Order of sovereign states, which emerged as a way of coping with confessional diversity under dramatically changed material conditions (the starting point for a functional genealogy of the state). For each state's claim to sovereignty to be effective, it had to be recognized as such, setting off a chain of reciprocation that defined the state as the unit of international affairs.[37] In consequence, a shared understanding of a territorial political community's governance—state sovereignty—acted as a convention-like focal point helping to avoid war on religious grounds among reasonably well-defined actors (states), and within the Germanic Empire.

As a spontaneous (not designed) Order of sovereign states seeking peaceful coexistence through a shifting balance of power took shape, the law of nations developed to institutionalize certain norms and practices and was propelled

---

37. For example, the Hanseatic League struggled to get recognized at Westphalia. See Spruyt, *Sovereign State*.

forward by the revolutions driving the rise of commercial society. Doctrines laid out in the still-famous treatises—of Grotius, Vattel, and so on, each adapting to the problems faced by their times—acted like a supplementary set of game-theoretic focal points for coordinating the conduct of nations and peoples. This was, then, a world of Order and initially thin Society seeking some new kind of thick Society via shared norms of conduct.

By the time Vattel was documenting that in the middle of the eighteenth century, the stage was being set for a move toward a nineteenth-century System that, partly through colonialism, aimed or claimed to be universal, but on other continents was rarely more than transactional, and often much worse. Back in Europe, meanwhile, the missing ingredient was sustained peace.

## A Mid-Nineteenth-Century World of Designed Institutions

That came when the end of the Napoleonic Wars changed everything. Driven by a shared repugnance of the human and material costs of the long-drawn-out conflict and, perhaps decisively, an interest in maintaining domestic order (which is to say, avoiding revolution), the leading states deliberately put some structure around the peace. The reciprocity at the heart of the Concert of Europe's collective security apparatus operated not as a sequence of discrete de facto bargains but, rather, as the honoring of collective strategic promises.[38] Because the Great Powers expected pledges to be kept, they conducted themselves accordingly, with two effects. They did not automatically defect when they had to wait for payback of some kind. And the range of potentially resolvable issues expanded because any necessary exchange of concessions did not need to be simultaneous. In other words, an element of System appeared, with a de facto hierarchy of states now formalized in the legally recognized roles of the Great Powers.[39]

From the middle of the century, this dynamic of System began to spread beyond war and peace. Slowly, three tracks became apparent: economic, moral, and geographic or civilizational.

On the first, propelled by the industrialization of commercial society, network externalities drove an economic turn in international law's orientation,

---

38. Tolerance for minor skirmishes and risks varied. With greater geographical security and internal political stability, Britain was less risk averse than, say, Austria, a multinational quasi-state bordering the Ottoman, Russian, and rising Prussian empires. Jervis, "Cooperation under the Security Dilemma."

39. Simpson, *Great Powers*, pp. 93–115.

with agreements covering trade, technical conventions for cross-border communications infrastructure, and binding (but voluntary) arbitration—all told in chapter 2. This was very much emergent System with thin Society.

### The Moral Track: Natural Law's Slow Revival

The second track was quite different. Back in Vienna, the Powers had confronted the slave trade, declaring it a "scourge which has so long desolated Africa, degraded Europe, and afflicted humanity"—the language of delegitimation, driven partly by transnational campaigning and public opinion. William Wilberforce urged that those who persisted be exposed to "shame and scandal"—the language of social norms.[40]

More than a generation later, the failed 1848 bourgeois revolutions, the carnage in Crimea, and the Franco-Prussian War generated new kinds of activity: multilateral agreements on humanitarian conduct during wars (starting with the Geneva Conventions) and a search for peace via law. This was reviving, while adapting to the new world of positive law, the moral concerns of the old natural law, and so was summoning the spirit of a thick Society's shared norms of decency.

The international lawyers who established the field's first journals (chapter 2) thought of themselves as buttressing and advancing liberalism: freedom in speech, opinion, association, trade, confessional allegiance, and so on.[41] Their self-conscious program was, in some respects, politically progressive in its aims and embryonically cosmopolitan in tone. Article 1 of their association's founding statute declared international law (translated into English) "the legal conscience of the civilized world."[42] Here one finds the idea of law as both constraint and project, and a European intellectual elite who, by tapping into what they saw as the better parts of public opinion, held themselves to be the arbiters and carriers of civilized values and conduct (priests with different garments). This has jurists as actors, law as policy, and international law as rather more than rules of the game for states' diplomatic entanglements and their merchants' transactional commercial relations.

Some decades later, a young Hersch Lauterpacht, longtime editor of one of the key English-language international law textbooks (and also, it should

---

40. I. Clark, *International Legitimacy and World Society*, pp. 54–55.
41. Drawing on Koskenniemi, *Gentle Civilizer*, chap. 1.
42. Quoted in Koskenniemi, *Gentle Civilizer*, p. 41.

be said, on his way to becoming a great man), promoted the idea of peace as "pre-eminently a legal postulate," and the League of Nations' covenant as a "fundamental charter of the international society."[43]

## The Universalist Track: Derailed but Not Destroyed

The third track, combining geopolitics with commercial interests and a public version of the new morality, emerged in fits and starts. A change of sorts was marked when, after Crimea, the Ottoman Empire was admitted to the formal inner circle of European diplomacy.[44]

But was policy toward other states and civilizations arm's length or missionary? These were old debates, and not just about afar. In the Concert's heyday, while Metternich's goals had included sustaining absolutist monarchy, Castlereagh's commitments were relatively thin, as evidenced in the quote at the chapter head. Later, Lord Aberdeen wanted Britain merely to hold the peace, but Palmerston stood ready to act as a defender of constitutional liberty elsewhere (when confident he could prevail). Toward the end of the nineteenth century, some Europeans did conceive of their international legal norms as constituting a *system* of law that could and should be taken up elsewhere, but that supposedly civilizing and so patronizing mission was to be subordinated to interests in commercial empire. Whatever their intentions, however, any notion of Europe as the vanguard of a universalizing liberalism was shattered by World War I and the Russian Revolution.

With the United States' long-awaited arrival as a leading state, broadly the same ambitions were revived after the conflict, but now animated—for a while, at least—by a more idealistic Wilsonian vision of peoples' rights, informing efforts to construct the League of Nations. Conferences now sometimes led to documented regimes (although still not in the monetary arena).

They were also attended by more countries. Already, before World War I, China, Japan, the Porte, Persia, and Siam had participated in the first Hague peace conference, instigated by Russia, in 1899.[45] Now others were invited into the tent. As after Crimea, in intent this was System with renewed aspirations to a slightly thicker Society. But it was still a System with few international

43. Quoted in Koskenniemi, *Gentle Civilizer*, pp. 365, 376.

44. While the Porte had already been a party to treaties with European powers, admission to the Concert was to enter System-Society, reflected in the 1856 Paris Treaty's striking language, "declare the Sublime Porte admitted to participate in the advantages of the *Public Law and System* (Concert) of Europe" (Article 7 [my emphasis]).

45. Donnelly, "Human Rights," p. 9.

organizations, which were limited to the Hague's arbitral tribunal, the League's Geneva secretariat and new permanent (but, again, voluntary) court, the International Labour Organization, and the limited-function Bank for International Settlements in Basel. More important, it utterly failed, at every level of the moral register—other than, perhaps, eventually but not insignificantly, fostering some solidarity among what became the Allies.

### The Post–World War II System of International Policy Regimes and Organizations

Something more like an overall regime change—akin to a constitutional moment—occurred after World War II, as foreshadowed by the culture of American-led planning during the conflict itself. With the operative words being "design" and "leadership," the decisive shifts were basing System on the agency of international organizations, some degree of universality for their membership, and, vitally, moving toward a regime of legally articulated rights for the individual. Five things should be said about this, which has been *our* world. It has been very different from what came before, centered on organizations rather than old-style international law, openly reliant on power to keep the peace, complex, and organically hierarchical.

First, the new arrangements marked a significant departure from the earlier, more classically liberal era.[46] That had been blown apart by the crimes against humanity perpetrated by a Nazified Germany—symbolically significant as the home of both the Christian Reformation and one strand of the European Enlightenment—and its collaborators in various occupied or Axis countries. Nor could the old order of things be sustained by the authority of Europe's two key victorious states, Britain and France, given economic bankruptcy and calls for self-determination across Asia and Africa.

Thus, the manifest moral shortcomings in Europe's long period of global leadership meant that, after the war, multilateralism was to be broadened, human rights declared, and the old institution of international law subordinated to collective policy via organizations that were designed, in the first place, by (mainly) American victors.

Second, the reflex response to almost any new collective-action problem was to set up an organization or extend the role of an existing one. Cooperation was to be secured—or at least attempted—not only through pooling but by delegating authority. As time passed, this drove an increase in the number of

46. Koskenniemi, *Gentle Civilizer*.

bodies or tribunals claiming the last word on various matters: the UN Security Council, the WTO's Appellate Body, some human rights courts, and, within Europe, the European Court of Justice. Significantly for us, this was purporting to introduce into international affairs a norm of authoritative finality, and as such it was a direct challenge to the idea of anarchic international relations via the politics of diplomacy, even though none of these bodies commanded enforcement machinery in the manner of a state's executive branch.[47]

Third, in contrast to the idealistic aspirations of the prewar League of Nations, basic order in the world as a whole has been sustained not through formal pledges or declarations of virtue but, rather, by American military might and its leadership of the free world: first through a binary balance of power with the Soviet Union, and later, for a short while, through unrivaled power. In other words, even while stability has been taken for granted by participants in the plentitude of peacetime economic regimes, System has clearly depended on the raw forces of basic Order.

Even so, peace and stability have not been enjoyed everywhere. While the American-led Order has avoided armed conflict among the powers and has kept the sea-lanes open, just as the Pax Britannica did in an earlier era (until it didn't), it has not established a general peace, with a whole series of humanitarian disasters perpetrated by civil wars and proxy wars. Thus, not all states and peoples have had an opportunity to benefit from the international System operating under the American Order's protection.

Fourth, the post–World War II System has been complex: a series of field-specific regimes (trade, banking, monetary, environment, human rights, health, etc.), each with its own membership, governance, and power dynamics. In structure, this is not at all the international analogue of a holistic domestic state, in which trade-offs between possible policies can be resolved ex ante through political hierarchy, and conflicts between laws are adjudicated ex post by a judicial hierarchy. From the 1960s and 1970s onward, it became more than clear that the UN General Assembly and the ICJ are not a world parliament and court. As others have observed, despite the rhetoric, there has not been a single rules-based order or system in any straightforward sense but, rather, a much more complex setup (chapter 3).[48]

Finally, the organizational turn was somehow to be, in time, universal but nevertheless hierarchical—informally. At its inception, the new System's inner members were limited to World War II's victorious North Atlantic allies (and

47. Milner, "Assumption of Anarchy."
48. Chalmers, "Which Rules?"

their then–Southern Hemisphere dominions). While Bonn's early reentry could be compared to that of Paris after 1815, Japan's—based on its meteoric economic rise—amounted to a profound, albeit initially fractious, watershed in the development of System with thin Society (chapter 16).

When, a couple of decades later, during the 1990s, South Korea and Mexico joined the OECD club of industrialized nations, the entry ticket seemed to be a certain combination of growth and liberalization. But that gave way to something both more pragmatic and, perhaps, deliberately idealistic: granting entry to states that were industrializing and might, with some encouragement, liberalize politically. This operated largely through expanding informal groupings (the G20), which became a way of adapting hierarchy without changing the law (next chapter).

Whatever the motives, the new fora quickly came under pressure. At one level this was about security, as first Russia and then the PRC surprised a foreign policy elite by not embracing moves toward Western-style constitutionalism. More prosaically, the new globalist machinery could not mask or resolve divergent interests. During environmental negotiations (Kyoto onward), large developing economies stressed the legacy problems created by the West's much earlier, very dirty industrialization. When, later, the terms of trade between China and the United States became politically salient, even the thin norms needed for an international economic system were called into question.

Solving those collective-action problems has been one source of difficulty, challenging the credibility of System. Other cleavages arguably go far deeper: to Society.

### Societal Tensions: A New Standard of Civilization?

When an older Lauterpacht, leaving the schoolroom to advise British prosecutors at the Nuremberg trials, succeeded in persuading the Powers to recognize crimes against humanity, the world's ethical axis turned.[49] That his ideas gained traction depended on the war's Western victors embracing a new set of norms for political morality: power in the service of humanity. While the regimes governing international commerce can in principle subsist with only thin Society, the broader System's formal commitment to human rights demanded rather more: at the least, a thick Society of shared institutionalized values, but maybe even that participating states subscribe to the autonomy and dignity of the individual (very European terms).

49. Hathaway and Shapiro, *Internationalists and Their Plan*, chaps. 11 and 12.

As the institutionalization of human rights and commitments to humanitarian intervention proceeded in the post–Cold War world, something akin to a new standard of civilization seemed to be emerging. Compared with the late nineteenth-century standard (chapter 2), the new one was not thin, because it was not indifferent to other states' systems of government; nor to their relationship with their citizen-subjects.[50] For some, this erosion of sovereignty was welcome because that had been "born as a legal doctrine and international norm in early modern Europe as a way to prevent the intrusion of transnational religious and imperial authority into newly evolving nation-states" and so, impliedly, was past its sell-by date.[51] But this, an authentic voice of American liberal internationalism, risked overlooking the possibility of other cultures viewing the doctrine as the imposition of a modern reincarnation of religious and imperial authority. As rising states felt able to flex their muscles, it became a glaring point of contention.

For those reasons, except in its thinnest (just beyond myopic transactionalist) mode, the very idea of "international society" can seem to have civilizational undertones, drawing on the history of European customary law, an ICJ statute framed at the moment of maximal American power, and ideas of the dignity of individual people from Cicero to Kant and onward.[52] In other words, how far has the vision really been of an international society fashioned according to the norms and values of Euro-America? If that's it, sustaining it is not going to prove straightforward since China and India—developing economies with distinctive and rich civilizational histories—have become the preeminent rising states.

And so, I suggest, the categories of Order, System, and Society (in degrees of thickness and depth) help make sense of the past and provide a framework for thinking about the present.

## Looking Ahead: Humes's Knaves' Giant Cousins

Some earlier loose ends have now been threaded into the fabric of the book's argument, but others are still obviously dangling. One big clutch, still waiting until part IV, concerns the legitimacy of the norms that in some sense constitute any Society.

---

50. Donnelly, "Human Rights"; Fidler, "Return of the Standard."

51. Ikenberry, *Liberal Leviathan*, pp. 249–50.

52. On civilizational standards in international law, see Fidler, "Return of the Standard." On the history of a European idea, see Rosen, *Dignity*, esp. pp. 11–31.

Another, to which we turn next, is whether the basic mechanism of an international Order—a balance (and dynamic rebalancing) of power, or a hegemonic superpower—affects the nature and reach of any System of international regimes and the membership of Society. As we turn to hard power, part II concludes by introducing the thuggish cousins of Hume's knave.

Readers will recall that the sensible knave declines to join some collective agreements, reneges on others, and free rides on various social norms—all on the basis that others will not follow suit, so that she can continue to profit from their fidelity (chapter 5). Given that the benefits of norms are like a common good—available to all, but liable to be eroded when defections pass a self-fulfilling tipping point—their traction depends on waverers caring about the reputational and other costs that will be heaped on them if they cross the line too frequently or glaringly. They desire cooperation's collective benefits, and perhaps want to be thought to fit in.

By implicitly assuming a group of actors with roughly equally power, however, Hume's picture struggles with the harmless knave's giant cousins, who might be benign but might not be. If unsocial, they are in effect Giant Knaves—of different varieties. One is a powerful rising figure who does not much like the status quo, especially its hierarchy. Another is the current leading citizen, who is fed up with bearing more than their fair share of keeping things in order. If *they* defect, the show may be over. Some knaves, being much bigger than others, might think they can thrive without cooperation or esteem. A third, feeling no shame, a deliberate disrupter, lies beyond the pale.[53]

In the international realm, they exist today in China, elements within the United States, and Russia. With Beijing asserting itself, and Moscow disregarding Ukrainian and other borders, recall that at the outset of World War I the then-established powers' normative expectations were confounded when Germany invaded *neutral* Belgium.[54] Part II's framework gets us only so far. We must shift perspective.

53. As identified in Applebaum, "Bad Guys."

54. Myerson, "Game Theory." While some violation (through the Ardennes) was not unexpected, its extent was. On the other side, French president Raymond Poincaré had rejected a defensive violation of Belgium's neutrality for fear of alienating British public opinion. See C. Clark, *Sleepwalkers*, pp. 306–7, 494.

# PART III

# Geopolitics with Geoeconomics

## ORDER, "CIVILIZATIONAL" TENSIONS, AND A DISLOCATED INTERNATIONAL SYSTEM

When we go to war with America, I would like Europe to remain neutral.

YAN XUETONG IN THE 2000S, QUOTED IN LEONARD, "WHAT DOES THE NEW CHINA THINK?"

# 8

# Varieties of Order and System

## THE CONTINGENT SOCIETAL STABILITY OF AN INSTITUTIONALIZED HIERARCHY WITH AMERICAN EUROPEAN ROOTS

Hereafter . . . those countries may grow stronger, or those of Europe may grow weaker, and the inhabitants of all the different quarters of the world may arrive at the equality of courage and force which, by inspiring mutual fear, can alone overawe the injustice of independent nations into some sort of respect for the rights of one another. But nothing seems more likely to establish this equality of force than that mutual communication of knowledge and of all sorts of improvements which an extensive commerce . . . carries along with it.

ADAM SMITH, *THE WEALTH OF NATIONS*, 1776[1]

As its relative power increases, a rising state attempts to change the rules governing the international system, the division of the spheres of influence, and, most important of all, the international distribution of territory. In response, the dominant power counters this challenge through changes in its policies that attempt to restore equilibrium in the system. The historical record reveals that if it fails in this attempt, the disequilibrium will be resolved by war.

ROBERT GILPIN, *WAR AND CHANGE IN WORLD POLITICS*[2]

1. A. Smith, *Wealth of Nations*, IV.vii.iii, para. 81, pp. 209–10.
2. Gilpin, *War and Change*, p. 187.

IF, AS PART II ARGUED, any international System of regimes, including for international commerce, depends on some kind of international Order, then the conditions necessary for an Order to prevail obviously matter a lot.

International order is fragile, at best, if states teeter on the edge of hostilities, or are expected to do so. To achieve order without imperial excess, states need to be able to rub along with each other without jeopardizing their most basic interests. System sometimes helps by institutionalizing dos and don'ts, reducing misunderstandings, even engendering limited trust. But its terms also affect the barriers to entry facing rising states, and thus their attitudes to the prevailing Order and the regimes it helped spawn.

Part III traces how this structures current relations between the West and the PRC, giving rise to hugely divergent possible scenarios for commercial and other relations (the book's Four Scenarios). It begins in this chapter by examining a vital feature of the post–World War II Order-System: that from the beginning, it has been based on hierarchy.

One group of states (broadly, the Western allies) has had more institutionalized power than others. And despite being markedly unequal in their material capabilities, that leadership group's members have mostly accepted an inner hierarchy in some spheres, notably security.[3] That poses two questions: what kind of bargain or relationship sustained the leadership group, and whether new rising powers can buy into it. An inquiry into System's regimes and organizations needs, therefore, to look at how Order among great powers is typically maintained, and its effects on the supply of global public goods beyond peace itself.

## Types of Order: Balance, Dominant Hegemony, and Voluntary Hierarchy

For Order to be achieved, states capable of projecting power into the world (regionally or globally) need to be able to live with the power of their peers and potential rivals, meaning both that each power is not intending to vanquish or undermine others' power (the truth), and that each is confident that

---

3. Simpson, *Great Powers and Outlaw States* (also focusing on the treatment of weak states as "outlaws").

its stance is reciprocated and so it does not need to ready its defenses (the perception).

Historians discern two broad sets of circumstances under which those conditions tend to prevail.[4] One is a balance of power among a handful of leading states, none of which is confident of being capable on its own of overwhelming or subduing the others acting together. That, more or less, was the case in Europe on and off during the eighteenth and nineteenth centuries, and globally during the half-century Cold War between the United States and the Soviet Union. The other is hegemony, where a leading state preserves order (on its terms) given material capabilities that are unrivaled for the time being: the Pax Romana; Tang and, later, Ming China's tribute system (next chapter); the Pax Britannica outside Europe for a while after the Napoleonic Wars; and the Pax Americana for a while after the Cold War.[5]

Those two ordering mechanisms are complex, dynamic, and not mutually exclusive, and they have profound implications for the provision of global public goods. In the first place, balance and hegemony can coexist, depending on the geographical scope of a particular Order. Thus, during much of the nineteenth century, Britain truly was the (marginally) dominant power on the high seas, even as peace within Europe itself continued to depend on precarious balancing with the continental powers (France, Russia, Austria, and Prussia). In modern times, the United States has been the leading (at times hegemonic) power within the free world while, until 1989, a precarious global peace depended on a balance of power (via fear of mutual destruction) with the Soviet bloc.

Second, the dance of balanced power is inherently dynamic, with alliances and pacts shifting around as first one, then another of the aspiring superpowers tries to break free of the constraint presented by its peers. That is part of the story of classical Greece, with famous and not-so-famous city-states sometimes balancing against Persia, a kind of ancient super-state, but at other times against one of their own, as discussed in Hume's essay on power balancing. It is also part of the story of ancient China during much the same period, until, like

---

4. For a nontechnical survey, see Ikenberry, *Liberal Leviathan*, pp. 47–61.

5. The proposition that a balance of power or a hegemon has, as fact, sometimes helped preserve order is distinct from theories holding either that states inevitably and inexorably gravitate toward balance under (narrow) anarchy or that only a hegemon can maintain a lasting peace and so inevitably emerges. For a literature review, see Paul, "Enduring Axioms." On doubting whether balance, as opposed to hierarchy, was the dominant Order in the East or ancient West, see Wohlforth et al., "Testing Balance-of-Power Theory."

the Macedonians, the Qin succeeded, in 221 BCE, in sowing division (a thought to hold on to) and sweeping all before them—creating hegemonic empires subsequently hoovered up by, respectively, the Romans and the Han.[6]

Jumping more than one and a half millennia, the story of post-Reformation Europe can be told as one of countries collectively prevailing against bids for supremacy by, successively, Habsburg Spain, Bourbon followed by revolutionary France, and finally the Prussian Reich.[7] It is a history with instructive lessons. After its victories in the mid-eighteenth-century Seven Years' War, Britain lost interest in continental affairs and alliances for a while, notably standing back as Poland was carved up among Austria, Prussia, and Russia.[8] With its naval dominance bothering others, this detachment left it with no allies during the American War of Independence. In effect, it was as if London thought it had achieved some kind of enduring preeminence when, in fact, it had not—a lesson that might have been useful for Washington after the Cold War.

Despite frequently being the balancer, Britain needed help at other times too. During the 1850s Crimean War, together with France it entered into alliance with the Ottomans in order to buttress opposition against Russia's incursions into southern central Asia (precious gateways to the Indian subcontinent). There are parallels with Washington's courting Beijing when, in the early 1970s, Richard Nixon and Henry Kissinger wanted to put a wedge between the two leading communist empires. The lesson is to remain open-minded about whose friendship or help you might need.

Third, both balance and hegemony often incorporate relationships with weaker states that sit somewhere between alliance and followership. These can be uncomfortable, insecure, and more important than they seem, as another British example illustrates. On the whole, Emmerich de Vattel reported in his famous treatise, smaller European states felt happier with Britain, given its limited continental ambitions, than with its peers.[9] But when, as just described, Britain's interest in balancing waned for a while during the eighteenth century, the liberty of the smaller German states was threatened, and Habsburg

6. Wohlforth et al., "Testing Balance-of-Power Theory"; Hume, "Balance of Power," in *Political Essays*, pp. 154–60; Yan, *Leadership and the Rise*, pp. 177–80.

7. From the early eighteenth to the mid-nineteenth century, British legislation authorizing a military routinely recited the cause of preserving a balance of power in Europe. A. Vagts and Vagts, "Balance of Power," p. 561.

8. Drawing on Simms, *Britain's Europe*, pp. 69–77.

9. Whatmore, "Vattel, Britain and Peace."

leadership in central Europe compromised. That turn of events risked jeopardizing the security of the Low Countries and so indirectly threatened Britain itself. Maintaining a balancing Order relies on leading states having far and wide vision. That was underlined in the first decade or so of the current century when the United States seemed occasionally to take its eye off central Asia and parts of the Middle East, and hence Eurasia as a whole, leaving doors ajar for both existing and new rivals (Russia and the PRC).

That matters because the acquiescence of smaller states in a balancing or hegemonic Order can be merely expedient. History is replete with examples of their changing camp or abandoning passive neutrality for an aspiring hegemon's bandwagon. And very occasionally, an ambitious rising state might be biding time before seeking to tilt power away from the leading states, toward themselves.

### Balance of Power versus Hegemony: Global Public Goods and System Itself

Those various dynamics combine in what, for us, matters most: the profoundly different incentives that balancing and hegemonic Orders generate for the provision of global or international public goods.

Under a balance of power, some kind of voluntary agreement is needed where the supply of a public good requires contributions from all the main states. Powers will bargain with an anxious eye to how the distribution of costs and benefits might affect their relative power (and their other eye on who stands to win or lose at home). If there are many powers (multipolarity), design will be an uphill struggle. Any kind of universal System might emerge only organically from the effects of bilateral pacts, with questions of broader cooperation thrashed out in conferences open to whoever counts as a current or coming power, and with organizations limited to providing simple network benefits plus voluntary arbitral machinery for handling nonexistential disputes: exactly the pattern of the later nineteenth century (chapter 2). Within a bipolar balance-Order, by contrast, a more ambitious system of regimes, with more active design, could operate within the blocs, shaped by each bloc's leader, as indeed during the Cold War (chapter 3).

Under hegemony, whether regional or global, the big issue is whether System's design is imposed or accepted. The hegemon might be capable of coercing others to help provide public goods, but at the risk of damaging its authority if it relies too heavily on imperial power. Forgoing coercion entirely, however, might expose it to exploitation (chapter 5): free riding by others on those public goods it provides (largely) alone. In attempting to fashion a co-operative System in its own image, how far a hegemon needs to make concessions will depend on the circumstances. The more others need it during the design phase, the more it can award itself veto powers in international regimes and organizations, waving the power of its sword to entrench the power of its pen: an approximation of post–World War II regime building. In the other direction, the more the hegemon looks to the future and the possibility of rising rivals, the more it will desire a rules-based system acceptable to secondary states in order to build a reputation as a benign leader that others should stick with.

Those different System dynamics under balancing versus hegemonic Order plainly matter a lot if, today, the world is transitioning from a US hegemony to precarious balancing between Washington and Beijing: *Superpower Struggle* or *New Cold War*. In those scenarios, China should be expected to want to retreat to a world of multilateral diplomacy and conferences until such time as it could reshape a global System in line with its own preferences and norms. But under what conditions could it do that? To make progress, it helps to look more closely at whether the US Order-cum-System has been based on a shadow of coercive dominance or, alternatively, on some kind of legitimate hierarchy, with Washington voluntarily sharing or ceding power in some fields in order to secure genuine acquiescence.[10]

## Hierarchy in International Relations

The notion that spontaneous balancing (and dynamic rebalancing) between roughly equal powers and, alternatively, hegemonic dominance are the only conditions under which peaceful coexistence (Order) and, hence, cooperative System can prevail is a stylization that is more limiting than illuminating. As political scientist David Lake has usefully summarized, there is a spectrum of security relations between a leading state and others:[11]

10. Compare I. Clark, *Hegemony in International Society* (but I focus more on regimes outside the security sphere).

11. Adapted from Lake, *Entangling Relations*, table 2.1, p. 28. The important distinction Lake draws between informal and formal empires applies to the other types of security relationships. (Empire can accommodate gradations, with local sovereignty but an accepted duty to aid the wider group on its leader's command—for example, medieval kings and the emperor. Hinsley, *Sovereignty*, p. 89.)

| Relationship | Defining characteristics |
| --- | --- |
| Alliance | Weaker parties retain full decision-taking autonomy |
| Sphere of influence | Subordinate states are restrained from entering security relationships with third parties |
| Protectorate | Subordinate states cede foreign policy to leading state |
| Informal empire | Subordinate states de facto cede foreign policy and some domestic policy decisions to leading state, but formally conduct relations with other states as sovereign equals |
| Empire | Subordinate states are not sovereign |

A broadly analogous spectrum could be drawn up for economic relations between a leading state and others, spanning trade, regulation, and monetary affairs. Absent hierarchy, states trade as formal equals, and with autonomous domestic regulatory and monetary systems. Under hierarchy, the spectrum of their possible relationships ranges from, at one end, joint membership of a "free-trade" area under terms largely set by the leader of the club; through a combination of those trading arrangements with a regulatory order under which subordinate states align their domestic regulations with the leader's regimes; and, at the far end of the spectrum, their also adopting the leading state's currency and banks.

Whether in security, economic affairs, or other fields, leader-follower relationships are characterized by how far lesser states are free to choose.[12] The post–World War II Order-System is hierarchical but incorporated some voluntarism and gave significant voice to states other than the United States.

### An International System with Institutionalized Hierarchy

It can provisionally be labeled *institutionalized hierarchy*.[13] One that is complex, being neither uniform, nor fixed, nor especially flexible. First, states have equality before the law (where they accept an international tribunal's jurisdiction) but not in the making of law and policy (see chapter 11 on sovereignty).

Second, formalized hierarchy is most evident where stability is at stake (security and the international monetary order) and lends itself to single-shot

12. On the significance of whether the glue is coercive, I am with Ikenberry, *Liberal Leviathan*, p. 56n28 (but I emphasize acquiescence and legitimation rather than consent [part IV]).

13. Simpson, whose focus is international law, terms it "legalized hierarchies" (*Great Powers*, chap. 3). I prefer to emphasize "institutionalized" because it connotes reliance on informal norms as well as law, and flags the associated legitimacy questions.

supply, rather than where states and peoples seek non-zero-sum mutual opportunities (notably in trade) or to contain bads not associated with stability (piracy). Indeed, it seems that where international stability (order) is clearly at stake, lesser powers accept that they cannot insist on sovereign equality in policy-making because they are not themselves capable of providing the public goods at stake, and often do not even need to contribute to them.

Third, even in those fields, the leadership group has not been a simple function of material power. The United States has hugely greater military power than France or Britain, but each holds a veto in the UN Security Council. Even at the IMF, where the United States is the only state with enough votes to veto motions on its own, the European members have more than enough votes to apply a veto when acting together, which has underpinned their capacity to hold on to the IMF's top job (the managing director).

Fourth, leadership groups vary across international organizations, reflecting which states matter in particular fields: plural hierarchies, not a monolithic, System-wide hierarchy. Banking-stability policy provides a striking example. The initial (mid-1970s) lineup of the Basel supervisors' committee included Belgium, the Netherlands, and Switzerland, none of which had its own dedicated seat at the IMF board, but all of which were home to major international banks or critical-infrastructure providers.

Fifth, that variable geometry across the core regimes functioned under something like an *informal core* leadership group. Given the Security Council quickly atrophied during the Cold War, this top table grew out of economic interdependencies and so was not static. During the late 1990s, Basel brought leading emerging market economies into its inner sanctums,[14] and the regular meetings of important finance ministers and central bankers expanded into what became the G20 (chapter 3). Then, when the 2008/9 crisis posed problems beyond economic policymakers' paygrade, meetings held at head-of-government level effectively heralded a new informal institution: the annual summit of the world's main states, ranging ever wider as the

---

14. After the 1990s Asian crises, major emerging-market central banks joined the Basel Tower's leadership group well before their commercial banks were of global systemic significance. The credit goes largely to the late Andrew Crocket (Bank for International Settlements [BIS] general manager from 1994 to 2003) and the late Hans Tietmeyer (former Bundesbank president and later chair of the BIS board), who recommended the establishment in Basel, with wide membership, of the Financial Stability Forum (the Financial Stability Board's predecessor).

years passed, and so attended by an expanding parade of international-organization bosses.[15]

This began to stutter even before Russia's European war. As technology blurred the distinctions between economic and security policy (most obviously through cyber hacking or dependencies), there was a retreat away from the G20 as some kind of all-purpose running-the-world club. Instead, with skips and starts, Washington and some other G7 states promoted the possibility of a new free-world top table, in which the post–World War II North Atlantic and Pacific allies are joined by India, a multicultural nuclear power with a record of navigating a studious geopolitical neutrality during the first Cold War, and whose democracy has survived emergency rule, sectional strife, and other problems.

But rising states had themselves developed reservations about the current setup, given the *formal* leadership groups of many international organizations—most obviously the IMF and the World Bank—are uncannily similar to half a century ago. This poses the question of whether, cutting to the chase, the post–World War II System has always been American hegemony in disguise. I think not quite, which is terribly important for where this book is heading.

## The United States and Europe: System Predicated on What?

As the quote at the chapter head from Robert Gilpin illustrates, some hold that international System invariably relies on the dominance of a leading state capable of policing the prevailing Order, that the rules of any System accordingly reflect the hegemon's interests, and that "shifts in the distribution of power among states give rise to new challenger states that eventually engage the leading-state in hegemonic war."[16]

That line of thinking—like much International Relations theory, proclaimed as a universal law of motion, as though it were physics—invites the question

15. G. Smith, "G7 to G8 to G20." Initially, the international organizations attending the summit were limited to the financial bodies (IMF, World Bank, Financial Stability Forum) plus the UN but have for some years now included the WTO, the OECD, and others.

16. Ikenberry, *Liberal Leviathan*, p. 57, discussing Gilpin's views, which drew on Charles Kindleberger's earlier suggestion that the twentieth century's interwar economic unraveling was down to the unwillingness of the arriving hegemon (the United States) and the incapacity of the outgoing one (Britain).

of why, after it had recovered from World War II, Europe did not challenge US leadership, and whether the explanation offers a window into relations with today's rising states. Those answers must turn on whether secondary and rising states, including Europe after its decline, experience institutionalized hierarchy as useful and acceptable or as dominance; and on whether the leader gets enough out of leadership—keeping the sea-lanes open, providing the reserve currency—to accept the costs of qualified followership.

### Europe's Edgy Volunteerism within Post–World War II US Hegemony

The US-European relationship has neither involved unqualified dominance, nor been entirely smooth. Even immediately after World War II, when Europe's states were bankrupt or broken, the United States had to acquiesce in their capitals' unpalatable domestic-policy preferences to get the postwar Order going at all. Among the war's victors, Britain nationalized industries and France pursued state-led investment planning, both significantly at odds with America's more free-market creed. But US leaders prioritized security policy (balancing the Soviets by keeping Western Europe within its own sphere of influence) over spreading their own economic model (chapter 3)—an example of taking the long view.[17]

Differences did not end there. In the security field, while NATO countries participated in the Korean War during the early 1950s, a decade or so later Paris and London declined to join the United States (and its Australasian and Southeast Asian allies) in Vietnam.[18] At other times, by contrast, leadership was unceremoniously asserted, notably over Suez in 1956, when France and especially Britain were still economically bereft.[19] But Washington did not try to maintain their weakness. If anything, by allowing Britain and France to acquire nuclear capability, and by pushing for some kind of European union (small $u$), the United States created conditions where partners could become rivals.

17. Steil, *Marshall Plan*, pp. 348–50, and chap. 13 generally.

18. Technically, and so significantly for the gap between System and Order, Vietnam was an undeclared war and simply bypassed the UN (where the different sides all had veto rights).

19. During this episode, Washington sold sterling (Kirshner, *Currency and Coercion*, pp. 63–82) and threatened to table a UN motion sanctioning the Europeans (J. Barr, *Lords of the Desert*, pp. 245–46).

Today, of course, Europe is rich again, and has been for decades. Not only rich per capita but rich in aggregate since it is populous (around 450 million people in the European Union [EU], plus about one hundred million across the EU's immediate advanced-economy neighbors). Europe is, therefore, latently capable of projecting more hard power than it does. Nevertheless, a solid if occasionally fractious alliance has been sustained. Europe as a whole supported the United States in the first Iraq war, and instinctively stood by Washington in its "war against terror" after the 9/11 atrocities. But there have also continued to be significant examples of Europe challenging, or simply ignoring, the United States. France and Germany rejected the case for the second Iraq war, openly (and correctly) disputing the reliability of US (and British) statements on weapons of mass destruction.

## Europe's Influence within the System

Away from security, Europe has been even less reticent. While it has not mounted a concerted challenge against the dollar's role as the world's premier reserve currency (and is in no position to do so until it completes its economic and monetary union), it has become something of a regulatory superpower, harnessing its vast internal market to techniques of international and transnational law and regulation to increase its leverage.[20]

This is not abstract. The EU continues to tax imports of some American foodstuffs (I think at root because of concerns about an endogenous decline in tastes and standards liable to be triggered by importing the United States' lower-cost produce). To date, it has been somewhat tougher with the US-domiciled technology-cum-media platforms, partly because of different values around privacy, decency, and private political power. And, at a higher level, it seems to have inspired the widespread judicialization of international regimes described in chapter 3.[21]

Despite those and other tensions, the institutionalized hierarchy of power has sustained itself for three-quarters of a century. So why does the United States put up with Europe? And why didn't European capitals aim for greater power once its Cold War security blanket briefly seemed less necessary?

Part of the answer is probably a prudent inertia: do not lightly jettison what has worked tolerably well when you do not know what lies ahead. That might

20. Bradford, *Brussels Effect*.
21. On judicialization, see Alter, "Multiplication of International Courts."

explain why, despite the predictions-cum-urgings of not a few American International Relations realists, Washington did not fold NATO after the Cold War.[22] But I think a more fundamental part of the answer is that, in a dangerous world, neither the United States nor Europe has represented a threat to the other, with that in turn rooted in something deeper: a loosely shared way of life.

### Threats versus Inconveniences

As a general matter, it seems likely that the response of established powers to rising states turns on what might change. Hobbesian International Relations realists tell us states want, above all else, to survive.[23] That seems right—at least of a state's leading officials—but it leaves much unsaid. Survive as what: as a state, the leading superpower, a prestigious leader, a materially prosperous political community, or a community with particular institutions and ways of life?

When one Order gives way to another, the precise circumstances of transition determine whether the new leading powers trash most of what has gone before or are constrained to work with the grain of at least some of the old Order's internalized values. The history of Christendom, the European balance of power, and US hegemony is, in this crucial sense, continuous. The post–World War II Order-System jettisoned some of the previous Order's baggage, notably colonialism, but there has been a great deal of continuity in its underlying aspirations. While there have been tensions and not a little hypocrisy, the United States–led Order-System has (most of the time) involved more than the thinnest possible international Society among its leadership group.

This helps make sense of Washington's relationship with Europe. If the test is whether a rising state poses a threat to the survival of the leading states' autonomy or prosperity, then just as the ascendency of the United States had not been much more than an (aggravating) inconvenience for Britain, so Europe's postwar recovery and confederation were hardly serious threats to the

22. E.g., Waltz, "Structural Realism after the Cold War." Many such essays hovered ambiguously (and instructively) between prediction (so far, wrong) and prescription (probably ill-judged).

23. Among International Relations realists, this is often rooted in Hobbes's belief, in his stripped-down natural-law account of politics, that survival is the elemental goal and right of each and every one of us.

United States.[24] That is partly because continental European capitals embarked on a strategy of breaking the link between being a hard-power top dog and a welfare top dog. The post–World War II Order-System has, in short, been good for Europe, freeing it to pursue greater regional interdependence and prosperity.[25] We see that in the *European Dream*, which acts as a magnet for many people in the former Soviet republics, such as Ukraine. A longing for freedom no longer requires a boat journey to America.

### The Grand Bargain: "Guns and Butter" or Prestige and Ways of Life?

That makes it sound, at least for Europeans, like the "guns versus butter" choice: whether to expend resources on consumption (and investing for greater future consumption) or, instead, on the military in order to ensure that the state and its people survive to consume in the future.[26] Europe has persistently chosen standard of living (leisure, a social-security safety net, consumption, and the cultivation of taste) over the pursuit of international leadership.[27]

But surely more was going on than different welfare preferences. At least for the eastern Atlantic, close relations—including volatile acquiescence in empowered followership—were buttressed by perceptions that Americans were and are, when it comes to it, either "like us" (deep Society) or, at least, governed via institutions instantiating shared political values: a modern, qualified kind of thick Society.[28] It really does matter that the US founding fathers were steeped in, among many others, Locke, Montesquieu, and Hume.

24. Britain abjured the temptation to secure Southern secession in the 1860s partly because of public opinion (against slavery), and gained a long-run protector of its liberties. For an International Relations realist stressing the balance of *threats* (probably closer to Hobbes himself), see Walt, *Origins of Alliances*.

25. Waltz, *Theory of International Politics*, p. 71, would cast this ambition as freedom to take more risks.

26. The phrase might be Lyndon Johnson's. Powell, "Guns versus Butter."

27. European living standards have been closer to those of the United States (in per capita gross domestic product terms) once adjustments are made for patterns of output (less on military, more on consumption goods) and leisure. Gordon, "Two Centuries."

28. Khong, "American Tributary System," argues the US-led system of international relations is structurally similar to China's old tribute system (next chapter). But the European and (in colonial origin) Anglo-Saxon states and peoples identified as the hegemon's "closest tributaries" do not regard the United States as the origin or authoritative exemplar of "European" civilization, culture, political institutions, and values, as opposed to being one rather grand and,

What about the United States: why does it go along with Europe's prefer-ences? Partly, it might be the shared liberalism embedded in the System's sin-ews.[29] But there are also concrete returns to Americans: top-dog prestige (for top officials), pride or even honor (for some citizen-subjects), wide-ranging soft power, and the harder power of tilting transnational initiatives toward its own interests. Whether that suffices for citizens is another matter, parked for now.

This, then, is chapter 1's *grand bargain*: European followership and acqui-escence in US prestige in exchange for an American security blanket and a sizable presence at an institutionalized hierarchy's top table. That is not only a matter of System—the design and workings of international regimes—but of the underlying Order. While, as US officials fairly point out, Europe plainly could bear a much bigger part of the burden of defending itself (and now, at last, looks set to do so), the possible effects of parity in effort would include the emergence of another great power (with hard power), changing the im-plicit bargain.

## Institutionally Constrained Hierarchy

The post–World War II Order and System evolved, therefore, into a highly tuned institutional hierarchy, with the United States a *constrained leader* (so long as it grasped and followed the construct's implicit bargains).

For the Europeans, international power was to be gathered and exercised through international organizations created, initially, on Washington's initia-tive. Indeed, if any part of the world truly embraces international law as the glue and modality of interstate relations, surely it is the EU and its member states—drawing on traditions going back to the Holy Roman Empire and, further still, to the jus gentium of Rome itself (chapter 2). This has seemed to suit Washington so long as it could embed a version of its worldview in the rules.[30] By accepting that it should address the moral-hazard risks implicit in hegemony, it in effect acquiesces in self-binding as a long-term strategy.[31]

---

inevitably, sometimes perverse manifestation of them, as well as being the source of a cul-tural efflorescence that cannot be traced to the free settlers (e.g., jazz, the blues, and their offspring).

29. Ikenberry, *Liberal Leviathan*.

30. Rabkin, *Law without Nations?*, pp. 3–4, rages against this, implicitly assuming US domi-nance is secure for the foreseeable future without conviction allies.

31. This might seem to be at odds with the United States' formal absence from the UN Conven-tion on the Law of the Sea treaty regime. Reconciliation, of sorts, comes via most US administrations

For other states and peoples, meanwhile, this construct placed the leadership group as a whole under some constraints that, in spirit, are not wholly dissimilar to the contestability that characterizes a republic. To give just three examples, IMF decisions and policies can be questioned in its governing bodies; WTO policymaking operates by consensus (meaning veto); and the UN General Assembly can protest against, although not overturn, decisions of the Security Council.

It is, then, an *institutionalized constrained hierarchy*. Although plenty of commentators would tighten the constraints—a big issue picked up in part IV's discussion of legitimation principles—the post–World War II Order-cum-System has operated, by and large, as a set of institutionalized political relationships existing in the space between (narrow) anarchy and coercive hegemony.[32]

## Making Sense of Rising Powers in a Noisy World

But is the notion of institutionally constrained leadership misleading, a product of Europe's twentieth-century moral horrors, its colonial history, current riches, and civilizational homogeneity (or at least connection) with the United States? Even if its moral standing in the world has recovered somewhat, might Europe's empowered followership, and hence the durability of the postwar System's institutionalized hierarchy, have depended all along on modern North America's cultural origins and outlook (or at least on European perceptions of them)? And if there is something in that, has the apparent equilibrium of constrained leadership and hierarchy been an artifact of Europe's having been for decades by far the richest part of the world after North America, and therefore the key counterweight in much international policymaking?

To the extent those contingencies have mattered, the reemergence of Asian powers, and already one superpower, outside the network of US security pacts changes the background conditions for the international Order-System that has shaped contemporary commercial society. Has the System's liberal orientation been contingent and temporary?

---

holding that the third regime codifies customary law, making ratification less momentous: see Rosenne and Gebhard, "Conferences on the Law."

32. A version of this argument, deploying republican accounts of security, is advanced in Deudney, *Bounding Power* (but with prescriptions for world republican government).

That is what makes the arrival at and near the top table of, respectively, Japan and South Korea so very interesting and important. These are Confucian-heritage states that, since World War II, have adopted and, at their own pace, adapted constitutionalism, forms of liberal democracy, and open markets. Rather like the EU in Western Europe, on a grander canvas these developments seemed to live up to Adam Smith's optimistic prescription quoted at the chapter head: let peace and justice follow from commerce and convergence toward republican government. Thinking about it like that helps make sense of Washington's optimistic policy toward Beijing's opening up after the Cold War: surely, they could only travel a similar liberalizing path (chapters 17 and 18).

Setting aside what induced that spasm of delusional hubris, sharing in "thickish society" is hardly the first thing the PRC's rise brings to mind. As discussed in the next chapter, whatever norms and values the PRC's leaders embrace, they do not obviously include constitutional democracy, civil society, a market economy, a free press, or certain basic rights. Of itself, that does not make China a threat, but it does underline the importance of gauging what the Communist Party of China (the Party) wants and, perhaps more straightforwardly, what it is actively against.

## Hazards of Observational Equivalence

In the real world, uncertainty about others' dispositions and intentions is a hazard in itself. While a commonplace in security circles, the problem is not confined to making sense of potential rivals' military capabilities and plans.

Imagine a government with vast net external assets, beyond anything needed to support its exchange rate.[33] Rationally, one would expect the investment policy to give great weight to geographical diversification, perhaps with some concentration in sectors where the country has great expertise, let's say various types of infrastructure. The result—high investment in critical physical and information-technology infrastructure all over the world—would be driven by economics. Now imagine a rising power that seeks to build a network of technical and economic, and so political, dependencies around the world that increase its capability to challenge the incumbent hegemon. The resulting investment policy would be much the same. Economists call this observational

---

33. Investment is assumed to be under the control of government (not disaggregated private firms and households constrained only by laws on transparency, fair dealing, and so on).

equivalence: the incumbent power cannot immediately tell which motive dominates.

Let's now turn to the rising power's perceptions of the incumbent. It will not be straightforward to distinguish between, on the one hand, genuinely held grievances about the rising state's terms of access to the international economic system and, on the other hand, a determined strategy of containing its economic and material power. Since neither power can be sure of the other's true motives, and since those motives might change over time, it might be prudent for each to give some weight to the malevolent interpretation and act accordingly. Those defensive actions themselves give signals, which might lend credence to any presumption of malevolence, and so take states further toward hostilities.

The structure of this problem is as old as can be. In circumstances where the stakes were also very high, it was described by the British Foreign Office official Eyre Crowe in a famous memo to ministers at the beginning of the twentieth century on the rise of the still recently unified Germany: "The element of danger [to Britain] present as a visible factor in one case [German confrontation], also enters, though under some disguise, into the second [nonaggressive pursuit of interests]; and against such danger, whether actual or contingent, the same general line of conduct seems prescribed."[34] International Relations scholars call this arm's race dynamic the security dilemma.[35] What matters for us is that economic policies and actions can be part of the feedback process, and a component of geopolitical strategy, which was partly why Hume decried the jealousy of trade (chapter 2, and chapter 4 on geoeconomics).

In general, a transparency regime—conventions on public or bilateral disclosure and so on—can help avoid misleading or false signals.[36] But in geopolitics, such regimes will frequently not be self-enforcing (chapters 6 and 7). Worse, there are incentives to exploit any international norm of truthfulness

34. Kissinger, *On China*, pp. 518–20. C. Clark, *Sleepwalkers*, dwells on Crowe's anti-German sentiment (pp. 162–66). Compared, however, with making sense of France and Russia, established global powers, it was surely harder for London to disentangle the manifestations of Germany's economic catch-up from its policy—a signal-noise extraction problem.

35. Jervis, "Cooperation under the Security Dilemma." But see Fearon, "Cooperation, Conflict," for similar results without a signal-extraction problem.

36. Economic activity is littered with this problem—for example, whether to rely on statements by central bankers, publicly quoted companies, or the person with whom you are trying to negotiate a transaction. Transparency and disclosure regimes accordingly run through economic policy and law.

or fidelity, precisely to get away with false signals. Where an Order itself is at stake, it is harder for System's regimes to be part of the solution rather than part of the problem.

## Summary

At the beginning of the twentieth century, the Second Hague Peace Conference, held in 1907, got derailed over whether power hierarchies could be reconciled with a strong conception of sovereign equality. Second-tier powers wanted an equal say in the making of policy and law, including in the composition of a proposed permanent international court. The great powers of the day would not go along with that, and the construction of a much more ambitious international System stalled.

A striking thing about this story, compellingly told in Gerry Simpson's *Great Powers and Outlaw States*, is that the aspirant powers banging on the door were Latin American.[37] At the time, Brazil and Argentina were among the largest economies in the world. Over the following decades all that changed, and their claims dropped away.

Some hierarchy of material power is inevitable, not only between great powers and other states but among the great powers themselves. System tames that somewhat, at least among those who find themselves at the top table. The accommodations between the United States, Canada, Europe, and Japan put that on display over the past seventy-five years.

But that has been a top table of states with similar systems of government, underpinned by similar institutional values. China's rise portends something very different; something not seen since the standoff between Britain and France during their long eighteenth century. Including disputed territory (Taiwan) within its definition of "core interests" is hardly a signal suffering from observational equivalence.

So, bringing together two themes of this book, it matters greatly that the serious challenge presented by China's rise to the post–World War II System's institutionalized hierarchy has gathered steam just as the leaders of that System were moving, through policies on human rights and humanitarian intervention, back toward making the shared moral values of a thick international Society a condition for inclusion. In other words, just as China has been banging the drum for sovereignty, nonintervention, and autonomy in states' choice of

37. Simpson, *Great Powers*, chap. 5.

domestic political regime, the entrenched leaders of the prevailing international Order-System seemed to be moving in the opposite direction.

Well, that is until the rash of Western authoritarian-style populism broke out after the Global Financial Crisis. But although those populists initially appeared not to care much about basic rights, they were no happier with China than were establishment liberals. It was, they said, taking away their peoples' jobs. We need to turn to China.

# 9

# Rising Powers, Norms, and Geopolitics

## PARTY-LED CHINA'S SELF-IDENTITY AND US POLITICAL NATIVISM AS RISKS TO SYSTEM AND ORDER

There are people who create order; there are no rules [*fa*] that create order.

XUNZI, 313–238 BCE[1]

The international system is an anarchical system. . . . We do not need economic cooperation alone: we also need to cooperate [bilaterally] in politics, security, culture, etc.

YAN XUETONG, "COOPERATION BETWEEN CHINA AND HUNGARY," JANUARY 2017[2]

AT THE TIME I heard the second statement, from one of contemporary China's leading International Relations theorists, as *There is no such thing as an international system. Only states pursuing their interests.*[3] The substance is the same (given

---

1. Tiwald, "On the View," p. 80. "People" here means gentlemen (elite). Angle's translation in *Sagehood* is, "There is only governance by men, not governance by *fa* [laws and institutions]" (p. 187).

2. Yan, "Cooperation between China and Hungary," pp. 65, 67. Yan is a realist who emphasizes norms, international hierarchy, and allies, as well as being a nationalist who believes the quality of personal leadership is key to international relations among otherwise similarly capable states.

3. I was at the Budapest conference, hosted by the Hungarian central bank, to mark the award to Jacques de Larosière of the Lamfalussy Prize, named after a former Bank for

the anarchy jargon), but the rhetorical effect rather stronger. It seemed different from Leader Xi Jinping's declaration, only a few days earlier, that "we should pro-actively manage economic globalization. . . . This is our unshirkable responsibility as leaders of our times"; that "we should pursue a well-coordinated and inter-connected approach to develop a model of open and win-win cooperation"; and that "we should honor promises and abide by rules." Those are hardly sentiments overtly embracing anarchic international relations, and of course they went down well with the crowd at Davos, where Xi was speaking.[4]

Whom should we take more seriously, the incumbent leader or the bold theo-rist? Yan could be read as implying something along the lines of the following: great powers cannot be held to the rules of the game, China is becoming a great power, and therefore China shall (and should) no more be part of any System than America has been. Or, going only a bit further: might is right, and China now has might. But a middle-way interpretation might also make sense. This would hold that while for some decades there has been an international system operat-ing under an American security umbrella, it will be abandoned, formally sus-pended, or displaced as the foundations of international order are reconfigured and a new great power pursues a system redesigned in its image. This construction might fit with Xi's observation during the same Davos speech, with a hat tip to Mao Zedong's attempts to lead the old Third World, that "the global governance system has not embraced [the rise of emerging market and developing countries] and is therefore inadequate in terms of representation and inclusiveness."

This chapter accordingly explores how China might think of itself, what it might want, and how Beijing and Washington approach international law and institutions.

## Some Implications of China's Rise for Order, System, and Society

Returning to Thucydides (chapter 1), rising powers almost inevitably perturb the equilibrium prevailing among incumbents, but it matters how. Take the late nineteenth century. After Prussia defeated France (1870) and, later, Japan

---

International Settlements head who had fled his native Hungary to escape communism. It ended up being combined with an event on China's Belt and Road Strategy, at which Hungarian prime minister Viktor Orbán attacked Western European values, and Yan urged European states to contract with Beijing bilaterally, not via the European Union.

4. Xi, "Jointly Shoulder Responsibility."

vanquished Russia in Manchuria (1905), the dynamics of balancing among Britain, France, Russia, and Austria-Hungary in, variously, the Far East, central Asia, the Middle East, North Africa, and the Balkans was dislocated, setting off a volatile and sometimes opaque reconfiguration of accommodations and alliances.

Even without the British succumbing to Thucydidean jealousy, the equilibrium would have changed.[5] How it played out turned partly on the Order-System of the day. The second German Reich—proclaimed in Versailles's Hall of Mirrors, God help us—entered the imperial contest largely unable to settle disputes with the standard (if ugly) currency of swapping distant territories, reducing the utility of bargaining and fueling Berlin's imperial ambitions (via the Scramble for Africa).

Fast-forwarding to today, the PRC's rise has come not through war but commerce, and the tradeable currency of international power is no longer swappable territories but, partly, the pecking order in institutionalized hierarchies, helping to explain Beijing's preoccupation with its voting weight at the IMF and other tables. Not unlike Berlin over a century ago, almost by definition Beijing has nothing of that kind to exchange. But concessions by the established powers—to help maintain peaceful coexistence—are less likely if they think Beijing hankers after deep change in a System that reflects a worldview anathema to its conception of itself and its proper role in the world.

We will argue that given Confucianism, its old Tribute System of international relations, and its long history of unitary hierarchical rule, China does have a distinct political conception of itself: an identity quite different from those of states that emerged out of Europe or that, for good or ill, have been more heavily influenced by European constitutionalism.

### Domestic Society: Conceptions of the Individual in Christian and Confucian Traditions

The gap between existing and rising powers will be most deep-seated (but not necessarily most alarming) where the latter reject some supposedly preemptory norms. That seems to be the position today with the PRC, which rejects universal human rights that can trump the authority of the state over its citizens and so justify humanitarian intervention (see below). While not alone, China has perhaps been most vociferous in rejecting those norms as peculiarly Western in origin and conception, and in maintaining that international

---

5. C. Clark, *Sleepwalkers*, especially chap. 3.

attempts to uphold them violate the doctrine (and ideal) of state sovereignty inscribed by the UN Charter into the international Order.[6] None of this is new or surprising. As one historian puts it, neither Mao, nor his Kuomintang predecessor Chiang Kai-shek, believed "a modern state was the same thing as a liberal state. Drawing inspiration from Lenin, both parties recognized and accepted the use of terror as part of the mechanism of control."[7]

Perhaps that can be attributed to different conceptions of the individual: how individuals fit into society, and in particular into the political community. One variant of this view goes roughly as follows. Christianity conceives of individual sinners as having a direct relationship with God, and so implicitly singles out each of us as of equal worth.[8] While Enlightenment thinkers dispensed with the religion, they (notably Kant) preserved for a demystified world the doctrine that each individual has inalienable rights to dignity and autonomy, and hence to various civil and political rights.[9]

By contrast, so this account goes, Confucianism starts not with self-asserting or self-realizing individuality but, rather, with the way each person is constituted by their multiple social roles.[10] Normatively, China's Confucian traditions emphasize the harmony and order embedded in and achievable through lifelong striving for private and public virtue (to Westernize the idea), entailing duty to family, community, and the state's leaders: hierarchy with reciprocity.

### Governance: Institutionalized Constraints versus Nurtured Virtuous Character

Chinese rulers rule under the Mandate of Heaven, an innovation of the Western Zhou (roughly 1050–750 BCE) to help justify ejecting the established but corrupted Shang. Periodically revived by much later dynasties, it evolved into

6. E.g., joint statement with Russia, *Promotion of International Law*, June 25, 2016. Perhaps at odds with its 2005 support for Responsibility to Protect, this reflects the 1950s nonaligned movement's Five Principles of Peaceful Existence (chapter 3), recited in the Chinese state constitution's preamble.

7. Mitter, *China's War with Japan*, p. 297.

8. Siedentop, *Inventing the Individual*.

9. Rosen, *Dignity*.

10. Confucius (551–479 BCE) lived during the Spring and Autumn Period (or Eastern Zhou). Other major figures include Mencius and Xunzi (see below). Under the Tang (618–907 CE) and Song (960–1279), there was a revival known as Neo-Confucianism, which was important under the Ming (1361–1644). For works comparing Confucianism's kinship order to European "corporation" trust systems (guilds, towns), see Greif and Tabellini, "Cultural and Institutional Bifurcation" and "Clan and the Corporation."

a desacralized form of legitimacy.[11] Short of disaster (famine, conquest, lethal pandemic) signaling the mandate's withdrawal, it seems to make little room for individuals to challenge the state, because to do so would violate the value of benevolent hierarchy—a value with intrinsic, not only instrumental, worth.

That contrast underlines the significance of the Party's still-recent restoration of Confucianism. Reaffirmed as a vital element of China's heritage and meaning, Party, state, and people are no longer tied to Mao's mid-twentieth-century modernist opposition of Past and Present but, adapting a dexterous initiative of Singapore's late leader Lee Kuan Yew, can now deploy Confucianism in a constructed civilizational opposition of East versus West.[12]

Beyond resetting the stage of ideational struggle—picking and framing a soft-power fight—these two worlds' apparently contrasting attitudes to hierarchy and authority are significant insofar as they reflect (and affect) profound differences in the state itself: its legitimation, structure, and geographical reach.

Heaven's Mandate revolves around what social scientists call output (or performance) legitimacy: governing well via virtuous conduct, benevolent rule, and good results.[13] When things go awry, this requires discerning between bad luck, incompetence, neglect, and malfeasance. In stark contrast, for reasons of history, the European tradition fell back on institutional checks and balances, an element of input legitimacy: if you cannot discern virtue in advance (adverse selection), or if virtue might abandon its post (moral hazard), better try to frame incentives. That was precisely Hume's point about the utility of contriving constitutions on the false assumption than men and women are knaves, or worse (chapter 6).

It marks a profound contrast with Xunzi, quoted at the chapter head, who, taking a dark view of humanity, prescribed norms (rites) and training to tame destructive instincts.[14] Nurturing virtue among future leaders and administrators is not foreign to the West (or any established order), but education

11. Initially conferred by the sky god. Not all later conquerors initially cared so much about the Mandate—for example, the Yuan Kublai Khan (he of Xanadu)—but it was definitely claimed by the Ming (ethnic Han).

12. Puett, "Who Is Confucius?"

13. Zhao, "Mandate of Heaven."

14. Unlike Mencius, Xunzi (a name not Latinized by the Jesuits) believed people were not inherently good (because of self-regarding appetites in conditions of scarcity): see Yan, *Ancient Chinese Thought*, pp. 92–93. Sometimes compared to Hobbes, Xunzi's stress on norms distinguishes him from most recent International Relations realists.

might need buttressing once a person is in power. Institutionalized checks and balances can channel the force of background norms grounded in virtue ethics. Xunzi's prescription is risky when left to stand alone.

Centuries later, the late Ming/early Qing writer Huang Zongxi (1610–95), detaching himself from the Neo-Confucian mainstream, advocated a stronger position for the chief minister in order to create an internal check on the Son of Heaven. He did not prevail.[15] With one heaven goes one leader. From the emperor there descended graduated hierarchies of land and gown, unchecked by an independent priesthood, giving way in the twentieth century to the Party leader from whom descend hierarchies of party and state, unchecked by an independent judiciary.

Again, Western Europe's history (and therefore North America's) is deeply different. As discussed in chapter 2 (and this was the purpose of doing so), the premodern parallel hierarchies and authorities of emperor and pope—with medieval investiture struggles (who crowns and can depose whom), excommunications (of mighty figures such as the thirteenth-century Hohenstaufen emperor Frederick II, as well as lesser local rulers such as England's King John), and imperial sackings of Rome, ending only after the post-Reformation confessional-cum-political wars gave rise to an order of sovereign states—are echoed, structurally, in today's parallel hierarchies and authorities of elected government, and an independent judiciary invigilating a regime of individual rights that places some constraints on government. Even putting aside the republican traditions of Athens, Rome, and Italy's early medieval city-states, in Western Europe the secular sovereign's sovereignty has nearly always been qualified, fractured, or, as today, formally separated. If government pursues welfare and therefore popularity, another group of European power holders have been guardians of divine and, later, natural law, and today of legalized rights (chapter 3).[16]

This difference can be summed up using Francis Fukuyama's threefold characterization of political order: a central state capable of wielding power across

15. Angle, *Sagehood*, p. 188; Tiwald, "On the View."

16. Hinsley, *Sovereignty*, esp. chap. 3. Western dual-control norms (and rivalries) go back to Pope Gelasius's late fifth-century letter to Emperor Anastasius, and to older New Testament distinctions between sacred and secular authority. In Europe's wider geographical history, China's fusion of top-down state control with Confucian/Neo-Confucian morality is closer to the setup in Byzantium, where the orthodox church partly operated as an arm of the state, and legitimated it. They are both like caesaro-moralist state systems.

its territory, rule of law, and accountability. While Western states took different paths to all three, for China the destination is different.[17] Central state power, exercised at times via law, developed millennia ago, but the rule *of* law (as opposed to rule *by* law) does not prevail, and accountability is atrophied, working through the special channels of the Party and its need to maintain public confidence that things are improving (Heaven's modern mandate).[18]

As often suggested, these differences probably owe something to geography, technology, and norms of succession. Even though Charlemagne reestablished empire in the West, the lack of primogeniture saw it divvied up among his grandsons, and thereafter geography impeded reunification. Local rule facilitated challenge and accountability, but a multiplicity of political units confronted each other tensely, often in war. By contrast, China's vast plains were more conducive to unified rule, with less interstate conflict because there were fewer states. The flip side of distant rule was weak accountability, frequent internal wars (as when the Ming were toppled and Beijing sacked in 1644), and more oppression.[19] When, in contrast to Europe, Confucian agrarian society was reconsolidated in the premodern era rather than giving way to private commerce—the Ming's fateful choice—the power of the landed elite was not diluted by rising local merchants.[20]

On that story, liberalism and authoritarianism are deep in the soil of today's main political societies. But it does not imply irradicable differences between "West" and "East." The peoples of South Korea, Taiwan, and to some degree Japan all have Confucian heritage, but their constitutional systems make space, in public law, for an independent judiciary and, in particular, for judicial review

17. Fukuyama, *Political Order and Political Decay*.

18. "Rule *by* law" captures the short-lived Qin dynasty's Legalism. Wang, *Rise and Fall*, suggests the prerevolution Chinese state's capacity did not match its durability, partly because, after the Tang, geographically fractured elites maintaining local order obstructed central tax collection without being able to challenge the throne.

19. For striking charts on the location of wars, see Dincecco and Wang, "Violent Conflict." Chinese emperors, including the Ming, did not all resort to heavy taxation or centrally directed oppression (Fukuyama, *Origins of Political Order*, chap. 21). But none was constrained by the rule of law or institutionalized accountability, leaving a "bad emperor problem," which was occasionally addressed through dynastic change, including outside peoples (Mongol Yuan and the Manchu Qing).

20. Glahn, "Political Economy," p. 49. (Among other things, some China-Japan trade was conducted via Western intermediaries; and under the Ming and Qing, indigenous coastal traders lost autonomy or were expelled.)

of executive government's decisions and actions.[21] Indeed, various modern scholars, typically writing outside mainland China, maintain that Confucianism is compatible with human rights, and even with various elements and interpretations of the Universal Declaration of Human Rights.[22]

Certainly Confucianism does not preclude compassion for strangers or civil fairness. Mengzi (to Westerners, Mencius, 372–289 BCE) famously observes our altruistic concern for a stranger's child falling into a nearby well; and, arguably, offers cautious authority for the people to withdraw obedience from wicked rulers and to support a benevolent outsider in overthrowing them (perhaps anticipating Locke by a couple of millennia).[23]

Seen thus, civilizational differences recede. Even the idea of the good ruler striving for sagacity is not a million miles away from Aristotle's ideal of virtuous political leadership.[24] Human rights can reemerge—not with metaphysical grounding, but as a practical way of guarding against the risk of abuses of political power when leaders do not live up to the standards properly demanded of them in their society's particular conditions.[25]

## The PRC and Institutionalized Rights

It is, however, hard to know what to make of claims about values latently available in a political community's ideological hinterland when they have rarely, if ever, been embedded in the structure of its governing institutions, meaning they are not available to memory as something lost or taken away.

In any case, there can be no doubt that today's Party-state rejects such structural protections, as evidenced, for example, by the 2017 remark of Wang Qishan, a central figure in the regime, that "there is no such thing as separation

21. Stone Sweet and Mathews, "Proportionality and Rights Protection."

22. E.g., Chan, "Confucianism and Human Rights"; Angle, "Human Rights in Chinese Tradition"; and, from within morality-first political philosophy, J. Cohen, "Minimalism about Human Rights."

23. Mencius, *Mengzi*, 2A.6, on a natural tendency to feel non-self-regarding compassion (the sprout of benevolence) for the stranger's child; and 1B.6 and 1B.8 on legitimate rebellion, which might be about the people subsequently legitimating rather than having a right to initiate a virtuous new ruler kicking out a degenerate one (2B.8.2). See Tiwald, "Right of Rebellion?"

24. Angle, "Virtue Ethics."

25. In Western thought, this is akin to accounts of human rights as basic political rights rooted in politics, as opposed to natural rights rooted in a common human nature: see Malcolm, *Human Rights and Political Wrongs*, chap. 5.

between the party and the government. There is only a division of functions."[26] Or as the October 2014 decision of the Fourth Plenum of the Eighteenth Party Congress declared, "The leadership of the Party is the most essential trait of Socialism with Chinese characteristics, and is the most fundamental principle for Socialist rule of law. . . . Party leadership and Socialist rule of law are identical."[27] Rather like some of Europe's seventeenth-century absolute monarchs, the Party cannot be subject to the law.[28] This was put beyond doubt in 2013—the year after Leader Xi's elevation—when the Central Committee's leaked "Document 9" exhorted cadres to "conscientiously strengthen management of the ideological battlefield" on the basis of the "seven No's," as they have become known. No to promoting constitutional democracy, universal values (see below), civil society (individual rights, challenging the Party's social foundation and its leadership of the masses), neoliberalism (total marketization), the Western idea of journalism via freedom of the press (contrary to Party discipline), historical nihilism against the history of the Party and New China, and No to any questioning of the socialist nature of socialism with Chinese characteristics.[29]

Somewhat farther reaching than the West's ill-conceived Washington Consensus (chapter 4), the Party's guidance is confined neither to the relative merits of economic models nor to the deleterious effects of Western constitutionalism but extends, significantly, to substantive doctrines of political morality, in ways expressly linked to the PRC's system of government. The promotion of so-called universal values—in the communiqué's words, defying time and space, transcending nation and class, and applying to all humanity—is condemned as, among other things, a threat to the Party's leadership and socialism.[30] (One cannot help wondering how many of the Davos throng offering rapturous applause in 2017 even knew of Document 9's existence.)

26. Quoted in McGregor, *Xi Jinping*, pp. 25, 117n20.

27. Quoted in Alford, "Does Law Matter in China?," p. 214.

28. In 1999 Chen, "Toward a Legal Enlightenment," argued this question, and whether China could develop a system of administrative law permitting legal challenges against the state, could not be avoided at some point (pp. 148–49). For the moment, those questions are answered.

29. ChinaFile, "Document 9." (Somewhat similar sentiments were prosecuted by Pope Pius IX [declaring papal infallibility in his war against liberalism] and Bismarckians in the 1860s and 1870s: Rosenblatt, *Lost History*, chap. 5.)

30. ChinaFile. Tracking China's recent history, Pils, "Human Rights," argues that the idea, perhaps in particular free speech, cannot be separated from Western political traditions.

This was no rhetorical flourish. Like any well-drilled bureaucracy, the Party-state followed up with instructions to universities and the media, as well as to foreign nongovernmental organizations (which have to register with a sponsoring government department).[31] That it amounts to rather more than words and censorship—a lot more than a comprehensible exercise in asserting East Asia's place in world history—is, for many, put beyond doubt by the detention camps in Xinjiang Province (although see below on the United States).

China's rise accordingly alerts us to the potential significance of political systems that not only are different but root and celebrate those differences in deep civilizational difference.[32]

### International Society: The Confucian Tribute System of International Relations

When the Western powers (Europeans in the eighteenth century and famously the US commodore Perry in the nineteenth) turned up in East Asia and demanded trading arrangements and political concord on their terms, they displaced a centuries-old system for structuring relations between governments and peoples in that part of the world. This is the famous Tribute System discerned by early Western scholars: the Celestial Empire exercising the Mandate of Heaven beyond its core territory. It was marked by periodically performed rituals and ceremonials through which overlordship could be acknowledged in suitably deferential terms and trade conducted in a beneficent (and controlled) manner.

In terms of the previous chapter's spectrum of security relationships, this lay somewhere between protectorate and informal empire, or what Westerners might call suzerainty: more or less autonomous government in internal affairs, but accepting leadership on external matters. In a hierarchy of closeness and obeisance,[33] Korea typically came first (entailing, or entitling it to, most frequent performance of tribute, with trade), followed by Vietnam (Annam), and only then offshore

---

31. Economy, *Third Revolution*, pp. 37–42.

32. Coker, *Civilizational State.*

33. Big picture, tributary structure "interstate" relations were not unique to China. The states of Hindu India traditionally pursued—and some successor Persianate states adopted—a not dissimilar strategy of *mandala*, comprising a dynastic heartland, an inner circle of subordinate provinces, a middle ring of semiautonomous allies, and an outer ring of tributary states: see Eaton, *India*, pp. 24–29, 124–25. China's heartland was, however, vast (although, like Rome, at various points it was a "capstone" state whose culturally distinct elite ruled over communities it did not penetrate deeply: see Morris, *Modern State*, p. 30).

Japan, which could thank the blessings (or curse) of water for a self-conception somewhat at odds with Beijing's perspective. But all of them came ahead of those lesser vassals-cum-aliens in the northern and central Asian steppes, which were not recognizably Confucian states administered by scholar-bureaucrats.[34]

In some respects, this is not wholly unrecognizable to Europeans (and so most North Americans) given our pre-Reformation history, with its complex juridical hierarchy (chapter 2). But even while that lasted, local political centers had a good deal of autonomy, becoming more or less absolute in the fragmented world that succeeded medieval Christendom. This seems to have had profound effects on the continent's development. With traces of hegemony kicked away, the kind of central state control and censorship of learning applied in Manchu China was infeasible across Europe's borders. That certainly did not impede, and might have fostered, the culture of inquiry and innovation that in time gave Europeans overwhelming superiority in material power, even overcoming the tyranny of distance as they pushed into East Asia.[35]

But in that case, surely it must matter that Western Europe's own hierarchy fizzled out centuries ago through *internal* pressures and struggles rather than, as happened to China and its neighbors, being upended by armed commercial invaders from another part of the world who then proceeded to induct local rulers into their foreign system of international law. With a lot of mess along the way, we owned our own revolution.

So today, it very much matters how China thinks about the Order that has prevailed since World War II. The concrete will shape the abstract, and vice versa.

## Self-Conceptions and History Telling

In this, the stories China tells itself—meaning the stories the Party-state apparatus tells its citizen-subjects and permits them to tell each other—matter greatly, as will our (Western) understanding of those stories. Was the old tribute system entirely voluntary, accepted by the near and far as the natural and

34. Japan's system of government was also less thoroughly Confucian—e.g., its emperors claimed to rule by divine descent rather than mandate. Kang, *East Asia*; Coe and Wolford, "East Asian History."

35. Mokyr, *Culture of Growth* (chaps. 16 and 17 on China), attributes science and industrialization partly to the cultural effects of Europe's fragmentation, noting Hume made a similar point in one of his essays (p. 290). Also, the Mongol (1279–1361/68) and Manchu (1644–1912) conquests might have prompted a conservative indigenous elite to try to preserve old ways (as during the intervening Ming).

right order of things?[36] Or did it reflect a realist accommodation by neighboring states of China's hugely greater might, internalization of its norms being a rational response to incipient threat?[37] Just as important, is it true that China was, in contrast to Western states, uniquely peaceful in its conduct of foreign relations?

We know the answer to at least the last of those questions. After Mongol world conquest stalled, the Ming's project combined local revivalism with efforts to maintain regional security.[38] Then, during the later seventeenth and eighteenth centuries, Qing China waged wars of conquest or domination over the frontier lands of Tibet, Xinjiang, and Taiwan, which, according to recent scholarship, it sought to entrench by frontier garrison settlements and some co-opting of local elites.[39] Nor, it seems, was the Qing regime itself as completely assimilated into Han etiquette and protocol as might casually be imagined given the impressive continuities in the Chinese state.[40] Alongside the mandarin structure of the Han state apparatus over which the new dynasty presided, they maintained the "Banner" security-garrison system of their Manchu forebears, which among other things exempted elite Manchu from the jurisdiction of local courts (akin to the Western system of extraterritoriality) and barred them from marrying regular Han (whose families had not been admitted, for loyal service, into a Banner).[41]

36. The view of Kang, *East Asia*. But Choson Korea switched horses to the Manchu Qing a decade before they vanquished the Ming. Robinson, "Ming Empire," p. 557.

37. Perdue, "Tenacious Tributary System."

38. Robinson, "Ming Empire."

39. Lately applauded by today's regime: see *Economist*, "Chinese Communist Party's Model Emperor."

40. Han administrative and cultural absorption of foreign dynasties (most famously the Yuan and, later, Qing) is rightly famous. From Western history, it brings to mind Egypt's Ptolemaic dynasty, which lasted around three hundred years (similar to the Qing), ruling and building partly in the Egyptian style. But the comparison goes only so far: in contrast to the steppe Manchus, those Hellenistic Egyptians drew on their own urban civilization and maintained their "home" culture in coastal Alexandria, a long way from the Nile's religious and ceremonial centers. A closer comparator might be the Persianization of the central Asian Turkic peoples, who, like the Mongols and Manchu, had been pastoral, cavalry peoples (and different branches of whom went on to rule South Asia and the East Mediterranean): see Eaton, *India in the Persianate Age*.

41. Taiwan became a formal province in 1866, having been a frontier area in the eighteenth century: see Kang, *East Asia*, p. 156. On the Manchus, see Kang, *East Asia*, p. 152; Cassel, *Grounds of Judgment*, p. 10; and Perdue, "China and Other Colonial Systems." On the Bannermen, including distinct Mongol and Han divisions, see Crossley, "Qing Empire" (note: she has been criticized-denounced by some PRC-based scholars).

Some of this is contested among specialists. But the point here is the necessity of recognizing without inhaling our respective constituting myths: presiding over a hierarchy of peoples is part of China's as much as a Westphalian moment of transformation from universal hierarchy and feudal complexity into a society of sovereign states is part of ours. At a deeper level, just as aspects of Rome and Athens live through the modern West, the East plainly is profoundly imbued with ancient and early medieval Chinese culture and civilization.

That does not mean either that we should accept the Chinese empire's rise was entirely peaceful or that we must acquiesce in the perception that the West's political history was uniformly violent (when, for example, the early modern consolidation of Habsburg authority in Europe was achieved very largely through dynastic marriages). Reciprocally, however, the West should not expect China to accept our self-conception of liberal progress toward enlightened humanitarianism on our terms, given for example the United States' treatment of its indigenous peoples and descendants of trafficked slaves, and Europe's colonial past and twentieth-century crimes against humanity.

While some mutual skepticism might be in order, it matters whether the great powers—their elites and peoples—permit their histories and identity-affirming myths to become stakes in national or even civilizational rivalries. What they say to themselves, as well as to each other, can constrain their options.

## What Might China Want?

What, then, might China want? An imponderable generating endless opinion, one view is that while Beijing might seek regional hegemony, nothing in its history implies more.[42] That might be the central case, but it is hard to believe that even the Chinese themselves can know what they will want as their power grows—the United States was studiously backward in coming forward until after World War II—so this is about the evaluation of risk (next chapter).

### Respect in the Shadow of Humiliation

For starters, it seems highly likely the country and its leaders want respect. At the beginning of the twentieth century, Sun Yat-sen's principles for Chinese government included nationalism.[43] During World War II, feeling marginalized

---

42. E.g., Johnston, "China in a World"; and recently Letwin, *China vs. America*.

43. The others were social welfare and democracy (people's power, now manifest in Party rule).

by Franklin D. Roosevelt and especially Winston Churchill, Chiang Kai-shek told his diary that "the next generation should understand the difficulty of building the country up from its past shame."[44]

In some ways, even that can be overblown: Chinese state capacity, measured by its tax take, was underdeveloped before Western imperialists turned up.[45] But we must take seriously the "century of humiliation." It culminated in the abuses inflicted by Japan during its mid-twentieth-century occupation.[46] It commenced, broadly speaking, with the Opium Wars, which, for good reasons, are perceived as having been fought so that Western merchants could be free to poison Chinese people (although they were also about broader trading rights and diplomatic equality).[47] After the Old Summer Palace was burned down and Beijing capitulated, a chain of coastal enclaves, including much of Shanghai, was ceded and so excluded from Chinese sovereignty, becoming subject instead to extraterritorial foreign rule and law—partly, it was held, on civilizational grounds, given objections to torture as an evidential instrument (chapter 2).

That kind of system, which included fixed tariffs for trade, was not unique to Western imperialism: the Italian peninsula's city-states had traded through exclusive enclaves in the Byzantine Empire, and Qing China had used something like consular jurisdiction in its conquered central Asian territories. It was imposed on Korea by its East Asian neighbors (first Japan, then China) and from 1871 operated voluntarily between those two powers. The Western states' unequal treaties also included constraints: initially their citizens could not travel into the Chinese interior, and when, after the second Opium War, they could do so, they were subject to Chinese law and policing. In some ways, this echoed premodern systems of law governing people and groups, and depended on cooperation with Qing officials.[48]

Be that as it may, it is striking how long it lasted. Whereas the equivalent arrangements in Japan ended in 1894 (following the "westernizing" reforms of 1868's Meiji restoration) and for the Ottoman Empire in 1923 (after war), extraterritorial jurisdiction in China actually expanded in the early twentieth

44. Quoted in Mitter, *China's War with Japan*, p. 243.

45. Wang, *Rise and Fall*.

46. Mitter, *China's War with Japan*.

47. As it happens, in Britain adults could buy opium without a doctor's prescription until the 1920s (*Economist*, December 19, 2017, quoted in Coker, *Civilizational State*, p. 100). That excuses nothing: opium was illegal in China but Britain helped traders resist enforcement (Horowitz, "Opium Wars").

48. Drawing on Cassel, *Grounds of Judgment*.

century, when there were almost one hundred treaty ports, and did not finally end until World War II (1943). Perhaps that was initially because the Chinese system's Manchu privileges impeded reform, and later due to internal political turmoil before and after the 1911 revolution (overthrowing the Qing). But whatever the reasons, for many decades Chinese residents of the treaty ports were effectively foreigners in their own land, living under locally applied regimes of Western law.

This is live stuff: bad things happened, and for the moment China's leaders want their people to remember them. It matters that the humiliations were brought into the school curriculum a few years ago (just as it matters that Britons of my generation were taught about our country's heroic time-saving resistance to rampant Nazi power in the interval between the fall of France and the entry of the United States).[49]

## Respect and Regional Power

A demand for respect is, therefore, inevitable and more than comprehensible, making some concrete goals extremely likely. At the least, China's leaders will want the country to be an unchallenged regional power, and hence will want the United States out of their backyard, East Asia. While it is too much to claim that the very survival of the Chinese state depends on American retreat, their historical self-conception requires their being at the top of the regional power tree, and that means their leadership being heard, understood, and accepted beyond the region (including in international organizations).[50] The aim here could be the restoration of regional hierarchy, perhaps without Beijing's neighbors having the kind of license exercised by European states toward the United States under the current Order-System (chapter 8).

Achieving that will not be easy for the PRC, as they surely realize, given America's regional ties and naval strength, and their own complicated, sometimes fractious, history and relations with many of their neighbors (including India,

49. I do not know whether the PRC curriculum includes the American and British support for the Chinese currency, perhaps vital to survival, during the 1930s and 1940s war. See Kirshner, *Currency and Coercion*, pp. 51–63.

50. Drawing on Mearsheimer, "Can China Rise Peacefully?," which back in 2014 anticipated much of what followed. His "offensive realism" is framed in terms of what *any* rising power in that part of the world would want given a posited primordial struggle for survival. My emphasis is on what would be wanted by the real-world China with its particular history (and geography), and its current Party-led system of communist-capitalist government. For a not dissimilar classical realist take, see Kirshner, "Tragedy of Offensive Realism."

Japan, South Korea, and Vietnam, not to say Taiwan).[51] This is more than a product of so-called structural relationships. To use today's idiom, not a few of those nation-states self-identify as democracies. What I called voluntary followership when describing Europe's relationship with the United States seems most unlikely between China and its neighbors unless they find there is no other choice: *coercive voluntary followership.*

In consequence, driving America out of the South and East China Seas (or even, maybe, the Asian side of the Pacific) might plausibly entail taking the struggle to where the United States' authority or leadership has hitherto been unchallenged, including Latin America (the realm of the Monroe Doctrine), Europe, Africa, and the Middle East. The point would be that if the United States could be stretched in its own backyard, it might abandon China's neighborhood, leaving its current allies to realign and reconceive themselves.

## More?

But if that is what plays out—and border skirmishes with India suggest both the strategy and its hazards—the question will be whether China's ultimate goal is, merely, to be one among very few superpowers (a regional hegemon with the capacity to project power more or less anywhere on the planet) or, going further, to be the preeminent global power in whose image or interests any international System must be reconstructed if order is to be preserved.

The question is not idle. Former Australian prime minister Kevin Rudd, a longtime observer, concluded an early 2020 catalog of China's perceived priorities with, "Xi wants to reshape the global Order so that it is more accommodating of Chinese values and interests."[52] Meanwhile, Yan Xuetong wants Beijing to aspire to a world leadership role where, in contrast to a hegemony rooted in might and strategic credibility (his take on US practice), it exercises a humane authority through stewardship of universal but hierarchical norms.[53]

51. Westerners are often surprised the 1960s/1970s Vietnam War seems to preoccupy Vietnamese people less than much older conflicts with China.

52. Rudd, "Coronavirus and Xi Jinping's Worldview." His first nine discerned priorities were preserving the Party's unrivaled leadership; maintaining national unity; achieving economic growth; increasing environmental sustainability; building the military; securing compliant relationships with China's neighbors; pushing the United States beyond the "second island chain"; securing the Eurasian landmass, including Western Europe, as a key market; and building China's influence and connections elsewhere in the world.

53. Yan, *Ancient Chinese Thought*, pp. 104–6, and, on Mencius's distinction, pp. 208–12; Yan, *Leadership and the Rise*, pp. 48–51.

This would be a kind of tribute system, without the old trappings and adapted, perhaps, to the formalities of modernity's sovereign equality (chapter 11).

### China's Exercise of Geoeconomic Power

That this is not fantasy finds some support in the PRC's use of geoeconomic measures (chapter 4). While partly tactical (initiating or responding to events), many seem strategic, beginning with a defensive security-centered course when the PRC first reentered the international economy, but moving on over the past decade or so to a policy that includes offensive measures.[54]

Among the former are steps taken from the 1990s onward to acquire stakes in foreign agricultural and energy producers as insulation against its dependence on external supplies; the Eurasian land-route element of the Belt and Road Strategy (BRS), since it is less vulnerable to the United States' continuing control of the world's key sea-lanes; and some BRS investments in foreign seaports, which might protect the PRC's maritime trade during an intensified struggle.

More offensive measures include banning the export of rare earths to Japan for a while in the 1990s (before substitutes were discovered elsewhere); putting the Philippines under pressure, in the context of disputed claims to the Scarborough Shoal (rocks and reefs), by suspending some critical trade and perhaps launching cyberattacks; reminding the Spanish, after campaigners protested over Chinese human rights, that the PRC held around 20 percent of Madrid's public debt; and blocking Australian trade after it called for an independent investigation into Wuhan's possible connection to COVID-19.[55]

## Chinese and US Attitudes toward International Law and Regimes

Those actions, some highly coercive, pose the question of whether China's approach toward international regimes and law differs from that of the United States.[56] In fact, both maintain a schizophrenic, cherry-picking approach to

54. Drawing on Friedberg, "Globalisation and Chinese Grand Strategy" (citing mainland Chinese commentators); and Economy, *Third Revolution*.

55. Friedberg, "Globalisation and Chinese Grand Strategy"; Economy, *Third Revolution*; Blackwill and Harris, *War by Other Means*; *Economist*, "China Punishes Australia."

56. For a prescient review before the Global Financial Crisis, see Posner and Yoo, "International Law."

the international system. As chapter 3 described, neither has submitted to compulsory adjudication by the ICJ, or the International Criminal Court. And, reflecting their respective domestic approaches to political and economic freedoms, China has not ratified the UN convention on civil and political rights, while the United States stepped aside from the convention on economic and social rights.

## China: Parallel Institutions and Norms

More specifically, for some time, Beijing has been convening international groups or establishing organizations that occupy similar space to the more universal multilateral institutions. Perhaps the most notable are the Shanghai Cooperation Organization (mandated, among other things, to seek common foreign policies) and the Asian Infrastructure Investment Bank (shifting the flow of development finance away from the post–World War II bodies). Various indicators suggest that, unlike the European Union, this is not just regionalism tucked under a more universal umbrella. The key provision in the Shanghai Cooperation Organization's mission is to promote, among a membership that includes Russia, "a new international political and economic order."[57] On the economic front, despite being the largest official creditor to developing countries, Beijing has not joined the long-established Paris Club of sovereign lenders, which coordinates public-debt rescheduling when a country cannot pay its debts as they fall due (chapter 4).

At a more fundamental level, while increasingly prepared to participate in UN peacekeeping operations, Beijing has long sought to downgrade the third (potentially coercive) pillar of Responsibility to Protect (chapter 3), on grounds of state sovereignty.[58] And it snubbed the Hague arbitral tribunal when the Philippines challenged the legality, under the UN Convention on the Law of the Sea (chapter 3), of China's nine-dash line and a claimed economic zone around the Scarborough Shoal used by Philippine fishermen. Having denied the tribunal's jurisdiction (but still publishing an opinion on the matter), Beijing responded to the tribunal unanimously finding in favor of the Philippines by declaring the decision "invalid and [of] no binding force." That was true in the sense the tribunal has no navy to police the seas,

---

57. Shanghai Cooperation Organization Secretariat, "About the Shanghai Cooperation Organisation."

58. Garwood-Gowers, "China and the Responsibility."

and China could veto any UN Security Council enforcement motion.[59] Coming just a few months before Xi's Davos excursion, it perhaps signaled an approach to the international system not far away from Yan's.

The case marks an interesting contrast with one roughly a century earlier between a then-rising power, the United States, and the Netherlands. They went to arbitration, also at The Hague, over title to the island of Palmas near the Philippines, which had been ceded by Spain to the United States at the end of the nineteenth century. The arbitrator concluded it fell under the Dutch East Indies (now Indonesia), which had been sovereign on the island since the seventeenth century.[60] The United States accepted the result, and the case established principles that contiguity is not relevant and discovery not decisive in establishing sovereignty.[61] It seems that, at least while it was rising, Washington felt somewhat bound by international law.

But as chapter 3 related, when during its pomp the United States was taken to the ICJ over its Nicaraguan interventions, it responded not so differently from Beijing on the South China Sea case. Washington withdrew from the proceedings and revoked its routine acceptance of the court's jurisdiction, falling back on its charter right to accept or reject case by case.[62] When the court found against it—concluding, among other things, it was "in breach of its obligations under customary international law not to use force against another state"—the United States blocked enforcement at the UN Security Council.[63] So an important question is whether Washington's approach in the 1980s created a (political) precedent for Beijing thirty years later. Maybe in geopolitics you reap what you sow.

### The United States Goes Rogue, or Just a Temporary Problem of Credibility and Competence?

Even before the Trump years, the United States was going much further, suggesting a long-running ratchet. In the early 1990s, Washington declined to ratify the UN Convention on the Law of the Sea, perhaps the most detailed

59. Perlez, "Tribunal Rejects Beijing's Claims."

60. Today, the Indonesian island takes its local name, Pulau Miangas.

61. Ginsburg and McAdams, "Adjudicating in Anarchy," pp. 1297–300.

62. See the letter from Secretary of State George Shultz, revoking President Harry Truman's 1946 acceptance of compulsory jurisdiction (except in, among other things, "domestic" matters): Shultz, "United States."

63. *Nicaragua* case (chapter 3). The ICJ based its jurisdiction on customary law. In the UN Security Council, France and the United Kingdom abstained, as did Thailand.

international code, even after it and other industrialized states gained concessions on deep-sea mining. Since the convention affects claims in the Arctic
(from Russia among others) and the South China Sea (from the PRC), it was
an interesting choice.

In 2003, not only did the United States go into Iraq without a clear UN
mandate, but it then conducted the war in, let's say, a particular way. Com-
menting on George W. Bush's law officers, the late Tom Bingham, Britain's
former leading judge, described a "cynical lack of concern for international
legality."[64] Given his international standing, this lashing was no small thing,
evidencing self-inflicted harm to the leading state's soft power.[65]

Against that awkward background, the Trump family government's
conduct—erratic commentary on NATO, tantrums over the WTO while dropping out of the Trans-Pacific Partnership, walking away from the Paris climate
talks, and "national security" tariffs on allies, to cite only a few examples—and
its obscure relationship with Russia's rulers inevitably raised questions about
the longer-term reliability of the United States as guardian of the post–World
War II Order-System. Coming after earlier underperformance, it was not irrational to query Washington's strategic and tactical competence.

Those concerns persisted after the Biden administration's abrupt exit from
Afghanistan and its blindsiding Paris, an active presence in Southeast Asia,
from its 2021 nuclear deal with Australia. Notwithstanding having also failed
to deter Putin's 2022 invasion of Ukraine, they were, however, somewhat assuaged by the well-coordinated response, based on apparently revived intelligence and diplomatic capabilities. But the worries will not be put to rest so
long as a Trumpian-comeback of some kind remains possible; something having happened shows it can happen.

## Summary

Two centuries ago, the Anglo-Irish politician-cum-commentator Edmund
Burke, a friend of American independence and scourge of Warren Hastings's
abuses in India, spearheaded the war of ideas against the French Revolution.
His problem was that France had become the wrong kind of power, jeopardizing international order. Today, while the jealousy of trade unquestionably adds

64. Bingham, *Rule of Law*, p. 127.

65. Roberts, "With Blinders On?" (summarizing *Is International Law International?*), attributes this to US law schools teaching international law as an adjunct of the domestic law of
foreign affairs.

spice to Washington and Beijing's rivalry, it matters more that the West views China as the wrong kind of power: a party-dominated authoritarian state openly rejecting supposedly universal norms. As Elizabeth Economy puts it, "China is an illiberal state seeking leadership in a liberal world order."[66]

The response of the United States, essentially unchanged since first articulated by then–vice president Mike Pence, is firm in its mixture of regret and concern.[67] Both sides are under pressure. Beijing is certainly a revisionist power. But, notwithstanding 2022's shifts, depending on who contests the 2024 election, so might be the incumbent.

66. Economy, *Third Revolution*, p. 17.
67. Pence, "Remarks Delivered."

# 10

# Wishful Thinking

## POLICY ROBUSTNESS, RESILIENCE, AND LEGITIMACY

There are risks and costs to economic statecraft, and using it properly is a careful balancing act. . . . The United States should seek to coordinate internationally where possible.

FORMER US TREASURY SECRETARY JACK LEW, 2018[1]

OVER THE COURSE of parts II and III, we saw that while institutions and norms cannot prevent aggression, they might focus and speed up a collective response to it. The point is hardly mysterious. In a village, the existence of a community council and a local norm against fights hardly prevents a person punching someone else in the face, but they might guide a robust and rapid community response, and so act as a bit of a deterrent, without guaranteeing safety.[2] The test of whether institutions matter is not whether they reign supreme. That became apparent during Russia's invasion of Ukraine. For global order, it is apt because, as the previous chapter argued, it would be prudent to assume that China wants the United States out of its backyard; that it will want to be a regional hegemon or, more ambitiously, a leader capable of projecting power across the planet; and that it might one day seek

---

1. Lew and Nephew, "Use and Misuse," pp. 141, 149.
2. For similar points, see Walt, "International Relations Theory Guide."

235

to be a global hegemon even if that is not its plan today. Taken together, all this has major implications for how to think about strategy and institutions in a contested Order-System.

## The Four Scenarios Redux

In the first place, we can now say more about the four geopolitical-economic scenarios introduced in chapter 4. At a high level, the provision of international and global goods would differ: crudely, selectively continuing under a *Lingering Status Quo*, stuttering under *Superpower Struggle*, mostly bloc based under *New Cold War*, and reconceived under *Reshaped World Order*. What follows, as in chapter 4, are characterizations rather than predictions.

### Lingering Status Quo

This scenario, under which Washington continues to keep the sea-lanes open and provide the main reserve currency, is sustainable only if the United States somehow heals its internal strife, rebuilding broad-based support for its core institutions and so the soft norms that sustain its domestic guardrails.[3] Successive administrations would need to exercise power prudently (a realist virtue stressed by Tacitus), and its economy would need to perform well (part IV).

Geopolitically, prudence means sometimes accommodating the interests of other major powers and perceiving how they play back into one's own interests. For example, Washington would quit flirting with divide-and-rule toward Europe—practiced by the Trump administration, and not infrequently urged by others—since that is Beijing's script. This is, then, a scenario in which the United States rediscovers (because it would need to) the norms of international law, and in which little heed is paid to commentators pressing the view that the hegemon can disregard what others care about. Reciprocally, Europe would bear more of the burden of its defense without displacing US leadership.

Even then, the status quo might survive only if the PRC stumbles, whether through internal economic imbalances, fractured relations with Belt and Road Strategy (BRS) recipients, tensions within the Party, or all that and more.

---

3. Levitsky and Ziblatt, *How Democracies Die*.

## Superpower Struggle

In this tense world, with a fragile peace, the balance of advantage between the two superpowers would turn on the relative stability of their domestic politics, success in technological innovation, the breadth and depth of their alliances and friendly relations, and avoiding egregious mistakes.[4]

As they vie for influence and clout beyond their natural constituencies, currency, commercial, and security politics blur. Domestic regulation and sovereign wealth funds become overt policy instruments. Critical overdependencies would be reduced, the pace set by events. Beijing's BRS would face serious, if perhaps only sporadic, competition from joint private-public initiatives sponsored by free-world capitals.

Drawn-out attrition might eventually favor the West given the PRC's aging demographics, leaving Party leaders with incentives to push the contest's pace, including militarily. Short of that, it would seek regional hegemony by harassment, dependency, and the veneer of inevitability. The East Asian seas, and perhaps the Indian Ocean, would be a cauldron. Sooner or later, perhaps only after a scary run-in, Beijing would agree to deescalation protocols.

Lesser powers would seek tactical advantage in the interests of local clout (or survival), some seeking to play one superpower against the other. Even after the free world reduces its dependence on fossil fuels, there would be intense competition for relations with Gulf states, which would be faced with judging whether Beijing would provide an alternative security blanket if they effectively abandoned the dollar (chapter 16). Provided each remains stable, India and Russia would be strategic actors, albeit on different trajectories. Japan might plausibly rearm while remaining in alliance with Washington.

Stretched globally, the United States would press Europe not only to take even greater responsibility for its defense but also to cut its dependence on Russian energy (if not already complete) and to be more restrictive in its commercial relations with China. Europe, meanwhile, would be reluctant to impair its living standards (including leisure time) and the leverage of its market until scared. Despite strains, the North Atlantic alliance would hold, with Europe expecting to be treated consistently as a strategic ally in trade and other negotiations rather than just one more transactional counterpart.

4. Yan regards allies as vital for transforming strategic into comprehensive capability. See Yan, *Leadership and the Rise*, p. 41.

International Society, conceived globally, would be at the thin end of thin. Universal-treaty initiatives would become a thing of the past, their eventual revival signaling the world was somehow renormalizing. Procedural norms of customary law would be honored for non-zero-sum pacts. *Jus cogens* norms might be in jeopardy if under-pressure powers became less sensitive to normative constraint.

## New Cold War

Under this scenario, sooner or later the PRC would seek regional hegemony by force. The United States—and if it had rearmed, Europe—would be faced with deciding just how far to go to preserve Japan, South Korea, Australia, and others as part of the free world. Against them would stand a collection of authoritarian states.[5] Already Moscow attempts to tilt east European regional issues its way, signaling its existence in a parade of insecurity. Rising states like India, Indonesia, and Turkey would become, to different degrees, swing states. But any revived nonaligned movement would, as things stand, be unlikely to be led by Delhi, given its tense history with Beijing.

The outcome might turn on how badly the United States and its allies were stretched elsewhere on the planet by the PRC (and partners) fomenting conflict in any or all of the Americas, the Middle East, and central Europe. A move on Taiwan might well coincide with yet more Russian aggression in the west. Proxy struggles and conflicts would abound. The UN building would provide an important place where diplomats could meet or signal via others that they wished to meet: no small thing.

Otherwise, the international System of regimes would bifurcate, somehow, as commercial autarky progressed. The G20 could no longer operate as the informal pinnacle of System's hierarchy (chapter 8). Only those international organizations addressing existential needs without geopolitical risk would have a chance of meaningful existence. Perhaps, therefore, the WHO—if it survives the aftermath of COVID-19—might continue, since exposure to deadly pathogens depends on the weakest link (chapter 5), but one can equally imagine bloc-based organizations competing to help poor states: two worlds, two WHOs. Similarly, it would be even harder than now to find a joined-up approach to climate change, at least until its crystalizing costs displaced the allure of glorious struggle.

5. Applebaum, "Bad Guys Are Winning."

The obstacles impeding cooperation would be even greater if, through turbulent domestic politics, Washington had retreated from the world. That is so far away from its interests, it would be unlikely to last long, however dramatic things were over four or eight years. Others, however, heeding worst-case possibilities, would not count on that.

By definition, international Society would fracture. *Jus cogens* norms would likely be dishonored, standing as history's measure.

### Reshaped World Order

With a new top table, some kind of international Society would reemerge. But whether it was thin or thick—and if thick, which values were shared, and so which vistas opened up—would turn on whether the new Order resulted from decline of one or both of the current superpowers (chapter 4), the flexing of power by others, and the response to any horrors committed during the struggle.

Given the longer-term prospect of multipolarity, we should expect rising states to pursue foreign policies that mark out space for their independent voices. That is already apparent in Delhi's issue-specific choices between neutrality (Ukraine) and alignment (India-Pacific security).

### How Does Russia's War Affect the Scenarios?

The dynamics of those scenarios for the contest between constitutional democracies and the Communist Party of China have been affected, for the time being, by Russia's war on Ukraine. In the first place, Europe's main capitals having been stirred, they will be somewhat better prepared if Russia broadens its attack to NATO members as and when Beijing moves to seize Taiwan; the authoritarian axis has given away some optionality. Second, the probability of arriving at *New Cold War* via a leap rather than incremental disengagement has risen, given the sharpness and breadth of participation in the sanctions against Russia and its various hangers-on (plausibly punished in order, at last, to start cleansing Western capitals of dirty money). That prospect would ratchet sharply if Beijing assists Moscow, and the free world responds with secondary sanctions that deprive China of their markets. But, short of such drama, it will in any case be fueled by efforts in Beijing and elsewhere to trade (invoice and pay) without the dollar. Third, for that reason there will be a contest for the ear of Saudi Arabia (over energy production, invoicing, and more), complicating

its foreign relations just as its leaders seek to unpick their long-standing accommodation of radical Wahhabi clerics (chapter 1).

For those reasons and others, as of this writing (mid-March 2022) China is
faced with a choice between studied public neutrality (amounting to acquiescing in Putin's aggression), living by its long-standing line on sovereignty and
noninterference (abandoning Putin), and standing by its "no limits" friendship
with Moscow. Like all superpowers, it might taste hypocrisy, symbolic retreat,
or both; only a quick victory for Moscow could have spared Beijing discomfort. But none of that affects the book's core premise: it is extremely unlikely
that the path of the Ukrainian war, even if it spreads, will affect China's capacity
to act as a superpower over the next half century or so. That would change only
if Putin were replaced by a more liberal and Western-friendly regime that
proved successful (three Ifs).

## Statecraft as Prudential *Realpolitik*: From Tail-Risk
## Robustness via Resilience to Legitimacy

In navigating those possibilities, questions of grand strategy are legion but, as
others have pointed out, slogans like "strategic competition" don't say much.[6]

Some precepts are standard but no less important for that. As leading game
theorists emphasize, effective use of power requires a well-judged combination
of resolve and restraint.[7] That is no less true for the coercive edge of geoeconomic power than for military interventions. The United States has often
found both hard. The Syrian redlines episode reveals the challenges of sticking
to a declared course, and the Trump administration's scattergun use of sanctions
hardly exemplified restraint, as highlighted in the chapter head, from former
US treasury secretary Jack Lew.[8] The widely coordinated response to Russia's
European war was quite different, but still left the question of whether any

6. Campbell and Sullivan, "Competition without Catastrophe." (Both now work in the
Biden administration.)

7. Myerson, *Force and Restraint*. (The concept of restraint being central to power is often
attributed by US leaders to Thucydides, but he did not say it. Pity.)

8. The Obama administration's insistence on using SWIFT's payments-messaging system
for security purposes found acceptance among European politicians but worried their unelected
central bankers who, understanding this vital piece of network infrastructure, grasped a box was
being opened. (Farrell and Newman, "Weaponized Interdependence," pp. 65–70, gets the political debate but not the technocratic unease.)

deterrent effect from sanctions was diluted by waiting until after Vladimir Putin had crossed his rubicon.

### Robustness in Policy: Against Wishful Thinking

Restraint and resolve bear on the application of general policy, not its orientation. I want to suggest that the only sane approach in a discordant environment is to adopt a "robust" policy. Also known as minimax, this means seeking to minimize the costs from the maximum plausible bad outcomes while trying to avoid unnecessarily making them more likely after weighing strategic interactions.[9] It reminds us that some circles of hell are worse than others and helps to clarify the objective of policy measures. For example, the debate about the effectiveness of sanctions typically focuses on whether they deliver some near-term goal, but perhaps they are sometimes better thought of as reducing an unfriendly state's prosperity, and therefore its capacity to threaten others, over the medium term. Would the Russian army have performed better in Ukraine if Russia had been free of sanctions over the previous decade?

More generally, robustness in policy can be viewed as a modern rendering of the old adage, found in Thucydides, against wishful thinking (chapter 1). That is more useful than other precepts extracted from the ancient historian, notably the cut-the-crap International Relations realist line notoriously attributed to Athenian commanders giving the island of Melos a choice between surrender and slaughter: "The strong do what they can, while the weak suffer what they must."[10] Well, it depends. With the Athenians themselves succumbing to wishful thinking—first in assuming the war would be short; later in the arrogance of their ill-fated Syracusan adventure and alliances sustained by power and fear—the Melian episode tells us as much about the importance of judgment as it does about raw power.

9. Economics adopted this from engineering. Neither "realist" calls to abolish NATO after the Cold War nor their laying responsibility for Russia invading Ukraine at Washington's door obviously pass a minimax test, since Putinesque aggression was always plausible. For their case, see Mearsheimer, "Why the Ukraine Crisis" (which does not contemplate still worse circles of hell).

10. Thucydides, *History*, V.84–116, pp. 400–408. (It is not obvious why the Melians would trust the Athenians' offer of clemency; those proclaiming the right of might are typically not in the trustworthiness business. The Melian men chose slaughter, but we do not hear whether, as the Athenians had claimed, that fortified their empire: domination-cum-extermination is not obviously a robust strategy in a repeat game with multiple players. The Melian women's slavery resonates in Euripides's *Women of Troy*.)

Even so, Western capitals have lately seemed to embrace wishful thinking, in both grand strategy and System design. At one level this has been geopolitical, such as seeming to forget that central Asia matters, or adopting Middle Eastern policies that proved time-inconsistent (proclaimed redlines over Syrian use of chemical weapons). Both missteps helped Russia reemerge as a power, which, given its European frontierland and four-thousand-plus-kilometer border with the PRC (and another three thousand with Mongolia), is hardly without significance. But surely the most glaring bit of wishful thinking was to place all the chips on the PRC liberalizing as its economy caught up. As it turned out, with its geoeconomic assertiveness, military buildup, and rejection of human rights, Beijing is hardly yet the "responsible stakeholder" US officials had in mind.[11]

Among other things, then, a robust strategy for the United States will assume that an illiberal China continues to catch up in economic and material power, becoming by far the largest economy in the world, and so capable of pursuing the most ambitious goals imaginable. Conversely, a robust strategy for China will assume that it does not catch up (in per capita terms). And a robust strategy for each of them would place weight on resilient domestic systems while also giving considerable weight to the prospect of other countries emerging as international powers during the course of their long struggle.

That might seem little more than adding a demand for competence (no small thing) to a standard International Relations realist prescription for states to pursue their interests without distraction, but in current circumstances it is quite a lot more. Perhaps the most reckless take I've encountered in American policy and scholarly circles is that the United States can prevail (whatever that means) alone. Maybe so over a horizon of a few years, but it is not compellingly robust for a horizon of, say, twenty-five or fifty years when, if the PRC were to achieve anything like parity in per capita incomes, its economy would be three to four times larger. Wishful thinking aside, the United States was slow to recognize its need for friends and allies.

## Resilience: In International Connectivity and at Home

If policy is to be robust to plausible worst outcomes, regimes and systems must be resilient rather than brittle: able to bounce back rather than collapse or unravel under stress.[12] This—a familiar thought for central bankers—has major

11. Zoellick, "Whither China."
12. Brunnermeier, *Resilient Society*.

implications for domestic and international policy. Some while ago Xi Jinping saw the importance of avoiding overdependence.[13] It is symmetric, and by no means limited to real-economy interdependencies. The West can hardly afford to be the source of another global financial crisis. And, as belatedly recognized, major European states should not depend on Russian gas.

While economic resilience runs through part V's prescriptions, here I want to underline a higher-level form of resilience: in a state's domestic system of government, and in the basic framework for international relations among states. If decision-making and delivery systems flake under pressure, *talk* of robust policy is just that. As well as influencing the set of feasible goals for international cooperation, this makes it impossible to dodge the significance of norms, values, and identities, and their relationship to interests. Prudent statecraft is more than crude power politics (*Machtpolitik*, in its Germanic rendering). Realistic statecraft (*Realpolitik*) cannot escape the forces of opinion within states and among them.[14] This is better approached through the lens of legitimacy than by jumping straight to morality because rulers' first challenge is who they need to carry and who to avoid alienating or provoking.

## From Respect to Legitimacy

The previous chapter's discussion of Beijing's demands for respect elided an important distinction. Is it respect in the sense of formal recognition in the institutions of international system (thin society), or respect as a form of esteem (thicker society)?[15] Those are very different things: the former turning on what is demanded by international law, the latter summoning esteem for the character of a state's governing regime and conduct, and for its historical achievements.

If respect-as-recognition is intended, it turns on legal and nonlegal facts (statehood, size, and so on) but comes bundled with understandings of how, under the current Order-System, sovereignty fits with basic rights (chapter 11).[16] If it means respect-as-esteem, things run deeper. In the familiar

---

13. Gewirtz, "Chinese Reassessment."

14. Bew, *Realpolitik*, esp. pp. 38–46, finds that thought in one of its early nineteenth-century Germanic fathers, Ludwig von Rochau.

15. Darwell, "Two Kinds of Respect."

16. On contested norms governing relations between states, princes, or peoples, recall that eighteenth-century Britain resisted kowtowing because they thought it, and having to conduct negotiations via regional officials, dishonored them as a sovereign equal. Likewise, they and

vernacular of respect among persons, if A wants others' esteem for its own sake, A is accepting the value of their point of view and buying into their normative criteria. If, on the other hand, A wants their respect merely because it would be instrumentally useful in some way, A still cannot deny the validity of their perspective. Soft power can help shape the grounds of normative assessments. It is not straightforward, then, for the PRC to reject human rights and demand or seek respect from constitutional democracies.

But whether or not sought, if esteem is not volunteered by established states, their formal recognition of rising states in international institutions is liable to be at the minimalist end of permissible interpretations of law and mores. In consequence, if a rising state takes a path that minimizes normative respect, it risks relying on the shadow of conflict to achieve its goals. As the German theorist Axel Honneth observes, "The desire to have one's own collective identity recognized by other peoples can be used to legitimate both an aggressive policy of conquest and a deescalating policy of reconciliation."[17]

## Values: Concerns about PRC Authoritarianism

This apparently high-minded distinction between thin respect and thicker esteem is no small matter. At the heart of Western concerns about China is the authoritarian nature and conduct of its system of government. Over recent years, this has been on display in censorship, surveillance, educational internment in Xinjiang, threats to the rule of law (as understood in the West) in Hong Kong, commercial sanctions against critical foreign actors (including members and managers of sports teams), and high-profile tacit support for Muscovite aggression against neighbors. Rather than merely taking a nondemocratic path, China has been living its illiberal creed.

Further centralizing power in Beijing, Xi's political Thought has been given constitutional status, and his predecessors' term limits no longer apply. But perhaps this should not be surprising after the 1989 Tiananmen Square events: Party leaders must do whatever it takes to maintain supremacy, as when, reasserting Leninist orthodoxy, they ditched an avant-garde separation of Party general secretary and state president.

---

others thought their dignity-cum-honor was impugned when designated *yi* (sometimes translated as "barbarian"). Horowitz, "Opium Wars."

17. Honneth, "Recognition between States," p. 32.

## Legitimacy at Home and Abroad

We might ask whether "humane authority"—as ideal or lodestar (chapter 9)—can really involve internment camps for maybe a million people. But attending to ourselves, we do better to recognize that the harsh edge of Party rule has violated norms that are meaningful for many people. That matters because alliances matter for any robust policy. The flip side is an expectation that to be secure in maintaining its own ties and influence, Washington will need to conduct itself in line with international law as the leading member of some kind of international Society.

But sensitivity to international norms needs to work at home. As Xi put it shortly after becoming leader, "If [a regime's] ideological defences are breached, other defences become very difficult to hold."[18] While articulated for Party cadres, it probably captures Beijing's (and Moscow's) take on Western vulnerabilities. We are beyond interests narrowly conceived. Values are interests too, shaping a political community's way of life.

## On to Part IV

The book has reached a junction. Parts II and III repeatedly got stuck. Initially, when exploring the political mechanics of international cooperation, we ended up not merely with conventions but with norms as internalized values—because, absent fear, something else is needed to render many institutions self-enforcing. Then, when turning to power, we found states having an interest not only in mere survival but also in the persistence of their way of life and having to be attentive to other states' values whenever they needed allies and friends to survive meaningfully at all.

Recapping, any international System of planned cooperative regimes depends on both an Order of some kind and Society in some degree. It is one of the defining marks of our time that the great Eastern Confucian states embarked on joining modernity's international System and its associated Society during a period when the West's rights tradition was at a relatively low ebb, overshadowed by the then-prevailing stress on national self-determination, state sovereignty, and the associated doctrine of nonintervention. Lurking behind that late nineteenth-century edifice's focus on property rights was an older tradition, harking back to the post-Reformation natural lawyers, the

18. Xi Jinping, August 2013, quoted in Economy, *Third Revolution*, p. 42.

earlier canon law of Christendom, and the Roman Stoics. Today it has resurfaced in the "just war"–like right of neutrals to help a state defend itself against aggression, in what our era calls the human rights of the individual, and in the humanitarian rights of minority groups.

In consequence, geopolitical dislocation brings uncertainty about how to manage institutional and organizational redesign without losing ourselves. This is about more than maintaining or reconstructing some kind of Order that permits cooperative System. It is also about whether a much thinner international Society is capable of combining a globalized economy's Utilitarian calculus with deep ideological-cum-civilizational differences.

The book's central thesis is that constitutional democracies—in the West, the Far East, and elsewhere—will not be able to navigate this without identifying the boundaries for System-Society implied by our deep political values. These are questions of legitimacy.

# PART IV

# Legitimacy

## VALUES AND PRINCIPLES FOR INTERNATIONAL ORDER AND SYSTEM

The people are the most important, the [state is] next, and the ruler is the least important.

MENCIUS, FOURTH–THIRD CENTURY BCE

# 11

# Sovereignty and the Globalization Trilemma

UNIVERSALIST VERSUS PLURALIST
INTERNATIONAL LAW AND SYSTEM IN
A WORLD OF CIVILIZATIONAL STATES

We can have at most two out of the three. If we want hyperglobalization and democracy, we must give up on the nation state. If we must keep the nation state and want hyperglobalization too, then we must forget about democracy. And if we want to combine democracy with the nation state, then it is bye-bye deep globalization.

DANI RODRIK, *THE GLOBALIZATION PARADOX*[1]

If people see their local system of justice and legitimate authority as flowing directly from the fundamental nature of the world, as directly authorized by the divine Creator of the Universe, then they may expect that people everywhere should naturally accept the same principles of justice and legitimate authority. Such perceptions can be a fundamental source of inconsistent beliefs in international relations. When international coordination is required in new areas, where internationally recognized limits have not yet been defined, the people in each society over-estimate the probability that their local principles of justice and legitimate authority will be accepted by people in other societies.

ROGER MYERSON, NOBEL ECONOMIST[2]

1. Rodrik, *Globalization Paradox*, p. 200. (The stress on *hyper*globalization signals a trilemma among idealized versions of its three horns.)
2. Myerson, "Game-Theoretic Consistency," p. 430.

IF THE BOTTOM LINE of part II was that international cooperation is feasible and sometimes happens, and that international organizations can make a difference, part III cautioned that all that relies on a more basic order prevailing among states, with shifting geopolitics capable of disturbing the constellation of forces sustaining an Order, not least when there is a clash of values and identities.

Maybe the key legitimation principle is sovereignty, an idea that works as a coordinating convention inscribed into the law of nations (part II). Some commentators and theorists hold or assume that international cooperation forces us to choose between preserving and surrendering sovereignty, period. This chapter takes that seriously but concludes it is not a wholly adequate lens for unraveling the big issues or for shaping strategy.

## What Is Sovereignty?

By Europe's early modern period, sovereignty was understood as "supreme authority within a territory."[3] This has three components: an unqualified right to govern within the territory, a right to territorial integrity, and juridical equality with other sovereign states. As one introduction to international law defines it, "The independent sovereign state is . . . subject to the authority of no other body, and . . . its relations with other groups are a matter of consent and agreement rather than of obligation and direction by some other body to which it is subordinate."[4] No longer inchoate customary law, as chapter 3 reported, since World War II sovereignty has been enshrined in the UN Charter's bar against threatening states' "territorial integrity or political independence" (Article 2[4]) and its promise not to interfere in internal affairs (Article 2[7]).

Political science has tried to unbundle those claims. In a landmark book, Stephen Krasner suggested sovereignty has no fewer than four aspects:[5]

- *International legal sovereignty:* Flowing from the mutual recognition of juridically independent (and so equal) states[6]

3. Philpott, "Sovereignty."

4. Lowe, *International Law*, p. 4.

5. Krasner, *Sovereignty*, pp. 3–4.

6. With South American states fearing not being recognized by some powers, the Americas' 1933 Montevideo convention articulated criteria: permanent population, defined territory, self-governing, and capacity for international relations (Ratner, *Thin Justice*, p. 186).

- *Westphalian sovereignty:* The exclusion from domestic governance of foreign states and actors
- *Domestic sovereignty:* The capacity of domestic government to rule its territory
- *Interdependence sovereignty:* The capacity of states to regulate cross-border flows of people, goods, services, capital, ideas, and, with rather more difficulty, pathogens and pollutants

Krasner's purpose, signaled in the subtitle, *Organized Hypocrisy*, was to demonstrate with wide-ranging examples, drawn across time and geography, that, in each and every of its four facets, sovereignty is myth. A compelling demolition of the notion that some purist idea of sovereignty reigns in practice at all times, it does not penetrate the thought that sovereignty is a high-level regulative norm materially shaping the world in which we live.[7]

### Sovereign Equality and Hierarchy in International Law

Taking sovereignty's legal dimension seriously, Gerry Simpson lifted the lid to reveal a pervasive element of hierarchy subsisting alongside equality, by distinguishing between "formal equality," "legislative equality," and "existential equality" as distinct concepts operating within the practice and doctrines of international law.[8]

The first amounts to states being treated as equal by international law tribunals (most importantly the ICJ) when they go or are taken to law. This is what we mean when, in a domestic context, we say citizens (and companies and other types of association) are equal under the law, which importantly does not entail that they are equal in the making of the law. Legislative equality, by contrast, entails all states having an equal say in the making of international law (and policy), which is true in neither form nor substance: the UN Security Council alone can mandate war, its permanent members have a veto, IMF voting is weighted, EU Council voting is weighted for some policy fields, and so on. In other words, there are hierarchies in the making of international law. Modern sovereignty does not preclude that, and indeed was defined (in the UN Charter) alongside formal lawmaking inequalities (chapter 3).

---

7. It operates like a Humean metaconvention (chapter 6; Sabl, *Hume's Politics*, pp. 139–51) insofar as repeated violations do not, of themselves, establish a new norm; see the response to the Ukrainian invasion.

8. Simpson, *Great Powers*, pp. 25–61.

Simpson's final type of legal equality—existential—reaches for something rather different, looking inward into the state as well as outward to the making and application of particular international laws. This type of equality goes to a state's right to make its own way in the world. As such, it is the legal union of all four of Krasner's de facto aspects of sovereignty, and if it prevails it is, as Simpson stresses, both a manifestation of and the formal basis for an international system predicated on and committed to pluralism. As well as territorial integrity and various immunities and rights, it emphasizes sovereign independence rather than equality as such.[9] It is consistent with a hierarchy of international law and policymaking, but not with a higher international legal order that prescribes to existentially sovereign states how they should govern themselves or which international institutions they must join. Nor, perhaps, is it easily consistent with a universalism extending beyond thin norms of good faith and the like.

### *Sovereignty as Constitutional Independence*

A strong version of that had been advanced some years earlier by the English political historian and theorist Noel Malcolm when he defined sovereignty as "constitutional independence."[10]

Writing against then–leading British politicians debunking sovereignty as outmoded and impractical in the Europe of the 1970s and 1980s, Malcolm pointed out that this confused sovereignty with power, arguing that ideas of "economic sovereignty" were irrelevant to the idea and value of sovereignty properly understood, and that the heart of the matter was authority, in the sense of legalized political authority.[11] That legal order was inherently domestic, underpinned by the political authority of the state's regime of government. As Malcolm put it, if the rules for exercising domestic authority "include the subjection of that authority to some higher political authority in some higher legal order, then the state is not sovereign."[12] In other words, sovereignty is conceived as a legal institution in pursuit of a political value.

Internationally, on this account a constitutionally independent (and so sovereign) state is one that is free to enter or not enter into agreements with other

---

9. Simpson, *Great Powers*, pp. 53–54. "Existential equality" needs two legs: (1) a right to exist and, given that, (2) a state's freedom to determine its own constitutional system.

10. Malcolm, *Sense on Sovereignty* (drawing on Alan James). Thanks to David Dyzenhaus for the reference and exchanges.

11. The power vs. authority distinction had been advanced by the earlier British conservative theorist Michael Oakshott.

12. Malcolm, *Sense on Sovereignty*, pp. 19–20.

states as a matter of independent choice; it does not need permission from some higher authority.[13] But this capacity depends on sovereign states recognizing each other as such. However one conceives of that recognition—as some kind of society of states conferring sovereignty, or discerning it, a fraught issue for legal theorists—lack of recognition plainly constrains a (budding) state's options for cooperation and exchange.[14] Not least, it affects how a state and its actions are treated under foreign states' domestic law (including immunity for its diplomats), and its eligibility to join certain international organizations.

Malcolm is clear that sovereignty is binary; conceptually, there can be no gradations (a slightly nervous conservativism). Limitations on government, including the executive's foreign policy, are permissible but must come from inside a particular state's constitutional system.[15] In consequence, a state's sovereignty may be neither delegated nor pooled internationally.

That does not preclude delegating the exercise of competences (as, for example, to NATO). It can also be consistent, Malcolm continues, with international organizations in which competence and power *seem* to be pooled, provided each state has a right of veto on every matter, or any majority voting is confined to matters where not much is at stake.[16] But incrementally expansive delegations or poolings could, eventually, create a higher-level legal order.

Summarizing, the conception of state sovereignty as constitutional independence is illuminating. It moderates wilder suggestions that any international pact or delegation of anything entails "sovereignty costs."[17] And it helps to clarify some of the uncertainties and tensions around international Order, System, and Society laid out in part II.

13. Independence as the essence of sovereignty had been stressed, in the 1960s, by leading twentieth-century legal theorist Herbert Hart, but without defining the zone of necessary independence as the constitutional (*Concept of Law*, pp. 217–18). Impliedly, the state was sovereign in whichever areas it was independent, conceptually allowing for degrees of sovereignty, which fits with Lake's catalog of security relations (chapter 8).

14. Even where a budding state appears to meet the Montevideo conditions and has relations of sorts with other states, it can face meaningful constraints if not formally recognized—e.g., Taiwan.

15. Malcolm, *Sense on Sovereignty*, pp. 23–25.

16. Malcolm, *Sense on Sovereignty*, pp. 25–29. (At this point, his analysis twists and turns in order to impale the EU's venality but, as he points out, the European Court of Justice [ECJ] had effectively proclaimed a higher-level legal order in a 1964 landmark decision.)

17. From Abbott and Snidal, "Hard and Soft Law." (Contrast Hathaway, "International Delegation.")

## The Globalization Trilemma: A Dilemma around Sovereign Autonomy

There is a striking connection here to the *globalization trilemma* made famous by Harvard social scientist Dani Rodrik: we cannot have all three of globalization (with supranational governance), the state, and democracy. But since global democracy is unlikely on any foreseeable time horizon, does that mean either globalization or state autonomy has to give?

That frames the question from *our* point of view. If there is a trilemma, it confronts nondemocratic states too. A communist state would face a trilemma among globalization, state autonomy, and communism, with one way out being globalization under a Communist Party–led world government (which, as it happens, was a goal of the Communist International during the early twentieth century).[18] As such, the trilemma is really a dilemma between unrestricted globalization and the autonomous state, raising two questions: whether autonomy can survive delegation, and whether there are unavoidable or intolerable trade-offs.

On the first, we find instruction within the democratic state itself. If democracy were defined wholly in terms of electing decision makers, there would be no room in domestic democratic governance for agencies whose policymakers are unelected, such as independent central bankers. But as I have argued elsewhere, there is a more than respectable case that such delegations are necessary to preserve some constitutional values (the separation of powers).[19] We do not insist everything is decided by elected ministers or plebiscite, for democracy-preserving reasons.

Such voluntary self-binding has a long pedigree, its utility having been identified when Jean Bodin first articulated sovereignty (chapter 2). By analogy, this book's question—at *this* stage of its argument—might be framed as whether there are conditions under which a state's *autonomy* (constitutional independence) could be underpinned by pooling or delegating to international bodies.

---

18. The Second Congress of the Communist International resolved to "struggle by all available means, including armed force, for the overthrow of the international bourgeoisie and *the creation of an international Soviet republic as a transition stage to the complete abolition of the state*" (Wikipedia, "Communist International" [my emphasis]).

19. Otherwise the executive could use money printing to sidestep the legislature's taxation prerogatives. Tucker, *Unelected Power*, pp. 287–90.

## Consent and Sovereignty

One implication of thinking of sovereignty as constitutional independence is that insofar as international law binds a state, it can do so only as a matter of the state's will (or, less metaphysically, its voluntary choice). Similarly, citizen-subjects cannot obtain rights against their state in defiance of its objections.

Such generalities mask the enormous range of what states might consent to internationally. It might be a specific act (or inaction), with short-lived effects, so that those deciding will be in office when the effects become clear (e.g., some UN Security Council and IMF decisions). It might be a specific rule or policy, as when the EU Council of Ministers votes on rules for banks proposed by Basel. It might be a whole policy regime, as when states agreed to establish the GATT and, later, the WTO. Or it might be a set of codified metarules to help make such lower-level regimes possible, as with ratifications of the Vienna treaty on treaties.[20] And finally, it might be the background set of societal norms, some manifest in general international law, that are preconditions for any kind of System of regimes and wider interstate or transnational cooperation (where, giving the game away, acquiescence seems more apposite than consent).

As that list proceeds, the effects stretch out in time and space, to future generations, and to states that do not yet exist, none of which get to do much overt consenting.[21] Yes, they can reject a tribunal's jurisdiction in a case brought against them—the place where consent lives most clearly in our states-based Order (chapter 3)—but that merely constrains formal enforcement, not informally imposed costs. The big action is accordingly in background norms, whether codified or not; and in regimes, especially those with majority voting of any kind, meaning a consenting state could lose on big issues.

If voluntary consent means ongoing consent (next chapter), it would have to be possible for a state to cast off those norms, or exit the regimes—just as Bodin's sovereign could shed the self-binding. For some background norms, that might be really hard. For regimes, exit might not always be easy. Even where a state joined a regime with deliberately high exit costs to increase the credibility of its commitment to the particular policy or scheme (chapter 5),

20. Neff, "Consent," makes these distinctions (without differentiating field-specific and metaregimes).

21. On consent not doing all or even any of the work, see Beitz, *Political Theory*, pp. 75–79; Goldsmith and Posner, *Limits of International Law*, pp. 189–93; and Buchanan, *Justice, Legitimacy, and Self-Determination*, pp. 301–14.

it might later become disaffected with the results only to find exiting even more costly than remaining. While in some narrow sense continuing is rational, it is hard to reconcile being stuck with anything other than an impoverished constitutional independence. The dissatisfied state's effective policy space has shrunk: at the highest level, away from, say, free-market liberalism toward social democracy, or vice versa.[22]

## Distinguishing the Claims, Value, and Effectiveness of Sovereignty

While constitutional independence neatly captures the claims of sovereignty, a state needs to be capable of making those claims good for it to amount to more than an empty slogan (or a domestic propaganda strategy). As constitutional theorist Nick Barber describes, sovereignty needs to be effective if it is to amount to much.[23]

Some tensions of that kind are inscribed into the prevailing Order-System. For example, international law (the Vienna treaty on treaties) stipulates a state may withdraw only from those treaties catering expressly for withdrawal. Some do not, the most notable being the UN Charter. That is no small thing because, as stressed in chapter 3, formal Security Council decisions can create obligations for the whole of the membership: a case of pooling, no exit, and delegation. On the binary view of sovereignty, either constitutional independence is consistent with that (how?), or it has been violated for everyone except those states with a permanent veto.

Alternatively, maybe some states have acquiesced, during the late 1940s and since, in a qualified sovereignty because they have thought it helps procure peace, and thus helps them exercise their *residual* sovereignty. But that changes the grounds of the argument.

More broadly, there are three especially fraught kinds of clash between sovereignty's claims and internationalism, each discussed below. The first is where a particular international regime-cum-organization is, in effect, the only game in town for the relevant policy field, needed by all or most states given their

22. Palley, "Fallacy of the Globalization Trilemma" (but overdoing an asymmetric probability of the dominating international order being neoliberal rather than social democratic or whatever).

23. Barber, *Principles of Constitutionalism*, chap. 2, distinguishing among the claims of sovereignty, conditions for its being effective, and its value.

own aims and projects. The second arises where tackling a vital global-commons problem requires everyone, or everyone within some class of states, to participate (chapter 5's weakest-link production technology). And the third concerns the emergence of norms of a putative thick international society that are held to trump all else, even though some states disagree.

While the first is about loss of control over policy, the second and third arise from *other* states declaring some projects or norms to be universal in the sense of being either owed to all (*erga omnes*) or peremptorily binding (*jus cogens*), or both, and so in effect resurrect, for the modern world, the late medieval world's natural-law-like doctrines of universal legislation (chapter 2). Both brands of universalism challenge the meaning of existential equality. A dissenting state, insisting on inviolable sovereignty, faces a choice between isolation (perhaps incurring sanctions for defecting from standards and projects) and norms it never accepted. This is dissent as a triumph of ineffectiveness—except where, as part II's discussion of the sensible knave's thuggish cousins revealed, the "out-law" is so powerful it can ignore others' views and deter their sanctions.

## Losing Control: Delegation and Sovereignty

Loss of control can happen in almost any multilateral regime-organization that is the only game in town, such as, probably, the WTO and Basel. Up to a point, because such regimes are needed by a member state given *its* interests and objectives, the drama is reduced to debates and struggles over outputs and processes. But that leaves plenty of scope for friction. If decisions are taken by majority voting or among a leadership group, the regime might become increasingly alien for minorities; if subject to each state's veto, increasingly objectionable for willing coalitions.

Loss of control can be glaring where dispute resolution has been put at arm's length from a regime's parties. This is most serious, since states have nowhere else to go, where a judiciary interprets and applies a regime's provisions in ways that develop or recast general policy but are strongly opposed by a particular member state or group of states. Here, the substitution of law for diplomacy has taken the regime beyond the control of its members. It was, perhaps, made more likely when the Vienna treaty on treaties stipulated that interpretation should be guided by a regime's object and purpose (chapter 3), marking a shift from an earlier doctrine-cum-practice of interpreting so as to minimize constraints on sovereign states' sovereignty. This is central to chapter 17's discussion of the WTO.

## *The Global Commons: Existential Harms and Sovereignty*

Of the two varieties of universalism, the more straightforward to grasp—not solve—is the global-public-goods problem, which might lead states, under duress or popular pressure, to cast aside any idea or norm of consent (and hence a sovereignty of voluntarism) because they feel threatened unless some unwilling state participates.[24] Potential examples include addressing climate change and eradicating lethal, highly contagious pathogens. The production technology of such global public goods (chapter 5) requires participation by, respectively, all big economies or every single state and territory, with the rich helping the poor if necessary.

If the stakes are high enough—existential—participating states might agree to penalize or even physically coerce recalcitrant free riders irrespective of whether they are permitted to do so by any explicit agreement. In those circumstances, one state's sovereignty simply clashes with the imperatives of the rest of the world. An issue initially highlighted in chapter 5 now takes on a new guise. At the level of System-Society, a strong norm of consent—meaning universal veto rights consistent with sovereignty as constitutional independence—is fundamentally at odds with a capacity to address some types of global public harms. At the level of Order, some vital goods are simply not supplied if the holdouts are great powers. Taken together, those two propositions imply a sovereignty of effectiveness for the few.

## *Higher Authority: Moral Law versus Sovereignty?*

The other challenge posed by universalism for state sovereignty arises where a tribunal or court holds that a particular norm, law, or body of law formally trumps national law or treaty law, without an opt-out.[25] That happened when, during the 2000s, the Inter-American Court of Human Rights and the EU Court held that various provisions of human rights conventions have the status of preemptory norms (*jus cogens*).

In such cases, the international tribunal is, in both effect and doctrine, asserting and, by its lights, operating a higher legal order. In those circumstances, if states insist on sovereignty as constitutional independence, there are in effect

---

24. Krisch, "Decay of Consent."

25. So formally distinct from the ECJ declaring EU law to be directly binding on member states, which, given the exit option, was closer to a loss-of-control problem.

parallel universes in which international law asserts a hierarchical order while, meanwhile, states proceed as if all and any international law depends on their consent and voluntary compliance.[26] For the domestic adherent of sovereignty in a constitutional state, all hinges on whether its local courts recognize the higher authority claimed by international law.

This can easily get bogged down in doctrinal issues over the relations between legal orders: whether wholly autonomous (constitutional independence can live) or hierarchical (not so). They can be left to the schoolroom and the passage of time to resolve or dissolve. What concerns us are circumstances where international law—possibly together with the internal law (and domestic opinion) in some states—asserts that certain norms are universally binding when, in fact, they are not accepted by all the major states on which any kind of Order and globalized System depends. This is so serious it needs unpacking.

## Human Rights and Sovereignty: Civilizational Differences

In a momentous 2008 judgment, the ECJ ruled that, given local human rights law, the European Commission could not require EU organs and member states to implement a formal decision of the UN Security Council subjecting a list of individuals to criminal-like sanctions (because of connections with terrorist networks).[27] An assertion of regional constitutional independence, the court's reason was that the individuals concerned had not been granted an opportunity to respond before the Security Council's decision was finalized.

In effect, the court held that irrespective of the Security Council's own view of its jurisdiction, it had fallen short of a higher law (an echo of natural-law traditions). In an illuminating discussion, legal theorist David Dyzenhaus

---

26. Analytically, this is a debate between two ways of conceiving law as a whole: monism and dualism. International legal monism deems all law to be part of a single, coherent system descending from the highest level of international law. Domestic monism deems the only real law to be the various autonomous systems of domestic law, with what is referred to as international law being merely for-the-time-being effects of agreements entered into by states operating under their own legal systems. Dualism, by contrast, posits a kind of gestalt, with parallel autonomous universes of domestic sovereignty and international law.

27. *Kadi et al. v. European Commission*, ECJ, C-402/05, 2008.

highlighted the tension between, on the one hand, the binding obligation to implement Security Council decisions and, on the other hand, what he describes as "the generally agreed . . . universal norm of legality, which requires that no one should be subject to sanctions which affect important rights and interests unless one has first had an appropriate opportunity to contest the case against one before an impartial tribunal."[28]

But while that is the view in Europe and so was at the heart of the problem facing the ECJ, Dyzenhaus's description of due process as a *generally agreed universal* norm of legality cannot be correct as a matter of fact. While it might, now and around here, be required for *legitimate legality* (which is, I think, his meaning), it is not even accepted as a *domestic* legal norm by two members of the Security Council, including the world's new superpower, China; and a third, the incumbent superpower, might not regard it as available to aliens on foreign soil. In other words, claims to universalism are liable to collide with the deep moral and political pluralism inherent in the emerging world of powerful civilizational states.

For a state or people holding to a conception of sovereignty as constitutional independence, such pluralism is fine. Whatever others say, such a state would simply not accept the universality of certain norms, other than through a process of ongoing consent. At this point, sovereignty is barely consistent with any kind of System that extends beyond transactional good faith; System with thick Society, as chapter 7 termed it, is off the agenda.

### Wicked Constitutional Provisions or Practices: Humanitarian Intervention?

Left there, sovereign consent simply narrows the realm of feasible cooperative endeavor (to some, not all, non-zero-sum projects). But things are not nearly so straightforward. A state that conceives of itself as constitutionally independent, politically decent, and potentially cooperative faces a question about what kind of relationship, if any, to have with other states that fall short of its own standards of decency.

Imagine that the (written) constitution of a sovereign state empowers or, worse, commits its government to do terrible things. Imagine, that is to say, that the state exercises its constitutional independence via constitutional provisions along the lines of the following:

28. Dyzenhaus, *Long Arc of Legality*, p. 262.

1. The executive may torture people suspected of crimes against the state; or
2. The executive shall eliminate or incarcerate indefinitely, under whatever conditions are deemed appropriate, any citizen-subjects believed to be actual or potential enemies of the state; or
3. The government may use whatever means it deems appropriate to defend the territory or interests of the state, including preemptively; or
4. The government shall endeavor, employing any means deemed useful, to expand the territorial boundaries of the state or to subordinate other territories or peoples to the interests of the state, including via overlordship and conquest.

The final pair, (3) and (4), would obviously be unacceptable to other states. Constitutional independence would have been deployed to construct a pariah state, threatening the interests and constitutional independence of other states. This would threaten order, and so the equilibrium delivered by the prevailing Order. The international community (not a crazy concept here) would try to avoid recognizing the legitimacy of such a state in international affairs and might take steps to contain the offensive activities or even transform the nature of the offending state. If that is so, constitutional independence cannot simply be a matter of self-declaration. Which is more or less what the UN Charter says. So sovereignty as constitutional independence begins to look like either a gift from other states or a status available only to superpowers.

The earlier pair of controversial constitutional provisions or practices poses deeper issues about relations with authoritarian or autocratic states that do not interfere with or threaten their neighbors and peers. The first, (1), makes no distinction between the tyrannical state's citizens, residents, and visitors. At the least, other states will want assurances that their own citizens will not be tortured, and will have at their disposal the levers of direct retaliation (if the tyranny permits its subjects to travel), plus sanctions of other kinds. But what of (2)? Where a tyranny has obliged itself to oppress citizen-subject dissenters, do other states look away, or do they seek, somehow, to enforce their idea of humane values?

More realistically, what if tyranny is not on the face of the constitution? What if the parchment text reads benignly but the practice is horrendous (by the standards of other states and peoples)? Under what conditions can other states permit themselves to recognize the sovereignty (the constitutional independence) of the tyrannous state? Should they treat the state as equal and independent, or what?

The point of those questions-cum-provocations is that they go to whether compliance with a set of norms and values bears on the terms on which states recognize other states' claims to sovereignty—perhaps admitting them into some kind of "society of states" or, alternatively, permitting them only to live autonomously in conditions of economic and political autarky. And beyond questions of recognition, these issues go to the grave matter of whether there are any conditions under which humanitarian intervention by force can be warranted to relieve the individuals or groups being intolerably oppressed.

If, as some hold, international law permits recognition to be denied, and intervention to be warranted under some conditions (Responsibility to Protect, chapter 3), then existential equality is conditional. Sovereignty is not, then, a condition that licenses a state to exercise constitutional independence however it wishes. While highly topical at the turn of the millennium, the thought is not new. In the middle of the eighteenth century, Emmerich de Vattel, the Enlightenment's codifier of sovereignty (chapter 2), held that, while Grotian-style penal wars were illegal, a state could, when asked, "help a brave people who are defending their liberties against an oppressor."[29]

## Challenges to the Core Value of State Sovereignty: Cosmopolitanism

Some want to go much further, rejecting state sovereignty. It is not incoherent to accept (effective) constitutional independence as the best conception of sovereignty but reject its value. The most distant normative perspective is cosmopolitanism. Very broadly, this prioritizes the value of each and every individual person, equally, irrespective of where in the world they live and work, and holds that all political life—from hamlet to cosmos—should be ordered accordingly. It draws on some of the oldest elements in the natural-law tradition, the Stoics having conceived the world as a *kosmopolis*.[30]

Its modern incarnation comes in two broad varieties. The most far reaching calls for the state to be swept away. Existing international organizations, such as the IMF and the WTO, would be overhauled and made accountable to a

29. Vattel, *Law of Nations*, III.iii.56, quoted in Tuck, *Rights of War and Peace*, p. 194.
30. Nussbaum, *Cosmopolitan Tradition*.

world assembly of some kind.[31] The other main vision-cum-program shies away from world government, calling instead for a society of states that exercise their powers in line with cosmopolitan morality, including ideas of global justice.

This is not all daydreaming far from the corridors of power. Some twenty years ago, a landmark article by the then UN secretary general, Kofi Annan, argued that sovereignty was being redefined by changing values and globalization. A decade later, speaking from retirement, this became a declaration that "sovereignty has evolved to include a demand that a state should govern under the rule of law with full respect for human rights."[32]

In part II's terms, the question is whether that could be incentive compatible. Given the problems it helped solve after the Thirty Years' War, it is easy to see how the institution of sovereign states subject to a convention-norm of nonintervention developed in Europe, and how it has remained (more or less) self-enforcing so long as accompanied by an exception for self-defense (individually or collectively). Taking a step further, it is not so hard to see how an equilibrium could include a license to intervene in foreign states where conditions of internal disorder jeopardize, possibly through mass migration, order elsewhere. But absent universally shared thick values, and perhaps even then, it is a bigger step to imagine a license to intervene in unpleasant states' governance except where they are weak, entailing one law for them and another for powers. However many people applaud Annan's sentiment, the norm of consent has not formally been put aside (i.e., via ongoing consent), and some very powerful states—notably the PRC and sporadically the United States—remain wedded to an older model whatever others might want. This seems to set up a live contest-cum-struggle between absolute and qualified notions of sovereignty.

## Summary: Turning toward Legitimacy

This chapter has shown that it won't do simply to deploy "sovereignty" as the decisive move in debates about international Order and System.

First, we needed to distinguish between what sovereignty claims, whether it is (or can be) effective, and its value. For those who accept the state as a fact of life under modernity, understanding sovereignty's claim as an assertion of

31. Caney, *Justice beyond Borders*, pp. 161–62.
32. Annan, "Two Concepts of Sovereignty"; Annan, "Sovereignty," p. 2.

constitutional independence helps to bring out the challenges to its effectiveness in a world where order, let alone prosperity or existential safety, might depend on cooperation of various kinds.

Second, it is not obvious that a constitutionally independent sovereign can do just anything it feels like to its citizen-subjects; put another way, that it can self-authorize unconstrained powers. In the West, this was the great step away from Hobbes taken by John Locke. While his account was grounded in natural rights, ours need not be. What matters is the inherited opinion—now and around here, but not everywhere—that people have a right to rise up against tyranny, and therefore that government should respect certain basic liberties.[33] Once rulers can no longer self-authorize, sovereignty is predicated on legitimacy: legitimate versus claimed sovereignty.

Once we put these two points together—peaceful existence among states whose local sovereignty relies on legitimacy—we face discomforting questions about how people (or, more realistically, top officials) living in a constitutionally independent state should treat states whose claim to the same seems disturbing if not horrific. If ruling elites cannot, in our tradition, self-legitimate, why can sovereign regimes in foreign states appear to do so? Perhaps international law can help by establishing standards, but that seems to generate a paradox. If external sovereignty turns, juridically, on recognition by other states as a matter of international law, how can international law itself depend for its existence and authority on the consent of autonomous states?

### An Early Twentieth-Century Debate Lives On

Those various tensions were at the center of one of the great intellectual and moral engagements of the early twentieth century, resonating into our own times: between the Nazi political and legal theorist Carl Schmitt and the Austrian jurist Hans Kelsen.[34] Broadly, Schmitt held the idea of binding law, and certainly international law, to be vacuous myth, bunkum, because when it truly matters, there is only power, the capacity and will of the executive to act: "He who decides the state of exception is the true sovereign."[35] Kelsen, meanwhile,

33. Ryan, *On Politics*, pp. 464–72. (This qualification to sovereignty fits with the account of necessary constraints on the state in Malcolm, *Human Rights and Political Wrongs*.)

34. For a summary, see Dyzenhaus, introduction to *Sovereignty*.

35. Quoted in Dyzenhaus, introduction to *Sovereignty*, p. 7. (Today, too many flirt with detaching Schmitt's writings, which included "The Fuhrer as the Guardian of Our Law," from his active Nazism. Lilla, *Reckless Mind*, chap. 2.)

argued any system of municipal (national, regional) law is law in virtue of being recognized as such by a higher-level, universal international legal order that regulates relations not only among states but between states and their citizen-subjects.

While one dismissed international law as mirage, the other elevated it to the font of all authority. The particular is pitched against the universal, local expediency against morality: "The attempt to square the circle of statehood and international law was doomed to fail on logical grounds. Either the State was sovereign—and there was really no binding international order. Or there was a binding international order—in which case no state could be truly sovereign."[36]

## Norms and Self-Enforcing Institutions Redux: On to Legitimacy and Legitimation

But the logical rigor is exaggerated. If, as suggested above, sovereignty is usefully thought of as a legal institution dedicated to a political value, then it can be self-enforcing as a *political*-social practice *within and among* states only if its norms are internalized (as values).[37] Put like that, we can see that if the norms that make a domestic constitutional order self-enforcing are essentially the same as those underpinning an international legal order, no tension would arise. It becomes a question of fact: Are those various norms congruent or in conflict?

This is not ethereal. The state officials who negotiate internationally need authorization to make bargains and agreements, and they are (in degree) accountable back home for their outputs and conduct. While that works through domestic power structures, infused by the local battle of interests, it is also framed by a state's political and legal system (in a constitutional state). Those at the international table need to give weight, therefore, to two types of consideration: their own domestic constraints and objectives (public and political opinion, etc.) and their peers' positions, which means tuning in to each other's domestic constraints.[38] They might clash.

At the chapter head, Nobel economist Roger Myerson identified the scope for deadlock or conflict when states fail to grasp that their counterparts do not

---

36. Koskenniemi, *Gentle Civilizer*, p. 240.

37. Broadly the position of another Weimar legal theorist, Hermann Heller: see Dyzenhaus, introduction to *Sovereignty*.

38. Known as a two-level game: see Putnam, "Diplomacy and Domestic Politics"; and, linking to normative issues, Savage and Weale, "Political Representation."

share some bedrock norms. Importantly, the same hazard arises when they *do* see the normative conflict but cannot compromise because the norms in question cannot be questioned (because they sustain their own constitutional setup). What they need to give up internationally cannot be given up at home. International bargaining's two dimensions can bring a normative tug-of-war, revealing that sovereignty's value calls on something lying further back: legitimation.[39] We can coherently ask whether sovereignty is legitimate, but not whether legitimacy is sovereign.

39. The implicit story (material and ideational) of Hinsley, *Sovereignty*.

# 12

# Legitimacy and Legitimation

## A HUMEAN-WILLIAMSIAN FRAMEWORK

It is therefore, on opinion only that government is founded; and this maxim extends to the most despotic and most military governments, as well as the most free and most popular.

DAVID HUME, "OF THE FIRST PRINCIPLES
OF GOVERNMENT," 1741[1]

The "first" political question . . . securing . . . order, protection, safety, trust, and the conditions of cooperation . . . is the condition of solving, indeed posing, any others. . . . The Basic Legitimation Demand implies . . . the state . . . hav[ing] to offer a justification of its power to each subject.

BERNARD WILLIAMS, *IN THE BEGINNING WAS THE DEED*[2]

IN THIS CHAPTER we change gear, embarking on an argument that will produce *Principles for Participation and Delegation* in international System.

To get going, we need a position on why legitimacy matters, and what the legitimacy of authority implies (or demands), before moving on to what generates or grounds legitimation principles and norms as a general matter, and how that plays out in the specific context of the modern *liberal* state. As the argument proceeds through those four stages, something will be said about the read across to states' international engagements. Rather than advocating universal principles for international relations and cooperation, applicable in

---

1. Hume, "First Principles of Government," in *Political Essays*, p. 16.
2. Williams, in *In the Beginning*, pp. 3–4.

all times and places, I shall argue that what matters for those of us living in the West and parts of the East, now, are legitimation precepts that can guide constitutional democracies.

The approach is "realist" in an important sense. It is not a *morality-first* account deriving duties, rights, and legitimation principles from fundamental, externally given, universal principles, with some kind of morality system providing ultimate foundations.[3] But nor does it consign moral values to the sidelines, so it is distinct from contemporary Hobbesian International Relations realism. Recalling chapter 2's matrix of top-down/bottom-up authority and sociability/hostility, it lives in the fourth cell: sociability with path-dependent, problem-solving norms, which leaves something to be said about the sources or mechanisms of normativity.

The aim is to tie legitimacy to part II's account of self-enforcing institutions, and to an account of normativity that makes sense on the ground. Hume is useful for the first, and Williams, in a striking way, for the second: incentives and values (of some kind) come together. Despite the abstraction, this sheds light on the intractability of geopolitical contests that, as now, are definitely ideological and can be presented as civilizational. In terms of our scenarios, *Superpower Struggle* or *New Cold War* becomes almost inevitable; for *Lingering Status Quo* to prevail, something will have to give.

## Why the State?

As the quote from Williams at the chapter head brings out, there is something distinctive and special about the level of government—whether local, national-territorial, regional, or global—that produces or preserves security and stability, since they are preconditions for cooperative endeavors among small or large groups. Solving that problem is, as he put it, the *First Political Question*.[4]

In conditions of modernity, as a matter of fact that role has been fulfilled (where it has been) by the state, since within its territory it has a monopoly

---

3. As noted in chapter 1, this distinguishes my account from others accepting the central role of states and taking institutions seriously. While some conclusions are shared, mine do not rely on a "natural duty of justice" (Buchanan) or "morally mandatory aims" (Christiano). Thanks to Allen Buchanan for reading this and the next chapter, and Ed Hall for looking at some passages on Williams.

4. Hume, quoting Cicero, makes a similar point: "*Salus populi suprema Lex*, the safety of the people is the supreme law. This maxim is agreeable to the sentiments of mankind in all ages" ("Of Passive Obedience," in *Political Essays*, p. 202).

over coercion and the final say over cooperation's modalities. The sovereign state emerged, partly through Westphalia, as a self-enforcing equilibrium institution for maintaining security both internally and externally (through a balance with other similarly endowed states; chapter 7).[5]

That helps to pin down some matters outstanding from the previous chapter. First, while thinking of sovereignty as constitutional independence remains useful, it becomes clear that one minimum condition for sovereignty to be effective is that a state is able to maintain security and stability within its borders through its own efforts, without ditching its constitution. Another is that it is able to maintain external security either on its own or via security relationships that do not force or otherwise generate unwelcome internal constitutional reforms.

Second, however much weight is given to cosmopolitan values, they cannot wholly override the value of the state so long as the capacity meaningfully to pursue cosmopolitan justice depends on internal security and stability prevailing somewhere, and that stability depends, as a matter of contingent fact, on the state of some territory. To hold otherwise is to gamble with stability, and hence with the possibility of justice at "home" in the hope of achieving some wider justice.[6]

## Why Legitimacy Matters

Only a political order benefiting from legitimacy is in a position to supply security, stability, and conditions for cooperation without excessive reliance on coercion.

Compared with princely personal rule, an Order of states breaks this down into the legitimacy of a state itself as a territorial political community (which any secessionists reject), the legitimacy of a state's system of government, and (for some such systems, including representative democracy) the legitimacy of the incumbent government.[7] Each has an international counterpart: the legitimacy of a state's relations with other states; the legitimacy of any system for international cooperation; and the legitimacy of specific regimes and organizations.

None of them—from a state to an international organization—can rely entirely on good outcomes, because outcomes will sometimes be poor, harming

---

5. Spruyt, *Sovereign State.*

6. Nagel, "Problem of Global Justice" (which otherwise seems like a morality-led political theory).

7. That delayering likely forms part of any vindicatory, not merely explanatory, genealogy of the state.

the people and communities supposedly protected or served. In those circumstances, people might have reasons to kick over their rulers or governors.[8] Instead, an Order-System's higher-level institutions, whether spontaneous or designed, need to be self-enforcing even when under pressure from degrees of failure, citizen-subjects' frustration with onerous demands, or external threat. Legitimacy is a precondition for a political order or governance institutions to be self-enforcing. Legitimacy is glue. Why?

### The Hobbesian Problem: Authoritative Governance with Excessive Coercion

Providing an adequate answer is the central weakness in the Hobbesian vision of a sovereign power whose authority stems from the self-interested rational calculus of the political community's members. Faced with the prospect of abject failure, individual members of the community have incentives to defect, withdrawing their cooperation or obedience, but that is liable to set off a run for the exits that brings down the regime and beckons disorder—restrained only by the prospective costs of transitioning to a new regime or order. (Think of the television coverage of the fall of the Berlin Wall in 1989, where transition costs were lowered by the prospective availability of the West German regime.)

For Hobbesians, the answer lies—and can lie only—in the shadow of coercion. Members do not run for the exits because they will be obstructed or punished. In principle, this coercion need not be a state's physical policing but in other contexts, including international regimes, could include decentralized punitive or retaliatory measures.[9]

The problem with this shadow-and-fist-of-coercion account of authority is, in its own terms, that it is very inefficient. Because policing and punishment are resource intensive, the governing regime will not be able to do much: policies that depend on solving collective-action problems will, perforce, be few. This is so whether the coercive power is centralized (and monopolized, as in a state) or decentralized (as in many international policy regimes), although the costs manifest themselves in different ways.

---

8. I.e., while necessary, what political scientists call output legitimacy cannot suffice to hold a regime together, because outcomes will never be consistently good, and sometimes aggravatingly poor. Output legitimacy (Scharpf, *Governing in Europe*) is akin to "performance legitimacy" in Zhao, "Mandate of Heaven," but with the latter focusing on outturns.

9. Hadfield and Weingast, "Microfoundations of the Rule of Law" (chapter 6).

In the centralized case (a state), unless the authority relying entirely on coercion is credibly oppressive (and so its policing capability overwhelmingly strong), the governing elite cannot expect to contain or deter resistance. But if tested, resorting to oppression is liable to undermine the legitimacy of its coercive power, fueling the possibility of revolt.

In the decentralized case (international law, regimes, and organizations), members of the relevant community will find that the costs of continually punishing defectors begin to exceed the benefits, leading them to give up, and so effectively join the defectors via abstention. In a mixed case where a few leading members of the community police the regime, they may face revolt from other participants. In an international Order of states, in the limit this means interstate conflict of some kind.

Hobbesians can overcome this tension between excessive coercion and defection only by stipulating that members of the community should realize, if thinking and acting rationally, that they *must* not resist the authority that provides order and stability. They should always obey. Further, as Thomas Hobbes himself famously spotted, since there cannot be any confusion about where any such supreme authority lies, power must be centralized. This has profound implications. In the first place, while Hobbes's account of natural law can accommodate duties, and hence undertakings, among states (princes),[10] there is nothing to make them stick, no sovereign. Since international authorities and regimes cannot rely on decentralized enforcement, international System is infeasible because there is no higher power to keep the peace and enforce contracts other than a coincidence of perceived interests. As chapter 5 argued, this does not in fact demonstrate infeasibility.

But even in a domestic setting, the response to Hobbesian sovereign authority might be: Why on earth should I obey an oppressive, abusive, or incompetent absolute power? Here, fear of order-maintaining power competes with fear of disorder.[11] This is the elemental basis for Williams's *Basic Legitimation Demand* (see the chapter head). An adequate answer to the First Political Question cannot be or become part of the problem it purports to solve.[12] As

---

10. Malcolm, "Hobbes's Theory."

11. Separating Hobbesians from Judith Shklar's "Liberalism of Fear" (to which Williams genuflects: see *In the Beginning*, p. 3, and chap. 5).

12. Williams, *In the Beginning*, pp. 4–5. If not initially solved, the possible outcomes are reform, more coercion, and breakdown. For an international setting, see Reus-Smit, "International Crises of Legitimacy" (omitting retreat to autarkic standoff).

he puts it, legitimate authority is the condition of politics itself, as opposed to tyranny, disorder, and other states of affairs that can hardly be described as political (see next chapter).[13]

That legitimation demand is not confined to the highest level of any political order. Domestically, subordinate institutions, such as central banks and regional governments, need to be legitimate so as not to rely on excessive coercion from above. Nor is it limited to domestic governance. Even where they do not directly exercise coercive power, international law, regimes, and organizations (including adjudicatory tribunals) claim *normative authority*: to set rules or standards, to resolve disagreements without conflict, and to decide other matters, all in ways that guide members or participants, and affect people around the world. In chapter 10's terms, legitimacy enhances the resilience of all such institutions.

## The Kantian Problem: Justice before Legitimacy

Kantians start in a different place: with justice. But if a legitimate order is a precondition for a political community embarking on ambitious cooperative endeavors, legitimate institutions are a precondition for justice in large and complex communities. Without them, neither public deliberation about what justice entails nor steps to pursue justice (on some conception) can get going, let alone gain traction. The pursuit of justice is a (loosely coordinated) cooperative endeavor for which order maintained by legitimate authority is a necessary (but not sufficient) condition.[14]

On achieving and sustaining a legitimate order, Kantians reach an impasse no less than their Hobbesian opponents. They articulate a moral imperative to comply with authority given what, through reason, we *must* recognize we owe to each other, as beings to be treated as ends, not means. To which the response might be: but what if some actors don't recognize that, or let down

---

13. Hence the earlier qualification that legitimacy is a precondition for a *political* order being self-enforcing. It is not sufficient for legitimation simply to be offered; it might be insincere, or sincere but comprehensively rejected. For politics, the authority needs to keep on trying—and adjusting—as otherwise resistance and still more coercion appear. (This seems to lie between Sleat, and Hall, *Value, Conflict, and Order*, pp. 141, 203–4n2.) Reflection suggests that a totalitarian order, reaching into life's every nook and cranny, abolishing distinctions between public and private, can be self-enforcing via sublimated fear (chapter 6). On comparing totalitarianism with authoritarianism and tyranny, see Arendt, "What Is Authority?"

14. Similarly, Pettit, *On the People's Terms*, p. 133, and chap. 3.

their better selves? As with the Hobbesian account, denying a right to disobedience does not cure the problem of resistance. We can whisper "should" and "must" only so many times.

If the problem with the Hobbesian account is lack of glue, the Kantians look to heavenly glue descending from Reason, and so lack the resources to contain the disruptive forces Hobbes observed in the world. I want to suggest that, where things do happen to hold together, attachment is provided partly by those of our values, beliefs, and commitments embedded in a community's habits and practices (its way of life). They shape how we evaluate outcomes, and how tolerant we are of failure, frustration, and threats; meaning legitimacy amounts to more than expedience, more than simply that "it seems to work for now." Part of this account, developed next, will be in the spirit of Hume, who criticized Hobbes for promoting tyranny (and left Kant in a lather that propelled him to one of the Enlightenment's towering achievements).[15]

## What Legitimacy Demands of the
## Members of a Community

To pursue cooperative ventures facilitated by order, a putative authority's policies and rules, and especially its laws, need to have some normative force with the community it claims to govern: they need to be taken as a reason for a person to do or refrain from doing something that presumptively preempts their own reasoning.[16] This commonly leads to the claim that the counterpart of legitimate authority is an obligation to obey each and every policy, rule, or law that is properly passed—meaning a moral obligation of some kind, with the only (moral) let out being the immorality of a particular law.[17] We saw this was central to the Hobbesian account: obey the sovereign in all.

---

15. Hume, *History of England*, vol. 6, p. 153. Like some Brexiters, Hobbes disliked the common law because judges (famously Sir Edward Coke) could stand up to the king, whereas Hume could embrace both statutory and common law.

16. Raz, *Morality of Freedom* (explicating authority but not legitimation).

17. The idea of various duties to obey is sometimes associated with Hohfeld, *Fundamental Legal Conceptions*, decomposing a right to rule into a claim-right to impose obligations, a power-right to create liabilities, a right to immunities, and a permissive right to a monopoly of coercion, each entailing correlate legal duties for members of the ruled community. But from a legal claim-right to impose legal duties, it is a leap to infer moral or political obligations to obey each and every law (as opposed to correlate duties *under the law*). The problem lies in equating an

## An Obligation to Obey versus a Responsibility
## Not to Undermine

I think this mistaken, and in any case more than necessary to generate an account of legitimacy that makes sense. It is mistaken because it is hard to see how a moral obligation to obey each and every law or rule can arise without ongoing, freely given, overt consent to the authority or system of governance. But while such overt and ongoing formal consent might (sometimes) obtain in smallish clubs and other entirely voluntary associations with low exit costs, it hardly operates in state-based political regimes typically thought legitimate.[18]

More important for us, overt, ongoing, and freely given consent as the key to generating a moral obligation to obey authority goes further than is necessary for legitimacy conceived as glue helping to hold a regime together during episodes of disappointment and failure. Instead, what is necessary is that the members of the relevant community (or, rather, sufficient of them) accept and act on the basis that they should not undermine the regime or resist its rights of enforcement. As a matter of prudence, this responsibility might involve most people going along with most laws most of the time.[19]

That makes space for case-by-case noncompliance. In the setting of a national state with legitimacy, citizen-subjects who break the law as part of opposing some other (actual or proposed) rule or law accept that they can be punished for doing so and, therefore, do not resist the process of adjudication and enforcement. In effect, they acquiesce in their political society's system of governance by accepting the punishment for their, willfully, breaking the law as part of their protest; they accept the law is the law while not equating that with a (presumptive) moral obligation to obey each and every law.[20] If, going

---

analysis of legal rights and obligations, tied to legal remedies, with an account of morally grounded political rights and obligations.

18. Lockean consent-based arguments are exactingly analyzed in Simmons, *Justification and Legitimacy* (and earlier work), concluding that, since there is no such overt and ongoing consent, almost no state is legitimate. This makes the fact of many states' orderly political life without oppressive coercion hard to fathom, implying they are benefiting from something that, while short of "consent-legitimacy," is doing a lot of work to deliver voluntary compliance notwithstanding frequent disappointments. I stick with calling that legitimacy.

19. I.e., not a presumptive moral obligation to obey. Political morality enters when we say to a person or group: that's going too far, you will bring the whole thing down if you carry on like that.

20. This distinction between legal and moral obligations is especially important for liberal states permitting freedom of conscience, expression, and assembly.

much further, some citizen-subjects resist the adjudication and enforcement, or otherwise try to bring down the system, when most others accept the system's legitimacy, they are exposed to harsher sanctions. This is the distinction between civil disobedience and outright resistance.[21]

That suggests the legitimacy of a state's claim to a right to enforce its laws (including laws creating organizations, rights, and so on) is the kernel of its viability as a means for sustaining order and providing conditions for cooperation.[22] It provides room for commonsense distinctions between a disgusting law, a horrible government, and an abhorrent and disgusting regime (system of government). If legality were coterminous with legitimacy, those distinctions would become harder to sustain, with the illegitimacy of the particular entailing (or at least risking) illegitimacy of the whole since government would be enforcing things called "laws" that were not, properly speaking, laws.

## Allegiance to Government as a Humean Self-Enforcing Equilibrium Institution

As described in part II, social conventions and norms develop to help communities, small and large, survive, and the institutions they comprise and underpin sometimes help those communities to thrive by overcoming other problems, and to fashion new peaks to climb (think science). Those norms and conventions assist this surviving and thriving (when they do) by effecting, in Hume's words, "an alteration in [the] direction" of self-interest.[23] Crucially, he goes on, the members of a political community become attached to those institutions (*their* institutions), almost for their own sake, through habits of practice (and, as we shall see, justification): "Such is the effect of custom, that it not only reconciles us to anything we have long enjoy'd, but it even gives us an affection for it, and makes us prefer it to other objects, which may be more valuable, but are less well known to us."[24] That attachment to institutions, partly via internalizing their value (chapter 7), becomes more important as the political community expands and as time passes, he says, because the origins (and, in some sense, arbitrariness) of the underlying conventions are lost to memory. This vindicatory genealogy, of the kind flagged in chapter 1, is

---

21. Similarly, Pettit, *On the People's Terms*, pp. 137–38.
22. Part of the burden of Nagel, "Problem of Global Justice" (e.g., pp. 115–17).
23. Hume, *Treatise*, III.ii.ii, p. 492.
24. Hume, *Treatise*, III.ii.iii, p. 503.

obviously a big deal. By simultaneously forging and reflecting our values, the development and performance of government can leave political communities exhibiting, in Hume's own terms, "allegiance."[25]

Rather than the thin relations of some arbitrary problem-solving convention, we have the somewhat thicker and deeper relations of a shared way of life through which a particular set of conventions and institutions evolved, informing how a political community thinks (normatively) of itself. In other words, values become part of the fabric of a political community: Society rather than merely Order and System. Disagreements rather than hostile conflicts.

The endogeneity in this genealogy of domestic legitimacy does not mean that values or values-based institutions are a veil; epiphenomenal, as it were (chapter 5). Once evolved and embedded in a community's way of life, they constrain and enable action. Sometimes as an absolute check.[26] Sometimes guiding the choice of solutions.

## A Humean Genealogy of Law as a Legitimate Coordinating Institution

We are now equipped with resources to make sense of law, including customary law, as an institution, which will prove important in our discussion of international Society and System (mainly in the next chapter).

Part II's analysis of self-enforcing institutions left two puzzles concerning why and when a convention becomes enshrined in law: which customs warrant the imprimatur of law, and what is the source of their authority once (somehow) incorporated into law?

The first part of a Humean account is that customs are incorporated into law when they need the authority of the law in order to serve as coordinating devices (focal points and so on). A particular custom might not be self-enforcing in itself, but it, or something like it, might be judged useful (or necessary) to avoid or resolve disputes of some particular kind without their tipping

---

25. Hume, *Treatise*, III.ii.viii–x, pp. 539–67. Along with fidelity to promises and respecting property rights, allegiance to government is one of Hume's artificial virtues (chapter 5). They can be thought of as qualities attributed to people corresponding to counterpart social norms and institutions.

26. Hume's approach does not preclude imperatives, but they are not categorical: see Blackburn, *Ruling Passions*, pp. 257–58.

into conflict, or cure problems of a particular kind, and those disputes or problems are judged to need (or be worth) resolving and avoiding.[27]

Centering on the function of law, this provides a criterion of identification: there is no point (and some cost) in incorporating into law those established customs and practices that are both self-enforcing and broadly accepted as among a decent set of possible customs of the relevant kind. But where a self-enforcing custom needs changing, or where a convention is wanted but has not arisen organically, the mechanism might be judicial lawmaking, collective legislation (internationally, a treaty), or whatever, with the political society's choice turning on still-higher-level background norms and the particular circumstances of the problem.

The second part of the Humean account, therefore, is that those various judgments—that issue X should be addressed, that a custom-convention would help do so, that any such convention needs higher-level assistance to become self-enforcing, and that some specific articulation of a convention (maybe tweaking a custom) will do the trick for now—need to be made via adjudicatory or legislative institutions that enjoy legitimacy in the relevant communities, meaning they enjoy acquiescence and are supported by a background norm that they should not be systematically resisted or undermined.

That separates identification criteria (e.g., which customs became law) from questions of authority, which are about adjudicatory and legislative institutions.[28] By doing so, the illusory allure of consent as *the* answer, and the irremediable

---

27. For an argument of this kind for law in general, see Basu, *Republic of Beliefs*, esp. chaps. 3 and 4, and chap. 5, sec. 5.5. (It offers a cleaner route to elements of Murphy, "Law beyond the State," sec. 3, with incisive commentary in Moellers, "Law beyond the State.")

28. This addresses some puzzles in the literature on customary law. Not all customs are solving coordination problems. Practices are the raw material for coordinating customs, sometimes more compellingly than others. They might be long standing, but not necessarily: a short-lived practice might plainly be a functioning or incipient convention but be in need of some higher-level support to become a sustained equilibrium. Whether that lawmaking action would be feasible would turn on the legitimacy of the tribunal (or other higher-level institution). Thus, UN General Assembly motions are not compelling sources of customary international law where resisted by states integral to the coordination issue at hand. Tribunals will make law where one of a number of rival focal points needs to be chosen or embedded, constrained by their legitimation conditions. And so on. For some similar points, without game-theoretic framing, see Bradley, "Customary International Law."

tension in notions of tacit consent (as opposed to tacit acquiescence), slip away, saving us from equating source (in the sense of identification criteria) with warrants for normative authority.[29]

But this account also underlines law's endogeneity to the kind of society (thin, thick, or deep) it serves. In a pluralist community, more will need to find its way into law because some older customary moral norms will no longer be self-enforcing on their own. Codification is a mark of a society that either is thin or badly needs to turn a moral-political corner. New or reconfigured political communities need to write things down in codified constitutions.[30]

### Taking the Humean Account to the International Sphere: Consent or Acquiescence?

Turning to the international, that helps make sense both of various elementary norms—notably, "don't break formal promises"—becoming codified in modern international law (the Vienna metatreaty) in the middle of the twentieth century, after many new states had been created, and of nuanced and contested ideas on the "responsibilities of states" being left in advisory documents for tribunals to draw on incrementally.

Otherwise, things are different here since consent plays a more obvious role, partly because it can be feasible. Compared with a country of millions of individuals, there are far fewer states, they have organizational capacity individuals lack, and opting out and exiting from *some* international regimes and norms is both materially and formally feasible (part I). Citizen-subjects have none of those opt-out rights and capacities under domestic law.

Even so, as the previous chapter discussed, it is not practicable for most states to opt out of some regimes, new states were not around to object to customary laws, and *jus cogens* norms (claim to) trump all, so express consent cannot do all the work. Nor, again, does tacit consent come to the rescue. Just as it is unrealistic for most individual citizen-subjects to up sticks and leave their state, it would be hard for most states to extricate themselves from the

---

29. The idea of consenting to customary law is commonly traced back to Justinian's *Digest* (1.3.35): "tacita civium conventio," often translated as "silent civic agreement," connoting active normative opinion. But it can be read as unspoken community convention, perhaps closer to habitual tacit willingness.

30. This makes sense of Germany's Basic Law needing a democracy clause, whereas Britain has not, so far. (The United States could do with one.)

international System as a whole without embracing a kind of isolationist autarky.[31]

It is best to think of the question of the legitimacy (or not) of states' international engagements as operating at two levels: a level of express consent to new initiatives or reforms effected via treaties and other pacts, whether codifying law, establishing regimes and organizational powers, or applying them; and a level of Humean acquiescence in background norms and institutions, including general international law, and regimes and organizations from which it is impossible, in practice, for a state to detach itself. Since any obligations under the former are generated by norms operating in the latter, we arrive at an analogue of subject-citizens' responsibility not to resist a legitimate state's system of government.

Having acquiesced, if they have, in the background norms, and having overtly consented (within living political memory) to some cooperative agreements and endeavors, it becomes incumbent on a state (its political leaders, officials, and people) not to undermine the international System. As with domestic-system legitimacy, this is the kind of consideration associated with Society of some kind. If (with stress on *if*) the participants-cum-members of international System treat it as legitimate, then they are in effect acquiescing to some social norms.

One is "No damaging disorderly exit." Another is that when a state has breached or disregarded an international law or rule, it (and its domestic legitimation audience) accepts the ex post jurisdiction of any *preagreed* adjudication process, and the result of any such adjudication. Where a state voluntarily signed up to an adjudication process but later rejects its authority, it is challenging the legitimacy of a particular regime and maybe, depending on the circumstances, even the wider System—a kind of rebellion against other members of any Society.

Of course, quite unlike the domestic state, the international equilibrium has included a formal right for states to opt out of the jurisdiction of some adjudicative and decentralized-enforcement machinery. But the laws of war developed to stigmatize outright aggression against other states, and thus the Order-System as a whole.

---

31. *Autarky*, already mentioned few times, comes from the Greek for "self-sufficiency." It was prized by Aristotle as the mark of the *polis* (city-state), a slightly crazy thought unless he means capability rather than optimality.

It now becomes clearer that as Order develops into System, to the point where interdependences among states and their peoples run so broad and deep that changing course abruptly could well jeopardize internal or external stability, part II's functional social norms of fidelity and good faith in negotiations extend to include some kind of mutualized responsibility in international politics—conceived as politics, not incipient war—not to bring the edifice crashing down: taken together, Good Faith in capital letters. Chapter 13 will provide this important proposition with more underpinning.

## On Legitimation Principles in General

On the account given so far, legitimacy matters beyond the schoolroom.[32] Starting with the Hobbesian-flavored First Political Question—achieving stability and security as a precondition for broader cooperative endeavors—does not signify, however, that the test of legitimacy is solely whether internal and external security are preserved. The Basic Legitimation Demand is framed as a demand because it holds that an Order's sustainability depends on adequate justifications-cum-explanations for its system of normative authority (and, if a state, coercive monopoly) being available to those affected. That is necessary to drive a wedge between disagreement and hostile conflict. As Williams puts it, "*Something* has to be said to explain (to the less empowered, to concerned bystanders, to children being educated in this structure, etc.) what the difference is between the solution and the problem, and that cannot simply be an account of successful domination."[33] That leaves open the legitimating community's composition, what legitimation principles look like, and how the account needs adapting to international relations (mostly deferred to the next chapter).

### Legitimation Communities and Audiences

Justification needs to operate for whichever groups are necessary for peaceful coexistence and rule (normative authority) without excessive coercion, so certainly those capable of meaningful resistance. In a narrow sense, in some times and places, that might be only an extended elite group that cannot easily

---

32. So only half the story is captured in Humean accounts relying on the force of conventions without the glue of legitimacy provided by values and opinions (legitimation principles).

33. Williams, *In the Beginning*, p. 5.

be coerced: domestically, those a ruler cannot rule without; internationally, those held in a balance of power, or essential hegemonic allies.[34] In such circumstances, the justifications amount to the stories leadership group members tell themselves about the conventions and norms maintaining equilibrium among them.

But unless an Order is peculiarly benign for those outside its de facto leadership or has extraordinarily efficient coercive machinery (one way of thinking about tyranny's technology), some kind of justification needs to be addressed to a wider population. For a modern state, that means citizen-subjects, since they can, at least, passively resist its system of government from within—reducing the rulers' returns from ruling. This becomes clear when thinking about the gravest demand made of citizen-subjects: conscription into the military to fight a war (to keep things tolerably straightforward, let's say a defensive war in which the conscripting state is not morally culpable). To resist is to risk undermining the state. To comply is to put one's life in jeopardy (hardly the security they were promised). While some people will travel far away to fight for a cause (as in the 1930s Spanish Civil War struggle against fascism), most people in a legitimate state are not inclined to respond to a call to arms by foreign states but do accept such calls from their own state. What drives this is obviously profound: some combination of patriotism, loyalty to fellow citizens, identity, and more.[35] When individuals, and their families and friends, have to choose whether to accept a state's ultimate call to duty, there can be little doubt that legitimation judgments do not, in reality, lie solely in the hands of governing elites. Legitimacy is more than fair-weather acquiescence: it must be internalized: in Humean terms, it is a useful social practice with internalized value.[36]

34. As Hume put it for the domestic case, "The soldan of Egypt, or the emperor of Rome, might drive his harmless subjects, like brute beasts, against their sentiments and inclination: but he must, at least, have led his marmalukes, or praetorian bands, like men, by their opinion" ("First Principles of Government," in *Political Essays*, p. 16).

35. War memorials testify to this. For this Brit, one can only kneel in awed gratitude for the sacrifice represented by the magnificent Anzac memorial in Canberra. (On motives for sacrifice, see Ferguson, "The Death Instinct," in *Pity of War*.)

36. A state peremptorily shooting retreating soldiers to get them to advance against the enemy—as the Soviets did in the Battle of Stalingrad against the Nazis—underlines how much is at stake. On internalizing functionally useful duties, see Craig, "Genealogies and the State," pp. 199–200.

For international institutions, the same thought suggests states themselves—all or some, depending on the context—comprise a diffuse legitimation community; a complex one involving each state's leaders, those of its agencies participating in international regimes, and its people. The legitimation audience prudently also includes those materially affected people around the world whose passive or active resistance could stymie or undermine the purpose or functionality of a particular international institution, or the Order-System as a whole (next chapter).

## Legitimation Principles: Scope and Nonperfectionist Holism

In the standard cases (states and empowered organizations), legitimacy conditions have the structure, "If X is going to have normative authority or a monopoly over coercive power in order to maintain order, then the putative authority's establishment, structure, processes, and so on need to fulfill criteria *xyz*, including delivering outcomes *abc*." Internationally, things are slightly different. Absent world government (anarchy), conditions for accepting or acquiescing in conventions and norms governing relations among states replace conditions for acquiescing in a formalized monopoly over coercive power, and conditions for normative authority apply to pooling and delegations of power in international organizations.

Such legitimation conditions need not be overtly expressed in such terms—*xyz* processes, *abc* outcomes—by all members of legitimation audiences, but can be distilled from social practices and debates (below). To function, they have to be internalized as legitimation norms, making sense alongside other beliefs, opinions, and values (chapter 7). They stand higher than other internalized norms since, by underpinning order without excessive coercion, they separate disagreement (resolved or sidelined) from hostile conflict notwithstanding occasional or recurrent conflicts among various norms.

Hypothetically, in a purely outcomes-based approach, *xyz* would be blank, and similarly *abc* in a purely procedural approach. In practice, for the highest-level institutions, such as the state or an international balance of power, they must cover security and safety and so on, and possibly means for handling disagreement. Otherwise, the content of *xyz* and *abc* depends partly on where a specific institution comes in a political community's network of institutions.

Legitimacy conditions need not be restricted to what is necessary for a legitimate Order because once established, order widens a community's sense of possibilities: it can aim for order with other goods. Being free from fear is hugely valuable in itself, but also useful for what, once released, we are able to contemplate and pursue. Domestically, the state will attempt, permit, or constrain various kinds of endeavors beyond those of a Hobbesian minimal state; as Hume puts it, "Thus bridges are built; ramparts rais'd; canals form'd."[37] Internationally, the opportunities and challenges of cooperation are summoned.

While lower-level institutions face their own specific legitimation demands, they do not have to be perfect so long as the whole fits together tolerably well, with capacity for improvement.[38] They cannot fall so far short of unit legitimacy that they jeopardize the legitimacy of the order-sustaining higher-level institutions themselves. But conversely, they can bolster the overall Order-system's legitimacy.[39]

Separately, at the level of the system as a whole (domestic or international), gaps in a network of institutions can undermine what otherwise might be sustainable. Imagine democracy unfettered from the disciplines of law; or a world of states without norms-cum-laws of war and peace. This highfalutin point has mighty implications for the international monetary order given its various holes (chapter 16).

## Endogeneity and Path Dependency

The cooperative projects made possible by order will generate new legitimation principles, or qualify or reframe old ones. Legitimation becomes endogenous to what a state's provision of a legitimate basic order, its other projects, its failures and successes make feasible or bring into view. However compelling a genealogy for a particular institution, its functionalist origins only loosely tether the justifications later required to meet a basic legitimation demand: opinion, as Hume termed it, is obviously affected by utility, but not only that. This is no less so in the international realm.

All that being so, it is clear that the values that matter most for legitimacy assessments are the values that actually animate the justificatory community. Of course, the prevailing technology (economic and cultural) will have influenced the evolution of those values, as will, crucially, events (wars, revolutions,

---

37. Hume, *Treatise*, III.ii.vii, p. 539.

38. Stressed in Buchanan, *Heart of Human Rights*, chap. 5.

39. Domestically, for example, better monetary policy delivered by *constrained* independent central banks can enhance economic performance without undermining constitutional democracy.

famines, etc.). But the values will have some influence on governing institutions—precisely through legitimation. In equilibrium, a political community's deep political values are those embedded in its core governance institutions (even when falling short of them).

As Williams put it, what we are contemplating is the legitimacy of authority for a community "now and around here" given its particular convictions about, and commitments to, ways of living together in a political community. In other words, legitimacy given its particular history.[40] It follows that legitimation principles might vary, at least in emphases, *within* a political community, and more notably across time and place.

Across time, this creates room for change. Moral theorizing about justice can be thought of as a kind of campaign to shift a political society's legitimation principles or audiences. Those principles might also sometimes play catch-up when particular government initiatives (maybe European liberalism's welfare state) prove so widely popular they become, in effect, required.[41] All of which fits with a Humean account so long as the high-level institutions remain self-enforcing.

Across space, the kind of justification offered to a citizen-subject of, say, the United States or the PRC will not be the same because the structure, reach, modalities, and history of state power differ profoundly in those two nation-states. This is one of the reasons chapter 9 discussed Confucian thinking: even if, as some eloquently argue, it does not preclude human-rights commitments, which do find a place in some other East Asian states, nothing like them is embedded in the history of mainland China's political institutions. Further, relying on a modernized output-based Heaven's Mandate, performance

---

40. Williams, *In the Beginning*, p. 8. This relates to Williams's earlier account, in *Ethics and the Limits*, of thick and thin evaluative concepts (chapter 7) and his broader attack on the "morality system," with its exclusive emphasis on obligation rather than an ethical outlook (reprising Aristotelian preoccupations with how to live, which for most people is mainly local). Thin evaluative concepts (good, wrong) are characteristic of highly generalized morality systems (whether Kantian or Utilitarian) that claim to lay down the moral law on the basis of some higher principles (specific obligations derived, somehow, from more general obligations). Williams hardly wants to banish thin evaluations, but is recovering the thought that they are reached at the end of thicker debates (within an ethical form of life). His target is abstract: universal governing principles, sourced in a point of view completely outside the context of how people make sense of the world they move in.

41. Nagel, "Problem of Global Justice," argues legitimacy risk-taking is sometimes warranted (p. 146), a point picked up in chapter 20.

(results and conduct) becomes the linchpin, creating incentives for opacity and secrecy, and perhaps introducing brittleness if outturns were ever seriously to disappoint. (On the other side, the West is exposed to erosion in the background norms oiling its checks and balances, and electoral systems of representation.)

### States' Legitimation Principles and International Relations

This legitimacy framework's relevance for a state's international relations and engagement in cooperative endeavors can be captured in three broad propositions (developed in the next two chapters).

First, a state's internal legitimacy will be in jeopardy if, given feasible alternatives, its external security relies on other states' protection under conditions that are excessively coercive or unacceptably redirect its way of life (a reorientation of chapter 11's sovereignty as constitutional independence).

Second, a state needs to avoid its capacity adequately to answer the First Political Question being undermined by cross-border flows of goods, services, people, capital, or waste matter. While a much higher threshold than people disliking a regime, it is still significant given lessons offered by Trumpian America and some other rich democracies.

Third, since the Basic Legitimation Demand for justification-cum-explanation of the structure and disposition of authority applies to power pooled or delegated by states in international organizations, those organizations themselves need legitimation stories that are generally accepted.[42] Where they fail, states' own legitimacy might be impaired. But where they succeed, states might take legitimacy risks if, by not participating, they forgo welfare or other benefits their people care about.

## A Sociological *and* Normative Approach to Legitimacy

My Hume-meets-Williams account has a good deal in common with that of the late British political sociologist David Beetham, who argued that in practice legitimate power depends on three conditions: (1) being established and

---

42. The burden of I. Hurd, "Legitimacy and Authority," with coercion, interests, and legitimacy distinct bases for the exercise of power (followed in Wendt, *Social Theory*, and Doshi, *Long Game*). (The third in the triad should be values, with legitimacy emerging as glue that, sometimes, binds and aligns the three into an incentives-values-compatible equilibrium.)

exercised by legally valid means; (2) being under laws, norms, and conventions that conform to a society's deep values and normative beliefs about governance; and (3) meeting with expressions of de facto recognition, acknowledgment, or engagement through the actions and cooperation of the people. In his words, "A given power relationship is not legitimate because people believe in its legitimacy, but because it can be *justified in terms of* their beliefs. This may seem a fine distinction, but it is a fundamental one."[43]

My account might therefore seem emptily sociological, with no normative grounds or bite.[44] Plainly, opinions concerning an institution's legitimacy are normative, practical judgments in the sense that they guide our individual and collective conduct, and do so because, like a coordinating focal point, we usually know whether our opinions are broadly shared by others.[45] They therefore help select among functional solutions to problems and opportunities, and give a system of governance a degree of coherence (chapter 7).

But do those opinions withstand examination: Is there a test of whether legitimacy is deserved that avoids slipping into idealism? One route might be to stipulate that opinions on legitimacy, which almost inevitably reflect the actions and outcomes of government, not just its proffered justifications, withstand reflection. For that to be worthwhile, they need to be reached without brainwashing or coercion.[46] But for normativity of operating *social* norms, a governance system needs to make space for reasonably unconstrained ongoing debate among citizen-subjects on its own characteristics and quality, including

43. Beetham, *Legitimation of Power*, p. 11. This is not Max Weber's raw belief, but closer to opinion in Hume's sense.

44. It is certainly distinct from accounts of legitimacy taking an external (more idealist) point of view, often revolving around Rawls's Neo-Kantian "Liberal Principle of Legitimacy," under which political institutions are legitimate if they can be justified with reasons that all citizens might reasonably be expected to endorse given principles and ideals acceptable to common human reason (or, in another formulation, advanced by T. M. Scanlon, which no one could reasonably reject). Rawls, *Political Liberalism*, p. 137, and Lecture VI. Although the word "justification" is shared, its meaning has slipped. The Rawlsian canon promotes a stipulated legitimacy, somehow judged by high priests: "public reason" without a public.

45. Zaum, "Legitimacy." Buchanan's metacoordination account of legitimacy is anchored partly in a "virtue of law-abidingness" ("Institutional Legitimacy," p. 63), which seems like Hume's artificial virtues.

46. On reflexivity in Hume (applied to virtues), see *Treatise*, III.iii.vi.3, p. 619; and Cohon, *Hume's Morality*, pp. 260–62. For legitimation, Williams adds a Critical Theory Principle (*In the Beginning*, pp. 6, 27; *Truth and Truthfulness*, pp. 219–32), setting aside acquiescence delivered through power structures (propaganda, brain washing, or whatever), but not persuasion.

its performance, alternative policies and procedures, reform, and so on. Where those conditions hold and a regime or authority is legitimate sociologically—delivering the resilience institutions need in the face of adversity—we can also say that normativity has entered through some kind of communal self-reflection (however unstructured or sporadic, and without members of the public needing to think about it in these terms).[47]

This is not, then, a matter of seeking timeless, universally applicable moral criteria for legitimate or just governance. It is a realist account rather than idealist declaration; the relevant moral considerations are internal, rather than prior, to the practice of politics. It rejects a sociological versus normative dichotomy.[48] Normativity is a special subset of the sociological.

That has a number of implications for our inquiry. First, rooting normativity in public reflection might seem to tilt the scales in favor of liberalism. Maybe, as a matter of fact, conditions for critical collective self-examination do obtain only in broadly liberal states, but it would be a liberal conceit simply to assume that. This matters because where conditions for public self-examination and opinion formation seem to prevail over time elsewhere, another state's internal legitimacy should carry some weight with outsiders—that is, us, even when we do not admire it; perhaps even when we think it horrible. But consequently, while we can try to refrain from judging another state's institutions or, going a step further, its community's legitimation principles, we might not be able to avoid making judgments about the adequacy of the public debates or deliberation via which those legitimation principles are articulated, sustained, tested, and applied. Chapter 13 returns to this pressing practical issue.

Second, under a realist account of legitimation principles, perfection is not demanded; legitimacy is not binary. Authority can be legitimate if it is the best realistically available (including taking account of the costs of transitioning to

---

47. A broadly similar argument is made in Gaus, "Why the Conventionalist," although bundled, I think unnecessarily, with metaphorical contractualism. It also relates to Christine Korsgaard's important *Sources of Normativity* (including discussion of Hume and Williams, and the latter's response) but applied to political relations and stripped, I hope, of Kantian overreach. A reflexivity standard can draw on genealogies of norms, exploring whether, for at least their circumstances, they survive reflection. While members of a community can gain critical distance from local norms (and thus vindicate or reject them), it is not possible for them to escape what counts as an argument in their community: what they say has to make sense (as an argument) to people they are trying to persuade or dissuade (and to themselves).

48. E.g., Buchanan and Keohane, "Legitimacy of Global Governance Institutions."

alternatives), holds out the prospect of things getting better rather than worse, and does not violate or undermine a community's deep political values.[49]

Third, the norms that are most obviously central to legitimation are those that are *institutionalized*, rather than merely talked about or found in books. Where legitimacy prevails, institutionalized political values plainly have some hold over people, and people think (having thought) that they should. The values that animate a political community's core institutions accordingly set the menu for other institutions, including those that involve pooling or delegating power internationally.

## Legitimation for *Liberal* States and Their Peoples

For *us*, Western-style constitutional democracies, now and around here, that means seeking to meet legitimation norms that are, in some broad sense, liberal.[50]

Since *our* political history matters, Locke, Montesquieu, and other luminaries matter. In Locke's case, this is because his writings informed Britain's 1688 institutional revolution, the US founding fathers, and the aims of the US Constitution (if not, as it turned out, the incentives set up by its detailed design), and because *we*, around here, have held on to some of his core insights (while, for the most part, discarding his appeal to divinely grounded natural law).[51] In consequence, as will become apparent, much (but not all) of the substance of the book's legitimation principles would be shared by morality-first approaches.

### A Legitimation Robustness Test for Plural Political Communities

Given, however, that in liberal political communities each and every person's allegiance to their local system of government is not explicable in identical terms, this means recognizing the pluralism *within* Western-style

---

49. Similarly, Buchanan, "Institutional Legitimacy."

50. For the moment, "liberal" covers, rather loosely, political systems that, as Williams puts it, "aim to combine the rule of law with a liberty more extensive than in most earlier societies, a disposition to toleration, and a commitment to some kinds of equality" (*Truth and Truthfulness*, p. 264).

51. This is a Humean view of why Lockean thought matters: because it helped his country, and then others, find solutions to big problems. The method is not rationalist as in the Grotian-Lockean tradition, because being inductive rather than deductive—Hume was writing after Francis Bacon and Isaac Newton—there is not a unique answer but contingency.

states. The legitimation principles at stake will not be monolithic—the product of one mind—since they must reflect, somehow, the opinions of millions of *citizens*. Nor can they be a simple union of what each citizen cares about, precisely because they disagree profoundly about some things. For society to hold, citizens need to be able to disagree without falling into hostile conflict.

Legitimation principles need to pass a "robustness test," meaning that authority needs to square with those values and norms that matter particularly to parts of the community and can be tolerated by others, even though they themselves would not prioritize the same list.[52] In a legitimate community, we find the answer by looking at what both animates and is instantiated in its core institutions.

For constitutional democracies, this goes deeper than welfare outcomes versus processes. As Williams points out, political authority interrupts primitive freedom in order to deliver order, leaving the question of how much coercion is too much hinging on how a political community think about and value liberty or freedom.[53] In *our* traditions, two conceptions of liberty run through our history: the liberal idea of liberty as noninterference, and the republican idea of liberty as nondomination (not being under the control of a master or mistress, however benign). If liberalism revolves around individuals' rights to pursue their personal projects and goals so long as they don't excessively undermine others' projects (such as not recklessly infecting them with deadly diseases), *republicanism* emphasizes political citizenship, self-government via a capacity to check and steer those in power, and power being dispersed (across groups and over time).[54]

---

52. On the idea of legitimation robustness tests, see Tucker, *Unelected Power*, pp. 161–63, and chap. 9. It is not a lowest common denominator, and so not the same as Rawls's "overlapping consensus" conceived thus.

53. On debates about liberty being part of our political history, see Williams, "From Freedom to Liberty: The Construction of a Political Value," in *In the Beginning*.

54. The leading accounts of republican liberty in modern political philosophy and the history of ideas are, respectively, Pettit, *On the People's Terms*, and Skinner, *Liberty before Liberalism*. In the modern world, the realization of liberal and republican ideals is intertwined, one bringing an emphasis on rights, the other a stress on participation and challenge, and both wanting to guard against abuses of power. Thus, Williams, expressly liberal, makes a point about domination: "The basic sense of being unfree is being in someone else's power. . . . (Note how this conception coincides neither with 'negative' nor with 'positive' freedom.)" ("Liberalism of Fear," in *In the Beginning*, p. 61.)

Those two ideas of liberty can plainly be applied to relations among states and peoples as well as within states: hence aspirations for a liberal international order or a nondominating one (see the next chapter). But in the spirit of a realist theory of politics, the relevant benchmarks are the standards prevailing and institutionalized (even while not always wholly met) back home.

Other parts of our political hinterland introduce other conditions for a structure of international cooperation or engagement to be legitimate at home. For example, *social democrats* demand domestic regimes, such as a welfare state, designed to mitigate the costs to individuals and groups of exposure to international market forces (known as *embedded liberalism*).[55]

Meanwhile, *conservatism* values stability in social institutions, with organic change. Its *prescriptive* legitimacy accordingly lies in established practices that form part of a community's way of life. It would be jeopardized if international pooling and delegation, economic globalization, or geopolitical reforms threatened abrupt or revolutionary change.

Notwithstanding their quotidian contest, the core values associated with each of those political traditions need to be satisfied by any international Order-System.

## Summary

Throughout this book we have encountered a contest between three broad schools of thought about how international relations work. International Relations realists have it that it is all, ultimately but always, about power (relative or absolute), and that sooner or later even the most determined idealists either bend to that reality or find themselves overwhelmed by it. By contrast, liberal institutionalists maintain that international relations revolve around trying to solve or mitigate collective-action problems through carefully designed international regimes that, at least in expectation, leave no participating country worse off and many better off. And finally, constructivists hold that, at root, international relations turn on ideas and values, which shape a country's preferences and goals, so that a mutually beneficial international society can result where states' and peoples' norms and values are aligned or converging, but friction or disorder are unavoidable where they collide.

Much of that debate seems to be in the grip of a picture in which one but only one foundational story—reducing everything to power, welfare, or ideas

---

55. Ruggie, "International Regimes."

and identities—must be true.[56] We need to escape from that picture, and can help ourselves by moving toward the spirit of Kant's near contemporary Hume. This sees social institutions, including the structure and role of the state and government—and so relations among states and peoples—developing through efforts and initiatives fashioned by need, the ebb and flow of power, experience, and the evolution of ideas via problem solving and debate.[57] Conventions emerge as solutions to practical coordination problems but can beget social norms that open a door to cooperation. As those norms are internalized, adapt, and thicken, they can foster society, even a way of life.

Hume's naturalistic approach to authority will, for some, still seem merely expedient, lacking normative (moral) force that rises above habit. The political realism articulated by Williams late in his life brings back moral arguments while discarding morality-first foundational approaches to political obligation. Since those in authority need, if only as a matter of prudence, to offer a justification for their claims to normative authority in order to avoid systemic resistance, legitimacy matters, providing glue in the face of adversity and a sense of responsibility not to undermine the whole show. Those justifications must make sense, fitting alongside opinions and values they do not displace (chapter 7). For any community, many will have roots in Humean norms and institutions, and so in its history.

Williams therefore helps us recognize that legitimacy is a (maybe the) defining feature of political relations.[58] While a political community's legitimation principles will be contingent, they will have deeper normative force to the extent that they survive ongoing, reflective debate: whether we think they provide an appropriate or decent standard for legitimacy in *our* political and material circumstances. They become values, not just tools. Hume's natural history of collective problem solving meets a people's reflective history of ideas and values.

We accordingly have an account of sustainable institutions in terms of *incentives-values compatibility*. At some level, institutions need to be self-enforcing,

56. Wittgenstein, *Philosophical Investigations*, sec. 115: "A picture held us captive. And we could not get outside it, for it lay in our language and language seemed to repeat it to us inexorably."

57. Hume, *Treatise*, bk. III, e.g., pp. 539–67.

58. Profoundly different from the crypto-fascist accounts of politics in terms of friends and enemies promulgated by Nazi apologist and abettor Carl Schmitt and inhaled by his twenty-first-century scholarly fans (see the next chapter).

so they must be legitimate as otherwise they would wilt under pressure. This is what constitutional norms, conventions, and other high-level institutions are for. They cannot lightly be undermined, whether by casual domestic innovations, or via international delegation, pooling, or subordination.

In ways explored later, this account pinpoints the potential tug-of-war between domestic legitimacy and legitimation for international institutions. Liberal societies—perennially exposed to being undone by navel gazing and, mislaying the republican part of their heritage, by a tendency to grow aristocracies of wealth or education—face this tension in terms of amplified domestic fractures, at times seeking remedies via a welfare safety net or redistribution at home and escape hatches abroad (chapter 3). The PRC, and some US conservatives, experience the tension in terms of compromised sovereignty.

History does not end. Our account of legitimation norms—their production, significance, and effects; whether thin, thick, or deep—does not preclude reform or evolution as a means to reconciliation. It is not history as destiny. A Humean vindicatory genealogy can be viewed as having staggered (notional) time periods: in the shorter run, the emergence via problem solving of conventions to aid collective action; over the medium run, some of those conventions and norms being internalized as values that guide and constrain conduct, projects, and so on; and over the longer run, those norms and values being tested, and maybe morphing, as quite new problems are encountered.[59] His metaconventions (chapter 6) exist—whether by evolution or incentive-compatible design—to enable change in institutions, including the highest-level ones. He is neither revolutionary nor conservative.

Living amid some of the eighteenth century's most vital flows, Hume saw that politics generates norm-challenging moments, but commercial society could lead to a less abrupt opening or broadening: a proposition expressly extended to relations among "several distinct societies."[60] This is captured in political theorist Anna Stilz's paraphrase:

> Artificial virtues come about not through the imposition of rules that refer to some exterior and universal standard of value, as natural law, or revealed

---

59. In contrast to Williams, Hume might have held that norms forged (and internalized) through trial and error take us toward the good or right in some teleological sense: see Sagar, "Minding the Gap." Russell, "Hume's Optimism and Williams' Pessimism," offers a different take. Chapter 20 returns to this.

60. Hume, *Enquiry*, III.21, p. 26.

religion. Since justice is the offspring of accumulated experience, it requires reference to history to understand it. But neither is justice static or particularist—it presupposes a certain degree of change which occurs through interaction with new and wider sets of communities. . . .

We become capable of impartiality not through renouncing our particular perspectives, but by marshalling the resources already contained within these perspectives to accommodate new and previously unconsidered people and situations. *We* create universality, not in abstraction from particularity, but through a broadening of it.[61]

Anticipating the note on which the book closes, we are offered an optimism rooted in the outward-looking perspective of commercial society (search for markets and trusty counterparts, fostering some limited mutual comprehension). But first, as Hume and Williams never overlooked, there must be order, a precondition for all else. For the first time in a very long while, liberal states need a framework for policy toward illiberal superpowers not sealed off in their own autarkic bloc. Armed with a politically realist account of legitimacy, the next chapter can now turn to that.

---

61. Stilz, "Hume, Modern Patriotism," pp. 22, 31. Perhaps the classic example in English history is the Elizabethan Thirty-Nine Articles of Anglican faith: the answer to whether they are Protestant or Catholic is, yes.

# 13

# Political Realism in International Relations

## ORDER VERSUS SYSTEM IN A WORLD OF CONCENTRIC LEGITIMATION CIRCLES

[Canning] thinks that all other States must protest against such an attempt to place them under subjection; . . . and that the people of this country may be taught to look with great jealousy for their liberties, if our Court [government] is engaged in meetings with great despotic monarchs, deliberating upon what degree of revolutionary spirit may endanger the public security, and therefore require the interference of the Alliance.

LETTER TO CASTLEREAGH ON THE
CONCERT OF EUROPE, 1818[1]

Constitutional liberty will be best worked out by those who aspire to freedom by their own efforts. You will only overload it by your help, by your principle of interference.

FORMER PRIME MINISTER ROBERT PEEL, OPPOSING
PALMERSTON'S POLICY, HOUSE OF COMMONS, 1850[2]

---

1. From Lord Bathurst, British secretary of state for war and the colonies while at the Alliance's Aix-la-Chappelle conference (D. Hurd and Young, *Choose Your Weapons*, p. 41). Castlereagh wrote to the prime minister that he was striving to get "legitime" and "constitutionelle" expunged from the communiqué (pp. 42–43).

2. D. Hurd and Young, *Choose Your Weapons*, p. 97. The debate was prompted by the Don Pacifico affair, when Britain sent gunboats into Piraeus Harbor as an act of reprisal after Greece deprived a British passport holder of legal rights. (The following day, Peel fell from his horse, passing away shortly afterward.) Similar sentiments were expressed a few years later by Mill, "A Few Words."

"Stability" has commonly resulted not from a quest for peace but from a generally accepted legitimacy ... [which] means no more than an international agreement about the nature of workable arrangements and about the permissible aims and methods of foreign policy. . . . An order whose structure is accepted by all major powers is "legitimate."

HENRY KISSINGER, *A WORLD RESTORED*, 1957[3]

FRESH FROM SETTLING the aftermath of the Napoleonic Wars, Castlereagh is being implored not to get into bed—regular, scheduled meetings of the Concert of Europe—with illiberal regimes, and to beware the dangers of hierarchy for those states outside the leadership group. The great statesman was not deterred from buttressing the balance of power with machinery, but the debate did not go away. A few decades later, former prime minister Peel is arguing, against future prime minister Palmerston, that it is a mistake to intervene in countries to promote liberalism, as it will have no roots unless they find their own way toward liberty. Fast-forward a couple of centuries, and it is easy to find analogues in post-1989 concerns about US hegemony, the roles of the G7 and the G20, maintaining order in a world of rising illiberal powers, and the stumbling "democratization" phase of US foreign policy. The periodic recurrence of such difficult choices in statecraft is instructive.

This is the first of two chapters applying our politically realist account of legitimacy to international relations and institutions, generating pragmatic principles for the participation of constitutional democracies in Order and System. It opens with what is, perhaps, the most notable recent account of how liberal states should approach international affairs—from the late twentieth century's most influential political philosopher, John Rawls. That will provide a foil for an alternative account that engages with the world's complexity, including great power rivalry, and existential threats. What emerges will not be one single, liberal international society but something more like a world of concentric and overlapping circles.

3. Kissinger, *World Restored*, pp. 1, 145.

# John Rawls's Principles for a Society of States

Toward the end of his career, Rawls articulated norms for relations between liberal peoples and illiberal but decent states, comprising what he called a Society of Peoples.[4] Roundly rejected by cosmopolitan theorists and campaigners for selling short important moral ideals, his account can also be examined from a realist perspective; not the power-is-all "realism" of some International Relations punditry but the richer political realism of David Hume and Bernard Williams. I argue that Rawls's principles are wanting in three respects: in not paying sufficient attention to the demands of Order, in not contemplating the necessity of some cooperation with states that lie beyond the pale (for Rawls, and perhaps for us), and in not confronting the need for different principles for different types of cooperation. Each is rooted in the variety of states and peoples occupying our shared planet.

## Rawls's Precis of Contemporary Liberal International Law

Rawls held that his purportedly utopian but realistic society of liberal and decent states would—meaning, in his Kantian hands, *should*—be guided by the following:

1. Peoples are free and independent, and their freedom and independence are to be respected by other peoples.
2. Peoples are to observe treaties and undertakings.
3. Peoples are equal and are parties to the agreements that bind them.
4. Peoples are to observe a duty of non-intervention [subject to (5) and (6)].
5. Peoples have the right of self-defense but no right to instigate war for reasons other than self-defense.
6. Peoples are to honor urgent human rights.[5]
7. Peoples are to observe certain specified restrictions in the conduct of war.

4. Rawls, *Law of Peoples*, which "proceeds from the international political world as we see it" (pp. 82–83). For followers' regret, see, e.g., Beitz, "Rawls's Law of Peoples."

5. Including "freedom from slavery and serfdom, liberty (but not equal liberty) of conscience, and security of ethnic groups from mass murder and genocide" (Rawls, *Law of Peoples*, p. 79). (Note: not including freedom of expression or association.)

8. Peoples have a duty to assist other peoples living under unfavorable conditions that prevent their having a just or decent political and social regime.[6]

These principles would, Rawls maintained, be rationally chosen by the representatives of liberal peoples in conclave behind a veil of ignorance (broadly, not knowing their particular circumstances). In fact, as he recognized, they are pretty much the state of international law and institutions as forged and developed since World War II by an international hierarchy led by Western states.[7] As such, they are principles that, as Williams would put it, might make sense for *us* now and around here—a liberal state's view of norms for international relations. Whether they do in fact make sense, however, turns partly on who is in and who out, on what it means to be on the outside, and (crucially) on whether they suffice for addressing the problems we currently or prospectively face (a Humean thought).

### Rawls's Criteria for Inclusion and Exclusion

Rawls approached exclusion from his society of states and peoples by setting principled tests for inclusion. A state neither liberal nor democratic could be admitted where, paraphrasing, (1) it does not attack or threaten us and (2) it does not abuse its citizen-subjects' human rights, permits them some degree of political free speech (enabling public consultation), and operates something like a system of generally applicable law supporting the common good.[8] Rawls maintained that, in contrast to "outlaw states" (below), we should tolerate such basically decent states, not force them toward liberalism or democracy, and be ready to cooperate with them.[9]

---

6. Rawls, *Law of Peoples*, p. 37. His "principles of justice among free and democratic peoples" are initially framed as a foreign policy for "a reasonably just liberal people" (p. 10) but are extended to "decent" peoples (pp. 68–69). While emphasizing "peoples," the principles are in fact for peoples organized into states: see Buchanan, "Rawls's Law of Peoples," p. 699.

7. The "original position" is not doing much work (and not only because, unless certain binding norms are already assumed, the pact might not be incentive compatible once peoples learn their endowments and circumstances). The same thought experiment two hundred years ago (Kant, "Perpetual Peace," in *Political Writings*) or in two hundred years' time would deliver different principles.

8. "Decent hierarchical peoples." Rawls, *Law of Peoples*, pp. 64–67, 71–72, 78–80.

9. Rawls, *Law of Peoples*, p. 59. Rawls divides states into five categories. The first and second, liberal and decent hierarchical, comprise "well-ordered peoples." The others are benevolent

While leaving a good deal hanging in the air—what counts as a threat, what suffices to comply with basic rights, what fields warrant cooperation, how far is delegating to international organizations OK, and so on—there is also the bigger question of how to approach states that are excluded (because they are not, in Rawls's terms, "well-ordered").

On states that are currently or prospectively threatening, or that systematically abuse their people, Rawls is clear. We should not extend toleration toward them. Instead, we should aim actively to bring them around to human rights and decency, using international institutions to do so; we should exclude them from various cooperative regimes; and we should be ready justly to intervene in some circumstances, their having forfeited traditional rights of self-defense. All this because "outlaw states are aggressive and dangerous; all peoples are safer and more secure if such states change, or are forced to change, their ways."[10]

But as guides for addressing our problems and pursuing our goals, Rawls's principles are too strict, and incomplete.

### *Membership: The Unrealism of Vanquishing "Nondecent" States*

It will help to bring back the categories Order, System, and Society. On Rawls's criteria, "outlaw states" plainly lie outside society, but can *we* sensibly exclude them from *all* cooperative regimes (from every corner of System), or from the conventions of war and peace (from Order)?[11] And what about states that do not threaten us and are not terrible abusers of human rights but do not permit free speech (say, on the ruling regime), or do not operate what we would recognize as a system of general law? These might be Rawls's "benevolent absolutisms," but he does not elaborate on whether we are ever allowed to cooperate with them.

---

absolutisms (not aggressive and honoring most human rights, but not "well-ordered"), burdened peoples (so poor and disorderly as to lack capabilities necessary to be any kind of effective state), and outlaw states (pp. 4, 63).

10. Rawls, *Law of Peoples*, pp. 80–81, 92–93.

11. Rawls seems to say (p. 92) that "outlaw" states are not entitled to rely on rights of self-defense, but what if they were invaded to grab territory or resources? (Conventions-cum-norms that might remain useful in relations with "outlaw" states are not nothing if Rawls's well-ordered states wish to live without disorder.)

It is immediately clear that a binary "in or out" is unsatisfactory for deciding which states can participate in specific international regimes. Their purpose and the nature of interdependence matter.

Topically, when it comes to the spread of deadly infectious diseases, eradication and containment need universal cooperation, however unstable or vile some states might be, as outcomes turn on the weakest link (chapter 5). When it comes to climate change, all the big pollution-generating economies need to be included, however offensive to our notions of basic decency their treatment of citizen-subjects or minorities, or, indeed, however much we might perceive them as a threat or strategic rival. Finally, we would need to be sure that peaceful coexistence with states outside Rawlsian society can be maintained only by a balance of force, without conventions and norms doing any work. In other words, Rawls's setup does not cater for a subcategory of "outlaw" states whose participation might be necessary for tackling some existential endeavors (possibly including peace), and more generally does not succeed in justifying cooperation being limited to the members of (in our terms) a thickish Society.

That is linked to what he says about respect among states: liberal states and peoples are to respect decent hierarchical states and peoples, since mutual respect aids their self-respect, which is good and useful, but impliedly not benevolent absolutisms or outlaw states.[12] But that elides the distinction between the two types of respect emphasized in chapter 10: respect as recognition and respect as admiration. It is not clear that we can always afford to withhold recognition-respect from states we happen not to esteem. There is complacency in a buried assumption that liberal democracies are secure in being able to choose our relations with the rest of the world, including helping some benighted states, just so long as we at least stick together in a Society of decent states. If only that were so.

## Do International Order and System Require Legitimacy in Themselves?

I am going to offer an alternative approach that, while not wholly at odds with Rawls's, starts in a different place: with questions of peaceful coexistence. I ask whether there is an international version of the First Political Question (of

12. Rawls, *Law of Peoples*, pp. 35, 45, 61–62.

basic order), and then whether this beckons an international equivalent of the Basic Legitimation Demand.

## The First International Political Question

The First Political Question needs unpacking to see whether each of its elements makes sense in an international setting and, separately, whether they are all necessary to what we might term the First *International* Political Question. As articulated by Williams, those elements are order, protection, safety, trust, and conditions for cooperation.

As to whether each can make sense in international terms, order (as a state of affairs) obviously does. It equates to peace prevailing across much of the world: no wars among powers, and external (including border) stability for most states, so that the world is not full of chaos and fear. Continuing by analogy with the domestic case:

- "Protection" would mean that some states protect others against invasions, peoples living in weak states from external hostility, and perhaps even peoples living under oppressive government from their own state. Absent strict isolationism, this would also include conventions-cum-norms among states around the safety of travelers in foreign lands (the doctrine of a "minimum standard of protection" for diplomats, merchants, investments, and so on described in part I).
- What counts as "safety" depends, I suggest, on what people think it is reasonable to expect or demand, but today might mean something like ensuring that peoples are not unduly exposed to lethal and highly contagious pathogens or environmental toxins flowing from other states and regions, or to severe degradation in the fabric of the earth on which all rely for life itself.
- "Trust" would make sense even if limited to only those things integral to maintaining order, protection, and safety. This would cover not perceiving other states and peoples as threatening; a social norm of good faith around any (formal) promises (trustworthiness); and means for resolving disputes affecting order, safety, and protection that were accepted by states as fair and de facto final (which, by analogy, is provided domestically by state-administered private law). The last of those works to separate disagreement from hostile conflict.

- Finally, "conditions of cooperation" make sense in an international setting because trustworthiness (over some domain of interactions) can itself facilitate cooperation, and because decentralized means for enforcing promises might support conventions around order, safety, and protection. Most obviously, conditions of cooperation would be needed to equip groups of states collectively to face up to hostile parties outside their Order: rampant piracy in the eighteenth and early nineteenth centuries, and today order-threatening organized crime (real-world versions of SPECTRE in the Bond movies).

Even though each of order, protection, safety, trust, and conditions for coop-eration makes sense in an international setting, it does not follow that they are all always *necessary* to answer the First International Political Question. Up to a point, that will vary across states.

All states and their peoples need order (peace), existential safety, and some trust (e.g., in promises not to attack some others) in order to enjoy the fruits of their *domestic* cooperative endeavors. Protection is more complicated. On the one hand, small states need it for external security but great powers do not. While it might serve a power's interests selectively to protect some smaller states to help maintain a balance of power with peers, it is not imperative for them in the way that some minimum level of protection is necessary for all individual citizen-subjects to live without fear within a state, as Rousseau shrewdly ob-served (chapter 7). On the other hand, absent strict autarky, all states benefit from norms of protection for their citizen-subjects abroad. So pretty much all states want protection for their people if not for themselves.

The necessity of conditions for cooperation is even more nuanced. Absent existential threats to safety that states cannot address alone, conditions for cooperation among states need to extend beyond the elementary only if states seek to cooperate in order to widen their peoples' possibilities: in Rous-seau's terms, to hunt stags together rather than hares alone (chapter 5). Whereas domestically the state providing order, protection, and so on simply *is* also the enabler of local cooperation (government), securing order among states does not of itself deliver machinery—organizational capability—for more ambitious international endeavors.

Having said that, order and protection (for smaller states) are both linked with trust and conditions for cooperation in important ways. If leading states (selectively) protect weaker states, they would rationally wish to make their protection predictable in order to deter other powers from opportunistic predation. But that means avoiding the risk of themselves sending hostile signals to peers when intervening to protect a weaker state from a middling power. They need, therefore, to coalesce around some conventions for any balance of power—for example, around no-fly zones, nonproliferation, and, even more basically, territorial borders. Even an isolationist state needs others to know and respect its boundaries.

Stepping back, a basic international Order plainly incorporates conventions and norms. They include conventions for what is a state (or, more generally, for the units of international politics), for what counts as its territory, for mutual recognition, and also, therefore, norms around keeping promises and around the treatment of different kinds of travelers (emissaries, merchants, pleasure-seekers, and so on). In its (Humean) orientation toward problem solving—most elementally, the problem of peaceful and tolerable coexistence—this is the origin and core of international law.[13] All this is familiar from parts II and III.

It becomes clear, though, that the necessary conditions for Order provide the most elementary conditions for cooperation irrespective of whether states and peoples do in fact seek to cooperate. And if there are shared existential threats, they might change their minds. Order prevails at the threshold of System (however thin it turns out to be).

### An International Basic Legitimation Demand: Order

This brings us to legitimacy. If, whether via a spontaneous Order alone or in tandem with some element of designed System, a plurality of states does seek to resolve the First International Political Question, the next question is whether a basic legitimation demand arises here too. Expanding on the previous chapter, in the most elemental sense it obviously does because order, safety, and so on among states might be achieved only with excessive coercion or oppression, so that (analogously with the domestic case) the purported institutional answer to the First International Political Question becomes part of the problem. A *legitimate* Order places international relations within the realm of a politics of recognized authorities rather than excessive coercion, domination,

---

13. Hume lists some (then) provisions of customary law: "the sacredness of the person of ambassadors, the declaration of war, the abstaining from poison'd arms, with other duties of the kind, which are evidently calculated for the commerce, that is peculiar to different societies" (*Treatise*, III.ii.xi, p. 567).

and fear, creating and framing conditions for degrees of cooperation. As Williams says, "The situation of one lot of people terrorizing another lot of people is not per se a political situation: it is, rather, the situation which the existence of the political is in the first place supposed to alleviate (replace)."[14]

Where they exist, essentially political relations among states are plainly different from those within them. There is no analogous formalized normative hierarchy putting those at the pinnacle of power in a position to seek legitimation by justifying the system (and, within it, their powers) to global subject-citizens. But, as the previous chapter discussed, the possibility of resistance to international authority exists, and so legitimacy makes sense conceived as acquiescence in a distribution of international (and transnational) power and authority, characterized partly by the political relations of diplomacy rather than solely by the power relations of war, coercion, and fear. Likewise, legitimation continues, conceived as those exercising international power seeking to justify themselves to themselves, sometimes to each other, and to multiple affected communities, including at home. Conventions and norms for relations among states need to make sense to leaders, and to be capable of making sense—when justified—to their domestic citizen-subjects.

English School accounts typically frame such conventions-cum-norms as criteria for membership of international society (excluding, for example, real-world Bond villains), and for proper conduct within Society.[15] Taken straight, that risks obscuring the possibility of gradations of participatory cooperation—of thin, thick, and even deep Society, in various degrees—as chapter 7's distinction between Order and System helps highlight.

14. Williams, "Realism and Moralism in Political Theory," in *In the Beginning*, p. 5; and also "slavery . . . is a form of internalized warfare" (p. 5). The political, then, is defined by where legitimacy, rather than excessive coercion or domination, creates and frames conditions for cooperation. This is not only a world away from Carl Schmitt's "friends v. enemies" (previous chapter), it is also quite different from Hans Morgenthau's early (1933) characterization of politics. After attacking Schmitt (good), he lands on the idea that politics concerns "the will to power," which rather saps one's will to live—except as a chilling window into the appalling world the young Morgenthau was struggling to comprehend, and thankfully escaped (Morgenthau, *Concept of the Political*, pp. 96, 118–20). Neither Schmitt nor, sadly, Morgenthau nails tyrannical or totalitarian governance as the perversion of politics. Sweeping aside or subverting the legitimate rules of the game (and background norms) for politics is the triumph of power over politics. (Hall, "Bernard Williams," pp. 477–78.)

15. I. Clark, *Legitimacy in International Society*, pp. 12–30. While mid-twentieth-century "classical realists" (Raymond Aron, E. H. Carr, Morgenthau, Kissinger) addressed legitimacy, later International Relations realists lost interest.

For basic order itself, one key test is whether the great powers (if plural) of the day accept the modalities of the prevailing Order, including mechanisms for containing the escalation of disagreements, since otherwise order persists under siege, on the brink of hostilities.[16] This is the legitimacy of the eighteenth-century balance of power, the Concert of Europe, and the Cold War's period of détente. As underlined by the quote at the chapter head, it is the legitimacy that preoccupied Henry Kissinger as scholar and policymaker. Picking up chapter 7's potential Giant Knaves, it is not clear this condition holds today. In different ways and perhaps degrees, Beijing and Moscow want to return to spheres of influence: a road to *New Cold War*.

A second test is whether other states find the Order oppressive compared with realistically available alternatives. If destabilizing or passive resistance is to be avoided, the leading states need to be able to justify to other states the extent and modalities of any coercion they use to maintain order between and among states, and any arrangements for protection and safety.[17]

For that second test to be adequately met, an Order's modalities cannot leave some states dominating many others, or actively deprive normal states and peoples from being partial commanders of their own destiny. While that does not preclude consensual defense pacts that create hierarchical, quasi-contractual security relationships (chapter 8), it might limit the way that the Order is enforced. For example, there could not be a free-for-all in using geo-economic instruments against states that had merely irritated or inconvenienced a power (a fraught issue picked up below).

While those thoughts are about the legitimacy of security relations among states, an international Order also gives us reason to care about legitimacy *in* other states, especially those that are crucial to maintaining order (and conditions of cooperation, etc.). For starters, powers will be interested in each

16. Broadly, that is analogous to the legitimacy demands facing the collective leadership of a local oligarchic Order, whether a hereditary aristocracy, or a single-party state where the party's leadership group must rule in equilibrium with each other and their various factions (see previous chapter).

17. This bears on debates about whether legitimation norms are held and operate at the level of individual people, state-societies, or the international order-system-society. Waltz (*Theory of International Politics*, pp. 62–63) observed that Morgenthau and Kissinger located the shared norms at the level of states, so they could not stem from the balance of power, a system-level phenomenon (I. Clark, *Legitimacy in International Society*, pp. 167–69). This is slightly mad: only people hold opinions, but sometimes they hold those opinions due to material circumstances and the company they must keep.

other's stability, since internal instability in any of them could spill over into the international arena; this was part of Edmund Burke's concern about revolutionary France. Similarly, under a legitimate hegemonic Order, states will sensibly care about stability *within* the hegemon, and in those allied second-tier states vital to its role. Today, this gives us reason not to dismiss America's social tensions as their problem (and, from the past, shines unflattering light on US treasury secretary John Connally's comments quoted in chapter 1). Rather, since those dislocations affect where the burdens of international leadership—on the public finances, military recruitment, and so on—would become too much, they concern anyone who regards the prevailing Order-System as legitimate (bearing in mind plausible alternatives).

But concern for order elsewhere is not confined to the powers being orderly. There is a basic-order interest in other states' treatment of their citizen-subjects not being so grim as to trigger disorderly flows of escapee-migrants that would overwhelm the capacity, and hence potentially the local legitimacy, of destination and transit states. Thus, something like Responsibility to Protect (R2P)—its first two pillars (chapter 3)—can be cast as an equilibrium responsibility of states to each other, emerging not from moral duties but, functionally, from the utility of states not being so badly or oppressively governed as to damage other states and peoples.

Given that mass migration—whether spontaneous or weaponized—might prove the greatest source of twenty-first-century disorder, this responsibility is no small matter, and bridges to System. Where an oppressive or incapable state does not meet its responsibility for answering the First Political Question legitimately, a policy of turning away distressed migrants can be sustained—without second-round destabilizing and delegitimizing horrors—only if they have somewhere else stable and decent to reside. That creates a collective-action problem that, quite apart from moral issues, spurs attempts to agree to accords-cum-norms on refugees (as in 1951: see chapter 3).[18]

### An International Basic Legitimation Demand: System

A shift in degree, perhaps in kind, occurs when we turn to the legitimacy conditions for designed cooperative policy regimes. As a rule, legitimation principles are likely to be more demanding, the more ambitious the System's purposes, the more it incorporates pooling and delegation in international

18. Kumm, "Sovereignty and the Right to Be Left Alone," pp. 250–51, makes a similar point.

organizations, and the more some regimes reach "beyond the border" into the domestic rights and obligations of states' citizen-subjects. The greater the scope for disagreement, the broader the need for mechanisms avoiding hostile escalation. In the language of the Basic Legitimation Demand, there is more to be justified because there are more claims to normative authority needing presumptive acceptance or toleration.[19]

Issues of membership and conduct still arise, but now with richer and subtler inflections, not least because although some regimes will clearly have leadership groups, the composition of such groups might vary somewhat across policy fields, while collectively forming some kind of informal top table (chapter 8). Some principles will be relevant for only leading states, some for everyone else, and others for all, big or small. In contrast to the previous chapter's state-solipsistic approach, the orientation here is to System-level legitimation posing a special kind of collective-action problem.

Starting with a general consideration, it is hard to see how specific regimes or System as a whole could be accepted if, as a rule, they preclude states from choosing to cooperate more deeply with a selection of others. This follows from the value of sovereignty conceived as constitutional independence (chapter 11), which entails that, subject to constraints of orderliness, collective existential safety, and the most basic decency (below), states view each other as free to decide where, how, and how far to constrain themselves. This seemingly innocuous proposition has bite, including for international trade (chapters 17 and 18).

Second, leading states will need assurance that each can live with the regimes that make up the System. This means accepting the terms of various formalized hierarchies (at the IMF, the World Bank, Basel, etc.), which is plainly a major issue today in monetary affairs given the way the dollar's role underpins Washington's wider leadership (chapters 15 and 16). Similarly, the Powers need to be confident each will accept the authority of various dispute-resolution mechanisms, since they are central to maintaining political rather than conflictual relations. A trade war conducted outside WTO structures

19. This might help cut through important differences between Aron (arguing that the conditions for coexistence included shared culture and values) and Kissinger (holding that consensus among the powers' leaders was sufficient): see I. Clark, *Legitimacy in International Society*, pp. 16–17. For thin System merely supporting a basic Order, Kissinger seems right, but the more states and peoples extend the scope and ambition of cooperation, the more Society needs to thicken, as per Aron.

walks away from politics, unless there is a route to a diplomatic table (chapters 17 and 18). And they need to acquiesce in the multitude of regimes taken as a whole, and in the composition and modalities of any de facto oversight groupings (G7, G20, and so on).

Third, for states outside regime-leadership groups to regard any Order-cum-System as legitimate, they will need to regard its more powerful leaders as sufficiently benign, limited, or accountable in the eyes of (enough of) the rest of the world. This is chapter 8's *constrained* leadership of institutionalized hierarchy recast as a condition for legitimacy rather than, merely, expedience. It draws on the West's republican traditions of checking domination.[20]

Those traditions bear on substance as well as process. Alongside, obviously, the direct outcomes of specific regimes (trade, parts of the law of the sea, and so on), enough nonleading states need to consider the overall System's diffuse effects on the way the world works tolerable compared with feasible alternatives. They will not be tolerable if, reprising the previous chapter, they undermine the local order. I shall call such System spillovers "basic-order externalities" since they are felt by any states not represented in the groups that design and operate the System's core regimes. Where such spillovers are widespread, they will (rationally) bother leading states to the extent they threaten to undermine the legitimacy of the System as a whole, or even the wider basic Order on which it relies. These are all legitimacy externalities or, as I shall term them, adverse *legitimacy spillovers*.[21]

## System Unpopularity versus Illegitimacy: A Liberal Background Norm

The hazard of basic-order externalities is not coterminous with some states or peoples intensely disliking the outcomes or modalities of an Order-System. Such dislike can stem from the unplanned actions of millions of individuals, from the intentional actions of states, or, somewhat differently perhaps, the design and operation of regimes themselves.

20. Deudney, *Bounding Power*: "Three of the most powerful ideas in contemporary international Liberalism, democratic peace, commercial peace, and international unions, are the legacies of Enlightenment republican security theory" (p. 269).

21. On the distinct but related idea of justice externalities, see Kumm, "Sovereignty and the Right" (starting from moral imperatives given by reason).

The simplest examples are new, more efficient production techniques being adopted abroad but not at home, with cheaper imports knocking out local suppliers. At the international level, these are good luck/bad luck spillovers.[22] Local adjustment (including mitigating hardship) is left to individual states, with a collective safety net (via the IMF and Paris Club) for economies tipped into default (a much higher threshold than for the help provided to citizens by domestic welfare states).

International intentionality enters, by contrast, in the example of most of the world, including most of the rich West, suffering serious economic harms, knocking onto domestic politics, from the Organization of Petroleum Exporting Countries' oil price hikes during the 1970s. In that case, adjustment in rich states was left to them, with banking rescues domestically and drawn-out sovereign rescues internationally. Where a global shock hurts the poorest states, discretionary aid is sometimes provided (by development banks and bilaterally). It is not scripted in the manner of domestic automatic fiscal stabilizers, although there are legitimacy arguments for moving to such a regime (provided it could be made incentive compatible for donors).

Those diverse kinds of examples are sometimes distinguished from the rules of the game themselves stacking the cards against some states and peoples. Whereas domestically the "basic structure" is over time sensitive, in democracies, to free and fair elections, that is not so internationally. There, the basic structure is in some sense organic, partly reflecting choices (including abstention) over time by individual powers: System initially follows the terms of Order (chapter 7). A big question is where and how far this is domination, robbing System of widespread legitimacy.

Say large states A and B (imagine the United States and EU members) decide to adopt low-tariff trade and liberalized capital flows. Must state C follow suit? No, not *must*, even though it might be difficult to avoid if A and B's pact diverts trade and investment away from it: C's feasible policy space has shifted.[23] It is hard to argue, however, that in consequence A and B should not be free to enter into their bilateral scheme. Instead, other things being equal

---

22. This is akin to economists' pecuniary externalities, working through the price system, such as when a surge in demand for oranges relative to apples is bad for the incomes of specialist apple growers and merchants. (In welfare terms, the costs and benefits of pecuniary externalities cancel out under complete markets—meaning no resource misallocation via the price system—but not otherwise, in the real world.)

23. Palley, "Fallacy of the Globalization Trilemma."

(no threats to order), C needs to be given options, including joining the regime lock, stock, and barrel now; joining later; or alternatively entering into parts of the regime so long as that does not undermine A and B's project.

There is a background norm of liberalism at work here, entailing a principle that multilateral regimes should leave states with a menu of realistic choices. In aspiration, it is freedom for A and B without domination of C. A socialist state is not dominated simply because much of the rest of the world wishes to adopt market-based international production and exchange.[24] It might be dominated if, even though nonaggressive, it were presented with a take-it-or-leave-it option, if it were subjected to extra barriers to trade because of its political ideology, or if it were starved of some essential materials.

The purpose of that story was to draw attention to the background norm: a kind of constrained liberalism for a world of constitutionally independent (sovereign) states.

### Where System Meets Order: Legitimacy and Production Technology for Vital Global Public Goods

More awkwardly, nondomination needs to be reconciled, somehow, with overcoming hold-up problems in collectively curing global public harms. The nature and degree of the legitimation challenge will vary with the relevant public goods' production technology—whether single shot, weakest link, or aggregate (chapters 5 and 11)—and, crucially, with the severity of the prospective harm.[25]

Starting with the production side, for weakest-link technology, if the recalcitrant happen to be weaker states, the powers need to find modes of persuasion, assistance, and coercion that can be justified to other states in general. Where assistance (funding, with some know-how) would suffice, the problem flips to

24. Laborde, "Republicanism and Global Justice," argues this kind of setup amounts to systematic or structural domination, and as such is illegitimate. But symmetrically, would there be domination if, instead, the world comprised largely (internally legitimate) socialist states, which steered the allocation of resources internationally and in consequence constrained the choices and policy space of a couple of (internally legitimate and law-abiding) medium-size states that held out for, and between themselves practiced, market-based liberalism? It plainly would be domination if the socialist states withheld essential resources from the liberal states or declined to trade on any terms.

25. Articulated (without the Order/System distinction) in Bodansky, "What's in a Concept?"

one of inaction among the rich and powerful because they lack a preagreed, incentive-compatible way of sharing the burden. Development banks, with constrained delegation to management, might offer an institutional solution given that most can borrow cheaply, reducing the upfront costs.[26]

The same kinds of considerations apply to aggregate-technology public goods where delivery is blocked by states whose contribution is essential but that are not integral to maintaining international peace and order (they are not powers). If they are capable but unwilling, coercion or inducement (including the incidence and any sharing of costs) must be legitimated.

As flagged in our discussion of sovereignty, things are more complicated where a holdout state is a power, since coercive peer pressure might then jeopardize the terms of Order itself. It might be possible to shift incentives by embedding, say, the climate-change collective-action problem within the regime for trade, with tariffs taxing inaction on the environment.[27] But the trade "game" is, in turn, embedded in the still-higher-level game of order and peaceful coexistence: Would tariffs trigger hostilities?

The first political questions, domestic and international, help make sense of this tension, introduced in chapter 11, between sovereign consent and global public goods. Contrary to arguments for state consent based on the doubly flawed analogy with individuals entering into a domestic social contract, it is better to think in terms of norms—of a responsibility not to bring the ceiling down and so on—associated with states acquiescing in a particular international Order being a tolerable answer to the First International Political Question, and consenting up front to specific regimes under that Order's umbrella, *given* the conditions of how each has answered (if they have) the first domestic political question. If a state withholds consent from some international measure, that might sometimes be because it believes the measure would jeopardize domestic order. If that could simply be brushed aside, other states would in effect be passing judgment on the value of the state's domestic order and stability. So a veto or opt-out norm *of some kind* seems, in general, to fit with states being the vehicle via which order, safety, protection, and so on are, as a matter of fact, maintained in territories around the world.

But that line of argument falters when confronted by the distinction between, at one end of the spectrum, nice-to-have global public goods and, at

26. As proposed by Okonjo-Iweala et al., *Global Deal.*
27. Nordhaus, "Climate Clubs."

the other, common "existential" threats that can be overcome only through some type of cooperation. Truly existential harms implicate the First International Political Question: the peace in peaceful coexistence presumes existence.

Setting aside sincere disagreements about the gravity of a threat, this marks a profound shift in the analysis of the relationship between Order and System. While Order can mostly be thought of as creating conditions for interstate cooperation, some kinds of existential hazard, possibly climate change, make a cooperative regime necessary. Truly existential global harms press the utility of System with even the thinnest possible Society (Rawls's framework made no room for that).

The crunch comes where, given stubborn holdouts, individual powers perceive themselves as faced with a horrendous choice (for them): of whether to act alone (possibly with friends and allies) to save the world but at the cost of falling behind in the economic race to maintain or achieve military parity or supremacy.

Consistent with this book's underlying theme, pulling a deontological precept off some high shelf—by asserting a holdout power simply *must*, morally, play its part—is not always going to help. This is the essence of the Western-Chinese dynamic around climate change. Instead, resolution is likely to come down to Humean norm formation via the opinions of people scattered across the world: whether the stigma of holding out has tangible costs quickly enough to dominate its benefits.

It is hardly sensible, however, to appeal to "world opinion" in terms of international System itself. It seems uncontroversial to say that most individuals in most states feel little or no Humean allegiance to international institutions or the international community; few would feel duty bound to respond to a call to arms from an international authority, meaning there is no such authority. In the phrase of British television series asking, "what the Romans [or Victorians] did for us," few people would have a sense of international System doing anything for them, however much it might actually do. Nor is there an international civil society corresponding to the domestic civil society of liberal states.[28] Instead, any pressure from world opinion will be issue specific. Hence Greta Thunberg: celebrity operates as a kind of focal point.

---

28. Christiano, "Democratic Legitimacy and International Institutions." Compared with domestic counterparts, international nongovernmental organizations are freer to roam beyond public opinion.

## Order-System without a Demos: From Tug-of-War to Relegitimation Moments

While leaders of international organizations can and do engage in legitimacy promotion, the legitimating community is not, then, some global demos. This has all sorts of consequences. In the absence of deepish Society, it is unlikely states and peoples will cooperate on projects of designed distributive justice (mandated net resource transfers among states).

While leaving a System unattractive in some eyes, that does not render it illegitimate. Though thin international Society lacks a shared conception of justice beyond complying with basic property rights (in treaties and so on), that does not prevent rich states acting alone or together, and some come under domestic pressure to do so. They might, for example, contingently forgive debt or, more systematically, contribute to development projects and programs—as, indeed, they do via various competing development banks (chapter 15).

Separately, given the legitimating community is largely the population of states themselves, legitimation operates at two intermingled levels: the high officials of the state, in their stewardship of relations with the rest of the world; and the people of each state insofar as they observe and respond to effects of international cooperation on their lives, on the state that protects them, and on any cosmopolitan things some of them care about.

Among the first, international legal and policy professionals within the state are plainly important. Caring about their reputation among their foreign peers would create something like a thick transnational community of specialists within the realm of international affairs.[29] But they also need to carry their domestic colleagues, some of whom (politicians) are sensitive to the eddies of domestic opinion (and legitimacy). This can set up the normative tug-of-war with which chapter 11 concluded: What happens if there is a conflict between norms operating among states and norms underpinning or framing the relationship between a state's system of government and its people? As Hume pointed out, domestic ties are typically more binding, since people can hardly subsist day-to-day without a structure of local authority, whereas states themselves are closer to being able to do so without international cooperation.[30] Hence, in a different manifestation of the Giant Knave problem, we see Washington, faced

---

29. A professional caste's internalization of international law's values is the explanation for compliance advanced in Yale scholar and former US State Department counsel Harold Koh's "Transnational Legal Process."

30. Hume, *Treatise*, III.ii.xi, p. 569.

with internal threats to domestic tranquility, sporadically thrashing out at elements of a System it largely created, in the process jeopardizing the international leadership on which some of its domestic prosperity depends.

That legitimacy tug-of-war favors domestic forces until states realize they cannot comfortably subsist in international disorder. After wars, states' leaders and their peoples become acutely conscious of the costs of enmity, the value of peace, and the utility of institutions that help preserve order. It is no wonder that the great international institution-building moments have followed wars: Westphalia, Utrecht, Vienna, Versailles (abject failure), and above all World War II (chapters 2, 3, and 8). At some such moments, legitimation principles for participation and conduct get reshaped, or reinforced, by the victorious coalition and their allies.[31]

Indeed, the most significant struggles and wars are in a sense about the legitimation principles bearing on basic order: as in early modern Europe's confessional struggles, in the wars with absolutist and then revolutionary France, in the modern Cold War, and also in the civil wars of England, the United States, and China. Such historical shifts are in effect *relegitimation moments*, when things need recodifying to establish new focal points for maintaining order, conditions of cooperation, and so on.

Such new legitimations have to include those losers that are not vanquished, as otherwise dissatisfied elements will resist (Versailles's failure).[32] Where reincorporated into an international hierarchy's leadership group (France after 1815, Germany and Japan after 1945), they become, in effect, renaissance states.

Before any such hostilities and consequent Order-System reconfiguration, the more a *Lingering Status Quo* is taken for granted, the less likely it is to prevail. As time passes, memories of order's contingencies fade, leaving incumbent leading states liable to make unforced strategic errors, and frustrated rising states to bide their time.

### When Other States Have Other Values: Legitimacy with Civilizational Competition?

In thinking about legitimation principles for System, then, we cannot duck the possibility—the reality—of other states holding to values and institutions that offend our notions of what is right and decent, and which might or might not

---

31. I. Clark, *Legitimacy in International Society*, p. 13; Ikenberry, *After Victory*.

32. Applied to international relations, this follows from the general approach of Myerson, "Fundamental Theory of Institutions."

represent a threat to us. In his neo-republican variant of a "law of peoples" centered on freedom as nondomination, the political philosopher Philip Pettit suggests that

> International order [meaning order-with-system in our terms] *will be legitimate* in so far as two conditions are fulfilled: it is designed to maximize the number of peoples who live under domestically legitimate governments; and it conducts the business of protecting legitimate states against domination, and securing other collective benefits, in a manner that gives *legitimate* states equal and effective control over how it operates.[33]

Mostly, that seems broadly correct but, as my italicized words signal, legitimate in whose eyes? Pettit means under republican principles. By contrast, the previous chapter argued that if we accept the historical contingency of our own liberalism (with its republican features), then we should recognize that other peoples and states have traveled down different paths to their own systems of legitimate authority—if legitimate they are under their own local principles and traditions. It is a line of thinking that can seem to slide into nihilistic relativism, maybe serving only the interests of commerce.

But that would be mistaken because even if we accept that another state is legitimate to itself, we have to decide whether (or in what fields) it is legitimate for us, now and around here, to treat with it. As Williams observed in a discussion of toleration,

> The distinction between the use of power which can reasonably claim authority, and the arbitrary use of power, tyranny or mere terror, applies for instance to historical formations, such as medieval kingdoms, whose claims and practices could not be acceptable to us. *When those other states exist now, in our world, of course other questions arise, of our moral and political relations to illiberal regimes.*[34]

That is to say, in contrast with the distant past of our own or other societies, we cannot duck choosing what kind of relationship to have with other, very different states: absent a stable *New Cold War* autarky so ingrained it leaves everyone securely safe, we cannot afford to indulge in what he called the "relativism of

---

33. Pettit, "Legitimate International Institutions," p. 155 (my emphases). (His "Republican Law of Peoples" classifies states, in a two-by-two matrix, into effective/ineffective and representative/nonrepresentative.)

34. Williams, "Toleration," in *In the Beginning*, p. 135 (my emphasis).

distance."[35] This means deciding how far in our international relations we can, as a matter of politics, tolerate (in the minimal sense of go along with) states that are illiberal, undemocratic, authoritarian, tyrannous, and so on. Commitment to the legitimacy of local legitimation does not bind our hands.

### The Basic Legitimation Demand without a Relativism of Distance: The Liberalism of Fear

We can find a way through by returning to Rawls's two-pronged test for outright exclusion (threatening to us and tyrannizing its own people), but now in the light of political realism's Basic Legitimation Demand. Systematic violations of basic human rights plainly signify excessive coercion, with the offending state having become part of the problem rather than the solution to maintaining order.[36] Rather than departing from the significance of local legitimation in evaluating the sustainability of order in other states, this is saying that it is hard to see how we could sincerely hold the view that a state produced order without excessive force in the view of a local legitimation community if they (or people they care about or just know about) were routinely exposed to torture, random arrest, political trials without an opportunity to make one's case, and such like.

In the background here is the importance of *living without fear*. If people, or parts of a people, live in fear because of state actions (or deliberate inaction, or menacing threats), then their state is, on the face of it, part of the problem. This makes it easier to see that in the real world of responsible political judgment and action, Rawls's two tests for exclusion from his international society can be linked. Namely, where a state is feared by its subjects because it routinely or systematically violates their most basic rights, would it not be prudent to adopt a default assumption that it would have even less respect for the citizen-subjects and peoples of other states? Put more simply, if a state attacks (some of) its own subjects, why wouldn't it attack us if it thought it could prevail (or at least get away with it)? As post–World War II US "realist"

---

35. Williams, *Ethics and the Limits*, chap. 9, esp. pp. 178–80.

36. Williams, "Human Rights and Relativism," in *In the Beginning*, p. 63. For legitimation judgments, the violated "rights" here could be, in the opinion of people, moral (e.g., natural) rights, without having to be inscribed in law; we can just be horrified by their violation, and make prudential calculations. But to take that into international relations in a systematic way, they have to be reflected in positive rights of some kind (below).

George Kennan put it in a discussion of what could reasonably be demanded of the Soviet Union, "Excess of internal authority leads inevitably to unsocial and aggressive conduct as a government among governments, and is a matter of concern to the international community."[37]

Perhaps, on examining specific cases, a prudent statesperson would conclude that, on more than a balance of probabilities, a particular state would not attack or threaten us given the circumstances (say, relative material power). But that would be a contingent judgment on the state's orientation and capabilities, rather than a general argument against prudence. In other words, we should be wary, for our own sake, of very powerful states that, by our lights, oppress or abuse their people or some of their people.

Those judgments do have to be about and for the present. That state (and people) X used to do really bad things need not of itself affect our relations with that state today. We need to make judgments about the past only insofar as they materially affect the present (through institutions, norms, values, embedded habits, and so on). Thus, in assessing, say, Russia's or the PRC's treatment of its subjects, it is no good simply looking back to the Gulag, the mass starvation of Mao's Great Leap Forward, or the randomized tyranny of his Cultural Revolution, just as we would maintain it is not relevant to look back to Britain's 1819 Peterloo Massacre. Instead, we have to make judgments about whether those histories still shape the boundaries of their states' conduct and so are relevant to us, today.[38] In that spirit, we surely worry (for ourselves) about recent executions on British soil, the Ukrainian invasion, turmoil in other border states, Tiananmen, political censorship, large-scale internment, disapperances, and so on.

So even though some states might now reject the universalism of human rights on the grounds—not completely solid (chapter 3)—that they were codified under liberal Western hegemony, those norms can still be viewed as having made clear, to ourselves as well as to others, the basis on which we believe international relations should proceed—at least *with us*.

To be usable systematically rather than episodically, the relevant tests must be positive rights; natural rights or moral precepts alone cannot suffice since,

---

37. Kennan, "America and the Russian Future" pp. 358–59. ("Inevitably" is too strong.)

38. To be clear, the past sometimes embeds norms and conduct that are shocking today. E.g., the nineteenth- and twentieth-century US institutions of slavery and segregation pose the question of whether their dismal domestic legacy materially affects current US attitudes to relations with other peoples.

on this earth, they are talk, however important that talk, and we cannot be confident different states and peoples mean the same things when they talk. Moreover, they need to be positive rights enjoying wide-based support among the peoples of, at least, constitutional democracies (so that they enjoy broad-based legitimacy in those states and communities). As positive rights, crucially, they come bundled together with adjudicatory machinery, which brings us back to the political nature of human rights. Not only do basic rights have the purpose of checking and guiding political power, but also their effectiveness depends on the authority of the courts, commissions, or whatever that pass judgment on states (or their officers). In other words, since the adjudicators must exercise political judgment, the machinery for policing legitimacy must itself be legitimate (among and beyond constitutional democracies).[39]

Such political realism about rights as minimal considerations bearing on the membership of international society might be thought somewhat undermined by the capaciousness of the catalog of positive rights that has gathered in international legal documents and doctrine. The question of whether we should treat a state differently because, say, it does not provide for education to children over a certain age (just that raw fact) is distinct—or so I want to argue—from whether we should treat it differently because, say, it routinely conducts random arrests and torture, or pursues genocide against minorities, or other horrors.

I mean *basic* human rights found, as a matter of institutionalized practice, in international law's list of *jus cogens* norms (chapter 3). They are by no means the same as a set of liberal values, but they have emerged (in a Humean way) as the world confronted big practical questions, not least at and after Nuremburg, about which, if any, norms should prevail universally without let-outs.[40]

Respect for those norms is, I am suggesting, a minimum necessary consideration bearing on cooperation in nonexistential endeavors, because they concern whether we can bring ourselves to accept that some other, nonliberal state can meet the Basic Legitimation Demand on its own terms, and also (less conclusively) whether we should fear it.[41]

---

39. For a discussion of Williams on this, see Hall and Tsarapatsanis, "Human Rights."

40. The Humean story is that we have come to react with abject horror to such atrocities (aided by things bringing them closer: eyewitness accounts, photographs, newsreels, art), and that those sentiments are reinforced by reflection, partly through recognizing that fear of recurrence obstructs basic trust and cooperation; we find a functional purpose—pre-conditions for living together—in our horror.

41. The landing place is not dissimilar to that of Buchanan, *Justice, Legitimacy, and Self-Determination*, p. 267, but he offers a universal moral conclusion given a Natural Duty of Justice,

Such minimal considerations hardly exhaust the preconditions for ventures with other states. We might want, for example, to set somewhat more demanding tests for cooperating on certain things with law-abiding, illiberal states; and still higher thresholds, reflecting liberal and possibly also democratic values, for certain deeper kinds of cooperative relationships with other liberal states.[42] As Williams puts essentially the same point, "If indeed primary freedoms are secured, and basic fears are assuaged, then the attentions of the liberalism of fear will move to more sophisticated conceptions of freedom, and other forms of fear, other ways in which the asymmetries of power and powerlessness work to the disadvantage of the latter."[43] We have, then, a route toward a complex Order-cum-System that, from our perspective, would comprise concentric (and overlapping) circles. For basic Order (peace), pragmatic considerations cannot sanely be dodged. Much the same goes for existential threats that can be overcome only by cooperating with states that are threatening, internally tyrannous, or both. Then we can begin to make choices. Where, as a practical matter, an endeavor can be expected to succeed only where some thick values are shared, then it could be opened only to members of a thickish Society, and perhaps would contribute to constituting that society as such.

Reprising our criticism of Rawls's single set of principles for a society of liberal and decent states, the problem is that it is binary (in or out) when, as a matter of fact, the spillovers from states' and peoples' choices and actions toward other states and peoples are myriad, and hugely variable in their significance. The world is complicated, which cannot be ducked by any legitimation principles that need to make sense and be useful (to us, among others).

## Precepts for Liberal States Participating in a System of International Regimes

Drawing also on chapters 10 and 12, we now pull together some basic precepts to guide how liberal states should approach international cooperative regimes, the first installment of our *Principles for Participation and Delegation*. They begin with elementary conventions and norms that any state—liberal,

---

whereas I reach a conclusion for *us*, given *our* values, in making *political* decisions about our international relations. Reflecting that, his list of basic rights is more expansive.

42. That is essentially what the EU has faced in deciding how to respond to illiberal institutional developments in some Central and Eastern European member states.

43. Williams, "Liberalism of Fear," in *In the Beginning*, p. 60.

democratic, decent, or not—needs to believe will hold, before moving on to others specific to liberal states.

## Preconditions: Not Order Threatening

States need to believe that participating in particular regimes (or in System generally) will not threaten external or internal order, or otherwise materially endanger their local legitimacy. For that reason, they will need to coalesce around conventions for recognizing each other, including their respective areas of jurisdiction, and so on.

## Order's Background Norms: Some Macro-reciprocity

For any kind of Order to provide conditions of cooperation, there need to be convention-norms that establish macro-reciprocity. These include the existing evolved immunities and "minimum standard of protection," which oil the wheels of political and economic commerce. The credibility of such norms is necessary for interstate relations to be political—diplomatic rather than rawly anarchic.

## System's Background Pragmatic Norms: Good Faith

When Society is thin, System's most basic norm is Good Faith (chapters 7 and 12). There must, therefore, be a widely shared understanding of what counts as a formal promise between and among states because, for System *without* thick or deep Society, participants cannot call on common understandings or a shared way of life acting as checks on defection.

While the post–World War II Vienna treaty on treaties (chapter 3) codifies conventions of good-faith promising, making it easier for new states to join in, it needs a strong background norm that treaties themselves should be followed: *pacta sunt servanda*, a convention-cum-norm that is part of customary international law, deriving authority from usage, and legitimacy from reflective internalization.

## Background Pragmatic Norms: Orderly Exit

Since no state's leaders or people can foresee the future, including whether they or their successors will change their minds about the merits of a particular international regime, participants need to be able to rely on each other not to disrupt it by abruptly walking away. In other words, there needs to be a social norm of *orderly exit*, made manifest by agreements setting out formal arrangements for such exit.

That amounts to a corollary of the principle-cum-norm of *Good Faith*: a state should enter into international System with a commitment not willfully to upend specific regimes or disrupt the System as a whole, because each state needs that.

### Background Pragmatic Norms: Formalized Hierarchy Not Precluded, So Long as Constrained

It is a fact of the world that international order is often preserved via some kind of hierarchy (a balance of power among leading states, or a hegemon of some kind), which cascades down to the power structures of some of System's regimes and organizations. This is not at odds with legitimacy when widely understood and accepted as necessary to sustain an Order. Applied to the permanent UN Security Council members' veto power, the issue is whether it can be satisfactorily explained in terms of no great power, capable unilaterally of upending global order, being exposed to having the totality of other states formally act against it through the UN. That makes China's membership a fortuitous historical accident, and suggests that changes should be approached cautiously. (The monetary order's hierarchy is addressed in part V.)

Regime-specific and System-wide hierarchies need to be constrained, in order to help contain grievances among weaker states (Castlereagh's colleague's worry after 1815). For liberal states (inside or outside any leadership group), that entails transparency and voice. Hence the necessity for something like the UN General Assembly and the WTO assembly.

### Liberal States Need a Jus Cogens Criterion for Nonexistential Cooperation

If constitutional democracies and other liberal states and their peoples are committed to the basic human rights institutionalized in international law's *jus cogens* norms, then they should set a high bar for cooperating with states that violate those norms. The tests might be the necessity of certain measures to maintain peaceful existence, indirectly to help the oppressed in an oppressive state, or to address shared existential threats that require joint action. Each involves balancing risks—for example, whether welfare, decency, or even security considerations are trumped by a need for collective action with other states and powers irrespective of their values, practices, and systems of government.[44]

## A Liberal Bias toward Universalism and Openness, Constrained by the Need to Preserve Order

Otherwise, liberal states might usefully and properly have a bias toward universalism in multilateral regimes, since that can help to limit an international System's effects on the policy space of nonleading and outsider states, underlining the liberal credentials of liberal states.

That disposition is properly qualified by a number of pragmatic and defensive considerations. Pragmatically, when universal consent is unobtainable, liberal states need to think of themselves as free to construct narrower membership regimes rather than accept nothing. In the same vein, liberal states should resist a regime precluding subsets of members cooperating more deeply with each other in the relevant field, so long as that does not undermine the umbrella regime. In consequence, standard-setting regimes with something approaching (or open to) universal membership should stick to articulating and policing minimum standards in the relevant field, except where the subject matter dictates otherwise.

That might sometimes amount to acting as a kind of vanguard, in which case the door to others reopens later. The point is that groups of states should not be prevented from thickening or deepening their cooperation because others do not wish to. It is relevant to funding poor states' efforts to contain deadly pathogens (above), but also to trade and many other fields (chapters 17 and 18).

## Avoiding Domination and Promoting Resilience in the Terms and Modalities of Policy Regimes

Away from weakest-link existential harms, universalism should be tempered where it could lead to some states dominating others (or other threats to domestic order and legitimacy). As well as being contrary to the (republican) values of some citizens of constitutional democracies, domination is counterproductive to sustaining cooperative endeavors given the possibility

---

44. Existential threats overlap with but are conceptually (and sometimes practically) distinct from the "moral mandatory aims" for collective action in Christiano, "Legitimacy of International Institutions," pp. 388–90.

of relative-power shifts: those dominated today may be tomorrow's potential dominators.

For essentially those reasons, powerful liberal states also need to exercise cautious self-restraint in applying economic sanctions, especially where their capability to do so depends on the continuing legitimacy of the provision of an international public good (e.g., a reserve currency) or when such action is not supported by friends and allies whose interests in the underlying Order are otherwise aligned (chapter 10). That does not preclude using sanctions to help preserve order.

Similarly, powerful liberal states should be cautious in claiming extraterritorial jurisdiction for their domestic laws. That does not preclude a state from using domestic regulatory powers to deny access to its markets and infrastructure to individuals or firms whose conduct in foreign jurisdictions is inappropriate (or worse) by domestic standards (chapter 18).

The incentive for states (vanguards and holdouts) to restrain themselves can improve if nondomination operates as a social norm. But conversely, it underlines the value of states building resilience, especially against order-threatening shocks, disturbances, and intrusions, so covering at least defense, parts of health care, and financial stability (chapters 16 and 19). By promoting resilience, regimes can mitigate domination risks.

### Open Universalism Moderated by a Principle of Subsidiarity: Respect for Thick Ethical Communities

Another constraint on the mechanical pursuit of universalism arises where the value of states' local or internal legitimacy is rooted in a thick community of ethics (chapter 7). It is not in the interests of democracies for globalization to trample over this, even as it inevitably thins out the bonds that hold people together in pursuit of otherwise unobtainable goods.

Drawing on the history of European civil law and governance, liberal democracies need to promote a principle of subsidiarity: pursue cooperative endeavors at the lowest level of politics feasible for their (net) benefits to be realized. This means pooling and delegating power internationally only where the costs to the thick relations and ways of life in home communities are weighed alongside the gains from cooperation at a higher level.[45]

---

45. This relates to weighing the value of self-determination (emphasized in Buchanan and Powell, "Constitutional Democracy").

### Not Endangering Liberalism or Democracy in Constitutional Democracies

That, if you like, communitarian check on universalist internationalism is as relevant for liberal powers as for weaker states. Particularizing our first precept, liberal democracies need to avoid participating in regimes (or on terms) liable to generate basic-order externalities *for them*—for example, by damaging or undermining liberal or democratic institutions and values (next chapter).

Further, consistent with limiting cooperation with *jus cogens* violators, liberal states will want to participate in international organizations on terms that permit their being used, when not counterproductive, to deter such violations; for example, via economic sanctions (chapters 3 and 4) or the terms of aid and credit.[46] But with great powers exhibiting deep differences on values and individuals' basic rights, constitutional democracies should not expect multilateral organizations to promote democracy itself.

That does not prevent liberal states acting alone, or together outside global organizations, to promote democracy (while weighing Peel's caution about likely effectiveness). And the suggested bar would not apply under a *New Cold War* if existing international regimes bifurcated, leaving bloc-based organizations free to promote their members' values, tempered by the risks of counterproductive effects in particular circumstances.

## A *Mere* International Modus Vivendi versus a Society of States: Circles of Legitimacy

Those precepts make for neither a mere modus vivendi nor a universal thick society of states and peoples. It is not a *mere* modus vivendi, as Rawls termed it, because order is not to be sniffed at: war and instability are quite a lot worse, as is fear of them.[47] Drawing on the most basic attributes Williams finds in the conditions of politics—order, protection, safety, trust, conditions for

---

46. Argued for human rights generally in Fabre, *Economic Statecraft*.

47. Rawls was dismissive of a "mere" modus vivendi as falling well short of a political community constituted by principles of justice: see *Political Liberalism*, pp. 145–49. In an international context, his modus vivendi resting on a "balance of forces" is somewhat akin to our Order (*Law of Peoples*, pp. 44–45) but without the sense that, to be credible and hence sustainable, its terms must find acceptance (relative to realistic alternatives). Instead Rawls draws a distinction with peace and order sustained by "the right reasons," which sounds Kantian, but adds that people can grow into the underlying norms (p. 44), which seems Humean.

cooperation, and legitimacy—we might say an international modus vivendi is a state of affairs where the first three prevail, where trust holds across only a narrow domain, where conditions for cooperation are latent but undeveloped, and where legitimacy is up for grabs. Where legitimate (given available alternatives), a modus vivendi amounts to, in our terms, a sustainable Order, but with the politics of diplomacy, not more.[48]

Since our precepts cater for circumstances where some states do not comply with the most basic *jus cogens* norms, they address a world that is neither a thick Society nor held together by uniformly shared liberal values. More generally, the precepts do not travel with the antipluralist drift toward moral universalism in the couple of decades after the end of the Cold War.[49] They make room for civilizational difference, while articulating legitimacy constraints on liberal states' choice of partners.

But the precepts do not preclude liberal states (or others) going further together.[50] They contemplate a world of different legitimacy circles, corresponding to—and, by helping deliver equilibrium, enabling—different degrees of cooperation. Moving from the outermost circle inward, each ratchet into closer cooperation brings more demanding legitimation principles, because more issues need to be kept within the bounds of resolvable or tolerable disagreement; the disagreement-conflict divide is shaped by which legitimation norms are shared. The membership and leadership of Order and System coincide, with a single top table, only where all the powers of the day find themselves in the same legitimacy circle.

## Concentric Circles Legitimating Ever-Deeper Cooperation

The outermost circle is a world of states seeking no more than to live in peaceful coexistence—quite possibly a strained and potentially unstable coexistence. It obtains only where at least one of the powers critical to global order of some kind does not pass the *jus cogens* test for cooperative relations with states inhabiting inner circles. Given coincident interests (in peace, or at least

48. Sleat, "Modus Vivendi and Legitimacy," which, fortifying my views, argues, mainly in a domestic context, that the legitimacy of the means of maintaining security and stability might be sufficient as well as necessary for a modus vivendi, whereas it will not be sufficient in a political community attempting rather more.

49. On liberal antipluralism versus UN Charter liberalism, see Simpson, "Two Liberalisms."

50. That might distinguish my approach from modus vivendi liberalism's manifesto: see Gray, *Two Faces of Liberalism.*

in not embarking on wars they might well not win), there would be some elemental conventions concerning things like territorial boundaries, various
protections and immunities (notably for diplomats), and illicit wartime conduct, with some codified, to reduce misunderstandings.

Any weak states not participating even here, existing beyond the pale, might
forcibly be held to certain of those standards. Indeed, occupants of inner circles, and perhaps this outermost circle, would probably try to insist the laws
of war apply to those who exit (recently Russia, after one Ukrainian invasion
too many). Even where enforced only via victors' justice, laws on the conduct
of war claim intrinsic universality. They can be thought of as conventions
forged during peacetime (when memories of disorder are fresh) that seek to
embed norms that will constrain leaders, commanders, and troops during the
incipient or actual disorder of war. As such, they aim to retain a residue of the
political during the breakdown of regular politics, partly by looking forward
to the eventual restoration of order, when politics as diplomacy resumes and
accounting for crimes sometimes begins. But whereas that frames the laws of
war as operating through the shadow of the future, their force in the heat
of combat—soldiers thinking, "no, this is wrong"—calls upon the nurturing
of moral instincts aligned with war's conventions.

Otherwise, if global order depends on peaceful coexistence among powers
living by diametrically opposed basic norms, the security top table of wary,
distrustful states will be distinct from leadership hierarchies overseeing any
bloc-based alliances and cooperative-regime systems. That would not preclude
collective action against shared existential threats, nor thin multilateral regimes for commerce so long as they did not expose parties to overdependence in anything materially or socially essential. Other than those final
possible components, the outermost circle is close to an Order of self-
enforcing conventions. In terms of our two modes of respect (above), it entails
no more than respect as formal recognition. It is rather Hobbesian, but with
elements recognizable to Emmerich de Vattel's nineteenth-century successors.

Moving inward only one notch, but significantly, the next legitimation
circle (for us) is, to adapt political theorist Richard Bellamy, a kind of "*thin*
cosmopolitan internationalist statism" where states grant individuals and
groups basic rights intended to protect them from fear (the *jus cogens* norms)
and conduct themselves by the norm of Good Faith.[51] Multilateralism operates,

---

51. Bellamy, *Republican Europe of States*, pp. 47–51, where the treatment is more EU-centric
and sets aside security problems.

but only to establish minimum standards, and states remain cautious about overdependence.

This second circle is distinct from the world of nineteenth-century imperialism as it treats some basic rights as universal. For denizens of inner circles, it is a fairly thin System-Society.[52] For those in the outermost ring—and beyond—it is an unacceptably thick Society challenging sovereignty as unqualified internal autonomy. Inward-looking nationalist (but basic-rights-respecting) states find themselves here, since for them more extensive cooperation risks loss of autonomy-cum-identity (which they might call sovereignty). In a time-traveling history of international legal thought, Vattel begins to meet Grotius.

I shall call those first two circles the outer circles. They are different in kind from what lies inside, where legitimation principles gradually thicken and deepen, and states cooperate more and more closely (or even agglomerate).[53] The third would incorporate some basic liberal rights—perhaps no more than the previous chapter's bare-bones liberalism—and somewhat closer commercial ties.[54] Accepting degrees of convergence in economic structure, more ambitious regimes could be tucked under the umbrella of the second circle's global minimum standards (for example, the preferential trade agreements discussed in chapter 18).

Going further, some inner legitimation circles might amount to regional or intercontinental forms of "*local* cosmopolitan statism" (another term adapted from Bellamy), involving states variously making increased use of pooling and delegation in international organizations, accepting or seeking greater interdependence, and codifying more extensive catalogs of human rights: the EU demands more of its members than, say, the IMF or the WTO.[55] For some such circles, the term "member" would be more apt than "participant," and questions of distributional justice across a community might gain traction.

52. Akin to the "thin standard of justice" for international relations and law advocated in Ratner, *Thin Justice*, which (p. 90) deploys the idea of thin- versus thick-morality communities (citing Walzer rather than the Oxford origins: see chapter 7).

53. The outer circles bear a family resemblance to the "practical association" of international law, and some inner-circle endeavors to the "purposive associations" of Nardin, *Law, Morality, and the Relations of States*, pp. 308–24.

54. It might approximate to Rawls's Society of Peoples, depending on how one parses "urgent rights" (on which, see Beitz, *Idea of Human Rights*, pp. 97–98).

55. Applications are restricted to European states that, among other things, respect the values of "human dignity, freedom, democracy, equality, the rule of law and respect for human rights, including the rights of persons belonging to minorities" (Articles 2 and 49, Treaty on EU).

Samuel Pufendorf might start to find himself at home somewhere around here. Cosmopolitan Kantians might regard it as a tolerable base camp for ascending to the kingdom of Rights. Hobbesians, if they woke up here, would initially deny its reality, before condemning it as an abomination (all the more so if they thought it was run by Kantians).

Summarizing, each circle is held together not only by shared material interests (order for the outer rings, and various cooperative purposes in inner rings) but also by common legitimation principles (thin through thick and on to deep). The circles are the normative manifestation of thin, thickening, thick, and ultimately deep Society among different groups of states. The geometry of the circles is perspectival: I have described them from the perspective of a liberal, constitutionalist democracy. But there will be other systems of concentric circles for other states, drawing on their normative traditions and civilizational histories: that is what the old Chinese Tribute System amounted to. While the outcome looks like variable geometry, that obscures the constraints legitimation places, sooner or later, on cooperation.

## International Law in a World of Concentric Legitimation Circles

Thinking of the world in terms of concentric legitimation circles helps make sense of international law's trajectory and tensions. On the one hand, some want it to institutionalize the values of thickish society, claiming universal authority but with noncompliant states regarded as beyond the pale (Rawls). On the other hand, it can aim for something like a semipragmatic pluralism, with globalization's commercial imperatives a vital forcing variable.

Seeking some form of universalism (moral or practical), general international law hovers at the interface of the two outer circles, institutionalizing formal promises (and other indispensable pragmatic conventions) and seeking to demand basic rights. For denizens of those circles, the emphasis will be on essential coordination problems, whereas those inhabiting inner circles will be looking for more.

Already, this pinpoints the significance of various senior US officials and scholar-commentators having, over recent decades, rejected the authority of international law *tout court* (chapters 4 and 9). It was a nonnegligible strategic mistake given that the country has no capacity to achieve and sustain a hegemonic dominium so absolute its reliability would be irrelevant; little capacity on its own—that is, without allies and friends—to maintain a balancing equilibrium with China unless the rising power's economy happens to plateau roughly where it is now; and, once its people's welfare is brought in, little interest in retreating to autarky, which is what a casual disregard for interstate promises would ultimately beckon.[56] In a nutshell, wishful thinking.

Meanwhile, denizens of inner circles try to push things in a quite different direction. Never mind the outermost circle's purely pragmatic coordinating conventions, they do not want to settle for the second circle's basic rights. In effect, their international-human-rights-law project is trying to pull all states toward the norms of their legitimation circle. A program for reform, it leads to unavoidable tension over what outer-circle and inner-circle inhabitants regard as properly universal.[57] On the one hand, outer-circle denizens cannot preclude hard or soft law being employed to cement thicker relationships in the inner circles. On the other hand, the more the organs of international law articulate norms that, in practice, are accepted and broadly respected only by the participant-members of inner circles, the more law detaches itself from the thin norms of the outer circles and instead seeks to impose or promote particular (civilizational?) values. That is one way of making sense of the liberal internationalist project: as System-Order rather than Order-System.[58]

Drawing an analogy between the UN's capacious human rights conventions and the Bill of Rights splendidly tacked on to the newly united United States' Constitution, it is useful to remember the latter rights governed only federal law and government, not the states themselves, and that a good deal of the Supreme Court's late twentieth-century jurisprudence was devoted to finding ways of reading the Bill of Rights into the constitutional norms binding states, sometimes stretching republican order.[59] One moral of the story is that declarations of rights do not give them bite—parties sometimes sign things they do not believe in. But rights declarations do provide focal points for

56. Hence my verdict on Goldsmith and Posner's *Limits of International Law* is that it did not grasp the utility to the United States of building a reputation for keeping formal promises, and so of taking seriously the internalization by its counterparts of core norms of international law.

57. This can shed some light on scholarly debates (triggered by H. Hart, *Concept of Law*, chap. 10) about whether international law comprises a legal *system*, in the sense of a more or less coherent system of interlocking legal norms generated via institutions recognized as authoritative. For inner-circle participants or members, the answer will be broadly yes, whereas for denizens of the outer circles (and certainly the outermost) it will be no. Denizens of the outermost circle assert sovereignty over law, whereas those of the inner circles do not (chapter 11).

58. For example, Deudney and Ikenberry, "Nature and Sources."

59. Gerstle, *Liberty and Coercion*.

diffusion by campaigners and policy entrepreneurs, so long as order and system legitimacy hold in the background.

## Campaigns for Cosmopolitan Justice

Viewed thus, campaigns and measures seeking to alter the terms of international coexistence and cooperation are often trying, in our terms, to shift a circle's legitimation norms. If a liberal state's citizens care greatly about pursuing cosmopolitan ends, its legitimacy at home will end up depending somewhat on whether it takes—and permits its people to take—those issues to international policy tables and fora.

Seen thus, those political and legal theorists and commentators who hold that, ideally, the world should be organized around cosmopolitan values (chapter 11) are best thought of as intellectual campaigners—engaging in debates to shift public opinion domestically and elsewhere.[60] The same goes for libertarians, nationalists, socialists, and so on.

What I think advocates for, say, global redistributive justice cannot reasonably claim is that, absent the realization of their own favored brand of cosmopolitan values, the existing system of states and their relations lacks legitimacy if, in the terms set out in the previous chapter, the governments (and, via them, citizen-subjects) of particular states acquiesce in international regime-cum-organizations' coercive powers, normative authority, and right to act as stewards for cooperative endeavors. Critics might not like the results but, as discussed above, that is different. They, in turn, can be pressed on the incentive compatibility of their proposed transformations, but they can respond that it will depend on changing hearts and minds (norms).

All this does depend, however, on the feasibility of justice issues being debated openly and publicly. That, after all, is part of the value of stability: why the capacity to produce and maintain order legitimately is, sanely, the First Political Question. Just as conditions for cooperation are latent but

60. E.g., some morality-first political theorists already mentioned (Charles Beitz, Simon Caney, and Cecile Laborde), plus others who argue for versions of cosmopolitan ends or means (including Thomas Pogge, attributing moral responsibility for world poverty to the background global economic order and rejecting the state as generating special local moral duties; and Mathias Risse, accepting that justice within states matters but holding that the world is the common property of all). Such writings tend to be awash with (stipulated) moral duties and obligations without addressing whether and how they would be incentive compatible, or the conditions of politics within and among states and peoples.

underdeveloped in a modus vivendi, so conditions for debating and pursuing justice, including distributional justice, are latent in at least those inner circles of cooperation that rely on and foster thicker (or even deeper) Society. Even a System of states with only very thin Society does not bar campaigns for justice (in its very different manifestations). The UN General Assembly realizes the value of each recognized state having a public voice (as in March 2022's emergency session on Ukraine) and provides a focus for nonstate campaigners; its declarations do not need to be binding for that to be so.

This is a kind of metapluralism, which does not commit states to thick or deep cooperation but does not preclude it. Conceivable outcomes include what is sometimes termed solidarism but only if it arises from convergence of values, interests, and identities toward deep Society (chapter 7)—not as some kind of deontological imperative. Other than states and peoples whose conduct and institutionalized values place them in what, from *our* perspective, are the outer circles (and beyond), the account presented here merely has liberal states holding that it is legitimate for different states and their peoples to live by differing legitimation norms, creating conditions for different levels of cooperative collective action and shared ethics (ways of life). For liberal states and peoples to hold otherwise would be to seek to dominate other states and peoples. But that leaves open the possibility of time, through problems faced and public debate, broadening a community's sense of justice, by broadening its sense of *we*.

## Humanitarian Intervention

Finally, in case it be doubted, the approach taken here does not preclude humanitarian intervention, but underlines that it is a political choice—albeit a morally informed one—rather than a moral imperative of some kind.

Drawing on long-standing debates in moral philosophy about individuals' responsibilities to come to each other's aid, Williams argued that such intervention can be warranted only if, among other things, it is sufficiently likely to be effective in helping the oppressed, and the costs and risks are not unreasonably high.[61] But he went on, obviously correctly, that humanitarian intervention

---

61. Williams, "Humanitarianism," in *In the Beginning*, pp. 145–53. These principles are not novel but illustrate that realist political theory can address such issues. For a variant badged consequentialist liberalism, where states' rights are a matter of positive convention, see Ryan, "Liberal Imperialism." For a review of the approaches of John Stuart Mill and, forty years ago, Michael Walzer, see Doyle, "A Few Words on Mill."

is more complex than intervening to address a horror in private life, because such choices are made by a state's government on behalf of its people, and can entail putting those people in harm's way (directly and immediately for the military, and indirectly and with uncertain timing for civilians).

What is more, there is also the matter of which states decide. As Williams observed, decisions to intervene will generally be taken by the most powerful states, which for us means the United States (and its leading allies).[62] That implicates the US state's relationship—the sustainability of its legitimacy—with the American people; and with its allies, and their own legitimacy with their peoples.

It is important, as Williams underlined but still perhaps did not make enough of, that the leaders who decide to intervene will not be the people who execute the intervention, and so are at risk.[63] In one sense, that is a triumph of constitutional democracy: civilian authority over the military. But there is also a legitimacy risk here; one that has, I suspect, been pertinent in the United States over recent decades. Comparing the Pax Britannica with the Pax Americana, one striking difference is how few members of the United States' civilian *executive* branch elite have served in the armed forces or have close family in the military. Whatever the madness of World War I, it is equally striking that, as testified by church memorials around Britain and elsewhere, many of the lieutenants who led their men "over the top" were drawn from the same parts of society as those making the decisions (the "ruling classes," as they were then known). It was, in complex ways, shared sacrifice. This plainly did not inject sanity into decision-making but, together with postwar actions to broaden the franchise, it might have helped hold the country together. Too many US troops come from what is, shockingly, sometimes referred to disparagingly as "flyover country." As Williams puts it, "The risk of being killed had better be rightfully imposed, and in a democratic state this requires at least that it be justifiable to the public."[64] But a proffered justification might be more compelling or easier to accept—because more likely to be sincere, and so truthful—if the exposure to sacrifice is shared. In other words, deciding to intervene in another state's oppressions is a special kind of domestic political question.[65]

62. Williams, "Humanitarianism," p. 148.

63. Williams, "Humanitarianism," p. 150.

64. Williams, "Humanitarianism," p. 150.

65. This differs from Nagel's "minimal humanitarian morality," which "require[s] us ... to relieve them [other people] from extreme threats and obstacles to such freedom if we can do

This affects how we should think about Responsibility to Protect (chapter 3). Focusing on the duty of states to protect their citizen-subjects from atrocities, it is a putative norm for domestic governance that fits with a realist recognition of the First Political Question being the maintenance of security and stability without excessive coercion.[66] As argued above, that matters for realist reasons: to stem refugee migrations that would stretch states' capacities and their peoples' tolerance. But nor, given *jus cogens* norms, can liberal states casually accept oppression as the device that shields them from migrants seeking to escape persecution or dire hardship.

While the West and others have promoted the R2P norm, it is not, in fact, universally accepted, and there is no prospect of our trying to enforce it against, hypothetically, China. Likewise, it seems most unlikely that it would be used uninvited were large-scale humanitarian tragedy to follow the intensification of sectarian politics in India, which (whether rightly or wrongly) does not have a UN Security Council veto but is a nuclear power, and a vital actor in the new geopolitics. Nor, looking back a few decades, were European states ever in a position to do anything about the deep racial segregation and deprivation of political and civil rights that persisted in the United States after World War II. Indeed, we Europeans took our external security from the United States while disapproving of some seemingly de facto structural features of its governance: our society has been, in some ways, thickish but not deep.

This way of approaching humanitarian issues is not destined for moral bankruptcy. Humanitarian intervention is part of the menu because some in the West and, importantly, elsewhere believe it should be, but it will always face the hurdles of domestic public acquiescence, threats to international order from rival powers (or their friends), and, loosely, coalitions of the willing. Today, R2P could become customary law (operating in the widest outer circle) only if a reformed China agreed.[67]

---

so *without serious sacrifice of our own ends*" ("Problem of Global Justice," p. 131 [my emphasis]). While a few hundred military deaths might not sacrifice a state's ends, it might sacrifice its legitimacy if part of the population concluded political leaders were reckless with their lives. On wars affecting US elections, see Kriner and Shen, "Battlefield Casualties."

66. Sleat, "Politics and Morality."

67. Bearing on the argument between legality and legitimacy for context-dependent humanitarian intervention in Ratner, *Thin Justice*, chap. 9.

# Summing Up: Legitimacy, Statecraft, and Robust Policy toward International Regimes

Realist international political theory steers us away from oversimplified, morality-first approaches to international cooperation. Departing from Rawls's in-or-out conception of international society, we adopted a picture of legitimacy circles, which caters for the compromises sometimes needed for peaceful coexistence or to combat existential threats without giving up the important thought that ambitious cooperation can be easier among states sharing elements of thick society. The outer circles amount to an Order and thin System of diverse states seeking peaceful coexistence and some commerce, whereas inward circles might constitute a somewhat less thin society of civilizational states and the innermost various local civilizational societies.

We can accept, as a general matter, that institutionalized interdependence can entail mutual and reciprocal political responsibilities, but framed politically rather than as unqualified moral obligations. They increase with the ambition of collective projects not merely because of increased interdependence but because those projects depend on and (maybe) promote shared norms.[68] While obviously an abstract image, the legitimation-circles framework represents real choices faced by states: With whom can we cooperate on what in ways that manage disagreement instead of letting it get out of control?

## Statecraft and Legitimacy

Conceived thus, international relations are partly shaped by the structures of power but also partly defined (constituted even) in their legitimation principles.[69] This becomes obvious when, going further than a norm of Good Faith, we wish to impose entry barriers to cooperation on states that (we think) threaten us, or systematically abuse the most basic human rights of their

68. Going with the grain of J. Cohen and Sabel, "Extra Rempublicam Nulla Justitia?" (against Nagel, "Problem of Global Justice"), that interdependence and institutions can take states and peoples into a space between minimal humanitarian concerns and domestic social justice, but framing that space in terms of Humean politics and legitimacy conditions rather than Kantian imperatives.

69. E.g., one way of thinking about Brexit is that too few British citizens accepted legitimation of some collective lawmaking via the EU, whereas, for example, France, Europe's other historically unitary state, has in effect recast its internal legitimation principles in terms of *the Republic within Europe.*

citizen-subjects, or fall short in some other way of what *we* need to maintain *our* legitimacy.

That is anything but straightforward. The chapter's precepts entail trade-offs. In the real world, unavoidable political judgments involve compromises, and sometimes cut across background norms. Statecraft is anything but banished.[70] To pick a hypothetical but grave example, imagine the West contemplated penalizing, say, India for not doing enough on climate change. That would have to be balanced against the risk of alienating Delhi, a democracy and rising power. Politics is not a subdiscipline of ethics, but overlaps.

Nevertheless, the legitimation norms governing whom a state can decently hang out with for what purposes act as a kind of anchor—to ourselves. Constitutional democracies' international policies will be less sustainable, because their domestic legitimacy less secure, if they are careless about where they cohabit.

The European project provides an illuminating example. In our terms, it is, broadly, a regional order-system that starts with an outer-circle security alliance and then, traveling inward, moves through a customs union (a still-thin society), on to a regulatory union (an internal market, necessitating its own legal order, and thus thickish society), to an innermost circle of monetary and fiscal union (entailing full mobility in all factors of production, and hence broadly shared ways of life). This helps clarify some of Europe's challenges. One is where labor mobility properly fits.[71] Another is whether Hungary and Poland fit in a regulatory union given their opposition to its thick-society values. If their governing parties dismantle pillars of constitutionalism, it is awkward, at home, for other European states to carry on (including sending subsidies) as though nothing is awry.

One of this book's central issues is not dissimilar. If a prominent state (say, the PRC) does not respect basic human rights as understood by us, that makes it harder, at home, for constitutional democracies to treat the states at the top table as homogeneous: for the thin respect of formal recognition to be accompanied by the thicker respect of esteem. The point here is political—the shared political morality internal to liberal states (Rawls's big point).

---

70. Rawls accepted that: "What to do . . . is . . . essentially a matter of political judgment" (*Law of Peoples*, p. 93)—offering insights on purposes and constraints (pp. 97–103).

71. In terms of standard economics, a commitment to mobility of labor is vital to an innermost-circle monetary union but not to an internal market-cum-regulatory union (Pisani-Ferry et al., *Europe after Brexit*).

Hence our four scenarios (chapters 4 and 10) can be recast in terms of legitimation circles. *Superpower Struggle* amounts to a normative fracture, which *New Cold War* cements. A *Reshaped World Order* is characterized by whatever basic norms are shared at its new top table, and however its members got there. But *Lingering Status Quo* depends on the values of constitutional democracy prevailing, somehow.

Discarding any relativism of distance, we make judgments about the legitimacy of other states, and the different elements of an international Order and System. The legitimation principles a state shares (broadly) with others can, at the margin, orient its foreign policy. For example, expressed in Rawls's terms, "liberal and decent states" might have a long-run aim of bringing "outlaw and benighted states" into their society. We—constitutional democracies—rationally do not want to leave states in the outermost circle of peaceful coexistence (a stable modus vivendi) or worse. We want to try to get them into, at least, the thinnest circle of cooperation and legitimation (respecting the most basic rights).

For that reason, in the event of conflict or combat, Rawls rightly says, "difficult though it may be, the present enemy must be seen as a future associate in a shared and just peace."[72] Rationally, we would not want those states' peoples to lose themselves—their sense of their own history and traditions. That the post-Napoleonic and post–World War II settlements fared better than Versailles (chapter 2) suggests there is something to a pluralist liberalism of accommodation and toleration.

### Making Our Way in an International Society of Civilizational States

In finding a way through those thickets, we have to call on our own local political, material, and moral resources. Our constitutional democracies probably are capable of inhabiting a world of concentric circles. At one level, this would entail giving up promoting a thick universalist morality, while also exercising enough self-restraint to avoid a perilous autarky. At an altogether more demanding level, it might involve deciding whether to accept or even promote moves toward a limited version of *New Cold War* in order to free (our bloc's) international organizations to promote our core values and other interests. Those choices demand a statecraft embracing robustness, and so balancing the costs of proxy wars against the benefits of disentanglement.

72. Rawls, *Law of Peoples*, p. 101.

It also requires attention to the current System's terms. Our circle's need for friends entails being sensitive to legitimacy spillovers hurting other states. Separately, in the scenario of prolonged *Superpower Struggle*, the Great Powers meeting normatively in only the outermost circle might benefit from new conventions catching up with the new technology. For example, on when cyberattacks will be treated as acts of war rather than unfriendly maneuvers in the game of peace—perhaps because a state closed off elementally vital supplies or communications connectivity.[73] It seems unlikely any such reform will happen until something goes so much too far that it causes outrage, regret, or even shame—partly because overreach helps clarify where self-enforcing lines could be drawn.

More prosaically, where constitutional democracies do wish to cooperate, this means deciding which of our local governance legitimation principles need to apply, transitively, in the international realm. Those are conditions for our participation, determining the legitimation circle in which specific regimes and organizations belong (with incentives-values compatibility). It is the subject of the next chapter.

73. NATO has already stated that its members could in principle invoke Article 5 (an attack on one is an attack on all) in response to cyber interference judged to be an attack; para. 32, summit communiqué, June 14, 2021.

# 14

# Principles for Constitutional Democracies Legitimately Delegating to International Organizations

The accumulation of all powers, legislative, executive and judiciary, in the same hands . . . may justly be pronounced the very definition of tyranny.

JAMES MADISON, FEDERALIST NO. 47, 1788[1]

WHILE CHAPTER 11 posed globalization as a problem for *autonomous* states, it has since been reconceived as a navigation challenge for *legitimate* states. Once participating in international System (subject to the previous chapter's constraints), what confronts representative democracies is a quadruple (even quintuple) chain of delegations. From the people to their elected assembly and executive (two steps in parliamentary systems); from them, together with their peers in other states, to the governing bodies of international organizations (via treaties, founding instruments, etc.); from them to organizations' boards; and from them to board committees, management, staff (under the organizations' statutes), and so on.

Somehow, the deep values operating at that very first stage cannot be so betrayed, or so tested by adverse legitimacy spillovers, as to undermine the whole show. After considering which of those values are clearly transitive,

---

1. Hamilton et al., *Federalist* no. 47, 1788.

this chapter offers the second installment of our *Principles for Participation and Delegation.*[2]

## Legitimation Norms in Constitutional Democracies: Transitivity of Institutionalized Political Values

The core legitimation principles of a legitimate political community are best found in the values animating the high-level institutions that provide security, stability, and means for cooperating. For constitutional democracies, that means the rule of law, constitutionalism, and democracy.

They cannot be treated as monolithic in conception or justification. Different people hold different conceptions of these values-cum-institutions and subscribe to different justifications of them.[3] In the first place, any of them might receive a warrant for either instrumental or intrinsic reasons. To take the most obvious example, some people surely value democracy because it expresses and constitutes values they hold dear, such as political freedom or a certain kind of political equality. Others, by contrast, may value democracy and our other political institutions for instrumental reasons: because they believe constitutional democracy provides the best means of delivering whatever it is they most care about, which might be welfare (for themselves, their family, or some broader community) or, again, freedom or political respect for all. They might have quite different time horizons, degrees of confidence, or views of how democracy works. But they think it is the best means of delivering or enabling whatever it is that they care about the state delivering and enabling. To gauge what constraints these value-laden and value-carrying institutions imply for international delegation, we must, therefore, look at them more closely.

### Law as a Commitment Device

It is easiest to start with one of law's elemental features and functions. Earlier sections of this book underlined the importance of commitment in international relations: promises between states, international standards, normative conventions, and so on need to be credible if they are to guide conduct and so serve

2. Compare Tucker, *Unelected Power*, on domestic delegation, typically involving only two steps: from people to representatives, and on to central bankers and independent regulators.
3. Tucker, *Unelected Power*, chaps. 8, 9, and 11.

their purpose. In the world of government and politics, law is the most basic commitment device. Otherwise, government officials could turn up for work each morning and shift policy about, this way or that, however they chose.

That constrains the processes via which law is enunciated and changed. In a domestic setting, legislated law is open to change only via formal amendment or repeal, with politicians exposed to audience costs if those procedures are set aside (chapter 5). The Vienna treaty on treaties aims to achieve similar effects for formal agreements between two or more states.

Up to a point, an equivalent set of standards applies to judge-made law—that is, for it to count as law rather than a series of observations. Whether domestically or internationally, if judicial adjudications are to deliver focal points that help law to function in its role as a coordination device (chapter 6), there need to be norms and standards for identifying judicial conduct as such. These might amount to what the leading mid-twentieth-century legal theorist Herbert Hart called rules of recognition (in a legal system). To bite, departures from them—by, say, discarding precedent or giving "reasons" that seem not to have the characteristics of reasons—need to create audience costs for the errant or rogue judges among the community of lawyers, the associated commentariat, and beyond.[4]

## The Rule of Law

Commitment problems also drive some of the values of the rule *of* law, distinguishing it from rule *by* law. They are generally taken to have three elements.

First, the laws themselves should be general, forward looking (not retroactive), publicly announced, internally consistent, reasonably stable over time, and capable of being followed: these are attributes we can associate with seeking to make credible a commitment to maintain a stable policy generated through stable processes (lawmaking). Second, the law of a state should apply equally to all, including the officers and machinery of government: the king is subject to the law (incentivizing better lawmaking, which gives this value a functional genealogy). Third, the laws should be applied fairly and consistently, and should be seen to be applied fairly and consistently.[5]

4. H. Hart, *Concept of Law*, chap. 6. (In chapter 6's terms, a rule of recognition is a self-enforcing institution, with legitimacy.)

5. The first group is associated with Lon Fuller, although, as he stressed (*Morality of Law*, p. 242), they are found in Aquinas, and so run through the rationalist natural-law tradition.

Fair procedures are necessary, in our societies, for courts to adjudicate with *finality*, meaning the outcomes are accepted as bringing closure to a dispute even where, on the merits, disagreement might persist. What counts as "fair" shifts over time, but a fair hearing is today typically held to entail either a balanced and open investigation by the inquiring judge (civil law systems) or, more broadly, reliance on evidence and arguments available to and challengeable by specialist professionals on both sides, a capacity to contest the applicability of the relevant laws, and adjudicating judges giving reasons for their findings so that they, in turn, can be challenged in a higher court. This condition for legitimacy finds a strong echo in social psychologists' research into what members of the public demand of the administration of law: fairness at every stage of the process, from policing to courtroom (implying a naturalistic account of procedural fairness).[6]

More generally, in a Humean vein, we can view these values as norms that evolved to help sizable political communities use law to help solve problems and expand their possibilities. Their use as (apparently) rationalist norms and political values goes hand in hand: an example of the vital incentives-values compatibility emphasized in chapter 12.[7]

All of these values seem to carry through, by transitivity, to the establishment and operation of international organizations. Otherwise, they could be circumvented by transferring power abroad.

### Democracy

Turning to democracy, the form in which it mainly operates is representative democracy, combined with an occasional plebiscite or referendum. Core representative democracy has many aspects, each instantiating a distinct set

---

Predictability is also emphasized by Hayek, *Road to Serfdom*, p. 80. The second and third elements are most associated with Dicey (*Law of the Constitution*) and older Anglo traditions.

6. Tyler, *Why People Obey*. It is not simply about process (form). Imagine a state where trials seemed to follow rule-of-law values, but the accused was *always* found guilty. To avoid Potemkin rule of law, we judge a process's integrity partly via (learned) priors about what range of outcomes is reasonable given the relevant laws' content, evidence presented, and so on.

7. Hadfield and Weingast, "Microfoundations of the Rule of Law," reports work modeling a legal regime with decentralized enforcement in which such norms emerge as a product of rational instrumentalism.

of political commitments and values. Here are a few, none excluding the others:[8]

- *Democracy as voting for competing parties*: This conception, the thinnest, claims that in reality democracy is merely a contest between rival elite groups who are periodically mandated by the public, and applauds that as combining modern efficiency (letting people get on with their private lives) with a scheduled check on incompetence, failure, and mendacity.
- *Democracy as public debate and deliberation*: At almost the other end of the spectrum, this sees democracy as a process through which a political community governs itself through seeking consensus via (genuine) public reason.
- *Democracy as challenge, accountability, and watchfulness*: This emphasizes ongoing accountability (not only at elections) and the transparency necessary to make accountability feasible, with the members of the community becoming a disaggregated check on officeholders (and each other).[9]
- *Democracy as trial-and-error exploration of means, but also ends*: This amounts not only to testing the *means* of achieving fixed ends but also to exploring, reviewing, and revising some of those ends, objectives, and goals; a way in which a political society evolves by trial and error, and is never done.
- *Democracy as participation*: Harking back to ideas of direct democracy inspired by classical Athens, this emphasizes the active involvement of individual citizens.

Part of the purpose of that catalog is to lean against the reflex thought that whatever other virtues international institutions need to exhibit, democracy cannot be one them. For sure, few states and their peoples would sign up to world government with majoritarian decision-taking given the risk of finding

8. In the academy, these conceptions are associated with, respectively, Joseph Schumpeter; John Rawls and Jürgen Habermas (but with a strain of elite rule in the former); Britain (the country); John Dewey; and radical Left democrats.

9. Democracy as watchfulness is analogous to the three guards checking on each other in Hurwicz, "Who Will Guard the Guardians?" (It operates without the mad controller of Jeremy Bentham's Panopticon, which is more appealing to authoritarian states harnessing the new technology.)

themselves in a minority on things central to their interests and sense of themselves. Nevertheless, aside from a global demos regularly electing the leaders of international organizations, the spirit of many of the other political values served or instantiated by democracy can be carried across to international policymaking, lawmaking, adjudication, and arbitration.

## Constitutionalism: The Structuring of Power and Administrative Law

The work done by the "constitutional" part of constitutional democracy is to structure power (democratic or not) and to place it within and under constraints. Constitutional values call for clarity in who holds which powers, what procedural or substantive constraints apply to the exercise of those powers, which of those constraints are entrenched (hard, or even formally impossible, to change), and, more broadly, which powers are to be exercised at arm's length (insulated) from the day-to-day pressures and exigencies of electoral politics (such as monetary policy).[10]

In other words, constitutions provide the rules of the game for political government, partly stipulating and partly structuring the incentives that generate the substructures of politics (e.g., parties) and governance (civil service). Altering the rules of the game is, accordingly, a form of higher politics, reconstituting rather than merely realizing or playing out a given structure through the development and implementation of policy. All legal constitutionalism summons some kind of political constitutionalism, whether in the foreground (as in Britain) or, as more often today, in the form of background norms helping to make the codified institution self-enforcing.[11]

Constitutional thinking, norms, and conventions are neither new nor unique to democracy or the liberal state, let alone the post-Enlightenment West. From ancient and medieval times, the design of polities—from city-states to great land empires—has been continuously debated, with core precepts ranging from spreading and sharing power across different groups in the political community to delineating the functional purpose and powers of distinct government institutions. From the Enlightenment onward, the stress, in theory and practice, in the Western tradition has been on a functional distribution of powers across three canonical branches: legislature, executive, and

---

10. Codified constitutions expressly confer powers, but the same purpose is served by uncodified constitutions manifested in superstatutes and conventions recognized as law.

11. Bellamy, *Political Constitutionalism*.

independent judiciary. This is the *separation of powers* articulated by the eighteenth-century French liberal political scientist Montesquieu.

While the doctrine's detailed application varies across advanced-economy democracies, they each seek to realize its animating values, which include (1) no person being a judge in their own cause, motivating a judiciary that stands independent of the lawmakers; (2) the benefits to efficiency and effectiveness, and thus to the people's welfare, of a division of institutional labor; and (3) avoiding concentrations of power, for the reasons famously urged by American founding father James Madison.

At one end of the spectrum, the legislature delivers, subject to constitutional constraints, most of the rules (the laws of the land) for our everyday collective life, while at the other end the courts apply the law through fair procedures that respect our equality before the law. One is the embodiment of quotidian politics, the other (in intention) the opposite. As the only 24/7 branch, the executive sits in between, administering the law in all the many millions of actions and choices that never end up in a courtroom; deciding which cases to take to court, and subsequently enforcing the courts' decisions; increasingly through the twentieth century, fleshing out the law through regulations and ordinances; and, drawing on that rich experience, proposing initiatives or amendments to the legislature. Far from being mechanical, this catalog of functions entails discretionary choices, and so policymaking by executive government.

During the twentieth century, government evolved to include delegation to domestic agencies of various kinds that apply rules, sometimes write them, manage parts of the state's balance sheet, and more. This presented two challenges. First, and very obviously during a period of discordant geopolitics, joined-up foreign policy must somehow be reconciled with some agencies, notably central banks, being insulated from day-to-day politics. Second, the modalities of delegated lawmaking and policy cannot undermine the norms that underpin our system of government (the subject of *Unelected Power*).

Domestically, even though some regulatory agencies span legislative, executive, and adjudicatory functions, that does not entail abandoning the values underlying the canonical separation of powers. As leading legal scholar Jeremy Waldron puts it, those delegations must maintain "articulated government through successive phases of governance each of which maintains its own integrity."[12]

International delegations must somehow live up to a similar standard because, in some respects, international organizations are akin to a dispersed

12. Waldron, "Separation of Powers," p. 467.

international executive branch. Arguably, fragmented international administration helps to realize some of the values of the separation of powers, but it leaves the exercise of power within individual organizations less tethered to, and so checked by, higher-level powers.

At home, given the general hazards involved (chapter 6), delegated administration, lawmaking, and adjudication are subjected to rule-of-law standards via what is known as administrative law. As Britain's former most senior judge the late Lord Bingham put it, the executive branch and agencies "must exercise the powers conferred on them in good faith, fairly, for the purpose for which the powers were conferred, without exceeding the limits of such powers and not unreasonably."[13]

In most advanced-economy constitutional democracies, an aggrieved party might, as a broad generalization, be able to bring a legal challenge against executive or administrative action on any of the following counts:

- The purported exercise of the power lay beyond the boundaries of the delegated power (*vires*).
- The power was exercised in a way that did not comply with prescribed or fair procedures (*natural justice* or, in terms more familiar in the United States, due process).
- Not all relevant or some irrelevant considerations were taken into account.
- The power was exercised in a deeply *unfair*, biased, *unreasonable*, irrational, or *disproportionate* way.

It will be observed (the italicized words) that, again, some of the dispositions of the old natural-law tradition make a comeback here.

While not necessarily institutionalized via a hierarchy of courts conducting judicial review, similar values and constraints should apply, somehow, to the exercise of powers delegated by constitutional democracies to international organizations. Otherwise we would hold international and transnational power to a lower standard even when it affected the lives of citizen-subjects, and states themselves, in similar ways. While framed in a particular way, that is also the burden of the *Global Administrative Law* movement.[14]

---

13. Bingham, *Rule of Law*, p. 60. (Administrative law serves constitutionalist values even when not formally part of constitutional law.)

14. Its US branch is headquartered at New York University: see Kingsbury et al., "Emergence of Global Administrative Law"; and Kingsbury, "Concept of 'Law.'" Advocating US domestic administrative law as a model, it has a flavor of Grotian rationalist (even Kantian) universalism.

PRINCIPLES FOR CONSTITUTIONAL DEMOCRACIES   345

## Constitutionalism with Democracy

Much of that could apply to a liberal constitutionalist state that was not demo-cratic (the old Hong Kong, for example). In combining constitutionalism with democracy, constitutional democracies are not relying on elite rulers being adequately constrained by checks and balances operated by functionally sepa-rated elite groups (legislators and courts) because, whether for reasons of cul-tural cohesion or raw material interest, they could collude.

Instrumentally, elections act as a useful third-party check (an argument, echoing chapter 9's imaginary exchange between Xunzi and Hume, that can be leveled against modern nondemocratic meritocratic rule: the party mandarins had better be virtuous, or lucky). Normatively, democracy also places a political system's higher-level rules of the game within the people's reach. This has im-plications for international institutions at three levels.

First, it implies states should distinguish agreements that reach back into their domestic legal order in ways that, to use English framing, (1) condition the legal relationship between citizen and state in some general, overarching manner or (2) materially alter the scope of what are regarded (locally) as fun-damental constitutional rights.[15]

The second implication concerns the division of labor between interna-tional courts and states. A corollary of the first implication, it says that where disputes between and among states under an international regime are adjudi-cated by an arm's-length judiciary, such courts and court-like bodies cannot properly—that is, without jeopardizing legitimacy—alter the fundamentals of the regime itself, since that was agreed on at the political level, entailing the requisite domestic democratic (plebiscite) or representative (e.g., supermajority) processes in participating states. Going back to chapter 6's instrumental ac-count of international agreements as, inevitably, incomplete contracts that are partly filled in case-by-case by courts, generating interpretations and doctrines that act as coordinating focal points, the values of constitutional democracy say, unequivocally, that there are normative limits to that vital role.[16] The limits come

15. The late Lord Justice Laws (*Thorburn v. Sunderland City Council*, 2003), quoted with approval extrajudicially in Phillips, "Art of the Possible" (while president of the UK Supreme Court).

16. At a high level of generality, this is akin to principles constraining the exercise of judges' law-developing powers in common-law systems: see, e.g., Bingham, "Judge as Lawmaker," in *Business of Judging*, p. 31 (including "where . . . there is no consensus within the community").

when the agreement needs, for legitimacy's sake, to be taken back to its makers or, alternatively, just left incomplete: a gap in the regime (chapter 17).

That line—between regime articulation and rewriting—cannot easily be drawn. Nor, domestically, is it always enough—although it is important to try—to rely on the formal constitutional-amendment machinery kicking in when many would want it to; we know from the United States that such processes can atrophy, making rulers of the justices. So in addition to making provision for regime amendment by participants, our deep political values call for *self-restraint* among insulated adjudicators (and technocrats).[17] It is not safe to rely on their regime-transforming excesses always being undone through diplomacy.

The third implication of this fundamental principle of constitutionalism—that decisions should lie within reach of the people—is that powers and responsibilities should be held at the level of government that puts them within reach of those most affected. Whereas in chapter 13 this principle of *subsidiarity* was motivated by the legitimacy demands of thick ethical communities, now, in democracies, it has traction even if the political community is socially thin.[18]

## Ready to Go

With that unpacking of the various values of the rule of law, democracy, and constitutionalism embedded in the basic institutions of our domestic governance, we can return to finding a way through the tension between sovereignty as constitutional independence and cooperative international endeavors. By helping liberal democracies safeguard their own legitimacy, our precepts summon Western-style constitutionalist values without relying on a program of global constitutionalism (chapter 1) being incorporated into general international law.[19]

These principles come under three headings: necessary processes for upfront, formal consent; criteria for whether to delegate power to international organizations, including via hierarchical policymaking and arm's-length adjudication

---

17. Famously urged on US Supreme Court justices by Yale professor Alexander Bickel in the early 1960s (*Least Dangerous Branch*), to no avail. And on today's central bankers in Tucker, *Unelected Power*, pp. 556–57.

18. On subsidiarity, see Barber, *Principles of Constitutionalism*, chap. 7.

19. Contrasting with Paulus, "International Legal System."

or operation; and design precepts for how such international organizations should be structured and operated.[20]

## Consent: Via Appropriate Constitutional Processes and Public Debate

In a democracy, two broad things are needed for the grant of upfront formal consent: domestic standards for where a formal process is needed and what it should be, and public debate exposing justification to examination and challenge.

### Formal Processes

On the former, consent should be given at the right level by the relevant organs of government. That, broadly, is recognized in the Vienna treaty on treaties, and constitutional states typically have local codes for how far the executive branch can proceed, under delegated authority, before it needs the assembly's sanction.

Within that general approach, any international agreement that materially alters the local constitutional regime requires whatever process a particular state employs to change constitutional rights and duties. Otherwise international law intrudes on a state's constitutional democracy in ways that could jeopardize the legitimacy of one or the other, or both.[21] Reverting to chapter 11's discussion, meaning is thereby given to sovereignty via the way constitutionalism's values are instantiated in particular states.

### Public Justification and Debate

Where primary legislation is needed, an element of formal debate is automatic. But even where it is not, a justification needs to be offered in public and exposed to debate.

First, this needs to address the subsidiarity principle: "We are loosening our, and therefore your (citizens'), grip on the reins of power, because this can

20. For similar exercises taking a morality-first approach, see Buchanan and Keohane, "Legitimacy of Global Governance Institutions,"; Buchanan, "Legitimacy of International Law"; and Christiano, "Legitimacy of International Institutions." For a public-administration approach, see Woods, "Good Governance."

21. Buchanan and Powell, "Constitutional Democracy."

deliver *abc*." That need not preclude democracies from having other-regarding motives for joining regimes; for example, "Since a clear majority of you [the people] want to help developing countries, it is much more effective for our state to pursue that via international agency X"—so long as that withstands examination. Given that different states (for example, Germany and Britain) live by subsidiarity in very different ways, the justificatory stories will have a different texture in different places.

Second, the depth of the explanation-cum-justification, and the intensity of public debate, will need to vary according to whether joining the regime would bring about a material shift in the domestic legal order, placing it within or under a higher one.[22]

Third, public deliberation needs to be more thorough, the harder it will be to amend or exit a specific regime.

None of that is easy. The substance of international pacts or initiatives is often dry and technical. Factions within a state's elites, whose voices are most easily heard by citizens, may have vested interests in rejecting or joining international endeavors: some will deny the utility or even decency of international institutions because they are not themselves part of that governance world, while others (Davos denizens) will insist there is no sane choice other than to be part of international System, because it is where they thrive.[23] But while the stakes might sometimes be higher, this is not qualitatively different from the noise that runs through public debate of purely domestic measures in a democratic republic.

## Criteria for *Whether* to Delegate Authority to International Organizations

Next come broad tests for *whether* liberal democracies can decently cede power to a hierarchy headed by some of their peers, to the policy staff of an international organization, or to arm's-length adjudicators.[24]

---

22. In Britain, neither at entry nor during the mid-1970s referendum were the public clearly informed that, following European court decisions in the early 1960s, the (then) Common Market had elements of a higher legal order, a legitimacy stain with consequences. Similarly, in the exit referendum forty years later, it was not clear what the new regime would be. Our precepts would have prescribed two referenda, a second being held on the terms of exit if the first favored exit (which a two-stage process would have made more likely).

23. Not a bad way of predicting establishment versus elite votes in the Brexit referendum.

24. They are not dissimilar to but more granular than the "complex standard for legitimacy" of Buchanan and Keohane, "Legitimacy of Global Governance Institutions." (Applied to the

First is the standard test of whether the benefits are expected to exceed the costs, but with an assessment of risks. More than with even very important domestic legislation, the assessment needs to be capacious. A state should satisfy itself that the regime will not so alter international relations as to become a source of disorder or deplete its own resilience in dangerous ways. It needs to form a view on whether its people will be left materially worse off than otherwise (in some relevant sense) if the regime works much less well than expected. This includes judging whether a regime would likely entail net transfers to other peoples or states, or lead to smaller gains than some of its peers, and how it feels about that.

Irrespective of whether it ends up as a net beneficiary or transferor, a state needs to satisfy itself that it would retain the capacity to offset any adverse distributional effects *within* its society (to the extent expected or demanded by its people). Given its electoral institutions are the mechanism for making decisions about and pursuing justice, and elections often turn partly on distributive issues, a democratic state could jeopardize its legitimacy if it lost its formal power or practical capacity to address perceived local inequalities and injustices.

Moving on, where the purpose and objectives of a regime are unclear, a liberal state should want power be pooled among participants rather than formally delegated to an international organization's arm's-length management or staff.

Such delegations can be justified (against democracy's norms) only where they are needed to overcome a problem of credibly committing to a purpose important to a people's welfare.

In that spirit, constitutional democracies should not empower an international organization's management and staff to make ex ante policy choices that have big effects on the distribution of the regime's benefits and costs across the policy regime's members or that, more broadly, materially change the balance of power among states. Behind this lies a profoundly important point, partly prefigured above. It is possible to imagine a world in which an international organization of some kind decides that there shall be net transfers from the peoples in territories A, B, and C to those in X, Y, and Z, either as a one-off or a continuing flow, and not necessarily with the agreement of A, B, or C. That is the kind of redistributive policy operated by many states, but international

---

international activities of independent domestic agencies in Tucker, *Unelected Power*, pp. 283–85.)

organizations should not be able to make such decisions without the consent of their member states, because they could not base their exercise of power on an express delegation from some transnational demos.[25]

In a similar spirit but concerning a different class of international officials, compulsory adjudication should be ceded to arm's-length judges only where a regime's terms are sufficiently precise and complete that the adjudicators are not expected to be able to decide or shape high policy via their case-by-case decisions. Dispute settlement via bilateral diplomacy (or voluntary arbitration) should be retained where a regime is open-ended or vague, so that each dispute becomes, in effect, a matter of bargaining over policy in front of experts.

Nor should constitutional democracies accept hard international lawmaking from international organizations whose members are state agencies that are independent domestically. Instead, such international organizations should, as necessary, be confined to proposing standards and norms that have to be turned into domestic hard law through each member state's particular processes. Whether that means domestic primary legislation or delegated regulatory rule-making is for individual states.

Finally, states should be reluctant to have international standards set by international organizations comprising independent agencies unless those agencies (their delegated powers and modes of operation) are legitimate domestically. Otherwise, the world could effectively be ruled by groups of experts with shaky legitimacy at home.

## Design Precepts for *How* International Organizations Exercise Their Power

When power and responsibility are pooled in or delegated to an international organization or tribunal, it matters hugely how. Design must carefully align incentives with values. Constitutional democracies should (try to) insist on the following (the main driving values are indicated in parentheses).[26]

---

25. Nagel, "Problem of Global Justice," p. 140 (deploying a moral account of the institutional basis for a system of [distributive] justice).

26. "Must" and "should" are not used categorically, but as prudential maxims for avoiding legitimacy mistakes and so forth. (For detailed robustness-test derivations of some of these precepts for a domestic setting, see Tucker, *Unelected Power*, chap. 11.)

## Legal Relationships, Including Financing

The nature of the legal relationship between member-participants and the regime or organization needs to be clear (constitutionalism). Most significantly, it needs to be clear whether rights to issue legally binding obligations are being conferred on the body. (For Basel, for example, plainly not, and so its standards are not issued under a legal relationship with its members.)

Where formal legal powers are used to impose obligations or restrictions on states or others, there should be provision for voting (democracy). Unanimity should be required only if the regime provides for subsets of its members to go further, by, for example, setting merely minimum standards (liberalism).

Where an organization's core mission is to provide vital public goods to the world or a specific region, it should not rely on project-specific or other voluntary funding, including from the private sector and nongovernmental organizations. Such reliance deprives the organization of agency and risks capture, compounding the problem of supplying public goods (chapter 5). Instead, the regime's charter should fix members' contributions. (This entails fundamental reform of the WHO.)[27]

## Mandate and Powers

The harder it is to exit a regime, the narrower should be its mandate (sovereignty).

Whatever the mandate, an international organization's powers should be as clear as possible (constitutionalism). That includes any powers for addressing noncompliance, coordinating decentralized enforcement, and handling orderly and disorderly exit. And it should be clear, formally, which organs of the organization hold which powers, and what specific constraints apply to them.

## Pooling

Hierarchical pooling—with legal authorities formally delegated to a subset of a regime's participants or members (a leadership group)—should be adopted only where either the means for executing the organization's decisions (for

27. Okonjo-Iweala et al., Global Deal, para. 85.

example, hard power, financial resources) are held disproportionately by those states, or they are disproportionately exposed to the issues addressed by the regime—that is, the regime is dependent on them or exists largely for them.

In such settings, the default should be that there is some kind of system under which those at the policy table represent constituencies of members that are not (democracy). Those constituencies should be constructed on the basis of broadly shared interests in the relevant regime's field. Even where that does not make sense given a regime's core purpose—for example, security— the leadership group should be accountable in some way to the wider membership (constitutionalism, democracy).

Those are default precepts for those regimes not integral to an Order itself, where neither constituencies nor universal participation would make sense in the context of an actual or incipient balance of power maintaining peaceful coexistence (the mistake of the League of Nations' architects; chapter 2).

## Delegation

Where there is delegation to management or dispute-settlement bodies, it must be clear whether those officials are intended to be independent (i.e., insulated from day-to-day politics among and within states). Where so, the relevant office-holding officials should have freedom (formal and de facto) to exercise their delegated powers, some budgetary autonomy, and job security (but not necessarily indefinite tenure, which creates a caste of insulated rulers).

Any such group of independent officials should have staggered terms. To avoid any possibility of conflicts, they should not have any other roles. They should be appointed via processes designed to avoid proxy political battlegrounds. To that end, appointment panels could have a majority of state representatives but include distinguished, retired members of the relevant technocratic or adjudicatory community, who could alert the world if the process's integrity were compromised.

Where arm's-length management and staff are delegated power in order to lend credibility to the member states' policy purpose—a trustee role (chapter 6)—the objective must be clear and monitorable. That way, their trusteeship can be monitored reasonably objectively by communities of outside experts, and so the wider transnational public (sovereignty, democracy).

## Independent Adjudication in Specific Regimes

Where an arm's-length adjudicatory body might materially develop the substance of a regime's general policy, or even its high-policy principles and purposes, there should be provision for the membership to revise that new general policy in a forward-looking way, without overriding the dispute panel's determination of particular cases or compromising pending cases (constitutionalism).

In consequence, where a regime's policymaking assembly atrophies for some reason, adjudicators, finding themselves in the position of a constitutional court for the regime in question, should exercise strong *self-restraint* in developing law and general policy—a nod to virtue ethics, and hence to Xunzi (chapter 9). Absent such self-restraint, they become the rulers in the relevant fields, endangering not only their own legitimacy but that of the regime in question, and even international System more generally (constitutionalism, democracy). (This matters to the WTO: see chapter 17.)

## Policy Outputs: Operating Principles

Wherever formal mandates leave gaps, ambiguity, or discretion, international organizations should make clear their general policies (rule of law). When applied to particular cases, there should not be a big surprise for those directly affected.

In particular, where a leadership group or management and staff have delegated authority to flesh out the regime or to apply it to particular cases, their operating principles for how they plan to exercise their discretion should be promulgated. This helps promote constrained rather than open-ended discretion (constitutionalism).

Where an organization departs from its published but nonbinding operational principles in particular cases, it should publish an account of why and hold itself accountable to the membership as a whole. (This matters to the IMF: see chapter 16.)

## Policymaking Procedures: Integrity and Deliberation

Undue concentrations of power in just a few office-holding individuals should be avoided (republicanism, constitutionalism). An organization's policy bodies should be deliberative (democracy, instrumental and intrinsic). This is especially important for arm's-length bodies (policy or adjudicatory), which should be small enough to help deliberation.

More generally, an organization's processes must help to deliver the values of the rule of law in its rule-making, adjudications, and other actions. Structures for applying laws, rules, or policies to particular cases, or for adjudicating disputes, should have degrees of separation from the policymaking process; and each distinct phase of policymaking through to application and enforcement should have its own integrity. (This matters for the Bilateral Investment Treaties order: see chapter 18.)

In the same spirit, international organizations should conduct themselves as though bound by international human-rights laws binding on all (especially *jus cogens* norms), even if technically not formally subjects of such law (constitutionalism).

## Transparency and Accountability

Organizations should be transparent when preparing general policies, consulting widely, and openly, on important initiatives (democracy).

Such consultations should be balanced and fair (democracy). Organizations should not grant access to, say, multinational firms, or an industry for which they set standards, or particular lobbyists for or against such industries, without being open about doing so, and without granting broadly equivalent access to other groups with different perspectives and, potentially, opposing views. (This matters for Basel: see chapter 19.)

The leadership group (under hierarchical pooling) or management group (under arm's-length delegation) should, at least annually, give an account to a general assembly of members for major issues to be aired and so on (constitutionalism, democracy). (This matters for bilateral investment treaties.)

## Legality versus Legitimacy Norms

Those final few items raise an important question. In constitutional states, such norms have been incorporated into the law of the land and are applied by judicial review. By analogy, the Global Administrative Law movement beckons, sometimes implicitly, a unified system of global judicial review applied by a hierarchy of international courts.[28] It would be a bigger change than it might sound.

28. Surfaced by Moellers, "Constitutional Foundations of Global Administration."

In theory, the ICJ could be given jurisdiction to review international organizations and specialist-regime tribunals, and perhaps to take appeals on questions (only) of general international law.[29] To avoid arbitrary variations in how those directly affected by such bodies were treated, that would entail moving to a system of universal compulsory jurisdiction, dropping the voluntarism that, arguably, is a mark of a states-based Order (chapter 11).[30] So legitimacy issues—incentives and values—are to the fore.

Currently, the ICJ operates only modestly beyond the system of permanent arbitration that preceded it (and continues). While, in chapter 6's terms, the court is certainly more than a controlled agent and, in settling questions of general international law, closer to guardian than regime trustee, it is only a part-time guardian, performing as and when it suits disputing states. A move to international judicial review would be a meaningful step toward a true world court. That would be problematic without a counterpart legislative assembly of some kind to reset forward-looking law when necessary. But if a global assembly of states operated on one state, one vote, it would displace the current hierarchical Order on which peaceful coexistence, and hence international System, ultimately rely (chapters 7, 8, and 12).[31] And if, for that reason, an assembly operated weighted voting, it would give the powers even more clout than they have now. More positively, the status quo fragmentation across regimes avoids the risk of a universal guardian becoming a wayward ruler (or even more ignored than now).

There seems to be a paradox here: the standard constitutional machinery for safeguarding the values of constitutionalism and the rule of law could almost certainly not be legitimated, at the international level, short of an implausible revolution away from a states-based Order. Rather than give up, some of those values have to be detached from their familiar juridical habitat, becoming internalized by those running and overseeing international organizations. In effect, that means international agencies being organized for legitimacy without the backing force of legality. If it is claimed the Kosovo interventions

29. This composite reform would involve giving ICJ jurisdiction over international organizations and permitting a wider population of subjects of international law (including individuals and corporations) to seek judicial review.

30. There would still be incentives to reshape "organizations" into soft-law bodies or clubs without legal personality.

31. Nor is ICJ itself immune from legitimacy issues: e.g., with fifteen members (to represent a spectrum of world opinion), it is probably too large to deliberate, and justices can work as arbitrators.

were illegal but legitimate (chapter 3), the risk with (and for) international organizations is that their conduct might sometimes be legal but corrosively illegitimate.

## Wrapping Up Part IV and the Book's Framework

To maintain peaceful coexistence, international relations need to accommodate inevitable disagreement without slipping into conflict, especially armed conflict. That means finding ways of getting through, or around, disagreements in ways states (and peoples) can live with. Our *Principles for Participation and Delegation* (cataloged in the appendix) stake out the ground that constitutional democracies should insist on to avoid sacrificing *our* deep domestic norms: to remain who *we* are.

Reminding us not to mislay or surrender the jewels of constitutional democracy, the *Principles* can help liberal states navigate the globalization trilemma-cum-dilemma (chapter 11). But others are also navigating it, so we encounter different, rival redlines, drawing on different traditions. While many of our *Principles* draw on Lockean values, they are reached in a Humean way—because they reflect *our* history—and so do not assert a universality of right reason (in the tradition running through Aquinas to early modern natural lawyers and their contemporary avatars). A profoundly important question, therefore, is whether non-Western constitutional democracies could find common cause in something like the *Principles*. The work of, perhaps especially, Japanese and Korean, and separately Indian, writers and leaders is crucial to this. If I have not delved far into their living fusions of Confucian, Sanskrit-Persianate, and other traditions with liberal democracy, that is partly because it is hardly for me. But the West should have no doubt that if we are to avoid losing ourselves, the same goes for them.[32]

Thinking in terms of the previous chapter's concentric legitimation circles helps. The liberal openness espoused there does not simply project our values but is useful, including for us, in ensuring developing and emerging-market countries have options. It goes hand in hand with insisting that where unanimity (universal veto) provisions end up blocking change, clubs or coalitions can proceed alone (under the umbrella of any universal minimum standards). In severely adverse circumstances—where the international Order was transformed—that would mean trying to maintain our institutionalized values

32. In that spirit, see Onuma, *International Law in a Transcivilizational World*.

within narrower spheres of cooperation and endeavor. It would likely confine some ambitious projects (Rousseau's stag hunting) to circles of aligned and broadly like-minded states, and so the *Principles* to those regimes and organizations serving a loose free-world community (or *New Cold War* bloc): an international commercial society with the rule of law and basic rights.

Thus equipped, we can apply the *Principles* to real-world institutions. That could mean any of the world's international regimes and organizations but, reflecting my earlier career, I focus on four of the main economic ones. What follows is prosaic in comparison with part IV but brings us to earth by exploring whether the *Principles* would make a difference.

# PART V

# Applications

## REFORMS TO THE INTERNATIONAL ECONOMIC SYSTEM DURING SHIFTING GEOPOLITICS

Is he not the true monarch of the world, who carries on its trade?

LAURENT ANGLIVIEL DE LA BEAUMELLE, WRITER AND
SOMETIME ADVISER TO FREDERICK THE GREAT, 1751

Create an international reserve currency that is disconnected from individual nations. . . . The SDR [Special Drawing Right] has the features and potential to act as a super-sovereign reserve currency.

ZHOU XIAOCHUAN, GOVERNOR OF THE
PEOPLE'S BANK OF CHINA, 2009

# 15

# Legitimacy for a Fragile International Economic System Facing Fractured Geopolitics

Commerce is a perpetual and peaceable war of wit and energy among all nations.

JEAN-BAPTISTE COLBERT TO LOUIS XIV, 1669[1]

MUCH OF THE constitutionalism on which part IV's *Principles for Participation and Delegation* draw is a product of the eighteenth century, an age uncannily like ours in many ways. Montesquieu, as well as coining the separation of powers, accepted the pluralism of different civilizations, offering "doux commerce" as its salve. Peace was not inevitable, with various ancient enmities rooted in ambition, jealousy, religion, and manners.[2] But commerce could help. Its mobile wealth (bills of exchange) checked the power of absolute sovereigns. By strengthening the hand of merchants and others, it promoted republican government without the ancient and medieval republics' pathological aggression. And it generated a need for conventions (laws), which, because they could not just incorporate one party's protocols, had to fall back on reason (a residue of natural law, which an otherwise admiring Hume didn't enjoy).[3] This provides a nice (but not deterministic) dynamic general equilibrium story for how Immanuel Kant's later vision might be realized.

1. Hont, *Jealousy of Trade*, p. 23.
2. Montesquieu, *Spirit of the Laws*.
3. Hume, *Enquiry*, III.ii, p. 29n12.

There were hazards, though. One was the perversion of government—including through commercial society corrupting and capturing those in power and vice versa (which helps make sense of the abject failure of Russia's post-Soviet big-bang economic reforms).[4] Separated powers and the rule of law helped protect against that.

Another hazard was war. To maintain a balance of power, a military was needed. But unless government's authorities were separated, leaders might succumb to the allure of war's glory. So internal and external checks worked in tandem, allowing commerce to do its gentle work.[5]

A third was money, but only if sovereigns violated the disciplines entailed by exchange in precious metals. Even happening to control the world's supply of gold and silver was as much curse as boon, as Montesquieu illustrated with Habsburg Spain's inflationary problems. As the century progressed, Hume recognized gold's anchor demanded symmetric adjustment to economic shocks (chapter 2), taking monetary policy out of the front line of international power politics. Trade and credit's jealousies played out against a backdrop of price stability. That all changed, however, when gold's ties were relaxed, wreaking havoc during the twentieth century's interwar years, introducing competition in monetary laxity, and culminating in the introduction's story of US treasury secretary John Connally's desire to screw his European allies.

If a single fact sums up the changes in the world since then, it is that the Pax Americana's guardian has run gigantic external and fiscal deficits without a run on the dollar or escalating debt-servicing costs dictating an excruciating domestic economic crunch. The explanation lies in a technical but profound change in monetary technology (chapter 16). Exaggerating, if the contemporary hegemon has an unknowing headquarters, it is the Federal Reserve building in Washington, DC.

Maybe it will be dislodged by China's digital currency (where part V closes) or dominance in trade (chapter 17). The contest is hardly friendly, as Colbert understood about Louis XIV's. Likewise, Adam Smith tempered his criticisms of Britain's empire (a rent-extraction machine for merchants) with a nod to the

---

4. On Montesquieu's approach to such dangers, see Shklar, "Political Theory." Unusually among then policymakers, Bank of England governor Robin Leigh-Pemberton argued Russia's economic reforms would fail unless the rule of law was embedded, and that would take time.

5. On Montesquieu, see Hirschman, *Passions and the Interests*, pp. 70–81; Rosow, "Commerce, Power and Justice"; and Howse, "Montesquieu on Commerce" (heralding world government).

wider struggle. Excluding a rival from markets can make sense when rela-tive (zero-sum) rather than absolute gains matter most (chapters 6 and 7).[6] In the face of grave risks, policy needs to be robust, which, remember, includes not unnecessarily making things worse (chapter 10). With nothing guaranteed, we have to hang on to what we know about ourselves (our way of life) and the risks of wishful thinking, underlining the importance of resilient institutions that reflect our *Principles for Participation and Delegation*.

To see where resilience is needed—shielding us from spillovers to security, welfare, and legitimacy—this chapter fills in some necessary background on the prevailing economic order's vulnerabilities and tensions. It then adds economic substance to the Four Scenarios—*Lingering Status Quo, Superpower Struggle, New Cold War,* and *Reshaped World Order*.[7]

## Tensions and Fault Lines in the International Economic System

Our first task, introductory, is to unbundle six sets of issues: the moral and pragmatic reasons for development aid, now a competitive marketplace; the costs and benefits of international commerce, the territory of regimes for trade, tax, mergers, and investment; the drivers and consequences of *net* capi-tal flows, the terrain of macroeconomic policy; the hazards of the underlying *gross* capital flows, a macrofinancial policy nightmare; the interconnections among internationally active financial intermediaries, the arena of regulation; and finally, the provision of the world's premier reserve currency, which is where monetary economics meets geopolitics in capital letters. Those six fields are characterized by politics that are, respectively, agonized, salient, impotent, angry, obscure, and explosive—and that is before each is affected by the hos-tile politics of sanctions.

### *The Agonized, Now Competitive Politics of Development Policy*

Beginning with a field not elaborated on later, development policy is besieged by contested moral debates (whether or not rich states owe duties to poor peoples) and sad implementation hazards (help being misdirected or captured

---

6. Weingast, "War, Trade, and Mercantilism."
7. Thanks to Larry Summers for reading the final draft of this and the next chapter.

by local elites). That has not deterred a multiplication in the number of development banks (to scores, arguably hundreds). Competition to help the poor is today sometimes little more than a polite face of geoeconomic rivalry, reflecting frustrations with asymmetric power in the long-established bodies.[8]

If approached, however, in terms of this book's concern with order as a precondition for collective endeavors at home and abroad, aid and development policy reemerge as instruments for tackling shared existential threats. Quite how depends on the nature of the hazard. One, already touched on (chapter 13), is that rich states have an interest in helping poor states overcome weakest-link global public harms, notably deadly pathogens. But it would be a mistake to reconceive the whole of development policy in those terms, because rich states also have a local interest in avoiding the mass migration caused by endemic domestic disorder or abject poverty. Rich states' involvement can, then, be motivated in terms of long-term risks to their own local legitimacy without any deontological moral imperatives.

Since pathogens, climate change, and mass migration represent serious threats to order, this argues for some reorientation of development policy and agencies, making them less dependent on annual discretionary choices. That would need to be explained at home in ways that make sense to citizen-subjects.

## The Salient Domestic Politics of International Commerce

While globalized commerce has long faced all sorts of challenges from opponents of market-based exchange and advocates of cosmopolitan governance, few have gained wide salience for long periods. Active concerns about, for example, cross-border investment treaties or multinational mergers have largely remained confined to specialists and campaigners. But there are exceptions. One, building over the past couple of decades, has been the capacity of multinational businesses to avoid (or evade) tax on a grand scale. The other is trade itself.

Since the end of the Cold War, the international trade regime has ridden a rollercoaster: from the highs of former communist-bloc states' joining, through the 1999 Seattle riots for "fair" trade, to growing disenchantment with China's trade practices culminating, briefly, in a US administration that junked the very idea of a rules-based regime. Behind those tensions lies a profound feature of the post–World War II System. Neither the original GATT nor the

8. Pratt, "Angling for Influence."

reformed WTO regime catered for a giant economy with a completely different economic and political model: state-sponsored capitalism, with subsidies to
export-oriented and import-competing businesses, and a single-party authoritarian government that can, among many other things, control and direct the
economy (chapter 17).

At one level, this has generated concerns about security hazards: whether
the free world is too dependent on unfriendly states for essentials, including
energy (from Russia). At another, despite the arcana—subsidies, technology
transfer (and piracy), and so on—trade relationships have become politically
salient, especially in the United States, where economists have documented
adverse effects from Chinese competition on wages and employment in
import-competing localities (essentially because local firms cannot sustain the
cost cuts necessary to remain competitive).[9] Feelings around this have fueled a view, held strongly by former president Trump but not only by him, that
the United States' persistent trade deficit—in particular, bilaterally with
China—reflects adverse terms of trade, and must be repaired via tariffs and
quotas. This popular view of trade's evils deprives the United States of political
license to join regional pacts even when they might serve its longer-term strategic interests. It is Hume's jealousy of trade unleashed—in ways that might
change the world.

In fact, however, one of the things nearly all economists agree on is that the
trade balance should be assessed in aggregate, not bilaterally. A country's deficit with one other state might be more than covered by surpluses with others;
and an aggregate deficit does not automatically generate hardship. The drivers
of a state's overall external balance reflect macroeconomic policies, not only
microeconomic factors.

### The Impotent International Politics of Global Current Account Imbalances

Not that all has been well on the macro side. In the years running up to the
2007–9 financial crisis, the world economy was plagued by persistent imbalances.[10] Big picture, the United States, along with some other Western nations, ran persistent external deficits, while China and others ran massive

9. Autor et al., "China Syndrome." (It happens within countries too, but states can adopt
regional policies.)

10. Bernanke, "Global Savings Glut."

surpluses. The counterparts were, by definition, in domestic savings and investment imbalances.[11] While the expansion of domestic investment in China during this period was extraordinary, it could not keep up with the growth in domestic savings.

Rather than letting its currency appreciate, which might have kept the country's external position closer to balance, the Chinese state intervened to hold down its value against the dollar and other currencies, accumulating a vast portfolio of foreign exchange reserves in the process. Many economists regarded all this as the height of irrationality, but as pointed out in chapter 4, mercantilism works for the mercantilists.

In any case, this was not just about China. Any summary of international gatherings in the years before the 2008 crisis would mention the strictures on Germany to consume more, the pleas for the United States to save more (which is to say, shop less), and the urgings for southern Europe to liberalize services and labor markets.

The story's moral is that surplus and deficit countries rarely see their shared interests, and even when their leaders do so, it is hard for them to convey that to their domestic constituencies. Attempts to break through this during the 2000s were an abject failure (chapter 16). It is not fanciful to think that we will go around the course again in a few years' time (if and) when India or some other long-slumbering giant full of potential grows to be a major part of the global economy, and its leaders find themselves trading off development imperatives against the country's longer-term interest in internal economic balance and global macroeconomic health.

Truly unsustainable imbalances resolve themselves in ugly ways. Current account deficits have to be financed; external surpluses have to be employed. These financing items are *net* capital flows into or out of an economy. A country that runs persistent deficits on its trade (and investment income) accumulates external debts. One running surpluses acquires assets around the world. If a deficit country's debt burden becomes so big that it cannot repay, it has to default in some way; its problems are fundamental, not illiquidity (see below). History is littered with the politics of sovereign default, which is why it matters that China, whose interstate lending terms are opaque and perhaps onerous,

---

11. It is an identity that, ex post, the external account (deficit or surplus) equals the difference between domestic savings and investment. A country with very low national saving relative to investment runs an external deficit, which is akin to borrowing productive capacity from abroad.

has stayed outside the Paris Club for coordinating reschedulings (chapters 9 and 16).[12]

With US public debt having rocketed in response to COVID-19, it is, therefore, worth underlining that the country is already heavily indebted to China, Japan, and the oil-producing countries. This could end up being an important factor in any twenty-first-century rebalancing of power. Whereas the United Kingdom's post–World War II debt-servicing problems led to friction between allies (chapter 3), a debt standoff between the United States and China would be a lot worse.

So to sum up, this is a field in which the biggest economies in the world are persistently irritated with each other, but no one has an easy cure.

### The Angry International Politics of Global Capital Flows

That is a long-fuse risk. Meanwhile, the *composition* of capital flows prompts all sorts of other political frictions.[13] When sovereign wealth funds or state enterprises acquire controlling stakes in companies, there are sometimes concerns about foreign governments controlling strategic sectors or facilities. When surplus countries or central banks invest massively in low-risk sovereign securities, there are concerns about stability spillovers as downward pressure on yields prompts other asset managers to scramble for better returns in other asset classes.[14]

This rich-country search for yield can be especially galling for the rest of the world. Before the Global Financial Crisis and again since, very low interest rates in the United States and Europe sent capital hurtling toward the magnet of higher returns in emerging-market economies, pushing up their exchange rates and asset values, and leading to easy internal credit conditions that it was hard for them to offset with tighter monetary policy without adding gravitational pull to the forces driving hot money toward them. Worse, as decades of

12. For granular analysis, see Gelpern et al., *How China Lends.*

13. Obstfeld, "Global Capital Market Reconsidered."

14. This could be sparked in three ways: an ex ante world savings imbalance, driving down the equilibrium real interest rate (the infamous $r^*$); increased *demand* for safe assets, as in the PRC and others buying US treasuries; and reduced *supply* of safe assets, as via central banks' quantitative easing (the latter two compressing the "term premium" compensating investors for locking up their funds). Falling risk-free yields then prompt some (irrational) investors to seek extra yield in *supposedly* low-risk asset classes.

misfortune underlines, there is sometimes an abrupt and disruptive rotation from one set of "opportunities" to others—game over, move on. Even with sound fundamentals, as in some East Asian states during the late 1990s, the end result can be a liquidity crisis that lands on the desks of the IMF and the US treasury secretary (see the next chapter).

But the politics is also frayed in states that have been spared or shielded themselves against external-financing crunches. That has been manifest in sporadic diplomatic flare-ups, as when a Brazilian finance minister complained about Federal Reserve policy during 2013, and also in technocratic challenges, as from the then-governor of the Indian central bank a year later. Raghuram Rajan argued the Fed should place greater weight on the effects of its policy choices on the rest of the world not only because of spillbacks into the US economy but because the dominant reserve-currency issuer impliedly owes something (morally, or politically?) to the world: "Even if a central bank has a purely domestic mandate, the country's international *responsibilities* do not allow it to arbitrarily impose costs on the rest of the world."[15] In our terms, that is better seen as explicitly questioning the international legitimacy of the monetary hegemon's authority: angry, constitutional politics.

## The Obscure Politics of the International Financial System

In comparison, our catalog's fifth element—the world of finance—is so technical, its international politics are opaque to the point of being wholly obscure to outsiders.

Crudely, a financial system comprises three elements: instruments that are held and traded (bonds, equities, currencies); intermediaries that move them about (banks, dealers, insurance companies, funds, and so on); and the platforms and tubes—infrastructure—through which agreements are struck and instruments transferred. Given the ubiquity of internationally active financial firms, the range and scale of capital flows, and the prevalence of transnational infrastructure providers, national authorities are hugely dependent on each other to keep finance safe and sound.

Many prefer, on the whole, not to admit that to domestic audiences. Others maintain international cooperation is rarely sustained when it matters: taxpayer bailouts have almost invariably fallen to financial groups' home-country

---

15. Rajan, "Competitive Monetary Easing" (my emphasis). A practical manifestation of J. Cohen and Sabel, "Extra Rempublicam Nulla Justitia?" (chapter 13).

governments. As former Bank of England governor Mervyn King memorably put it, the biggest banks and dealers have proved international in life but national in death. Yet no major jurisdiction has embraced that pessimism. Notwithstanding some partial ring-fencing of local units, no one has moved to anything like financial autarky.

Up to now, those issues have played out largely among advanced economies with deep fiscal capacity (including the euro area, taken as a whole) and close security relations, because that is where the so-called systemically important financial institutions (SIFIs, to the cognoscenti) are domiciled. Things will become even more difficult when globally systemic intermediaries start emerging from economies that are still developing or that have cool or worse relations with the United States, Europe, and Japan.

Even before we get there, the step-by-step weaponization of the financial system, and its vulnerability to attacks, has transformed the terrain. Does the current plumbing give the Western allies an upper hand in applying sanctions? Does it furnish them with sensitive information on people from around the world? And, the other way around, is the infrastructure on which global finance and commerce depend exposed to cyberattack from hostile actors? Those issues are hardly conducive to frank exchanges at the G20 table.

But nor are all the tensions limited to superpower rivalry. Europeans have at times been so uncomfortable with Washington's approach to financial sanctions that, like Beijing and Moscow, Brussels has explored a segmented payments infrastructure, enabling European businesses to transact beyond the reach of a US regulatory state that sometimes substitutes for Washington's security apparatus.[16]

This shades into a similarly awkward, although to date slightly less fraught, issue around the territorial reach of national regulatory policy. Whether or not strictly accurate, there is a perception that if an entity in, say, Melbourne trades in a dollar-denominated contract with an entity in, say, Manilla, the US authorities might claim jurisdiction for some purposes given that the dollars must ultimately, at the end of a long chain, be settled across accounts in the United States. That may make sense, but it is not obvious that American legislators, policymakers, and commentators would applaud if, in the future, a rival nation with a rival reserve currency claimed jurisdiction over trades

16. In 2019 the European authorities created INSTEX—Instrument in Support of Trade Exchanges—a special-purpose vehicle to facilitate non-dollar transactions with Iran outside the SWIFT payments-messaging system.

denominated in their currency between parties in, say, Massachusetts and Tennessee. National security and basic-order issues aside, jurisdictional modesty might have longer-term benefits.

## The Explosive Politics of the World's Reserve Currency

Many of the political tensions associated with those various hazards—around trade and investment, global macroeconomic imbalances, volatile capital development flows, and financial system fragility—are linked to the role played by the dominant reserve currency. There is nothing new about this. As long ago as the 1960s, French finance minister (later president) Valéry Giscard d'Estaing summed up Paris's frustrations with the dollar's exorbitant privilege.

Part of that is straightforwardly financial: a running annuity for US companies, banks, and taxpayers. Corporations can borrow more cheaply in liquid markets. With direct access to the Fed, US banks can expand internationally, confident they can raise any local currency in exchange for dollars. And the country as a whole can run larger external and fiscal deficits than otherwise, enabling some combination of lower taxes and higher spending, including on the projection of power. But it works both ways: Washington's widespread security blanket sponsors dollar use, and is sometimes offered to do just that.[17] The military-industrial complex, as President Dwight Eisenhower called it, and the monetary-finance machine are linked.

Pulling things together, the endowments—subsidies to American consumers and businesses—can be viewed as enjoyed in exchange for providing a security blanket to friends and allies, open sea-lanes, and dollar liquidity insurance. Quite apart from whether rising states like that grand bargain (chapter 1), it presses the question of whether the privilege comes bundled with a curse.

### The Bargain's Buried Burdens: The Modern Triffin Problem

During the Bretton Woods era, the Belgian American economist Robert Triffin articulated his eponymous dilemma: that since the reserve-currency issuer must meet international demand for its currency, it is destined to run current account deficits that cumulatively become so great that, eventually, structural demand flips into a dash for the exits in the mother of all crises.[18]

17. Norrlof, *America's Global Advantage*.

18. Triffin, *Gold and the Dollar Crisis*. The mechanics vary according to whether the big economies operate fixed or floating exchange rates, with or without capital controls. Today (see main text), both current account and "banking" channels are relevant.

Writing in a world with capital controls, Triffin focused on how expanding world trade would drive increasing demand for the dollar, a process that, as it turned out, was amplified by its use in invoicing (where the international monetary system and international price system mesh).[19]

Today, by contrast, the demand for dollar-denominated instruments also comes from states insuring themselves against volatile capital flows, and from businesses, especially financial intermediaries, needing to hold low-risk assets to use as collateral to cover all sorts of counterparty credit exposures (not least in derivative markets). Similarly, while Triffin saw his dilemma crystallizing through unsustainable trade deficits (net capital flows), in today's world things could come to a head through financial-system instability (gross capital flows).

The central point here is that, with capital-flow freedom, the national balance sheet of the reserve-currency issuer comes to resemble that of a bank or hedge fund. Not only the state but parts of the private sector issue short-term liquid claims—ostensibly safe assets—to external buyers, with the proceeds recycled back into the world as longer-term loans and investments.[20] To the extent that net issuance of Treasury bills and bonds (after Federal Reserve purchases) does not satisfy demand for safe assets, the private sector acts to fill the vacuum, incentivized by the availability of cheap financing. The world becomes one great carry trade.

The engine for supplying those privately issued safe assets is the banking industry. But where there are regulatory constraints on the size of bank balance sheets (so that banks cannot frictionlessly meet unsatisfied demand for low-risk dollar instruments), unregulated shadow banks emerge to plug the gap. At this point the safety of "safe assets" becomes moot. Think of them, generically, as those instruments that users (investors, traders, intermediaries) feel no need to analyze, and so do not: they are, as economists put it, information insensitive. Like money, they enjoy network economies and so are liquid: as Hume observed, "Public securities are with us become a kind of money," but today, with alchemy, it goes much wider. Until, that is, some revelation shatters an illusion, there is a run for the exits, and supposedly safe assets become, in a flash, illiquid, or worse.[21]

19. Gopinath, "International Price System"; Gourinchas, "Dollar Hegemon."

20. Pierre-Olivier Gourinchas and Helene Re documented this in the mid-2000s. (States that are not the monetary hegemon can have a national external balance sheet with a similar structure but in foreign currencies, notably if, like the United Kingdom, they host a major international financial center.)

21. Holmstrom, "Understanding the Role"; Hume, "Of Public Credit," in *Political Essays*, p. 168.

This is the monetary hegemon's first problem: inherently fragile domestic banking-like vehicles and structures issuing ostensibly money-like claims but lacking (ex ante) access to a liquidity safety net. Given they almost inevitably overreach, their subsequent explosive unraveling might undermine confidence in dollar monetary instruments, and so conceivably the dollar itself, if they are simply allowed to collapse.[22]

Since some of the implosions will be in foreign states, the hegemon's second problem is painful monetary diplomacy. Given the greater liquidity of dollar-denominated capital markets, short-sighted foreign entrepreneurs and businesses finance themselves in dollars even where they lack matching dollar-denominated income sources. When the music stops, the United States finds itself having to act as the de facto lender of last resort to the world as a whole, with the proximate objective of ensuring dollar liquidity problems elsewhere do not destabilize the international economy and financial system. If Washington rejected this burden, it would undermine demand for its currency, and so its leadership role. This possibility—long familiar to my old central bank from its own history—has been labeled an "exorbitant duty."[23]

## The World Liquidity Insurer's Big Macro Privilege

Notwithstanding those burdens, which are sometimes—myopically given the broader geopolitics—resented in Washington, leading states are unlikely voluntarily to forgo an opportunity to provide the world's reserve currency. That is because, I suggest, the most important economic benefits of monetary hegemony are not annuity-like but, rather, that issuing the world's bedrock safe assets provides a state with highly valuable insurance against big economic shocks, reducing their local costs and hence the domestic political fallout from crises.[24]

Even during the 2008/9 phase of the national and international crisis sparked by the United States' subprime mortgage improvidence, with incompetence and venality on naked display, far from US Treasury bonds collapsing, they rallied, reducing the cost of government debt just as fiscal support was automatically provided to cushion the blow to the American people. Having such a shock absorber to help their country get through what was then their

---

22. For a model of this and other international monetary order vulnerabilities, see Farhi and Maggiori, "China versus the United States." For a review, see Ilzetzki et al., "Rethinking Exchange Rate Regimes."

23. Gourinchas et al., "International Monetary and Financial System," and earlier articles.

24. B. Cohen, "Macrofoundation of Monetary Power."

biggest domestic economic and financial crisis for nearly eighty years must have struck US officials as providence indeed. It can hardly have failed to have been noticed in the capitals of the main rising powers.

It would, indeed, be surprising if Beijing did not entertain the prospect of the renminbi one day enjoying similar blessings: when we mess up so massively it infects the whole world, the world shelters under our currency. That fits with its efforts to develop infrastructure for offshore renminbi transactions and trading, with its anxiety for the renminbi to be included in the IMF's Special Drawing Right basket even though it was not yet convertible, and with former central bank governor Zhou's public musings about a radically reformed international monetary system.[25] But, as the Party must realize, efforts to displace the dollar are potentially explosive, since the knock-on effects would extend well beyond finance—into security alliances and the whole architecture of the prevailing System.

This directs us toward the demands of supplying the major reserve currency. It should alert US policymakers to the long-term costs of powerful domestic lobbies resisting measures to come to grips with the country's shadow-banking habit. It underlines just how much turns on the integrity of the Federal Reserve's independence and commitment to internal monetary-system stability. And, going to a tension at the heart of this book, it reveals the geopolitical importance of the American state's legitimacy at home, since that is a precondition for navigating the inevitable sequence of shocks, stumbles, and disappointments that beset an Order-System's leading power.

## The Four Scenarios Redux: Filling Out the Economic Dimension

Armed with that survey of some of the international economy's and so commercial society's fractures and sore points, we can return to the Four Scenarios introduced in chapter 4 and elaborated in chapter 10, now fleshing out what they mean for economic order and system.

### Lingering Status Quo

This first scenario depends on the United States performing well economically. That means continuing to be the world's engine of technical innovations that drive productivity improvements; avoiding macroeconomic boom and bust,

25. Zhou, "Reform the International Monetary System."

especially another US-concocted global financial crisis; and maintaining long-run fiscal and external sustainability, so that, even when stretched, the country can sustain the costs of the Pax Americana without harsh domestic adjustment. Likewise, this scenario depends on Europe avoiding crisis, including any renewed euro-area fractures.

It is a world in which most of the major oil suppliers continue to invoice in dollars, avoiding a new structural demand for renminbi (or other currencies) and the network effects of producers turning their backs on dollar capital markets. That means navigating among the various Sunni and Shia powers, in competition with Beijing and Moscow.

Elsewhere, Washington would need to be careful to avoid allies, friends, and neutrals accumulating short-term dollar-denominated obligations unless it is prepared to support them with dollar liquidity reinsurance if and when a run occurs. In policing those hazards, it will also need to be careful not to drive states into the hands of alternative sources of liquidity help and protection.

As for the international organizations, this is a world in which, somehow, the World Bank remains relevant, especially in helping with global public goods; in which the IMF comes up with viable policies to help insulate members from volatile capital flows (chapter 16); in which the WTO somehow resolves the big problems currently undermining its rules-and-judge-based system (chapter 17); in which international investment law is no longer perceived as sheltering conspiracy behind opacity; and in which Basel addresses glaring fault lines in the international financial system (chapter 19). Those are big asks.

## Superpower Struggle

Under this scenario, there is some economic decoupling; a process Beijing embarked on during Leader Xi's second term.[26] Some commercial supply chains fracture, but well short of fully fledged deglobalization. Multinationals are subject to intensified cyber espionage and attacks. They might well be required to firewall data sets in certain foreign operations, and to follow a stipulated set of technical standards (to give their "side" network-economy opportunities and protections).[27]

26. Rudd, "Xi Jinping's Pivot."
27. Already in train in the PRC according to Leonard, "New China Shock."

On the monetary front, the main currency issuers would seek to keep others tied to them by encouraging wide use of their currency.[28] There would be intense pressure on key energy suppliers to move away from invoicing in dollars, linked to deals over security. The US Congress would back off its historical opposition to the Fed providing liquidity reinsurance to foreigners, and instead the two superpowers' monetary authorities would fall over each other to reward potential friends and, crucially, neutrals with liquidity lines (whether via swaps or other facilities)—a practice Beijing sensibly began around a decade ago. In contrast to the Global Financial Crisis (preface), geopolitical sensitivity of that kind was apparent in the Fed's 2020 facilities to help foreign states liquify their US Treasury bonds during the COVID-19 pandemic.

In other words, trade officials would weigh geopolitics alongside their habitually narrower concerns, and some monetary officials would become international monetary diplomats of a kind familiar before and during Bretton Woods. A world Paul Volcker and Jacques de Larosière would have recognized.

As for the international organizations, the WTO would atrophy, perhaps becoming a thin umbrella for thicker "regional" free-trade pacts among allies and friends (chapter 18). Development banks would become even more obviously aligned geopolitically. The IMF would struggle to maintain ideological neutrality in its programs, giving it incentives to talk more about issues peripheral to its core mission (already?). Sheltered in the Basel Tower, the central bankers' collective endeavors would become even more obscure. That is, unless kicking countries out of the plumbing—SWIFT and so on—becomes the door through which the world enters cold war (a looming prospect while signing off this text in spring 2022).

### New Cold War

Commercially, businesses would find themselves having to pick sides; Stockholm syndrome (the desire of multinationals to please powerful hosts), a feature of the first two scenarios, and already apparent, would largely pass, albeit in a parade of discomfort. Depending on the speed with which the trade shutters came down, there would be divestment, asset seizures, write-offs, and dislocated supply chains. Asset managers would find themselves implementing a

---

28. During the 1930s, when seeking to displace Britain, Washington urged the Republic of China to peg to the dollar: see Conway, *Summit*, p. 125.

geopolitical-bloc version of home bias in their investment choices. Sanctions policing would mushroom until interbloc commerce shrank. But deglobalization—undoing the dispersed production chains described in chapter 1—would not be complete, especially if many states were carefully neutral or nonaligned (admittedly an obstacle course).

On the monetary front, the public good of a shared financial infrastructure would unravel as each side sought to insulate itself from cyber infection, intrusion, and sanctions. There would be a single numeraire and common medium of exchange (the dollar) for natural-resource transactions only if the United States preserved close relations with nearly all the major energy producers. Otherwise, some states—perhaps Iran, Russia, and conceivably Saudi Arabia if they dispensed with Washington's security umbrella—would transact in renminbi, while others stuck to Western currencies. Efforts to launch a multilateral currency would get nowhere until and unless the conflict was resolved— dramatically, or through symmetric exhaustion.

Meanwhile, the main international economic organizations would either become irrelevant bystanders or, more likely, reinvent themselves for one or other of the blocs, perhaps alongside a set of doppelgängers, each with its own institutional top table and hierarchy. Up to a point, this is already apparent in the development field. Our *Principles* would more easily prevail within our bloc's regimes, but it would be no less important to try to sustain them in any truly global organizations.

### Reshaped World Order

The economic shape of this new world might turn on the fortunes and choices of states with such large populations that they will acquire economic and political clout if only they manage to grow fairly rapidly, without crises, for a number of years. To the extent they succeed, their rise could cause the world to revisit mercantilism's tensions, but that is not inevitable.

It is a world in which, via consensus among the new Order's powers, the trade regime would either revert to liberalism or embrace state capitalism, and in which, by design, there would be changes to the international monetary order and financial system. Depending on how the new Order came about, there would be efforts to replace the dollar, either with a system of parallel reserve currencies or with some kind of internationally issued and collectively controlled currency. Such dreams have long circulated, which the important speech by former PRC central bank governor Zhou was tapping into. None of this would be straightforward technically (chapter 16).

At the international economic institutions, there would be efforts to check the superpowers' geoeconomic capabilities. That would probably require codified rules of the road, in order to clarify what counted as impermissible geoeconomic aggression. If monitoring became feasible, certain types of egregious cyber interference would become the leading candidates, but the credibility of such norms might depend on whether the new Order was hegemonic or multipolar.

## Turning to the Dos and Don'ts of Reform

That sets the stage for our case studies of the main international economic regimes and organizations. They are not intended to be exhaustive but to illustrate the bite in part IV's *Principles for Participation and Delegation* and, in doing so, the demands and pitfalls of the international commercial society entertained by Hume, Montesquieu, and Smith. Addressing those vulnerabilities and hazards is necessary to realize those luminaries' hopes, and hence to buttress our world.

As well as addressing whether the various international regimes and organizations are the product of spontaneous order or deliberate design, and whether they provide a global public, common, or club good (part II), each case study is centered on a specific legitimacy shortfall relative to the *Principles*. For the IMF, it is overreach in intruding into the deep political choices of program countries. For the WTO, judicial overreach. In the bilateral investment treaty regime, rule of law. And for Basel, unbalanced and opaque access to policymakers, with bankers and fund managers benefiting relative to activists with different points of view. Along the way, we will propose measures to make the international economic system more resilient, which would help both to protect the autonomy of individual states and to enhance the platform for cooperation among states: order as a precondition for System.

# 16

# The International Monetary Fund and the International Monetary Order

## AN EXERCISE IN EXCESSIVE DISCRETION WITH MISSING REGIMES?

[The] Fund is designed for a special purpose, and that purpose is to prevent competitive depreciation of currencies.

HARRY DEXTER WHITE DURING 1944
BRETTON WOODS NEGOTIATIONS[1]

[The IMF] shall oversee the international monetary system in order to ensure its effective operation, and shall oversee the compliance of each member with its obligations.

IMF ARTICLE IV.3(A)

NEITHER OF THOSE propositions has held. There is no longer a system. For some rising states, currency policy has served the ends of trade policy. The domestic monetary policies of large economies sometimes spill over onto other states. And the IMF arguably blinked rather than exercise its powers in the face of shifts in the balance of power.

Meanwhile, there is no doubt that the world's premier reserve currency, the US dollar, provides a global public good (nonrivalrous and, sanctions aside,

---

1. Steil, *Battle of Bretton Woods*, p. 208.

barely excludable). And the IMF (sometimes in this chapter called the Fund) supplies public goods ranging from the mundane publication of data on its members' economies and policy regimes to its benchmark forecasts.[2] Its crisis-management services might deliver either private goods to states, as when the benefits accrue entirely locally, or global goods if they stave off system-wide collapse. Finally, the IMF promotes (but does not develop all) standards and codes for economic resilience, which are certainly public goods, while not always being any good. During prolonged periods of stability, there is typically a good deal of angst-ridden head-scratching about the IMF's role in the world, only for that to be laid aside once crisis resumes.

Taking its various roles together, one could say the IMF's mission is to achieve a weakest-link good—resilience—by promoting certain practices via the carrot of positive assessments (a weak force for large states) and the stick of conditions attached to rescue finance. It would itself want to say it promotes general equilibrium—balance—in the world economy, but that, no small thing, is largely illusory. Finally, the IMF is an interesting vehicle for delivering aid to developing countries through its peculiar and opaque Special Drawing Right (SDR) (see below).

Adding a few more episodes of international monetary history to those described earlier, this chapter uses part IV's legitimacy *Principles for Participation and Delegation* to develop prescriptions for how constitutional democracies should approach questions about reserve currencies and the IMF, contextualizing them with the book's Four Scenarios.

## A Monetary Nonsystem within a Wider Order-System

The Bretton Woods international monetary regime was most definitely designed, but the world of floating exchange rates that followed its unraveling is better thought of as an evolved monetary *order*—a nonsystem, as some international monetary titans call it.[3] That transformed the role and relevance of the IMF, leading to legitimation problems that, around the turn of the millennium, almost engulfed it.

---

2. Joyce and Sandler, "IMF Retrospective and Prospective." On multilateral surveillance helping states see which coordination and cooperation situations they are in, see Frankel, "International Coordination."

3. Larosière, "Demise of the Bretton-Woods."

As chapter 3 emphasized, the 1944 agreement was crafted as part of the scaffolding for a System intended to avoid revisiting the interwar trade protectionism that had exacerbated the world's many problems. With memories still fresh of the gold-exchange standard's collapse, and subsequent sterling and dollar depreciations triggering Belgian and French tariffs and import quotas, the rebuilt trade system needed buttressing with guardrails against competitive currency devaluations.[4]

Fortunately given the values associated with the separation of powers (chapter 14), the architects did not entrust both trade and monetary affairs to the same organization, choosing instead to cater for the possibility of conflict. First, a country could use trade restrictions to address a balance-of-payments problem only if the IMF formally determined that macroeconomic measures could not suffice (Article XV of GATT).[5]

Second, the new monetary system's fixed exchange rates were adjustable, helping members avoid having to depress their economies to accommodate shocks that would otherwise lead to chronic current account imbalances. That needed either an impartial umpire (too powerful), or a collective process informed by economic analysis that was, so far as possible, independent of the affected countries. Enter the IMF.

Initially, the US veto made sense, as otherwise, given their postwar predicament, the Europeans could have coordinated voting for each to devalue. But as Europe (and other parts of the world) recovered through the 1950s and into the 1960s, it was less reasonable for the United States to be able to block dollar revaluation, transmitting the burden of adjustment elsewhere. Then, when the United States itself fell into persistent deficits, the others were in a position to exercise a de facto collective veto against dollar devaluations, creating the tensions recalled in chapter 1.

In other words, finding a fair and workable process for parity adjustments proved elusive—even among allies. Efforts to solve the riddle got nowhere, despite the expertise of those involved.[6] Initially, the general float led to

4. Eichengreen, *Globalizing Capital*, pp. 88–91.

5. On receiving a complaint, the GATT/WTO secretariat formally consults the IMF, where management submit a staff analysis and a recommendation to its executive board, with the conclusion relayed back to the GATT/WTO. If the IMF says there is no macroeconomic option, GATT/WTO machinery then vets the trade measures. Shaffer and Waibel, "(Mis)alignment of the Trade."

6. The Committee of 20 Deputies charged with recommending a new system was chaired by Bank of England director Jeremy Morse (unlucky not to become governor) supported by a young Eddie George (who did).

runaway inflation in most of the advanced economies, whose monetary authorities were no longer tethered by any kind of anchor, and whose politicians did not reject a silent form of taxation as they confronted oil price shocks and other social disturbances. Over the next thirty or more years, they discovered, via uncomfortable trial-and-error experiments, that independent central banks could maintain internal price stability without an external anchor. Converging on a regime for *domestic* monetary policy known as inflation targeting, central bankers themselves became the institutionalized anchor, without mechanical rules or IMF say-so (chapter 15's momentous technology shift).[7]

Later I will suggest those developments massively affect prospects for transplanting the dollar, absent severe geopolitical dislocation. For now, what matters is that their passage was eased by the wider international System having become firmly embedded before the monetary regime experimentation got under way. By the 1980s and 1990s, full-on protectionism and trade wars seemed consigned to the past, against a security background in which the Cold War's North Atlantic and East Asian alliances were solid. Those were circumstances in which monetary affairs could be parceled out to specialists without geopolitics looming over them.

That international Order-System saw plenty of monetary scraps, but they were containable. The 1980s squabbles around the dollar-yen and dollar-deutschmark exchange rates—leading to two rounds of coordinated foreign exchange market intervention, known as Plaza and Louvre, after the New York hotel and the Paris palatial museum where they were agreed—remained disagreements among Cold War allies, to be addressed rather than escalated (chapter 3). Aside from the IMF being a bystander and the episode advertising the pitfalls of active currency management,[8] the thing that resonates four decades later is that, at Plaza, the US Treasury was trying to take the steam out of protectionist initiatives in Congress against Japan's rising (but friendly) economic powerhouse. I recall Washington and London negotiating with Tokyo over their respective banks and dealers having reciprocal access to each other's financial centers, rather than have Japanese banks eat everyone's lunch. No similar process occurred with Beijing in the early twenty-first century—the tip of a by-then already visible iceberg.

---

7. Invented in New Zealand; analytically formalized by a Swede (Lars Svensson).

8. Less than two years after Plaza (G5, September 1985), a slightly larger group was trying to keep the dollar *up* (G7, February 1987). Eichengreen, *Globalizing Capital*, pp. 146–52.

## *The Renminbi Exchange Rate Standoff: Bretton Woods II*

The post–Bretton Woods monetary order was jolted when China became a large part of the world economy but did not want to float. The new nonsystem, mixing floating and managed exchange rates, became known as Bretton Woods II.[9] Since a state can avoid currency appreciation by printing its own money (which it then sterilizes to avoid inflation), while amassing foreign exchange reserves, no law of nature stood in Beijing's way. But what about international law?

True to the spirit of the White Mountains' regime, in 1978 the IMF Articles had been amended to outlaw "manipulating exchange rates or the international monetary system in order to prevent effective balance of payments adjustment or to gain an unfair competitive advantage" (Article IV[1][iii]). Not the very best drafting, perhaps: it is potentially offensive to the accused ("manipulating") and also places the burden of proof on demonstrating intent ("in order"). Fine things when codifying crimes against the person, but not especially when trying to design a self-enforcing regime for international commerce. For a mercantilist, emerging power, any substantive costs in conceding a breach were compounded by the implied loss of face.

High-stakes pantomime ensued.[10] IMF staff initially tried to articulate a rules-like framework for assessing "external stability" and "fundamental misalignment," only to find themselves in a dense interpretative quagmire. Channeling the specter of past crises, emerging-market members from Latin America and elsewhere resisted anything that could enable interference in their own domestic policies that was not matched by adjustment in, for want of a better term, the first world.

Even when the Fund landed a framework, nothing happened. Its senior management (appointed by Washington) concluded the dollar was not fundamentally misaligned. The PRC stalled in providing information, stressing that any notion of finding their currency fundamentally misaligned, triggering possible WTO trade sanctions, was "totally unacceptable." Here we see power, not economics; states digging in, not cooperating via international organizations.[11]

9. Dooley et al., "Revived Bretton Woods System."

10. Drawing on Blustein, "A Flop and a Debacle." (Some DC antics read more like an episode of *Homeland* in which an inept, ambitious White House staffer gets an inexperienced president to declare war via an impromptu address to the nation.)

11. Blustein, "A Flop and a Debacle," pp. 17–23. By the time new managing director Dominic Strauss-Kahn found an approach not completely ducking the substance, Lehman had failed. Drift costs.

Meanwhile, the US Congress passed retaliatory legislation, which had been serially resisted by administrations that prioritized inducting China into the international system gradually and peaceably. Looking back, Washington might have done better to bring a formal proceeding to the WTO, requiring the Fund to reach a formal view through the process described above. If it had succeeded, that would have authorized the United States (and any other parties) to impose tariffs on trade in goods with China.[12] Instead, a decade later, the Trump administration threw everything out the window (chapter 17).

## The Monetary Trilemma: Capital Flows and Capital Account Crises

If that first set of fault lines in international monetary geopolitics revolves around exchange rate adjustments and net capital flows, the second concerns gross capital flows and national balance-sheet vulnerabilities, and creates some deeper issues. It is rooted in inadequate handling of the liberalization of capital flows that began during the 1970s (chapters 3 and 15).

The "globalization trilemma," which chapter 11 partly dissolved, takes its name from a less easily dodged trilemma of international monetary affairs: a country cannot combine complete national control over domestic monetary policy, a fixed exchange rate, and liberalized capital flows. After World War II, most countries reconciled a dollar standard with some monetary autonomy by controlling capital flows. That way, they avoided giving up the capacity for economic stabilization that only a few decades earlier they had painfully discovered was necessary, under full-franchise democracy, to maintain public acquiescence (Hume's legitimacy) in state authority.

With Bretton Woods' demise, the monetary trilemma's constraints shifted. By floating their exchange rates, states could now enjoy domestic monetary autonomy without controlling the inflow and outflow of capital.[13] Gradually, capital controls were relaxed. This changed the world, initially, again, via a spontaneous process rather than design.[14]

---

12. But not services because, oddly, the GATT's Article XV provisions (above, main text) were not replicated in the mid-2000s trade-in-services treaty.

13. Ignoring the intra-European system of fixed exchange rates, bringing design to a subsystem of the broader monetary order.

14. During the mid-1980s, Washington pressed Tokyo to liberalize its capital account, hoping to strengthen the yen. In fact, previously trapped domestic capital flowed out, pushing the yen down (Eichengreen, *Globalizing Capital*, p. 148, citing Jeff Frankel).

## Liberalization: Voluntary but Promoted

By the end of the 1980s, the industrialized nations, as they were then known, were changing gear. They revised the OECD's capital movements code to include a *nonbinding* commitment to liberalize short-term flows (chapter 3). While merely codifying what the major economies had already done rather than pushing them into it, this still marked a big shift from the late 1950s, when they had been openly concerned about "hot money."[15] It reflected a view that, at least for them, domestic money markets were now (again) deep enough to absorb abrupt swings in inflows and outflows.

But the same was not so obviously true for emerging-market economies, which shines uncomfortable light on the mid-1990s initiative of IMF staff, management, and some leading members to amend the Fund's articles to include capital-account liberalization among its *legal* objectives, and oversight of capital flows in its *legal* powers. This meant liberalization could be included among the conditions attached to support programs, effectively depriving ailing states of autonomy in this area.[16]

Whether a grab for power, relevance, or both, the campaign crumbled when the late 1990s' Asian crises advertised the grim reality of contagious capital flight. The post–Bretton Woods monetary order had proved disorderly for many newly emerging economies, which in aggregate were now big enough to matter in rich capitals (as well as to their own people and neighbors). While some in the West were bothered for cosmopolitan-type reasons, others were discombobulated by the costs of bailing out the crisis-hit countries. The marginal voters in the US Congress insisted the Clinton administration veto the proposed amendment to the Fund's articles before they would vote through an increase in its resources.

Even with that policy bullet dodged, the crisis itself highlighted difficult, even grave issues. We consider four: two at the nexus of economics and political morality (or responsibility), and two concerning what national and international macrofinancial resilience might look like in a world of interdependent but not friendly sovereign states.

---

15. Abdelal, *Capital Rules*, pp. 11–12, 101–6. (While agreeing with Abdelal that most accounts attribute too much to Anglo-Saxon "neoliberals," I am not persuaded it was a French initiative with US officials largely indifferent.)

16. Abdelal, *Capital Rules*, pp. 123–61.

## IMF Conditionality as Constitutional Reform

Partly on the back of prudent fiscal policies (the Fund's reflex traffic light), the East Asian economies had grown rapidly for years, attracting capital inflows of all kinds. They included lots of short-term claims denominated in dollars. So long as states could maintain their then-pegged exchange rates against the dollar, all looked good (maybe), but they were underwater if they could not. When confidence cracked, hot money fled, and the pegs broke, in what in many cases was more analogous to a self-fulfilling run on a bank than to a standard balance-of-payments crisis caused by unsustainable economic fundamentals (previous chapter). Revisiting interventions barely contemplated since the 1980s Latin American crisis, Western central bankers urged their banks to provide time by rolling over claims on Korean counterparts, and the IMF provided assistance.

But the Fund overreached. In some of its programs (most significantly for Indonesia), it required restructuring of real-economy markets in ways that not only were microscopic (for outsiders) but also intruded on matters of basic political choice (for Indonesians). Most egregious were the edicts to liberalize the monopolies operating on some of the archipelago's spice islands. Quite apart from the, to put it lightly, tension with European powers having battled for centuries to control those monopolies during the age of discovery (as it was for us), it was hard to insist that liberalization was the country's *only* route to external stability. Even if one thought growth was the primary goal, or that the monopolies greased the wheels of corruption, the IMF was laying down the law on what it thought best rather than providing a menu of options for stability.[17]

That was a legitimacy issue, as leading economists pointed out.[18] Whereas, under international law, a state may not use coercive measures to interfere with another state's basic choices about its economic or social system,[19] it turned out the IMF was at liberty to require changes in a member's economic structure as a condition for a rescue: coercion without "aggression." It was a moment when the IMF appeared as an instrument or organ of supranational governance rather than an agent of international cooperation, and we return to it below.

---

17. On the then president's family controlling the clove-distribution monopoly, see Schoenberger, "Two Faces."

18. Notably, Feldstein, "Refocusing the IMF."

19. As laid down in the ICJ's *Nicaragua* judgment (chapters 3 and 9).

Meanwhile, not everyone took the Fund's medicine. While most of the afflicted countries immediately floated their exchange rates and accepted IMF terms, one adopted a different course. After rejecting the Fund's prescriptions (and arresting its finance minister), Malaysia escaped the worst of the contagion by barring capital outflows, thereby exercising discretion it enjoyed (in international law) only because the amendment to the Fund's articles had not already been passed.[20] Its actions were roundly condemned as likely to make international capital even more flighty in the future, because lenders would fear the shutters coming down at the first sign of trouble. In fact, the episode sparked revisionist thinking about capital controls.

### Capital Controls and the Liberalism of Fear: Freedom and Its Abuses

Before getting to that, this book cannot duck deeper questions about how such controls fit with liberal values. Bans on moving resources abroad are the milder cousin of barring citizen-subjects leaving a territory. Turning this around, the ability to flee—bodily, please God,[21] but also financially for those lucky enough to have mobile resources—can be a check on tyranny. Reprising earlier themes, the liberalism of fear (chapter 13) precedes the liberalism of commercial society. For liberal states, this suggests that, whatever their economic doctrines, they should condone outflow controls only for temporary financial emergencies. Where rich countries do permanently operate tight outflow controls, the liberal parts of the world are entitled to weigh that in assessments of local legitimacy.

On the other side, while capital freedom might impede or even deter creeping persecution, an open door can also be used by dirty money, with its culture of bribery and corruption, and for endemic international tax arbitrage. Together, those two poisons have eaten away at the legitimacy of the international System as a whole and fueled domestic cynicism about government in some major democracies. When capital flows were liberalized, the network of regimes needed filling out. Thanks to the OECD's efforts, that might now,

20. Malaysia's then–central bank markets director, Zeti Aziz, later became governor and today is an elder stateswoman of the central banking world.

21. Human Rights Declaration, Article 13 (reiterated in Article 12, 1966 Covenant on Civil and Political Rights, not yet ratified by the PRC), proclaims, "Everyone has a right to leave any country, including their own."

forty years on, be happening for corporate taxation. Meanwhile, the Financial Action Task Force, also serviced from the OECD's Paris offices, existed for over thirty years (chapter 3) without managing to check dirty money's rise. Despite repeated warnings, only the Ukrainian war gave salience to the way Putin-regime associates had inveigled their way into Western commerce, politics, and civil society (chapter 18).[22] Missing regimes catch up with us, eventually.

## National Balance-Sheet Resilience

More prosaically, there are the economic vulnerabilities generated by flighty capital flows. During the 1990s Asian crises, the epicenter of each country's problems varied according to which sector had accumulated excessive short-term, foreign-currency obligations—in Thailand, it was the government; in South Korea, the banks; in Indonesia, the nonfinancial corporate sector—but the problem's structure was essentially the same. External-financing runs are not, however, confined to emerging economies or states with pegged exchange rates, even though they might be especially vulnerable. The remedies, which must be distinguished from those for more fundamental macroeconomic problems, come in three broad varieties: international regime change, self-insurance against external liquidity shocks, and external liquidity insurance.

On the first, former IMF chief economist Olivier Blanchard and his then team promoted the idea of countries routinely controlling inflows of short-term debt.[23] Quite apart from the inevitability of eventually being undermined by loopholes and abuses of the kinds familiar from the 1960s and 1970s, there was a certain irony in the IMF, within a generation, flipping from promoting universal capital liberalization (above) to championing capital controls. Changing tack should obviously not taint an idea, but both pole positions get too close to wanting to interfere unduly with states' freedoms. If states want to maintain inflow controls, international organizations should generally not stand in their way, but nor should they seek to prescribe them.

The most determined example of self-insurance comes, unsurprisingly, from East Asian states wishing never again to have to turn to the IMF for help. Many accumulated massive defensive foreign exchange reserves, which, when

22. Financial Action Task Force assessments found both the United States and the United Kingdom need to do more to comply with its standards. Putin's Ukrainian invasion might prompt action.

23. Ostry et al., "Capital Inflows."

combined with Chinese mercantilism, added to the downward pressure on safe world interest rates that, by inflating collateral values, helped fuel the debt-financed consumption binge in the West during the 2000s. In other words, comprehensible self-help heralded mixed blessings for the international system as a whole.

Another kind of self-help is to be more careful about vulnerabilities accumulating in the first place: *national balance-sheet* monitoring and management. The best examples come from rich states. Throughout the early 2000s, neither the United States nor the United Kingdom—hosting the two main international financial centers, and each running a national balance sheet resembling that of a giant hedge fund—seems to have asked itself the essential but crude question: If China does not change course, what national savings or other policy should each adopt to contain its own accumulating vulnerabilities? It is hard to believe that the range of sane answers included carrying on shopping with an international credit card—especially a card supplied by a securitization industry feeding flaky synthesized "safe assets" to a hungry world (summoning chapter 15's modern Triffin problem).

Risk-management measures might include taxing hot inflows à la Blanchard, but only when *stocks* of short-term or foreign-currency-denominated obligations become a threat. As a dynamic targeted policy rather than a static blanket one, this substitutes the hazards of discretion—acting too late or too indiscriminately—for those of endemic regulatory arbitrage. The IMF would therefore need to recommend publication by national authorities of how they plan to deliver such a policy, and to put it at the center of their own surveillance. They might at last be moving toward that.[24]

Quite how resilient a national balance sheet needs to be depends partly on whether a state has liquid local capital markets, and partly on its access to external liquidity insurance. In a measure of *collective* self-help, some East Asian states provide foreign-currency insurance to each other.[25] The big question always, however, is the availability of liquidity insurance in the primary world

24. In 2014 David Li (China) and I advised the IMF, "No Article IV or FSAP [Financial Sector Assessment Program] report should be approved if it does not contain [a national balance-sheet analysis]" (*2014 Triennial Surveillance Review*, paras. 30–35, reprising post-Asian crises recommendations by a group chaired by Mario Draghi [on which I served]).

25. Some Association of Southeast Asian Nations members initiated a network of currency-swap agreements, effectively pooling some foreign currency reserves (the Chiang-Mai initiative).

reserve currency, and therefore ultimately from its issuer, the problem with which the preface began.

## Global Liquidity and International Liquidity Insurance

The need for a swap line (or other facility) from the Fed is related to the availability of liquidity insurance from markets, and hence to the nebulous concept of global liquidity.[26] I shall try to make it sufficiently concrete to be operationalized. As with domestic monetary liquidity, a good starting point is to think of global liquidity as the stock of instruments treated, internationally, as "safe" (previous chapter) *plus* the capacity and willingness of those instruments' issuers to supply more, elastically, to meet surges in demand.[27] In monitoring that, the job of the authorities should include making judgments about whether the supposedly safe instruments (and hence the suppliers of liquidity insurance) are, with very high likelihood, in fact safe, warranting the market's own lack of ongoing analysis.[28] Cast thus, the analysis of global liquidity conditions becomes an arm of macroprudential policy (chapter 19) and feeds into central banks' choices about their own provision of liquidity insurance, domestically and across borders to their peers.

Concretely, in the context of national balance-sheet management, the prudent boundary for foreign currency (currently, mainly dollar) mismatches depends on whether a state has preagreed swap lines with the Fed, the European Central Bank, and other internationally used currencies' central banks. Where they do not, a country should curtail the foreign-currency obligations of its financial system, government, and real economy. If, however, its economy is large enough or its banks highly active internationally, such a country might play moral-hazard chicken with the Fed (and others), gambling on their

---

26. Landau, "Global Liquidity."

27. The domestic analogue is the broad money stock (currency and deposits with banks) *plus* committed lines of credit (overdraft facilities) from banks, which they can provide because (and only so long as) their liabilities are treated as money.

28. This is different from simply tracking stocks and flows of cross-border credit (the current practice, so far as there is one), because the issues around global liquidity are not sensibly about regular credit flows or debt vulnerabilities. They are about the availability of supposedly safe assets and of credit (liquidity) on demand, including in adverse circumstances, and therefore about the resilience of the suppliers of such services, including shadow banks (chapter 19). Credit flows and stocks are pointers to where the job begins (of assessing the suppliers), not more.

having to provide dollars ex post. Such brinkmanship should be called out by the IMF.[29]

The global liquidity insurer—today the United States, tomorrow maybe others—faces a similar constraint, but one that is not apparent until its spell at the summit is manifestly ending. Parochially, as the United States enters a period during which swap-line shopping will be part of the geoeconomics of *Superpower Struggle* or *New Cold War*, tempting it to accommodate states in order to sustain a dollar-based international economic system, the country will need to ensure the sustainability of its finances and the resilience of its banking system.[30] Among other things, that will mean grasping that its burgeoning shadow-banking vehicles represent a potential threat to its geopolitical role (chapter 19).

## Currency Politics: Topple the Dollar?

That brings us to the big issue where international economics and geopolitics are inseparable: Will the reserve currency change?

The first episode summarized above—around global current account imbalances and real exchange rate disequilibria—revealed IMF surveillance to be essentially toothless where the stakes are highest. A couple of decades ago, the G20 tried to make progress via discussions among the economic powers: failure. Later, after the Global Financial Crisis, alongside all the concrete stuff on banks, derivatives infrastructure and so on, they had another go: again failure, slowly. Officials got stuck on the central issue of how to get to a world of more symmetric adjustment between surplus and deficit countries. Guess what, the surplus countries did not want to play ball.

There was nothing new in this. In the run-up to Bretton Woods itself, Harry Dexter White (for a United States in surplus: oh, for the old days) and John Maynard Keynes (for a painfully in-deficit declining power) had promoted fundamentally different designs. Of course the United States prevailed, as Britain simply owed it too much money, having mortgaged its very being to provide a platform for the fight for civilization and liberty (in history's annals, not a bad way to vacate the summit, as Spartan shades testify).

With White's scheme later imploding under its own relentless logic, the shift to floating rates could provide a lasting remedy only if decentralized enforcement of a norm barring exchange management by large countries did not

---

29. On surveillance, see Eichengreen and Woods, "IMF's Unmet Challenges."
30. Farhi and Maggiori, "China versus the United States."

destabilize international relations more widely. Taken with the other spillovers from a unipolar reserves standard (previous chapter), this motivates perennial efforts by the great, good, and cranky to devise a pristine international monetary system, heralding a new dawn of symmetric adjustment, smoother monetary policy transmission, and "safe" assets that are truly safe rather than this season's shadow-banking cocktail. I will pour cold water on three of them: a return to IMF-approved parities; gold; and a souped-up, perhaps digitalized SDR, which has been touted by the PRC itself. (Since the first two options overlap—fixing parities, and what acts as the anchor—I will deal with each issue only once.)

### A Return to Adjustable Exchange-Rate Pegs: A Problem of Decision-Making

Some experts and commentators advocate a return to a system of fixed (but adjustable) exchange rates. Except perhaps in the wake of a horrible but decisive conflict, I do not see how the decision-making process could work given that, unlike after World War II, today's great powers are most definitely not allies.

The PRC would hardly agree to a regime where the United States had a veto over its exchange rates but not vice versa, while the United States would hardly agree to a quota increase that gave China a veto over the dollar's exchange rates.

Going in the other direction, getting rid of vetoes altogether just flips the political risk exposure to which of the great powers proved most effective in assembling monetary coalitions for coordinated voting in the new IMF board. It is not going to happen—short of a *Reshaped World Order*.

### Returning to Gold: The Problem of Giving Up Stabilization Policy When There Is No Need To

A different approach starts with what should be the international reserve asset. Rejecting any of the powers' currencies, some suggest a return to the old, nineteenth-century variant of the gold standard, where currencies pegged to gold and reserves were held (wholly) in gold too. *If* compliance could be ensured, this could reintroduce a norm of symmetric adjustment to shocks.[31]

---

31. For commentary from a Nobel economist, see Mundell, "International Monetary System."

Even if authoritarian states could stomach the aggressive cyclical swings entailed in economic activity and jobs, which in China seems unlikely given Heaven's outcome-based mandate (chapter 9), liberal states could not. In a break from the past too infrequently noticed, monetary officials no longer need a metallic standard to maintain price stability (and even when they did, credibility relied on a particular distribution of political power: to Hume's merchants and away from Machiavelli's princes). Even if they tried gold again, the availability of a credible escape hatch—central banking—would undermine protestations of commitment to gold's rod. At root, a domestic legitimacy constraint would dominate international legitimacy considerations.

### A New, Collective Reserve Currency Unit?

What, then, of something novel, or at least untried? Three-quarters of a century ago, during the preparations for the Bretton Woods conference, Keynes offered a radical solution to asymmetry: Bancor, an international unit of account and medium of international settlement among governments, but not a mobile store of value for the private sector. Members would have held Bancor-denominated payments accounts with the Fund. Those running surpluses would have received a submarket interest rate on their balances (a de facto penalty), incentivizing them to adjust their national savings policies.[32]

Rather like John F. Kennedy's Camelot, the hope this inspires generates serial imitators, not least turning the Fund's orphan SDR into the fulcrum of a newly designed system for international monetary exchange. While conjuring variations on this theme has long been a pastime among monetary aficionados, it garnered new significance when, in 2009, with the financial world wobbling, then–People's Bank of China governor Zhou Xiaochuan launched his call to shift away from international monetary exchange via credit currencies (i.e., national fiat currencies such as the dollar), toward an SDR system.[33] A few years later, others, including IMF senior staff, combining hypermodernity with fundamental reform, aired the possibility of a digital basket currency.[34] I have been left befuddled, for narrow and deeper reasons.

32. Eichengreen, *Globalizing Capital*, pp. 96–97.

33. Triffin International Foundation, *Using the SDR*; Zhou, "Reform the International Monetary System" (seemingly advocating a basket of credit currencies).

34. IMF, *Considerations on the Role*. At the board, most (not all) were skeptics (chair's summing up, meeting 18/27, March 30, 2018, released April 6, 2018). Subsequently, a digital SDR was

The SDR comprises a (weighted) basket of dollars, euros, sterling, renminbi, and so on. It is not money but, in the jargon, a "reserve asset." Since that is hardly transparent, think of the SDR as a gift voucher entitling the holder to some international helicopter money. When allotted, IMF member states can unbundle them via the main central banks, receiving dollars and other currencies (in exchange for a low fee to the Fund).[35] This can be useful during a crisis, as it strengthens the reserves of countries struggling to cope. Of itself, it does nothing to induce future prudence if they believe they will be helped whenever crisis hits again. (That is similar to bailing out bankers, albeit mostly for a better cause.)

But a basket of fiat (credit) currencies cannot escape its nature. The main action is still in the underlying currencies. There is no liquid market in the SDR, and no swap line with the IMF, which is *not* a monetary institution capable of elastically supplying its own currency. For sure, converting the IMF into a currency-issuing central bank would cure those technical obstacles, but even a hint of world monetary government would kill the idea before people spilled onto the streets.

More deeply, it is not clear why any reincarnation of Bancor would deliver the grail of symmetric adjustment to nasty global imbalances. Why would a great power running an external surplus stick to the rules and bear half of any necessary macroeconomic adjustment rather than, when it suited its geoeconomic purposes, tell its commercial counterparts to settle in its own currency? Too much rests on the conviction that a better-designed monetary system could cure international macroeconomic imbalances and financial crises.[36]

The underlying problem is that whereas a deficit country faces an immovable object in the need to borrow externally to finance itself, a surplus country does not face a correspondingly irresistible force. Symmetric adjustment during the nineteenth century was a by-product of underdeveloped domestic

---

floated in Adrian, "Stablecoins, Central Bank," and Carney, "Growing Challenges," calling for a "synthetic hegemonic currency," perhaps responding to the possibility of a Facebook private hegemonic digital currency (chapter 19).

35. With the added intermediate step of the gift voucher, this is like a central bank sending cash to part of the population, then deciding whether to offset the addition to the overall money supply in order to avoid inflation. For the recipients, it is close to a gift.

36. For a domestic analogy, imagine a single, large, autarkic country that suffers a nasty internal economic shock. Lower interest rates help debtors somewhat and induce those in surplus to save less. But they do not force savers to spend more, and they do not save all debtors from bankruptcy. Hence domestic distributional fiscal policies, bankruptcy laws, and so on.

monetary technology combined with rule by property owners in leading states. Where property was increasingly in merchant hands (Hume's commercial society), states prized the benefits for trade of external currency stability: interests and technical constraint were aligned. By contrast, today the most a rules-based system could do is, perhaps, raise the social costs of defection *if* any new regime could be agreed on at all.

If that seems like a dead end, it is also important to keep in mind that symmetric adjustment would not have vanquished the West's current internal political problems. Had the PRC let its currency float twenty-odd years ago, its lower production costs would still have dislocated Western economies—just more slowly, which is not nothing but not a panacea.

## Multipolar Reserve Currencies

If design is overambitious, what is left, as many point out, is competition among multiple contending reserve currencies.[37] This too should not be surprising. Whereas Bretton Woods itself was a Hobbesian moment of compact writing and swearing, the underlying monetary order has generally been Humean: the product of path-dependent habits and network effects, kicked off by wider forces. The Hobbesian dollar-exchange standard was feasible in 1944/45 only because the dollar was already widely used as a reserve currency, sterling was no longer secure, and any responsibility for keeping the sea-lanes open had plainly shifted from London to Washington.

Precisely because monetary order is Humean, it is contestable. While the dollar begins with the advantages of incumbency—strong positive network externalities in invoicing, payment systems, and capital markets (chapters 5 and 15)—it is not impregnable, as history makes more than clear. This, then, is the territory of the first three of our geoeconomic-cum-political scenarios: *Lingering Status Quo*, *Superpower Struggle*, and *New Cold War*, marking a progression or descent—depending on where one sits—from continued US centrality through prolonged currency competition to monetary autarky. Thinking of this as mere competition—the winner emerging in due course through some combination of luck and skill—would, however, fall into the trap of conceiving it as contested among friends. UK-US competition nearly a century ago was ugly enough, as the history of the Middle East testifies, but

37. Eichengreen, "Managing a Multiple Reserve Currency World."

that was a village squabble in comparison.[38] This will be uglier. Whichever of the three scenarios prevails, it will rely on internalized constraints (norms) to achieve some kind of equilibrium without tipping into open conflict.

We can now expand on some of the book's earlier prescriptions for Europe, the United States, and the PRC. Unless European capitals wish to reemerge as a collective hard power—a superpower pole in their own right—they need to temper their currency ambitions.[39] Toppling the dollar might well impair Washington's capacity to provide its continent with a security umbrella: efforts to improve the System part of an Order-System that end up undermining the Order itself are counterproductive when the alternatives are plausibly worse.[40] The condition for such European self-restraint is, of course, the awkward one of believing that US leadership remains durably credible and broadly liberal (in the sense of chapter 13), a matter that might reasonably be in doubt for the next couple of presidential election cycles.

However well it maintains peaceful transfers of power domestically, the United States needs a course change in monetary diplomacy, beginning with being clearer about the provision of dollar liquidity insurance to other states, which in degree might be under way. It also needs to be less trigger happy with sanctions and extraterritorial regulatory claims, without being any less robust when its own security or world order is at stake (chapters 10 and 15).

There is a general principle here. If providing the principal reserve currency enhances the issuer's autonomy, as it does, that should not be used to diminish the autonomy of others who represent no threat to order or wider peaceful coexistence (chapter 13). It would be useful for an informal international norm along those lines to emerge, as a world with multiple superpower reserve currencies will be one in which sanctions are a tempting instrument of coercive competition. If the hard edge of sanctions has become obvious in recent decades, not least after Russia invaded Ukraine, the dog that has not yet barked is a cyberattack incapacitating a major state's payments infrastructure. Perhaps we can thank deterrence: mutually assured economic decapitation. Whatever, Washington, Moscow, and Beijing will at some point share an interest in barring unprovoked cyber interventions to disable the core domestic financial and communications infrastructure of another state, perhaps designating such

38. J. Barr, *Lords of the Desert*.

39. E.g., European Parliament, "Strengthening the International Role," para. 18.

40. On this dimension of monetary leadership, see Norrlof et al., "Global Monetary Order"; and Norrlof, "Dollar Hegemony."

actions "aggression" under the UN Charter. As NATO has made clear (chapter 13), the charter could be construed that way already, but a dedicated pact would signal the norm to the world. Even under a tense *New Cold War*, that might help contain the scope of any hostilities, but it will be realistic only if public verification becomes feasible.

## The IMF as an International Organization

Turning, finally, to the organization supposedly at the center of all this, I have cast the IMF as a monitor of monitors, but it is actions, not words, that underpin its influence. Genuflecting to that, the organization is often tagged "It's Mostly Fiscal." Partly a joke among central bankers keen to get the Fund off their monetary turf, it does capture an important post–Bretton Woods truth since IMF programs almost invariably revolve around fiscal reform—except, as we saw, it is more awkward than that.

### A Political-Economy Change Agent

Unlike bankrupt businesses, states unable to service their debts cannot simply disappear through a liquidation of their assets. Instead, even if creditors take a hit, an ailing state must adjust somehow, if only to retain access to imported goods and services. Such adjustments are, in effect, coordinated by the Fund, putting it in the political-economy business—inevitably but uncomfortably. Inevitably, because sustained or repeated external financing problems, whether generated by flawed or malfunctioning regimes for fiscal, monetary, or banking policy, are almost always rooted in a state being unable to find its own way to any of the technical solutions. That in turn is almost always a product of domestic political actors' incentives given local constitutional, social, and economic institutions.[41] Frayed legitimacy obviously exacerbates institutional frictions—most obviously, making it harder to collect higher taxes—but, reciprocally, stubborn crises erode legitimacy, whether by revealing institutional disfunction or elite mendacity.

If crises often implicate local institutions, acting as an outside political-economy reformer is, putting it mildly, uncomfortable. It entails the Fund steering a state toward reforms that might have big distributional effects or,

41. E.g., Britain's IMF program in the mid-1970s, notwithstanding a floating exchange rate and its own central bank, given sclerosis in cabinet and labor relations.

more profoundly, reshape its economic structure and political society. If anything, the institutional turn in economics has made these dilemmas harder to
dodge by exposing the deeper pathologies of many external-financing problems. Where it seems such vulnerabilities will recur unless national institutions
are reformed (Argentina?), there is something slightly frivolous in relying,
abstemiously, on national-savings-enhancing public spending cuts or tax rises
as the core of any adjustment program's conditions.

Here we revisit the important distinction between policies to avoid hot-
money runs and deeper problems. It hardly interferes with a state's freedoms
to require it to avoid a national balance sheet with massive short-run liabilities
(by strengthening bank regulation, say). But demanding fundamental reform
to the structure of the real economy is close to ruling without local legitimation. For reasons rooted in part IV's analysis, neither IMF management nor its
board of directors can take it upon themselves to make those legitimacy judgments about states' governance.[42] While the individual states sitting at the
board can of course do so, a system that combines weighted voting with
constituency representation is designed for financial, not constitutional,
conditionality.

That raises tough higher-order issues. The IMF's purposes include to
"facilitate the expansion and *balanced* growth of international trade, and to
contribute thereby to the promotion and maintenance of high levels of employment and real income and to the *development of the productive resources of
all members* as primary objectives of economic policy" (Article I[ii]; my emphasis). It is not obvious, however, that this licenses the IMF to presume each
member prioritizes growth above all else, including its way of life. Nor is it
plain that it would be decent for the Fund, using the kind of cliff-edge leverage
available to bankruptcy practitioners, to promote convergence toward a particular *kind* of international society. Even if doing so lies within its legal vires, it is
a legitimacy graveyard. Therein lies the deep problem, beyond the technocratic hubris of the 1990s Washington Consensus.

Turning that around, what to do if a crisis-hit state's government has insufficient will to reform, or prefers solutions that will leave the rich rich while the
mass of citizen-subjects are poor? And what to do if it seems likely that a particular state will hit crisis again, and again, if it does not swallow some fundamental reforms? One can, for example, make a respectable case that if the

42. Similarly, Eichengreen and Woods, "IMF's Unmet Challenges," but in terms of
sovereignty.

Fund properly stays away from constitutional reform, it will eventually face the choice of letting Argentina default. While that might usefully shift the incentives of the country's rulers, and of the myopic investors who, after each dismal episode, return for another quick buck, the choice should turn on the fateful judgment of whether nonfundamental (and hence legitimate) program conditions can cure a deeper malaise.

## Operating Principles for Program Conditions

Consistent with those arguments, our *Principles* for delegating power to international organizations (chapter 14) push in the direction of the Fund's published program guidelines applying clearer constraints. The imposition of society-transforming conditions should be out of bounds, meaning Fund staff should be under a duty to try to find solutions that will not alter a state's way of life, even where its choice might leave it poorer. Measures already taken by the Fund itself, sensitized by its wobbly legitimation history, already go in that direction.[43] They leave in the air, however, the future crunch issue of when to say no because, in particular cases, macrofinance measures are sticking plaster.

If they grip, such operating principles have implications for rich states. Unless a regime for orderly sovereign bankruptcy can be devised (and perhaps even if it were), their banks and other financial intermediaries would be left more exposed where a stricken country chose to adopt only partial remedies to its underlying problems. That would sharpen rich states' incentives to ensure their banks do not become overexposed, whether directly or via funds they support with liquidity insurance. This is stability before growth.

## Governance and Quota Reform

Finally, there is the Fund's (and World Bank's) contentious governance. The distribution of voting power can be criticized for not reflecting the balance of economic activity in the world. It can be defended, broadly, for reflecting the reality of America's role in international monetary affairs given the dollar's preeminence. For rising powers, that is objectionable because it seems self-fulfilling: *Lingering Status Quo* nailed down.

The bigger truth is that where, due to threatening geopolitical and ideological rivalries, peaceful coexistence among the major economies is not secure,

43. IMF, "Guidelines on Conditionality," which stress local ownership, including local support (paras. 3–4), and a macrofinance focus (para. 7[b]).

it is unrealistic to expect incumbent leading states to give up current privileges. Those are circumstances where, in the limit, the semiautarkic arrangements of the *New Cold War* scenario might need to be accepted rather than wished away. In practice, it means that the United States and Europe would be unwise to agree to fundamental reform until the current geopolitical competition has played out somewhat further. That this is not the moment to embark on constructing a new top table—the beginnings of *Reshaped World Order*—needs to be explained and justified to neutral states.

## Summary

The international monetary order is destined to stay outside the clutches of design until and unless some calamity, possibly war, forces the construction of a new institutional equilibrium. This is the field where, through the power of security relationships and network effects, a *Lingering Status Quo*—in the form of dollar dominance—is likely to be part of the scene for some time.

But that is not destiny, and the dollar's preeminence will be challenged during *Superpower Struggle*, not least by the advent of digital central bank currencies, which might spread across borders with much greater ease than paper money. Even without technological change, the United States might well find itself on the uncomfortable end of dollar-invoicing-for-more-security rebargaining with Gulf energy powers, but that is no less true for Beijing. Separately, Washington and its friends will need to get serious about the modern Triffin problem, which means ensuring the resilience of national balance sheets, and monitoring "global liquidity" conditions in terms of vulnerabilities in the supply of "safe" assets denominated in dollars (and other reserve currencies). Both the digital revolution and putting safe-asset supply at the heart of policy tie IMF surveillance to the geoeconomics of central bank swap lines and the obscure business of the Basel Tower (chapter 19).

Concessions on the balance of formal power at the IMF, inevitable and proper in the long run, will wait until it is clear the PRC (and others) can find a comfortable place in a thin society of states credibly committed to peace with basic human rights (chapter 13's second legitimation circle). It is strange for actors from the free world to call for reform of the Bretton Woods institutions before then.

Meanwhile, a self-restrained IMF needs to pursue stability with legitimacy. The answer does not lie in management proselytizing good causes—such as on climate change and inequality, massively important though they are—in order to ingratiate themselves with strands of public opinion and activist nongovernmental organizations. However effective in the short term, that exposes the Fund over the longer run if it distracts the organization from what only it can do. To harness management and staff to the core mission, their reputation and standing must depend on respect for delivering it, not on popularity. The only good answer, as one of my old bosses (Eddie George) used to say about the analogous predicament of central bankers, is a relentless focus on stability, stability, stability.

Combining that with legitimacy will not be easy. When the economic waters seem calm, the Fund typically returns to promoting practices and policies via its bilateral and multilateral surveillance. Certainly, it is important to plug the missing-regime gaps discussed in this chapter: in the Fund's case, on national balance-sheet vulnerabilities, just as the OECD is trying to help advanced-economy democracies address corporate tax arbitrage and dirty money. But, in its post–Bretton Woods existence, the Fund's core business is crisis management. Its exhortations to do (or avoid doing) this or that are merely the for-the-time-being opinions of either its leading staff or main shareholders, and do not directly bind states in the way that, say, bank regulation binds banks.

It matters, therefore, that IMF rescue terms, even for repeat "customers," seem to bear little or no relation to whether or not a state has complied with the Fund's standards and codes or its options for sensible macro-finance policy regimes. In the limit, any such connection cannot sanely be watertight since the size and terms of a rescue depend on the severity of spillovers elsewhere, and inevitably on geopolitics too. Somehow, though, the Fund's promulgated practices do need to feed back from its harder-edged program policies, and vice versa. If a crisis-stricken state followed the Fund's advice, why should a program require reform unless those prescriptions were wanting? On the other hand, a state's wanton neglect of IMF advice could reasonably influence the board's rescue terms (incentives), subject to their not forcibly changing a people's constitutional structure or way of life (values). As well as reflecting that legitimacy constraint, crisis-prevention and crisis-management policies need to cohere and reinforce each other more than now. That might usefully redirect the incentives of not only vulnerable states, but also the Fund staff and members who shape policies for good and bad times (a theme revisited, for banking businesses, in chapter 19).

# 17

# The World Trade Organization and the System for International Trade

## IS JUDICIALIZED UNIVERSALISM UNSUSTAINABLE BECAUSE ILLEGITIMATE?

The encrease of riches and commerce in any one nation, instead of hurting, commonly promotes the riches and commerce of all its neighbours; and . . . a state can scarcely carry its trade and industry very far, where all the surrounding states are buried in ignorance, sloth, and barbarism.

DAVID HUME, "OF THE JEALOUSY OF TRADE," 1758[1]

The economist's case for free trade is essentially a unilateral case: a country serves its own interests by pursuing free trade regardless of what other countries may do.

PAUL KRUGMAN, NOBEL ECONOMIST[2]

HISTORY WILL REMEMBER the antiprotectionist sentiments of the G20 summits held in late 2008 and through 2009 as the international community grappled with the Global Financial Crisis. In effect, the leaders held hands and

1. Hume, "Jealousy of Trade," in *Political Essays*, p. 150.
2. Krugman, "What Should Trade Negotiators Negotiate About?," p. 113.

committed not to repeat the protectionist mistakes of the 1930s. It was something only they could do, and it was their biggest contribution to the postcrisis world. But it didn't last. On March 25, 2011, the Appellate Body of the WTO made a decision so momentous, in its awkward context, that it may have altered the course of world history.

In terms of our Four Scenarios, trade already lies between *Lingering Status Quo* and *Superpower Struggle*: the WTO regime is intact but in trouble. Unlike monetary affairs, there are no network economies bestowing incumbency on Washington. The PRC already has the largest share of global trade.[3]

That awkward case, brought by the PRC against the United States, turned on whether Chinese state-owned enterprises were illegally subsidizing firms engaged in international trade.[4] The US side argued they were entitled, under international law, to retaliate with countermeasures of various kinds where such subsidies distorted the pattern of trade. The court concluded that subsidies from state-owned enterprises were not automatically subsidies from the state, and so not covered by the WTO's ban.[5] In effect, the Chinese state was free to subsidize exporters and import-competing firms, provided it worked through businesses or other organs that could be held, as a matter of law, to be at arm's length. It was a big blow to Washington (and other market economies) because, from their perspective, it meant private-sector firms domiciled or operating in their states were not competing on a level playing field but, instead, against the financial might of the Chinese state-economy.[6]

This was international System at its most paradoxically potent, potentially undoing itself in the process. One great power's interests were, in effect, subordinated to those of another via the adjudicatory authority, delegated by

---

3. Thanks to Petros Mavroidis and Andre Sapir for comments.

4. *US—Anti-dumping and Countervailing Measures (China)*, DS379, 2011.

5. Under the WTO Agreement on Subsidies and Countervailing Measures, a subsidy is a "financial contribution by a government or any public body," and under certain conditions it may meet with immediate countervailing duties, increasing effective import prices (Hoekman and Mavroidis, *World Trade Organization*, pp. 40–42, 51–52). Addressing whether state-owned enterprises are caught, the Appellate Body construed "public body" as an entity that "possesses, exercises, or is vested with, governmental authority" and concluded PRC state-owned enterprises did not satisfy that description.

6. For a narrative, see Blustein, "China Inc." In one extraordinary moment, shining light on how DC infighting breeds incompetence, the American judge at the WTO misses an important case meeting because she is being told over coffee that the United States will not support her renewal (pp. 11–12).

treaty, of a group of trade lawyers insulated from day-to-day politics but whose decisions frame high-level rules of the game for international commerce and, therefore, politics. These were judges acting on the international stage with the same kind of structuring power that Supreme Court justices wield within the United States itself.

The subsidies case throws up massive substantive and design issues. On the former, as Harvard Law professor Mark Wu prominently argued, the underlying problem is that neither the GATT nor the broader WTO regime caters for the arrival of a very large economy structured completely differently from the market-based and mixed economies that established them—a point since underlined by Leader Xi having cracked down on large businesses not owned by the state.[7] On design, the move from the old GATT's essentially diplomatic system of dispute resolution to the WTO's essentially court-based system proved, as some had always understood, to be a change not of degree but in kind; a constitutional reform with far-reaching consequences.

Substance and design collided in an explosive fusion in the countermeasures case because there was something, to put it lightly, awry in casting the question as whether or not Chinese subsidies could properly be attributed to the state when, as explained in chapter 9, the Party stands above the state; indeed, above everything.[8] That was not corrected when, in a subsequent case, the Appellate Body partly switched course on the crucial term "public body."[9] The underlying problem was and remains elemental. If the Party is lord of all it surveys, does that mean that everything that goes on in the PRC is governmental, or attributable to state policy or actions? There simply is no sensible answer to this that fits into the usual principles of market exchange.

While the next chapter addresses the equally vexed issue of technology transfers, this one explores whether part IV's *Principles* can help make

7. Wu, "'China, Inc.' Challenge"; Rudd, "Xi Jinping's Pivot." Recall the Soviet Union had been declined GATT membership because it was not a market economy (chapter 3).

8. Blusten, "China Inc.," p. 15, implies the US side did not develop questions about the Party's role until after the case, which, if true, is as extraordinary as a seventeenth- or eighteenth-century European diplomat negotiating with France or Prussia but neglecting to ask about Louis XIV's or Frederick the Great's policy. If true, it illustrates this book's thesis that, during transformational geopolitics, subject specialists need to reach beyond their specialism.

9. *US—Countervailing Measures (China)*, DS437, 2015 (mainly on how the United States had assessed the alleged subsidy). Remarkably, the later judgment does not explain why the court develops (overrules?) its earlier "public body" doctrine. An eloquent minority opinion explains the underlying difficulties.

sense of what has happened on state-capitalist subsidies, and what it means for the WTO.

## From Hierarchical but Pluralist to Flatter but Universalist Trade Liberalism: Intended or Inadvertent Revolution?

Those subsidies cases raise issues that go to the heart of how to think about the substance and politics of the trade regime, including the benefits and costs of international commerce, and the role of judges versus diplomats in resolving disputes and developing policy.

### The Spirit of the GATT

Almost everything about Washington and Beijing's dispute seems at odds with the spirit of the original GATT, which aimed to provide a playing field for trade among states without interfering with their choice of social and economic model, and by leaving disputes to structured diplomacy. In going about that, four formal elements were vital, especially when combined with a particular policymaking practice.

The first formal provision was the incorporation, in Article I, of the most favored nation (MFN) commitment adopted by Britain and France in the nineteenth century (chapter 2). A quintessentially multilateral measure, this guards against states A and B agreeing to a particular set of tariffs only for one of them, A, to go and agree still-lower tariffs with C, thereby diverting trade away from B. MFN provisions are commitment devices intended to reduce the attractions of defection and so make trade agreements more feasible. In terms of institutional equilibria (chapter 6), they are incentive compatible (so long as the umbrella Order holds). In terms of norms of legitimacy for interstate relations, they embody a spirit of Good Faith (chapters 12 and 13). Incentives and values are, therefore, aligned.

Just as important, in its second vital provision (Article III), the GATT freed signatories to set their own domestic regulations, duties, and subsidies as they saw fit, provided only that domestic producers were not effectively preferred over foreign competitors: barriers might be erected at borders, but not within them. In other words, sovereignty (chapter 11) was to remain effective within a regime of coordinated reductions of barriers to trade, and nondiscriminatory regulation.

That was also the burden of, third, provisions permitting states to depart from those commitments during emergencies of various kinds, including irreparable damage to domestic production, threats to public order, risks to national security, and so forth (chapter 3). This was consistent with Bernard Williams's First Political Question—security, safety, and order—trumping those cooperative ventures that depend on its having a legitimate answer (chapter 12).

Fourth, a policy regime approaching trade as a matter of free, ongoing cooperation embodied that very principle in its arrangements for handling disputes, which were essentially voluntary at each and every step.

In making sense of this, it seems reasonable to infer that the GATT's architects and early curators assumed the regime was for trade among states that, while wishing to govern themselves and allocate resources in somewhat different ways, were at root broadly similar in outlook. That outlook was liberal and, moreover, a pluralist liberalism not insisting on homogeneity across the membership, because, within limits, it did not need to.[10]

While general policy was, in practice, to be decided by consensus (meaning veto), sclerosis did not result. New rounds of liberalization were concluded even though, with European colonialism gradually ending, developing countries very different from the leadership-group states were joining; the number of participants quadrupled by the mid-1960s. The key to this, as persuasively argued by leading trade economist Richard Baldwin, was the emergence of a set of practices and provisions that gave poorer countries asymmetric benefits and obligations: they gained from the large states' MFN obligations without having to reduce their own tariffs and barriers in tandem. In effect: don't object to our proposed regime extensions, because you don't have to obey.[11]

During the mid-1960s, nonreciprocity was embedded in the regime (Article XXXVI). A decade later, in 1979, an "Enabling Clause" was added excusing developing countries more completely from the regime's MFN and other core provisions.[12] The old GATT was, in other words, a limited-scope trading

10. Similarly, Mavroidis and Sapir, *China and the WTO*, chap. 5. On two approaches to liberalism in international law, see chapter 8; and Simpson, *Great Powers*.

11. Baldwin, "Understanding the GATT's Wins," appendix; Baldwin, *Great Convergence*, pp. 69–75.

12. Argentine economist Raul Prebisch argued, while serving as the UN Conference on Trade and Development's first director, that developing economies do not benefit symmetrically from trade and should adopt targeted import-substitution policies (which Peronist Argentina did on a grand scale). In 1958 a group of economists chaired by free trader Gottfried

regime of pluralist liberalism, with an institutionalized hierarchy comprising, loosely, a leadership group of industrialized and industrializing nations, to-gether with a less empowered layer of poorer states subject to fewer binding constraints.[13] In contrast to what followed, the GATT harnessed incentives from the wider self-enforcing international Order.

### The Mid-1990s "Universalist Liberal" Revolution and Its Aftermath

Much of that changed when the WTO treaty was passed during the first rush of post–Cold War optimism. It demanded more from nearly everyone, in ways that were not foreseen, and changed the regime's underlying principle from pluralist to universalist liberalism.

Part of this flowed from a profound change in the nature of the bargain with developing economies. Because the advanced-economy leadership group wanted to avoid the developing world opting out wholesale from various new subregimes (for intellectual property, services, and so on), they framed the agreement as all or nothing. Poorer states' preexisting GATT rights could be retained only by signing up to the WTO lock, stock, and barrel (a single undertaking: nothing is agreed until everything is agreed). But by expanding the population of states whose participation mattered to the regime's effectiveness, disputes could no longer be left to diplomacy and voluntarism.[14] In consequence, the WTO moved to the judicialized system with which this chapter opened. In chapter 6's terms, the Appellate Body became the regime's trustee.

For what ensued, substantive reforms mattered too. The Marrakesh treaty demanded more alignment in domestic regulatory regimes so as to reduce what are known as "behind-the-border barriers," which are just that: domestic regulatory and other policies that might indirectly favor local businesses over their foreign competitors. Especially when combined with various bespoke trade and investment arrangements (next chapter) and competition to host

---

Haberler proposed that underdeveloped countries be freed to maintain barriers to help industrialization and so reduce reliance on commodity exports. Baldwin, "Understanding the GATT's Wins"; Hoekman and Mavroidis, *World Trade Organization*, pp. 110–13.

13. Not the same as saying the regime was good for all less developed economies.

14. Sometimes framed as diplomacy versus law, but better thought of as diplomats versus lawyers given the latter's interpretative discretion. Arguing for judicialization of lower-level panels, Weiler, "Rule of Lawyers," draws parallels with the European Court of Justice's role in the EU. But the analogy is stretched because the EU still passes ordinary legislation and, even occasionally, treaties: de facto high-policy development does not reside solely with judges.

parts of global supply chains, the new WTO regime pushed or incentivized emerging-market and even developing countries to liberalize their economies in the manner of North America and Western Europe.

Finally, with the arrival of large emerging economies, notably the PRC, a long-standing feature of the trading regime became hugely more significant under the new dispensation of judicial, not diplomatic, policymaking. Who counts as a "developing country" continued to be, largely, a matter of self-identification; in other words, the category of a state's membership was not rules based even though the policy regimes for different categories of members ostensibly were.[15] This was supposedly motivated by a principle of sovereignty, but it is not clear how one state's self-election as "developing" can be consistent with free choice for others if their obligations and rights are materially affected. Instead of free choice being collectively consistent, there is a cooperation problem under which every state that can half-plausibly claim to be "developing" will do so even where that is prejudicial to the interests of other states.

This story invites an important challenge: How, big picture, could such a state of affairs possibly be prejudicial to the rich and powerful? The answer is that it could become so in circumstances where even though the average (per capita) income of a state's citizen-subjects is well below that of rich countries (implying a developing economy), a huge population means the state's aggregate income is of the same order of magnitude or exceeds that of per capita–rich states. From the latter's perspective, it might seem inequitable to be required by international law to trade on terms that, in effect, subsidize a state that has accumulated enough resources to pose, if it wishes, a potential threat to their security and safety.

The China case is, therefore, different from more routine trade frictions with other subsidizing states. Crudely, from the perspective of market-based

15. For most purposes, WTO membership has three categories: developed, developing, and least developed. The last is conferred by the UN (Article XI.2, WTO Agreement), but "developing" is neither defined nor conferred by an arm's-length process. Although there has not yet been a formal complaint, during the 2021 Trade Policy Review of China (WTO Doc. WT/TPR/M/415/Add.1, December 22, 2021, pp. 164–65), the United States, the EU, and other members, including India and Indonesia, criticized China's invocation of developing-country status. Separately, GATT (Article VI) lowers the bar for states taking countermeasures against dumping or subsidies from what *they* regard as a nonmarket economy (NME). China's accession protocol dubbed it an NME until 2016. Since then, members maintaining the designation, including the EU and United States, would need to justify it in any WTO case: see Mavroidis and Sapir, *China and the WTO*, p. 41.

constitutional democracies, the forces of Hume and Adam Smith's commercial society might not have time to work their magic before tables are turned. This puts flesh on the bones of part II's argument that System without thick or deep Society can, in some circumstances, become strained to the point of jeopardizing the very Order on which it depends. In the jargon for describing strategic interaction, since the trade and other policy games are embedded in a higher-level security game, the short-term costs of trade concessions or combatting climate change might be compared with those of, say, building an aircraft carrier.

## The Underlying Assumption of Liberal Convergence, and the Awakening

Around Marrakesh, such risks were either unrecognized or deemed too unlikely to bother about. Looking back, it is fairly clear that by the mid-1990s, with the Cold War apparently in the past, the American foreign policy community had inhaled optimism about the gravitational pull of the West's system of government and way of life. Compared with the mid-1940s, or even the 1970s, the background assumption became that states were either already liberal or on a trajectory to become like us, politically.

In those happy circumstances, pretty much all that was left to do was to place administration of the trading regime's rules in the hands of judges, while continuing to extend its application across different parts of states' economic life. Whether or not pundits really believed this, policymakers conducted themselves as though we had reached the terminus of international politics—forgetting Thucydides's warnings against wishful thinking.

In fact, as chapter 9 summarized, the PRC has been on no such liberal trajectory, which was abundantly clear from the late 1980s. When complaints about economic inequalities in the United States became salient, the China question was no longer just for chambers of commerce and seminar rooms. Shortly after taking office in early 2017, the Trump administration threw everything out the window. In a raging wave of protectionist measures, it invoked "national security" concerns against its ally Canada (a NATO member) and its neighbor Mexico, hurled findings of "unreasonable or discriminatory" conduct against China, and maintained the Obama policy of blocking appointments to the WTO's Appellate Body (triggering a sharp drop in cases going through the system, although, as of this writing, not quite to zero).

## The WTO as International Organization

The concluding chapter of the 2016 edition of one of the textbooks I used in writing this book opens with the declaration, "The WTO is one of the most successful multilateral institutions of the post-1945 period."[16] It was too early to tell. Regimes get tested when circumstances change. The Bretton Woods monetary system unraveled after a quarter century, and it has never been replaced. Successful, self-enforcing institutions are not brittle, but the WTO has seemed precisely that since the background security Order got questioned. Any lack of resilience is partly a problem of design.

### The Constitutionalist Problem in the WTO's Constitution

As an organization, the WTO is not directly coercive or dominating. As a regime, it supplies coordinating focal points for decentralized enforcement (chapter 5). Since, to be sustainably self-enforcing, it needs to be legitimate among states, the question for us is whether its constitutional structure and modalities conform with our legitimation principles, and if not, whether that matters to our states' domestic legitimacy. Put thus, the striking thing about the subsidies cases is that, in the broader light of international relations during an era of geopolitical competition, the WTO judges were simply operating beyond their pay grade: trustees had morphed into all-powerful guardians (chapter 6).

That is one of the great hazards of judicialization. Much the same could be said of some domestic constitutional courts. When, for example, US Supreme Court justices rule on campaign finance in ways that materially shift the dynamics of the republic's system of representative democracy, they too are out of their depth. It is a mistake to pretend otherwise.[17] The comparison is instructive because the underlying problem in the US system is that the constitutional processes for formally amending the Constitution have long been inoperable, turning the justices into something like ancient Sparta's ephors—standing over the

---

16. Hoekman and Mavroidis, *World Trade Organization*, p. 129.

17. Another example is the court's facilitating private armies. This creates a special kind of problem: Why should citizens respect a body that operates beyond its innate competence? The answer, at the heart of this book, can only be that not doing so would be even more likely to bring the house down, taking us back to political judgment and practice.

kings, backstop leaders in whose hands the system's integrity is entrusted.[18] The effect is elite rule of the hierarchical kind favored by Friedrich Hayek in his longing for "the dethronement of politics."[19] But rule by judges merely shifts the locus of constitutional politics to the process for appointing the judges—that is, in what concerns us here, to the selection of the Appellate Body, which effectively rules the realm of world trade. Ephors, after all, were elected annually.

Seen thus, the WTO problem is that, in practice, there is no longer room for politics to assert itself over judicialization *within* the regime itself. Unable, under its rules, to operate via diplomacy (bargaining), raw politics asserts itself through exit or disruption. This, frankly, reflects nonrobust design (chapter 10), rooted in an implicit assumption that nothing very big could find its way to the judges, or that consensus decision-making could cure any problems, or both. With the rise of a great power holding to a completely different political, social, and economic model, any such assumptions have been trashed: there are big issues, but there is no thick Society to settle them.

## Possible Remedies: Restoring the Role of Diplomacy in the Regime's Basic Parameters

What, then, should be done? One route, advocated by some leading trade economists and lawyers, is for the United States to return—this time with friends and allies—to prosecuting the rules of the game via the WTO's existing adjudicatory machinery: by bringing some kind of jumbo case that puts the central doctrinal issues on the table at once.[20]

That might work, and it would underline renewed commitment to a certain brand of multilateralism. But what if they try and fail (not a bad question for policymakers to ask)? If commitment to the rules-based regime depended on winning, that's not much of a commitment. Symmetrically, where, after all the comings and goings—a cost of the court's doctrinal flip-flopping and fuzziness—would a loss leave Beijing or other rising powers?

As stressed in chapter 6, because the rules of any designed regime will be incomplete, machinery of some kind must address gaps. Our legitimacy *Principles for Participation and Delegation* preclude that role lying solely with

18. Cartledge, *Spartans*, pp. 49–50.

19. Hayek, *Law, Legislation and Liberty*, pp. 455–58, 481–85.

20. Lawrence, "How the United States"; Hillman, "Best Way" (the former, not-renewed US WTO judge).

arm's-length judges, since some gaps might turn out to be fundamental in the eyes of participating states (and their peoples). Some room needs to be recovered, therefore, for the WTO membership to set high policy, including resets in the wake of Appellate Body decisions based on policy principles that are highly contested.

In principle, this could be done in a series of ways *within* the regime. One would be for the membership to agree to a rule that dispute-settlement panels and the Appellate Body should decline to adjudicate on fundamental questions for which no answer can be found in the treaties. This fits with the value of judicial self-restraint (chapter 14). A second option would be for the membership to have a regular (say, annual) meeting to vote (on some majoritarian basis) on such fundamental questions.[21]

Although not mutually exclusive, those two routes adopt fundamentally different approaches to constitutionalism. Under the first, complaining states would be entitled to erect barriers against trade with counterparts pursuing what they regarded as harmful practices so long as the treaties had been held to be silent. In this chapter's core example, the PRC might run a system of comprehensive state subsidies for exporters, and the United States would be free to erect barriers in return. Strategically, it allows gaps back into the law, potentially creating incentives for states to return to the bargaining table to complete the contract. In principle, the judges themselves could adopt this doctrinal course.[22]

Under the second option, by contrast, answers on legality might always be generated from within the regime, but when judicial decisions created doctrine widely opposed among the membership, *forward-looking* policy would be reset at the diplomatic table. This would be issue-by-issue legislative development of the kind seen in some parliamentary democracies. But that analogy pinpoints the difficulty of finding a new voting rule that would command universal support when introduced, and ongoing acquiescence in its use.

The same goes for a third, more ambitious because nonincrementalist option: to rejig the regime more holistically, with a view to reaffirming the

21. Technically, the Appellate Body submits opinions to a members' assembly (Article 14, Dispute Settlement text). But unanimity is needed to overturn an opinion, so it is a sham (in terms of consent).

22. For a similar proposal to leave gaps in the law (known to international lawyers as *non liquet*), see Hoekman and Mavroidis, "Preventing the Bad from Getting Worse," sec. 5.1.

centrality of trade being conducted on commercial terms.[23] In the spirit of sustaining System with thin Society, that seems worth trying. It might help avert the *New Cold War* scenario, leaving things poised somewhere between *Lingering Status Quo* and *Reshaped World Order*.

Incentives in any such renegotiation could be shaped by building a more limited-membership liberal trade regime under the umbrella of the WTO's universal minimum standards (consistent with chapter 13's contribution to the legitimacy principles). If successful, that might even prove an organic route back to the WTO as the principal substantive regime. Bearing in mind liberal states are not the only actors, that possibility is discussed in the next chapter. First we must address a curiosity. Why is anyone objecting to lower prices from Chinese subsidies when, surely, they are good for households?

## Domestic Commercial Policy, Geopolitics, and Legitimacy

The standard political economy account of trade pacts, going back to John Stuart Mill, casts them as a response to collective-action problems (chapter 5). States, especially those with a material share of world markets, have incentives to adopt distorting measures in order to tilt the terms of trade (the ratio of export prices to import prices) in their favor. But others have mirror-image incentives, meaning they retaliate, leaving everyone worse off. Trade pacts arise so that all can bind themselves to the mast of not embarking on the inferior-equilibrium course.

That argument addresses the risk of universally higher import prices, but it does not explain why anyone should want to combat *lower* prices.[24] One persuasive answer is that import-competing businesses, being few and so capable of coordinating, have more lobbying power than the widely dispersed consumers who benefit directly from increased disposable incomes. Another possibility, not turning on political inefficiency, looks to trade's effects on ways of life, and so legitimacy.

23. For a variant, see Mavroidis and Sapir, *China and the WTO*, chap. 6. They prioritize trade-Quad (Canada, EU, Japan, and US) negotiations involving the PRC, but without ruling out a bottom-up strategy.

24. Grossmann and Horn, "Why the WTO?," 4.5.10, 4.5.11.

### *"Social Dumping" via Superpower-State-Sponsored Capitalism*

In that spirit, Dani Rodrik has influentially argued that states should be free to counteract not only regular dumping (selling excess supply into international markets at lower prices) but also "social dumping" that risks undermining domestic regulatory arrangements.[25]

Stepping back, some states' export businesses are internationally competitive because, unlike foreign counterparts, they are not required by law to incur costs on health and safety, medical insurance, pensions, and so on. In other words, the state's social model gives them an edge. Rodrik's target is those foreign firms that are cheaper through "abuse of worker rights (including, say, the absence of collective bargaining, or freedom of association)."[26] Proposing that the trade regime free states to preserve their higher-cost social models, he seeks not to protect domestic firms for their own sake but, rather, to avoid their seeking to restore competitiveness by lobbying their governments to abandon such rights for their own peoples.

The orthodox response, perhaps most eloquently from Nobel Prize winner and pundit Paul Krugman (quoted at the chapter head), is that the gains from trade do not depend on why a country's consumers enjoy cheaper imports. It is the same whether foreign producers are more efficient, have lower labor costs because their economy is still in the "catch-up" phase of development, or are not burdened by overheads stemming from government social policy. Comparative advantage is, straightforwardly, good for consumers.[27]

That ducks the political economy of trade relations, as Krugman himself stressed, never mind their geopolitics, or the need to sustain local legitimacy. Local communities sometimes struggle to adjust to competing with lower-cost labor elsewhere.[28] The policy question is whether that should be left to domestic government or addressed by the international regime, and if the

---

25. Rodrik, "New Rules," in *Straight Talk on Trade*, pp. 231–35.

26. Rodrik, "New Rules," p. 231.

27. In principle, comparative advantage's fruits can be exhausted. Samuelson, "Where Ricardo and Mill," showed (in a two-country model) that an economy can suffer permanent aggregate welfare losses when other states' productive efficiency catches up across the board. Where fair, losing-state policymakers should rely on domestic measures (e.g., spending on retraining). Things are different where—as Samuelson signposted—the losses flow from forced or purloined technology transfer (next chapter).

28. Acknowledged in Krugman, "Globalization."

latter, how to prevent countermeasures becoming part of a state's offensive geoeconomic armory (chapter 4). For Rodrik, "there is an important difference . . . between using trade policy to prevent undermining of domestic standards and the use of trade policy to export our standards to other countries. The first is legitimate; the second much less so."[29]

## Competition Policy and the Terms of Trade

This opens quite a door, since not only social policies have unwelcome spillovers. In what might seem a million miles away, the terms and intensity of competition policy (antitrust in the United States) can operate as a complex substitute, mitigant, or complement to trade policy.[30] For example, a state running trade deficits might toughen antitrust policy to drive local firms to be more competitive, or (if large enough to influence world prices) reduce gains available to foreigners while helping local consumers. More important here, a large economy might adopt *lax* merger policies to foster national champions that can take massive economies of scale to foreign markets: a form of hyper-technocratic mercantilism.

In consequence, it might be argued, Washington's pro-merger and pro-acquisitions policy has been a boon to many exporting businesses.[31] In that case, could geopolitical rivals reasonably argue the WTO regime should permit them to employ countervailing measures to shield themselves from monopoly-friendly policies that act like a subsidy unless they adopt a similar domestic regime? To make sense of this, a view would be needed on whether states were free to choose their own antitrust regime, including whether to have one at all. If so, it might also be subject to Rodrik's argument, since antitrust affects a state's social model by enabling or impeding private power. Europe's aversion to such concentrations is rooted in its twentieth-century political history: a desire to attain modernity without beckoning oppression. It would not want to take the same risks as the United States, but does the

29. Rodrik, "New Rules," p. 233.

30. While trade policy addresses barriers erected by governments, barriers and subsidies can also arise from private cartels and mergers: see Buthe, "Politics of Market Competition."

31. Chicago School antitrust policy, pressed by judges, not legislation, approves mergers and cartels expected to reduce prices for consumers. Unlike in earlier twentieth-century US policy or European ordo-liberal policy, weight is not given to more diffuse costs, including concentrated economic power begetting concentrated private political power.

trade regime make that an expensive choice? No doubt spillovers could be pinned on other policy fields too.

### Political Morality via Political Realism

The question becomes whether a defensible line can be drawn on taking countervailing measures to protect local practices and preferences. Rodrik offers guidance in a formulation focusing on trade's threats to "norms embodied in our institutional arrangements."[32] But any old norms or institutions?

Perhaps we could frame it as a pluralist liberal proposition that all states should be free to determine their own social model, subject to not *directly* interfering materially with others' choices. In consequence, individual states would be free to impose trade barriers where, via trade, one state's social model would otherwise undermine another's. But that still seems too loose, as shifts in technology or in patterns of commerce among some states can materially affect others.

This book's political realism suggests the focus should be those norms that are integral to whether a state satisfies its basic legitimation demand (chapter 12). In the West, by no means all norms running through the regulatory-cum-welfare state are foundational to domestic legitimacy but, very differently, are part of what we vote about in general elections. Illiberal and undemocratic states have their own distinct sets of core versus contestable norms and institutions.

Those considerations lead to a higher threshold than Rodrik's: that countermeasures could be taken only when the effects of commerce would undermine the local legitimacy of the afflicted state's system of government (chapter 13). Perhaps that way of approaching adverse legitimacy spillovers could be tucked under the GATT's existing exceptions for public order and national security. Whatever the legal mechanism, its application entails political judgment about legitimacy thresholds.

The problem now becomes, who decides and adjudicates? Rodrik (for his lower test) argues it cannot be judges or technocrats but must involve democratic deliberation (in the afflicted state).[33] But say, following such deliberation (with its real-world underside of logrolling), the United States (or whoever) introduced a particular measure, insisting it was necessary to protect workers'

32. Rodrik, "New Rules," p. 230.
33. Rodrik, "New Rules," p. 233.

rights. China might respond with a barrage of points: That these Western "rights" are not recognized by Chinese traditions, let alone Xi Jinping Thought, but are contingent positive rights the West has no (higher) right to impose as preconditions for protection-free trade.[34] Getting close to the bone, they might continue by challenging the idea that US domestic legitimacy depended on those specific rights; Washington was just trying to avoid the quotidian political cost of legislating more redistributive policies or structural reforms to promote dynamism. And perhaps most intractably, they might argue that the problem was symmetric: the United States was trying to engineer a trade regime that indirectly pressured Beijing to trade off slower development and living standards against maintaining access to foreign markets by granting broadly Western rights to their own workers and subject-citizens.

It is not clear how an arm's-length Appellate Body could possibly resolve that. Even more than the subsidies case with which the chapter began, laying down criteria for the legality of legitimacy-protecting actions, and then adjudicating case by case, would amount to ruling on the integrity of domestic political judgments about threats to a state's social cohesion and system of governance.[35] Worse, given the geopolitical stakes, the shadow of the future—working via reputational costs—would be weak (chapters 5 and 7). If the judges struck down a countervailing measure that the losing side sincerely believed was essential to safeguarding domestic legitimacy, it would need to ignore the court. The core difficulty is that a rational state would sensibly take preventative measures well before that point had been reached, but they would be harder to defend as indispensable. These complications are not so abstract given apparent discontent within the United States over the past decade.

### Reconfiguring the Regime

The underlying issue is that multilateral universalism is a stretch when the world's largest trading nations have rival political systems, gains from trade are sometimes lopsided, and relative economic performance might affect the prevailing Order-System's sustainability. In those circumstances, the gaps in incomplete contracts are not technical issues best left to specialists. If the trade

34. E.g., should the EU apply tariffs to US goods and services because its citizens have much weaker welfare and group rights, eroding our European way of life, which up to a point it has? No (not blanket-wise).

35. Bearing on proposals in Lehman, Rodrik, et al., *US-China Trade Relations*.

regime is to be reset, that bargain has to be struck at the table of diplomacy. It would turn on a trade-off between less trade and more local resilience for all the powers, some of whose economies, notably the United States' and the PRC's, would need to achieve a closer balance of domestic demand and supply.

With other rising powers on the horizon, that kind of bargained reduction in economic imbalances and overdependencies might even be thought a useful step toward a *Reshaped World Order*. But it is not yet obvious who would sit at the new top table. Nor are circumstances yet tense enough for nearly two hundred weaker states to surrender their existing veto power over the WTO regime. In that case, an organic solution will need, somehow, to emerge from plurilateral initiatives, with more or less mess on the way (next chapter). Whether examining the WTO against constitutionalist values or "social dumping" through the lens of local legitimacy, we end up in much the same place.

## Summing Up Trade So Far

Can commerce only be peaceable war between the West and China, as Louis XIV's adviser viewed the protracted struggle between eighteenth-century France and Britain? Or, better, in the spirit of Hume, the prophet of liberalism via commercial society, can the early twenty-first-century's powers find their way to an Order where their enormous economies enrich each other without seriously threatening each other's systems of government and ways of life?

The eighteenth-century powers' attempts to find a safe space where trade could thrive without geopolitics largely failed.[36] Nothing much has changed. Today, the WTO's Appellate Body seems to work tolerably well where the parties are a big and a small state, or two big states sharing some semblance of thick Society (e.g., Washington and Brussel's fractious aeroengine cases). But it falters when the parties are rival powers, the law is unclear, and the dispute's stakes high.

This challenges Hume's optimism. As our other guiding spirit, Bernard Williams, observed, commercial society does not exhaust the resources and commitments of liberal society, with its distinctively critical approach to more or less everything, including its own history.[37] For modern liberal societies, the ethical presumptions and inducements of international commerce are less

36. Shovlin, *Trading with the Enemy*, pp. 288–89.
37. Williams, *Truth and Truthfulness*, p. 265.

easily segmented from domestic legitimation norms than in Hume's day. That does not make things easy, but it is who we are (or have become).

Thick Society's endogeneity underlines the hazards in the WTO's unanimity procedures, sometimes defended as embodying the values of Pareto efficiency and justice. Fair dos, so long as the initial compact is complete and the signatories clear-sighted over possible future developments in preferences, interests, values, capabilities, and domestic constraints. Hobbesian mythmaking of efficiency-through-binding-unanimity is in denial about the inevitability of disagreement and the Hobbesian risk of conflict.

Maybe, though, Hume's optimism can be rescued by his organic problem-solving mechanisms. As well as signaling WTO malaise, mushrooming regional trade agreements conceivably help us toward a new equilibrium in international politics. The next chapter considers them alongside the framework for cross-border investment, transformed global production structures, and technology transfer and security.

# 18

# Preferential Trade Pacts and Bilateral Investment Treaties

## SECURITY FIRST, OR GLOBALIZATION VIA MIMESIS?

I am inclined to the belief that . . . a greater measure of national self-sufficiency and economic isolation among countries than existed in 1914 may tend to serve the cause of peace, rather than otherwise. At any rate, the age of economic internationalization was not particularly successful in avoiding war.

JOHN MAYNARD KEYNES, RECANTING, 1933[1]

ECONOMIC POLICY MULTILATERALISM came under strain well before geopolitical tensions resumed. This had roots in the shift, described in the previous chapter, away from the old GATT's institutionalized hierarchy. No longer operating under a de facto regime of "don't object because you don't have to obey," developing and poorer country members could veto new proposals, dislocating the dynamics of trade rounds. Nothing has been agreed since the Doha Round, addressing a score of issues, opened in late 2001, over twenty years ago.[2]

Instead, club deals, most famously the EU's Single Market and NAFTA (and its successor), have become trade policy's vanguard. Looking back, the

---

1. Keynes, "National Self-Sufficiency." With hindsight a remarkable mix of wisdom and folly, it was delivered a few months after the new Nazi government opened its first camp, made "non-Aryans" leave public service and universities, and held book burnings.

2. Baldwin, "World Trade Organization."

multilateral regime took a critical step during the 1950s when, perhaps to harness European recovery at the outset of the Cold War, the GATT—and hence, consistent with part III's account of voluntary hierarchy, Washington—cleared the European Coal and Steel Community even though it was not obviously compliant. Ever since, there have been few challenges against similar arrangements.[3] There are now hundreds of preferential trade agreements (PTAs), which go beyond WTO terms but are permitted-cum-tolerated.[4] Together with bilateral investment treaties (BITs), these highly technical exercises accompanied the growth of globalized supply chains.

That has not been uncontroversial, generating complaints about Western hegemony and the legitimacy of specific institutions, notably BIT arbitrations conducted away from the public eye. Nor, from liberal states' own perspective, have these regimes cured hazardous technology transfers to potentially unfriendly states. With the allure of its giant market, Beijing has been able to insist on bespoke terms in its own investment treaties (e.g., requiring most inward investment via joint ventures), to shrug off limited WTO obligations, and to escape legal challenge given the burdens of assembling concrete, usable evidence (and the risk of complainants triggering cases against their home states). These issues are entangled with the previous chapter's insofar as demands for technology transfers often work through state-owned enterprises.[5]

After outlining how that fits into the recent history of economic liberalism and geoeconomics, this chapter identifies possible national-security measures for reconciling the demands of Order and economic System, and uses our legitimacy *Principles for Participation and Delegation* to prescribe some institutional reforms.[6]

---

3. Mavroidis, *Regulation of International Trade*, 1.6.4.3–4. Under GATT Article XXIV, preferential trade agreements must comply with conditions, including covering substantially all trade among club members.

4. There are two PTA variants: a free-trade agreement with zero tariffs internally but individual-member tariffs externally, and, less frequently, a customs union (e.g., the EU) with a common external-tariff schedule. Free-trade agreements have become common since the 1990s. Hoekman and Mavroidis, *World Trade Organization*, pp. 57–61; Krueger, *International Trade*, chap. 14.

5. On PRC practices, see Branstetter, "China's Forced Technology Transfer," pp. 2–3. On holes in the international legal framework, see Mavroidis and Sapir, *China and the WTO*, pp. 90–105.

6. Thanks to Petros Mavroidis, Andre Sapir, and Michael Waibel for comments.

## Offensive and Defensive International Liberalism via Trade and Investment Agreements

The shift from multilateralism to geopolitical economic strategy has moved through four phases or modes.

### Liberalism Proselytized via Global Supply Chains

The first is associated with the development of global supply chains (chapter 1), which could not happen in a legal vacuum. Multinational companies not only needed permission to establish outlets in foreign states, they wanted assurances their assets would not be seized or treated differently from those of domestic businesses. They chose locations on the basis of those protections plus the tariffs and other barriers affecting imported inputs and exported outputs. In other words, the regimes for cross-border investment and trade could make or break globalized production and value chains. Once some developing countries lowered barriers, others rushed to join them in a scramble to attract capital and capabilities.[7]

In the background were some fairly profound changes in high policy, and an interesting extension of a long-standing principle of international law. For many developing countries, opening up to foreign direct investment (FDI) marked a pronounced shift in their development model: from using trade barriers to protect domestic producers (import substitution, as economists call it), to opening up to benefit from transfers of technology and know-how. For developed economies, it marked a shift in bargaining strategy from, as Richard Baldwin captures it, "my market for yours" to "my factories for your reform."[8]

In international law, this amounted to modernity's version of the old customary laws protecting diplomats and treaties insisting merchants be subject to their home laws and legal processes (chapter 2). By suspending sovereign authority to interfere with foreigners' local property rights, customary law's international minimum standard of state responsibility was resurrected for globalized commercial society.

That is best seen in cross-border investment law. Whereas the GATT (and later WTO) approached trade multilaterally, repeated attempts to create an

7. Baldwin, *Great Convergence*, pp. 98–106.
8. Baldwin, "World Trade Organization," p. 111.

equivalent regime and organization for international investment had failed (chapter 3). Instead, as globalization accelerated after the relaxation of capital controls, BITs skyrocketed. Except for those with the most attractive new markets or most determined hosts (e.g., China, India), they evolved to incorporate a catalog of protections—notably, bars on capital-outflow controls and prejudicial treatment of almost any kind—with investors able to go to arbitration to seek redress from host states for perceived violations.[9] Recalling our discussion of sovereignty (chapter 11), a state could not adopt constitutional amendments discriminating against foreign investors so long as it remained a BIT signatory, and even after exiting it could not violate customary law's minimum standard—so far as international law is concerned.

Over roughly the same period, rich countries' PTAs with many emerging and developing economies began reaching behind borders. Adding to WTO Uruguay-round protections on intellectual property and trade-related services, PTAs required hosts to open up to international telecom and other infrastructural services, eschew state aid to local firms, and embrace Western-style competition policies. With cross-border provision of services growing, rich states also led processes—largely in specialist fora outside the WTO—to agree to common minimum (precautionary) standards. Compared with the relative simplicity of antiprotectionist tariff reductions, globalized trade begat hierarchical international standard setting.[10]

In some respects, these trends worked with the grain of the 1990s Washington Consensus for macroeconomic policy (chapters 4 and 16), but with different implications for political economy and legitimacy (incentives and values). Whereas the IMF's liberalizing conditions were applied under the duress of dire need, it is harder to mount that argument here. Yes, poorer economies faced losing inward investment if they rejected the advanced economies' terms, but that was a matter of rational calculation of prospective costs and benefits, which is not the same thing as the comprehensive disorder that could engulf a financially distressed state if the Fund walked away. Further, since most BITs provide for withdrawal, accepting their terms could be a move

9. Bonnitcha et al., *Political Economy*, chaps. 1–4.

10. Baldwin, *Great Convergence*, table 5, p. 106. On protection versus precaution, see Lamy, *New World of Trade*. Consistent with a minimum standard, there can be meaningful differences among states—e.g., between competition policy in the EU and the United States, where a domestic commercial (and political) aristocracy was fostered.

within trial-and-error governance.[11] Against that, hosts have to weigh the costs (and benefits) of losing policy space, and how that might affect future domestic legitimacy.

### Liberalism Buttressed via Commercial Society

The second mode of commercial liberalism's modern diffusion came partly in response to deadlock in the WTO's Doha Round talks. Advanced and (generally) highly developed emerging economies entered into trade agreements to increase trade interlinkages in the absence of a full-blown universal pact. The whole world did not need to embrace deeper economic policy convergence in order for coalitions of the willing to do so. As such, the liberal integrationist program was to be buttressed by thickening commercial relations among those opting in, with some PTA measures covering territory so far left blank by the WTO.[12]

Initially relatively local or regional, these projects became seriously plurilateral (in the jargon) with the talks on the Trans-Pacific Partnership and the Transatlantic Trade and Investment Partnership. Delayed by the 2007–9 financial crisis and set back by various substantive disagreements, including concerns about the investment chapters, they were derailed by the Trump administration's general withdrawal from affairs. In a climactic moment, the other parties to the Pacific venture went ahead with a variant in 2018 (the Comprehensive and Progressive Agreement for Trans-Pacific Partnership, or CPTPP).[13]

### Liberalism Defended with Geoeconomics

Ironically, by the time Donald Trump walked away from those talks, they had become much more than technical exercises for specialists. The third phase or mode was marked by geoeconomic defense of a beleaguered liberalism, with megaregional trade clubs viewed as a means to thicken more than commercial

---

11. Bearing on normative criticisms of BITs given empirical uncertainty about whether they attract FDI or promote economic development: if not working for them, hosts can pull out.

12. On how EU and US PTAs did that, see H. Horn et al., *Beyond the WTO?*

13. It includes Canada and Mexico, is substantively similar to the draft Trans-Pacific Partnership, and has formal entry conditions and processes, including incumbent veto rights. (As I write, Britain is trying to join, and China might.)

ties, while incentivizing the PRC to alter course. This makes sense of the Pacific pact talks in terms of part IV's legitimation-norm circles, until Washington mislaid its own longer-term interests.

The sheer complexity of the new geopolitics-cum-geoeconomics, with its updated eighteenth-century-style jealousies of trade and pressures for middling powers to maintain tolerable relations with their neighboring superpower, was displayed on both sides of the world. Shortly after agreeing on their rich Pacific pact (without the United States), seven participating states, including Australia, entered into a somewhat thinner pact with the PRC itself (plus half a dozen other East Asian countries, including Indonesia and South Korea). Like CPTPP, it provides for additional members.[14] Meanwhile, in the eastern Pacific, a revised agreement among Canada, Mexico, and the United States introduced a provision to the effect that if any of them entered into a free-trade agreement with a nonmarket economy (as designated by any of them), their trilateral agreement was terminated, to be replaced by revised bilateral pacts. With a similar provision featuring in US proposals for other free-trade agreements, a strong signal had been sent that its trade partners should be cautious in trade relations with illiberal state-capitalist economies.[15]

### Geoeconomic Overdependence, Resilience, and Security

That geoeconomic orientation to international integration took a new turn in the wake of the COVID-19 pandemic, which in the early months of 2020 left most advanced economies—and, of course, much poorer states and peoples—scrambling for essential medical and other supplies. At the most mundane level, production and inventory policies were overwhelmed by surges in demand and undermined by fractures in international supply chains as countries shut down and international cargo transportation froze. Having been the hallmark of business efficiency for decades, just-in-time practices

14. Regional Comprehensive Economic Partnership, November 2020, commencing 2022. Differences with CPTPP concern state-owned enterprises, subsidies, government procurement, and intellectual property.

15. US-Canada-Mexico Trade Agreement, Article 32.10(1), which might affect any PRC application to join CPTPP. Vidigal, "Really Big Button." The revised "NAFTA" also jettisoned the previous arbitral system for resolving investment disputes: see Poulsen and Gertz, *Reforming the Investment Treaty*, p. 2n2.

were exposed as delivering nothing like an economist's idea of efficiency, which contemplates terrible as well as good states of the world.

In consequence, just as the 2007–9 Global Financial Crisis drove demands for much more resilient financial intermediaries and infrastructure providers (next chapter), so the pandemic shortages triggered a desire, associated with the new slogan "just in case," for more resilient and secure provision of essential goods. But unlike those financial system reforms, the new emphasis on *secure* supply also reflected geopolitics, since leaders no longer wanted to rely on vaccine capacity (or whatever) in unfriendly states; a sentiment fortified by the Ukraine war. As the quote from Keynes at the chapter head suggests, one possible response would be self-sufficiency in essentials. Another would be to try to ensure that key links in vital supply chains are located in friendly (if not formally allied) states. Again, unlike financial reform, there is no international machinery for pursuing that.

In terms of part II's account of cooperation's political economy, 2020 unpacked the ambiguity of "interdependence"—a watchword of liberal institutionalism—into safe dependence and reckless overdependence. In effect, liberalism is reconfiguring as governments regrasp System's reliance on peaceful coexistence among great powers. But those forces are symmetric—explaining why, for example, the PRC might ration exports of rare earths used in instruments that could be turned against it.

Two other questions confront policy and law. How far should advanced-economy states adopt, and more generally promote, measures guarding against the transfer or purloinment of technology potentially integral to their longer-term security? Separately, what changes are important to enhancing the legitimacy of preferential trade and cross-border investment agreements?

## Technology Transfer and National Security

The security issue is affected by a particular collective-action problem in liberal states. On the one hand, businesses are far better placed than governments to make judgments about commercial opportunities and risks in new markets, implying the state should keep out of outward FDI decisions. On the other hand, those very same businesses have incentives to grant concessions of all kinds to gain entry into especially big or rapidly growing markets, particularly given their short horizons (stretching out a few years at most). While in most (not all) sectors not much harm will be done by any one firm transferring proprietary technology and know-how, that is not so in aggregate.

Multinationals' incentives and horizons potentially jeopardize the longer-run interests of their home states and peoples.

The issues run across a two-by-two matrix: outward versus inward investment (FDI and portfolio); and problematic technology transfers via theft or preconditions for doing business.

On outward investment to Russia (once back in the circle of peaceful co-existence), the PRC, or wherever, one possible solution to the incentives hazard would be to constrain multinationals to investing in unfriendly states via subsidiaries that are, in relevant ways, ring-fenced from other parts of their group, with the aim of impeding inadvertent transfers of nonlocally held technology, data, and so on. Another, with costs as well as benefits, would be to bar Western-domiciled groups entering into joint ventures with firms in unfriendly states. In other words, if the PRC demands joint ventures, which it is surely free to do, other states have the wherewithal to say a collective no. Going further, Western states could bar their groups from complying with local licensing conditions that require technology transfers. Further still, they could bar ventures with state-owned enterprises (although other businesses are hardly free of Party influence).[16]

Controls on inward investment already exist, typically operated by statutory bodies applying national-security tests.[17] Similar care (in places, overdue) needs to be taken on funding and control of universities, research institutes, think tanks, political parties, and media outlets. The challenge is to ensure that machinery for protecting national security is subject to checks and balances so that it does not become a riot of indiscriminate favoritism and arbitrary power, undermining the very liberalism it seeks to guard. Depending on the course of events, local measures might need coordinating, as during the old Cold War for arms exports (at the Coordinating Committee on Export Controls, and subsequently via the Wassenaar Arrangement: chapter 3).

The goal would be to contain threats to local order—and so to the legitimacy of our constitutional system of government and way of life—without completely choking off commerce among rival ideological blocs: to avoid *Superpower Struggle* tipping into a fully fledged *New Cold War*. In part IV's terms, that would entail the thinnest circle of prudent and legitimate engagement with states that are a potential threat and have or may have violated *jus cogens*

---

16. Branstetter, "China's Forced Technology Transfer."

17. US Committee on Foreign Investments. The EU established a regime only in 2019, Britain in 2021.

norms. On that count, Germany's Nordstream2 energy deal with Russia exemplified costly wishful thinking given its failure to temper Moscow's nervous aggression.

## Legitimacy Challenges for Bottom-Up
## Trade and Investment Regimes

Separately, constitutional democracies face legitimacy issues around the legal frameworks for trade and investment, which are different in important respects.

Whereas PTAs operate under the broad umbrella of the WTO treaties, there is no equivalent multilateral regime for most cross-border investments. Whereas trade disputes are between states, investment disputes are between aggrieved investors and host states. Whereas some PTAs incorporate judicialized adjudication of disputes (notably in the EU, via its Court of Justice), BIT disputes are settled via arbitration. Whereas trade disputes are largely transparent, investment disputes are somewhat opaque.[18] But in case the drift seems one way, whereas plurilateral PTAs are hard to revise given the number of parties, BITs might in principle be easier to reform.

### PTAs: Constitutionalism and Conditional Openness

Having already discussed the WTO, I will make only three points highlighting what our *Principles* entail for constitutional democracies' participation in PTAs. First, they should incorporate a binding judicial dispute-adjudication system only if there is also a *workable* procedure for members to revise their treaty's provisions or guide their application where judicial constructions (in settling backward-looking disputes) clash with members' collective forward-looking wishes. In other words, diplomacy needs to retain a foothold alongside law as a means of giving states and peoples an ongoing say in law.[19]

Second, the club-like nature of PTAs needs to be consistent with the broader approach of advanced-economy democracies to the developing world.

18. The 2015 Mauritius Transparency Convention subjected signatories' existing BITs to the 2014 Rules on Transparency developed by the UN Commission on International Trade Law (UNCITRAL). But as of March 2022, only nine signatories had ratified.

19. Technically, the Vienna Convention provides for interpretative agreements, as specifically do some PTAs, notably NAFTA (old and new): see Roberts, "Power and Persuasion."

The doors cannot be bolted shut, but need to be open to those states that can meet the terms of a club-regime and fit into its broader, longer-run aims without disturbing the wider Order or System in ways that jeopardize the legitimacy of the existing members' systems of governance.

In consequence, third, membership can prudently be extended to authoritarian states only where they are not breaching *jus cogens* norms and where decentralized enforcement of the regime's provisions (for example, against forced technology transfers) is credible. This could accommodate, say, Vietnam but not, currently, the authoritarian superpowers.[20]

## Institutionalized Cross-Border Investment Law: Arbitration versus Judicialization

The issues around BITs are distinct. Despite sequential attempts at Havana and by the OECD and WTO (chapter 3), there is no multilateral regime or organization. Nor is there a soft-law standard for the content of BITs promoted via the kind of structure Basel employs for financial policy. But there is not a vacuum. Customary international law's minimum standard of protection does some work in the background, and various forces promote a degree of convergence, producing something like an order (spontaneous, informal coordination).

First, many large economies, including Washington and Beijing, use model investment treaties as the basis for bilateral pacts. Second, through where investing subsidiaries and funds are domiciled, multinational businesses and asset managers can select which BIT will govern particular foreign investments. Third, in addition to diffusion via copycatting, the standard inclusion of most-favored-nation provisions creates gravitational pull toward similar templates via a somewhat precedent-sensitive arbitration process. In our terms, this is an investment order, not a designed system.[21]

---

20. For PTAs among nonpowers that are a mixture of liberal and illiberal states, such as CPTPP, this points to refusing the authoritarian power on values grounds, and the more liberal power on incentives grounds (unless they wish to take sides).

21. Bonnitcha et al., *Political Economy*, pp. 95–104. Schill, *Multilateralization of International Investment*, goes too far in arguing convergence delivers multilateralism. Also, while constraining constitutional (and other) discrimination, BITs do not introduce constitutional constraints because exit and renegotiation are not unrealistic.

## Decentralized Informal Judicial Review?

Avoiding the diplomatic complexities of state-to-state disputes, plus any hazards from litigating in a host's domestic courts, the norm is investor-state arbitration, mostly serviced by the World Bank's International Centre for the Settlement of Investment Disputes (ICSID).[22] Operating under public international law, ICSID arbitral outcomes cannot be overturned by domestic courts, but signatory states are bound, if necessary, to enforce them via local law.

That national self-binding suggests an analogy with domestic judicial review of executive and legislative actions. There are, however, many differences. At the level of design, there is no appeal process;[23] there is no fixed panel of arbitrators, who are better thought of as ad hoc independent neutral agents rather than system trustees constrained by a common trust deed (chapter 6);[24] the parties help select arbitrators, who are paid lots (conceivably affecting their incentives); the proceedings are private, as can be the outcomes if the parties wish;[25] and so on.

All that has generated a good deal of criticism, especially as the open-ended texture of most BITs gives arbitrators—especially those frequently appointed—room to develop norms to the extent they eye past decisions. To pick an important example, "fair and equitable treatment" is especially vague, marking a potential gamut of procedural or substantive abuses and leaving tribunals to decide what standard to apply in determining whether host conduct is arbitrary, unreasonable, or contrary to legitimate expectations. This matters more if the decisions affect not only the parties to a dispute, and at one remove potential future disputants, but also local and foreign bystanders (chapters 12 and 13).[26]

---

22. Bonnitcha et al., *Political Economy*, pp. 22–30. UNCITRAL provides a rival venue.

23. ICSID Article 52 provides a process for annulment but on grounds of bias and so on, rather than manifest mistakes of law or fact, which some believe have occurred: see Comella, *Constitution of Arbitration*, pp. 146–48.

24. Departing from the view of Roberts, "Power and Persuasion," that, positively, they are like trustees for disputants, but subordinate agents for signatory states in law development.

25. Under ICSID, arbitrators must give reasons, but publication is up to the parties. The parallel UNCITRAL terms require publication, possibly contributing to its lower use. Comella, *Constitution of Arbitration*, p. 144.

26. Crawford, *Brownlie's Principles*, p. 600, notes four fair-and-equitable-treatment variants, affecting the fit with customary law's minimum standard of protection for foreigners (chapter 2). On spillovers and hence transnational public interest, see Schill, "Developing a Framework."

For some years, complaints about the BITs order have been under discussion at the UN Commission on International Trade Law, with very different reform preferences articulated by large states (the EU, the United States, the PRC, Brazil, and South Africa) as well as smaller ones.[27] The startlingly wide range of proposals includes vanilla measures such as establishing a permanent arbitral tribunal to promote consistency; returns to ideas for a multilateral treaty or an investment court; extends to requiring investors to litigate in hosts' domestic legal systems, or moving to state-to-state dispute settlement of some kind; and culminates in proposals to give investors obligations to aid development and preserve human rights. As of this writing, there is no agreement.

## The Legitimacy Constraints of Constitutionalism, Rule of Law, and Democracy

The objective here is not to offer a first-best structure, which would be at odds with Humean political realism, but to use part IV's *Principles* to suggest some conditions for incentive- and values-compatible reforms. Heeding incentives, any reforms must recognize the capacity—arguably rooted in liberal norms— for large multinational investors to revert to contract-based arbitration if that became more attractive than proceeding under any treaty.

On values compatibility, a democratic host state's self-binding should not formally be tighter (in kind) than that applied by ordinary domestic legislation. Just as ordinary legislation puts obstacles in the way of course changes without preventing them, so it should be possible to exit a cross-border investment treaty. This makes a case for BITs rather than a formally multilateral WTO-style universal investment treaty, since exit from the latter would be much harder.[28]

Second, repeating my conclusions on the WTO and PTAs, an international investment court could be placed in charge only if it were combined with some kind of process for states to coordinate forward-looking treaty amendments. This would be more pressing if any such court was accompanied by a new multilateral investment treaty codifying minimum standards for all member states. But even absent such a treaty (and associated international organization), moving to a system of doctrinal development by arm's-length judges

27. Roberts, "Incremental, Systemic, and Paradigmatic Reform."

28. Recent research suggests host states do renegotiate or terminate BITs to create more regulatory space: see Thompson et al., "Once Bitten, Twice Shy?"

would throw grit in the wheels of the diplomatic evolution of bilateral treaties in the light of lessons learned from past cases, changing tastes and objectives, structural changes in the economy and geopolitics, and so on. While a global economic libertarian might applaud such constraints, they would implicitly be making particular assumptions about the nature of the international Order that enables System, and about the solidity of domestic legitimacy. For that reason, while a relatively thick European society has included a court system in some of its bilateral treaties with similar states (e.g., Canada), it is quite different for the EU to propose an international court for a very thin international society struggling to maintain peaceful coexistence.

Third, other values test the existing reliance on jobbing arbitrators. A case can be made for ICSID to operate with a panel of arbitrators paid a fixed salary, barred from nonacademic work, and serving for lengthy terms. Owing duties to the system, they would be closer to regime trustees than their current role as impartial ad hoc agents for disputants.[29]

In the same vein, fourth, the current system's opacity sits ill with the values of both the rule of law and democracy given the transformation in the scale, scope, and nature of cross-border investment. Where people around the world cannot see how the law of international investment develops and is applied, their capacity to track the adequacy and degrees of freedom of their own government's policies is impaired, at odds with a republican value.

As well as greater transparency, states need to have a say in the development of the arbitral community's de facto jurisprudence. This might be helped by some kind of annual assembly meeting to air issues, creating all the familiar (but, given democratic values, desirable) problems of separating wheat from chaff. Beyond that, treaty counterparts could try to promulgate statements documenting the interpretations they want arbitrators to follow or avoid.[30]

Fifth, our values can inform the tribunals' standard of review. Almost any action taken by a host government against a foreign investor could be taken against a local investor. If arbitral tribunals employ a more demanding standard

---

29. The *normative* thrust of Roberts, "Power and Persuasion." The UNCITRAL talks currently include a draft code for arbitrators.

30. Poulsen and Gertz, *Reforming the Investment Treaty*, advocates something like this, but at a plurilateral level, whereas it might sometimes be easier for it to emerge organically. In addition to the point that such statements are compatible with general international law, treaty partners could tacitly agree simply not to rehire arbitrators who ignored mutually favored interpretations.

in protecting foreign investors than domestic courts use, the upshot would be that a measure intended to protect foreigners from discrimination resulted in discrimination against home investors, eating away at domestic legitimacy.

The proper response, I suggest, is for international investment tribunals to track the standard of review prevailing in the host state, subject to satisfying themselves that a state has a broadly satisfactory system of judicial review (in practice).[31] Otherwise, domestic corporations and asset managers have incentives to invest at home via a foreign subsidiary that can benefit from its host state's BIT with their own country.[32] In some regulated sectors, including international banking, if ever a host state loses a cross-border investment case, rational domestic investors could well adopt that model, which would be highly perverse.

Sixth, on substance, constitutional democracies should distinguish between preestablishment and postestablishment provisions. A legal right of entry is distinct from a legal right to nondiscriminatory treatment having been granted permission to enter. There is an important asymmetry here. Citizens (and thus local businesses) are entitled to the benefit of the doubt about their not representing a threat to local order and stability (except where there is evidence to the contrary). Outsiders are not entitled to a similar benefit of the doubt, precisely because they are not citizens. There is a need to strike a balance between the benefits of openness and avoidable risks to order, and where to strike that balance is a political judgment. Committing in treaties to generalized preestablishment rights deprives a state of the capacity to make case-by-case exceptions, other than by overtly incurring the costs of relying on national security considerations. Regional or megaregional investment pacts that grant such rights implicitly depend on alignment or convergence in values and interests, which is obviously fine where it prevails, but should not be a generalized obligation in international law.

## Summing Up

Discordant geopolitics hang over these issues. Regional trade pacts, with their overlapping memberships, might in time generate a dynamic back toward the universalist WTO, but probably not soon. For similar reasons, establishing a

---

31. For a not dissimilar proposal, arrived at differently, see Aisbett and Bonnitcha, "Pareto-Improving Compensation."

32. Lithuania-Ukraine and Isle of Man–Russia cases delivered that: see Bonnitcha et al., *Political Economy*, pp. 54–55.

new international investment organization while existing multilateral regimes are wilting seems like wishful thinking. Steps to reduce the BIT order's frailties are worth trying given its legitimacy strains.

The goal should be to provide a basic legal infrastructure for international commerce while underpinning (or at least not undermining) liberalism, not jeopardizing the domestic order and legitimacy of constitutional democracies, and embracing a constrained pluralism rather than a hegemonic universalism (ours today, someone else's the day after tomorrow).

The constraint on pluralism, reflected here in the stress on customary law's *minimum* standard for the protection of foreigners, is important. It stems from the book's argument (chapter 13) that constitutional democracies should favor the transnational application of norms against a state's ongoing consent only where necessary to satisfy some basic threshold of human decency (*jus cogens*), to keep us safe, or, as here, to maintain the thinnest possible kind of international Society needed for a System of cooperative regimes to be feasible.

# 19

# Basel and the International Financial System

## ARE THE TOWER'S DENIZENS TOO POWERFUL?

Financial globalization makes cooperation between central banks and regulators all the more important.

JACQUES DE LAROSIÈRE, 2006[1]

If we want to achieve international monetary cooperation, governments will have something to say about it. Inevitably, it is not a matter for central bankers alone.

PAUL VOLCKER, 2006[2]

WHEN WE TURN to international finance, things change. Here we do meet a system based on designed regimes, but one that relies on informal standard setting, largely in the Basel Tower, and something closer to club membership than universality.

This chapter offers an account of how central banks, hosted by the Bank for International Settlements (BIS) in Basel, emerged as potent international standard setters. It then proposes reforms for making the financial system more resilient given discordant geopolitics, and to help the Tower avoid being

1. Bank for International Settlements, *Past and Future*, p. 12.
2. Bank for International Settlements, *Past and Future*, p. 17.

compromised by its confidential dialogue with the industry (international finance) it is meant to oversee, not serve.[3]

To kick off, a story illustrating that Basel is nothing like the barbed environment inhabited by government negotiators. Sometime in 2009 I was chairing a meeting of a G20 Financial Stability Board (FSB) group charged with overcoming the difficulties that, during 2008's banking collapse, had impeded cooperation between the authorities of the jurisdictions where banking groups were headquartered (home authorities) and those of the many jurisdictions where they had foreign operations (host authorities). We were a bit stuck, atmospherically as well as substantively. On the spur of the moment, I asked for hands up among significant host authorities who did not really trust home authorities to cooperate during a crisis. After a pause, Mexico put up its hand. Others followed, including me. I then asked which home authorities did not really trust host authorities to cooperate. The United States and some others put up their hands, and I did so again, explaining I raised my hand both times because London was the home of some significant internationally active banks but also host to many foreign banks' international outlets (branches and subsidiaries), some gigantic in their own right. I suggested that to crack the problem, we had to come up with a regime that was incentive compatible for all parties, meaning commitments made ex ante would be honored ex post, in the midst of crisis.

Those few minutes changed the group's dynamics. Much of the credit goes to Pascual O'Dogherty, the senior Banco de Mexico official who decided to answer honestly even though it meant sending an awkward signal to powerful home authorities of banks operating in Mexico. As it happens, we did come up with an incentive-compatible policy, but that can wait because the important point is that the outbreak of candor was, I believe, made possible by an ethic (strong social norm) of cooperation that is a hallmark of the community of central bankers meeting in Basel. I am not convinced people feel obliged to volunteer bad news (although I witnessed that too), but they rarely dissemble when an issue is squarely put.

For our group, not only did the answers reveal information, they created a positive atmosphere, almost like the (usually phony) bonding moments management gurus go on about. In this book's terms, it was Good Faith in action,

3. Thanks to Svein Andresen, Gavin Bingham, and Steve Cecchetti for reading through the final draft of this chapter.

which can be powerful in a thick society, bound together by more than expedience or a shared technical language. That is what Basel is.

## Responding to Problems: How Basel Became a Powerful Standard Setter

Having in previous chapters seen global trade agreements freeze after the
mid-1980s Uruguay Round, and sequential attempts at multilateral investment pacts come to nothing, it is useful to ask why Basel could still strike
agreements after it was expanded to include the large Asian, Latin American,
and African economies. Is it that soft-law agreements do not really matter
or are easier to exit, and so are entered into lightly? Is it something to do
with the Basel community and process, or with the nature of banking? The
answer has a flavor of all that, as well as path dependence and the power of
incumbency.

From its creation in the mid-1970s up until the mid-1980s, the members of
the Basel Committee on Banking Supervision (BCBS) did little more than
exchange views on how to supervise banking safety, and pronounce publicly
(the 1975 Basel Concordat) how they would try to maintain an effective division of labor in supervising internationally active banks with outlets in
more than one country. That was not so different from the informal cooperation agreements that exist today among some of the main competition
authorities.[4] There was no commitment to act or refrain from acting in
particular ways, and no commitment to promote laws or issue regulations
of specific kinds.

How that changed is instructive. When, during the mid-1980s, the Fed and
the Bank of England started talking about a common approach to their banks'
capital adequacy (soundness), the initial target was to find a way for bank
supervisors to cope with some new innovations (roughly, off-balance-sheet
derivatives): Humean problem solving. With that technical exercise making
rapid progress, Paul Volcker and Robin Leigh-Pemberton ratcheted up their
ambition to agreeing a joint approach to *all* the risk-taking business of *all*
major internationally active banks, which meant taking a prototype to the
Basel committee (then a club comprising the G10 plus Switzerland).[5]

4. Papaconstantinou and Pisani-Ferry, "New Rules for a New World."
5. Disclosure: I was the most junior member of the initial Bank of England team. Under
Brian Quinn, the others were Richard Farrant and Carol Sergeant.

Motivations varied as this elaborate dance progressed. At the outset, it was mutual dependence: because New York and, especially, London were open international financial centers, an intervention by only one could not work. When the exercise embraced on-balance-sheet business, achieving a level playing field with other countries mattered, especially to Washington, and the Japanese authorities (led by their Ministry of Finance) were invited to a secret meeting in London. Only once Tokyo was on board could an international standard be imagined.

Under the skillful chairmanship of Peter Cooke, who had not been part of the Bank of England's negotiating team, the BCBS agreed a *voluntary minimum* standard. No state had international-law obligations to implement it, but there was little doubt they would, via their domestic hard-law (primary, secondary, or regulatory) and, mostly, democratically sensitive processes. Thus, the Basel standards became "soft law"—informal but credible commitments.[6]

### The Explosion of Standards and Codes: Enter the International Monetary Fund and World Bank

A decade later (1998), the BCBS compiled and codified, again informally, core principles for effective banking supervision, and in a critical step the IMF and the World Bank started tracking and reporting on compliance among their much larger membership. Whether or not this was sensible, it set off a process that engulfed international finance after the late 1990s crises in developed-economy capital markets (triggered by a failing hedge fund, Long-Term Capital Management) and, as already discussed, in East Asian emerging market economies. The high authorities (G7) established a new umbrella body (the Financial Stability Forum),[7] charging it with overseeing a more complete set of standards and codes to preserve stability.[8]

Coming only a few years after the WTO's inception, these developments fueled a perception among scholars and commentators that the world was in

---

6. Brummer, "Why Soft Law Dominates."

7. Bringing together finance ministries, central bankers, financial regulators, standard setters (e.g., the BCBS, the International Organization of Securities Commissions [IOSCO]), international organizations (e.g., the IMF, the BIS in its own right), and so on.

8. Twelve initial codes and standards have since evolved into twelve headings, with more standards underneath.

the throes of a profound transition from the intergovernmental diplomacy of multilateral treaties to governance via transnational expert networks operating via soft law (chapter 1). But this was exaggeration. For good or ill, some international regulatory bodies had nothing like Basel's influence.[9] That began to change only after the 2007–9 crisis when, notwithstanding the second Basel capital accord's inadequacies being laid bare, G20 leaders doubled up on their investment in Basel, upgrading the Financial Stability Forum into the new Financial Stability Board. Why?

## Basel as Stability Policy's Center: A Vindicatory Genealogy

Part of the explanation is the rise, during the 1980s and 1990s, of central bankers as core macroeconomic policymakers—manifested in over-the-top accolades, and perhaps declining confidence among treasury officials. But that explains only why others would give them space, not why they were capable of using it (in the sense of producing results, whether good or bad).

The answer turns on the way Basel consensus building flips between groups of different size, composition, and authority, and on the history of central banking (as absorbed by central bankers). So what follows is, in the spirit of Hume and Bernard Williams, a vindicatory genealogy of social norms fostered by calamities faced collectively.

### A Social Norm of Gubernatorial Collegiality

The culture is strongest among a fairly small group, as another story illustrates. Around 2012, Mervyn King, as chair of the BCBS's governing body— Governors and Heads of Supervision (GHOS)—declined to table a proposed new Liquidity Coverage Ratio requirement for approval until satisfied none of the major central banks was going to try to derail it. Instead, its substance

---

9. E.g., IOSCO: partly because the US Securities and Exchange Commission has rarely embraced international cooperation—perhaps because it is not insulated from day-to-day congressional politics or staff interests. Singer, *Regulating Capital*, chap. 5. Disclosure: I cochaired a joint IOSCO-Basel group on financial infrastructure, greatly enjoying working with securities counterparts (whose world I briefly shared in the late 1980s when helping redesign Hong Kong's regime).

was discussed in the Tower's core informal gathering of a dozen or so governors (the Economic Consultative Committee [ECC]).[10] That inner group— smallish but including nearly all the most important central bankers, who have repeat business with each other on lots of issues and also sit as directors of the BIS itself—has a strong spirit of avoiding disagreement; the social costs of holding out are potentially high. While it took more than one ECC session, spread over a few months, a tweaked liquidity requirement was signed off. The ECC could not have driven through something opposed by other regulators, but it could avoid the risk of non-ECC GHOS members bandwagoning on the back of one of its own.

Similar stories could be told of how, under Mario Draghi, the FSB Steering Committee, then comprising mainly central bankers, cleared away obstacles facing the formal standard setters. Even when, a few years later, BCBS chair Stefan Ingves faced all sorts of lobbying and opposition, including from big governors, on the Basel 3 capital reforms, he got them across the line.

The Tower's denizens have, to date, proved adept at avoiding sclerosis by exploiting variable geometry decision-making to harness a strong norm prevailing among a de facto leadership group (chapter 8). This, however, merely again relocates the puzzle: to why a bunch of central bank governors, some of them occasionally novices in monetary affairs, feel the norm's pull.

### Beggar-Thyself or Common Resource Problem?

The secret ingredient is, I think, a sense among generations of central bankers—embedded in their organizations—that they are in it together, somehow. In my preferred terms, they grasp that they serve as (constrained) collective trustees for a global financial commons. As Dani Rodrik has pointed out, unlike the atmosphere, the global economy's financial system is not a natural commons. Financial crises are, on this view, rooted in lax home regulation, a form of self-harm—a "beggar-thyself" pathology rather than a beggar-thy-neighbor vicious circle.[11] Certainly, that is part of the problem. Basel minimum

---

10. The ECC is, roughly, the old G10 governors plus peers from the European Central Bank, Brazil, China, India, and Mexico. Disclosure: During this period, I was the Bank of England member of the GHOS, and the bank's deputy in Basel, attending the ECC.

11. Rodrik, "What Will Not Work," in *Straight Talk on Trade*, pp. 206–13, 218–21.

standards are a mechanism for national self-binding in the face of an internationally mobile banking industry with potent local lobbying power.

There is more to it than that, however. An international financial commons
arises through policy choices to permit cross-border flows of capital and risk,
giving rise to deep and complex interlinkages. Countries that are the home or
host to internationally active banks (and other intermediaries) cannot achieve
domestic financial stability on their own. If one center implodes, the shock
waves spread everywhere, washing some away. The greater the variations in
states' resilience requirements, the more activity migrates to those with the
weakest standards, leaving everyone more exposed.

Those mutual dependencies are amplified by any airgaps—intra-day credit
or liquidity exposures—coded into the international infrastructure (clearing
houses, payment systems, and securities-transfer systems) used by banks and
others to transact and settle claims on each other. Just as railways and telecoms
are essential to commerce in general, so the financial infrastructure is essential
to finance. The plumbing serving the biggest markets and the most actively
used currencies is especially important.

Crucially, finally, those interdependencies are compounded by a special
kind of problem. The more people believe the financial system as a whole is
resilient—and hence, paradoxically, the more policymakers publicly declare
it is highly resilient—the more individual firms, like Hume's sensible knave,
have incentives to take more risk, which when aggregated diminishes the very
resilience on which each firm is relying. The system's resilience is a common
resource: available to all but exposed to erosion if any authorities permit their
local firms to exploit its blessings (chapter 5).[12] Individual states face a choice
between some degree of financial autarky (via capital controls and segmenta-
tion of domestic intermediation from foreign and entrepot activities) and
embracing, and policing, international minimum soundness standards. Basel
is not only a mechanism for self-binding, but one for binding other significant
banking jurisdictions.

Since the BIS was created in the 1930s, its leading lights have mostly understood that. Some might not be internationalists by temperament, but their
craft pushes them to international engagement through financial-system interdependences that enhance welfare so long as all goes well, but destroy
welfare when the system breaks down.

12. Tucker, *Design and Governance*, p. 26, applying the principles in Ostrom, *Governing the
Commons*, p. 90.

## The Bonds of Shared History

The Tower's denizens are, I believe, disposed to see things this way by virtue of their organizations' shared histories. On the monetary side, this is the history of the gold standard, and of Bretton Woods and its aftermath (chapters 3, 15, and 16). On the stability side, it is the history of calamities triggered by the collapse of Vienna's Credit Anstalt in 1931, of New York's Franklin National Bank and Germany's Bankhaus Herstatt in 1974, and of others since.

The institutional reverberations from Herstatt were profound, stretching over four decades. A small bank with an active foreign exchange business, when its doors closed it had already received the deutschmark leg of some trades during Europe's banking hours but not yet paid out the corresponding dollars it owed in New York, effectively defaulting on those obligations. Finance ministers and central bank governors were left grappling with a web of credit interdependences (rooted in deeply flawed infrastructure not fixed until the early 2000s!). Under pressure from finance ministers, and scrambling to maintain order in money markets, the G10 governors took two steps. With some foreboding, they issued a very short and somewhat cryptic statement on their role as lenders of last resort—a first, and a rarely repeated missive.[13]

Then, as 1974 was closing, the governors announced what became the BCBS, initially under Bank of England official (and later deputy governor) George Blunden. Each member had two seats, one for a central banker and one for a prudential supervisor, whether or not based in the central bank. As well as setting the supervisors' committee slightly apart from the Basel hierarchy, that established, with profound consequences, a precedent for the Tower hosting bodies led by central bankers but involving others: Humean problem solving had shifted the sense of the possible. Years later, therefore, it was not unthinkable for the FSB—an informal, partly intergovernmental body overseeing all international standard setting on financial-system stability, and reporting up to the G20—to be housed and supported in the Tower.

Meanwhile, in another post-Herstatt thread, the governors grasped the importance of the plumbing, especially when presented with various schemes for multilateral netting of interbank obligations. In 1980 they set up

---

13. Mid-1970s deliberations documented in Goodhart, *Basel Committee*, pp. 35–40.

an expert group on payments (again with Blunden as first chair), which developed into part of the permanent machinery. After the 2007–9 crisis, it issued its first standard in partnership with the International Organization of Securities Commissions. Since that covered clearing houses as well as settlement systems, it was subsequently renamed the Committee on Payments and Market Infrastructure, accurately signaling central banks' de facto responsibilities (given claims on clearing houses need to be safe).[14]

In summary, the secret of Basel is communal recognition that, so long as most countries maintain liberalized capital flows, no central bank can deliver domestic financial stability acting alone.[15] They are, as the cliché goes, in it together. For sure, to different degrees, but none—not even the mighty United States—is safe left to its own devices. That has been central bankers' shared history—of crises, and so, in a way, of failure.

## Institutional Amnesia

In effect, under this genealogy of the Basel process, individual governors get inducted into a culture of international-financial-system trusteeship through socialization into the community of central bankers; more elementally, a matter of their fitting in. The genealogy is vindicatory because it survives reflection, given available alternatives: with open capital flows, cooperation is necessary and cannot sanely be subject to universal vetoes given the costs to order of sclerosis, but it can operate via minimum standards that get incorporated into law locally.

But since active trusteeship is not formally entrenched, the culture depends on memorializing past crises. Long periods of stability are liable to lead to collective amnesia, compounding rather than checking the habitual myopia of market participants.[16] Since governors and their deputies are just people, the challenge becomes how to embed a sense of collective trusteeship even when memories of why it is needed are fading. Somehow, the policy regime itself needs to do this: by working backward from the end game.

---

14. My final act in Basel was to recommend to ECC governors that the Committee on Payment and Settlement Systems' mandate be reviewed (delivered under my successor, then–European Central Bank policymaker Benoît Coeuré).

15. Schoenmaker, *Governance of International Banking*.

16. That helps make sense of inadequate gubernatorial oversight of the BCBS during the drawn-out production of the disastrously flawed Basel 2.

## Regime Reform: System Resilience
## for Discordant Geopolitics

Much of the Tower's policy toward stability has had the wrong orientation: trying to prevent instability rather than curing it on terms that alter incentives. This needs some unpacking.

Most financial stability crises come about through the failure of banks and other intermediaries, which inflict costs on society at large through preemptive or forced sales of assets to generate liquidity (depressing wealth, and so spending), and by cutting back on the provision of services, including credit, to households and businesses (risking ruptures in the real economy). Since intermediaries' direct problems are illiquidity or insolvency, the thrust of policy has been to reduce their probability.

With the focus on prophylactic crisis prevention rather than crisis management, Basel's foundational Concordat—issued in 1975, updated for lessons from the failures of Banco Ambrosiano (the Vatican Bank, 1982, as in *Godfather III*) and the Bank of Credit and Commerce International (1991), and now (regrettably) absorbed into the mammothly long *Core Principles for Effective Banking Supervision*—never quite rose to the problem of whether an ex ante division of labor between home and host authorities can hold ex post when a banking operation is falling over. An incentive-*in*compatible cooperative regime is only the simulacrum of the real thing.[17]

When, decades later, Mervyn King proclaimed banks to be international in life but national in death (chapter 15), the important question was whether that was only contingently so there and then, or unavoidably so. In making sense of their predicament, part of the governors' problem is that the availability of a time-consistent international prudential regime depends on the policies and actions of lenders of last resort (a separate aspect of themselves), but also of resolution authorities (or bankruptcy practitioners and judges) who step in when a bank has had it. A concordat among supervisors alone is radically incomplete.

17. Absorbing the Concordat into the Core Principles was a mistake because promulgating a soft standard on best practices is different *in kind* from trying to commit to cross-border coordination before, during, and after a crisis. The initial work on the Concordat, led by Netherlands BCBS founding father Huib Muller, included a matrix crystallizing some of the big issues, but it was dropped from the versions going to the governors and the outside world. Goodhart, *Basel Committee*, pp. 97–98.

For decades, the governors hesitated to confront this. Habitually reluctant to discuss lender-of-last-resort policy even among themselves—crystallizing in the deeply flawed doctrine of "constructive ambiguity"—insolvency seems to have been regarded as too far afield, even after it was pointed out, in the early 2000s, that no one knew how to bring off an orderly wind-down of a large and complex financial institution.[18] To some extent, the government rescues of bust banks in late 2008 changed that, but not enough to have shifted supervisors' focus away from avoiding crises to containing them.

There is an alternative strategy rooted in this book's emphasis on avoiding wishful thinking, robust policy (catering for the worst without unnecessarily making it more likely), and resilient systems (chapter 10). This is not just some techy thing for monetary wonks. Given the fracturing world Order, the West and other market-based democracies cannot afford to be the source or epicenter of another international financial crisis for the foreseeable future. Were that to occur, it would be a geopolitical gift to Beijing, Moscow, and other unfriendly states, and further alienate the peoples of the West itself. In other words, the stakes for the Basel Tower's regime are higher than since, perhaps, the twentieth century's interwar years.

The alternative has two parts: comprehensive liquidity insurance for "safe assets," and ex ante cross-border coordination for handling insolvency.

### Complete Liquidity Insurance for "Safe Assets"

The current setup requires banks to cover a fraction of their liquid liabilities with liquid assets, and to issue a fraction of their liabilities in equity that absorbs losses ahead of deposit and other debt liabilities. Known as fractional reserve banking, it is inherently fragile because prone to self-fulfilling runs. Part of the solution is to require banks and shadow banks to cover 100 percent of their short-term liabilities with assets discountable at their central bank.[19] Turned around, the central bank would be committing, subject to prospective borrowers not being fundamentally insolvent, to provide comprehensive

---

18. In an unpublished but no longer secret report to G10 finance ministers and the Financial Stability Forum. At the time, serving on the group, I was powerfully struck by Fed staffer Molly Wassom's eloquence on this.

19. King, *End of Alchemy*, pp. 269–81; Tucker, "Is the Financial System?" For regulated firms, this probably leaves less scope for hidden actions than the current approach. Severe penalties would, however, be needed for officers of any vehicle that did not register for liquidity insurance but ended up receiving liquidity help to contain a crisis.

liquidity insurance against the security of designated assets, and protected by excess collateral requirements ("haircuts," which would be published).[20]

For unleveraged shadow banks such as money funds, investments would be safe (informationally insensitive)—and could be marketed as safe—only up to the discounted value of their assets.[21] For banks and other leveraged vehicles issuing instruments treated as "safe," policy on collateral and haircuts would drive capital requirements, because the excess collateral demanded has to be financed by some (stipulated) combination of common equity and long-term bonds (see below).

Central banks would be able to vary their collateral haircuts in the face of booms and busts—an instrument of dynamic macroprudential policy enabling central banks to respond to dangerous increases of leverage in trading markets (a massive missed opportunity over recent years). That would probably call for active information sharing and, perhaps, coordination among central banks, meaning Basel's machinery would need to adapt.[22] But that is far from the proposed regime's only international element.

### Swap Lines and the Modern Triffin Problem Redux

Each bank and shadow bank would need local liquidity insurance covering its short-term foreign currency liabilities. To the extent that a host state did not have enough reserves or swap-line facilities to provide that insurance, its international banking activities would have to shrink. As such, this policy finds a place within the broader one of national balance-sheet management advocated in chapter 16, and underlines the importance of swap-line decisions by reserve-currency-issuing central banks. There might be a role for the BIS here, selectively standing between those of its member central banks that, for some reason, cannot contract bilaterally, but where there exists a wider systemic case.[23] That might have made it easier to get liquidity to India during the 2008–9 phase of the Global Financial Crisis, avoiding the geopolitical fumbling in refusing Delhi bilateral lines (preface).

20. The "no fundamental problems of insolvency" proviso is vital in constitutional democracies, since lending to fundamentally bust firms is a fiscal action that distributes resources from longer-term to short-term creditors, and so should be reserved to elected politicians. Tucker, "Solvency as a Fundamental Constraint."

21. Thanks to Steve Cecchetti for exchanges.

22. Cecchetti and Tucker, "Is There Macro-prudential Policy?" (In contrast to monetary policy, there is no macroprudential equivalent to exchange rate changes.)

23. Cecchetti and I discussed this possibility many years ago.

More widely, by making the banking and, crucially, shadow-banking system more resilient to liquidity shocks, the regime would go some way to address the financial-system element of the international monetary order's modern Triffin dilemma (chapter 15): that excess international demand for dollar-denominated "safe assets" incentivizes the issuance of money-like instruments to the point where, eventually, the whole edifice collapses (illusory global liquidity). By taking the dollar toward an invisible tipping point, international shadow banking creates hazards not only for monetary officials but for foreign policy too. Action is necessary for the *Lingering Status Quo*'s vital monetary element to be robust. Ferocious lobbying against shadow-banking reform is at odds with US national interests, and for the rest of us a fault line in the US-led Order-System.

### Structuring Insolvency as a Cross-Border Corporate Finance Coordination Problem

What, though, when the proviso that a prospective borrower is fundamentally broken kicks in? In that case, if a taxpayer bailout is to be avoided, the distressed intermediary must go into a bankruptcy or special resolution process that does not unleash local, international, or global chaos. The authorities of home and host jurisdictions need to be able to commit to cooperate on a solution. Kicked into action by the 2008 banking rescues, the FSB came up with a plan to do that, which was endorsed by G20 leaders and is now reflected in the legal regimes of most major banking jurisdictions.[24] It seeks to channel King's "international only in life" quip into a course that avoids both international balkanization and national socialization.

Minimizing technical stuff, the resolution of a complex international intermediary group would involve two stages. In the first, any losses in a foreign subsidiary exceeding its equity would be transferred to its home-country holding company by converting into equity a super-subordinated debt instrument issued by the subsidiary to its parent. The host authorities would trigger this conversion instead of putting the subsidiary into a local resolution or bankruptcy process.[25]

---

24. Drawing on Tucker, "Resolution of Financial Institutions." Disclosure: I chaired the FSB committee.

25. The trigger would be something like the following: if the statutory conditions were met for host-country authorities to put the distressed subsidiary into a local liquidation or resolution, *they* could instead trigger the intragroup debt conversion. (If the home country controlled that trigger, host states would likely worry the trigger might not be pulled, incentivizing regional balkanization.)

That done, the subsidiary's health is restored (assuming a big enough intra-group convertible bond), but the losses are now sitting in the parent holding company. If, as a result, that is now bust, the second stage kicks in, with the home authorities triggering a process that converts externally issued bonds into equity. As a consequence, ownership of the group moves from its old equity holders—who have been wiped out (restoring to banking at least some of the values of a market economy: taking the downside as well as the upside)—to the holders of the converted bonds.

For our purposes, what matters is the reconstruction of host and home authority incentives. Where, for example, the viability of even a healthy subsidiary's business depends on the health of the group as a whole, host authorities will want to satisfy themselves that the group's home authorities are capable of resolving the holding company in an orderly way: that they have the powers, plans, professional know-how, and so on. Conversely, home authorities would want to be confident that a host authority would not be trigger happy. By being forced to choose whether to hardwire up front how they would coordinate the resolution of a global group, they find out ex ante whether they can cooperate rather than, as in past crises, only as distress erupts. Where the necessary partnership cannot be hardwired, a significant subsidiary needs to be balkanized, enabling it to stand alone in both life and death.

Taken together, the package of liquidity and resolution policies outlined here would give a harder edge to discussions among home and host authorities in supervisory and crisis-management colleges. The potential flip side to Basel's social norm of honesty in overt issues is carefully ducking awkward questions. Central bank governors need to impale themselves on credible stability policies if, as they must, they are to make their necessary contribution to maintaining international order and underpinning commercial society.

## Basel as International Organization and Venue: Servant of International Finance?

Basel, where such plans can be hatched, is a strange part of the international firmament. The treaty establishing and governing the BIS—the legal and physical manifestation of "Basel"—does almost no work in the Tower's outputs, other than, far from trivially, empowering the BIS to undertake market operations and income-generating activities. This gives it the wherewithal to host the venue and various secretariats, and makes it not only legally but practically self-standing. It also gives the BIS financial relationships with nearly all the world's central banks, so it was significant that, learning from its dreadful moral compromises during World War II, in spring 2022 it briefed journalists that it would "follow sanctions as applicable," implying it was suspending relations with the Russian central bank.[26]

## Basel's Need for Legitimacy

It would be hard to describe the Basel standard setters as inherently coercive: none of the Tower's organs has the tools, hard or soft, to enforce the various international standards issuing from its counsels. But it unquestionably exercises de facto normative authority over its members. And to the extent the IMF and World Bank apply its standards to the whole world, there is arguably some dominance of states not represented at the Basel tables. That is enough to generate a basic legitimation demand, with two separate legitimation audiences: states (and their peoples) at the table, and the rest of the world.

The Tower's standard setters were not formally delegated authority under international law, but they responded to the BIS shareholders' problems and calls for help from summit-level political leaders (many democratically elected). Operating via "soft law," each jurisdiction has to comply with local administrative law and processes when implementing Basel standards, helping to underpin legitimacy by generating arguments and pressures to diverge.

Nevertheless, all is not quite as it might be. One is whether the Tower can offer an adequate justification to states not represented at its tables. The other is whether its processes live up to chapter 14's *Principles for Participation and Delegation*.

## Membership: Softly Institutionalized Hierarchy and Outsiders

This might seem surprising, but of all the international bodies I researched in the course of writing this book, the one that most brought Basel to mind was the very first systemized international institution discussed in chapter 2: the Concert of Europe. Here is British foreign minister Castlereagh:

> The advantage of this mode of proceeding is that you treat the plenipotentiaries [the multiple-state Congress of Vienna] as a body with early and becoming respect. You keep the power by concert and management in your

own hands [the Great Powers], but without openly assuming authority to their exclusion. You obtain a sort of sanction from them for what you are determined at all events to do, which they cannot well withhold . . . and you entitle yourselves, without disrespect to them, to meet together for dispatch of business.[27]

Substitute "G10/ECC governors and deputies" for "Great Powers" and one has the Tower's underlying informal but institutionalized hierarchy. The analogy works because just as the early nineteenth century's balance of power turned on dynamics among the Powers, so the threats to and maintenance of stability long turned on cooperation among those sitting at the "G10" table, and that was recognized by others.

But—and this has been vital to the sustainability (so far) of Basel's mode of existence—just as the Concert's four initiating Powers needed to recognize the rightful place of others at their table (first France, later the Porte), so the G10 needed to recognize when their number no longer exhausted the jurisdictions indispensable to financial system resilience. In a field of weakest-link public goods (chapter 5), all the key links need to be there. Hence the addition of Brazil, China, India, and Mexico to the inner circle.

At the same time, the Tower embarked on a wider restructuring of authority. Broadly paralleling the GHOS's role in prudential supervision, the core governors created the Global Economy Meeting, which, despite sounding like a study group, is in effect an assembly for a wider group of central banks to vet key policies. When combined with the FSB's broad membership, and its regular consultations with regional groups of central banks that are not members, so far, so good. Indeed, the Tower looks capable of adapting to a *Reshaped World Order*'s new top table. Similarly, a somewhat thinned-down version of its role could survive under a weak *New Cold War* unless cybersecurity and other imperatives led to bloc-based monetary partition.

Even for some Global Economy Meeting participants, however, and certainly for states that do not attend Basel, there is the issue of why they should be subject to its various standards if they are not material to the resilience of the international financial commons. For Basel itself, the only proper answer is that there is no need for them to be, although the test cannot anymore be the old one of whether some of a state's banks are internationally active (the entry ticket to BCBS membership). It needs also to incorporate whether, all

27. Simpson, *Great Powers*, p. 99.

told, the implosion of a state's local financial system would create significant adverse spillovers for the international financial system.[28] Away from Basel itself, the question is whether the IMF and World Bank can justify universalizing Basel's standards, or whether it is at root a market-led process.

## Basel's Conduct: A Problem of Asymmetric Access

Legitimacy issues for the Tower itself surface when turning from membership and institutionalized hierarchy to conduct and processes. While its standard setters have embraced much of the Global Administrative Law movement's ethos (chapter 14),[29] there are gaps. Notably in the meetings that governors and deputy governors (joined, sometimes, by nonmonetary regulators) have with the leading banks, dealers, and asset managers. They take various forms, not all led or convened by the standard-setting committees, but a common theme is that they give the industry access to the Tower's informal leadership group.

Although opinions probably differ on whether the meetings are useful, they provide an opportunity for members of the industry to convey things they think the Tower's policymakers do not understand (not always true) or should hear before standards are finalized and various domestic formal consultation processes get under way (sometimes useful). One could, then, perhaps, put a tick against the *Principles'* requirement for "participation."

But that pinpoints the problem. While the Tower's staff (especially the FSB secretariat) see various "civil society" groups and parliamentarians, senior policymakers rarely gather to meet with users of financial services or the people who, as taxpayers, fund bailouts. Since the threshold for national rejection of Basel standards is high (although not infinite), that means the policy dialogue is asymmetric.

The costs should not be overstated. For years now, Basel standard setters have consulted publicly, with anyone free to submit written comments, and in addition the FSB provides a kind of mediated participation, via treasury departments, for those on the receiving end of financial failures. But good though

28. Under that test, various subsidized state-owned enterprises in the West, such as the German Landesbanken and the US government-sponsored housing intermediaries, both of which amplified excesses wreaking havoc in 2007/8, become objects of proper international interest. Chapter 17's state-owned enterprise problem appears in a different guise in finance.

29. M. Barr and Miller, "Global Administrative Law."

that might be, it misses a norm that has long bound the judicial realm: justice must be *seen* to be done. Equivalently, Basel needs to be *seen* to be impartial—a general norm that is given edge by the revolving door between high finance and monetary institutions.

The necessary remedy could take one of two forms. Asymmetric access could be maintained but made transparent: meetings with bankers and others would be livestreamed, or a video posted afterward, or a record published. Alternatively, access could become symmetric, with "civil society" allowed in, although it is not easy to identify who can properly represent the people (other than their elected politicians). A good answer might combine livestreaming consultations with lobbyists and activists from both (and more) points of view. The imperative is clear: high finance should not have (even the appearance of) privileged access to Basel policy counsels.

But nor should they be deprived of rights to a hearing, especially now Basel (BCBS and FSB) classifies the largest individual banking groups by degree of global systemic significance, entailing calibrated add-ons to the standard minimum capital requirements. The values of the rule of law demand that, in addition to public consultations on the general approach, the specific firms themselves should have a say, whether domestically, internationally, or both.[30]

## Digital Currencies and Geopolitics: Money, Finance, Trade, and Investment

Part V closes with something that not only is highly topical but, more important, could have massive consequences for geopolitics and domestic legitimacy: digital currencies.

Overexcitement about financial innovation is perennial, and mainly misplaced. The deep architecture of domestic monetary systems—private banking plus a state central bank—has not changed since the late eighteenth century when Francis Baring first wrote about the lender of last resort using a quill pen. By permitting fractional-reserve banking, under which banks maintain only a fraction of their assets in supersafe reserves at the central bank, states effectively separate credit-allocation decisions from government, since

30. The United States delivers this by the Fed applying the Basel classifications via a mechanical rule, adopted via standard notice-and-comment rule-making processes. Where, elsewhere, local authorities may exercise discretion, groups need rights to respond to their regulator's intentions or to appeal to another body.

it is determined via the market for bank loans, while allowing private banks to issue money-like liabilities.[31] This has the following consequences. It ensures the state does not have direct access to the banking details on every transaction entered into by citizen-subjects (privacy). In consequence, it prevents the state from exercising social control with that information. But it leaves the state with a problem of fending off and containing banking instability. That deeply buried political economy trade-off is up for grabs in a world of digital currency.

If a central bank makes a digital currency generally available, and especially if it pays interest on it (as the main central banks do today on banks' reserve balances but cannot, currently, with paper money), everything changes. Since this is, definitively, the only truly safe and liquid financial asset, people and businesses could move the entirety of their checking account balances from commercial banks and money funds into the digital currency (during a banking panic if not before). Other things being equal, private banking would shrink, and central banks expand (yes, to massively bigger than they have been under quantitative easing). Private banks would no longer be the engine room of credit supply and allocation, unless the central bank funded them. If it did not fund the banks, it would become the prime banker to the economy; if it did, the state would still have powerful indirect levers over the banks' credit decisions. Those levers were used to spur recovery from the Global Financial Crisis, but a digital currency could make them routine. So the state, via the central bank—now more like a central-state bank—would know a lot more than now, in liberal states, about every person's day-to-day life, and would have options to control the allocation of resources. In terms of chapter 14's tests of profound reforms, these would materially change the legal relationship between citizen and state in general, overarching ways.

The legitimacy issues for constitutional democracies are obvious, the geopolitical implications slightly less so. What might be objectionable across the West might seem useful to a single-party-led state—not least to assert its dominance over private-sector rivals, such as China's Alipay—leaving leaders free and eager to introduce and promote foreign use of a digital version of their currency. Since the technological changes will make it easier for people and governments to adopt another jurisdiction's digital currency (known as currency substitution), the prospect of the People's Bank and the Fed competing to provide swap lines (chapter 15) will involve foreign policy, not only economics. Ending where I began in the preface, those considerations are

---

31. Tucker, "Political Economy of Central Banking in the Digital Age."

mainly above the paygrade of central bankers and their Basel Tower refuge. Monetary politics is getting serious—perhaps for the first time since, a few decades before Baring's essay, Hume was pondering what London's financial revolution might hold in store for Britain's struggle with France. If liberal states wish to remain liberal, they will declare that any domestic digital currency will be designed (somehow) to preserve privacy and security, and to avoid state domination of credit allocation.

The international contest will not, however, be easy. A big question will be whether a values-compatible domestic framework for digital money can be sustained in the face of intense international competition. A big indicator of how that contest is going will be whether a digital renminbi is adopted in states that are not in any case dependent on China for security and investment, and whether doing so brings them into Beijing's orbit.

The art of strategic monetary diplomacy, embodied by the past titans to whom this book is dedicated, must be revived.

# 20

# Conclusions

## GLOBAL DISCORD: BETWEEN
## DISAGREEMENT AND CONFLICT

France and England may each of them have some reason to dread the increase
of the naval and military power of the other; but for either of them to envy
the internal happiness and prosperity of the other, the cultivation of its lands,
the advancement of its manufactures, the increase of its commerce, the security
and number of its ports and harbours, its proficiency in all the liberal arts and
sciences, is surely beneath the dignity of two such great nations. These are all
real improvements of the world we live in. . . . They are all proper objects of
national emulation, not of national prejudice or envy.

ADAM SMITH, *THE THEORY OF MORAL SENTIMENTS*, 1790[1]

Because the international realm is a decentralized environment of strategic
interaction, it is difficult to control the outcome of a policy initiative with
much precision; so there is seldom a justification for discounting worst-case
outcomes, and there is always reason to plan for outcomes that seem
antecedently unlikely.

CHARLES BEITZ, *POLITICAL THEORY AND
INTERNATIONAL RELATIONS*[2]

One thing that the liberalism of fear does is to remind people of what they
have got and how it might go away.

BERNARD WILLIAMS, *IN THE BEGINNING WAS THE DEED*[3]

1. A. Smith, *Theory of Moral Sentiments*, VI.ii.2. Initially written before *Wealth of Nations*,
*Theory of Moral Sentiments* was frequently revised, with a new part VI added to the final 1790
edition.
2. Beitz, *Political Theory*, p. 190, part of the 1999 edition's twentieth-anniversary afterword.
3. Williams, "Liberalism of Fear," in *In the Beginning*, p. 60.

THESE CONCLUDING THOUGHTS open with the words of Adam Smith, who needs no introduction, and Charles Beitz, who back in the late 1970s kicked off modern justice-based theorizing about international relations. Here both speak the language of prudence. For Smith, it is the prudence of accommodation; an optimistic affirmation of the utility of emulation over the jealousies of trade. For Beitz, it is the prudence of statesmen and women not inhaling their own habitual optimism: a practical rule of thumb operating in a different dimension from his morality-first goals and principles. Bernard Williams collapses those distinctions, reminding us the stakes are high: we can lose everything, more than our sense of ourselves, even our safety and security, if legitimate order is taken for granted. A "goals versus practice" separation principle makes no sense in politics.

Where might that leave values? Writing in retirement, the famous hard-headed US diplomat George Kennan, architect of Cold War containment policy, argued there is no room for morality in foreign policy: "Military security, the integrity of [a state's] political life and the well-being of its people . . . have no moral quality." Various pacts were mere parchment, "declaratory, not contractual." It was mistaken to assume "our moral standards are theirs as well, and to appeal to those standards as a source of our grievances." Instead, he urged "a policy that would seek the possibilities for service to morality primarily in our own behaviour, not in our judgment of others."[4] Rightly exhorting restraint's virtues, this misleads by exaggeration, and perhaps myopia.

The exaggeration is easy: surely Kennan did not believe a great power might exterminate its enemies and their citizen-subjects so long as there could be no reprisals (morality lives). The trap was flirting with the relativism of distance (chapter 13). Prudently, as Kennan himself had stressed decades before, we cannot avoid making judgments about other countries' treatment of their peoples when, taken with their capabilities, it bears on what they might do to us if they could.[5] Also, the stand we take on the gravest crimes will, because it

4. Kennan, "Morality and Foreign Policy," pp. 206, 207, 208, 217.

5. Kennan, "America and the Russian Future." Likewise, Yan, *Leadership and the Rise*, p. 50, observes, "The principle of humane authority also traditionally requires consistency between a ruler's international governance and his or her conduct of foreign affairs, known as *neisheng waiwang*." But there are other routes to consistency.

reveals something important about us, affect attitudes toward us, and so our capacity to make and keep friends and allies. Morality and statecraft are not so easily detached, but combining them is an exercise in politics (judgment), not a branch of ethical theory.[6] In what follows, I recap the book's framework, its principles for international collaboration, and whether they have a chance given, at best, fractious geopolitics.

## Framework: Realist Legitimacy for Thin and Thick Societies

Hobbesians can't help because, burdened by an attachment to obedience, they can't cope with decentralized enforcement or constrained power. Kantians can't help because they don't heed power enough: principles for liberal and decent societies don't suffice if those beyond the pale can't be kept there. What about the Grotian-Lockeans' natural-law jurisprudence, which offered a middle way for Hedley Bull and other English School writers (chapter 7)? One challenge is its ambition. Here is leading Grotian Hersch Lauterpacht, writing in 1946 while the Nuremberg trials on which he advised were under way:

> The subjection of the totality of international relations to the rule of law; the acceptance of the law of nature as an independent source of international law; the affirmation of the social nature of man as the basis of the law of nature; the recognition of the essential identity of states and individuals; the rejection of "reason of State"; the distinction between just and unjust war; the doctrine of qualified neutrality; the binding force of promises; the fundamental rights and freedoms of the individual; the idea of peace; and the tradition of idealism and progress.[7]

Even Lauterpacht himself went on, "Some of these elements . . . are still an aspiration." Another difficulty is the rationalists' tendency to declare unique, universal moral laws, sweeping aside others' civilizational histories. Hedley Bull wanted, instead, to emphasize consensus emerging from the practice of states, but did not offer a compelling account of how that might reconcile order with values and institutions.[8]

6. Similarly, see Nye, *Do Morals Matter?*

7. Lauterpacht, "Grotian Tradition," p. 43.

8. On Bull's departure from rationalism, see Hurrell's foreword in Bull, *Anarchical Society*, p. xxi.

### First Political Questions, Plural

Returning to basics, the First Political Question is whether security, safety, stability, and other preconditions for local cooperation can be maintained. That is in the image of Thomas Hobbes; what follows, drawing on Hume, Williams, and mechanism-design economics, is not. The institutions that deliver the answer must be self-enforcing somehow; there is no higher force. That work might be done solely by coercion, by blind expedience given limited alternatives, or by an acquiescence that survives reflection. The first is inefficient, liable to meet resistance unless it embraces tyranny, and thus liable to become part of the problem. The gap between the second and third is marked by legitimacy, a precondition for *political* society existing at all.

That goes for relations among states, as well as within them. There is, in other words, a first *international* political question, and the prevailing answer, whether a balance of power or hegemony, needs to be regarded as legitimate by sufficient of the population of states, and by all powers. Henry Kissinger drew a variant of that conclusion from the Concert of Europe and other periods of peaceful coexistence. It is the condition for an international politics of diplomacy.

Through stability and limited-scope trust, a legitimate Order provides conditions for deliberate, designed cooperation. This can affect peace itself. While nothing other than superior force can directly prevent or repel aggression, institutions and norms sometimes make it possible to coordinate and channel a collective response (as NATO showed in helping Ukraine resist Russia's 2022 invasion), and so potentially a deterrent. Institutions do matter, and design sometimes reinforces organic equilibria.

Once tolerably secure, there will be incentives to exploit peaceful coexistence where clearly mutually advantageous, and public calls to do so in the cause of heading off global harms. That sums up much of the past seventy-five years. While relying on a basic Order—first the Cold War's balance of power, then US hegemony—to keep the peace, the post–World War II System of designed international regimes and organizations has, reciprocally, affected the evolution of international relations: by enabling economic globalization; shifting the balance of hard and soft power among free states; shaping opinions about what is possible and necessary, good and bad; and arguably accelerating China's rise through access to world markets. If that all depended in some degree on the prevailing Order-System's legitimacy, it matters what legitimacy demands and entails.

## Basic Legitimation Demands, Plural: Histories Matter

Hume's account of legitimate authority is an extension of his genealogy of institutionalized norms. Communities come to internalize, as values, some of the norms that developed out of institutions and practices helping them cope with problems and seize opportunities.[9] When institutionalized, some such norms work at a higher level than others, as de facto or de jure metaconventions, facilitating innovation and reform in lower-level institutions, and even in themselves—constitutional change—provided, like Neurath's boat, not all the planks are removed at once.[10]

Among states, that function is performed by the conventions and norms of general international law, including keeping formal promises (treaties). By acquiescing (via opinion) in those background norms and in regimes they cannot exit, together with consenting (within living memory) to exitable regimes, states effectively take on a responsibility—to each other, and to their peoples—not to bring down the System as a whole. If they conduct themselves otherwise, they are exposed to a reputational hit that, in almost all circumstances, would have meaningful material consequences.

But for institutions to be sustainable under pressure, those internalized norms and opinions need to withstand scrutiny. Legitimacy, whether to rule or to exercise the normative authority of international organizations, presents itself as a demand for a justification-cum-explanation of why things are as they are. These are real justifications available to real people in a position, having reflected, to resist or acquiesce. As Williams stresses, these will often be local justificatory stories—legitimacy now and around here—so history matters. For that reason alone, legitimation principles might incorporate moral considerations beyond delivering good outcomes.

In liberal societies, they plainly do, including the values of the rule of law, democracy, and constitutionalism. While not monolithic, we mess with them at our peril: our way of life is an interest. Therefore, our participation in international regimes and organizations needs to be consistent with them, and certainly not put them in jeopardy.

---

9. For similar stress on internalization (without Hume), see Wendt, "Three Cultures of Anarchy," in *Social Theory*, pp. 310–11.

10. After Otto Neurath, the Vienna Circle philosopher and impresario.

### The Legitimacy Tug-of-War

Even without discordant geopolitics, that creates challenges. People will not feel allegiance to—and, hence, some responsibility not to undermine—international institutions just because their state participates, formally consented, or whatever. Acquiescence would turn, instead, on whether they were enduringly useful—part of the habits of day-to-day life, or even a visible precondition for a particular way of life—and justified in ways that make sense given other institutions, practices, and stories.

But whereas the domestic state and domestic politics are familiar parts of our lives, the same cannot be said—for most people most of the time—of international institutions. If any are useful, knowledge of that is largely confined to expert communities that interact with a particular organization—large exporting businesses for the WTO, some medics for the WHO, bankers for Basel, and so on. Domestic legislators lack incentives to remedy that. On the contrary, it can be in their interests to play down the role of international regimes and organizations, sometimes presenting as their own reforms that in fact emerged from international bodies. In consequence, except in the face of aggression, international Society is likely to be an elite appreciation, however real its wider benefits (and costs).

Statesmen and women accordingly operate in two legitimacy spaces—at home and abroad. The tug-of-war this generates was displayed in the British Brexit referendum, and more seriously in successive US administrations' nonchalant dismissal of international norms and processes. In hindsight, those were mere disagreements compared with the current state of things. Discordant geopolitics bring danger to the mix.

## Geopolitics and Legitimacy:
## From Disagreement to Conflict?

If, for good or ill, the high-water mark of Britain's role in shaping a liberal international order was, perhaps, the move to free trade under gold-anchored money in the middle of the nineteenth century, future generations might think America's was the transformation brought by the Nuremberg trials a century later. While victors' justice, it came packaged with help to reabsorb Germany and Japan into international commercial society. Confronting the horror that even a supposedly enlightened state could wantonly exterminate people, the trials drove norm-shaping innovations in international law; the moral predicament of the unconstrained state demanded nothing less. Sovereignty's recalibration qualified the conventions of noninterference and territorial integrity that had emerged from solutions to Europe's seventeenth-century confessional strife (chapters 2 and 11). Large parts of the West had, in effect, reembraced some of the natural-law traditions of their earlier history: that nonbelligerents are free to help each other against aggression, and that there are some higher moral laws that *must* find their way into positive law.

Shifting the norms for peaceful coexistence beckoned a new kind of strife with states that had joined the club when unqualified sovereignty was in its pomp, that were chaotically weak during the Order-System's postwar refounding, and that do not have a liberal history. No one much bothered about this until one of those states, the PRC, turned out, through the miracle of exponential economic growth, to be a superpower.

### Civilizational or Ideological Tensions?

When two peoples have different worldviews—different ethics and forms of deep society—it matters whether either is a real option for the other given their circumstances, including their history. It is a real option only "if they could live inside it in their actual historical circumstances and retain their hold on reality, not engage in extensive self-deception, and so on."[11]

In what way do today's rival states-cum-peoples have real options here? On the Western side, it is plain enough we could return to a more respectful mode of social life: a society of duties, not only of legal rights. But it is more or less impossible for us to take seriously the voluntary reimposition of authoritarian government: shedding that and so finding a way to escape domestic fear was, for the West, modernity's defining element.

On the Chinese side, it is, I venture, possible for Chinese people living in the PRC or its penumbra to contemplate (even if they reject) less authoritarian government without losing their sense of themselves. Judging from Japan, South Korea, and Taiwan (and the old Hong Kong), it is possible for Confucian-heritage societies to achieve a fusion of filial respect, older rituals, social duty, electoral democracy, and the rule of law. This is profoundly important. For the PRC,

---

11. Williams, *Ethics and the Limits*, p. 178.

and especially Party leaders, by contrast, relaxing control is a real option only in the narrow sense of being realistically imaginable—it was tried in the Soviet Union—but it is completely unacceptable; an option that must, somehow, be rendered unthinkable so that it is not, in fact, an option entertained by the people. This is evidenced in Beijing's reactions to Mikhail Gorbachev's reforms, and by Document 9's "Seven No's" to any kind of liberalism (chapter 9).

That helps explain the superpowers' mutual wariness. Today's geopolitical conjuncture is not like, say, nineteenth-century Britain's slow path toward a more egalitarian (French) version of liberalism, while on the other side France discovered that some of its radical Enlightenment dispositions could be embedded in constitutionalist structures (British-style). That all came after 1815. Today's situation is more like the late eighteenth-century confrontation between two great peoples-cum-powers holding to different views about how political life, domestically and internationally, should be organized and animated. At present and for the foreseeable future, liberal constitutionalism is an affront to the Party, and to its sense of how, under its leadership, China should find a place at the center of world affairs.

Even though, in the West, our local ways of living together have thinned out under pressure from the reflective examination triggered by what we call the Enlightenment (and by migrations), they are revealed to be thicker than we thought when confronted by something as different as the PRC's system of Party leadership (chapters 7 and 9), or by Moscow's aggression. It turns out that we—the thinned-out, highly transactional North Atlantic—do have a way of life after all, which includes the freedom of debate central for legitimation principles to be tested for normative weight. We need some confidence in that way of life, while respecting the confidence of Chinese people in their own. In our approach to international relations and institutions, we need to preserve what could be called the *integrity* of our way of life.[12]

That being so, commentators in the West who insist current tensions are not ideological—and should not be allowed to become so—are deeply mistaken, while nevertheless pressing an important practical question: What to do?

---

12. Playing off Williams's famous demolition of Utilitarianism's claim to be *the* normatively authoritative moral code: because there are situations where a person might lose their sense of the integrity of *their* life—as *they* have lived it—if they followed Utilitarian calculus.

## Robustness in Policy

Successive US administrations accommodated China's smooth entry into the international commercial system. With almost Marxist inevitability, their efforts aroused suspicion in Beijing.[13] Looking back, Washington seemed not to grasp that, as between Britain and France 250 years earlier, a strategic contest would be conducted between the United States and China across every single part of the planet, in every imaginable field, spanning almost all relationships. Less excusable was the conviction that absorbing the PRC into global trade, investment, and production would inexorably, through the emergence of a middle class, lead to liberalism, when that would threaten the Party's grip on power. As recently as 1989, its leaders had demonstrated they were committed to ruling almost whatever the price.

This book's strategic preference, following Thucydides in eschewing wishful thinking, is to combine conditionally open doors with robustness— catering for plausible worst outcomes while not unnecessarily making them more likely (minimax: chapter 10). Not taking excessive risks with order and legitimacy back home is a precondition for sustaining politics itself, and so the possibility of cooperative ambition.

## Pluralist Legitimation Circles

Toward the end of philosopher Thomas Nagel's important mid-2000s essay on global justice, he argues that *sometimes* the best thing for the world might be for institutions to reach beyond their established boundaries, leaving legitimacy playing catch-up. Right now, however, there are negligible chances of developing, in his words, supranational "global structures of power that are tolerable to the interests of the most powerful current nation states."[14]

Instead, if constitutional democracies are to subsist in a moderately orderly world, we need to revert to a somewhat more pluralistic liberalism; no longer prosecuting an absolutist liberalism that issues a stream of categorical imperatives for other peoples, but without surrendering our conviction that individuals

---

13. After Tiananmen, notwithstanding Congress having linked most-favored-nation trade status to human rights (chapter 3), President Bill Clinton continued to grant annual waivers, which were made permanent to enable WTO accession (finalized under George W. Bush). Irwin, *Clashing over Commerce*, pp. 663–72. Also see Doshi, *Long Game*, pp. 308–10.

14. Nagel, "Problem of Global Justice," p. 146.

everywhere should be free from fear of tyranny. Convergence in ways of life can only be organic, not imposed by schoolmen or international officials legislating the answer. We are free to hold on to parts of the Lockean-Grotian element of our heritage, and to engage in diffusion and persuasion, but without the declarative baggage (or insolence) of universal right reason.

That drove chapter 13's articulation of concentric legitimation circles: cooperating more with those with whom we share the most and whom we fear the least in the cause of sustaining internal and external legitimacy. The framework leaves general international law, especially general customary law, operating where relations are thin. But it also makes sense of seeking thicker relations with other states and peoples, and of simply having, via history, deeper relations with yet others. International law as project—for a thick society of universal morality—finds itself at odds with international law as thin normative glue evolved via problem-solving utility.

In short, there is in principle space for a diverse society of civilizational states, connected by thin liberal institutions, as opposed to the civilizational society pursued by late imperial Europe, and perhaps by the United States after the Cold War. Not everyone could be part of even that pluralist society, as opposed to the outermost circle's (perhaps precarious) peaceful coexistence.

## International Cooperation via Regimes and Organizations

So much for framework. What about the real world? Apart from war and horror, there are four broad scenarios: *Lingering Status Quo*, *Superpower Struggle*, *New Cold War*, and *Reshaped World Order*. Constitutional democracies generally would like the first, the superpowers are already embarked on the second while edging selectively toward the third, and the fourth could be brought forward by reconfigured alliances, decisive conflict, or expulsions from existing institutions.

The first three could obtain simultaneously, and in some degree already are (part V). On the monetary front, the dollar's incumbency is so deeply entrenched that, barring big mistakes (see below), there will be a lingering status quo for quite some time, albeit one challenged by initiatives to bypass sanctions and efforts to internationalize a digital renminbi. Meanwhile, the PRC is already the world's largest goods-trading nation, and operates a worldwide program of state-sponsored or directed investment, fueling eighteenth-century-style jealousies of trade and geoeconomic struggle. COVID-19 has prompted a modest shift toward "just-in-case" production in some sectors, but I would put more than a 50-50 chance on a combination of cyberattacks, infrastructure defense policies, sanctions evasion, and contested telecommunications and other tech standards (chapter 4) accelerating a retreat to moderately bloc-based economics. Under anything like those conditions, multinational businesses will find themselves painfully squeezed. And global governance organizations will struggle with their core missions, gravitating toward existential issues and justice, such as climate change and poverty, in order to protest their relevance.

All of which pushes the onus back onto groups of states sharing any thicker society. In the West they need, in ways hardly anticipated, to square the legitimacy of international institutions with legitimacy at home. Geopolitically, they need to identify just where their redlines will be if, other than after defeat in hostile conflict, they face growing pressure from around the world to reform the organizations they largely created.

### Principles for Participation and Delegation

Here the book's central analytical move kicks in. Sweepingly, incentive-compatible things happen; non-incentive-compatible things don't. Trivially, that underlines the importance of careful design of any pacts, regimes, or organizations intended to help address the world's various problems and opportunities. But incentive-compatible schemes might be incompatible with our values, which shows up eventually in legitimacy problems. For international System to be *incentives-values compatible*, for us, we need our leaders and officials to take our values with them to international tables, meaning the values actually embedded in our high-level domestic institutions, not an aspirational list.

To that end, part IV developed, for constitutional democracies, *Principles for Participation and Delegation* in international System (see the appendix). Some are high-level precepts guiding our approach to which states to cooperate with at all, including limiting the depth of relations and interdependencies with states judged to be aggressive or to have breached peremptory (*jus cogens*) norms.[15] Among more specific matters (below), this challenges the

---

15. Those judgments need a process. A Westminster parliamentary motion to that effect was voted down by the government in 2021. The United States has passed a law banning imports

role of globalization's current top table, the G20, since that relies on some degree of candor, trust, reliability, and decency. We cannot be indifferent to the participation of states prosecuting deep cyber interference, wars of aggression, and possible crimes against humanity. Yet the free world will still need fora for coordinating with emerging market economies and rising states, and for dialogue with nuclear powers.

Partly for that reason, the default position of liberal states should be to desire international regimes that are (conditionally) open to new members. Most elementally, that means the aftermath of any decisive conflict should be approached in the spirit of Vienna 1815 or Washington 1945, not Versailles after 1918. More prosaically, second, universal policy regimes should not preclude richer cooperation among coalitions of the willing: thin System must not block the way to thicker Society. This goes to whether regional trade pacts inherently betray multilateralism: they don't.

Third, constitutional democracies should strive to avoid participating in international regimes and organizations on terms that expose them (or those they need or want as friends) to adverse *legitimacy spillovers* (chapter 13). While those externalities might work through any number of channels, including hits to material well-being or domestic norms, they matter if they seriously strain public acquiescence in the local system of government. Neglect of this elemental truth has already dislocated some Western democracies. While they could do more domestically to cushion citizens from globalization's distributional costs, they should also be more vigilant about the design and operation of international regimes and organizations.

Sticking to those precepts may amount to choosing the legitimation circle in which a regime resides and operates. The more geopolitics moves away from the post–World War II Order-System, the crunchier those choices will become, unless *New Cold War*'s bifurcation of international organizations makes it easier to maintain our values in *our* bloc. In the meantime, the *Principles for Participation and Delegation* have to be applied in the light of current strains and vulnerabilities (part V). Headlines include that inchoate policies (IMF), rule by judges (WTO), invisible doctrines (the bilateral-investment-treaties order), and privileged access to policymakers for global financial services firms (Basel) fall short of who *we* say we are.

---

from Xinjiang Province unless importers prove forced labor was not used: see *Economist*, "Quiet Americans."

## Regime-Resilience Reforms

The trade and investment regimes have shown the limitations of judicialization, and the importance of self-restraint's virtue. If arm's-length tribunals adjudicate regimes with policy assemblies operating by veto (WTO), they rule—beyond their depth. If they arbitrate in private (bilateral investment treaties), only the cognoscenti know who rules, if anyone. But fixing that will not be enough. The real-economy regimes are going to need to accommodate more measures to avoid overdependence on potentially hostile rivals.

On the monetary-financial side, crisis prevention and management must be joined up. Short of the kind of watershed brought by decisive conflict, the tension-generating vulnerabilities in the international monetary and financial order (chapter 15) are not going to get resolved by a new reserve currency anytime soon. But that moment could be brought forward unless the United States (with others) addresses the illusory global liquidity created by finance spewing out "safe" assets that aren't. Rather than regulatory obscurantism, issues like "shadow banking" and "orderly resolution" are, in a world with free capital flows, part of the current monetary order's underbelly—a complex, modern Triffin problem creating a vulnerability for the whole Order-System (chapter 16). Practically, this would mean the major central banks extending liquidity insurance to issuers of safe assets, outing phony safety through the terms of that insurance, and preserving resilient national balance sheets (chapters 16 and 19). Every time US industry lobbyists resist reform, they are weakening their country and the Pax Americana.

Those proposals are driven by a conviction that, during *Superpower Struggle*, the West cannot afford to be the source or epicenter of another global financial crisis. Similar considerations apply to the problem of dirty money, which slips through holes in the economic system in ways that undermine local politics and legitimacy, and eventually sour relations among states. Likewise, given the prospect of currency competition, constitutional democracies need to agree principles for digital currencies that preserve privacy and security, avoid state domination of credit allocation, and do not unleash widespread currency substitution.

One theme shared by the real-economy and financial-economy sides is the need for a functioning diplomatic policy table, comprising the leading states, to address the big issues without locking out smaller and weaker states or voices outside the industries directly affected (an issue for Basel). The geopolitics make that harder, but more important. There might be common cause in shared mutual resilience. That could include measures to avoid order-threatening overdependence; the powers dipping their toes into bloc-based autarky in order to avoid the old Cold War's at times almost comprehensive bifurcation (chapter 2).

## No System without Order: Toward a New Cold War

There can be no meaningful cooperative System without Order; monetary affairs are intertwined with security relationships; commerce cannot thrive without peaceful existence. By the time this book is published, the PRC might have taken the plunge into *New Cold War* by openly coming to Moscow's aid, or even made its move to seize Taiwan. In those circumstances, the world's two great economic powers that do not currently project hard power, Europe and Japan, would face climactic choices if the United States applied primary or secondary sanctions on Beijing, or more. The world would cleave.

There are, however, voices counseling American withdrawal from the East, rendering to Beijing what is Beijing's, so to speak. Were they heeded, pretty much every other security relationship, obviously in East Asia but elsewhere too, would be called into question, and in due time tested. In stark contrast to mid-twentieth-century threats to global order, right now there is no equivalent of the US cavalry other than the United States itself, supported by whichever allies and partners it holds on to.

### Beijing's Inherent Brittleness

In some ways, Washington's preferred scenario—*Lingering Status Quo*—has been helped by Beijing and, perversely, Moscow. Had China's leaders been transparent over COVID—admitting mistakes, sharing information, offering help, asking for it—it might have been regarded differently today. Instead, presumably reflecting the Party's deep interests and instincts, Beijing embarked on a communications campaign that was not accepted as wholly truthful. Taken with strident wolf-warrior diplomacy, international ideological exercises seemed still to be the reflex response of a political regime that for decades has survived domestically partly through internal propaganda and censorship. Whether or not that was the intent, China's COVID strategy was, with a global audience watching, hardly deft cultivation of soft power, and perhaps left it already less admired when it (at least) implicitly backed Moscow's invasion of Ukraine.

It seems fair to surmise that the Party's leadership group is held together not only by internalized values but also, given recurrent purges, by fear—the darker force behind some self-enforcing institutions (chapter 6). The West should note but not rely on this: fear sometimes sustains itself. Similarly, while China's many internal problems could be enumerated—including a central-provincial fiscal structure that plausibly incentivizes debt-fueled real-estate excesses—a robust policy will not bet on China's economy stumbling. Likewise, while Xi Jinping's looking set to continue at the helm forever may well turn out to be a lucky break in disguise, we should not count on that. Just as we should not project onto Chinese people, their traditions, and extraordinary civilizational history whatever prudential and other judgments we make about the regime and its rulers.

### Fragile Domestic Legitimacy: Which Circle Does Washington Embrace?

If the PRC has not auditioned well for global leadership, nor for years on end did the United States, except it was not auditioning: it was already meant to be the preeminent global leader. Embarking on a discussion of state security, Montesquieu wrote, "If a republic is small, it is destroyed by a foreign force; if it is large, it is destroyed by an internal vice."[16] The United States is such a republic: one where idealistic belief in manifest destiny has twisted itself into pervasive discord.

Mr. Trump's political movement has ridden frustration created by globalization's dislocations, working people being fed opiates and dirty water, and a host of other things. Those problems preceded him, and were too often allowed to drift due to the incentives-values incompatibility at the heart of the US Constitution: an elected legislature, the cockpit of democracy, with incentives to leave their job to others. This is serious: unaddressed grudges displace hope, and risk worse. If underlying growth remains weak, domestic policymaking will be akin to a zero-sum distributional struggle, which is unlikely to improve the political weather as downward social mobility would carry absolute, not only relative, costs. And this before the new technology tangibly threatens to replace many of the white-collar jobs that from the late nineteenth century created a democracy-supporting middle class across the Western world.[17]

16. Montesquieu, *Spirit of the Laws*, II.ix.i, p. 131.
17. Wolf, "Hypocrisy and Confusion" (citing John Goldthorpe).

Unlike now-standard analogues to the current situation—Sparta versus rising Athens, late nineteenth-century Britain versus rising Germany—my preferred eighteenth-century Britain-France comparator is ambiguous about who maps onto whom. Washington needs to take care not to be felled by the domestic legitimacy problems that were part of Paris's undoing.[18] Legitimacy matters to the resilience of a system of government. Those claiming US foreign policy begins at home—in reestablishing competence, integrity, and results—are plainly right. But the world won't simply wait.

While hardly alone among liberal democracies in having problems, the United States' matter to all of us because the Pax Americana is what it says on the tin. The period of Trump-family government left friends and allies, and not only them, wondering whether something similar could happen again, soon. But as with the United States' domestic problems, those four years aggravated existing concerns rather than instigating the damage to Washington's international reputation. Among other mistakes, the legitimacy hit from the second Iraq war was a product not only of flawed strategy and execution, but also of apparently mendacious communication with its own citizens, disregard of challenges from key European allies (France and Germany) and UN weapons inspectors, and a desire to junk codified international norms.

All that made it easier for rising states to claim the US-led international system has been a sham, with tragic irony echoing its own patriotic "realists." Had the PRC's leaders embraced moves to political liberalism during this period, US leadership would already be in deep trouble. They didn't, and it is intact, helped recently by Vladimir Putin and signs of improved competence, including in Washington's intelligence agencies. But its standing is not as resilient or as unquestioned as a couple of generations ago.

Even if Beijing ends up backing away from Moscow after Ukraine, over the longer run Washington should expect to be stretched across the planet in every imaginable way—just as France and Britain did to each other a long time ago. Learning from history (part I), its leaders need consistently to stick to a risk-sensitive statecraft that allies realism with core values; neither naïve, nor unduly interfering, nor casually provocative. This entails attempting to navigate a relationship with China (and potential future superpowers) that leaves the door open to degrees of cooperation—for example, on some trade

18. Returning to Britain in 2014 after my first lengthy spell in the United States, the following was my response to friends asking what it was like: it's about 1770, French time. (I may have been out by a decade.)

or acting against climate change—*without* jeopardizing our security or way of life. No one outside government can write a cookbook for this, but its execution will demand skillful communication and zero delusions.[19]

Elsewhere, prudent statecraft means the pivot to Asia cannot neglect Eurasia (Moscow's backyard, and now also Beijing's) or preclude helping states and peoples across Latin America and Africa. It might also entail a renewed dollar oil-invoicing-for-security bargain to keep key Gulf states onside.

Among friends, it requires a kind of high-level reciprocity. Unless, embracing wishful thinking, Washington gambles on prevailing alone, its need for allies entails, among many other things, being sensitive to Europe's commitment to international law and other institutions. Reciprocally, Europe, when flirting with competing with the dollar or becoming a hard power again, needs to maintain a grip on the fact the United States keeps the sea-lanes open, and a lot else that matters to preserving global and regional order. Equivalent considerations apply to Washington's relations with Japan and other East Asian and Pacific allies, and with numerous friendly or nonhostile actors. Most important among the latter will be India, whose rise as the decades pass will likely be increasingly important to *Superpower Struggle* and the prospect of *Reshaped World Order* (preface).

## Optimism or Pessimism?

If Washington prepares for conflict, as it must, that inexorably feeds back into China's own choices through the age-old dynamics of the security dilemma (chapter 8). As they gain hold, the protagonists might usefully recall that the eventual beneficiary of Athens's struggle with Sparta was Macedonia (and then Rome), just as that of the past century's two world wars was not any of the Europeans or Japan but the United States. But maybe it won't come to direct armed conflict among the powers. Should we be optimistic or pessimistic? Other than Washington's military capabilities and the shadow of mutual destruction, there are four reasons for cautious optimism.

### Democracy's Secret Ingredient: Resilience through Adaptability

Representative democracy does not depend wholly on output (or performance) legitimacy, and to the extent it does, it has insulation. Its secret ingredient is the way it separates how we feel about the government of the day from

---

19. Similar to the spirit of a joint paper spanning different approaches to international relations: Rodrik and Walt, "How to Construct a New Global Order."

how we feel about the system of government.[20] In combination, democracy as 360-degree watchfulness, as trial-and-error policymaking, and as voting in (*and out*) our governors (chapter 14) make it easier for democracies to make course changes without the foundations of the state creaking. Learning, often haphazardly, is built into the system, which up to a point is therefore insulated from the incompetence or mendacity of particular administrations.

By contrast, the PRC combines a heavy emphasis on performance legiti-macy (Heaven's Mandate) with a system of government that fuses Party and State. This could prove brittle in the face of disappointment—a recurrent fea-ture of China's long history. It means Xi's capacity to override term-limit norms is not only a manifestation of power and an objective source of strength (he's plainly an able, farsighted man) but a source of fragility as time passes, for all sorts of reasons.

## Our Best Values Are a Strength

If representative democracy, with its peaceful power transfers, is a source of internal resilience, it does not exhaust our institutions' strengths. Constrained market economics helps drive technical innovation. Constitutionalism and the rule of law act as a check on domination by rulers, and on commercial society corrupting politics and so undoing itself (chapters 14–16). While Beijing runs campaigns against corruption, it is too early to tell whether, by following Xunzi's ancient wisdom (chapter 9) and forgoing the benefits of constitution-alism, this relies too heavily on the personal qualities of its leaders.

More generally, liberalism—especially a bedrock liberalism of fear—is a beacon of possibility, and so of hope, for those around the world facing fear. Apparent in the joined-up response to Putin's manifest aggression, it means constitutional democracies really must try hard to live by their own creed, helping to align domestic and foreign policies. Recent internal dissent and disturbances are a useful as well as a moral wake-up call.

## Confucian Liberal Democracies

Third, whether it be *Superpower Struggle* or *New Cold War*, this is not really about civilizations: Confucian hierarchy and duty versus European-American individualism and natural rights, or whatever. To repeat, South Korea, Japan, and Taiwan share parts of a civilizational history with mainland China, but

20. Tucker, *Unelected Power*, pp. 210, 548.

they are rule-of-law democracies. Nazi Germany shared a civilizational history with Britain but was an abomination in which we cannot recognize ourselves other than to glimpse the gates of hell.

While the long-run future will depend, because of their vast populations, on the fortunes and dispositions of India, maybe Indonesia, Brazil, and others, and on Europe (depending on how it gets its act together), those three Confucian-heritage states herald possibility. So, in a different way, does Vietnam, a socialist republic not queuing up to rejoin a Beijing tribute system. Together, they might promise an international society of civilizational societies of the kind contemplated above. Its feasibility depends, partly, on the West rediscovering the constrained pluralism embedded in its own various paths to its modern traditions and institutions: that, rather than unqualified sovereignty, is the lesson for today from Westphalia.

### Existential Global Public Goods as a Salve for Existential Geopolitics?

Finally, in a paradox of incipient tragedy, there is still some hope in common existential threats. Those that can be met only through common actions might offer some kind of opportunity: for the superpowers to redirect their interests into a gigantic effort—partly cooperative, partly competitive—against climate change, the ravages of pandemics, and no doubt more.

## Final Thoughts: Liberal Commercial Society without Wishful Thinking

Any such enlargement of interest would be very Humean. Whether the problem was political faction or religious tension, one of his recurrent themes was the utility of redirecting interest by broadening the issue.[21] Like his friend Adam Smith, he thought the cross-community relations generated by commerce, exposing us to other views and forms of life, will over time heal some ills. Although fretting about jealousies of trade and credit, Hume was a moral and political optimist.

Williams did not share Hume's sunny disposition but nevertheless heads off in the same direction: "Hope [for toleration, and hence peaceful coexistence]

---

21. Underlined by Anna Stilz (quoted in chapter 12) and Sabl, *Hume's Politics*, pp. 52–55, 263n29.

may lie rather in modernity itself, and in its principal creation, international commercial society. . . . One thing the modern international order does make less likely is the self-contained enforcement of opinion in one society over a long time . . . shielded from external influences."[22]

While, a quarter century on, the new technology enables rulers and elites—the Party in the East, tycoons in the West—to shield and shape opinion, the powers' societies are unlikely to become hermetically sealed short of capitals tyrannically policing a *New Cold War* (as Moscow is discovering as I write). Nevertheless, even if democracies do a better job on this, as they must, there are limits to how far or quickly commercial society can dissolve differences, and not only because of its darker ambiguities.

As Williams saw more clearly than most, some commitments, some incommensurable values and justificatory stories, run too deep to be given up—mislaid, cast aside, or surrendered—without dislocation. Some become part of a political community's makeup in unbearably tragic ways. The moral horrors of World War II enabled Europeans, finally, to see what they have in common and find their better selves (mostly). In the decades ahead, much will turn on whether people—especially leaders—handle geopolitical conflict and other existential issues in ways their descendants, and history more generally, can appreciate without adopting a relativism of distance toward atrocities committed or permitted.

In the meantime, at home in the West, many constitutional democracies are under strain from reexamining the *local* legacies of their imperial past. This is the latest manifestation of liberal political societies' critical relationship with their own history (and therefore, in degree, their present). If they are not broken by it,[23] this tendency toward self-criticism will prove a source of strength, and therefore of hope, because liberal reflection joins commercial exchange in broadening our sense of "we."

That rather extraordinary feature of liberal modernity is worth holding on to, without for one second warranting wishful thinking in a discordant world. Sheltering under prudently robust statecraft, this is a liberalism tempered by realism, and vice versa; one that cannot discount the possibility of sacrifice to keep fear at bay, and so to remain who we have managed to become without

22. Williams, "Toleration," p. 26. Toward the end of his life, Williams wryly noted, "I once had a great admiration for Hume. Now I think that he suffered from a somewhat terminal degree of optimism" ("Seminar," p. 256).

23. Echoing the final words of Williams's final book (*Truth and Truthfulness*, p. 269).

declaring the end of history. All of which underlines the importance of carefully attending the flaws and strains in the main international economic regimes, since they frame the terms on which, during peacetime, people from around the world—tourists, travelers, businesspeople, scholars, journalists, aid workers—meet, transact, sometimes get to know each other, and sometimes learn something about other traditions and peoples.

That came home to me some years ago while eating alone in a café in Hong Kong. At a nearby table, a group of young businesswomen were having a meeting—relaxed, informal but focused, in Cantonese. The dynamics and atmosphere felt very familiar. My thought sitting there was: This is *us*—plural.

# Principles for Constitutional Democracies Participating and Delegating in International System

THIS APPENDIX pulls together the various principles in chapters 13 and 14, drawing on the particular account of legitimacy offered in chapter 12. It assumes conditions for cooperation are created by some kind of international Order (balance of power, constrained hegemony) that maintains peaceful coexistence. The first section concerns preconditions for cooperation of any kind among states being incentive compatible, whereas the others concern constraints on liberal states. The words "must" and "should" are not categorical, given the inevitability of political judgment in making trade-offs. They address possible mistakes, wishful thinking, and moral horrors.

## Preconditions for Any States Participating in a System of International Policy Regimes

1. States need confidently to expect each other to conduct themselves in ways that do not undermine either peaceful coexistence (order) or the System as a whole.
   - Accordingly, cooperative regimes will, where not perverse, provide for orderly exit.
2. States need to believe that participating in a System's regimes will not endanger domestic order or legitimacy.
3. Participating states confidently expect each other to abide by a norm of Good Faith.

- This means delivering on uncoerced formal promises (*pacta sunt servanda*) and negotiating in good faith.
- States should, therefore, not sign up to regimes lightly, as doing so undermines the higher-level norm.

4. More particularly, states confidently expect each other to abide by certain common conventions concerning:
   - recognition of each other as states, and the delineation of their respective territories or areas of local jurisdiction
   - interactions in spaces under no state's jurisdiction
   - movements of people seeking safety or opportunity
   - what counts as a formal promise
   - certain immunities from local law for each other's representatives, to enable diplomatic discourse and exchange without fear
   - a minimum standard of protection and security for people and property under the jurisdiction of a foreign state that has permitted them to be there
   - mechanisms for resolving disputes that threaten the prevailing Order or, more widely, peaceful coexistence
   - grounds for forceful intervention, retaliation, or preemption, and constraints on the manner in which force is exercised (laws of war and peace)

5. Participating states accept that some regimes, and perhaps System as a whole, will have hierarchical formal decision-making where a necessary international public good is supplied by a particular state or states.
   - In particular, hierarchy will operate in parts of System where basic order and hence preconditions for cooperation are as a matter of fact maintained by equilibrium among a group of leading powers.

## Liberal States Participating in International System

1. Liberal states should restrict their formal cooperation with states violating international law's *jus cogens* norms to endeavors judged necessary to promote peaceful coexistence or to address shared existential threats.

2. Liberal states should avoid cooperating with other illiberal states in regimes on terms that either facilitate conduct or are likely to deliver

outcomes that could plausibly jeopardize their domestic legitimacy or the legitimacy of the System of cooperation as a whole.

3. Otherwise, liberal states should have a bias toward universalism in international regimes, but without constraining coalitions of the willing from entering into club-like regimes (both for relations among themselves and for assisting poor states). In consequence,

    a. regimes with more or less universal membership that prescribe standards in some field should limit themselves to minimum standards, and

    b. club-like regimes should leave the door open to other (nonthreatening) states able to meet reasonable entry criteria.

4. Any decision-making hierarchies must be formally constrained by a regime's terms.

5. In the application of international System, states should be treated as equal before the law in respect of the particular rights and obligations they happen to have under general international law and specific regimes.

    a. In a similar spirit, any minimum standard of protection and security for people (and property) should not discriminate between a state's subjects and those foreigners it has permitted to be (or hold property) there.

6. Liberal states should avoid participating in international System under terms that lead to other peaceable states being dominated in ways or degrees that jeopardize their internal legitimacy.

    a. In consequence, liberal powers should, among other things, exercise restraint in applying economic sanctions or their own laws extraterritorially.

7. Liberal states should generally promote a principle of subsidiarity, favoring cooperative endeavors at the lowest level of politics feasible for (net) benefits to be realized. This means:

    a. pooling and delegating power internationally only where the costs to the thick relations—or ways of life—in home communities are weighed alongside the gains from cooperation at that higher level; and

    b. adopting a policy of resilience at home and using international regimes to help promote resilience in other states and in the System as a whole.

8. In a world where great powers hold deeply different views on political values and individuals' basic rights, constitutional democracies should not expect global multilateral regimes and organizations to promote democracy.
   a. That does not prevent their acting alone or together to promote democracy (while avoiding wishful thinking).

## Criteria for Pooling or Delegating Authority in Specific Regimes and Organizations

1. *Consent and public justification.* Democratic states should join international regimes and organizations only where a public justification has been offered and debated, and consent has been expressed via the particular procedures of representative democracy.
   a. Where a regime's terms directly and materially alter the relationship between a state and its citizens under domestic law, the measures employed to deliver consent should be those employed to reform a particular state's constitution (whether codified or not).
   b. More generally, the depth of the explanation-cum-justification, and the intensity of public debate, will need to vary according to whether joining the regime would bring about a material shift in the domestic legal order, placing it within or under a higher one.
   c. Public deliberation also needs to be more thoroughgoing, the harder it will be to amend a specific regime or the higher the prospective costs of exiting if things do not work out well.
2. *Cost-benefit assessments, including distributional effects.* Assessments of whether benefits are expected to exceed the costs should be capacious, including due regard to risks.
   a. A state should satisfy itself that a regime's design (i) will prove resilient, without making liberal states less resilient; and (ii) is incentive compatible.
   b. It should satisfy itself that a regime's modalities or effects (i) will not so alter international relations as to become a source of disorder; and (ii) will not create order-threatening overdependence on states that are not secure friends.
   c. It should satisfy itself that its people(s) will not be left materially worse off than otherwise (in some relevant sense) if the regime

works much less well than expected. This includes judging whether
a regime would likely entail net transfers to other peoples or states,
or lead to smaller gains than for some of its peers, and how it feels
about that.

d. Irrespective of whether, ex post, a state ends up as a net material
   beneficiary or transferor, it needs to satisfy itself that it would have
   and retain the capacity to offset any adverse distributional effects
   *within* its society.

3. *Pooling versus delegation.* Where the purpose and objectives of a regime
   are unclear, a liberal state should want power to be pooled among
   participants rather than being formally delegated to an international
   organization's management or staff.

4. *Delegation.* Power to make policy should be delegated to the management and staff of an international organization only where that is
   needed to overcome a problem of credibly committing to the regime's
   purpose.

   a. An international organization's management and staff should not be
      empowered to make ex ante policy choices that have big effects on
      the distribution of the regime's benefits and costs across the policy
      regime's members or that, more broadly, materially change the
      balance of power among states.

5. *Arm's-length binding adjudication.* Compulsory adjudication should be
   ceded to arm's-length judges only where the regime's terms are sufficiently precise and complete that the adjudicators are not expected to
   be able to decide or shape high policy via their case-by-case decisions.

   a. Dispute settlement via bilateral diplomacy (or voluntary arbitra-
      tion) should be retained as an option where a regime is open-ended
      or vague, as some disputes are then effectively about high policy.

6. *International organizations or standard setters whose members are
   independent agencies.* Constitutional democracies should not accept
   hard international lawmaking from international organizations whose
   members are state agencies that are independent domestically. Instead,
   such international organizations should, as necessary, be confined to
   proposing standards and norms that have to be turned into domestic
   hard law through each member state's particular processes.

   a. Individual states should decide whether that means domestic
      primary legislation or delegated regulatory rule-making.

# Design Precepts for How International
# Organizations Exercise Their Power

1. *Legal relationships.* The nature of the legal relationship between member-participants and the regime or organization needs to be clear (constitutionalism).
   a. Most significantly, it needs to be clear whether rights to issue legally binding obligations are being conferred on the body.
2. *Governance.* Where formal legal powers are exercised in ways imposing obligations on or restricting states or others, there should be provision for voting (rule of law, democracy).
   a. Unanimity should be employed only if the regime does not preclude subsets of its members going further (liberalism).
3. *Financing.* Where an international organization is intended to provide vital global or regional public goods, it should not be financed ad hoc, by project-specific grants, or by nongovernmental organizations or other nonstate bodies.
4. *Mandate and powers.* The powers of the organization should be as clear as possible (constitutionalism). That includes any powers for addressing noncompliance, coordinating decentralized enforcement, and handling orderly and disorderly exit.
   a. The harder it is to exit a regime, the narrower should be its mandate (sovereignty).
   b. It should be clear, formally, which organs of the organization hold which powers, and the constraints on their exercise (constitutionalism).
5. *Pooling.* Where *legal* authorities are *formally* delegated to a subset of a regime's participants or members (a leadership group), they should be accountable in some way to the particular regime's wider membership (constitutionalism, democracy).
   a. In such settings, the default should be that there is some kind of system of representation under which those at the policy table represent constituencies of members that are not at the table (democracy). Those constituencies should be constructed on the basis of broadly shared interests in the relevant regime's field.
   b. That kind of leadership-group-based hierarchical structure should be adopted only where either the means for executing the organization's decisions (for example, hard power, financial resources)

are held disproportionately by those states or they are disproportionately exposed to the issues addressed by the regime—that
is, the regime is dependent on them or largely for them. In that
case, there needs to be some kind of full member-participant
assembly that can hold the decision-making body accountable,
even if the assembly's views are not binding.

   c. Those are default precepts for those regimes *not* integral to an
Order itself, where neither constituencies nor universal participation would make sense in the context of a dynamic balance of
power maintaining peaceful coexistence.

6. *Delegation.* Where powers are delegated to management or dispute-
settlement bodies, it must be clear whether those officials are intended
to be independent, which is to say insulated from day-to-day politics
among and within states.

7. *Delegation to independent management and staff.* Where power is
delegated to an arm's-length management and staff in order to achieve
credible commitment, the objective must be clear, so that their stewardship can be monitored reasonably objectively by members and a
community of outside experts (sovereignty, democracy).

   a. The relevant office-holding officials should have freedom to
exercise their delegated powers, some budgetary autonomy, and job
security (which does not mean indefinite tenure, since that creates
a cast of insulated rulers).

8. *Independent adjudication and high policy.* Where the substance of
general policy might be developed materially by an arm's-length body
that adjudicates or arbitrates disputes between members (or challenges from individuals, firms, or civil society), there should be
provision for the membership to revise that new general policy in a
forward-looking way, without overriding the dispute panel's determination in any particular cases (constitutionalism).

9. *Avoiding concentrated power in management or adjudication.* Where
power is delegated to an arm's-length management or adjudicator, this
should be to more than one person (republican constitutionalism).

   a. Any such group of independent officials should have staggered
terms.

   b. The appointment process should be designed to avoid its becoming
little more than a proxy political battleground. To that end, appointment panels could have a majority of state representatives but

include distinguished members of, for example, the adjudicatory community itself, so that they could lean against (or alert the world to) degradation in the process.

10. *Policy outputs: operating principles.* The general policies of international organizations should be clear so that, when applied to particular cases, there should not be a big surprise for those directly affected (rule of law).

   a. In particular, where the application of the regime to particular cases is delegated to a leadership group or to management and staff, their operating principles for how they plan to exercise their discretion should be promulgated.

   b. Where the organization departs from its published but nonbinding operational principles in particular cases, it should publish an account of why, and hold itself accountable to the membership as a whole.

11. *Policymaking procedures.* Processes for making decisions must have integrity, helping to deliver the values of the rule of law.

   a. The policy body or bodies of an international organization should be deliberative (democracy).

   b. Within any rule-writing activity, the structure for determining (adjudicating) individual cases should have degrees of separation from the policymaking process; and each distinct phase of activity—from determining policy through to application and enforcement—should have its own integrity (constitutionalism, rule of law).

   c. International organizations should conduct themselves as though bound by international human-rights laws binding on all (*jus cogens* norms), even if technically they are not formally subjects of such law (constitutionalism).

12. *Transparency and accountability.* International organizations should be transparent when preparing general policies (rule of law, democracy). They should consult widely, and openly, on important initiatives (democracy).

   a. They should be balanced and fair in consultations and access (democracy). Thus, they should not grant access to some parts of civil society (say, multinational firms or representatives of an industry for which they set standards) without being open about doing so, and without granting broadly equivalent access to other groups with different perspectives or interests.

    b. The leadership group (under delegated pooling) or management group (under arm's-length delegation) should, at least annually, give an account to a general assembly of members, so that major issues are aired and can be debated (constitutionalism, democracy).

13. *Self-restraint.* Where a regime's policymaking board or assembly atrophies for some reason, the management and any arm's-length adjudicators should exercise strong *self-restraint* in developing law and general policy (constitutionalism).

ACKNOWLEDGMENTS

HARVARD IS EXTRAORDINARY in the breadth of its depth. When embarking on this project, people across the university kindly advised on the literature: Christina Davis, Jeff Frieden, Jack Goldsmith, Robert Lawrence, Beth Simmons, Michael Szonyi, Richard Tuck, Steve Walt, and Michael Wu. So did three economists, Alberto Alesina, Richard Cooper, and Emmanuel Farhi, who very sadly passed away not long afterward.

Joel Trachtman (Tufts) provided similar early guidance, as did Andrew Hurrell, John Ikenberry, and Duncan Snidal during a visit to Oxford; Harold Koh and Tyler Pratt at Yale; Matthias Kumm in Berlin; and Albert Weale and Dominic Zaum in London.

Still in the early stages, Jeff Frankel's weekly Kennedy School international political economy lunch, including locals Carmen Reinhart, Dani Rodrik, and Arvind Subramanian, was helpful (before COVID). As were some Belfer Center events.

As I got going, Richard Baldwin and Doug Irwin fielded questions on trade, Matteo Maggiori on international macroeconomics, Jonathan Kirshner on International Relations (as a discipline), and Mark Kramer on Soviet-US bloc trade and finance. On applying game-theoretic ideas to institutions, part of the book's high road, I must thank Kaushik Basu, Roger Myerson, Peyton Young, and Luigi Zingales. On realist political theory (that road's other part) and more: Ed Hall, Paul Sagar, and Matt Sleat. On sovereignty: David Dyzenhaus. On sanctions supporting human rights: Cecile Fabre. For exchanges on neo-republicanism, beginning while writing my previous book: Philip Pettit. On myriad aspects of moral and political philosophy, special thanks to David Wiggins for a most enjoyable long lunch discussion (and to Dominic Shorthouse, who brought us together).

Away from academia, I had useful exchanges with various people engaged on current geopolitics and economics: Michael Birshan, Creon Butler, Chris Davidson, Jonathan Fenby, Anja Manuel, Simon Nixon, former NATO secretary general George Robertson, former Australian prime minster Kevin Rudd, and Martin Wolf. Big thanks also to Wendy Hyde for the 2016 Tacitus Lecture invitation, where the project began.

People from my previous career helped on macrofinance details including Jon Cunliffe, Diego Devos, Bill English, Sean Hagen, Bikas Joshi, Jean-Pierre Landau, Ceyla Pazarbasioglu, Carolyn Rogers, Michael Salib, James Sassoon, Larry Schembri, Hyun Shin, Tanjinder Singh, Mark Sobel, Dan Tarullo, Ted Truman, Philip Turner, Mark Van Der Weide, and Sam Woods (and Hugh Burns).

Some very old friends lent a helping hand: Nicky Dahrendorf (on real-life humanitarian operations), Rick Lewis (history chapters, and editorial advice), and Toby Wallis (with Greek and Latin, and Hegelian thinking on recognition).

On top of fielding questions, some experts generously read particular chapters: Svein Andresen, Joshua Bailey (about a quarter of the book), Gavin Bingham, Allen Buchanan (whom I had cited before meeting, by happy coincidence, while completing the manuscript), Steve Cecchetti, Petros Mavroidis, Stephen Neff, Andre Sapir, Larry Summers, and Michael Waibel. I could hardly be more grateful.

At Princeton University Press, many thanks to Joe Jackson (and initially Hannah Paul), Josh Drake, production editor John Donohue, copyeditor Ashley Moore, the design and marketing teams, and anonymous reviewers.

Special thanks are owed to Steve Cecchetti, for ongoing exchanges and support; and to Larry Summers, for doing more than anyone to make possible my attempt at a second professional life.

Writing a book, in its all-consuming mental displacement, asks a lot of family and close friends. During lockdown, multiply so. So my deepest thanks to them, most especially Sophie.

# BIBLIOGRAPHY

Abbott, Kenneth W., Robert O. Keohane, Andrew Moravcsik, Anne-Marie Slaughter, and Duncan Snidal. "The Concept of Legalization." *International Organization* 54(3) (Summer 2000), pp. 401–419.

Abbott, Kenneth W., and Duncan Snidal. "Hard and Soft Law in International Governance." *International Organization* 54(3) (Summer 2000), pp. 421–456.

———. "International 'Standards' and International Governance." *Journal of European Public Policy* 8(3) (2001), pp. 345–70.

Abdelal, Ravi. *Capital Rules: The Construction of Global Finance*. Cambridge, MA: Harvard University Press, 2007.

Adrian, Tobias. "Stablecoins, Central Bank Digital Currencies, and Cross-Border Payments: A New Look at the International Monetary System." International Monetary Fund, May 14, 2019. https://www.imf.org/en/News/Articles/2019/05/13/sp051419-stablecoins-central-bank-digital-currencies-and-cross-border-payments.

Aggarwal, Vinod K., and Cedric Dupont. "Collaboration and Coordination in the Global Political Economy." In *Global Political Economy*, edited by John Ravenhill, pp. 28–49. Oxford: Oxford University Press, 2005.

Aisbett, Emma, and Jonathan Bonnitcha. "A Pareto-Improving Compensation Rule for Investment Treaties." *Journal of International Economic Law* 24 (2021), pp. 181–202.

Alderson, Kai, and Andrew Hurrell, eds. *Hedley Bull on International Society*. Basingstoke, UK: Palgrave Macmillan, 2000.

Alexander, Kern. *Economic Sanctions: Law and Public Policy*. Basingstoke, UK: Palgrave Macmillan, 2009.

Alford, William P. "Does Law Matter in China?" In *The China Questions: Critical Insights into a Rising Power*, edited by Jennifer Ruddolph and Michael Szonyi, pp. 212–18. Cambridge, MA: Harvard University Press, 2018.

Allison, Graham. *Destined for War: Can America and China Escape Thucydides's Trap?* Boston: Houghton Mifflin Harcourt, 2017.

Alston, Philip. "Resisting the Merger and Acquisition of Human Rights by Trade Law: A Reply to Petersmann." *European Journal of International Law* 13 (2000), pp. 815–44.

Alter, Karen J. "The Multiplication of International Courts and Tribunals after the Cold War." In *The Oxford Handbook of International Adjudication*, edited by Cesare P. R. Romano, Karen J. Alter, and Yuval Shany, pp. 63–89. Oxford: Oxford University Press, 2014.

Alvarez, Jose E. *International Organizations as Law-Makers*. Oxford: Oxford University Press, 2005.

Angle, Stephen C. *Sagehood: The Contemporary Significance of Neo-Confucian Philosophy*. Oxford: Oxford University Press, 2009.

——. "Virtue Ethics, the Rule of Law, and the Need for Self-Restriction." In *The Philosophical Challenge from China*, edited by Brian Bruya, pp. 159–82. Cambridge, MA: MIT Press, 2015.

——. "Human Rights in Chinese Tradition." In *Handbook on Human Rights in China*, edited by Sarah Biddulph and Joshua Rosenzweig, pp. 14–31. Cheltenham, UK: Edward Elgar, 2019.

Annan, Kofi. "Two Concepts of Sovereignty." *Economist*, September 18, 1999. https://www.economist.com/international/1999/09/16/two-concepts-of-sovereignty.

——. "Sovereignty: The State and the Individual." Plenary Session I: Current Global Trends Affecting the Work of Ombudsmen, June 9, 2009. https://www.theioi.org/downloads/f1s7g/Stockholm%20Conference_04.%20Plenary%20Session%20I_Kofi%20Annan.pdf.

Anonymous. *The Longer Telegram: Toward a New American China Strategy*. Atlantic Council Strategy Papers. New York: Atlantic Council, 2021.

Applebaum, Anne. "The Bad Guys Are Winning." *The Atlantic*, November 15, 2021.

Arendt, Hannah. "What Is Authority?" In *The Portable Hannah Arendt*, edited by Peter Baehr, pp. 462–507. London: Penguin Books, 2000.

Aristotle. *Rhetoric*. Translated by W. Rhys Roberts. Edited by W. D. Ross. New York: Cosimo Classics, 2010.

Armitage, David. "Edmund Burke and Reason of State." *Journal of the History of Ideas* 61(4) (2000), pp. 617–34.

Autor, David H., David Dorn, and Gordon H. Hanson. "The China Syndrome: Local Labor Market Effects of Import Competition in the United States." *American Economic Review* 103(6) (2013), pp. 2121–68.

Axelrod, Robert. *The Evolution of Cooperation*. New York: Basic Books, 1984.

Baldwin, Richard. "Understanding the GATT's Wins and the WTO's Woes." *CEPR Policy Insight*, no. 49 (June 2010). https://cepr.org/active/publications/policy_insights/viewpi.php?pino=49.

——. *The Great Convergence: Information Technology and the New Globalization*. Cambridge, MA: Harvard University Press, 2016.

——. "The World Trade Organization and the Future of Multilateralism." *Journal of Economic Perspectives* 30(1) (2016), pp. 95–116.

Bank for International Settlements. *Past and Future of Central Bank Cooperation: Policy Panel Discussion*. BIS Papers, no. 27, February 2006. https://www.readcube.com/articles/10.2139%2Fssrn.1188802.

Barber, N. W. *The Principles of Constitutionalism*. Oxford: Oxford University Press, 2018.

Barnett, Robert. "China Is Building Entire Villages in Another Country's Territory." *Foreign Affairs*, May 7, 2021. https://foreignpolicy.com/2021/05/07/china-bhutan-border-villages-security-forces/.

Barr, James. *Lords of the Desert: Britain's Struggle with America to Dominate the Middle East*. London: Simon and Schuster, 2018.

Barr, Michael S., and Geoffrey P. Miller. "Global Administrative Law: The View from Basel." *European Journal of International Law* 17(1) (2006), pp. 15–46.

Barrett, Scott. *Why Cooperate? The Incentive to Provide Public Goods.* Oxford: Oxford University Press, 2007.

Basu, Kaushik. *The Republic of Beliefs: A New Approach to Law and Economics.* Princeton, NJ: Princeton University Press, 2018.

Baughan, Emily. Review of *Securing the World Economy: The Reinvention of the League of Nations, 1920–1946,* by Patricia Clavin. Reviews in History, review no. 1536, January 2014. https://reviews.history.ac.uk/review/1536.

Beetham, David. *The Legitimation of Power.* 2nd ed. Basingstoke, UK: Palgrave Macmillan, 2013.

Beitz, Charles R. *Political Theory and International Relations.* 2nd ed. Princeton, NJ: Princeton University Press, 1999.

———. "Rawls's Law of Peoples." *Ethics* 110(4) (2000), pp. 669–96.

———. *The Idea of Human Rights.* Oxford: Oxford University Press, 2009.

Bellamy, Richard. *Political Constitutionalism: A Republican Defence of the Constitutionality of Democracy.* Cambridge: Cambridge University Press, 2007.

———. *A Republican Europe of States: Cosmopolitan Intergovernmentalism and Democracy in the EU.* Cambridge: Cambridge University Press, 2019.

Bernanke, Ben S. "The Global Savings Glut and the US Current Account Deficit." Homer Jones Lecture, St. Louis, Missouri, April 14, 2005. Federal Reserve Board. https://www.federalreserve.gov/boarddocs/speeches/2005/200503102/.

Bew, John. *Realpolitik: A History.* Oxford: Oxford University Press, 2016.

Bicchieri, Cristina. *The Grammar of Society: The Nature and Dynamics of Social Norms.* New York: Cambridge University Press, 2006.

Bickel, Alexander M. *The Least Dangerous Branch: The Supreme Court at the Bar of Politics.* 2nd ed. New Haven, CT: Yale University Press, 1986.

Bingham, Tom. *The Business of Judging: Selected Essays and Speeches, 1985–1999.* Oxford: Oxford University Press, 2000.

———. *The Rule of Law.* London: Allen Lane, 2010.

Binmore, Ken. "David Hume: Grandfather of Modern Economics?" 2011. http://www.homepages.ucl.ac.uk/~uctpa97/Hume.tex%20typeset%20copy.pdf.

Blackburn, Simon. *Ruling Passions.* Oxford: Oxford University Press, 1998.

Blackwill, Robert D., and Jennifer M. Harris. *War by Other Means: Geo-economics and Statecraft.* Cambridge, MA: Harvard University Press, 2016.

Blustein, Paul. "A Flop and a Debacle: Inside the IMF's Global Rebalancing Acts." CIGI Papers, no. 4, Centre for International Governance Innovation, Waterloo, Ontario, June 2012. https://www.cigionline.org/sites/default/files/no.4.pdf.

———. "China Inc. in the WTO Dock: Tales from a System under Fire." CIGI Papers, no. 157, Centre for International Governance Innovation, Waterloo, Ontario, December 2017. https://www.cigionline.org/publications/china-inc-wto-dock-tales-system-under-fire/.

Bodansky, Daniel. "What's in a Concept? Global Public Goods, International Law, and Legitimacy." *European Journal of International Law* 23(3) (2012), pp. 651–68.

Bonnitcha, Jonathan, Lauge N. Skovgaard Poulsen, and Michael Waibel. *The Political Economy of the Investment Treaty Regime.* Oxford: Oxford University Press, 2017.

Boughton, James M. *Silent Revolution: The International Monetary Fund, 1979–1989.* Washington, DC: International Monetary Fund, 2001.

Bradford, Anu. *The Brussels Effect: How the European Union Rules the World*. Oxford: Oxford University Press, 2020.

Bradley, Curtis A. "Customary International Law Adjudication as Common Law Adjudication." In *Custom's Future: International Law in a Changing World*, edited by Curtis A. Bradley, pp. 34–61. Cambridge: Cambridge University Press, 2016.

Bradley, Curtis A., and Judith G. Kelley. "The Concept of International Delegation." *Law and Contemporary Problems* 71 (2008), pp. 1–36.

Branstetter, Lee G. "China's Forced Technology Transfer Problem, and What to Do about It." PIIE Policy Brief 18-13. Washington, DC: Peterson Institute for International Economics, 2018. https://www.piie.com/publications/policy-briefs/chinas-forced-technology-transfer -problem-and-what-do-about-it.

Brewster, Rachel. "Unpacking the State's Reputation." *Harvard International Law Journal* 50(2) (Summer 2009), pp. 231–69.

Brown, Andrew G. *Reluctant Partners: A History of Multilateral Trade Cooperation, 1850–2000*. Ann Arbor: University of Michigan Press, 2003.

Brummer, Chris. "Why Soft Law Dominates International Finance—and Not Trade." *Journal of International Economic Law* 13(3) (2010), pp. 623–43.

Brunnermeier, Markus. *The Resilient Society*. Colorado Springs, CO: Endeavor Literary Press, 2021.

Buchanan, Allen. "Rawls's Law of Peoples." *Ethics* 110(4) (2000), pp. 697–721.

———. *Justice, Legitimacy, and Self-Determination: Moral Foundations for International Law*. Oxford: Oxford University Press, 2004.

———. "The Legitimacy of International Law." In *The Philosophy of International Law*, edited by Samantha Besson and John Tasioulas, pp. 79–96. Oxford: Oxford University Press, 2010.

———. *The Heart of Human Rights*. Oxford: Oxford University Press, 2013.

———. "Institutional Legitimacy." In *Oxford Studies in Political Philosophy*, vol. 4, edited by David Sobel, Peter Vallentyne, and Stephen Wall, pp. 53–78. Oxford: Oxford University Press, 2018.

Buchanan, Allen, and Robert O. Keohane. "The Legitimacy of Global Governance Institutions." *Ethics and International Affairs* 20(4) (2006), pp. 405–37.

Buchanan, Allen, and Russell Powell. "Constitutional Democracy and the Rule of International Law: Are They Compatible?" *Journal of Political Philosophy* 16(3) (2008), pp. 326–49.

Bull, Hedley. "The Grotian Conception of International Society." In *Diplomatic Investigations*, edited by Herbert Butterfield and Martin Wight, pp. 51–73. London: George Allen and Unwin, 1966.

———. "Natural Law and International Relations." *British Journal of International Studies* 5(2) (1979), pp. 171–81.

———. *The Anarchical Society: A Study of Order in World Politics*. 4th ed. Basingstoke, UK: Palgrave Macmillan, 2012 [1997].

Buthe, Tim. "The Politics of Market Competition: Trade and Anti-trust in a Global Economy." In *The Oxford Handbook of the Political Economy of International Trade*, edited by Lisa L. Martin, pp. 213–32. Oxford: Oxford University Press, 2015.

Buzan, Barry. *From International to World Society? English School Theory and the Social Structure of Globalization*. Cambridge: Cambridge University Press, 2004.

Campbell, Kurt M., and Jake Sullivan. "Competition without Catastrophe: How America Can Both Challenge and Coexist with China." *Foreign Affairs*, September/October 2019. https://www.foreignaffairs.com/articles/china/competition-with-china-without-catastrophe.

Caney, Simon. *Justice beyond Borders: A Global Political Theory*. Oxford: Oxford University Press, 2005.

Carnegie, Allison. *Power Plays: How International Institutions Reshape Coercive Diplomacy*. Cambridge: Cambridge University Press, 2015.

Carney, Mark. "The Growing Challenges for Monetary Policy in the Current International Monetary and Financial System." Speech given at the Jackson Hole Symposium, Bank of England, August 23, 2019. https://www.bis.org/review/r190827b.pdf.

Carr, E. H. *The Twenty Years Crisis, 1919–1939*. With a new preface by Michael Fox. London: Palgrave Macmillan, 2016 [1939].

Carroll, Sean B. "Mission: Save the Environment." Project Syndicate, July 15, 2016. https://www.project-syndicate.org/commentary/smallpox-eradication-global-cooperation-by-sean-b--carroll-2016-07.

Cartledge, Paul. *The Spartans: An Epic History*. Oxford: Channel Four Books, 2002.

Cassel, Par Kristoffer. *Grounds of Judgment: Extraterritoriality and Imperial Power in Nineteenth-Century China and Japan*. Oxford: Oxford University Press, online edition, May 2012.

Cecchetti, Stephen G., and Paul M. W. Tucker. "Is There Macro-prudential Policy without International Cooperation?" CEPR Working Paper 11042, January 2016. http://people.brandeis.edu/~cecchett/WPpdf/2015_Cecchetti_Tucker.pdf.

Chalmers, Malcolm. "Which Rules? Why There Is No Single 'Rules-Based International System.'" Royal United Services Institute Occasional Paper, April 2019.

Chan, Joseph C. W. "Confucianism and Human Rights." In *Religion and Human Rights: An Introduction*, edited by John Witte and M. Christian Green, pp. 87–102. Oxford: Oxford University Press, 2011.

Chen, Albert H. Y. "Toward a Legal Enlightenment: Discussions in Contemporary China on the Rule of Law." *Pacific Basin Law Journal* 17 (1999), pp. 125–65.

Chesterman, Simon. "Asia's Ambivalence about International Law." In *The Oxford Handbook of International Law in Asia and the Pacific*, edited by Simon Chesterman, Hisashi Owada, and Ben Saul, pp. 16–36. Oxford: Oxford University Press, 2019.

———. "Responsibility to Protect and Humanitarian Intervention: From Apology to Utopia and Back Again." In *The Oxford Handbook of the International Law of Global Security*, edited by Robin Geiss and Nils Melzer, pp. 808–20. Oxford: Oxford University Press, 2021.

ChinaFile. "Document 9: A ChinaFile Translation." November 8, 2013. https://www.chinafile.com/document-9-chinafile-translation.

Christiano, Thomas. "Democratic Legitimacy and International Institutions." In *The Philosophy of International Law*, edited by Samantha Besson and John Tasioulas, pp. 119–37. Oxford: Oxford University Press, 2010.

———. "The Legitimacy of International Institutions." In *The Routledge Companion to the Philosophy of Law*, edited by Andrei Marmor, pp. 380–94. Oxford: Routledge, 2012.

Clark, Christopher. *The Sleepwalkers: How Europe Went to War in 1914*. London: Penguin Books, 2013.

Clark, Ian. *Legitimacy in International Society*. Oxford: Oxford University Press, 2005.

———. *International Legitimacy and World Society*. Oxford: Oxford University Press, 2007.

———. *Hegemony in International Society*. Oxford: Oxford University Press, 2011.

Clinton, David. "Tocqueville, Obligation, and the International System." *Review of International Studies* 19(3) (1993), pp. 227–43.

Coe, Andrew J., and Scott Wolford. "East Asian History and International Relations." In *East Asia in the World: Twelve Events That Shaped the Modern International Order*, edited by Stephen Haggard and David C. Kang, pp. 263–381. Cambridge: Cambridge University Press, 2020.

Cohen, Benjamin J. "The Macrofoundation of Monetary Power." In *International Monetary Power*, edited by David A. Andrews, 31–50. Ithaca, NY: Cornell University Press, 2006.

Cohen, Joshua. "Minimalism about Human Rights: The Most We Can Hope For?" *Journal of Political Philosophy* 12(2) (2004), pp. 190–213.

Cohen, Joshua, and Charles Sabel. "Extra Rempublicam Nulla Justitia?" *Philosophy and Public Affairs* 34(2) (2006), pp. 147–75.

Cohon, Rachel. *Hume's Morality: Feeling and Fabrication*. Oxford: Oxford University Press, 2008.

———. "Hume's Practice Theory of Promises and Its Dissimilar Descendants." *Synthese* 199, online ahead of print (May 16, 2020). https://doi.org/10.1007/s11229-020-02684-2.

Coker, Christopher. *The Rise of the Civilizational State*. Cambridge: Polity Press, 2019.

Comella, Victor Ferreres. *The Constitution of Arbitration*. Cambridge: Cambridge University Press, 2021.

Conway, Ed. *The Summit: The Biggest Battle of the Second World War—Fought behind Closed Doors*. London: Little, Brown, 2014.

Cooper, Richard N. "Macroeconomic Policy Adjustment in Interdependent Economies." *Quarterly Journal of Economics* 83(1) (1969), pp. 1–24.

———. "Almost a Century of Central Bank Cooperation." Working Paper 198, Bank for International Settlements, 2006.

Craig, Edward. "Genealogies and the State of Nature." In *Bernard Williams*, edited by Alan Thomas, pp. 181–200. Cambridge: Cambridge University Press, 2007.

Crawford, James. "Revising the Draft Articles on State Responsibility." *European Journal of International Law* 10(2) (1999), pp. 435–60.

———. "The Current Political Discourse Concerning International Law." *Modern Law Review* 81(1) (2018), pp. 1–22.

———. *Brownlie's Principles of International Law*. 9th ed. Oxford: Oxford University Press, 2019.

Crossley, Pamela K. "The Qing Empire: Three Governments in One State and the Stability of Manchu Rule." In *The Oxford World History of Empire*, vol. 2, *The History of Empires*, edited by Peter Fibiger Bang, C. A. Bayly, and Walter Scheidel, pp. 810–31. Oxford: Oxford University Press, 2021.

Darwell, Stephen L. "Two Kinds of Respect." *Ethics* 88(1) (1977), pp. 36–49.

Davis, Christina L., and Tyler Pratt. "The Forces of Attraction: How Security Interests Shape Membership in Economic Institutions." *Review of International Organizations* 16(4) (2020), pp. 903–29.

Deudney, Daniel H. *Bounding Power: Republican Security Theory from the Polis to the Global Village*. Princeton, NJ: Princeton University Press, 2007.

Deudney, Daniel H., and G. John Ikenberry. "The Nature and Sources of the Liberal International Order." *Review of International Studies* (25) (1999), pp. 179–96.

Dicey, A. V. *Introduction to the Study of the Law of the Constitution.* London: Macmillan, 1982.

Dickerson, Hollin. "Minimum Standards." In *Max Planck Encyclopedia of Public International Law,* edited by Anne Peters and Rüdiger Wolfrum. Oxford: Oxford University Press, online edition, last updated October 2010.

Dincecco, Mark, and Yuhua Wang. "Violent Conflict and Political Development over the Long Run: China versus Europe." *Annual Review of Political Science* 21(1) (2018), pp. 341–58.

Dixit, Avanish K. *The Making of Economic Policy: A Transactions-Cost Politics Perspective.* Cambridge, MA: MIT Press, 1996.

Dolzer, Rudolf. "Mixed Claims Commissions." In *Max Planck Encyclopedia of Public International Law,* edited by Anne Peters and Rüdiger Wolfrum. Oxford: Oxford University Press, online edition, last updated May 2011.

Donnelly, Jack. "Human Rights: A New Standard of Civilization?" *International Affairs* 74(1) (1998), pp. 1–23.

Donnelly, Jack, and Daniel J. Whelan. *International Human Rights: Dilemmas in World Politics.* 5th ed. London: Routledge, 2017.

Dooley, Michael P., David Folkerts-Landau, and Peter M. Garber. "The Revived Bretton Woods System: The Effects of Periphery Intervention and Reserve Management on Interest Rates and Exchange Rates in Center Countries." NBER Working Paper No. 10332, National Bureau of Economic Research, Cambridge, MA, March 2004.

Doshi, Rush. *The Long Game: China's Grand Strategy to Displace American Order.* Oxford: Oxford University Press, 2021.

Doshi, Rush, Emily de la Bruyere, Nathan Picarsic, and John Ferguson. *China as a "Cyber Great Power": Beijing's Two Voices in Telecommunications.* Brookings Foreign Policy. Washington, DC: Brookings, April 2021.

Doshi, Rush, and Kevin McGuiness. *Huawei Meets History: Great Powers and Telecommunications Risk, 1840–2021.* Brookings Foreign Policy. Washington, DC: Brookings Institution, March 2021.

Doyle, Michael W. "A Few Words on Mill, Walzer, and Nonintervention." *Ethics and International Affairs* 23(4) (2009), pp. 349–69.

Doyle, Michael W., and Geoffrey S. Carlson. "Silence of the Laws? Conceptions of International Relations and International Law in Hobbes, Kant, and Locke." *Columbia Journal of Transnational Law* 46(3) (2008), pp. 648–66.

Dunoff, Jeffrey L., and Joel P. Trachtman. "A Functional Approach to International Constitutionalization." In *Ruling the World? Constitutionalism, International Law, and Global Governance,* edited by Jeffrey L. Dunoff and Joel P. Trachtman, pp. 3–35. Cambridge: Cambridge University Press, 2009.

———, eds. *Ruling the World? Constitutionalism, International Law, and Global Governance.* Cambridge: Cambridge University Press, 2009.

Dyzenhaus, David. Introduction to *Sovereignty: A Contribution to the Theory of Public and International Law,* by Hermann Heller, pp. 1–59. Oxford: Oxford University Press, 2019 [1927].

———. *The Long Arc of Legality: Hobbes, Kelsen, Hart.* Cambridge: Cambridge University Press, 2022.

Eaton, Richard M. *India in the Persianate Age, 1000–1765*. London: Penguin Books, 2019.

*Economist*. "China Punishes Australia for Promoting an Inquiry." May 23, 2020.

———. "The Chinese Communist Party's Model Emperor." September 18, 2021.

———. "The Quiet Americans." January 1–7, 2022.

Economy, Elizabeth C. *The Third Revolution: Xi Jinping and the New Chinese State*. Oxford: Oxford University Press, 2018.

Eichengreen, Barry. *Globalizing Capital: A History of the International Monetary System*. Princeton, NJ: Princeton University Press, 1996.

———. "Managing a Multiple Reserve Currency World." In *The 21st Century International Monetary System*, edited by J. D. Sachs, M. Kawai, J.-W. Lee, and W. T. Woo. Manila: Asian Development Bank, 2010. http://emlab.berkeley.edu/~eichengr/managing_multiple_res_curr_world.pdf.

———. "International Policy Coordination: The Long View." In *Globalization in an Age of Crisis: Multilateral Economic Cooperation in the Twenty-First Century*, edited by Robert C. Feenstra and Alan M. Taylor, pp. 43–90. Chicago: University of Chicago Press, 2013.

———. "Versailles: The Economic Legacy." *International Affairs* 95(1) (2019), pp. 7–24.

Eichengreen, Barry, and Ngaire Woods. "The IMF's Unmet Challenges." *Journal of Economic Perspectives* 30(1) (2016), pp. 29–51.

Esty, Daniel C. "Bridging the Trade-Environment Divide." *Journal of Economic Perspectives* 15(3) (2001), pp. 113–30.

European Parliament. "Strengthening the International Role of the Euro." Committee on Economic and Monetary Affairs, A9-0043/2021, March 12, 2021.

Fabre, Cecile. *Economic Statecraft: Human Rights, Sanctions, and Conditionality*. Cambridge, MA: Harvard University Press, 2021.

Farhi, Emmanuel, and Matteo Maggiori. "China versus the United States: IMS Meets IPS." *AEA Papers and Proceedings* 109 (2019), pp. 476–81.

Farrell, Henry, and Abraham L. Newman. "Weaponized Interdependence: How Global Economic Networks Shape State Coercion." *International Society* 44(1) (2019), pp. 42–79.

Fearon, James D. "Rationalist Explanations for War." *International Organization* 49(3) (1995), pp. 379–414.

———. "Bargaining, Enforcement, and International Cooperation." *International Organization* 52(2) (1998), pp. 269–305.

———. "Cooperation, Conflict, and the Costs of Anarchy." *International Organization* 72(3) (2018), pp. 523–59.

Feldstein, Martin. "Refocusing the IMF." *Foreign Affairs* 77(2) (March/April 1998), pp. 20–33.

Ferguson, Niall. *Pity of War, 1914–1918*. London: Penguin Books, 1998.

Fidler, David P. "The Return of the Standard of Civilization." *Chicago Journal of International Law* 2(1) (2001), pp. 137–57.

Fischer, Stanley. "The Washington Consensus." In *Global Economics in Extraordinary Times: Essays in Honor of John Williamson*, edited by C. Fred Bergsten and C. Randall Henning, pp. 11–24. Washington, DC: Peterson Institute for International Economics, 2012.

Frankel, Jeffrey. "International Coordination." In *Policy Challenges in a Diverging Global Economy*, edited by Reuven Glick and Mark M. Spiegel, pp. 149–85. Proceedings of the Asia Economic

Policy Conference, San Francisco, November 19–20, 2015. San Francisco: Federal Reserve Bank of San Francisco, 2015.

Fraser, Henry S. "Sketch of the History of International Arbitration." *Cornell Law Review* 11 (1926), pp. 179–208.

Friedberg, Aaron L. "Globalisation and Chinese Grand Strategy." *Survival* 60(1) (2018), pp. 7–40.

Frieden, Jeffrey A., David A. Lake, and Kenneth A. Schultz. *World Politics: Interests, Interactions, Institutions*. 4th ed. New York: W. W. Norton, 2019.

Fukuyama, Francis. *The Origins of Political Order*. New York: Farrar, Straus and Giroux, 2011.

———. *Political Order and Political Decay*. New York: Farrar, Straus and Giroux, 2014.

Fuller, Lon L. *The Morality of Law*. Rev. ed. New Haven, CT: Yale University Press, 1969.

Garrett, Geoffrey, and Barry R. Weingast. "Ideas, Interests, and Institutions: Constructing the European Community's Internal Market." In *Ideas in Foreign Policy: Beliefs, Institutions, and Political Change*, edited by Judith Goldstein and Robert O. Keohane, pp. 173–206. Ithaca, NY: Cornell University Press, 1993.

Garwood-Gowers, Andrew. "China and the Responsibility to Protect." In *Handbook on Human Rights in China*, edited by Sarah Biddulph and Joshua Rosenzweig, pp. 103–18. Cheltenham, UK: Edward Elgar, 2019.

Gaus, Gerald. "Why the Conventionalist Needs the Social Contract (and Vice Versa)." *Rationality, Morality, Markets* 4 (2013), pp. 71–87.

Gelpern, Anna, Sebastian Horn, Scott Morris, Brad Parks, and Christoph Trebesch. *How China Lends: A Rare Look into 100 Debt Contracts with Foreign Governments*. Washington, DC: Peterson Institute for International Economics, 2021.

Gerstle, Gary. *Liberty and Coercion: The Paradox of American Government from the Founding to the Present*. Princeton, NJ: Princeton University Press, 2015.

Geuss, Raymond. "Thucydides, Nietzsche, and Williams." In *Outside Ethics*, pp. 219–33. Princeton, NJ: Princeton University Press, 2005.

Gewirtz, Julian. "The Chinese Reassessment of Interdependence." *China Leadership Monitor* 64 (Summer 2020). https://www.prcleader.org/gewirtz.

Giegerich, Thomas. "Retorsion." In *Max Planck Encyclopedia of Public International Law*, edited by Anne Peters and Rüdiger Wolfrum. Oxford: Oxford University Press, online edition, last updated September 2020.

Gilpin, Robert. *War and Change in World Politics*. Cambridge: Cambridge University Press, 1981.

Ginsburg, Tom, and Richard H. McAdams. "Adjudicating in Anarchy: An Expressive Theory of International Dispute Resolution." *William and Mary Law Review* 45(4) (2004), pp. 1229–339.

Glahn, Richard von. "The Political Economy of the East Asian Maritime World in the Sixteenth Century." In *East Asia in the World: Twelve Events That Shaped the Modern International Order*, edited by Stephen Haggard and David C. Kang, pp. 44–66. Cambridge: Cambridge University Press, 2020.

Goldsmith, Jack L., and Eric A. Posner. *The Limits of International Law*. Oxford: Oxford University Press, 2005.

Goodhart, Charles. *The Basel Committee on Banking Supervision: A History of the Early Years, 1974–1997*. Cambridge: Cambridge University Press, 2011.

Gopinath, Gita. "The International Price System." In *Inflation Dynamics and Monetary Policy: A Symposium*, pp. 71–150. Proceedings of the Federal Reserve Bank of Kansas City Symposium, Jackson Hole, WY, August 27–29, 2015. Kansas City, MO: Federal Reserve Bank of Kansas City, 2016.

Gordon, Robert. "Two Centuries of Economic Growth: Europe Chasing the American Frontier." NBER Working Paper 10662, National Bureau of Economic Research, Cambridge, MA, August 2004.

Gourinchas, Pierre-Olivier. "The Dollar Hegemon: Evidence and Implications for Policy Makers." Paper prepared for Sixth Asian Monetary Policy Forum. Version: May 16, 2019. https://www .parisschoolofeconomics.eu/IMG/pdf/chaire-bdf-sept-2019-speaker-gourinchas.pdf.

Gourinchas, Pierre-Olivier, Helene Re, and Maxime Sauzet. "The International Monetary and Financial System." *Annual Review of Economics* 11(1) (2019), pp. 859–93.

Gray, John. *The Two Faces of Liberalism*. Cambridge: Polity Press, 2000.

Greif, Avner. "Commitment, Coercion, and Markets: The Nature and Dynamics of Institutions Supporting Exchange." In *Handbook of New Institutional Economics*, edited by Claude Menard and Mary Shirley, pp. 727–86. Dordrecht, Netherlands: Springer, 2005.

Greif, Avner, and Christopher Kingston. "Institutions: Rules or Equilibria?" In *Political Economy of Institutions, Democracy and Voting*, edited by N. Schofield and G. Caballero, pp. 13–43. Berlin: Springer-Verlag, 2011.

Greif, Avner, and Guido Tabellini. "Cultural and Institutional Bifurcation: China and Europe Compared." *American Economic Review: Papers and Proceedings* 100(2) (2010), pp. 135–40.

———. "The Clan and the Corporation: Sustaining Cooperation in China and Europe." *Journal of Comparative Economics* 45(1) (2017), pp. 1–35.

Grieco, Joseph M. "Anarchy and the Limits of Cooperation: A Realist Critique of the Newest Liberal Institutionalism." *International Organization* 43(3) (1988), pp. 485–507.

Griffin, James. *On Human Rights*. Oxford: Oxford University Press, 2008.

Grossmann, Gene M., and Henrik Horn. "Why the WTO? An Introduction to the Economics of Trade Agreements." In *Legal and Economic Principles of World Trade Law*, edited by Henrik Horn and Petros Mavroidis, pp. 9–67. Cambridge: Cambridge University Press, 2013.

Guzman, Andrew T. *How International Law Works: A Rational Choice Theory*. Oxford: Oxford University Press, 2008.

Hadfield, Gillian K., and Barry R. Weingast. "Microfoundations of the Rule of Law." *Annual Review of Political Science* 17 (2014), pp. 21–42.

Hall, Edward. "Bernard Williams and the Basic Legitimation Demand: A Defence." *Political Studies* 63(2) (2015), pp. 466–80.

———. *Value, Conflict, and Order: Berlin, Hampshire, Williams, and the Realist Revival in Political Theory*. Chicago: University of Chicago Press, 2020.

Hall, Edward, and Dimitrios Tsarapatsanis. "Human Rights, Legitimacy, Political Judgement." *Res Publica* 27, online ahead of print (June 11, 2020), pp. 171–85. https://link.springer.com /article/10.1007/s11158-020-09470-4.

Hamilton, Alexander, James Madison, and John Jay. *The Federalist*. London: Phoenix Press, 2000.

Happold, Matthew. "Economic Sanctions and International Law: An Introduction." In *Economic Sanctions and International Law*, edited by Matthew Happold and Paul Eden, pp. 1–12. London: Hart, 2016.

Hardin, Russell. *Liberalism, Constitutionalism, and Democracy*. Oxford: Oxford University Press, 1999.

———. *David Hume: Moral and Political Theorist*. Oxford: Oxford University Press, 2007.

Harris, Ian. "Order and Justice in the 'Anarchical Society.'" *International Affairs* 69(4) (1993), pp. 725–41.

Hart, H.L.A. *The Concept of Law*. Oxford: Oxford University Press, 1961.

Hart, Oliver D. "Incomplete Contracts and the Theory of the Firm." *Journal of Law, Economics, and Organisation* 4(1) (1988), pp. 119–39.

Hathaway, Oona A. "International Delegation and State Sovereignty." *Law and Contemporary Problems* 71 (2008), pp. 115–49.

Hathaway, Oona A., and Scott J. Shapiro. *The Internationalists and Their Plan to Outlaw War*. New York: Allen Lane, 2017.

Hayek, F. A. *The Road to Serfdom*. Edited with a foreword and introduction by Bruce Caldwell. Chicago: University of Chicago Press, 1994.

———. *Law, Legislation and Liberty: A New Statement of the Liberal Principles of Justice and Political Economy*. 3 vols. in 1. London: Routledge, 2013.

Helfer, Lawrence R. "Taking Stock of Three Generations of Research on Treaty Exit." *Israel Law Review* 52(1) (2019), pp. 103–17.

Hillman, Jennifer. "The Best Way to Address China's Unfair Policies and Practices Is through a Big, Bold Multilateral Case at the WTO." Testimony to US-China Economic and Security Review Commission, Washington, DC, June 8, 2018. https://www.uscc.gov/sites/default /files/Hillman%20Testimony%20US%20China%20Comm%20w%20Appendix%20A.pdf ?mod=article_inline.

Hinsley, F. H. *Sovereignty*. 2nd ed. Cambridge: Cambridge University Press, 1986.

Hirschman, Albert O. *The Passions and the Interests: Political Arguments for Capitalism before Its Triumph*. Princeton, NJ: Princeton University Press, 2013.

Hirshleifer, Jack. "From Weakest-Link to Best-Shot: The Voluntary Provision of Public Goods." *Public Choice* 41(3) (1983), pp. 371–86.

Hobbes, Thomas. *Leviathan*. Edited by R. Tuck. Cambridge: Cambridge University Press, 1996 [1651].

Hoekman, Bernard M., and Petros C. Mavroidis. *The World Trade Organization: Law, Economics, and Politics*. 2nd ed. London: Routledge, 2016.

———. "Preventing the Bad from Getting Worse: The End of the World (Trade Organization) as We Know It?" Working Paper RSCAS 2020/06, Robert Schuman Centre for Advanced Studies, Global Governance Programme, European University Institute, Florence, Italy, June 2020.

Hohfeld, Wesley. *Fundamental Legal Conceptions as Applied in Judicial Reasoning*. New Haven, CT: Yale University Press, 1919.

Holmstrom, Bengt. "Moral Hazard and Observability." *Bell Journal of Economics* 10(1) (1979), pp. 74–91.

———. "Understanding the Role of Debt in the Financial System." BIS Working Paper no. 479, Bank for International Settlements, Basel, January 2015.

Honneth, Axel. "Recognition between States: On the Moral Substrate of International Relations." In *The International Politics of Recognition*, edited by Thomas Lindemann and Eric Ringmar, pp. 25–38. London: Routledge, 2016.

Hont, Istvan. *Jealousy of Trade: International Competition and the Nation-State in Historical Perspective*. Cambridge, MA: Harvard University Press, 2005.

Horn, Henrik, Petros C. Mavroidis, and Andre Sapir. *Beyond the WTO? An Anatomy of EU and US Preferential Trade Agreements*. Brussels: Bruegel Blueprint 7, 2009.

Horn, Sebastian, Carmen M. Reinhart, and Christoph Trebesch. "China's Overseas Lending." Kiel Working Paper no. 2132, Kiel Institute for the World Economy, Kiel, Germany, 2019, updated April 2020.

Horowitz, Richard S. "The Opium Wars of 1839–1860." In *East Asia in the World: Twelve Events That Shaped the Modern International Order*, edited by Stephen Haggard and David C. Kang, pp. 164–187. Cambridge: Cambridge University Press, 2020.

House, Edward M. "Interpretation of President Wilson's Fourteen Points." Accessed February 3, 2022. https://www.mtholyoke.edu/acad/intrel/doc31.htm.

Howse, Robert. "Montesquieu on Commerce, Conquest, War, and Peace." *Brooklyn Journal of International Law* 31(3) (2006), pp. 1–16.

Hume, David. *A Treatise of Human Nature*. Edited by L. A. Selby-Bigge and P. H. Nidditch. 2nd ed. Oxford: Oxford University Press, 1978 [1739/40].

———. *An Enquiry Concerning the Principles of Morals*. Edited by J. B. Schneewind. Indianapolis: Hackett, 1983 [1751].

———. *The History of England*. 6 vols. Edited by W. B. Todd. Indianapolis: Liberty Classics, 1983 [1778].

———. *Political Essays*. Edited by Knud Haakonssen. Cambridge: Cambridge University Press, 1994.

———. "Of the Populousness of Ancient Nations." In *Essays: Moral, Political, and Literary*, edited by Eugene F. Miller, pp. 377–464. Indianapolis: Liberty Classics, 2012.

Hurd, Douglas, and Edward Young. *Choose Your Weapons: The British Foreign Secretary, 200 Years of Argument, Success and Failure*. London: Weidenfeld and Nicolson, 2010.

Hurd, Ian. "Legitimacy and Authority in International Politics." *International Organization* 53(2) (1999), pp. 379–408.

———. *How to Do Things with International Law*. Princeton, NJ: Princeton University Press, 2017.

———. *International Organizations: Politics, Law, Practices*. 3rd ed. Cambridge: Cambridge University Press, 2018.

Hurrell, Andrew. *Global Order: Power, Values, and the Constitution of International Society*. Oxford: Oxford University Press, 2007.

Hurwicz, Leonid. "But Who Will Guard the Guardians?" Nobel Prize Lecture, December 8, 2007.

Ikenberry, G. John. "A World Economy Restored: Expert Consensus and the Anglo-American Postwar Settlement." *International Organization* 46(1) (1992), pp. 289–321.

———. *After Victory: Institutions, Strategic Restraint, and the Rebuilding of Order after Major Wars*. Princeton, NJ: Princeton University Press, 2001.

———. *Liberal Leviathan: The Origins, Crisis, and Transformation of the American World Order*. Princeton, NJ: Princeton University Press, 2011.

Ilzetzki, Ethan, Carmen M. Reinhart, and Kenneth S. Rogoff. "Rethinking Exchange Rate Regimes." In *Handbook of International Economics*, edited by Gita Gopinath, Elhanan Helpman, and Kenneth S. Rogoff, vol. 5. Elsevier: North-Holland, forthcoming.

Independent International Commission on Kosovo. *The Kosovo Report: Conflict, International Response, Lessons Learned*. Oxford: Oxford University Press, 2000.

International Military Tribunal, Nuremberg. *Trial of the Major War Criminals*. Nuremberg, Germany: published under the jurisdiction of the Allied Control Authority, 1947.

International Monetary Fund (IMF). "Guidelines on Conditionality." March 31, 2017.

———. *Considerations on the Role of the SDR*. Washington, DC: International Monetary Fund, April 2018.

Irwin, Douglas A. "The Nixon Shock after Forty Years: The Import Surcharge Revisited." *World Trade Review* 12(1) (2013), pp. 29–56.

———. *Clashing over Commerce: A History of US Trade Policy*. Chicago: University of Chicago Press, 2017.

James, Harold. *The End of Globalization: Lessons from the Great Depression*. Cambridge, MA: Harvard University Press, 2001.

Jervis, Robert. "Cooperation under the Security Dilemma." *World Politics* 30(2) (1978), pp. 167–214.

———. "Security Regimes." *International Organization* 36(2) (1982), pp. 357–78.

Johnston, Alastair Iain. "China in a World of Orders: Rethinking Compliance and Challenge in Beijing's International Relations." *International Security* 44(2) (2019), pp. 9–60.

Joyce, Joseph P., and Todd Sandler. "IMF Retrospective and Prospective: A Public Goods Viewpoint." *Review of International Organizations* 3(3) (2008), pp. 221–38.

Kadens, Emily. "Custom's Past." In *Custom's Future: International Law in a Changing World*, edited by Curtis A. Bradley, pp. 11–33. Cambridge: Cambridge University Press, 2016.

Kang, David C. *East Asia before the West: Five Centuries of Trade and Tribute*. New York: Columbia University Press, 2010.

Kant, Immanuel. *Political Writings*. Edited by H. S. Reiss. Cambridge: Cambridge University Press, 1991.

Kaplan, Robert D. *Asia's Cauldron: The South China Sea and the End of a Stable Pacific*. New York: Random House, 2014.

Kennan, George F. "America and the Russian Future." *Foreign Affairs* 29(3) (1951), pp. 351–70.

———. "Morality and Foreign Policy." *Foreign Affairs* 64(2) (1985), pp. 205–18.

Kennedy, Kevin C. "The Accession of the Soviet Union to GATT." *World Trade Law* 23 (1987), pp. 23–39.

Keohane, Robert O. *After Hegemony: Cooperation and Discord in the World Political Economy*. First Princeton classic ed. Princeton, NJ: Princeton University Press, 2005 [1984].

Keynes, John Maynard. "National Self-Sufficiency." *Yale Review* 22(4) (1933), pp. 755–69.

Khong, Yuen Foong. "The American Tributary System." *Chinese Journal of International Politics* 6 (2013), pp. 1–47.

King, Mervyn. *The End of Alchemy: Money, Banking and the Future of the Global Economy*. London: Little, Brown, 2016.

King, Stephen D. *Grave New World: The End of Globalization, The Return of History*. New Haven, CT: Yale University Press, 2017.

Kingsbury, Benedict. "The Concept of 'Law' in Global Administrative Law." *European Journal of International Law* 20(1) (2003), pp. 23–57.

Kingsbury, Benedict, Nico Krisch, and Richard B. Stewart. "The Emergence of Global Administrative Law." *Law and Contemporary Problems* 68(3/4) (2005), pp. 15–61.

Kingsbury, Benedict, and Benjamin Straumann. "State of Nature versus Commercial Society as the Basis of International Law: Reflections on the Roman Foundations and Current

Interpretations of the International Political and Legal Thought of Grotius, Hobbes, and Pufendorf." In *The Philosophy of International Law*, edited by Samantha Besson and John Tasioulas, pp. 33–51. Oxford: Oxford University Press, 2010.

Kirshner, Jonathan. *Currency and Coercion: The Political Economy of International Monetary Power*. Princeton, NJ: Princeton University Press, 1995.

———. "The Tragedy of Offensive Realism: Classical Realism and the Rise of China." *European Journal of International Relations* 18(1) (2010), pp. 53–75.

Kissinger, Henry. *A World Restored: Metternich, Castlereagh and the Problems of Peace, 1812–1822*. London: Weidenfeld and Nicolson, 1957.

———. *Diplomacy*. London: Simon and Schuster, 1994.

———. *On China*. New York: Penguin Books, 2012.

———. *World Order: Reflections on the Character of Nations and the Course of History*. New York: Penguin Books, 2014.

Klabbers, Jan. *Advanced Introduction to the Law of International Organizations*. Cheltenham, UK: Edward Elgar, 2015.

Koh, Harold H. "Transnational Legal Process." *Nebraska Law Review* 75 (1996), pp. 181–207.

Kolb, Melina. "What Is Globalization?" Peterson Institute for International Economics, last updated February 4, 2019. https://www.piie.com/microsites/globalization/what-is-globalization.

Koremenos, Barbara. *The Continent of International Law: Explaining Agreement Design*. Cambridge: Cambridge University Press, 2016.

Korsgaard, Christine M. *The Sources of Normativity*. Cambridge: Cambridge University Press, 1996.

Koskenniemi, Martti. *The Gentle Civilizer of Nations: The Rise and Fall of International Law, 1870–1960*. Cambridge: Cambridge University Press, 2001.

———. *Fragmentation of International Law: Difficulties Arising from the Diversification and Expansion of International Law*. Report of the Study Group of the International Law Commission. Geneva: United Nations, 2006.

Koslowski, Rey. "Global Mobility Regimes: A Conceptual Framework." In *Global Mobility Regimes*, edited by Rey Koslowski, pp. 1–25. New York: Palgrave Macmillan, 2011.

Krasner, Stephen D. "Structural Causes and Regime Consequences: Regimes as Intervening Variables." *International Organization* 36(2) (1982), pp. 185–205.

———. *Sovereignty: Organized Hypocrisy*. Princeton, NJ: Princeton University Press, 1999.

Kriner, Douglas, and Francis Shen. "Battlefield Casualties and Ballot Box Defeat: Did the Bush-Obama Wars Cost Clinton the White House?" *Political Science and Politics* 53(2) (2020), pp. 248–52.

Krisch, Nico. "The Decay of Consent: International Law in an Age of Global Public Goods." *American Journal of International Law* 108(1) (2014), pp. 1–40.

Krueger, Anne. *International Trade: What Everyone Needs to Know*. Oxford: Oxford University Press, 2020.

Krugman, Paul. "What Should Trade Negotiators Negotiate About?" *Journal of Economic Literature* 35 (1997), pp. 113–20.

———. "Globalization: What Did We Miss?" In *Meeting Globalization's Challenges: Policies to Make Trade Work for All*, edited by Luis A. V. Catao and Maurice Obstfeld, pp. 113–20. Princeton, NJ: Princeton University Press, 2019.

Kumm, Mattias. "Sovereignty and the Right to Be Left Alone: Subsidiarity, Justice-Sensitive Externalities, and the Proper Domain of the Consent Requirement in International Law." *Law and Contemporary Problems* 79(2) (2016), pp. 239–58.

Laborde, Cecile. "Republicanism and Global Justice." *European Journal of Political Theory* 9(1) (2010), pp. 48–69.

Lake, David A. *Entangling Relations: American Foreign Policy in Its Century*. Princeton, NJ: Princeton University Press, 1999.

Lamy, Pascal. *The New World of Trade*. Third Jan Tumlir Lecture. Tumlir Policy Essays No. 1. Brussels: European Centre for International Political Economy, 2015.

Landau, Jean-Pierre. "Global Liquidity: Public and Private." In *Proceedings of Jackson Hole Policy Symposium*, pp. 223–59. Kansas City, MO: Federal Reserve Bank of Kansas City, 2013.

Larosière, Jacques de. "The Demise of the Bretton-Woods System Explains Much of Our Current Financial Vulnerabilities." Speech given at the G7 High Level Conference "Bretton Woods: 75 Years Later." Banque de France, July 16, 2019.

Lauterpacht, Hersch. "The Grotian Tradition in International Law." *British Yearbook of International Law* 23 (1946), pp. 1–53.

Lawrence, Robert Z. "How the United States Should Confront China without Threatening the Global Trading System." Peterson Institute for International Economics Policy Brief, August 2018.

Le Corre, Philippe. *China's Rise as a Geoeconomic Influencer: Four European Case Studies*. Washington, DC: Carnegie Endowment for International Peace, 2018.

Lehman, Jeffrey S., Dani Rodrik, Yang Yao, Meredith A. Crowley, Robert L. Howse, Jiandong Ju, Feng Lu, et al. *US-China Trade Relations: A Way Forward*. Joint statement by US-China Trade Policy Working Group, October 27, 2019.

Lemnitzer, Jan Martin. "'That Moral League of Nations against the United States': The Origins of the 1856 Declaration of Paris." *International History Review* 36(5) (2013), pp. 1068–88.

Leonard, Mark. "What Does the New China Think?" In *China 3.0*, edited by Mark Leonard, pp. 9–24. London: European Council of Foreign Relations, 2012.

———. *The Age of Unpeace: How Connectivity Causes Conflict*. London: Bantam Press, 2021.

———. "The New China Shock." Project Syndicate, March 31, 2021. https://www.project-syndicate.org/commentary/the-new-china-shock-by-mark-leonard-2021-03.

Lesaffer, Randall C. H. "The Classical Law of Nations: 1500–1800." In *Research Handbook on the Theory and History of International Law*, edited by Alexander Orakhelashvili, pp. 408–40. London: Edward Elgar, 2011.

———. "Too Much History: From War as Sanction to the Sanction of War." In *The Oxford Handbook of the Use of Force in International Law*, edited by Marc Weller, pp. 35–55. Oxford: Oxford University Press, 2015.

———. "Roman Law and the Intellectual History of International Law." In *The Oxford Handbook of the Theory of International Law*, edited by Anne Orford and Florian Hoffman, pp. 38–58. Oxford: Oxford University Press, 2016.

Letwin, Oliver. *China vs. America: A Warning*. London: Biteback Publishing, 2021.

Levitsky, Steven, and Daniel Ziblatt. *How Democracies Die*. New York: Crown, 2018.

Lew, Jacob J., and Richard Nephew. "The Use and Misuse of Economic Statecraft: How Washington Is Abusing Its Financial Might." *Foreign Affairs*, November/December 2018, pp. 139–49.

Lewis, David. *Convention: A Philosophical Study*. Cambridge, MA: Harvard University Press, 1969.

Li, David Daokui, and Paul Tucker. *2014 Triennial Surveillance Review—External Study—Risks and Spillovers*. International Monetary Fund, July 30, 2014. https://www.imf.org/-/media/Websites/IMF/imported-full-text-pdf/external/np/pp/eng/2014/_073014e.ashx.

Lilla, Mark. *The Reckless Mind: Intellectuals in Politics*. New York: New York Review of Books, 2016.

Lipson, Charles. "International Cooperation in Economic and Security Affairs." *World Politics* 37(1) (1984), pp. 1–23.

Lohmann, Susanne. "Why Do Institutions Matter? An Audience-Cost Theory of Institutional Commitment." *Governance* 16(1) (2003), pp. 95–110.

Lowe, Vaughan. *International Law: A Very Short Introduction*. Oxford: Oxford University Press, 2015.

Lowe, Vaughan, and Antonios Tzanakopoulos. "Economic Warfare." In *Max Planck Encyclopedia of Public International Law*, edited by Anne Peters and Rüdiger Wolfrum. Oxford: Oxford University Press, online edition, last updated March 2013.

MacMillan, Margaret. *Paris 1919: Six Months That Changed the World*. New York: Random House, 2003.

Malcolm, Noel. *Sense on Sovereignty*. London: Centre for Policy Studies, 1991.

———. "Hobbes's Theory of International Relations." In *Aspects of Hobbes*, pp. 432–56. Oxford: Oxford University Press, 2002.

———. *Human Rights and Political Wrongs*. London: Policy Exchange, 2017.

Margalit, Avishai. *On Betrayal*. Cambridge, MA: Harvard University Press, 2017.

Marlow, Iain. "What Is the 'Quad' and Should China Fear It?" Bloomberg, March 26, 2021. https://www.bloomberg.com/news/articles/2021-03-26/what-is-the-quad-and-should-china-fear-it-quicktake.

Mavroidis, Petros C. *The Regulation of International Trade*. Vol. 1, *GATT*. Cambridge, MA: MIT Press, 2016.

Mavroidis, Petros C., and Andre Sapir. *China and the WTO: Why Multilateralism Matters*. Princeton, NJ: Princeton University Press, 2021.

Mazower, Mark. *Governing the World: The History of an Idea*. London: Allen Lane, 2012.

McGregor, Richard. *Xi Jinping: The Backlash*. Lowy Institute Paper. Docklands, Australia: Penguin Books, 2019.

———. "Increasingly Powerful, Xi's China Believes It No Longer Needs Washington—or Its Foreign Reporters." *Guardian*, March 19, 2020.

Mead, Walter Russell. *Special Providence: American Foreign Policy and How It Changed the World*. New York: Routledge, 2002.

Mearsheimer, John J. "The False Promise of International Institutions." *International Security* 19(3) (1994/95), pp. 5–49.

———. "Why the Ukraine Crisis Is the West's Fault: The Liberal Delusions that Provoked Putin." *Foreign Affairs*, September/October 2014.

———. "Can China Rise Peacefully?" *The National Interest*, October 25, 2014. https://nationalinterest.org/commentary/can-china-rise-peacefully-10204.

Mencius. *Mengzi*. Translated by Bryan W. Van Norden. Indianapolis: Hackett, 2008.

Milgrom, Paul R., Douglass C. North, and Barry R. Weingast. "The Role of Institutions in the Revival of Trade: The Law Merchant, Private Judges, and the Champagne Fairs." *Economics and Politics* 2(1) (1990), pp. 1–23.

Mill, John Stuart. "A Few Words on Non-intervention." *New England Review* 27(3) (2006), pp. 252–64 [1859].

Milner, Helen. "The Assumption of Anarchy in International Relations Theory: A Critique." *Review of International Studies* 17(1) (1991), pp. 67–85.

Mitter, Rana. *China's War with Japan, 1937–1945: The Struggle for Survival.* London: Penguin Books, 2014.

Moellers, Christoph. "Constitutional Foundations of Global Administration." In *Research Handbook of Administrative Law*, edited by Sabino Cassese, pp. 107–28. Cheltenham, UK: Edward Elgar, 2016.

———. "Law beyond the State: A Reply to Liam Murphy." *European Journal of International Law* 28(1) (2017), pp. 251–56.

Mokyr, Joel. *Culture of Growth: The Origins of the Modern Economy.* Princeton, NJ: Princeton University Press, 2017.

Momani, Bessana. "Gulf Cooperation Council Oil Exporters and the Future of the Dollar." *New Political Economy* 13(3) (2008), pp. 293–314.

Montesquieu, Baron. *The Spirit of the Laws.* Cambridge: Cambridge University Press, 1989 [1748].

Morgenthau, Hans J. *The Concept of the Political.* London: Palgrave Macmillan, 2012 [1933].

Morris, Christopher W. *An Essay on the Modern State.* Cambridge: Cambridge University Press, 1998.

Mulder, Nicholas. "The Rise and Fall of Euro-American Inter-state War." *Humanity* 10(1) (Spring 2019), pp. 133–53.

Mundell, Robert A. "The International Monetary System in the 21st Century: Could Gold Make a Comeback?" Lecture, March 12, 1997. http://www.ahamedkameel.com/wp-content/uploads/2014/01/RAMArticle.pdf.

Murphy, Liam. "Law beyond the State: Some Philosophical Questions." *European Journal of International Law* 28(1) (2017), pp. 203–32.

Myerson, Roger B. "Fundamental Theory of Institutions: A Lecture in Honor of Leo Hurwicz." Hurwicz Lecture, presented at the North American Meetings of the Econometric Society, University of Minnesota, June 22, 2006.

———. "Game-Theoretic Consistency and International Relations." *Journal of Theoretical Politics* 18(4) (2006), pp. 416–33.

———. *Force and Restraint in Strategic Deterrence: A Game-Theorist's Perspective.* Carlisle, PA: Strategic Studies Institute, US Army War College, 2007.

———. "Learning from Schelling's *Strategy of Conflict*." *Journal of Economic Literature* 47(4) (2009), pp. 1109–25.

———. "Game Theory and the First World War." Mimeograph, July 2021.

Nagel, Thomas. "The Problem of Global Justice." *Philosophy and Public Affairs* 33(2) (2005), pp. 113–47.

Nakano, Jane. *The Geopolitics of Critical Minerals Supply Chains.* Washington, DC: Center for Strategic and International Studies, 2021.

Nardin, Terry. *Law, Morality, and the Relations of States*. Princeton, NJ: Princeton University Press, 1983.

———. "The International Legal Order 1919–2019." *International Relations* 33(2) (2019), pp. 157–71.

Neff, Stephen C. *Friends but No Allies: Economic Liberalism and the Law of Nations*. New York: Columbia University Press, 1990.

———. "Peace and Prosperity: Commercial Aspects of Peacemaking." In *Peace Treaties and International Law in European History: From the Late Middle Ages to World War One*, edited by Randall Lesaffer, pp. 365–81. Cambridge: Cambridge University Press, 2004.

———. "A Short History of International Law." In *International Law*, 2nd ed., edited by Malcolm D. Evans, pp. 3–31. Oxford: Oxford University Press, 2006.

———. *Justice among Nations: A History of International Law*. Cambridge, MA: Harvard University Press, 2014.

———. "Consent." In *Concepts for International Law*, edited by Jean d'Aspremont and Sahib Singh, pp. 127–40. Cheltenham, UK: Edward Elgar, 2019.

———. "The Law of Armed Conflict." In *The Cambridge Companion to Hugo Grotius*, edited by Randall Lesaffer and Janne E. Nijman, pp. 457–76. Cambridge: Cambridge University Press, 2021.

Nixon, Simon. "Rival Superpowers Are Vying to End the Era of Dollar Supremacy." *Times* (London), July 9, 2020.

Nordhaus, William. "Climate Clubs: Overcoming Free-Riding in International Climate Policy." *American Economic Review* 105(4) (2015), pp. 1339–70.

Norrlof, Carla. *America's Global Advantage: US Hegemony and International Cooperation*. Cambridge: Cambridge University Press, 2010.

———. "Dollar Hegemony: A Power Analysis." *Review of International Political Economy* 21(5) (2014), pp. 1042–70.

Norrlof, Carla, Paul Poast, Benjamin J. Cohen, Sabreena Croteau, Aashna Khanna, Daniel McDowell, Hongying Wang, and W. Kindred Winecoff. "Global Monetary Order and the Liberal Order Debate." *International Studies Perspectives* 21 (2020), pp. 109–53.

North, Douglass C. *Institutions: Institutional Change and Economic Performance*. Cambridge: Cambridge University Press, 1990.

———. "Institutions." *Journal of Economic Perspectives* 5(1) (1991), pp. 97–112.

North, Douglass C., and Barry R. Weingast. "Constitutions and Commitment: The Evolution of Institutions Governing Public Choice in Seventeenth-Century England." *Journal of Economic History* 49(4) (1989): 803–32.

Nussbaum, Martha C. *The Cosmopolitan Tradition: A Noble but Flawed Ideal*. Cambridge, MA: Harvard University Press, 2019.

Nye, Joseph S. *The Future of Power*. New York: PublicAffairs, 2011.

———. *Do Morals Matter? Presidents and Foreign Policy from FDR to Trump*. New York: Oxford University Press, 2020.

Obstfeld, Maurice. "The Global Capital Market Reconsidered." *Oxford Review of Economic Policy* 37(4) (2021), pp. 690–706.

O'Connell, Mary Ellen, and Lenore VanderZee. "The History of International Adjudication." In *The Oxford Handbook of International Adjudication*, edited by Casare P. R. Romano, Karen J. Alter, and Yuval Shany, pp. 40–62. Oxford: Oxford University Press, 2014.

Okonjo-Iweala, Ngozi, Tharman Shanmugaratnam, and Lawrence H. Summers. *A Global Deal for Our Pandemic Age*. Report of G20 High Level Independent Panel on Financing the Global Commons for Pandemic Preparedness and Response, June 2021.

Olson, Mancur. *The Logic of Collective Action: Public Goods and the Theory of Groups*. Second printing, with new preface and appendix. Cambridge, MA: Harvard University Press, 1971.

Onuma, Yasuaki. "When Was the Law of International Relations Born? An Inquiry of the History of International Law from an Intercivilizational Perspective." *History of International Law* 2 (2000), pp. 1–66.

———. *International Law in a Transcivilizational World*. Cambridge: Cambridge University Press, 2017.

O'Rourke, Keven Hjortshoj. "Economic History and Contemporary Challenges to Globalization." *Journal of Economic History* 79(2) (2019), pp. 356–82.

Osiander, Andreas. "Sovereignty, International Relations, and the Westphalian Myth." *International Organization* 55(2) (Spring 2001), pp. 251–87.

Ostrom, Elinor. *Governing the Commons: The Evolution of Institutions for Collective Action*. New York: Cambridge University Press, 1990.

Ostry, Jonathan D., Atish R. Ghosh, Karl Habermeier, Marcos Chamon, Mahvash S. Qureshi, and Dennis B. S. Reinhardt. "Capital Inflows: The Role of Controls." IMF Staff Position Note, International Monetary Fund, February 19, 2010.

Paddeau, Frederia I. "Countermeasures." In *Max Planck Encyclopedia of Public International Law*, edited by Anne Peters and Rüdiger Wolfrum. Oxford: Oxford University Press, online edition, last updated September 2015.

Palley, Thomas I. "The Fallacy of the Globalization Trilemma: Reframing the Political Economy of Globalization and Implications for Democracy." FMM-Working Paper no. 8, Forum for Macroeconomics and Macroeconomic Policies, Hans-Böckler-Stiftung, Düsseldorf, Germany, July 2017.

Papaconstantinou, George, and Jean Pisani-Ferry. "New Rules for a New World: A Survival Kit." STG Policy Papers no. 9, School of Transnational Governance, European University Institute, 2021.

Paternotte, Cedric, and Jonathan Grose. "Social Norms and Game Theory: Harmony or Discord?" *British Journal of the Philosophy of Science* 64 (2013), pp. 551–87.

Paul, T. V. "The Enduring Axioms of Balance of Power Theory and Their Contemporary Relevance." In *Balance of Power: Theory and Practice in the 21st Century*, edited by T. V. Paul, James J. Wirtz, and Michael Fortmann, pp. 1–25. Stanford, CA: Stanford University Press, 2004.

Paulus, Andreas. "The International Legal System as a Constitution." In *Ruling the World? Constitutionalism, International Law, and Global Governance*, edited by Jeffrey L. Dunoff and Joel P. Trachtman, pp. 69–109. Cambridge: Cambridge University Press, 2009.

———. "International Adjudication." In *The Philosophy of International Law*, edited by Samantha Besson and John Tasioulas, pp. 207–24. Oxford: Oxford University Press, 2010.

Pauly, Louis W. "The League of Nations and the Foreshadowing of the International Monetary Fund." Essays in International Finance no. 201, Princeton University, 1996.

Pavel, Carmen E. "Hume's Dynamic Coordination and International Law." *Political Theory* 49(2), online ahead of print (May 16, 2020), pp. 1–28. https://doi.org/10.1177/00905 91720921831.

Pence, Mike. "Remarks Delivered on the Trump Administration's Policy towards China." Hudson Institute, October 4, 2018. https://trumpwhitehouse.archives.gov/briefings-statements/remarks-vice-president-pence-administrations-policy-toward-china/.

Perdue, Peter C. "China and Other Colonial Systems." *Journal of American-East Asian Relations* 16(1/2) (2009), pp. 85–103.

———. "The Tenacious Tributary System." *Journal of Contemporary China* 24(96) (2015), pp. 1002–14.

Perlez, Jane. "Tribunal Rejects Beijing's Claims in South China Sea." *New York Times,* July 12, 2016. https://www.nytimes.com/2016/07/13/world/asia/south-china-sea-hague-ruling-philippines.html.

Persson, Torsten, and Guido Tabellini. "Culture, Institutions and Policy." In *The Handbook of Historical Economics,* edited by Alberto Bisin and Giovanni Federico, pp. 463–90. London: Elsevier Science, 2021.

Petersmann, Ernst-Ulrich. "Justice in International Economic Law? From the 'International Law among States' to 'International Integration Law' and 'Constitutional Law.'" EUI Working Papers, Law 2006/46, European University Institute, 2006.

Pettit, Philip. "Legitimate International Institutions: A Neo-Republican Perspective." In *The Philosophy of International Law,* edited by Samantha Besson and John Tasioulas, pp. 139–60. Oxford: Oxford University Press, 2010.

———. "A Republican Law of Peoples." *European Journal of Political Theory* 9(1) (2010), pp. 70–94.

———. *On the People's Terms: A Republican Theory and Model of Democracy.* New York: Cambridge University Press, 2012.

Phillips, Lord. "The Art of the Possible: Statutory Interpretation and Human Rights." First Lord Alexander of Weedon Lecture, April 22, 2010.

Philpott, Daniel. "Sovereignty." In *The Stanford Encyclopedia of Philosophy,* edited by Edward Zalta. Last updated March 25, 2016. https://plato.stanford.edu/entries/sovereignty/.

Pils, Eva. "Human Rights and the Political System." In *Handbook on Human Rights in China,* edited by Sarah Biddulph and Joshua Rosenzweig, pp. 32–59. Cheltenham, UK: Edward Elgar, 2019.

Pincus, Steve. *1688: The First Modern Revolution.* New Haven, CT: Yale University Press, 2009.

Pisani-Ferry, Jean, Norbert Roettgen, Andre Sapir, Paul Tucker, and Guntram B. Wolf. *Europe after Brexit: A Proposal for a Continental Partnership.* Brussels: Bruegel, 2016.

Posner, Eric A., and John C. Yoo. "International Law and the Rise of China." Public Law and Legal Theory Working Paper no. 127, University of Chicago, 2006.

Poulsen, Lauge N. Skovgaard, and Geoffrey Gertz. *Reforming the Investment Treaty Regime: A "Backward-Looking" Approach.* Washington, DC: Brookings Institution, March 17, 2021.

Powell, Robert. "Absolute and Relative Gains in International Relations Theory." *American Political Science Review* 85(4) (1991), pp. 1303–20.

———. "Guns versus Butter." *American Political Science Review* 87(1) (1993), pp. 115–32.

Pratt, Tyler. "Angling for Influence: Institutional Proliferation in Development Banking." *International Studies Quarterly* 65(1) (2021), pp. 95–108.

Puett, Michael. "Who Is Confucius in Today's China?" In *The China Questions: Critical Insights into a Rising Power,* edited by Jennifer Ruddolph and Michael Szonyi, pp. 231–36. Cambridge, MA: Harvard University Press, 2018.

Putnam, R. D. "Diplomacy and Domestic Politics: The Logic of Two-Level Games." *International Organization* 42(3) (1988), pp. 427–60.

Queloz, Matthieu. "Williams's Pragmatic Genealogy and Self-Effacing Functionality." *Philosopher's Imprint* 18(17) (September 2018), pp. 1–20.

Rabkin, Jeremy A. *Law without Nations? Why Constitutional Government Requires Sovereign States.* Princeton, NJ: Princeton University Press, 2005.

Rajan, Raghuram. "Competitive Monetary Easing—Is It Yesterday Once More?" Remarks at the Brookings Institution, Washington, DC, April 10, 2014.

Rasilla, Ignazio de la. "A Very Short History of International Law Journals (1869–2018)." *European Journal of International Law* 29(1) (2018), pp. 137–68.

Ratner, Steven R. *The Thin Justice of International Law: A Moral Reckoning of the Law of Nations.* Oxford: Oxford University Press, 2015.

Rawls, John. *Political Liberalism.* New York: Columbia University Press, 1993.

———. *The Law of Peoples.* Cambridge, MA: Harvard University Press, 1999.

Raz, Joseph. *The Morality of Freedom.* New York: Oxford University Press, 1986.

Reus-Smit, Christian. "International Crises of Legitimacy." *International Politics* 44(2–3) (2007), pp. 157–74.

Reuters. "BIS Says Won't Be Avenue for Russia Sanctions to Be Circumvented." February 28, 2022. https://www.reuters.com/markets/europe/global-markets-bis-urgent-2022-02-28/.

Reynolds, David. *Summits: Six Meetings That Shaped the Twentieth Century.* London: Penguin Books, 2007.

Roberts, Anthea. "Power and Persuasion in Investment Treaty Interpretation: The Dual Role of States." *American Journal of International Law* 104(2) (2010), pp. 179–225.

———. "With Blinders On? How International Law Casebooks Teach Students in the United States." Just Security, October 11, 2017. https://www.justsecurity.org/45825/blinders-on-international-law-casebooks-teach-students-united-states/.

———. "Incremental, Systemic, and Paradigmatic Reform of Investor-State Arbitration." *American Journal of International Law* 112(3) (2018), pp. 410–32.

Robinson, David M. "The Ming Empire." In *The Oxford World History of Empire*, vol. 2, *The History of Empires*, edited by Peter Fibiger Bang, C. A. Bayly, and Walter Scheidel, pp. 533–70. Oxford: Oxford University Press, 2021.

Rodrik, Dani. *The Globalization Paradox: Why Global Markets, States, and Democracy Can't Coexist.* New York: Oxford University Press, 2011.

———. *Straight Talk on Trade: Ideas for a Sane World Economy.* Princeton, NJ: Princeton University Press, 2018.

Rodrik, Dani, and Stephen Walt. "How to Construct a New Global Order." Harvard Kennedy School, March 2021. https://drodrik.scholar.harvard.edu/files/dani-rodrik/files/new_global_order.pdf.

Rosen, Michael. *Dignity: Its History and Meaning.* Cambridge, MA: Harvard University Press, 2012.

Rosenblatt, Helena. *The Lost History of Liberalism: From Ancient Rome to the Twenty-First Century.* Princeton, NJ: Princeton University Press, 2018.

Rosenne, Shabtai. "Codification Revisited after 50 Years." In *Max Planck Yearbook of United Nations Law*, vol. 2, edited by Jochen A. Frowein, Rüdiger Wolfrum, and Christiane E. Philipp, pp. 1–22. Leiden: Brill, 1998.

Rosenne, Shabtai, and Julia Gebhard. "Conferences on the Law of the Sea." In *Max Planck Encyclopedia of Public International Law*, edited by Anne Peters and Rüdiger Wolfrum. Oxford: Oxford University Press, online edition, last updated May 2008.

Rosow, Stephen J. "Commerce, Power and Justice: Montesquieu on International Politics." *Review of Politics* 46(3) (1984), pp. 346–66.

Rossi, Enzo, and Matt Sleat. "Realism in Normative Political Theory." *Philosophy Compass* 9(10) (2014), pp. 689–701.

Rothwell, Donald R. "Sea Lanes." In *Max Planck Encyclopedia of Public International Law*, edited by Anne Peters and Rüdiger Wolfrum. Oxford: Oxford University Press, online edition, last updated June 2009.

Rousseau, Jean-Jacques. "The State of War." In *Basic Political Writings*, pp. 253–65. Indianapolis: Hackett, 2012.

Rudd, Kevin. "The Coronavirus and Xi Jinping's Worldview." Project Syndicate, February 8, 2020. https://www.project-syndicate.org/commentary/coronavirus-will-not-change-xi -jinping-china-governance-by-kevin-rudd-2020-02.

———. "Xi Jinping's Pivot to the State: The Impact of Ideology, Demography, and Decoupling on China's New Economic Policy Framework." Asia Society, September 8, 2021. https:// asiasociety.org/policy-institute/xi-jinpings-pivot-state.

Ruggie, John G. "International Regimes, Transactions, and Change: Embedded Liberalism in the Postwar Economic Order." *International Organization* 36(2) (1982), pp. 379–415.

Russell, Paul. "Hume's Optimism and Williams' Pessimism: From 'Science of Man' to Genealogical Critique." In *Ethics beyond the Limits: New Essays on Bernard Williams' "Ethics and the Limits of Philosophy,"* edited by Sophie Grace Chappell and Marcel van Ackeren, pp. 37–52. Abingdon, UK: Routledge, 2019.

Ryan, Alan. "Liberal Imperialism." In *The Making of Modern Liberalism*, pp. 107–22. Princeton, NJ: Princeton University Press, 2012.

———. *On Politics*. London: Penguin Books, 2012.

Sabl, Andrew W. *Hume's Politics: Coordination and Crisis in the "History of England."* Princeton, NJ: Princeton University Press, 2012.

Sagar, Paul. "Minding the Gap: Bernard Williams and David Hume on Living an Ethical Life." *Journal of Moral Philosophy* 11 (2014), pp. 615–38.

———. *The Opinion of Mankind: Sociability and the Theory of the State from Hobbes to Smith.* Princeton, NJ: Princeton University Press, 2018.

———. *Adam Smith Reconsidered: History, Liberty, and the Foundations of Modern Politics.* Princeton, NJ: Princeton University Press, 2022.

Sahasrabuddhe, Aditi. "Drawing the Line: The Politics of Federal Currency Swaps in the Global Financial Crisis." *Review of International Political Economy* 26(3) (2019), pp. 461–89.

Samuelson, Paul A. "Where Ricardo and Mill Rebut and Confirm Arguments of Mainstream Economists Supporting Globalization." *Journal of Economic Perspectives* 18(3) (2004), pp. 135–46.

Sand, Peter H. "The Evolution of International Environmental Law." In *The Oxford Handbook of International Environmental Law*, edited by Daniel Bodansky, Jutta Brunnee, and Ellen Hay, pp. 29–42. Oxford: Oxford University Press, 2007.

Sandler, Todd. *Global Collective Action*. Cambridge: Cambridge University Press, 2004.

Savage, Deborah, and Albert Weale. "Political Representation and the Normative Logic of Two-Level Games." *European Political Science Review* 1(1) (2009), pp. 63–81.

Scharpf, Fritz W. *Governing in Europe: Effective and Democratic?* Oxford: Oxford University Press, 1999.

Schelling, Thomas C. *The Strategy of Conflict.* Cambridge, MA: Harvard University Press, 1960.

Schill, Stephen W. *Multilateralization of International Investment Law.* Cambridge: Cambridge University Press, 2009.

———. "Developing a Framework for the Legitimacy of International Arbitration." In *Legitimacy: Myths, Realities, Challenges,* edited by A. J. van den Berg, pp. 789–827. International Council for Commercial Arbitration Congress 18. Alphen aan den Rijn, Netherlands: Wolters Kluwer, 2015.

Schoenberger, Karl. "Two Faces of Indonesia: Skyscapers and Squalor, Free-Market Capitalism and Sanctioned Monopoly Exist Side by Side." *Los Angeles Times,* June 1, 1992.

Schoenmaker, Dirk. *Governance of International Banking: The Financial Trilemma.* Oxford: Oxford University Press, 2013.

Schulz, Kenneth A., and Barry R. Weingast. "The Democratic Advantage: Institutional Foundations of Financial Power in International Competition." *International Organization* 57(1) (2003), pp. 3–42.

Shaffer, Gregory, and Michael Waibel. "The (Mis)alignment of the Trade and Monetary Legal Orders." In *Transnational Legal Orders,* edited by Terence C. Halliday and Gregory Shaffer, pp. 187–230. New York: Cambridge University Press, 2015.

Shanghai Cooperation Organization Secretariat. "About the Shanghai Cooperation Organisation." Accessed February 15, 2022. http://eng.sectsco.org/about_sco/.

Shelton, Dinah. "Normative Hierarchy in International Law." *American Journal of International Law* 100(2) (2006), pp. 291–323.

———. "Human Rights." In *The Oxford Handbook of International Organizations,* edited by Jacob Katz Cogan, Ian Hurd, and Ian Johnstone, pp. 249–80. Oxford: Oxford University Press, 2016.

Shklar, Judith. "Liberalism of Fear." In *Liberalism and the Moral Life,* edited by Nancy Rosenblum, pp. 21–38. Cambridge, MA: Harvard University Press, 1989.

———. "Political Theory and The Rule of Law." In *Political Thought and Political Thinkers,* edited by Stanley Hoffmann. Chicago: University of Chicago Press, 1998.

Shovlin, John. *Trading with the Enemy: Britain, France, and the 18th-Century Quest for a Peaceful World Order.* New Haven, CT: Yale University Press.

Shultz, George. "United States: Department of State Letter and Statement Concerning Termination of Acceptance of I.C.J. Compulsory Jurisdiction." *International Legal Materials* 24(6) (1985), pp. 1742–45. https://www.jstor.org/stable/20692919.

Siedentop, Larry. *Inventing the Individual: The Origins of Western Liberalism.* London: Penguin Books, 2015.

Sikkink, Kathryn. *Evidence for Hope: Making Human Rights Work in the 21st Century.* Princeton, NJ: Princeton University Press, 2017.

Simmons, A. John. *Justification and Legitimacy: Essays on Rights and Obligations.* Cambridge: Cambridge University Press, 2001.

Simms, Brendan. *Britain's Europe: A Thousand Years of Conflict and Cooperation.* London: Allen Lane, 2016.

Simpson, Gerry. "Two Liberalisms." *European Journal of International Law* 12(3) (2001), pp. 537–71.

———. *Great Powers and Outlaw States: Unequal Sovereigns in the International Legal Order.* Cambridge: Cambridge University Press, 2004.

Singer, David A. *Regulating Capital: Setting Standards for the International Financial System.* Ithaca, NY: Cornell University Press, 2007.

Skinner, Quentin. *Liberty before Liberalism.* Cambridge: Cambridge University Press, 1998.

Skyrms, Brian. "Trust, Risk, and the Social Contract." *Synthese* 160(1) (2008), pp. 21–25.

———. "Evolution and the Social Contract." In *The Tanner Lectures on Human Values 28*, ed. Grethe B. Peterson, pp. 49–69. Salt Lake City: University of Utah Press, 2009.

Slater, Martin. *The National Debt: A Short History.* London: Hurst, 2018.

Slaughter, Anne-Marie. *A New World Order.* Princeton, NJ: Princeton University Press, 2004.

Sleat, Matt. "The Politics and Morality of the Responsibility to Protect: Beyond the Realist/Liberal Impasse." *International Politics* 53(1) (2016), pp. 67–82.

———. "Modus Vivendi and Legitimacy: Some Sceptical Thoughts." In *The Political Theory of Modus Vivendi*, edited by John Horton, Manon Westphal, and Ulrich Willems, pp. 185–204. Cham, Switzerland: Springer, 2019.

Slobodian, Quinn. *The Globalists: The End of Empire and the Birth of Neoliberalism.* Cambridge, MA: Harvard University Press, 2018.

Smith, Adam. *The Wealth of Nations.* Bks. 4–5. Edited by Andrew Skinner. London: Penguin Books, 1999 [1776].

———. *The Theory of Moral Sentiments.* Edited by Knud Haakonssen. Cambridge: Cambridge University Press, 2002 [1759–90].

Smith, Gordon S. "G7 to G8 to G20: Evolution in Global Governance." CIGI G20 Papers no. 6, Centre for International Governance Innovation, May 2011.

Snidal, Duncan. "Coordination versus Prisoners' Dilemma: Implications for International Cooperation and Regimes." *American Political Science Review* 79(4) (1985), pp. 923–42.

Spruyt, Hendrik. *The Sovereign State and Its Competitors: An Analysis of Systems Change.* Princeton, NJ: Princeton University Press, 1994.

Steil, Benn. *The Battle of Bretton Woods: John Maynard Keynes, Harry Dexter White, and the Making of a New World Order.* Princeton, NJ: Princeton University Press, 2013.

———. *The Marshall Plan: Dawn of the Cold War.* New York: Simon and Schuster, 2018.

Steil, Benn, and Robert E. Litan. *Financial Statecraft: The Role of Financial Markets in American Foreign Policy.* New Haven, CT: Yale University Press. 2006.

Stein, Arthur A. "Coordination and Collaboration: Regimes in an Anarchic World." *International Organization* 36 (Spring 1982), pp. 299–324.

Stilz, Anna B. "Hume, Modern Patriotism, and Commercial Society." *History of European Ideas* 29 (2003), pp. 15–32.

Stollberg-Rilinger, Barbara. *The Holy Roman Empire: A Short History.* Princeton, NJ: Princeton University Press, 2018.

Stone Sweet, Alec, and Jud Mathews. "Proportionality and Rights Protection in Asia: Hong Kong, Malaysia, South Korea, Taiwan—Whither Singapore?" *Singapore Academy of Law Journal* 29 (2017), pp. 774–99.

Stoye, John. *Europe Unfolding: 1648–1688.* London: Fontana Press, 1969.

Stuart-Buttle, Tim. *From Moral Theology to Moral Philosophy: Cicero and Visions of Humanity from Locke to Hume*. Oxford: Oxford University Press, 2019.

Sugden, Robert. "Normative Expectations: The Simultaneous Evolution of Institutions and Norms." In *Economics, Values and Organization*, edited by Avner Ben-Nur and Louis Putterman, pp. 73–100. New York: Cambridge University Press, 1998.

Sully, Razeen. *Classical Liberalism and International Economic Order*. London: Routledge, 1998.

Tabellini, Guido. "The Scope of Cooperation: Values and Incentives." *Quarterly Journal of Economics* 123(3) (2008), pp. 905–50.

Thompson, Alexander, Tomer Broude, and Yoram Z. Haftel. "Once Bitten, Twice Shy? Investment Disputes, State Sovereignty, and Change in Treaty Design." *International Organization* 73(4) (2019), pp. 859–80.

Thompson, Helen. *Disorder: Hard Times in the 21st Century*. Oxford: Oxford University Press, 2022.

Thucydides. *History of the Peloponnesian War*. Translated by Rex Warner, with an introduction and notes by M. I. Finley. London: Penguin Books, 1972.

Tiwald, Justin. "A Right of Rebellion in the Mengzi?" *Dao* 7(3) (2008), pp. 269–82.

———. "On the View That People and Not Institutions Bear Primary Credit for Success in Governance: Confucian Arguments." *Journal of Confucian Philosophy and Culture* 32 (2019), pp. 65–97.

Tombs, Robert, and Isabel Tombs. *That Sweet Enemy: Britain and France, The History of a Love-Hate Relationship*. London: Pimlico, 2007.

Tooze, Adam. "John Mearsheimer and the Dark Origins of Realism." *New Statesman*, March 8, 2022.

Triffin, Robert. *Gold and the Dollar Crisis: The Future of Convertibility*. New Haven, CT: Yale University Press, 1961.

Triffin International Foundation. *Using the SDR as a Lever to Reform the International Financial System*. Report of an SDR Working Party, May 2014. https://www.triffininternational.eu/images/RTI/articles_papers/SDR-WP_Final-Report-May-2014.pdf.

Tuck, Richard. *The Rights of War and Peace: Political Thought and the International Order from Grotius to Kant*. Oxford: Oxford University Press, 1999.

Tucker, Paul. "Regulatory Reform, Stability, and Central Banking." Hutchins Center Working Paper no. 1, Hutchins Center on Fiscal and Monetary Policy, Brookings Institution, Washington, DC, 2014.

———. "The Resolution of Financial Institutions without Taxpayer Solvency Support: Seven Retrospective Clarifications and Elaborations." Delivered at European Symposium in Economic Theory, Gerzensee, Switzerland, July 3, 2014. https://cepr.org/sites/default/files/events/papers/6708_TUCKER%20Essay.pdf.

———. *The Design and Governance of Financial Stability Regimes: A Common Resource Problem That Challenges Technical Know-How, Democratic Accountability and International Coordination*. CIGI Essays on International Finance, vol. 3. Waterloo, ON: Centre for International Governance Innovation, 2016.

———. "The Geopolitics of the International Monetary and Financial System." Tacitus Lecture, Worshipful Company of World Traders, London, February 24, 2016. http://paultucker.me/675/.

———. "The Political Economy of Central Banking in the Digital Age." *SUERF Policy Note*, no. 13 (June 2017).

———. *Unelected Power: The Quest for Legitimacy in Central Banking and the Regulatory State.* Princeton, NJ: Princeton University Press, 2018.

———. "Is the Financial System Sufficiently Resilient?" BIS Working Paper no. 792, Bank for International Settlements, Basel, July 4, 2019.

———. "Solvency as a Fundamental Constraint on LOLR Policy for Independent Central Banks: Principles, History, Law." *Journal of Financial Crises* 2(2) (2020), pp. 1–33.

Tyler, Tom. *Why People Obey the Law.* Princeton, NJ: Princeton University Press, 2006.

Ullmann-Margalit, Edna. *The Emergence of Norms.* Oxford: Oxford University Press, 2015 [1977].

US Central Intelligence Agency. "Soviet International Banking and Insurance." Intelligence Memorandum ER IM 71-170, September 1971. Originally classified Secret. Sanitized copy approved for release March 5, 2010. CIA-RDP85T00875R0011700020023-3.

Vagts, Alfred, and Detlev F. Vagts. "The Balance of Power in International Law: A History of an Idea." *American Journal of International Law* 73(4) (1979), pp. 555–80.

Vagts, Detlev F. "International Economic Law and the American Journal of International Law." *American Journal of International Law* 100(4) (2006), pp. 769–82.

Vanderschraaf, Peter. "The Informal Game Theory in Hume's Account of Convention." *Economics and Philosophy* 14 (1998), pp. 215–47.

Vattel, Emmerich. *The Law of Nations: Or, Principles of the Law of Nature Applied to the Conduct of Affairs of Nations and Sovereigns.* Edited by Bela Kaposy and Richard Whatmore. Indianapolis: Liberty Classics, 2008 [1758].

Verosta, Stephan. "History of International Law, 1648 to 1815." In *Max Planck Encyclopedia of Public International Law*, edited by Anne Peters and Rüdiger Wolfrum. Oxford: Oxford University Press, online edition, last updated June 2007.

Vidigal, Geraldo. "A Really Big Button That Doesn't Do Anything? The Anti-NME Clause in US Trade Agreements between Law and Geo-economics." *Journal of International Economic Law* 23 (2020), pp. 45–64.

Volcker, Paul A., and Toyoo Gyohten. *Changing Fortunes: The World's Money and the Threat to American Leadership.* New York: Times Books, 1992.

Vrdoljak, Ana Filipa. "Human Rights and Genocide: The Work of Lauterpacht and Lemkin in Modern International Law." *European Journal of International Law* 20(4) (2010), pp. 1163–94.

Waldron, Jeremy. "Separation of Powers in Thought and Practice." *Boston College Law Review* 54(2) (2013), pp. 433–68.

Walt, Stephen M. *The Origins of Alliances.* Ithaca, NY: Cornell University Press, 1987.

———. "An International Relations Theory Guide to the War in Ukraine." *Foreign Policy*, March 8, 2022.

Waltz, Kenneth N. *Theory of International Politics.* Long Grove, IL: Waveland Press, 1979.

———. "Structural Realism after the Cold War." *International Security* 25(1) (2000), pp. 5–41.

Walzer, Michael. *Thick and Thin: Moral Argument at Home and Abroad.* Notre Dame, IN: University of Notre Dame Press, 1994.

———. "Mill's 'A Few Words on Non-intervention': A Commentary." In *Mill's Political Thought: A Bicentennial Reassessment*, edited by Nadia Urbinati and Alex Zakaras, pp. 347–56. Cambridge: Cambridge University Press, 2007.

Wang, Yuhua. *The Rise and Fall of Imperial China: The Social Origins of State Development*. Princeton, NJ: Princeton University Press, 2022.

Weiler, J.H.H. "Rule of Lawyers and Ethos of Diplomats: Reflections on the Internal and External Legitimacy of WTO Dispute Settlement." *Journal of World Trade* 35(2) (2001), pp. 191–207.

Weingast, Barry R. "A Rational Choice Perspective on the Role of Ideas: Shared Belief Systems and State Sovereignty in International Cooperation." *Politics and Society* 23(4) (1995), pp. 449–64.

———. "War, Trade, and Mercantilism: Reconciling Adam Smith's Three Theories of the British Empire." Working paper, Hoover Institution, Stanford University, 2017.

Wendt, Alexander. *Social Theory of International Politics*. Cambridge: Cambridge University Press, 1999.

Westerman, Pauline. "Hume's Reception of Grotius: A History of Historization." *Grotiana* 9(1) (1988), pp. 64–78.

Whatmore, Richard. "Vattel, Britain and Peace in Europe." *Grotiana* 31(1) (2010), pp. 85–107.

———. "Enlightenment Political Philosophy." In *The Oxford Handbook of the History of Political Philosophy*, edited by George Klosko, pp. 296–318. Oxford: Oxford University Press, 2011.

Wiggins, David. "Natural and Artificial Virtues: A Vindication of Hume's Scheme." In *How Should One Live? Essays on the Virtues*, edited by Roger Crisp, pp. 131–40. Oxford: Oxford University Press, 1996.

Wight, Martin. *International Relations and Political Philosophy*. Edited by David S. Yost. Oxford: Oxford University Press, 2022.

Wikipedia. "Communist International." Accessed October 9, 2020. https://en.wikipedia.org /wiki/Communist_International.

Williams, Bernard. "Conflicts of Values." In *Moral Luck: Philosophical Papers, 1973–1980*, pp. 71–82. Cambridge: Cambridge University Press, 1981.

———. *Shame and Necessity*. Berkeley: University of California Press, 1993.

———. "Toleration: An Impossible Virtue?" In *Toleration: An Elusive Virtue?*, edited by David Heyd, pp. 18–27. Princeton, NJ: Princeton University Press, 1996.

———. "Truth in Ethics." In *Truth in Ethics*, edited by Brad Hooker, pp. 227–42. Oxford: Blackwell, 1996.

———. "Seminar." KU Leuven, November 25, 1998. *Ethical Perspectives* 6(3) (1999), pp. 243–65.

———. *Truth and Truthfulness: An Essay in Genealogy*. Princeton, NJ: Princeton University Press, 2002.

———. *In the Beginning Was the Deed: Realism and Moralism in Political Argument*. Selected, edited, and with an introduction by Geoffrey Hawthorne. Princeton, NJ: Princeton University Press, 2005.

———. *Ethics and the Limits of Philosophy*. Abingdon, UK: Routledge, 2006 [1985].

———. *Philosophy as a Humanistic Discipline*. Princeton, NJ: Princeton University Press. 2006.

Williamson, John. "What Washington Means by Policy Reform." Washington, DC: Peterson Institute for International Economics, 1989.

Wirth, David A. "Environment." In *The Oxford Handbook of International Organizations*, edited by Jacob Katz Cogan, Ian Hurd, and Ian Johnstone, pp. 425–446. Oxford: Oxford University Press, 2016.

Wittgenstein, Ludwig. *Philosophical Investigations*. Translated by G.E.M. Anscombe. Oxford: Basil Blackwell, 1976 [1953].

Wohlforth, William C., Richard Little, Stuart J. Kaufman, David Kang, Charles A. Jones, Victoria Tin-Bor Hui, Arthur Eckstein, Daniel Deudney, and William L. Brenner. "Testing Balance-of-Power Theory in World History." *European Journal of International Relations* 13(2) (2007), pp. 155–85.

Wolf, Martin. "Hypocrisy and Confusion Distort the Debate on Social Mobility." *Financial Times*, May 2, 2019.

Woods, Ngaire. "Good Governance in International Organizations." *Global Governance* 5(1) (1999), pp. 39–61.

World Health Organization. "Frequently Asked Questions about the International Health Regulations (2005)." Accessed February 8, 2022. https://www.who.int/ihr/about/faq/en/#faq02.

Wu, Mark. "The 'China, Inc.' Challenge to Global Trade Governance." *Harvard International Law Journal* 57(2) (2016), pp. 261–324.

Xi Jinping. "Jointly Shoulder Responsibility of Our Times: Promote Global Growth." Speech given at the World Economic Forum, Davos, Switzerland, January 17, 2017. https://govt.chinadaily.com.cn/s/201701/17/WS5c0627d5498eefb3fe46e130/jointly-shoulder-responsibility-of-our-times-promote-global-growth.html.

Yale Law School. "Nuremberg Trial Proceedings Vol. 1. Indictment: Count Three." Avalon Project, Lillian Goldman Law Library, accessed June 21, 2020. https://avalon.law.yale.edu/imt/count3.asp.

Yan Xuetong. *Ancient Chinese Thought, Modern Chinese Power*. Princeton, NJ: Princeton University Press, 2011.

———. "Cooperation between China and Hungary." In *Can the Silk Road Tune Up Growth? Opportunities in the European-Asian Economic Cooperation*, pp. 65–68. Proceedings of the Fourth Conference of the Magyar Nemzeti Bank's Lamfalussy Lectures Conference Series, Budapest, January 23, 2017. Budapest: Magyar Nemzeti Bank, 2017.

———. *Leadership and the Rise of Great Powers*. Princeton, NJ: Princeton University Press, 2019.

Young, H. Peyton. "The Evolution of Social Norms." *Annual Review of Economics* 7(1), pp. 359–87.

Zaum, Dominic. "Legitimacy." In *The Oxford Handbook of International Organizations*, edited by Jacob Katz Cogan, Ian Hurd, and Ian Johnstone, pp. 1107–25. Oxford: Oxford University Press, 2016.

Zhao, Dingxin. "The Mandate of Heaven and Performance Legitimation in Historical and Contemporary China." *American Behavioral Scientist* 53(3) (2009), pp. 416–33.

Zhou Xiaochuan. "Reform the International Monetary System." Speech given at People's Bank of China, March 23, 2009. https://www.bis.org/review/r090402c.pdf.

Zoellick, Robert. "Whither China: From Membership to Responsibility?" Remarks to the National Committee on US-China Relations, New York, September 21, 2005. https://2001-2009.state.gov/s/d/former/zoellick/rem/53682.htm.

Zurn, Michael. *A Theory of Global Governance: Authority, Legitimacy, and Contestation*. Oxford: Oxford University Press, 2018.

Zurn, Michael, Martin Binder, and Matthias Ecker-Ehrhardt. "International Authority and Politicization." *International Theory* 4(1) (2012), pp. 69–106.

# NAME INDEX

Annan, Kofi, 263
Aquinas, Thomas, 35, 37n25, 38, 339–40
Aristotle, 27, 35, 221, 279n31

Baldwin, Richard, 6, 405, 421
Beitz, Charles, 329n60, 454–55
Bellamy, Richard, 325, 326
Bentham, Jeremy, 40, 156n25, 341n9
Bingham, Tom, 233, 344, 345n16
Blanchard, Olivier, 387, 388
Bodin, Jean, 31, 254, 255
Buchanan, Allen, 25n60, 163n39, 268n3,
  286n45, 317–18n41, 348n24
Bull, Hedley, 21, 166–67, 168n5, 170–72,
  175–76, 179, 180n32, 456
Burke, Edmund, 13, 233, 305
Bush, George H. W., 15n35, 95

Carr, E. H., 17, 303n15
Castlereagh, Lord, 32, 166, 186, 294, 295,
  448–49
Chiang Kai-shek, 72, 217, 227
Churchill, Winston, 83, 85, 227
Cicero, 35, 139, 268n4
Clark, Ian, 21, 303n15, 306n19, 313n31
Colbert, Jean-Baptiste, 52, 361, 362
Connally, John, 1–2, 305, 362
Crowe, Eyre, 211

Dyzenhaus, David, 252n10, 259–60

Gaulle, Charles de, 1–2, 15, 88n44
Gentili, Alberico, 37, 38n27, 49, 53, 170
Gilpin, Robert, 195, 203

Giscard d'Estaing, Valéry, 370
Grotius (Hugo de Groot), 21, 39, 48–49, 53,
  54, 139, 167, 170, 456; on law of the sea, 53;
  on law of war, 48–49; on natural and positive law, 29, 38, 49n59, 80; on sociability, 54

Hamilton, Alexander, 56, 83
Hart, H. L. A., 253n13, 328n57, 339
Hayek, Friedrich, 149n8, 168n4, 340n5, 410
Hobbes, Thomas, 18, 206n23, 207n24; First
  Political Question in image of, 457;
  Hobbes's Foole, 136, 139–40; Hume on, 273;
  on nonsociability undermining international law and authority, 34, 39, 41–42, 54,
  136, 139; on sovereign states, 40, 270–71
Holmstrom, Bengt, 158n31, 371n21
Hull, Cordell, 83
Hume, David, 18–19, 41, 55n75, 63, 268n4,
  288n51, 291, 362; on balance of power, 197;
  Bull and, 21, 170; on commercial society, 54,
  292–93, 417–18, 472; on common point of
  view, 173–74, 177; on habits, conventions,
  and social norms as means to cooperation,
  119, 121, 128, 130, 134–38, 143, 150, 163, 176;
  on institutions and legitimacy, 134–38,
  148–49, 267, 275–80, 281n34, 283, 286n43,
  291–93, 458; on international law and cooperation, 141, 302n13, 312; on jealousy of
  trade, 13, 54, 211, 365, 401; on Justinian's
  Digests, 34; on the natural lawyers, 139;
  on promising, 135–38; on public credit,
  13–14n31, 62, 371; on sympathy and the
  sensible knave, 138–40, 191, 218, 440
Hurwicz, Leonid, 147n4, 341n9

515

theory principle, 286n46; on First Political Question, the Basic Legitimation Demand, and legitimacy, 20, 267, 268, 271–72, 280, 289, 291, 293, 457; on genealogies, 20–21; history and, 284, 458; on humanitarian intervention, 330–32; on Hume's optimism, 473n22; on internalizing norms, 172; on liberalism, 288n50, 289n54; on liberalism of fear, 318, 454–55; on "morality system," 19, 174n18, 284n40, 461n12; on promising, 135; on shame, 133n22; on thick vs. thin evaluative concepts, 173n16, 176n25; on toleration, 314–15

Wilson, Woodrow, 65, 67, 68

Xi Jinping, 106, 112, 113, 215, 222, 229, 243, 244, 245, 374, 403, 416, 468, 471
Xunzi, 214, 217n10, 218–19, 345, 353, 471

Yan Xuetong, 111n10, 193, 214–15, 229, 232, 237n4, 455n5

Zhou Xiaochuan, 359, 373, 377, 392

# SUBJECT INDEX

aggression, 47–48, 49–51, 71, 396; institutions and norms to restrain, 235. *See also* war

anarchy in international relations, 19–20, 34–35, 128, 167; and Thucydides Trap, 12

arbitration, 58–59, 65, 429–32; Hague tribunal for, 59, 79, 187, 231–32

Association of Southeast Asian Nations (ASEAN), 95, 100, 100n75, 388n25

audience costs, 144, 164

Augsburg, Peace of (1555), 30

Australia, 87, 89–90, 113, 230, 424

Austria (Habsburg), 14, 32, 44n46, 197, 198–99, 216

autarky, 89–91, 238, 262, 279, 328, 440

authoritarian governments, 4, 13, 244, 428n20, 460

balance of payments, 63, 111, 365, 380

balance of power, 31–33, 151, 191, 197–200, 215–16, 302; as institution, 149, 151

Bank for International Settlements, 64, 91, 157, 187, 445, 447–48. *See also* Basel

Bank of England, 62, 133, 436–37, 441

bargaining, 127–28, 144, 153–54, 162

Basel, 434–53; asymmetric access to, 450–51; banking standards, 93, 125, 157, 351, 434, 436–40, 450; Basel Committee on Banking Supervision, 93, 157, 202, 436–39, 441, 449, 451; Basel Committee on Payments and Market Infrastructure, 157, 442; culture at, 436–42; hierarchy in, 448–50; legitimacy and, 377, 448, 450–51. *See also*

Bank for International Settlements; Financial Stability Board (Forum)

"beggar-thyself" policies, 439–40

Belt and Road Strategy (China), 11, 111–12, 215n3, 230, 236, 23

bilateral investment treaties, 8, 58, 93–94, 98, 102, 110, 419–33; arbitration of, 420, 427, 429–32; legitimacy of, 377, 427–28, 430–32; liberalism via, 421–25; reform of, 377, 430–32

Brazil, 10, 14, 212, 449, 472

Bretton Woods international monetary system, 90, 92, 109–10, 379–80, 383, 390–91, 409

Calvo Doctrine, 50n63, 57–58, 82, 93

Canada, 2n7, 90, 92n55, 93n58, 100, 408, 423n13

capital controls, 92, 93, 383, 422; liberalism of fear and, 386–87; security and, 426

capital flows, 7, 367–68, 371, 383–87; League of Nations and, 65n104, 66

central banking, 151–52, 373, 381, 389–90, 393, 438–42, 444–47; digital currencies and, 452; swap lines, 92, 389–90, 445–46, 452

checks and balances, 117–18, 218–19, 345, 426. *See also* separation of powers

China, 6, 7, 9–15, 19, 43, 61, 67n112, 68, 79, 109–115, 189–191, 196, 212–34, 230, 235–36, 244, 420, 460, 467–68, 471; and Bhutan, 113; century of humiliation of, 226–28; Document 9 on liberalism, 222; financial

retaliation, 130–32, 153. *See also* aggression; laws of war (and peace)

rising states: authoritarian, 4; civilizational competition with, 22–23, 190; geopolitics and, 10–12, 211–12, 214–34; globalization challenges with, 9; moral hazard for, 10–11; observational equivalence hazards with, 210–12; Order and System in, 195–203, 209–13, 214–34; respect for, 244; trade policy in, 405–7, 417, 419. *See also specific states*

robust policy (minimax), 241–42, 444, 462. *See also* resilience

Rome, 43–44, 60, 198; *jus gentium*, 36, 38n29, 53; Justinian's *Digests*, 34, 45, 278n29

rule of law, 24, 35, 55, 377, 451; China and, 220, 222, 244; as legitimation norm, 338, 339–40, 430–32; sovereignty governed by, 263

rules: and institutions, 146–47, 149, 150–51, 164, 215, 343; policy regime as body of, 150–51

Russia, 1, 7, 11–12, 32, 44n46, 66, 74, 85–86, 89, 95, 104, 108–9, 186, 189, 191, 197–199, 215, 241–42, 362, 387, 427; China's relations with, 12, 113, 239–40, 242, 467; economic sanctions against, 50, 102, 106, 239, 241; oil/gas industry in, 109, 243, 427. *See also* Cold War; Soviet Union; Ukraine

safe assets, 367n14, 371, 388, 389, 444–46, 452

SALT (Strategic Arms Limitation Talks), 88–89

Saudi Arabia, 7, 10, 93, 109, 239–40

security and security pacts, 32, 65, 72–82, 87–89, 95, 112–14, 200–201, 269, 300–302, 304, 405, 408, 425–27; Freedom of Navigation Operations and, 86, 113; Indo-Pacific Quad, 113; in leadership-based international system, 72–82, 87–89, 95; overdependence, technology, and, 114, 203, 425–27 (*see also* cyber attacks/interference)

security dilemma, 211; and observational equivalence, 210–12

self-defense, 51, 73, 103, 181, 298

separation of powers, 343–44, 380

shadow banking, 373, 390, 444–46. *See also* safe assets

slavery, 36n23, 44, 55n75, 59, 185, 296n5, 303n14, 316n38

sociability, 41–42, 54, 56, 139

social dumping, 413–14; compared with antitrust policy, 414–15

social norms, 16–17, 18, 136, 303, 319–20; conventions and, 24, 136n32, 137n33; cooperation via, 132–41, 142, 143, 144, 152, 435, 438–39; coordination via, 128, 163; institutions, regimes, and, 148, 150, 151n13, 152, 265–66, 275–78, 288, 458; instrumental vs. intrinsic value of, 171–72, 178–79; legitimacy and, 21–22, 190, 245, 249, 265–66, 273, 275–78, 286–88, 310–11, 415–16, 458; macro-reciprocity of, 319; morality and, 136n31, 138, 141; reputation and, 132–33; Society with shared, 170, 171–73, 176–82, 190; sovereignty and acceptance of, 257, 260, 265–66; sympathy and, 138–40. *See also* customary law; international law; normativity

Society, 18, 166–91; Christendom's, 183; civilizational standards for, 189–90, 284, 460; deep (shared justificatory doctrines), 173, 174–175, 178–79, 180, 207; human rights stance in, 174, 177, 178–79, 189–90; internalization of norms in, 171–72, 176, 177–78; international law and, 170–71, 175; legitimacy of, 456–59; legitimation circles and, 327; morality, ethics, and, 173–75, 176, 177, 178n29, 189; Order and, 179–82, 457; Pufendorf on international, 80, 327; Rawls's, 296–99; rising state challenges to, 215–26; social norms shared by, 170, 171–73, 176–82, 190; as society of state-societies, 179; System and, 166, 170, 174, 176–77, 179–82, 303; tensions in, 189–90; thick (shared evaluative resources), 173–175, 177–79, 180–82, 257, 456–59; thin, 173, 175–77, 180–82, 456–59. *See also* commercial society

## A NOTE ON THE TYPE

This book has been composed in Arno, an Old-style serif typeface in the classic Venetian tradition, designed by Robert Slimbach at Adobe.